English-Spanish
Spanish-English
Medical
Dictionary

Diccionario
Médico
inglés-español
español-inglés

NOTICE

Medicine is an ever-changing science. As new research and clinical experience broaden our knowledge, changes in treatment and drug therapy are required. The author and the publisher of this work have checked with sources believed to be reliable in their efforts to provide information that is complete and generally in accord with the standards accepted at the time of publication. However, in view of the possibility of human error or changes in medical sciences, neither the author nor the publisher nor any other party who has been involved in the preparation or publication of this work warrants that the information contained herein is in every respect accurate or complete, and they disclaim all responsibility for any errors or omissions or for the results obtained from use of the information contained in this work. Readers are encouraged to confirm the information contained herein with other sources. For example and in particular, readers are advised to check the product information sheet included in the package of each drug they plan to administer to be certain that the information contained in this work is accurate and that changes have not been made in the recommended dose or in the contraindications for administration. This recommendation is of particular importance in connection with new or infrequently used drugs.

Fourth Edition

English-Spanish
Spanish-English
Medical
Dictionary

Diccionario
Médico
inglés-español
español-inglés

Cuarta Edición

Glenn T. Rogers, MD

New York   Chicago   San Francisco   Athens   London   Madrid
Mexico City   Milan   New Delhi   Singapore   Sydney   Toronto

English-Spanish Spanish-English Medical Dictionary, Fourth Edition

1 2 3 4 5 6 7 8 9 0   DOC/DOC   18 17 16 15 14

ISBN 978-0-07-182911-3
MHID 0-07-182911-3

This book was set in Times Roman.
The editors were Sarah Henry and Robert Pancotti.
The production supervisor was Richard Ruzycka.
RR Donnelley was the printer and binder.

This book is printed on acid-free paper.

Library of Congress Cataloging-in-Publication Data
Rogers, Glenn T., author.
  English-Spanish, Spanish-English medical dictionary = Diccionario médico inglés-español, español-inglés / Glenn T. Rogers. — Fourth edition = "Cuarta edición".
    p. ; cm.
  Parallel title: Diccionario médico, inglés-español, español-inglés
  Medical dictionary
  ISBN 978-0-07-182911-3 (soft cover : alk. paper) — ISBN 0-07-182911-3 (soft cover : alk. paper)
  I. Title. II. Title: Diccionario médico, inglés-español, español-inglés. III. Title: Medical dictionary.
  [DNLM: 1. Medicine—Dictionary—English. 2. Medicine—Dictionary—Spanish. W 13]
  R121
  610.3—dc23
                                                                2014016281

To my wife, Cynda, and our children,

Valle and Casey

CONTENTS / MATERIAS

PREFACE TO THE FOURTH EDITION

Since it was first published in 1991 the primary aim of this book for English speakers has been to offer the health professional a lightweight, easy-to-use reference to be used in real time while communicating with Spanish-speaking patients. For this fourth edition every term was individually reviewed with an eye toward ensuring that the reader will understand and use effectively the terms she has looked up. Several thousand entries were expanded or improved, and about 2,000 new terms were added (4,000 if you count the terms in both English and Spanish). New procedures, concepts, and drugs account for many of the added terms, and the rest cover all fields. Mental health deserves mention because it is such an important component of overall health and may finally get more attention following passage of the Affordable Care Act. Many psychiatric terms have been added, and because providers need to know what their patients are feeling, I have added terms that describe human emotions. I have also added terms that involve the "mechanics" of medicine: scheduling of appointments, referrals, insurance issues, charting, advance directives, confidentiality, and the like.

For readers unfamiliar with this book, it is laid out simply. The front matter contains some tips on medical Spanish and a pronunciation guide, the text is straightforward and uncluttered, and at the back there is an appendix with sample conversations relating to medicine in general, nursing, pediatrics, dentistry, and radiology. The questions in these conversations are the questions my colleagues and I use in our daily practice and have been crafted over decades to be the best questions for eliciting the information desired. The appendix ends with a sample discussion of code status.

Choosing which terms to include in this dictionary has been a challenge. Highly technical terms that are unlikely to occur in conversations with patients have been excluded. Thanks to their Latin and Greek roots, most of these terms aren't that difficult. Few would fail to recognize "hemodinámico," "monoterapia," and "hepatectomía," and with a little practice one can become adept at translating this type of term in the other direction (English to Spanish). All other medically-related terms are potential candidates for inclusion, and over the years I have strived to maintain a list that is thorough, relevant, and concise. It should be hard to stump this little book. In particular, I have made a point of including many compound terms and phrases. These multi-word terms don't always translate literally and are often neglected in standard reference works. Examples include: acting out, breakthrough pain, case manager, comfort zone, coping mechanism, death with dignity, doctor-patient confidentiality, drug-eluting stent, durable power of attorney, flesh-eating, free-floating anxiety, life partner, noninvasive positive pressure ventilation, parenting workshop, patient-centered, patient service representative, peer pressure, point of care, ritonavir-boosted, secondhand smoke, self-fulfilling prophecy, shared decision making, sibling rivalry, skilled nursing facility, sliding scale, thin liquid diet, tight glucose control, to stay on task, to bite your nails, to suck your thumb, and upper limit of normal.

Other exceptional features of this book include its grammatical rigor and the extent to which the reader is guided toward correct use of a translation. Since its first printing the book has included parts of speech; notations of gender; indications of subject, region, and usage (formal, familiar, vulgar); irregular past participles; parenthetical disambiguations; example phrases and sentences; and editorial notes. Exceptional, too, is the inclusion of generic drug names. Along with the names of the 200 top-selling pharmaceuticals for 2012 I have included approximately 600 others chosen for their relevance to the Spanish-speaking population. Where appropriate, labels for International Nonproprietary Name (INN) and United States Adopted Names (USAN) are included (see the section "How to Use this Dictionary.")

Accuracy of translation has been a priority for this work. For all but the most straightforward translations, frequency analyses were performed on large data bases in both Spanish and English, some technical, some lay. The results were then vetted by myself and by José Francisco Durán Blanco, a Colombian physician who has an eagle eye for subtleties. The Spanish technical terms then are the terms used by researchers publishing in Spanish, and the lay terms are the terms most commonly used by Spanish-speaking people discussing their health. Regional variations often exist and are included, with labels. For the technical English terms I have relied heavily on the language used in the New England Journal of Medicine and Mayo Clinic Proceedings.

Very special thanks go to Dr. Durán. Without his help the ambitious goals I set for this revision could not have been accomplished. Thanks go to the team at McGraw-Hill for their continued support since this book's inception, now over 20 years ago, and thanks go to those readers who wrote to my publisher or otherwise tracked me down in order to express their appreciation and offer thoughts. Comments are appreciated and can be sent to: rogersdiccionario@gmail.com. Finally I would like to thank my family for their support as well as their patience with regard to my long work hours.

Glenn Rogers
Willits, CA

PRÓLOGO A LA CUARTA EDICIÓN

Desde su primera publicación en 1991, el propósito de este diccionario para los hispanohablantes ha sido brindar una referencia bilingüe práctica de la terminología médica utilizada en conversaciones con los pacientes. Los profesionales de la salud que quieran leer libros de texto o artículos en inglés apreciarán los términos técnicos aquí presentados. Además, debido a la inclusión exhaustiva de términos no técnicos, este libro ha de ser imprescindible para aquellos que tengan pacientes de habla inglesa.

Esta cuarta edición representa una gran revisión del texto. Cada artículo fue verificado de forma minuciosa con el fin de asegurar que el lector pueda entender bien y usar efectivamente los términos que busque. Varios miles de artículos fueron ampliados o mejorados y cerca de 2000 nuevos términos fueron agregados (4000 si se toma en cuenta el mismo término en inglés y en español). Muchos de los términos agregados corresponden a nuevos procedimientos, conceptos y medicamentos, y los demás abarcan todos los campos relacionados a la medicina. Cabe mencionar entre ellos la salud mental, cuya importancia con respecto a la salud general no se puede menospreciar. Muchos términos psiquiátricos han sido agregados y, como los practicantes deben saber lo que sus pacientes están sintiendo, se han incluido términos que describen emociones humanas. También se han agregado términos relacionados con la "mecánica" de la medicina: programación de citas, remisiones a especialistas, trámites de seguro, documentación, confidencialidad, documentos de voluntad anticipada y similares.

Para los lectores que no están familiarizados con este diccionario, se presenta de una manera sencilla: va al punto y no se extiende con información innecesaria. En la parte posterior se encuentra un apéndice con conversaciones de ejemplo relacionadas con la medicina en general, enfermería, pediatría, odontología y radiología. Las preguntas en estas conversaciones mis colegas y yo las utilizamos en el ejercicio médico, y han sido elaboradas durante décadas de práctica para ser la mejor forma de obtener la información deseada. El apéndice termina con una discusión de ejemplo sobre reanimación.

Escoger cuáles términos deberían ser incluidos en este diccionario ha sido un reto. Términos altamente técnicos que generalmente no se usan en conversaciones con pacientes han sido excluidos. Debido a sus raíces latinas y griegas, la mayoría de estos no representan mucha dificultad. Pocos serían incapaces de reconocer "hemodynamic", "monotherapy" y "hepatectomy," y con un poco de práctica uno puede volverse hábil en traducir al revés (del español al inglés). Todos los otros términos de relevancia médica son candidatos para ser incluidos, y a lo largo de los años me he esforzado por mantener una lista que sea completa, relevante y concisa. Será difícil encontrar términos de uso frecuente relacionados con la medicina que no estén en este pequeño libro. Además, he incluido muchos términos compuestos de varias palabras. Estos términos no siempre se traducen literalmente y frecuentemente se dejan a un lado en obras de referencia. Algunos ejemplos incluyen: ansiedad flotante centro de enfermería especializada, centro sociosanitario, chuparse el dedo, comerse las uñas, control estricto de la glucemia, dieta de fácil masticación, dispositivo de ayuda, dolor irruptivo, gestor -a de casos, humo ambiental del tabaco, límite superior normal, mecanismo de afrontamiento, muerte digna, pareja sentimental, potenciado con ritonavir, presión social, poder notarial duradero, profecía autocumplida, rivalidad fraterna, secreto médico, stent liberador de fármacos, taller de padres, ventilación no invasiva con presión positiva, zona de confort.

Otras características excepcionales de este libro incluyen su rigor gramatical y la extensión en las indicaciones al lector sobre el uso correcto de las traducciones. Desde su primera impresión, este libro ha incluido partes de la oración; indicaciones de sujeto, región y nivel de uso; participios irregulares; aclaraciones parentéticas; frases de ejemplo; y notas editoriales. Y como este libro se dedica al lenguaje hablado, se han incluido muchos coloquialismos. Los lectores que trabajan con pacientes que hablan inglés se alegrarán al entender lo que quieren expresar sus pacientes cuando dicen "I get charley horses," "You want me to quit cold turkey?" or "I threw my back out."

Excepcional también, es la inclusión de nombres genéricos de medicamentos. Aproximadamente 800 nombres de medicamentos están registrados, incluyendo todos los que alcanzaron los 200 primeros en ventas en 2012. En donde fuese apropiado, se incluyeron indicaciones de International Nonproprietary Name (INN) (Denominación Común Internacional) y United States Adopted Names (USAN) (Véase la sección "Cómo Usar este Diccionario.")

La precisión de las traducciones ha sido una prioridad en este trabajo. Para escoger las traducciones más puntuales, se realizaron análisis de frecuencia en grandes bases de datos en español e inglés, algunas técnicas, algunas informales. Los resultados fueron después revisados por mí y por José Francisco Durán Blanco, un médico colombiano con buen ojo para los detalles sutiles. Variantes regionales de términos en español fueron incluidas e indicadas de acuerdo a los países en donde aplican. Para los términos técnicos en inglés me he apoyado bastante en el lenguaje usado en el New England Journal of Medicine y Mayo Clinic Proceedings.

Quiero dar gracias especiales al Dr. Durán. Sin su ayuda, las metas ambiciosas que planteé para esta revisión no podrían haber sido alcanzadas. Gracias al equipo de McGraw-Hill por su continuo apoyo desde el origen de este libro, y gracias a aquellos lectores que le escribieron a mi editorial o a mí mismo para expresar sus apreciaciones y compartir ideas. Sus comentarios siempre son bienvenidos y pueden ser enviados a: rogersdiccionario@gmail.com. Finalmente, quisiera agradecer a mi familia por su apoyo así como por su paciencia con mis largas horas de trabajo.

Glenn Rogers
Willits, CA

HOW TO USE THIS DICTIONARY

For easy reference this guide is organized according to the different possible parts of a dictionary entry in the order in which they appear.

Entry-terms:
Entry-terms are listed in alphabetical order and are bolded. For the purpose of alphabetization, punctuation marks and spaces are ignored. Alphabetization of the Spanish-English side is identical to that of the English-Spanish side save for the inclusion of the letter *ñ*, which immediately follows *n*.

For terms with multiple meanings only those meanings relevant to medicine are translated. For instance, under *throw* the reader will find *to throw up* and *to throw one's back out*, but not the usual meaning of the word *throw*.

Chemical names consisting of more than one word are alphabetized according to the first word of the term. Also alphabetized this way are terms, such as *black widow,* which have meanings different from the sum of their parts. Other terms consisting of more than one word can generally be found as sub-entries under the dominant word of the term, usually a noun. This system lends itself to lists; for example, all the syndromes are listed under *syndrome* and all the arteries are listed under *artery.*

Abbreviations:
Abbreviations immediately follow the term they abbreviate and are enclosed in parentheses. English abbreviations are often used for Spanish terms; for example, *INR* is used far more often than *RNI* to abbreviate *razón normalizada internacional*. Where an abbreviation appears for an English term but not its Spanish counterpart, it can be assumed that the English abbreviation is the one most commonly used.

Grammatical Category:
Notations of grammatical category are italicized abbreviations which indicate the part of speech, number (singular or plural), and gender of the word they follow. Their meanings can be found in the "List of Abbreviations" that follows. The two that might give readers trouble are *mf*, which applies to Spanish nouns such as *cardiólogo -ga*, which are masculine or feminine according to context, and *m&f*, which applies to certain Spanish nouns, such as *enzima*, which may be treated as either masculine or feminine, irrespective of context.

Irregular inflections:
For English entries these include comparatives formed other than by adding -er or -r, superlatives formed other than by adding -est or -st, plurals formed other than by adding -s or -es, preterites and past participles formed other than by adding -d or -ed, and gerunds formed other than by adding -ing (possibly after dropping a silent e).

For Spanish entries these include plurals formed other than by adding -es to a terminal consonant, plurals which involve a change in the location of an accent, plurals of nouns which end in an accented vowel, and past participles which have endings other than -ado or -ido.

Restrictive labels:
Restrictive labels are italicized words or abbreviations enclosed in parentheses which indicate the region, field of relevance, level of usage, and other attributes of the term being translated. The label '(*form*)' applies to terms used frequently in writing but which may not be understood by patients; the label '(*fam*)' applies to terms used frequently in speech, but which might seem overly familiar or inappropriate in certain settings; and the label '(*vulg*)' applies to terms which should generally be avoided by health practitioners not thoroughly familiar with their usage and connotations. Restrictive labels are often used to discriminate between several meanings of an entry term, as in the following example:

raw *adj* (*food*) crudo; (*skin, mucous membrane*) excoriado (*form*), pelado, en carne viva

Translations:
Translations appear in order of preference taking into consideration level of usage (formal before lay), accuracy of translation, frequency of usage, and universality (application to all countries where Spanish is spoken). Translations of the same meaning of an entry term are separated by commas, while translations of different meanings are separated by semicolons (see the previous example under Restrictive Labels.)

For translations to Spanish it happens occasionally that the term preferred by the Real Academia Española (RAE) is not the preferred term according to the criteria previously mentioned. This situation is indicated as follows:

kinesiology *n* kinesiología, quinesiología (*RAE*)

Parentheses are used to set off portions of a translation which are either optional, alternative, or required in certain contexts, as in the following examples:

finger *n* dedo (de la mano)
sense *n* sentido; — **of balance** sentido de(l) equilibrio
adapt *vt, vi* adaptar(se)
generation *n* generación *f*; **first (second, third, latest, etc.)** — primera (segunda, tercera, última, etc.) generación
induce *vt* inducir, provocar; **exercise-induced** inducido (provocado) por el ejercicio

In the first example, if you are already talking about a finger you could simply use *dedo*, but out of context *dedo* could mean *toe* in which case you would want to use the full translation: *dedo de la mano*. In the second example the parentheses indicate that *sentido de equilibrio* and *sentido del equilibrio* are both acceptable translations. In the third example *se* is required for the translation of *adapt* as an intransitive verb but not as a transitive verb. The fourth example is an economical way of demonstrating a pattern of translations. In the fifth example *provocado* is an alternative to *inducido*.

Indications of gender:
In the Spanish-English section of the dictionary indications of gender are included in the notations of grammatical category. In the English-Spanish section indications of gender follow the first appearance of a noun translation which is not a masculine noun ending in *o* or a feminine noun ending in *a*. This rule does not apply if the gender of the noun is evident from a modifying adjective.

Disambiguations:
Disambiguations are italicized parenthetical words or phrases that serve to discriminate between different possible meanings of a translation, as in the following example:

báscula *f* scale (*for weighing*)

Examples:
These are bolded and separated from their non-bolded translations by double dots (..). Consecutive example-translation pairs are separated from one another by triple dots (...) as in the following example:

operate *vt, vi* operar; **to operate machinery**..operar maquinaria...**We need to operate on your leg**..Tenemos que operarle (de) la pierna.

<u>Sub-entries:</u>
For sub-entries the entry-term is replaced by a dash as in the following example:

suite *n* sala; **endoscopy** — sala de endoscopia

Dashes are not used to replace the entry-term when the entry-term is pluralized, inflected, or combined with another term by a hyphen. Sub-entries are listed in alphabetical order save that plurals are treated as though they were singular.

<u>Other:</u>
In most cases drug names conform to the International Nonproprietary Names (INN) list produced by the World Health Organization. INN names are only labeled as such when they do not appear as the first-listed term. When a United States Adopted Names (USAN) term appears ahead of an INN name, it is labeled, as in the following example:

glyburide (*USAN*), **glibenclamide** (*INN*) *n* gliburida, glibenclamida (*INN*)

CÓMO USAR ESTE DICCIONARIO

Para fácil referencia, esta guía está organizada teniendo en cuenta las diferentes partes posibles de un artículo en el orden en que aparecen.

Entradas:
Las entradas se encuentran en orden alfabético y están escritas en negritas. Para efectos de alfabetización, se ignoran los signos de puntuación y espacios. Si una entrada tiene múltiples acepciones, solo aquellas de relevancia médica son traducidas. Por ejemplo, bajo *throw* el lector encontrará *to throw up* y *to throw one's back out*, pero no la acepción usual de la palabra *throw* (arrojar).

Los nombres de sustancias químicas que consisten en más de una sola palabra son alfabetizados tomando en cuenta la primera palabra. Son alfabetizados así también términos como *viuda negra* que tienen acepciones diferentes a la suma de sus partes. Los demás términos que consisten en más de una sola palabra se encuentran generalmente como subentradas bajo la palabra dominante del término (en la mayoría de los casos, un sustantivo). Este sistema resulta en la formación de listas muy convenientes. Por ejemplo, todos los síndromes se encuentran bajo *síndrome* y todas las arterias se encuentran bajo *arteria*.

Abreviaturas:
Las abreviaturas están encerradas entre paréntesis y siguen inmediatamente los términos a los que se refieren. Los términos técnicos en español muchas veces se abrevian con la abreviatura del término en inglés. Por ejemplo, *INR* es de uso mucho más común que *RNI* para abreviar *razón normalizada internacional*. Cuando se incluye una abreviatura para un término en inglés, pero no para el término traducido al español, se puede suponer que la abreviatura en inglés es la más usada.

Marcas de categorización:
Las marcas de categorización son abreviaturas en letra cursiva que indican la parte de la oración, número (singular o plural) y género de las palabras que les anteceden. Sus significados se encuentran en la "Lista de Abreviaturas," más adelante. Las dos que pueden merecer clarificación son *'mf,'* que aplica a sustantivos en español como *cardiólogo -ga*, los cuales son masculino o femenino según el contexto, y *'m&f,'* que aplica a ciertos sustantivos en español como *enzima* que pueden ser tratados como masculinos o femeninos sin importar el contexto.

Flexiones irregulares:
Para entradas en inglés las flexiones irregulares incluyen comparativos formados al agregar algo diferente a -er o -r, superlativos formados al agregar algo diferente a -est o -st, plurales formados al agregar algo diferente a -s o -es, pretéritos perfectos y participios formados al agregar algo diferente a -d o -ed y gerundios formados al agregar algo diferente a -ing (después de eliminar una e silenciosa cuando la haya).

Para las entradas en español las flexiones irregulares incluyen plurales formados al agregar algo diferente a -es a una consonante final, plurales que ocasionan un cambio en la ubicación del acento, plurales de sustantivos que terminan en una vocal con acento y participios que terminan en algo diferente a -ado o -ido.

Etiquetas restrictivas:
Las etiquetas restrictivas son palabras o abreviaturas en letra cursiva y entre paréntesis que indican la zona geográfica de uso, campo de relevancia, nivel de uso y otros atributos de la entrada o subentrada. La etiqueta '(*form*)' aplica a términos usados frecuentemente en la literatura, pero que podrían no ser entendidos por los pacientes; la etiqueta '(*fam*)' aplica a términos usados frecuentemente en la lengua hablada, pero que podrían parecer muy informales o inapropiados en algunos contextos; y la etiqueta '(*vulg*)' aplica a términos que deberían generalmente ser evitados por lectores que no estén completamente familiarizados con su uso y connotaciones. Asimismo, las etiquetas restrictivas también sirven para distinguir entre varias acepciones de una entrada como en el siguiente ejemplo:

agudo -da *adj* (*enfermedad*) acute; (*dolor*) sharp; (*tono*) high-pitched

Traducciones:
Las traducciones aparecen en orden de preferencia teniendo en cuenta el nivel de formalidad, precisión de la traducción, frecuencia de uso y universalidad (aplicabilidad en todos los países donde se habla español). Las traducciones de la misma acepción de una entrada se separan por comas y las traducciones de distintas acepciones se separan por punto y coma. Acerca de las traducciones al español, ocurre ocasionalmente que el término preferido por la Real Academia Española (RAE) no es el término preferido de acuerdo a los criterios mencionados. Esta situación se indica así:

kinesiology *n* kinesiología, quinesiología (*RAE*)

Porciones de las traducciones que son opcionales, alternativas, o que se requiere sólo en ciertos contextos aparecen entre paréntesis como en los siguientes ejemplos:

consultorio *m* (doctor's) office
abotonar *vt, vr* to button (up)
adapt *vt, vi* adaptar(se)
articulación *f* joint; — **de la rodilla (tobillo, etc.)** knee (ankle, etc.) joint
induce *vt* inducir, provocar; **exercise-induced** inducido (provocado) por el ejercicio

En el primer ejemplo, si ya está hablando de un médico, será suficiente decir no más *office*, pero fuera de contexto *consultorio* se traduce como *doctor's office*. En el segundo ejemplo *to button* y *to button up* son traducciones equivalentes de *abotonar*. En el tercer ejemplo, es necesario incluir *'se'* para traducir la forma intransitiva de *adapt* (la cual corresponde a la forma reflexiva en español en este caso). El cuarto ejemplo demuestra un patrón de traducción. En el quinto ejemplo *provocado* es una alternativa a *inducido*.

Desambiguaciones:
Las desambiguaciones son palabras o frases en cursiva y entre paréntesis que sirven para distinguir entre diferentes acepciones de una traducción, como en el siguiente ejemplo:

hangnail *n* padrastro (*en el dedo*)

Ejemplos de uso:
Los ejemplos de uso se encuentran en negritas y separados de sus traducciones por doble punto (..). Los ejemplo-traducción consecutivos se separan el uno del otro con triple punto (…). P. ej.:

preocuparse *vr* to worry; **¿Está preocupado?**..Are you worried?...**No se preocupe**..Don't worry.

Subentradas:
Para las subentradas, el término de entrada es reemplazado por una raya como en los siguientes ejemplos:

suite *n* sala; **endoscopy** — sala de endoscopia

Las rayas no son usadas para reemplazar el término de entrada cuando este es pluralizado, flexionado o combinado con otro término por un guión. Las subentradas se encuentran incluidas en orden alfabético, a menos que los plurales sean tratados como si fueran singulares.

Otros:
Normalmente, los nombres de medicamentos provienen de la lista de la International Nonproprietary Names (INN) publicada por la Organización Mundial de la Salud. La etiqueta '(*INN*)' sólo aparece cuando el término INN no es el nombre preferido. Cuando un término de United States Adopted Names es preferido sobre uno del INN, lleva la etiqueta '(*USAN*),' como en el siguiente ejemplo:

glyburide (*USAN*), **glibenclamida** (*INN*) *n* gliburida, glibenclamida (*INN*)

MEDICAL SPANISH TIPS

- The most important advice I can give to anyone learning a foreign language is to try to master the pronunciation at an early stage. This has a double benefit. Not only will you be understood more easily, but you will be better able to identify and retain words and phrases of the foreign language as you hear them. This will greatly accelerate the learning process. As you hear the foreign language being spoken by a native speaker, repeat key phrases over and over in your mind—or even aloud if possible—comparing your pronunciation to the immediate memory of the correctly spoken sounds. Experiment with your tongue, lips, and palate to create sounds which may be unfamiliar to you. Take a deep breath and pronounce the soft 'i' of the English word 'sin,' then slowly modulate it to the 'ee' of 'seen.' Go back and forth between these two sounds. Somewhere in between is the '*i*' as it sounds in Spanish, for example in '*cinco*.' Pronounce the English 'd' sound over and over again and gradually modulate it to the 'th' of 'the.' Somewhere in between is the Spanish '*d*.' Pronounce the English 'h' sound over and over again and gradually modulate it to the English 'k.' Somewhere in between is a close facsimile of the Spanish '*j*.' Exercises like these will improve your pronunciation rapidly.

- On the subject of pronunciation, note that Spanish vowels are short and pure. Never linger on a vowel as in English. Say the sentence, "No way!" with feeling and notice how the vowel sounds are drawn out. This rarely happens in Spanish; Spanish is much more staccato in its delivery. Note also that there is no schwa sound in Spanish. The schwa sound is the 'uh' sound so often given to unaccented syllables in English. For example the first, third, and fifth syllables of 'acetazolamide' are schwa sounds. In Spanish, vowels retain their characteristic sounds whether or not they are accented. 'Acetazolamida' is pronounced ah-ceh-tah-zoh-lah-MEE-dah, not uh-ceh-tuh-zoh-luh-MEE-duh. It is often helpful first to practice a word without consonants. 'Acetazolamida' without consonants would be ah-eh-ah-oh-ah-EE-ah. When you have mastered the vowel changes for a given word, it is usually a simple matter to fill in the consonants. Learn to say *cah-BEH-sah*, not *cuh-BEH-suh*; *meh-dee-SEE-nah*, not *meh-duh-SEE-nuh*.

- When referring to a part of the body in Spanish, it is common to use the definite article instead of the possessive adjective, provided it is clear whose body is involved. The Spanish definite articles, recall, are *el* and *la*. *¿Le duele la cabeza?* is the best translation of "Does your head hurt?" *¿Le duele su cabeza?* is redundant in Spanish.

- The indirect object* is used much more often in Spanish than in English. Health workers are frequently doing things to patients and this often involves the use of *le* or, in familiar speech, *te*.

  > *Quiero tomarle el pulso*...I want to take your pulse.
  > *Voy a escucharle el corazón*...I'm going to listen to your heart.
  > *Tenemos que operarte la pierna*...We need to operate on your leg.

  This phrasing often sounds less brusque than *Quiero tomar su pulso, Voy a escuchar su corazón,* etc.

  * Recall that a *direct* object may be any type of object and receives the direct action of the verb, while the *indirect* object is always a person (or other living being) *to* whom or *for* whom the action is being performed.

- English-speaking people are often confused by the choices available for the direct object in Spanish. *Te* is always correct when speaking informally, for instance to a child.

  > *Voy a examinarte, hijo*..I'm going to examine you, young man.

  When speaking formally, most Spanish speakers use *lo* for males and *la* for females.

  > *Voy a examinarlo, señor*..I'm going to examine you, sir.
  > *Voy a examinarla, señora*..I'm going to examine you, ma'am.

  There are a few exceptions to this rule; for instance, the verb *pegar*, when it means 'to hit' takes *le* for a direct object.

  > *¿Le pegó?*..Did it hit you?

Some Spanish speakers will use *le* for *all* (formal) second person direct objects, male or female.

> *Voy a examinarle, señor*..I'm going to examine you, sir.
> *Voy a examinarle, señora*..I'm going to examine you, ma'am.

This style is common in Mexico.

- Some verbs require that the subject and object be inverted when translating between English and Spanish. The Spanish student is likely to encounter this for the first time when learning to translate the verb 'to like.' "I like coffee" would be *Me gusta el café*. The subject and object are inverted. This particular construction is a stumbling block to fluency and even advanced students often have to think for a couple seconds in order to conjugate the verb correctly and choose the correct object pronouns.

> *Me falta el aire*..I am short of breath.
> *Les falta el aire*..They are short of breath.
> *Me dieron náuseas*..I got nauseated.
> *¿Le salieron moretones?*..Did you get bruised?
> *Te falta hierro*..You're low on iron.

Notice that the English subject corresponds to the Spanish indirect object in all these cases.

- Many Spanish verbs are used in the reflexive form when applied to medicine. The use of the reflexive pronoun *se* turns the action of the verb back on the verb's subject.

> *Orinó*..He urinated.
> *Se orinó*..He urinated on himself.
>
> *Puede vestirla*..You can dress her.
> *Puede vestirse*..You can get dressed (literally 'dress yourself').
>
> *La enfermera le va a inyectar*..The nurse will give you an injection.
> *La enfermera le va a enseñar como inyectarse*..The nurse will teach you how to inject yourself.

A reflexive construction is often used when an English-speaking person would use the past participle preceded by 'to get' or 'to become.'

> *Se cansa*..He gets tired..He becomes tired.
> *Se mejoró*..She got better.
> *Se dislocó*..It became dislocated.
> *Se infectó*..It became infected..It got infected.

- Most Spanish nouns which end in *-o* are masculine and most which end in *-a* are feminine; however, there are some important exceptions in medical Spanish. For instance, many Spanish words which end in *-ma* are derived from Greek and retain their original masculine gender.

> *un problema médico*..a medical problem
> *el electrocardiograma*..the electrocardiogram

Other medical terms which end in *-a* and are masculine include *cólera* (the disease), *día, herbicida, insecticida, pesticida, raticida, espermaticida* and *vermicida*.

The word *mano*, which comes from the Latin *manus*, retains its original feminine gender despite the fact it ends in *-o*.

> *Tengo las manos frías*..My hands are cold.

A source of confusion to Spanish students is the construction '*el agua*.' Although *agua* is feminine (and requires feminine modifiers), *el* is used instead of *la* to avoid the awkward double *ah* sound of '*la agua*.' This rule applies to any word which begins with an accented *ah* sound.

> *tratar el asma*..to treat asthma
> *terapista del habla*..speech therapist

This rule also applies to the indefinite article.

> *un afta dolorosa*..a painful canker sore
> *un arma blanca*..a sharp weapon

This rule does not apply to plural forms, since the double *ah* sound is then broken up by an *s* sound.

las aftas dolorosas..painful canker sores
las armas blancas..sharp weapons

Other feminine medical Spanish terms which begin with an accented *ah* sound include *ámpula, área,* and *hambre.*

- When comparing quantities, use *de.*

   más de dos pastillas..more than two pills
   menos de una taza..less than a cup

In all other situations use *que.*

   más alto que tu hermano..taller than your brother
   menos que siempre..less than usual
   menos que nunca..less than ever

- Health practitioners should be aware that the Spanish word *alcohol* is often considered a synonym for 'hard liquor.' Many Hispanic beer and wine drinkers will answer no in all sincerity to the question *¿Toma alcohol?* A slightly broader question would be *¿Toma bebidas alcohólicas?* And then to avoid all misunderstandings, you could follow a negative answer with *¿cerveza?..¿vino?*

SPANISH PRONUNCIATION

a Like the English **a** in **father** (e.g., *padre*, *cama*).

b Similar to the English **b**. At the beginning of a breath group or following an *m* or *n*, the Spanish *b* sounds like the **b** in **bite** (e.g., *boca*, *embarasada*). In all other situations the Spanish *b* lies somewhere between the English **b** and the English **v** (e.g., *tubo*, *jarabe*). Allow a little air to escape between slightly parted lips as you make this latter sound.

c Like the English **c**. Before *a*, *o*, or *u* it is hard (e.g., *cara*); before *e* or *i* it is soft (e.g., *ácido*). (In Castilian Spanish, *c* preceding **e** or **i** is pronounced like the **th** in **bath**, but this form of Spanish is rarely spoken by Latin Americans.) The Spanish *ch* sounds like the English **ch** in **child**.

d Similar to the English **d**. At the beginning of a breath group or following *l* or *n*, the Spanish *d* sounds like the English **d** in **dizzy** (e.g., *dosis*, *venda*). In all other situations the Spanish *d* lies somewhere between the English **d** and the **th** in **there** (e.g., *mudo*, *nacido*). Allow a little air to escape between the tip of your tongue and upper teeth as you make the latter sound.

e Similar to the **ey** in **they** (e.g., *peso*, *absceso*), unless followed by a consonant in the same syllable, in which case it is closer to the **e** in **sepsis** (e.g., *esperma*, *recto*).

f Like the English **f**.

g When followed by *a*, *o*, *u*, or a consonant, the Spanish *g* is similar to the English **g** in **gout** (e.g., *gota*, *grasa*). Allow a little air to escape between your tongue and palate as you make this sound. When followed by *e* or *i*, the Spanish *g* is similar to the **h** in **hot** shaded slightly toward the English **k** (e.g., *gen*, *gingiva*).

h Silent (e.g., *hombre*, *almohada*).

i   Like the **i** in **saline** or **latrine** (e.g., *orina*, *signo*, *sifilis*). Preceding another vowel, the Spanish *i* sounds like the English **y**. *Siesta* is pronounced *SYES-tah*, *sodio* is pronounced *SO-dyoh*, *viudo* is pronounced *VYOO-doh*, etc. Following another vowel, *i* forms individual diphthongs: *ai* sounds like the **y** in **cry** (e.g., *aire*, *aislar*); *ei* sounds like the **ay** in **tray** (e.g., *aceite*, *afeitar*); *oi* sounds like the **oy** in **boy** (e.g., *toxoide*, *coloide*); and *ui* sounds like the **ui** in **suite** (e.g., *cuidado*, *ruido*).

j   The Spanish *j* is pronounced the same as the Spanish **g** in **gen** or **gingiva**. See above.

k   Like the English **k**. (*k* is not native to the Spanish alphabet and appears only in foreign words.)

l   Similar to the English **l** (e.g., *lado*, *pelo*). The Spanish *l* is articulated rapidly, never drawn out as in English. The Spanish *ll* is pronounced somewhere between the **ll** of **million** and the **y** of **yes**.

m   Like the English **m**.

n   Like the English **n**.

ñ   Like the **ni** in **bunion** (e.g., *baño*, *sueño*).

o   Similar to the English **o** in **coma**.

p   Like the English **p** in **spit**. Hold your hand in front of your mouth as you say **spit** and then **pit**. Note that less air is expelled in pronouncing **spit**. The Spanish *p* is not aspirated, which means little air should be expelled. It is a shorter, more explosive sound than the English **p**.

q   Like the English **k**. The Spanish *q* is always followed by *u*, but lacks the **w** sound of the English **qu**. *Quinina* is pronounced *kee-NEE-nah*, not *kwee-NEE-nah*. The **kw** sound of **quit** is represented in Spanish by *cu*, as in *cuarto*, *cuidado*, etc.

r   Similar to the **tt** of **butter**. At the beginning of a word the Spanish *r* is trilled. The Spanish *rr* is always trilled.

s   Like the English **s**. Before voiced consonants, the Spanish *s* sounds like the English **z** (e.g., *espasmo*).

t Like the English **t** in **stent**. Hold your hand in front of your mouth as you say **stent** and then **tent**. Note that less air is expelled in pronouncing **stent**. The Spanish *t* is not aspirated, which means little air should be expelled. It is a shorter, more explosive sound than the English **t**, made by quickly tapping the tip of the tongue against the back of the upper front teeth.

u Like the English **u** in **flu** or **rule**. Be sure not to pronounce it like **you** (unless it follows an *i*—see below). The Spanish *u* has a **w** sound when it precedes another vowel (e.g., *agua*, *cuello*), except in the case of *gue*, *gui*, *que*, and *qui*, when it is silent (e.g., *inguinal*, *quebrar*). The **w** sound is retained in *güe* and *güi* (e.g., *agüita*, *ungüento*). The diphthong *au* sounds like the **ow** of **brow** (e.g., *aura*, *trauma*). The diphthong *iu* sounds like the **u** in **acute** or **use** (e.g., *viudo*, *diurético*).

v Identical to the Spanish *b*. See above.

x Like the English **x** in **flex**. Before consonants, the Spanish *x* is often pronounced like the English **s** (e.g., *extra*, *expediente*).

y Similar to the English **y** (e.g., *yeso*, *yodo*). An exception is the word *y* (meaning **and**), which is pronounced like the **ee** in **see**.

z Like the English **s** (e.g., *nariz*, *brazo*).

ABBREVIATIONS / ABREVIATURAS

abbr	abbreviation	abreviatura
adj	adjective	adjetivo
adv	adverb	adverbio
Amer	Latin America	Latinoamérica
anat	anatomy	anatomía
Ang	Anglicism	anglicismo
ant	antiquated	anticuado
Arg	Argentina	Argentina
arith	arithmetic	aritmética
Bol	Bolivia	Bolivia
bot	botany	botánica
CA	Central America	Centroamérica
card	cardiology	cardiología
Carib	Caribbean	Caribe
chem	chemistry	química
Col	Colombia	Colombia
comp	comparative	comparativo
conj	conjunction	conjunción
dent	dentistry	odontología
derm	dermatology	dermatología
Dom	Dominican Republic	República Dominicana
Ecu	Ecuador	Ecuador
El Salv	El Salvador	El Salvador
esp.	especially	especialmente
Esp	Spain	España
euph	euphemism	eufemismo
f	feminine	femenino
fam	familiar	familiar
form	formal	formal
fpl	feminine plural	femenino plural
frec.	frequently	frecuentemente
ger	gerund	gerundio
Guat	Guatemala	Guatemala
Hond	Honduras	Honduras
gyn	gynecology	ginecología
interj	interjection	interjección
INN	International Non-proprietary Name	Denominación Común Internacional
inv	invariant	invariable
m	masculine	masculino
mf	masculine or feminine	masculino o femenino

m&f	masculine and feminine	masculino y femenino
mfpl	masculine or feminine, plural	masculino o femenino, plural
math	mathematics	matemáticas
Mex	Mexico	México
micro	microbiology	microbiología
mpl	masculine plural	masculino plural
n	noun	nombre (sustantivo)
neuro	neurology	neurología
Nic	Nicaragua	Nicaragua
npl	noun plural	nombre plural
obst	obstetrics	obstetricia
ophth	ophthalmology	oftalmología
ortho	orthopedics	ortopedia
path	pathology	patología
ped	pediatrics	pediatría
p. ej.	for example	por ejemplo
pharm	pharmacology	farmacología
physio	physiology	fisiología
pl	plural	plural
pp	past participle	participio
PR	Puerto Rico	Puerto Rico
pref	prefix	prefijo
prep	preposition	preposición
pret	preterite	pretérito
psych	psychology	psicología
rad	radiology	radiología
RAE	Real Academia Española	Real Academia Española
SA	South America	Sudamérica
stat	statistics	estadística
super	superlative	superlativo
surg	surgery	cirugía
US	United States	Estados Unidos
USAN	United States Adopted Names	United States Adopted Names
Ur	Uruguay	Uruguay
V.	See	Véase
Ven	Venezuela	Venezuela
vet	veterinary	veterinary
vi	verb, intransitive	verbo intransitivo
vr	verb, reflexive	verbo reflexivo
vt	verb, transitive	verbo transitivo
vulg	vulgar	vulgar
zool	zoology	zoología

ENGLISH-SPANISH

INGLÉS-ESPAÑOL

A

AA V. **Alcoholics Anonymous**.

abacavir n abacavir m

abdomen n abdomen m, barriga, estómago (fam)

abdominal adj abdominal

abdominoplasty n (pl -ties) abdominoplastia

ability n (pl -ties) capacidad f, habilidad f; — **to drive** capacidad para manejar

ablation n ablación f; **radiofrequency** — ablación por or con radiofrecuencia; **radioiodine** — ablación con yodo radiactivo

abnormal adj anormal

abnormality n (pl -ties) anormalidad f

abort vt, vi abortar

abortifacient adj & n abortivo

abortion n aborto provocado or inducido, aborto, interrupción voluntaria del embarazo; **habitual** — aborto habitual; **incomplete** — aborto incompleto; **partial birth** — aborto por nacimiento parcial; **spontaneous** — aborto espontáneo; **therapeutic** — aborto terapéutico; **threatened** — amenaza de aborto; **to have an** — tener un aborto

above adv arriba; prep encima de; (number) superior a, por encima de, arriba de; **Keep your feet elevated above the level of your heart**..Mantenga los pies elevados encima del nivel del corazón...**Your sugar is above 500**..Su azúcar está superior a (por encima de, arriba de) 500.

abrasion n abrasión f (form), raspadura

abrasive adj & n abrasivo

abruptio placentae n (form) desprendimiento prematuro de placenta

abscess n absceso

absence n ausencia, falta

absent adj ausente

absenteeism n absentismo, ausentismo (esp. Amer)

absent-minded adj distraído, despistado

absorb vt absorber

absorbable adj (suture) absorbible, reabsorbible (esp. Esp)

absorbent adj absorbente

absorption n absorción f

abstain vi abstenerse; **to** — **from sex** abstenerse del sexo

abstinence n abstinencia

abuse n abuso, maltrato; **child** — maltrato or abuso infantil, maltrato a (los) niños, abuso de (los) niños; **drug** — abuso de drogas; **drug of** — droga de abuso; **elder** — maltrato a (las) personas mayores, maltrato a (los) adultos mayores (Amer); **physical** — maltrato or abuso físico; **psychological** — maltrato or abuso psicológico; **sexual** — maltrato or abuso sexual; **substance** — abuso de sustancias, abuso de drogas o alcohol; vt abusar, maltratar; **to** — **drugs** abusar de drogas

abuser n abusador -ra mf; **drug** — drogadicto -ta mf, persona que abusa de drogas

abusive adj abusivo

acalculous adj alitiásico, acalculoso

acanthosis nigricans n acantosis f nigricans

acarbose n acarbosa

acceptance n (stage of grief, etc.) aceptación f (etapa del duelo, etc.)

access n acceso; — **to treatment** acceso a tratamiento; **venous** — acceso venoso; **wheelchair** — acceso para silla(s) de ruedas

accessible adj accesible; **wheelchair** — accesible para silla(s) de ruedas, con acceso para silla(s) de ruedas

accessory adj accesorio

accident n accidente m; **by** — sin querer; **cerebrovascular** — accidente cerebrovascular; **traffic** o **motor vehicle** — accidente de tránsito or tráfico, choque m (fam); **work-related** — accidente de

trabajo
accidental *adj* accidental; — **death** muerte *f* accidental
acclimated *adj* aclimatado; **to become —** aclimatarse
accumulate *vt, vi* acumular(se)
accumulation *n* acumulación *f*
accuracy *n* exactitud *f*, precisión *f*
accurate *adj* exacto, preciso
acellular *adj* acelular
acetabulum *n* acetábulo
acetaminophen *n* acetaminofén *m*, acetaminofeno, paracetamol *m* (*INN*)
acetate *n* acetato
acetazolamide *n* acetazolamida
acetic acid *n* ácido acético
acetone *n* acetona
acetylcysteine *n* acetilcisteína
acetylsalicylic acid *n* ácido acetilsalicílico
achalasia *n* acalasia
ache *n* dolor sordo, dolor persistente; **side** — dolor de costado, dolor en el costado; **stomach** — dolor de estómago; *vi* doler
achondroplasia *n* acondroplasia
acid *adj & n* ácido; **fatty** — ácido graso (*V.* también **fatty acid**); **gastric** *o* **stomach** — ácido gástrico *or* del estómago
acidity *n* acidez *f*
acidophilus *n* acidophilus *m*
aclidinium bromide *n* bromuro de aclidinio
ACLS *abbr* **advanced cardiac life support.** *V.* **support.**
acne *n* acné *m&f* — **rosacea** acné rosácea; **cystic** — acné quístico; [*Note: feminine usage is correct from historical and etymological viewpoints, but masculine usage has become the norm, save for the endings of the adjectives in* el acné rosácea *and* el acné conglobata. Acné rosácea *is sometimes preceded by* la, acné conglobata *rarely.*]
acoustic *adj* acústico
acquire *vt* adquirir
acrochordon *n* (*derm*) acrocordón *m*
acromegaly *n* acromegalia
acrophobia *n* acrofobia
acrylamide *n* acrilamida
acrylic *adj & n* acrílico
act *n* acto; *vi* (*persona*) comportarse; (*un*

medicamento) funcionar, actuar; **intermediate-acting** de acción intermedia; **fast-acting** (*fam*) de acción rápida; **long-acting** de acción prolongada; **rapid-acting** de acción rápida; **short-acting** de acción corta; **to — out** (*psych*) expresar emociones o impulsos reprimidos
ACTH *abbr* **adrenocorticotropic hormone.** *V.* **hormone.**
acting out *n* (*psych*) paso al acto, expresión *f* de emociones o impulsos reprimidos
actinic *adj* actínico
actinomycosis *n* actinomicosis *f*
action *n* acción *f*
activate *vt* activar
activator *n* activador *m*
active *adj* activo; **sexually —** sexualmente activo; **Are you sexually active?..**¿Es Ud. sexualmente activo?.. ¿Está teniendo relaciones sexuales?
activity *n* (*pl* -ties) actividad *f*; **activities of daily living** actividades cotidianas; **strenuous activities** actividades extenuantes
actualization *n* (*psych*) actualización *f*
actually *adv* en realidad, realmente
acuity *n* agudeza; **visual —** agudeza visual
acupressure *n* acupresión *f*, tipo de masaje empleando presión de los dedos sobre ciertas áreas con el fin de curar
acupuncture *n* acupuntura
acute *adj* agudo
acyclovir *n* aciclovir *m*
adalimumab *n* adalimumab *m*
Adam's apple *n* manzana *or* nuez *f* de Adán
adapalene *n* adapaleno
adapt *vt, vi* adaptar(se)
adaptation *n* adaptación *f*
add *vt* añadir, agregar; (*arith*) sumar; **Can you add 7 and 16?..**¿Puede sumar 7 y 16?
addict *n* adicto -ta *mf*; **drug —** drogadicto -ta *mf*; **heroin —** heroinómano -na *mf*, adicto a la heroína
addicted *adj* adicto; **addicted to prescription drugs..**adicto a los medicamentos recetados; **to get** *o* **become —** volverse adicto
addiction *n* adicción *f*; **drug —** droga-

dicción *f*; **heroin** — adicción a la heroína

addictive *adj* adictivo, que crea dependencia

additive *adj & n* aditivo

address *n* dirección *f*, domicilio; **e-mail** — dirección de correo electrónico

adefovir *n* adefovir *m*

adenitis *n* adenitis *f*

adenocarcinoma *n* adenocarcinoma *m*

adenoidectomy *n* (*pl* -mies) adenoidectomía

adenoids *npl* adenoides *fpl*

adenoma *n* adenoma *m*; **villous** — adenoma velloso

adenomatous *adj* adenomatoso

adenomyosis *n* adenomiosis *f*

adenosine *n* adenosina

adenovirus *n* adenovirus *m*

adequate *adj* adecuado, suficiente

ADHD *abbr* **attention deficit hyperactivity disorder.** *V.* **disorder.**

adherence *adj* adherencia; — **to treatment** adherencia al tratamiento

adherent *adj* adherido

adhesion *n* adherencia, brida

adhesive *adj & n* adhesivo

adjust *vt* ajustar; (*chiropractic*) realizar un ajuste; *vi* adaptar; **well-adjusted** bien adaptado

adjustable *adj* ajustable, regulable, graduable

adjustment *n* (*chiropractic, etc.*) ajuste *m*

adjuvant *adj* adyuvante

administer *vt* (*a drug, etc.*) administrar

administrate *vt* administrar

administration *n* administración *f*; **Food and Drug Administration (FDA)** Administración de Alimentos y Drogas

administrator *n* administrador -ra *mf*

admission *n* ingreso

admit *vt* (*pret & pp* **admitted**; *ger* **admitting**) (*to the hospital*) ingresar, admitir (*al hospital*); **We need to admit him**..Tenemos que ingresarlo.

adnexal *adj* anexial

adolescence *n* adolescencia

adolescent *adj & n* adolescente *mf*

adopt *vt* adoptar

adoption *n* adopción *f*

adoptive *adj* adoptivo; — **parents** padres adoptivos

adrenal *adj* suprarrenal; *n* (*fam*) glándula suprarrenal, suprarrenal *f* (*fam*)

adrenalectomy *n* (*pl* -ties) adrenalectomía, suprarrenalectomía

adrenaline *n* adrenalina

adsorbent *adj* adsorbente

adult *adj & n* adulto -ta *mf*

adulterated *adj* adulterado

adulthood *n* edad adulta

advanced *adj* avanzado

advance directive *n* documento de voluntad anticipada (*Amer*), documento de voluntades anticipadas (*Esp*), documento de instrucciones previas, documento que indica de antemano la atención médica deseada en caso de coma u otra incapacidad para expresarse; (*living will*) testamento vital

advantage *n* ventaja; **the advantages and disadvantages**..las ventajas e inconvenientes..las ventajas y desventajas

adverse *adj* adverso

advice *n* consejo

advise *vt* aconsejar

advisory *n* aviso; **(public) health** — aviso sanitario

advocate *n* defensor -ra *mf*; **patient** — defensor del paciente

AED *abbr* **automated external defibrillator.** *V.* **defibrillator.**

aerobic *adj* (*exercise*) aeróbico; (*micro*) aerobio

aerobics *npl* aeróbic *m*, aeróbics *mpl* (*esp. Mex*), aeróbicos (*esp. SA*); **low impact** — aeróbic (aeróbics, aeróbicos) de bajo impacto

aerosol *n* aerosol *m*

aerosolized *adj* en aerosol

affect *n* (*psych*) afecto; **blunted** — afecto embotado; **flat** — afecto aplanado; *vt* afectar; **affected by**..afectado por

affection *n* cariño, afecto

affectionate *adj* cariñoso, afectuoso

affliction *n* aflicción *f*, mal *m*, padecimiento

affordable *adj* asequible; **Affordable Care Act** (*US*) Ley *f* de Asistencia Asequible, ley aprobada en 2010 para reformar aspectos disfuncionales del sistema de salud de los EEUU

aflatoxin *n* aflatoxina

afraid *adj* **to be** — tener miedo, temer;

Are you afraid of needles?..¿Les tiene miedo a las agujas?...**I'm afraid that** ..Me temo que

after *adv* después (de); **after you eat**.. después de comer; *prep* después de; **after a week**..después de una semana; — **meals** después de las comidas; **the day** — el día después

afterbirth *n* secundinas, placenta y membranas expulsadas después del parto

aftercare *n* cuidado posterior; cuidado que sigue una cirugía, un procedimiento, una hospitalización, etc.

afternoon *n* tarde *f*

aftertaste *n* regusto, sabor *m* que deja la comida o medicamento, (*unpleasant*) resabio

against medical advice, en contra del consejo médico

agammaglobulinemia *n* agammaglobulinemia

age *n* edad *f*; **bone** — edad ósea; **childbearing** — edad fértil; **gestational** — edad gestacional; **middle** — mediana edad; **old** — vejez *f*, tercera edad (*euph*)

agency *n* (*pl* **-cies**) agencia

agent *n* agente *m*; **Agent Orange** agente naranja

aggravate *vt* agravar, empeorar

aggression *n* agresión *f*, hostilidad *f*

aggressive *adj* agresivo

agile *adj* ágil

aging *n* envejecimiento

agitated *adj* agitado; **to become** — agitarse

ago *adj & adv* **two weeks ago**..hace dos semanas

agonal *adj* agónico

agony *n* agonía, dolor intenso, angustia extrema

agoraphobia *n* agorafobia

agree *vi* **This pill didn't agree with me**.. Esta pastilla me cayó *or* sentó mal.

agricultural *adj* agrícola

aid *n* ayuda, auxilio, socorro; **hearing** — audífono; *vt* ayudar, asistir, auxiliar

aide *n* auxiliar *mf*, asistente *mf*, ayudante *mf*; **nurse** — auxiliar de enfermería

AIDS *abbr* **acquired immunodeficiency syndrome**. *V.* **syndrome**.

ailment *n* enfermedad *f*, achaque *m*, mal

m, molestia, padecimiento

air *n* aire *m*; **room** — aire ambiente

airbag *n* bolsa de aire, airbag *m* (*Ang*)

airborne *adj* (*polen, etc.*) transportado por el aire, suspendido en el aire; (*bacterias, virus*) de transmisión aérea

air conditioning *n* aire acondicionado

airsickness *n* mareo (en avión)

airway *n* vía aérea (*frec. pl*); **upper** — vía(s) aérea(s) superior(es); **lower** — vía(s) aérea(s) inferior(es)

akathisia *n* acatisia

alanine *n* alanina

alarm *n* alarma; **bed** — alarma de cama

albendazole *n* albendazol *m*

albinism *n* albinismo

albino *adj* albino; *n* (*pl* **-nos**) albino -na *mf*

albumin *n* albúmina

albuminuria *n* albuminuria

albuterol *n* salbutamol *m*, albuterol *m*

alcohol *n* alcohol *m*, bebidas alcohólicas (*incluyendo vino y cerveza*); **Do you drink alcohol?**..¿Toma Ud. bebidas alcohólicas? ¿vino? ¿cerveza?; **denatured** — alcohol desnaturalizado; **rubbing** — alcohol para fricciones, alcohol para frotar

alcoholic *adj & n* alcohólico -ca *mf*; **recovering** — alcohólico en recuperación

Alcoholics Anonymous (AA) *n* Alcohólicos Anónimos (AA)

alcoholism *n* alcoholismo

aldosterone *n* aldosterona

aldosteronism *n* aldosteronismo

alendronate, alendronate sodium (*USAN*), **alendronic acid** (*INN*) *n* alendronato, alendronato sódico, ácido alendrónico (*INN*)

alert *adj* alerta; *n* alerta; **health** — alerta sanitaria, alerta sobre peligro para la salud de una población

alertness *n* estado de alerta, vigilancia

alfalfa *n* (*bot*) alfalfa

alfuzosin *n* alfuzosina

alga *n* (*pl* **-gae**) (*frec. pl*) alga; **blue-green algae** algas verdeazuladas

alginate *n* alginato

alienated *adj* (*psych*) alienado, aislado emocionalmente

alienation *n* (*psych*) alienación *f*, aislamiento emocional

align *vt, vi* alinear(se)
alignment *n* alineación *f*
alimentary *adj* alimentario
alive *adj* vivo, con vida
alkaline *adj* alcalino; — **phosphatase** fosfatasa alcalina
alkalosis *n* alcalosis *f*
alkaptonuria *n* alcaptonuria
allergen *n* alérgeno *or* alergeno
allergic *adj* alérgico; **Are you allergic to any medicine?**..¿Es Ud. alérgico a algún medicamento?
allergist *n* alergólogo -ga *mf*, médico -ca *mf* especializado en alergias
allergy *n* (*pl* **-gies**) alergia; **seasonal —** alergia estacional
alleviate *vt* aliviar
allograft *n* aloinjerto
allopath *n* alópata *mf*
allopathic *adj* alopático
allopathy *n* alopatía
allopurinol *n* alopurinol *m*
allowance *n* **recommended daily —** (*ant*) ingesta diaria recomendada (*V. también* **intake**.)
all right *adj* bien; **Are you all right?**.. ¿Estás bien?
almotriptan *n* almotriptán *m*
aloe *n* (*bot*) aloe *or* áloe *m*, sábila, acíbar *m*
alone *adj* solo; **to feel —** sentirse solo; *adv* solo; **Do you live alone?**..¿Vive solo?
alopecia *n* alopecia
alpha *n* alfa; **— fetoprotein** alfa fetoproteína; **— galactosidase** alfa galactosidasa; **— hydroxy acids** ácidos alfa hidróxidos; **— methyldopa** alfa metildopa
alprazolam *n* alprazolam *m*
alternate *adj* alterno; **— days** días alternos; un día sí, un día no; *vt, vi* alternar
alternative *n* alternativa
altitude *n* altura, altitud *f*; **high —** gran altura *or* altitud; **at high —** en altura *or* altitud
alum *n* alumbre *m*
aluminum *n* aluminio; **— chloride** cloruro de aluminio; **— hydroxide** hidróxido de aluminio
alveolar proteinosis *n* proteinosis *f* alveolar
alveolus *n* (*pl* **-li**) alvéolo *or* alveolo

always *adv* siempre; **almost —** casi siempre
amalgam *n* (*dent*) amalgama
amantadine *n* amantadina
ambidextrous *adj* ambidiestro
ambivalence *n* ambivalencia
amblyopia *n* ambliopía, ojo perezoso *or* vago (*fam*), disminución *f* de la agudeza visual sin lesión orgánica del ojo
ambulance *n* ambulancia
ambulate *vi* (*form*) deambular, caminar
ambulation *n* deambulación *f*, ambulación *f*, (el) caminar
ambulatory *adj* ambulatorio
ameba *n* (*pl* **-bae** *o* **-bas**) ameba *or* amiba
amebiasis *n* amebiasis *or* amibiasis *f*
amebic *adj* amebiano *or* amibiano
amenorrhea *n* amenorrea
amiloride *n* amilorida
amino acid *n* aminoácido
amiodarone *n* amiodarona
amitriptyline *n* amitriptilina
amlodipine *n* amlodipino, amlodipina
ammonia *n* amoniaco *or* amoníaco
ammonium *n* amonio; **— carbonate** carbonato de amonio, carbonato amónico (*esp. Esp*)
amnesia *n* amnesia
amniocentesis *n* (*pl* **-ses**) amniocentesis *f*
amnionitis *n* amnionitis *f*
amniotic *adj* amniótico; **— fluid** líquido amniótico
amoeba *n* (*pl* **-bae** *o* **-bas**) ameba *or* amiba
amoebiasis *n* amebiasis *or* amibiasis *f*
amoebic *adj* amebiano *or* amibiano
amount *n* cantidad *f*
amoxicillin *n* amoxicilina
amphetamine *n* anfetamina
amphotericin B *n* anfotericina B
ampicillin *n* ampicilina
amprenavir *n* amprenavir *m*
ampule *n* ampolla, ámpula (*Mex, Cuba*)
ampulla of Vater *n* ampolla de Vater
amputate *vt* amputar
amputation *n* amputación *f*; **above-the-knee —** amputación por encima de la rodilla; **below-the-knee —** amputación por debajo de la rodilla
amputee *n* amputado -da *mf*
amygdala *n* amígdala (cerebral)

amylase *n* amilasa
amyloidosis *n* amiloidosis *f*
amyotrophic *adj* amiotrófico
ANA *abbr* **antinuclear antibody.** *V.* **antibody.**
anabolic *adj* anabolizante, anabólico
anaerobic *adj* (*esp. metabolism*) anaeróbico, (*organism*) anaerobio
anal *adj* anal
analgesia *n* analgesia, supresión *f* de sensación dolorosa en el paciente consciente; **patient-controlled** — analgesia controlada por el paciente
analgesic *adj & n* analgésico
analogue *n* análogo
analysis *n* (*pl* **-ses**) análisis *m*; (*psych, fam*) psicoanálisis *m*, análisis *m* (*fam*); **semen** — análisis de semen
analyst *n* (*psych, fam*) psicoanalista *mf*, analista *mf* (*fam*)
analyze *vt* analizar; (*psych, fam*) psicoanalizar, analizar (*fam*)
analyzer *n* analizador *m*
anaphylactic *adj* anafiláctico
anaphylactoid *adj* anafilactoide
anaphylaxis *n* anafilaxia, anafilaxis *f*
anastomosis *n* anastomosis *f*
anastrozole *n* anastrozol *m*
anatomical, anatomic *adj* anatómico
anatomy *n* anatomía
ancestor *n* antepasado
ancillary *adj* auxiliar
ancylostomiasis *n* anquilostomiasis *f*
androgen *n* andrógeno
androgyny *n* androginia
andropause *n* andropausia
anemia *n* anemia; **aplastic** — anemia aplásica; **hemolytic** — anemia hemolítica; **iron deficiency** — anemia ferropénica (*form*), anemia por deficiencia de hierro; **pernicious** — anemia perniciosa; **sickle cell** — anemia falciforme *or* drepanocítica *or* de células falciformes; **sideroblastic** — anemia sideroblástica
anemic *adj* anémico
anencephaly *n* anencefalia
anergy *n* anergia
anesthesia *n* anestesia; **epidural** — anestesia epidural; **general** — anestesia general; **local** — anestesia local; **regional** — anestesia regional; **spinal** — anestesia raquídea

anesthesiologist *n* anestesiólogo -ga *mf*, médico -ca *mf* especializado en anestesia, médico que duerme a los pacientes durante una cirugía
anesthesiology *n* anestesiología
anesthetic *adj & n* anestésico; **general** — anestésico general; **local** — anestésico local
anesthetist *V.* **nurse anesthetist.**
anesthetize *vt* anestesiar, quitar la sensación de dolor
aneurysm *n* aneurisma *m*; **abdominal aortic** — aneurisma aórtico abdominal, aneurisma de aorta abdominal; **dissecting** — aneurisma disecante; **mycotic** — aneurisma micótico
angelica *n* (*bot*) angélica
anger *n* ira, enojo; — **management** manejo de la ira *or* del enojo, control *m* de la ira *or* del enojo
angiitis *n* vasculitis *f*, angeítis *f*, angitis *f* (*RAE*)
angina *n* angina (de pecho); **unstable** — angina inestable; **variant** —, **Prinzmetal** —, **vasospastic** — angina variante *or* de Prinzmetal *or* vasoespástica; **Vincent's** — angina de Vincent
anginal *adj* anginoso
angiodysplasia *n* angiodisplasia
angioedema *n* angioedema *m*
angiogram *n* angiografía (*estudio*)
angiography *n* angiografía, arteriografía (*técnica*); **computed tomographic** — angiografía por tomografía computarizada
angioma *n* angioma *m*; **cherry** — hemangioma *m* capilar; **spider** — araña vascular, angioma aracniforme
angiomatosis *n* angiomatosis *f*; **bacillary** — angiomatosis bacilar
angioplasty *n* (*pl* **-ties**) angioplastia; **percutaneous transluminal coronary** — **(PTCA)** angioplastia coronaria transluminal percutánea (ACTP)
angiosarcoma *n* angiosarcoma *m*
angiotensin *n* angiotensina
angle *n* ángulo
angry *adj* enojado; **to get** — enojarse, enfadarse
anguish *n* angustia
anhedonia *n* (*psych*) anhedonia
aniline *n* anilina
animal *adj & n* animal *m*; **companion** —

animal de compañía; **service** — animal de servicio

ankle *n* tobillo; — **jerk** reflejo aquíleo

anklebone *n* hueso del tobillo

ankylosing spondylitis *n* espondilitis *f* anquilosante

ankylosis *n* anquilosis *f*

annoying *adj* molesto, fastidioso

annual *adj* anual

annular *adj* anular

anointing of the sick, unción *f* de los enfermos

anomaly *n* (*pl* -lies) anomalía; **congenital** — anomalía congénita

anomie *f* (*psych*) anomia

anorexia *n* anorexia; — **nervosa** anorexia nerviosa

anorexiant *adj & n* anorexígeno

anovulation *n* anovulación *f*

anovulatory *adj* anovulatorio

ant *n* hormiga

antacid *adj & n* antiácido

antagonist *n* antagonista *m*; **calcium** — antagonista del calcio; **CCR5** — antagonista del CCR5

anterior *adj* anterior

anthelmintic *adj & n* antihelmíntico

anthracosis *n* antracosis *f*

anthrax *n* carbunco, ántrax *m* (*Ang*)

antianginal *adj & n* antianginoso

antianxiety *adj* ansiolítico, que calma la ansiedad

antiarrhythmic *adj & n* antiarrítmico

antiasthmatic *adj & n* antiasmático

antibacterial *adj* antibacteriano

antibiotic *adj & n* antibiótico; **broad-spectrum** — antibiótico de amplio espectro

antibody *n* (*pl* -dies) anticuerpo; **antibodies against your own sperm**..anticuerpos contra sus propios espermatozoides; **antimitochondrial** — anticuerpo antimitocondrial; **antinuclear** — (**ANA**) anticuerpo antinuclear (**AAN**); **antiphospholipid** — anticuerpo antifosfolípido

anticancer *adj* antineoplásico (*form*), anticanceroso

anticholinergic *adj & n* anticolinérgico

anticoagulant *adj & n* anticoagulante *m*; **lupus** — anticoagulante lúpico

anticoagulate *vt* tratar con anticoagulante, anticoagular

anticonvulsant *adj & n* antiepiléptico, anticonvulsivante *m*

antidepressant *adj & n* antidepresivo; **tricyclic** — antidepresivo tricíclico

antidiarrheal *adj & n* antidiarreico

antidote *n* antídoto

antidrug *adj* antidroga

antiemetic *adj & n* antiemético

antiepileptic *adj & n* antiepiléptico

anti-flu *adj* antigripal

antifreeze *n* anticongelante *m*

antifungal *adj & n* antifúngico, antimicótico

antigas *adj* antigás, contra los gases

antigen *n* antígeno; **carcinoembryonic** — antígeno carcinoembrionario; **prostate-specific** — (**PSA**) antígeno prostático específico (APE)

antihistamine *adj & n* antihistamínico

antihistaminic *adj* antihistamínico

antihypertensive *adj & n* antihipertensivo

antiinflammatory *adj & n* antiinflamatorio

antimalarial *adj* antipalúdico, contra la malaria *or* el paludismo; *n* antipalúdico, medicamento para la malaria

antimicrobial *adj & n* antimicrobiano

antimonial *n* antimonial *m*

antioxidant *adj & n* antioxidante *m*

antiparasitic *adj* antiparasitario

antiperspirant *adj & n* antitranspirante *m*

antipsychotic *adj & n* antipsicótico

antipyretic *adj & n* antipirético, antitérmico

antireflux *adj* antirreflujo

antiretroviral *adj & n* antirretroviral *m*

antiseptic *adj & n* antiséptico

antiserum *n* (*pl* -ra) antisuero

antismoking *adj* contra el tabaco, antitabaco

antisocial *adj* antisocial

antispasmodic *adj & n* antiespasmódico

antithrombotic *adj & n* antitrombótico

antitoxin *n* antitoxina

antivenin, antivenom *n* antiveneno

antiviral *adj & n* antiviral *m*

anus *n* (*pl* anuses) ano

anxiety *n* ansiedad *f*, angustia; **performance** — ansiedad de ejecución *or* desempeño

anxiolitic *adj & n* ansiolítico

anxious *adj* ansioso, nervioso
aorta *n* aorta
aortic *adj* aórtico
apathetic *adj* apático
apathy *n* apatía
Apgar (*fam*) Apgar score. *V.* score.
aphasia *n* afasia, dificultad *f* para entender o para expresarse debida a una lesión del cerebro; **expressive** — afasia expresiva; **receptive** — afasia receptiva
apheresis *n* aféresis *f*
aphrodisiac *adj & n* afrodisíaco *or* afrodisiaco
aphthous *adj* aftoso
apixaban *n* apixabán *m*
aplastic *adj* aplásico
apnea *n* apnea; **obstructive sleep** — apnea obstructiva del sueño
apparatus *n* (*pl* -tuses) aparato
appear *vi* aparecer
appearance *n* apariencia, aspecto
appendectomy *n* (*pl* -mies) apendicectomía
appendicitis *n* apendicitis *f*
appendix *n* (*pl* -dices *o* -dixes) apéndice *m*
appetite *n* apetito
apple *n* manzana
appliance *n* (*dent, etc.*) aparato
application *n* aplicación *f*; (*for insurance, etc.*) solicitud *f*
applicator *n* aplicador *m*; **cotton** — aplicador de algodón
apply *vt* (*pret & pp* applied) aplicar; (*for insurance, etc.*) solicitar
appointment *n* cita
approach *n* abordaje *m*; **surgical** — abordaje quirúrgico
appropriate *adj* adecuado, apropiado
approximately *adv* aproximadamente
apraxia *n* apraxia
apron *n* delantal *m*; **lead** — delantal de plomo
aptitude *n* aptitud *f*
aqueous *adj* acuoso
arch *n* arco; — **of the foot** arco del pie; **fallen** — arco caído, pie plano
ARDS *abbr* adult respiratory distress syndrome. *V.* syndrome.
area *n* área, zona, región *f*, parte *f*
argatroban *n* argatroban *m*
arginine *n* arginina

argon *n* argón *m*
aripiprazole *n* aripiprazol *m*
arm *n* brazo; **upper** — parte *f* superior del brazo
armadillo *n* armadillo
armamentarium *n* arsenal terapéutico
armpit *n* (*fam*) axila, sobaco (*fam*)
armrest *n* reposabrazos *m*
arnica *n* (*bot*) árnica
aromatherapy *n* aromaterapia, uso del aroma de los aceites esenciales para curar
around *adv* alrededor; aproximadamente; *prep* alrededor de; **around your arm.**.alrededor de su brazo
arousal *n* (*from sleep*) (el) despertar; (*sexual*) excitación *f*
arouse *vt* (*from sleep*) despertar; (*sexually, etc.*) excitar
arrest *n* paro; **cardiac** — paro cardíaco; **cardiorespiratory** — paro cardiorrespiratorio; **respiratory** — paro respiratorio
arrhythmia *n* arritmia
arsenic *n* arsénico; — **trioxide** trióxido de arsénico
ART *abbr* antiretroviral therapy. *V.* therapy.
artemisinin *n* artemisinina
arterial *adj* arterial
arteriosclerosis *n* arteriosclerosis *or* arterioesclerosis *f*
arteriovenous *adj* arteriovenoso
arteritis *n* arteritis *f*; **giant cell** — arteritis de células gigantes; **Takayasu's** — arteritis de Takayasu; **temporal** — arteritis temporal
artery *n* (*pl* -ries) arteria; **brachial** — arteria braquial *or* humeral; (**common**) **carotid** — arteria carótida (común); **circumflex (coronary)** — arteria (coronaria) circunfleja; **coronary** — arteria coronaria; **femoral** — arteria femoral; **iliac** — arteria ilíaca *or* iliaca; **left anterior descending (coronary)** — arteria (coronaria) descendente anterior izquierda; **left (main) coronary** — arteria coronaria (principal) izquierda; (**superior, inferior**) **mesenteric** — arteria mesentérica (superior, inferior); **popliteal** — arteria poplítea; **radial** — arteria radial; **right coronary** — arteria coronaria derecha; **subclavian** —

arteria subclavia
arthritic *adj* artrítico
arthritis *n* artritis *f*; **juvenile —** artritis juvenil; **reactive —** artritis reactiva; **rheumatoid —** artritis reumatoide
arthrogram *n* artrografía (*estudio*)
arthrography *n* artrografía (*técnica*)
arthroplasty *n* (*pl* **-ties**) artroplastia
arthroscopic *adj* artroscópico
arthroscopy *n* (*pl* **-pies**) artroscopia
articular *adj* articular
artificial *adj* artificial
asbestos *n* asbesto, amianto
asbestosis *n* asbestosis *f*
ascariasis *n* ascariasis *f*
ascending *adj* ascendente
ascites *n* ascitis *f*
ascorbic acid *n* ácido ascórbico
ASCUS *abbr* **atypical squamous cells of undetermined significance.** *V.* **cell.**
ASD *abbr* **atrial septal defect.** *V.* **defect.**
aseptic *adj* aséptico, estéril
ashamed *adj* avergonzado
asleep *adj* dormido; **to fall —** dormirse, quedarse dormido; **My foot fell asleep** ..Se me durmió el pie; **to stay —** permanecer dormido, mantener el sueño
asparagine *n* asparagina
asparagus *n* espárrago
aspartame *n* aspartame *m*, aspartamo
aspect *n* (*anat*) cara
aspergillosis *n* aspergilosis *f*
asphyxia *n* asfixia
asphyxiate *vt, vi* asfixiar(se)
aspirate *vt* (*to inhale*) aspirar; (*to remove fluid with a syringe*) aspirar, sacar líquido con una jeringa
aspiration *n* aspiración *f*; **needle —** aspiración con aguja
aspirin *n* aspirina
assault *n* asalto, agresión *f*; **sexual —** agresión sexual
assay *n* ensayo, análisis *m*, prueba; **interferon gamma release —** ensayo de liberación de interferón gamma, prueba del interferón gamma (*fam*)
assertiveness *n* asertividad *f*, autoafirmación *f*
assessment *n* evaluación *f*, valoración *f*
assimilation *n* (*psych*) asimilación *f*
assist *vt* asistir; **computer-assisted, vacuum-assisted, etc.** asistido por computadora, asistido por vacío, etc.

assistance *n* asistencia, ayuda
assistant *n* asistente *mf*, auxiliar *mf*, ayudante *mf*; **certified nursing —** auxiliar de enfermería certificado; **medical —** asistente médico, persona entrenada para ayudar al médico en el consultorio o en la clínica; **nursing —** auxiliar de enfermería; **physician's —** asistente médico, persona entrenada para diagnosticar y tratar enfermedades comunes bajo la supervisión de un médico
assisted living *adj* sociosanitario; *n* vida asistida; **— facility** *o* **center** centro sociosanitario
assistive *adj* que asiste, asistivo (*Ang*)
associated *adj* asociado
association *n* (*psych, etc.*) asociación *f*; **free —** asociación libre
asthenia *n* (*ant*) astenia
asthma *n* asma
asthmatic *adj* & *n* asmático -ca *mf*
astigmatism *n* astigmatismo
astringent *adj* & *n* astringente *m*
asylum *n* asilo; **insane —** (*ant*) hospital psiquiátrico *or* mental, manicomio (*ant*)
asymptomatic *adj* asintomático
asystole *n* asistolia
ataxia *n* ataxia
ataxic *adj* atáxico
atazanavir *n* atazanavir *m*
ate *pret de* **eat**
atenolol *n* atenolol *m*
atheroma *n* ateroma *m*
atherosclerosis *n* aterosclerosis *or* ateroesclerosis *f*
athlete *n* atleta *mf*
athlete's foot *n* tinea pedis (*form*), pie *m* de atleta, infección *f* por hongos de los pies
athletic *adj* atlético; **— supporter** suspensorio
atomoxetine *n* atomoxetina
atopic *adj* atópico
atorvastatin *n* atorvastatina
atovaquone *n* atovacuona
atria *pl de* **atrium**
atrial *adj* auricular
atrioventricular *adj* auriculoventricular
atrium *n* (*pl* **atria**) (*of the heart*) aurícula
atrophy *n* atrofia; *vi* (*pret* & *pp* **-phied**)

(*también* **to become atrophied**) atrofiarse

atropine *n* atropina

attach *vt* ligar, conectar

attack *n* crisis *f* (*form*), ataque *m*; **anxiety** — crisis de ansiedad *or* angustia, ataque de ansiedad, ataque de nervios (*fam*); **asthma** — crisis asmática (*form*), ataque de asma; **heart** — infarto de miocardio (*form*), ataque cardíaco *or* al corazón; **panic** — ataque de pánico, ataque de nervios (*fam*); **transient ischemic** — (**TIA**) ataque isquémico transitorio (AIT)

attend *vt* (*a clinic, class, etc.*) asistir a; (*a patient*) atender, tratar, cuidar

attention *n* atención *f*; — **span** período de atención

attentive *adj* atento

attenuated *adj* atenuado

attitude *n* actitud *f*

atypical *adj* atípico

audiogram *n* audiograma *m*

audiologist *n* audiólogo -ga *mf*, especialista *mf* en audición

audiology *n* audiología, estudio de los trastornos de la audición

audiometer *n* audiómetro

audiometric *adj* audiométrico

audiometry *n* audiometría

auditory *adj* auditivo

augmentation *n* aumento; **breast** — aumento mamario *or* de senos

aunt *n* tía

aura *n* aura

autism *n* autismo

autistic *adj* autista; — **person** autista *mf*

autoclave *n* autoclave *f*

autoeczematization *n* autoeccematización *or* autoeczematización *f*, reacción *f* ide, dermatitis *f* por autosensibilización

autoimmune *adj* autoinmune

autoimmunity *n* autoinmunidad *f*

autoinjector *n* autoinyector *m*; **epinephrine** — autoinyector de epinefrina

autologous *adj* autólogo

automobile *n* automóvil *m*, coche *m*, carro

autonomy *n* autonomía; **patient** — autonomía del paciente

autopsy *n* (*pl* -**sies**) autopsia, necropsia

autosomal *adj* autosómico

autumn *n* otoño

auxiliary *adj* auxiliar

available *adj* disponible

average *adj* medio, promedio (*inv*); **the** — **height** la estatura media *or* promedio; *n* media, promedio; **above (the)** — superior a la media *or* al promedio, por encima de la media *or* del promedio; **below (the)** — inferior a la media *or* al promedio, por debajo de la media *or* del promedio; **on** — en promedio

aversion *n* aversión *f*

avocado *n* aguacate *m*

avoid *vt* evitar; **You should avoid salt..** Debe evitar la sal.

avoidance *n* evitación *f*, (el) evitar

awake *adj* despierto

aware *adj* consciente

awareness *n* concientización *f*, sensibilización *f*; **AIDS** — **week** semana de concientización *or* sensibilización del SIDA

axes *pl de* **axis**

axilla *n* (*pl* -**lae**) axila

axillary *adj* axilar

axis *n* (*pl* **axes**) eje *m*

azathioprine *n* azatioprina

azelaic acid *n* ácido azelaico

azelastine *n* azelastina

azithromycin *n* azitromicina

AZT *n* AZT *m&f*

B

babble (*ped*) *n* balbuceo; *vi* balbucear
babesiosis *n* babesiosis *f*
baby *n* (*pl* **-bies**) bebé *mf*, criatura (*fam*)
baby-sitter *n* niñero -ra *mf*, persona que cuida niños
bacille Calmette-Guérin (BCG) *n* bacilo de Calmette-Guérin (BCG)
bacillus *n* (*pl* **-li**) bacilo
bacitracin *n* bacitracina
back *adj* de atrás; *adv* hacia atrás; *n* espalda; **— of the hand** dorso (de la mano), parte *f* de atrás de la mano; **low — pain** dolor *m* lumbar, dolor de la espalda baja, dolor de la parte baja de la espalda; **to have a bad —** (*fam*) estar mal de la espalda (*fam*), tener dolor de espalda crónico; **upper —** parte alta de la espalda, espalda superior (*form*)
backache *n* dolor *m* de espalda
backbone *n* columna vertebral, columna (*fam*)
backup *n* respaldo; **surgical —** respaldo quirúrgico
backward *adv* hacia atrás
baclofen *n* baclofeno
bacteremia *n* bacteriemia
bacteria *pl de* **bacterium**
bacterial *adj* bacteriano
bactericidal *adj* bactericida
bacterium *n* (*pl* **-ria**) (*frec. pl*) bacteria; **resistant bacteria** bacterias resistentes
bad *adj* (*comp* **worse**; *super* **worst**) malo*, nocivo (*form*), dañino; **Salt is bad for you.**.La sal es mala para Ud...**bad for your health** nocivo *or* malo para su salud...**a bad cold**..un resfriado fuerte
*malo become *mal* before masculine nouns: *un mal cáncer* (a bad cancer)
bag *n* bolsa; **— of waters** bolsa de las aguas; **colostomy —** bolsa de colostomía; **doctor's —** maletín del médico; **hot-water —** bolsa de agua caliente; **to have bags under one's eyes** (*fam*) tener los ojos hinchados
bake *vt* hornear, cocer al horno
balance *n* equilibrio
balanced *adj* equilibrado, balanceado
balanitis *n* balanitis *f*

bald *adj* calvo
baldness *n* calvicie *f*; **frontal —** calvicie frontal; **vertex —** calvicie del vértice, calvicie de la parte superior de la cabeza
ball *n* pelota, balón *m*; (*of cotton*) torunda; (*fam o vulg, testicle*) testículo, huevo (*esp. Mex, fam or vulg*)
balloon *n* (*of a catheter*) balón *m* (*de una sonda*)
balm *n* bálsamo; **lip —** bálsamo *or* protector *m* labial
banana *n* plátano, banana (*Arg, Ecu, Esp*), banano (*Col*), guineo (*Carib*)
band *n* cinta, banda; (*orthodontics*) banda; **adjustable gastric —** banda gástrica ajustable
bandage *n* (*material*) venda, (*once placed*) vendaje *m*; **adhesive —** vendaje adhesivo, venda adhesiva, cura; (*small*) curita (*Amer*), tirita (*Esp*); **compression —** vendaje compresivo; **elastic —** venda elástica, vendaje elástico; **figure-of-eight —** vendaje en ocho; **pressure —** vendaje compresivo
Band-Aid *n* (*marca*) *V.* **small adhesive bandage** *bajo* **bandage**.
banding *n* banda; **laparoscopic adjustable gastric —** banda gástrica ajustable laparoscópica *or* por laparoscopía
bank *n* banco; **blood —** banco de sangre; **food —** banco de alimentos; **organ —** banco de órganos
bar *n* barra; **grab —** agarradera, barra de seguridad
barb *n* púa, lengüeta
barbed wire *n* alambre *m* de púas
barber *n* barbero, peluquero -ra *mf*
barbiturate *n* barbitúrico
bare *adj* desnudo, descubierto
barefoot *adj* descalzo
barf (*fam o vulg*) *V.* **vomit**.
bargaining *n* (*stage of grief*) negociación *f* (*etapa del duelo*)
bariatric *adj* bariátrico
barium *n* bario
bark *n* (*bot*) corteza
barotrauma *n* barotrauma *m*
barrel *n* (*of a syringe*) cilindro; **— chest**

tórax en tonel

barrier *n* barrera; **placental** — barrera placentaria

basal *adj* basal, (*at rest*) en reposo

basal ganglia *npl* ganglios basales

base *n* (*chem, pharm, etc.*) base *f*; (*of an ulcer*) base, fondo (*de una úlcera*); **data** — base de datos; **evidence-based** basado en la evidencia; **oil-based**, **water-based**, etc. a base de aceite, a base de agua, etc.

baseball *n* beisbol *m*

baseline *adj* basal; — **value** valor *m* basal; *n* (*something measured*) línea de base; (*behavior, physical exam*) estado habitual *or* normal

bashful *adj* tímido

basic *adj* básico

basin *n* vasija, palangana; **emesis** — riñonera, recipiente *m* para vómito(s)

basketball *n* (*sport*) baloncesto, basquetbol *m*

bassinet *n* moisés *m*, cuna portátil

bat *n* (*zool*) murciélago

bath *n* baño; **sitz** — baño de asiento; **sponge** — baño de esponja; **steam** — baño de vapor; **to take a** — bañarse

bathe *vt, vi* bañar(se)

bathroom *n* cuarto de baño, baño; **to go to the** — ir al baño

bathtub *n* bañera, tina (de baño), bañadera (*Cuba*)

battered *adj* golpeado, maltratado

battle *n* lucha; — **against cancer** lucha contra el cáncer

BCG *V.* bacille Calmette-Guérin.

beam *n* (*of light, X-rays, etc.*) haz *m*

beans *npl* frijoles *mpl*, judías (*Esp*)

bear *vt* (*pret* bore; *pp* borne) tolerar, aguantar, soportar; (*to give birth to*) dar a luz; **child-bearing age** edad fértil; **to** — **down** pujar; **Bear down as if you were having a bowel movement**.. Puje como si estuviera defecando (haciendo popó); **to** — **weight** soportar peso; **You shouldn't bear weight with your left leg for two weeks**..No debe soportar peso con su pierna izquierda durante semanas.

bearable *adj* soportable, tolerable

beard *n* barba

beat *n* (*of the heart*) latido; *vt* (*pret & pp* beat) (*fam*) superar; **He beat cancer**..

Superó el cáncer; *vi* (*one's heart*) latir

beclomethasone (*USAN*), **beclometasone** (*INN*) *n* beclometasona

become *vi* ponerse, volverse, (*permanently*) quedarse; (*inflamed, sick, etc.*) inflamarse, enfermarse, etc.; **If it becomes swollen**..Si se pone hinchado... **She became blind**..Se quedó ciega...**It became inflamed**..Se puso inflamado.. Se inflamó.

bed *n* cama, lecho; — **rest** reposo en cama; **hospital** — cama de hospital; **nail** — lecho ungueal; **sick** — lecho de enfermo, lecho; **to stay in** — guardar cama; **vascular** — lecho vascular

bedbug *n* chinche *f*

bedclothes *npl* ropa de cama

bedding *n* ropa de cama

bedpan *n* cuña, chata, bacinica *or* bacinilla

bedrail *n* barandilla, baranda

bedridden *adj* encamado, incapaz de abandonar la cama

bedroom *n* habitación *f*, dormitorio, recámara (*esp. Mex*)

bedsheet *n* sábana

bedside *adj* de cabecera; — **manner** actitud *f* (del médico) hacia el paciente; **at the** — a la cabecera

bedsore *n* úlcera de decúbito (*form*), úlcera por presión, llaga debida a permanecer mucho tiempo sentado o encamado sin cambiar de posición

bedtime *n* hora de acostarse

bed wetting *n* enuresis *f* (*form*), (el) orinarse en la cama, (el) mojar la cama

bee *n* abeja; **Africanized** — abeja africanizada; **killer** — abeja asesina

beef *n* carne *f* de vaca *or* res

beeper *n* buscapersonas *m*

beer *n* cerveza

before *adv* antes; **Have you ever had these pains before?**..¿Ha tenido estos dolores antes?; *conj* antes de que; **before you take this medicine**..antes de que tome esta medicina; *prep* antes de; — **meals** antes de comer

begin *vt, vi* comenzar, empezar

behavior *n* comportamiento, conducta

behind *adj* atrasado; **Is he behind in school?**..¿Está atrasado en sus estudios?; *n* (*fam, buttocks*) nalgas, trasero (*fam*); *prep* detrás de

being *n* ser *m*; **human —** ser humano
belch *vi* eructar
belief *n* creencia
belladonna *n* (*bot*) belladona
belly *n* (*pl* **-lies**) abdomen *m*, barriga, estómago (*fam*)
bellyache *n* dolor *m* de barriga
bellybutton *n* (*fam*) ombligo
below *adv* abajo; *prep* por debajo de; (*number*) inferior a, por debajo de; **below the waist**..por debajo de la cintura; **below 200**..inferior a 200..por debajo de 200
belt *n* cinturón *m*, cinto; **seat** *o* **safety —** cinturón *m* de seguridad, cinturón (*fam*)
benazepril *n* benazepril *m*
bend *n* curva, ángulo; **deep knee —** sentadilla; *vt* (*pret & pp* **bent**) doblar; **Bend your knee**.. Doble la rodilla; **to — one's head down** bajar *or* agachar la cabeza; *vi* doblarse; **to — over** *o* **down** inclinarse hacia adelante, doblarse, agacharse; **Bend over**..Inclínese hacia adelante.
bends, the *npl* enfermedad *f* por descompresión
beneficence *n* beneficencia
beneficial *adj* beneficioso
benefit *n* beneficio, bien *m*; **for your —** para su beneficio, por su bien
benign *adj* benigno
bent *pret & pp de* **bend**
benzatropine *n* benzatropina
benzene *n* benceno
benzoate *n* benzoato
benzodiazepine *n* benzodiazepina *or* benzodiacepina
benzoin *n* benzoína
benzonatate *n* benzonatato
benzoyl peroxide *n* peróxido de benzoílo
benztropine, benzatropine (*INN*) *n* benztropina, benzatropina (*INN*)
benzyl alcohol *n* alcohol bencílico
bereavement *n* luto, dolor *m* emocional por la pérdida de un ser amado
beriberi *n* beriberi *m*
bestiality *n* bestialidad *f*
beta *n* beta; **— blocker** beta-bloqueador *m*, beta-bloqueante *m*; **— carotene** betacaroteno; **beta-hemolytic** beta-hemolítico
betamethasone *n* betametasona

better (*comp de* **good** *y* **well**) *adj & adv* mejor; **to get —** (*patient*) recuperarse, (*pain*) aliviarse, (*wound*) sanar, (*illness, cough, etc.*) mejorar; **to make —** aliviar, mejorar
between *prep* entre; **between your teeth** ..entre sus dientes
bevel *n* (*of a needle, etc.*) bisel *m*
bezoar *n* bezoar *m*
bib *n* babero
bicarbonate *n* bicarbonato
biceps *n* bíceps *m*
bicuspid *adj & n* bicúspide *m*
bicycle *n* bicicleta; **stationary —** bicicleta estática; **to ride a —** ir *or* montar en bicicleta
bifocal *adj* bifocal; *npl* (*fam*) lentes *mpl or* gafas bifocales, bifocales *mpl or fpl* (*fam*)
big *adj* (*comp* **bigger**; *super* **biggest**) grande; (*fam, sibling*) mayor; **How big was it?**..¿Qué tan grande era?; **— sister** hermana mayor; **to get bigger** agrandarse, aumentar de tamaño
bilateral *adj* bilateral
bilberry *n* (*bot*) mirtilo, (tipo de) arándano
bile *n* bilis *f*
biliary *adj* biliar
bilirubin *n* bilirrubina
bill *n* (*statement of charges*) cuenta, factura
bind *vi* (*pret & pp* **bound**) (*clothing, etc.*) apretar
binge *n* (*alcohol*) borrachera (*esp. por varios días seguidos*); (*food*) atracón *m*, período de comer en exceso; **— eating** atracones de comida, (el) comer en exceso periódicamente; *vi* beber alcohol en exceso periódicamente; comer en exceso periódicamente
bioactive *adj* bioactivo
biochemical *adj* bioquímico
biochemistry *n* bioquímica
biodegradable *adj* biodegradable
bioengineering *n* bioingeniería
bioequivalence *n* bioequivalencia
bioequivalent *adj* bioequivalente
bioethics *n* bioética
biofeedback *n* biorretroalimentación *f*
biohazard *n* riesgo *or* peligro biológico
biohazardous *adj* biopeligroso, que presenta riesgo biológico

bioidentical *adj* bioidéntico
biologic, biological *adj* biológico; — **clock** reloj biológico; — **mother** madre biológica; *n (pharm)* biológico
biology *n* biología
biomechanics *n* biomecánica
biomedical *adj* biomédico
biopharmaceutical *n* biológico, biofármaco
bioprosthesis *n (pl -ses)* bioprótesis *f*
bioprosthetic *adj* bioprostésico
biopsy *n (pl -sies)* biopsia; **bone marrow** — biopsia de médula ósea; **breast** — biopsia de mama; **excisional** — biopsia escisional; **fine needle aspiration** — punción *f* aspiración con aguja fina; **incisional** — biopsia incisional; **liver** — biopsia de hígado; **prostate** — biopsia de próstata; **punch** — biopsia en sacabocados; **renal** — biopsia de riñón; **skin** — biopsia cutánea *or* de piel; **stereotactic** — biopsia estereotáxica
biorhythm *n* ritmo biológico
biostatistics *n* bioestadística
biotechnology *n* biotecnología
bioterrorism *n* bioterrorismo
BiPAP *(marca)* V. **bilevel positive airway pressure** *bajo* **pressure**.
biphasic *adj (pharm)* bifásico
bipolar *adj* bipolar
bird *n* ave *f*, pájaro
birth *n* nacimiento; *(childbirth)* parto; — **control** anticoncepción *f*, control *m* de la natalidad, método anticonceptivo; **Do you use birth control?**..¿Usa algún método anticonceptivo?; — **weight** peso al nacer; **breech** — parto de nalgas; **(blind, deaf, etc.) from** — (ciego, sordo, etc.) de nacimiento; **natural** — parto natural; **to give** — dar a luz, aliviarse *(Mex, fam)*, parir *(esp. Carib, fam)*; **She gave birth to a baby girl**..Dio a luz una niña.
birthday *n* cumpleaños *m*; **Happy birthday!**..¡Feliz cumpleaños!
birthing *n* parto asistido por un médico o partera con intervención mínima y en un ambiente natural y hogareño
birthmark *n* marca de nacimiento, antojo *(fam)*
bisacodyl *n* bisacodilo
bisexual *adj* bisexual

bismuth subsalicylate *n* subsalicilato de bismuto
bisoprolol *n* bisoprolol *m*
bisphenol A (BPA) *n* bisfenol A
bisphosphonate *n* bisfosfonato
bite *n (of food)* bocado; *(wound)* mordedura; *(of an insect)* picadura; *(dent)* mordida; *vt, vi (pret* bit; *pp* bitten *o* bit)* morder; *(insect)* picar; **Bite down**.. Apriete los dientes; **to** — **one's nails** comerse *or* morderse las uñas
bite block *n (dent)* bloque *m* de mordida
bitter *adj* amargo
black *adj* negro; **to** — **out** *(to lose consciousness)* desmayarse, perder el conocimiento *or* la conciencia; *(to suffer memory lapse)* sufrir una laguna mental, perder la memoria por un tiempo *(debido al alcohol)*
black-and-blue *adj (fam)* que tiene moretones
black cohosh *n (bot)* cimicífuga
black eye *n* ojo morado
blackhead *n* comedón *m (form)*, espinilla
blackish *adj* negruzco
blackout *n (loss of consciousness)* desmayo, pérdida de la conciencia *or* consciencia; *(memory lapse)* laguna mental, pérdida transitoria de la memoria *(debido al alcohol)*
black widow *n* viuda negra
bladder *n* vejiga; **neurogenic** — vejiga neurogénica, vejiga neurógena *(esp. Esp)*; **overactive** — vejiga hiperactiva
blade *n* hoja; **razor** — cuchilla (de afeitar), hoja de afeitar
bland *adj (food)* blanda
blanket *n* manta, frazada *(Amer)*, cobija *(esp. Mex)*, friza *(PR, SD)*; **electric** — manta eléctrica
blastomycosis *n* blastomicosis *f*
bleach *n* blanqueador *m*
bleed *n* hemorragia, sangrado; **(upper, lower) GI** — hemorragia digestiva (alta, baja), sangrado gastrointestinal (alto, bajo); *vi (pret & pp* bled)* sangrar
bleeding *adj* sangrante; — **ulcer** úlcera sangrante; *n* hemorragia, sangrado; **dysfunctional uterine** — hemorragia uterina disfuncional; **menstrual** — sangrado menstrual
bleomycin *n* bleomicina

blepharitis *n* blefaritis *f*

blepharoplasty *n* (*pl* **-ties**) blefaroplastia

blew *pret de* **blow**

blind *adj* ciego; — **person** ciego -ga *mf*

blindness *n* ceguera; **color** — daltonismo (*form*), dificultad *f* para diferenciar ciertos colores; **night** — ceguera nocturna

blind spot *n* escotoma *m* (*form*), área de ceguera en el campo visual; (*physiological*) punto ciego

blink *n* parpadeo; *vi* parpadear

blister *n* ampolla; **blood** — ampolla de sangre, ampolla que contiene sangre; **fever** — herpes *m* labial (*form*), fuego, calentura, erupción *f* en los labios (*debida al herpes*)

blister pack *n* envase *m* blister, blister *m* (*fam*)

bloated *adj* distendido, hinchado; **to feel** — sentirse hinchado, hincharse(*le*) (*a uno*) el estómago

bloating *n* distensión *f* abdominal, hinchazón *f* del estómago (*fam*)

block *n* bloqueo; **bundle branch** — bloqueo de rama; **heart** — bloqueo cardíaco; **nerve** — bloqueo nervioso; *vt* (*pharm, physio*) bloquear; (*anat, surg*) obstruir

blockage *n* obstrucción *f*, bloqueo

blocked *adj* obstruído (*form*), bloqueado, tapado (*fam*)

blocker *n* bloqueador *m,* bloqueante *m*; **angiotensin receptor** — bloqueador *or* antagonista *m* del receptor de angiotensina; **beta** — beta-bloqueador, beta-bloqueante; **calcium channel** — bloqueador *or* bloqueante de los canales del calcio; **H₂ blocker** bloqueador H₂; **neuromuscular** — bloqueador *or* bloqueante neuromuscular

blocking *n* (*psych*) bloqueo

blond *adj* rubio, güero (*Mex*); *n* rubio -bia *mf*, güe-ro -ra *mf*

blonde *adj* rubia, güera (*Mex*) *n* rubia, güera (*Mex*)

blood *n* sangre *f*; **arterial** — **gas** gasometría arterial, gases *mpl* arteriales; — **poisoning** (*ant*) septicemia (*form*), infección *f* de la sangre; — **pressure** *V.* **pressure**; — **pressure monitor** *V.* **monitor**; **cord** — sangre del cordón umbilical; **whole** — sangre total

bloodborne *adj* de transmisión sanguínea, transmitido por la sangre

bloodshot *adj* rojo (*el ojo*)

bloodstream *n* torrente sanguíneo

blood thinner *n* (*fam*) anticoagulante *m*

bloody *adj* sanguinolento (*form*), con sangre; — **discharge** secreción sanguinolenta, secreción con sangre; — **nose** (*fam*) hemorragia nasal (*form*), sangrado nasal *or* por la nariz; — **show** (*obst*) sangrado vaginal (*antes de la expulsión del feto*)

blot *n* blot *m*, tipo de prueba médica muy precisa; **Western (Southern, etc.)** — Western (Southern, etc.) blot; *vt* (*pret & pp* **blotted**; *ger* **blotting**) secar por presión con material absorbente

blotch *n* (*derm*) mancha, roncha

blouse *n* blusa

blow *n* golpe *m*; **psychological** — golpe psicológico; *vt, vi* (*pret* **blew**; *pp* **blown**) soplar; **Blow as hard as you can..**Sople lo más fuerte que pueda; **to** — **one's nose** sonarse la nariz, soplarse la nariz (*Carib*)

BLS *abbr* **basic life support**. *V.* **support**.

blue *adj* azul; (*fam, sad*) triste; **the blues** (*fam*) melancolía, tristeza

bluish *adj* azulado

blunt *adj* (*object*) romo, sin filo; (*trauma*) cerrado

blur *vi* (*pret & pp* **blurred**; *ger* **blurring**) (*one's vision*) nublarse, empañarse

blurred, blurry *adj* nublado, borroso; — **vision** visión nublada *or* borrosa

blush *vi* sonrojarse, ruborizarse

BM *V.* **bowel movement**.

BMI *abbr* **body mass index**. *V.* **index**.

board and care *n* (*US*) residencia para gente de edad avanzada o discapacitados en donde se ofrecen comidas y cuidados básicos como bañar, vestir, etc.

board-certified *adj* (*US*) que ha aprobado un examen estatal en su campo

boceprevir *n* boceprevir *m*

body *adj* corporal; *n* (*pl* **bodies**) cuerpo; — **heat** calor *m* corporal; — **language** lenguaje *m* corporal; — **odor** olor *m* corporal; **foreign** — cuerpo extraño; **out-of-body experience** experiencia extracorpórea *or* extracorporal; **upper — parte** *f* superior del cuerpo

bodybuilder *n* culturista *mf*, fisicoculturista *mf*

bodybuilding *n* culturismo, fisicoculturismo

bodywork *n* trabajo corporal

bodyworker *n* masajista *mf*, practicante *mf* de trabajo corporal

boil *n* forúnculo (*form*), nacido, absceso (de la piel), grano (grande); *vt* (*water*) hervir; (*vegetables, meat, etc.*) cocer, hervir; *vi* hervir

boiled *adj* (*water*) hervido; (*vegetables*) cocido, hervido

boiling *adj* hirviendo; **— water** agua hirviendo

bolus *n* bolo

bomb *n* bomba; **atomic —, atom —** (*fam*) bomba atómica; **time —** bomba de relojería, bomba de tiempo

bond (*obst, psych, etc.*) *n* vínculo (afectivo), lazo afectivo; *vi* establecer vínculos (afectivos), establecer un vínculo (afectivo)

bonding (*obst, psych*) *n* formación *f* de un vínculo *or* lazo afectivo

bone *adj* óseo; **— marrow** médula ósea; *n* hueso; (*of a fish*) espina; **ankle —** hueso del tobillo; **breast —** esternón *m* (*form*), hueso del pecho; **collar —** (*fam*) clavícula; **hip —** hueso de la cadera

boob *n* (*fam o vulg*) mama, seno, pecho

booger *n* (*fam o vulg*) moco (*esp. duro*)

booklet *n* folleto, libreta

boost *vt* (*one's immune system, etc.*) potenciar, reforzar, fortificar (*el sistema inmunitario, etc.*); **ritonavir-boosted darunavir** darunavir potenciado con ritonavir

booster *adj* de refuerzo; **— dose** dosis *f* de refuerzo; **— shot** (*fam*) vacuna de refuerzo, revacunación *f*

boot *n* bota; **Unna —** bota de Unna

booze *n* (*fam o vulg*) bebida alcohólica (*incluyendo vino y cerveza*)

border *n* (*edge, margin*) borde *m*, margen *m*

borderline *adj* (*psych*) límite; (*leprosy*) dimorfa; **— hypertension** prehipertensión *f*; **— diabetes** prediabetes *f*

bore *vt* aburrir

bore *pret de* **bear**

bored (*pp de* **bore**) *adj* aburrido; **to become —** aburrirse; **He gets bored easily**..Se aburre fácilmente.

boric acid *n* ácido bórico

born *adj* nacido; **to be —** nacer

borne *pp de* **bear**

borreliosis *n* borreliosis *f*; **Lyme —** borreliosis de Lyme

boss *n* jefe -fa *mf*, patrón -trona *mf*

botanical *adj* botánico; *n* medicina de origen botánico, planta medicinal

botch *vt* (*a surgery, etc.*) hacer mal (*una cirugía, etc.*)

bother *vt* molestar; **Is your neck bothering you?**..¿Le molesta el cuello?

bottle *n* botella; (*for pills*) botella, frasco, pomo (*Mex, CA*); **baby —** biberón *m*, mamadera (*Amer*), pacha (*CA*); **hot-water —** bolsa de agua caliente

bottom *n* fondo; (*fam, buttocks*) nalgas, trasero (*fam*)

botulinum toxin *n* toxina botulínica

botulism *n* botulismo

bound *pret & pp de* **bind**

bout *n* episodio, ataque *m*

bovine *adj* bovino

bowed *adj* (*curved*) encorvado, arqueado

bowel *n* intestino, tripa (*fam, frec. pl*); **large —** colon *m*, intestino grueso; **small —** intestino delgado

bowel movement (BM) *n* (*act*) defecación *f* (*form*), evacuación *f* (del intestino); (*stool*) heces *fpl* (*form*), popó (*fam*), caca (*esp. ped, fam or vulg*), deposición *f* (*Esp, SA; form*), evacuación *f*, excremento; **painful ——** defecación *or* evacuación dolorosa, dolor cuando va al baño; **to have a ——** defecar (*form*), ir al baño, hacer del baño (*Mex*), dar del cuerpo (*Carib*), hacer del cuerpo (*SA*), hacer popó (*fam*), hacer caca (*esp. ped, fam or vulg*); **When was the last time you had a bowel movement?**..¿Cuándo fue la última vez que defecó (fue al baño, etc.)?

bowlegged *adj* con genu varo (*form*), con las piernas arqueadas

boy *n* niño, muchacho, chico

boyfriend *n* novio

BPA *abbr* bisphenol A.

bra (*fam*) *V.* **brassiere.**

brace *n* órtesis *f* (*form*), aparato ortopédico (para estabilizar una articulación); **halo** — halo cervical, halo *m* (*fam*); **knee (ankle, etc.)** — órtesis de rodilla (tobillo, etc.); *npl* aparato (de ortodoncia), frenos *or* frenillos (*Amer, fam*)

bracelet *n* pulsera, brazalete *m*; **identification (ID)** — brazalete *or* pulsera de identificación; **medical alert** — brazalete *or* pulsera de alerta médica

brachial *adj* braquial

brachytherapy *n* braquiterapia

brackets *n* (*orthodontics*) brackets *mpl*

bradycardia *n* bradicardia

Braille *n* braille *m*, sistema *m* de escritura para ciegos

brain *n* cerebro; **brain-dead** con muerte *f* cerebral, que tiene muerte cerebral; — **death** muerte *f* cerebral

brainstem *n* tronco cerebral *or* encefálico, tallo cerebral *or* encefálico

bran *n* salvado

branch *n* rama

brassiere *n* sostén *m*, sujetador *m*

brave *adj* valiente; **Be brave!**..¡Sé valiente!

bread *n* pan *m*

break *n* (*ortho, fam*) fractura, quebradura (*fam*); *vt, vi* (*pret* **broke**; *pp* **broken**) (*ortho, etc.*) fracturar(se), romper(se) (*fam*); (*a fever*) quitar(se); **I broke my foot**..Me fracturé (rompí) el pie...**to break the fever**..quitar la fiebre; **to — out** (*one's skin*) salir(*le*) (*a uno*) granos; **When did your skin break out?** ..¿Cuándo le salieron granos?; **to — up** (*romance*) terminar, romper; **She broke up with him**..Ella terminó con él...**They broke up**..Terminaron.

breakdown *n* crisis *f*, colapso; **nervous** — crisis nerviosa, colapso nervioso; **skin** — ruptura de la piel, deterioro de la piel (*que puede preceder a una úlcera de decúbito*)

breakfast *n* desayuno; **to have** — desayunar(se)

breakthrough *adj* — **pain** dolor irruptivo, dolor que aparece a veces a pesar del medicamento tomado diariamente para controlarlo

breakup *n* (*romantic*) ruptura, separación *f*

breast *n* (*chest*) pecho; (*female*) mama, seno, pecho

breastbone esternón *m* (*form*), hueso del pecho

breastfeed *vt, vi* (*pret & pp* **-fed**) amamantar, lactar, dar el pecho, dar de mamar; **Are you breastfeeding her?**.. ¿Le amamanta (lacta, da el pecho, da de mamar)?

breastfeeding *n* lactancia materna, amamantamiento, (el) lactar, (el) dar el pecho, (el) dar de mamar; **Breastfeeding will help protect your baby against disease**..Amamantar a su bebé ayudará a protegerlo de enfermedades.

breath *n* aliento, respiración *f*; **bad** — mal aliento; — **test** prueba del aliento; **short of** — sin aire *or* aliento; **shortness of** — falta de aire *or* aliento, dificultad *f* para respirar, ahogo; **to be short of** — faltar(*le*) (*a uno*) el aire *or* aliento; **Do you get short of breath when you walk?**..¿Le falta el aire (aliento) cuando camina?...**How many blocks can you walk before you get short of breath?**..¿Cuántas cuadras puede caminar antes de que le falte el aire (aliento)?; **to hold one's** — contener *or* aguantar la respiración; **Hold your breath**..Contenga (Aguante) la respiración; **to take a deep** — respirar profundo *or* hondo; **Take a deep breath**..Respire profundo (hondo).

breathe *vt, vi* respirar; **Breathe quietly while I listen to your heart**.. Respire suavemente mientras le escucho el corazón; **to — in** inspirar (*form*), inhalar (*form*), respirar (*fam*), tomar aire (*fam*); **Breathe in**..Respire..Tome aire; **to — out** espirar (*form*), exhalar (*form*), sacar aire (*esp. Mex, CA; fam*), botar aire (*esp. Carib, SA; fam*)

bridge *n* (*dent, etc.*) puente *m*; — **of the nose** puente nasal *or* de la nariz

bring *vt* (*pret & pp* **brought**) **to — on** (*pain, etc.*) provocar

bristle *n* (*of a brush*) cerda; **soft-bristle** de cerda suave; **stiff-bristle** *o* **hard-bristle** de cerda dura

brittle *adj* (*nails, etc.*) frágil, quebradizo; (*diabetes*) difícil de controlar

broccoli *n* brócoli *m*, brécol *m*

broke *pret de* **break**

broken (*pp de* **break**) *adj* quebrado, roto

bromide *n* bromuro
bromine *n* bromo
bromocriptine *n* bromocriptina
bronchi *pl de* **bronchus**
bronchial *adj* bronquial
bronchiectasis *n* bronquiectasia
bronchiole *n* bronquiolo
bronchiolitis *n* bronquiolitis *f*; — **oblite-**
rans bronquiolitis obliterante
bronchitis *n* bronquitis *f*; **chronic** —
bronquitis crónica
bronchoalveolar *adj* broncoalveolar
bronchoconstriction *n* broncoconstricción *f*
bronchodilator *n* broncodilatador *m*
bronchogenic *adj* broncogénico, broncógeno
bronchoscope *n* broncoscopio
bronchoscopy *n* (*pl* -**pies**) broncoscopia
bronchospasm *n* broncoespasmo
bronchus *n* (*pl* -**chi**) bronquio
broth *n* caldo
brother *n* hermano
brother-in-law *n* (*pl* **brothers-in-law**)
cuñado
brought *pret & pp de* **bring**
brow *n* (*forehead*) frente *f*; (*eyebrow*)
ceja
brown *adj* castaño, de color café, marrón; (*eyes*) marrón, castaño; (*hair*)
castaño; (*sugar*) moreno; (*bread*) integral, moreno
brown recluse *V.* **spider**.
brucellosis *n* brucelosis *f*
bruise *n* moretón *m*; **stone** — (*fam*) dolor
m de la región metatarsal del pie; *vt*
causar *or* producir moretones; *vi* salir-
(*le*) *or* hacerse(*le*) (*a uno*) moretones;
Do you bruise easily?..¿Le salen moretones fácilmente?..Se le hacen moretones fácilmente?
bruised *adj* con moretón, con moretones
brush *n* cepillo; *vt* cepillar; **to** — **one's**
hair cepillarse el pelo; **to** — **one's**
teeth cepillarse los dientes
brushing *n* (*dent, etc.*) cepillado; **bron-**
chial — cepillado bronquial
bruxism *n* bruxismo
bubble *n* burbuja
bubo *n* (*pl* **buboes**) bubón *m*
bubonic *adj* bubónico
buckle *n* hebilla; *vt* abrochar(se)
bucktooth *n* (*pl* -**teeth**) diente salido

buddy tape *vt* fijar (*un dedo*) al dedo ad-
yacente con cinta adhesiva
budesonide *n* budesonida, budesónida
(*INN*)
buffer *n* tampón *m*
buffered *adj* amortiguado
bug *n* (*fam*) (*insect*) insecto, bicho; (*mi-*
crobe) microbio, virus *m*, bacteria; (*ill-*
ness) gripe *f*, resfriado, enfermedad *f*
de tipo gripal
build *n* contextura, físico, complexión *f*;
vt (*pret & pp* **built**) **to** — **up** (*one's*
strength, muscles, etc.) fortalecer, reforzar; *vi* **to** — **up** acumularse
buildup *n* depósito, acumulación *f*
bulbar *adj* bulbar
bulge *n* abultamiento, protuberancia; *vi*
(*también* **to** — **out**) abultar; **so that it**
doesn't bulge (out)..para que no
abulte; **bulging disc** disco abultado;
bulging fontanelle fontanela abultada
bulimia *n* bulimia
bulimic *adj* bulímico
bullet *n* bala
bully *vt* acosar, intimidar, hostigar
bullying *n* acoso, intimidación *f*, hostigamiento
bullous *adj* (*emphysema*) bulloso; (*pem-*
phigoid) ampolloso
bumetanide *n* bumetanida
bump *n* bulto, nódulo (*form*), bola, (*due*
to trauma, esp. about the head) chichón *m*
bunion *n* juanete *m*
buprenorphine *n* buprenorfina
bupropion *n* bupropión *m*
burden *n* carga; **tumor** — carga tumoral
burdock *n* (*bot*) bardana, lampazo (*esp.*
Esp)
burn *n* quemadura; **first (second, third)**
degree — quemadura de primer (segundo, tercer) grado; *vt* (*pret & pp*
burned) quemar; **Did you burn your**
hand?..¿Se quemó la mano?; **to** —
oneself *o* **to get burned** quemarse;
Did you burn yourself?..¿Se quemó?;
vi arder; **Does it burn when you uri-**
nate?..¿Le arde cuando orina?
burning (*pain*) *adj* quemante, ardiente; *n*
(*sensation*) ardor *m*, quemazón *f*
burnout *n* desgaste *m* (profesional), agotamiento (profesional)
burp *vt* (*a baby*) hacer eructar; **You**

should burp your baby after each meal..Debe hacerle eructar a su bebé después de cada comida; *vi* eructar
burrow *n* (*of scabies*) surco (*de la sarna*); *vi* hacer un surco, hacer surcos
bursa *n* bolsa
bursitis *n* bursitis *f*; **anserine** — bursitis anserina; **olecranon** — bursitis olecraneana *or* del olécranon; **prepatellar** — bursitis prerrotuliana *or* prepatelar; **subacromial** — bursitis subacromial; **trochanteric** — bursitis trocantérea *or* trocantérica
burst *vt, vi* (*pret & pp* **burst**) reventar(se)
buspirone *n* buspirona
bust *n* busto, pecho
busulfan *n* busulfán *m*, busulfano (*INN*)
butalbital *n* butalbital *m*
butt (*vulg*) **buttocks**. *V*. **buttock**.
butter *n* mantequilla
butterbur *n* (*bot*) petasita
buttock *n* nalga; *npl* nalgas, trasero (*fam*)

button *n* botón *m*; **call** — botón de llamada; **If you need the nurse, press the call button**..Si necesita a la enfermera, presione el botón de llamada; *vt* (*también* **to** — **up**) abotonar(se), abrochar(se); **to button one's shirt**.. abotonarse la camisa...**difficulty buttoning** ..dificultad para abotonar(se)
buzz *n* (*fam o vulg*) sensación placentera al tomar una cantidad modesta de una sustancia intoxicante
buzzing *n* zumbido
bypass *n* derivación *f*, bypass *m*; **cardiopulmonary** — derivación *or* bypass cardiopulmonar; **coronary artery** — **graft (CABG)** injerto de derivación arterial coronaria; **femoro-popliteal** — derivación femoropoplítea, bypass femoro-poplíteo; **gastric** — derivación gástrica, bypass gástrico; **triple (quadruple, etc.)** — derivación *or* bypass triple (cuádruple, etc.)
byssinosis *n* bisinosis *f*

C

CABG *abbr* **coronary artery bypass graft**. *V*. **graft**.
cactus *n* (*pl* **-ti**) cactus *m*, cacto
cadaver *n* cadáver *m*
cadaveric *adj* cadavérico, de cadáver
cadmium *n* cadmio
caffeine *n* cafeína
calamine *n* calamina
calcification *n* calcificación *f*
calcify *vi* (*pret & pp* **-fied**) calcificarse
calcinosis *n* calcinosis *f*
calciphylaxis *n* calcifilaxis *f*
calcipotriene *n* calcipotrieno
calcitonin *n* calcitonina
calcitriol *n* calcitriol *m*
calcium *n* calcio; — **carbonate** carbonato cálcico *or* de calcio; — **gluconate** gluconato de calcio
calculus *n* (*stone*) cálculo, piedra; (*dent*) cálculo, sarro (dental); **renal** — cálculo renal, piedra en el riñón
calf *n* (*pl* **calves**) (*anat*) pantorrilla
calibrate *vt* calibrar
calisthenics *n* calistenia
call *n* llamada; visita; **house** — visita domiciliaria, visita al paciente en su casa; **on** — de guardia; *vt, vi* llamar; **Call for the nurse**..Llame a la enfermera.
callus *n* (*pl* **-luses**) callo, (*thin*) callosidad *f*
calm *adj* tranquilo; *vt* calmar; *vi* **to** — **down** calmarse, tranquilizarse

calming *adj* calmante, tranquilizante
calorie *n* caloría
calves *pl de* **calf**
campaign *n* campaña; **anti-smoking** — campaña antitabaco, campaña contra el tabaco; **vaccination** — campaña de vacunación
camphor *n* alcanfor *m*
canagliflozin *n* canagliflozina
canal *n* canal *m*, conducto; **auditory** — conducto auditivo; **birth** — canal del parto; **semicircular** — conducto semicircular
cancel *vt* (*pret & pp* -**celed** *o* -**celled**; *ger* -**celing** *o* -**celling**) cancelar
cancer *n* cáncer *m*; **bladder** — cáncer vesical (*form*), cáncer de vejiga; **bone** — cáncer óseo *or* de hueso; **breast** — cáncer de mama *or* pecho; **cervical** — cáncer cervical; **colon** — cáncer de colon; **colorectal** — cáncer colorrectal; **esophageal** — cáncer de esófago; **gastric** — cáncer gástrico *or* de estómago; **head and neck** — cáncer de cabeza y cuello; **kidney** — (*fam*) cáncer renal *or* de riñón; **laryngeal** — cáncer laríngeo *or* de laringe; **liver** — cáncer de hígado; **lung** — cáncer pulmonar *or* de pulmón; **non-small-cell lung** — cáncer de pulmón de células no pequeñas; **ovarian** — cáncer de ovario; **pancreatic** — cáncer de páncreas; **prostate** — cáncer de próstata; **rectal** — cáncer de recto; **renal cell** — cáncer de células renales, cáncer de riñón (*fam*); **skin** — cáncer de piel *or* cutáneo; **small-cell lung** — cáncer de pulmón de células pequeñas; **stomach** — cáncer gástrico *or* de estómago; **thyroid** — cáncer tiroideo *or* de tiroides; **uterine** — cáncer uterino *or* de útero; [*Note: the definite article can be added to the translations above to personalize a statement:* Ud. tiene cáncer de la próstata..You have prostate cancer..You have cancer of your prostate.]
cancer-causing *adj* cancerígeno, que causa cáncer
cancerous *adj* canceroso
candesartan *n* candesartán *m*
candidate *n* candidato -ta *mf*; **candidate for a heart transplant**..candidato a trasplante de corazón

candidiasis *n* candidiasis *f*, infección *f* por hongos *or* levaduras
candy *n* (*pl* -**dies**) dulces *mpl*, caramelos; **a piece of candy**..un dulce...**Candy is bad for your teeth**..Los dulces son malos para los dientes.
cane *n* bastón *m*; **four-pronged** — bastón de cuatro patas *or* apoyos *or* puntos
canker sore *n* afta, pequeña úlcera en la boca
cannabinoid *adj & n* cannabinoide *m*; **synthetic** — cannabinoide sintético
cannabidiol (CBD) *n* cannabidiol *m* (CBD)
cannabis *n* cannabis *m*
cannula *n* cánula; **nasal** — cánula nasal, puntas nasales (*Mex*)
cap *n* (*of a bottle*) tapa; (*of a needle*) capuchón *m*; (*dent*) corona (*esp. una del color del diente*); (*head covering*) gorro; **shower** — gorro de baño; **cervical** — capuchón *m* cervical; **safety** — tapa de seguridad; **surgical** *o* **scrub** — gorro quirúrgico
capable *adj* capaz
capacity *n* (*pl* -**ties**) capacidad *f*; **forced vital** — capacidad vital forzada
CAPD *abbr* **continuous ambulatory peritoneal dialysis**. *V.* **dialysis**.
capecitabine *n* capecitabina
capillary *adj & n* (*pl* -**ries**) capilar *m*
capitation *n* capitación *f*, sistema *m* de seguro médico en el cual se les paga a los proveedores una cantidad fija por persona asegurada
capsaicin *n* capsaicina
capsule *n* cápsula
capsulitis *n* capsulitis *f*; **adhesive** — capsulitis adhesiva
captopril *n* captopril *m*
car *n* coche *m*, carro (*Amer*)
carat *n* quilate *m*; **14** — **gold** oro de 14 quilates
carb (*fam*) *V.* **carbohydrate**.
carbamazepine *n* carbamazepina
carbamide peroxide *n* peróxido de carbamida
carbidopa *n* carbidopa
carbohydrate *n* carbohidrato, hidrato de carbono; **complex** — carbohidrato complejo; **simple** — carbohidrato simple

carbon *n* (*element*) carbono; **— dioxide** dióxido de carbono; **— monoxide** monóxido de carbono; **— tetrachloride** tetracloruro de carbono
carbonate *n* carbonato
carbonated *adj* carbonatado
carboxymethylcellulose *n* carboximetilcelulosa
carbuncle *n* ántrax *m*, infección *f* de varios folículos pilosos cercanos
carcinogen *n* carcinógeno, cancerígeno, sustancia que causa cáncer
carcinogenic *adj* cancerígeno, que causa cáncer
carcinoid *adj & n* carcinoide *m*; **— tumor** tumor *m* carcinoide
carcinoma *n* carcinoma *m*; **basal cell —** carcinoma basocelular; **bronchogenic —** carcinoma broncogénico; **ductal — in situ** carcinoma ductal in situ; **hepatocellular —** carcinoma hepatocelular; **lobular —** carcinoma lobulillar *or* lobular; **non-small-cell —** carcinoma de células no pequeñas; **renal cell —** carcinoma de células renales; **small-cell —** carcinoma de células pequeñas; **squamous cell —** carcinoma escamocelular *or* de células escamosas; **transitional cell —** carcinoma de células transicionales
carcinomatosis *n* carcinomatosis *f*
card *n* (*business, insurance, etc.*) tarjeta
cardiac *adj* cardíaco *or* cardiaco
cardiogenic *adj* cardiogénico, cardiógeno
cardiologist *n* cardiólogo -ga *mf*, médico -ca *mf* especializado en el corazón y sus enfermedades, especialista *mf* del corazón
cardiology *n* cardiología, rama de la medicina que se ocupa del corazón y sus enfermedades
cardiomyopathy *n* (*pl* **-thies**) cardiomiopatía, miocardiopatía, cardiopatía; **dilated —** cardiomiopatía *or* miocardiopatía dilatada; **hypertrophic —** cardiomiopatía *or* miocardiopatía hipertrófica; **ischemic —** cardiopatía isquémica; **restrictive —** cardiomiopatía *or* miocardiopatía restrictiva; **stress-induced —, takotsubo —** cardiomiopatía *or* miocardiopatía por estrés, cardiomiopatía de takotsubo

cardiopulmonary *adj* cardiopulmonar
cardiorespiratory *adj* cardiorrespiratorio
cardiovascular *adj* cardiovascular
cardioversion *n* cardioversión *f*; **synchronized electrical —** cardioversión eléctrica sincronizada
cardioverter *n* cardioversor *m*
cardioverter-defibrillator *n* desfibrilador *m* cardioversor; **implantable — (ICD)** desfibrilador cardioversor implantable (DCI)
carditis *n* carditis *f*
care *n* cuidado (*frec. pl*), atención *f*; **The care in this hospital is excellent.**.La atención en este hospital es excelente; **after —** *V.* **aftercare**; **critical —** atención crítica, cuidado(s) crítico(s); **day —** cuidado durante el día (*para niños de madres que trabajan o para cualquier persona que no se puede dejar sola*); **foot —, skin —, wound —, etc.** cuidado del pie, cuidado de la piel, cuidado de la herida, etc.; **health —** *V.* **health care** *como artículo independiente*; **home —** atención domiciliaria, cuidado(s) en el hogar; **hospice —** atención paliativa para pacientes terminales; **intensive —** cuidado(s) intensivo(s), terapia intensiva; **long-term —** cuidado(s) prolongado(s), cuidado(s) a largo plazo; **nursing —** cuidado(s) de enfermería; **prenatal —** cuidado(s) prenatal(es), atención prenatal; **primary —** atención primaria; **respite —** cuidado de relevo *or* respiro, cuidado temporal para que los cuidadores habituales descansen; **tertiary —** atención terciaria, atención de tercer nivel (*esp. Mex*); **to take — of** cuidar de, atender a; **Who takes care of your mother?** ..¿Quién cuida de su madre? **to take — of oneself** cuidarse; **You should take better care of yourself.**.Debe cuidarse mejor; *vi* importar(*le*) (*a uno*); **Don't you care?**.¿No le importa?
careful *adj* cuidadoso; **to be —** tener cuidado. **Be careful with this medicine.**.Tenga cuidado con esta medicina.
caregiver *n* cuidador -ra *mf*, persona que cuida a un enfermo o discapacitado
careless *adj* descuidado

carelessness *n* descuido
caries *n* caries *f*
carisoprodol *n* carisoprodol *m*
carnitine *n* carnitina
carotene *n* caroteno
carotenoid *n* carotenoide *m*
carotid *adj* carotídeo, (*artery*) carótido
carpal *adj* carpiano
carrier *n* portador -ra *mf*; **asymptomatic** — portador asintomático; **hepatitis B carrier**..portador de hepatitis B.
carrot *n* zanahoria
carry *vt* (*pret & pp* **-ried**) (*a gene, etc.*) tener; **He carries the gene for color blindness**..El tiene el gen del daltonismo.
carsickness *n* mareo (en vehículo)
cartilage *n* cartílago
carvedilol *n* carvedilol *m*
cascara sagrada *n* (*bot*) cáscara sagrada
case *n* caso; **in 9 out of 10 cases**..en 9 de 10 casos; — **manager** gestor -ra *mf or* administrador -ra *mf* de casos; **just in** — por si acaso
cashew *n* anacardo
cast *n* (*ortho*) yeso, escayola, (*splint*) férula; (**inflatable**) **air cast** férula inflable, férula hinchable (*esp. Esp*); **removable** — escayola desmontable, yeso removible; **spica** — espica de yeso
castrate *vt* castrar
castration *n* castración *f*
CAT *abbr* **computerized axial tomography**. *V*. **tomography** *y* **scan**.
cat *n* gato
catabolic *adj* catabólico
cataplexy *n* cataplexia
cataract *n* catarata
catastrophe *n* catástrofe *f*
catatonia *n* catatonia
catatonic *adj* catatónico
catch *vt* (*pret & pp* **caught**) (*fam, a disease*) dar(*le*) (*a uno*), pegar(*le*) (*a uno*), coger*, agarrar, contraer (*form*); **I caught the flu**..Me dio (pegó) la gripe..Cogí la gripe; **to — one's breath** recuperar el aliento
**potentially offensive in Mexico and much of Central and South America*
catching (*fam*) *adj* infeccioso, contagioso (*fam*)
catgut *n* catgut *m*
cath (*fam*) *V*. **catheterization**.

catharsis *n* (*psych*) catarsis *f*
cathartic *adj* (*psych*) catártico; (*ant*) purgante, laxante; *n* (*ant*) purgante *m*, laxante *m*
catheter *n* (*venous, arterial*) catéter *m*; (*urinary*) sonda; **central venous** — catéter venoso central; **epidural** — catéter epidural; **Foley** — sonda Foley, sonda vesical; **Hickman** — catéter Hickman; **implantable** — catéter implantable; **peripherally-inserted central** — (**PICC**) catéter central de inserción periférica; **pulmonary artery** *o* **Swan-Ganz** — catéter de arteria pulmonar, catéter de Swan-Ganz; **urinary** — sonda *or* catéter vesical, sonda *or* catéter en la vejiga
catheterization *n* cateterismo, cateterización *f*, colocación *f* de un catéter; (*of the bladder*) sondaje *m*, cateterismo, colocación de una sonda *or* un catéter; **cardiac** — cateterismo cardíaco
catheterize *vt* (*arterial, venous*) cateterizar, colocar *or* introducir un catéter; (*bladder*) colocar *or* introducir una sonda *or* catéter
cat's claw *n* (*bot*) uña de gato
caught *pret & pp de* **catch**
cauliflower *n* coliflor *f*
causalgia *n* causalgia
cause *n* causa; *vt* causar
caustic *adj* cáustico
cauterization *n* cauterización *f*
cauterize *vt* cauterizar
cautery *n* cauterio
cavity *n* (*pl* **-ties**) cavidad *f*; (*dent*) hueco producido por caries; **You have a cavity**..Tiene un diente con caries..Tiene una carie (*fam*)..Tiene un diente picado (*fam*)...**You have cavities**..Tiene caries; [*Note: caries is a mass noun like the English word* decay, *therefore* una carie *is grammatically incorrect though commonly used.*]
CBC *abbr* **complete blood count**. *V*. **count**.
CBD *V*. **cannabidiol**.
cc *abbr* **cubic centimeter**. *V*. **centimeter**.
CDC *V*. **Centers for Disease Control and Prevention**.
cecum *n* ciego (del colon)
cefaclor *n* cefaclor *m*

cefazolin *n* cefazolina
cefdinir *n* cefdinir *m*
cefepime *n* cefepima
cefoperazone *n* cefoperazona
cefotaxime *n* cefotaxima
cefoxitin *n* cefoxitina
ceftazidime *n* ceftazidima
ceftriaxone *n* ceftriaxona
cefuroxime *n* cefuroxima
celecoxib *n* celecoxib *m*
celery *n* apio
celiac *adj* celíaco, celiaco
celibate *adj* célibe, que no tiene relaciones sexuales
cell *n* célula; **atypical squamous cells of undetermined significance (ASCUS)** células escamosas atípicas de significado indeterminado; **B** — célula B; **brain** — célula cerebral; **CD4** — célula CD4; **cytotoxic T** — célula T citotóxica; **helper T** — célula T auxiliar *or* colaboradora; **natural killer** — célula asesina natural; **packed red blood cells** concentrados de hematíes; **unit of packed red blood cells** concentrado de hematíes; **plasma** — célula plasmática; **red blood** — eritrocito (*form*), hematíe *m* (*form*), glóbulo rojo; **stem** — célula madre; **suppressor T** — célula T supresora; **T** — célula T; **transitional** — célula transicional; **white blood** — leucocito (*form*), glóbulo blanco
cellular *adj* celular
cellulite *n* celulitis *f*, depósitos de grasa detrás de los muslos
cellulitis *n* celulitis *f*, infección *f* del tejido debajo de la piel
Celsius *adj* Celsius; **37 degrees Celsius** ..37 grados Celsius
cement *n* (*dent, ortho*) cemento
center *n* centro; **Centers for Disease Control and Prevention (CDC)** Centros para el Control y la Prevención de Enfermedades (*US*); **day** — centro diurno *or* de día; **day-care** — guardería infantil; **fitness** — gimnasio, centro de acondicionamiento físico; **medical** — centro sanitario *or* médico; **Poison Control** — Centro de Control de Envenenamientos e Intoxicaciones (*US*); **surgery** — centro quirúrgico *or* de cirugía; **tertiary care** — centro terciario; **urgent care** — centro de urgen-

cias; **wellness** — centro de bienestar
centered *adj* centrado; (*emotionally*) centrado, relajado y con la mente despejada; **patient-centered** centrado en el paciente
Centigrade *adj* centígrado; **38 degrees Centigrade**..38 grados centígrados
centimeter (cm) *n* centímetro (cm); **cubic** — **(cc)** centímetro cúbico (cc)
central *adj* central
cephalexin *n* cefalexina
cephalic *adj* cefálico
cephalosporin *n* cefalosporina
ceramic *adj* (*dent, etc.*) cerámico
cerclage *n* cerclaje *m*
cereal *n* cereal *m*
cerebellar *adj* cerebeloso
cerebellum *n* cerebelo
cerebral *adj* cerebral; — **palsy** parálisis *f* cerebral
cerebrospinal *adj* cefalorraquídeo
cerebrovascular *adj* cerebrovascular
cerebrum *n* cerebro
certificate *n* certificado, acta, partida; **birth** — acta *or* partida de nacimiento; **death** — certificado de defunción
certified *adj* certificado, titulado
cerumen *n* cerumen *m*, cera de los oídos
cervical *adj* (*obst, ortho*) cervical
cervices *pl de* cervix
cervicitis *n* cervicitis *f*
cervix *n* (*pl* -vices *o* -vixes) cérvix *m&f*, cuello uterino
cesarean section *n* operación cesárea, cesárea (*fam*)
cessation *n* abandono; **smoking** — (el) dejar de fumar, abandono del tabaco, deshabituación tabáquica (*form*)
cetirizine *n* cetirizina
chafe *vt, vi* rozar
chain *n* cadena; **branched-chain** de cadena ramificada; — **of cold** cadena de frío; — **of custody** cadena de custodia; — **of survival** cadena de supervivencia; — **reaction** reacción *f* en cadena; **heavy** — cadena pesada; **light** — cadena ligera; **long-chain** de cadena larga; **medium-chain** de cadena media
chair *n* silla, sillón *m*; **dental** — sillón dental; **reclining** — silla reclinable
chalazion *n* (*pl* -zia) chalazión *m*
challenge *n* desafío, reto; provocación *f*; **methacholine** — provocación con me-

tacolina

chamber *n* cámara; **decompression —** cámara de descompresión; **hyperbaric —** cámara hiperbárica; **valved holding —** (*for metered-dose inhaler*) cámara espaciadora con válvula

chamomile *n* (*bot*) manzanilla

chance *n* posibilidad *f*; casualidad *f*; **There's maybe one chance in a hundred**..Puede haber una posibilidad entre cien; **by —** por casualidad

chancre *n* chancro; **soft —** chancro blando

chancroid *n* chancroide *m*

change *n* cambio; **bandage —** cambio de vendaje; **— of life** (*ant*) menopausia; **sex —** (*fam*) reasignación *f* de sexo *or* género, cambio de sexo (*fam*); *vt, vi* cambiar

chap *vi* (*pret & pp* **chapped**) agrietarse, partirse (*la piel o los labios*)

chaplain *n* capellán *m*, sacerdote *m*

chapped *adj* agrietado, partido (*la piel o los labios*)

Chap Stick *n* (*marca*) *V.* **lip balm** *bajo* **balm.**

characteristic *adj* característico; *n* característica, carácter *m*; **secondary sex —** carácter sexual secundario

charcoal *n* carbón *m*; **activated —** carbón activado

charge *n* (*frec. pl*) precio, costo, coste *m* (*esp. Esp*); *vt, vi* cobrar

charley horse *n* (*fam*) calambre *m* muscular de la pantorrilla

chart *n* gráfico *or* gráfica, tabla, carta; **medical —** historia clínica, historial médico, expediente clínico *or* médico (*esp. Mex*); **eye —** tabla *or* carta de Snellen, tabla de letras (*para evaluar la agudeza visual*)

check *vt* chequear, revisar

checkup *n* chequeo (médico), revisión (médica)

cheek *n* mejilla; (*fam, buttock*) nalga

cheekbone *n* pómulo

cheerful *adj* alegre

cheese *n* queso

cheilitis *n* queilitis *f*, inflamación *f* de los labios; **angular —** queilitis angular, boquera (*frec. pl*), agrietamiento e inflamación en los ángulos de la boca

chelating *adj* quelante; **— agent** quelante *m*, agente *m* quelante; **iron-chelating agent** quelante de(l) hierro

chelation *n* quelación *f*; **— therapy** terapia quelante

chemical *adj* químico; *n* sustancia química, producto químico

chemistry *n* química

chemo (*fam*) *V.* **chemotherapy.**

chemoprophylaxis *n* quimioprofilaxis *f*

chemotherapy *n* (*pl* **-pies**) quimioterapia; **adjuvant —** quimioterapia adyuvante; **consolidation —** quimioterapia de consolidación; **high-dose —** quimioterapia a dosis altas; **induction —** quimioterapia de inducción; **neoadjuvant —** quimioterapia neoadyuvante

chest *n* tórax *m* (*form*), pecho

chew *n* (*fam, chewing tobacco*) tabaco de mascar; *vt, vi* masticar; **to — one's nails** comerse *or* morderse las uñas

chewable *adj* masticable

chewing gum *n* chicle *m*

chicken *n* pollo

chickenpox *n* varicela

chickweed *n* (*bot*) pamplina, alsine *m*

chigger *n* ácaro de la cosecha, ácaro rojo, larva roja de ciertos ácaros

chigoe flea *n* nigua

chilblain *n* sabañón *m*; lesión inflamatoria producida por el frío

child *n* (*pl* **children**) niño -ña *mf*, hijo -ja *mf*; **foster —** niño acogido, hijo de crianza; **only —** hijo único; *npl* niños, hijos

childbearing *adj* fértil, reproductivo; **— age** edad fértil; **— years** años reproductivos; *n* maternidad *f*

childbirth *n* parto

childhood *n* niñez *f*, infancia

childproof *adj* a prueba de niños

children *pl de* **child**

chili pepper *n* chile *m*

chill *n* escalofrío

chimerism *n* quimerismo

chin *n* mentón *m*, barbilla

chip *n* astilla, pedacito; *vt, vi* (*pret & pp* **chipped**; *ger* **chipping**) quebrar(se) (un poco), astillar(se), desportillar(se)

chiropodist *V.* **podiatrist.**

chiropractic *n* quiropráctica

chiropractor *n* quiropráctico -ca *mf*

chlamydia *n* clamidia

chloral hydrate *n* hidrato de cloral**

chlorambucil *n* clorambucilo
chloramphenicol *n* cloranfenicol *m*
chlordane *n* clordano
chlorhexidine *n* clorhexidina
chloride *n* cloruro
chlorinated *adj* clorado
chlorination *n* cloración *f*
chlorine *n* cloro
chloroform *n* cloroformo
chloroquine *n* cloroquina
chlorpheniramine (*USAN*), chlorphenamine (*INN*) *n* clorfeniramina, clorfenamina (*INN*)
chlorthalidone *n* clortalidona
chocolate *n* chocolate *m*
choice *n* elección *f*; drug of — medicamento de elección; drug of first (second, third) — medicamento de primera (segunda, tercera) elección
choke *vt* estrangular; *vi* (*asphyxiate*)
asfixiarse (*form*), ahogarse; to — on
(*food, etc.*) atragantarse con
choking *n* (*asphyxia*) asfixia, ahogo; (*on
food, etc.*) atragantamiento
cholangiocarcinoma *n* colangiocarcinoma *m*
cholangiogram *n* colangiografía (*estudio*)
cholangiography *n* colangiografía (*técnica*); percutaneous transhepatic —
colangiografía transhepática percutánea
cholangitis *n* colangitis *f*
cholecystectomy *n* (*pl* -mies) colecistectomía
cholecystitis *n* colecistitis *f*; acalculous
— colecistitis alitiásica *or* acalculosa
choledochal *adj* colédoco
cholelithiasis *n* colelitiasis *f*
cholera *n* cólera *m*
cholestasis *n* colestasis *f*; intrahepatic
— of pregnancy colestasis intrahepática del embarazo
cholesteatoma *n* colesteatoma *m*
cholesterol *n* colesterol *m*; LDL (HDL,
etc.) — colesterol LDL (HDL, etc.);
total — colesterol total
cholestyramine *n* colestiramina
chondrocalcinosis *n* condrocalcinosis *f*
chondroitin sulfate *n* sulfato de condroitina
chondrosarcoma *n* condrosarcoma *m*
chorea *n* corea *m&f*; Huntington's —

corea de Huntington; [*Note: the RAE
lists* corea *as masculine, but it is commonly treated as feminine.*]
choriocarcinoma *n* coriocarcinoma *m*
chorioretinitis *n* coriorretinitis *f*
chromate *n* cromato
chromium *n* cromo
chromomycosis *n* cromomicosis *f*
chromosomal *adj* cromosómico
chromosome *n* cromosoma *m*
chronic *adj* crónico
chronically *adv* crónicamente
ciclopirox *n* ciclopirox *m*
cidofovir *n* cidofovir *m*
cigar *n* puro, tabaco (*esp. Carib*)
cigarette *n* cigarrillo, cigarro; electronic
—, e-cigarette (*fam*) cigarrillo *or* cigarro electrónico; filter — cigarrillo *or*
cigarro con filtro
cilostazol *n* cilostazol *m*
ciprofloxacin *n* ciprofloxacino, ciprofloxacina
circadian *adj* circadiano; — rhythm ritmo circadiano
circle *n* círculo; dark circles under
one's eyes ojeras; vicious — círculo
vicioso
circulate *vi* circular
circulation *n* circulación *f*; collateral —
circulación colateral; extracorporeal
— circulación extracorpórea; fetal —
circulación fetal; pulmonary — circulación pulmonar; systemic — circulación sistémica
circulatory *adj* circulatorio
circumcise *vt* circuncidar
circumcised *adj* circunciso
circumcision *n* circuncisión *f*
cirrhosis *n* cirrosis *f*; primary biliary —
cirrosis biliar primaria
cirrhotic *adj & n* cirrótico -ca *mf*
cisplatin *n* cisplatino
citalopram *n* citalopram *m*
citrate *n* citrato
citric *adj* cítrico
citrus fruit *n* (*pl* fruit *o* fruits) fruta cítrica
clammy *adj* pegajoso y frío (*piel, manos,
etc.*)
clamp *n* pinza; *vt* pinzar
clap *n* (*fam, ant*) gonorrea
clarithromycin *n* claritromicina
class *n* clase *f*

claudication *n* claudicación *f*; **intermittent** — claudicación intermitente
claustrophobia *n* claustrofobia
clavicle *n* clavícula
claw *n* garra, (*of a pet*) uña; *vt* arañar, desgarrar
clean *adj* limpio; — **and sober** limpio y sobrio, libre de drogas y alcohol; *vt* limpiar
cleaning *n* limpieza; **dental** — limpieza dental
cleanliness *n* limpieza
clear *adj* claro; *vt* **to** — **one's throat** aclarar la garganta, carraspear; *vi* **to** — **up** (*a rash, illness, etc.*) resolverse, quitarse
cleft *adj* hendido; — **lip** labio hendido; — **palate** paladar hendido
clench *vt* (*teeth, fist*) apretar fuerte (*los dientes, el puño*)
click *n* (*card*) chasquido
climacteric *n* climaterio
climate *n* clima *m*
climax *n* (*sexual*) orgasmo
clindamycin *n* clindamicina
clinic *n* clínica; **free** — clínica gratuita; **urgent care** — clínica de urgencias
clinical *adj* clínico
clinician *n* clínico -ca *mf*
clip (*surg*) *n* clip *m*; *vt* (*pret & pp* **clipped**; *ger* **clipping**) clipar, ligar (con clips), pinzar (con clips)
clippers *n* (*fam, for nails*) cortaúñas *m*
clitoris *n* clítoris *m*
clobetasol *n* clobetasol *m*
clofazimine *n* clofazimina
clofibrate *n* clofibrato
clogged *adj* (*fam*) obstruido, bloqueado, tapado (*fam*)
clomiphene (*USAN*), **clomifene** (*INN*) *n* clomifeno
clonazepam *n* clonazepam *m*
clone *n* clon *m*
clonic *adj* clónico
clonidine *n* clonidina
clonus *n* clonus *m*
clopidogrel *n* clopidogrel *m*
close *adj* cercano; — **friend** amigo -ga *mf* cercano; — **relative** pariente *mf* cercano; *adv* cerca; **close to your aorta**..cerca de su aorta
close *vt, vi* cerrar(se); **Close your eyes**.. Cierre los ojos...**the valve closes**..la

válvula se cierra
closure *n* (*psych*) cierre *m* emocional, sensación *f* de conclusión; (*surg*) cierre *m*; **vacuum-assisted** — cierre asistido por vacío
clot *n* coágulo; — **buster** (*fam*) trombolítico, medicamento que disuelve los coágulos; *vi* (*pret & pp* **clotted**; *ger* **clotting**) coagularse
clothes *npl* ropa
clothing *n* ropa
clotrimazole *n* clotrimazol *m*
clotting *n* coagulación *f*
cloudy *adj* (*comp* **-ier**; *super* **-iest**) (*urine, etc.*) turbio
clozapine *n* clozapina
club *n* club *m*; **health** — gimnasio, club de salud (*Ang*)
clubbing *n* hipocratismo digital (*form*), dedos en palillo de tambor
clubfoot *n* (*pl* **-feet**) pie zambo, malformación congénita del pie
clumsy *adj* torpe
cluster *n* agrupación *f*; **a cluster of cases of hepatitis B**..una agrupación de casos de hepatitis B
cm. *V.* **centimeter**.
CMV *V.* **cytomegalovirus**.
CNS *abbr* **central nervous system**. *V.* **system**.
coagulate *vt, vi* coagular(se)
coagulation *n* coagulación *f*; **disseminated intravascular — (DIC)** coagulación intravascular diseminada
coagulopathy *n* coagulopatía
coal *n* carbón *m*
coal tar *n* alquitrán *m* de hulla
coarctation *n* coartación *f*
coat *n* abrigo; *vt* cubrir; **coats the lining of your stomach**..cubre el revestimiento del estómago; **sugar-coated** azucarado, cubierto de azúcar
coating *n* (*of a tablet*) cubierta, capa, recubrimiento
cobalt *n* cobalto
Coban (*marca*) *V.* **self-adherent elastic wrap** *bajo* **wrap**.
coca *n* (*bot*) coca
cocaine *n* cocaína
coccidioidomycosis *n* coccidioidomicosis *f*
coccus *n* (*pl* **-ci**) coco
coccyx *n* cóccix *or* coxis *m*, colita (*Amer,*

fam), rabadilla (*Amer, fam*)
cochlea *n* (*pl* **-leae**) cóclea
cochlear *adj* coclear
cockroach *n* cucaracha
cocktail *n* (*of medications*) cóctel *or* coctel *m*, mezcla (*de medicamentos*)
cocoa butter *n* manteca de cacao
coconut *n* coco
coddle *vt* mimar, consentir
Code Blue *n* código azul (*Ang*), anuncio por parlante de emergencia solicitando a los médicos para realizar medidas de reanimación a un paciente en paro cardiorrespiratorio
codeine *n* codeína
codependency *n* codependencia
coenzyme *n* coenzima *m&f;* — **Q** coenzima Q; [*Note: the RAE lists* coenzima *as feminine, but as with* enzima, *masculine usage is common, particularly in Spain.*]
coffee *n* café *m*; — **grounds** posos *or* granos de café; **Did the vomit look as if it had coffee grounds in it?**..¿Se veía el vómito como si tuviera posos (granos) de café?
cognitive *adj* cognitivo
coinfection, co-infection *n* coinfección *or* co-infección *f*
coitus *n* coito; — **interruptus** coitus interruptus *m*, coito interrumpido
coke *n* (*fam*) cocaína, coca (*fam*)
colchicine *n* colchicina
cold *adj* frío; **to be** — tener frío, (*the weather*) hacer frío; **Are you cold?**.. ¿Tiene frío?; **to feel** — sentir frío; *n* frío; (*illness*) catarro, resfriado; **chest** — bronquitis (aguda), resfriado de pecho; **common** — catarro *or* resfriado común; **head** — resfriado de cabeza, catarro que afecta los senos paranasales; **to catch a** — resfriarse; **to have a** — estar resfriado, tener catarro
cold cream *n* crema fría, (tipo de) crema limpiadora
cold snap *n* (*fam*) ola de frío
cold sore *n* herpes *m* labial (*form*), fuego, calentura, erupción *f* en los labios (*debida al herpes*)
cold turkey *adv* (*fam*) de golpe, abruptamente y sin ayuda (*refiriéndose a la suspensión de un hábito o de una adicción*)

colectomy *n* (*pl* **-mies**) colectomía
colesevelam *n* colesevelam *m*
colestipol *n* colestipol *m*
colic *n* (*ped*) cólico (*frec. pl*); (*surg*) cólico
coliform *adj & n* coliforme *m*
colitis *n* colitis *f;* **ischemic** — colitis isquémica; **microscopic** — colitis microscópica; **pseudomembranous** — colitis seudomembranosa; **ulcerative** — colitis ulcerosa
collagen *n* colágeno
collapse *n* (*person*) desmayo, caída; (*lung, etc.*) colapso; *vi* (*person*) desmayarse, caerse, desplomarse; (*lung, etc.*) colapsarse
collar *n* (*ortho*) collarín *m*, collar *m*; **(rigid *o* hard, soft) cervical** — collarín *or* collar cervical (rígido, blando)
collarbone *n* (*fam*) clavícula
collateral *adj* colateral
colleague *n* colega *mf*
collect *vt* (*blood, stool sample, etc.*) recoger, recolectar (*sangre, muestra de heces, etc.*)
collection *n* recolección *f*, colección *f*; **blood** — recolección *or* colección de sangre
colloid *n* coloide *m*
colon *n* colon *m*; **ascending** — colon ascendente; **descending** — colon descendente; **sigmoid** — colon sigmoide *or* sigmoideo; **spastic** — (*ant*) síndrome *m* de intestino irritable, colon espástico (*ant*); **transverse** — colon transverso
colon cleansing *n* limpieza de colon (*para fines terapéuticos*)
colonic *adj* colónico, relativo al colon; *n* (*fam*) hidroterapia de colon
colonization *n* colonización *f*
colonoscope *n* colonoscopio
colonoscopy *n* (*pl* **-pies**) colonoscopia; **virtual** — colonoscopia virtual
color *n* color *m*
color-blind, colorblind *adj* daltónico (*form*), que no diferencia bien ciertos colores
colorectal *adj* colorrectal
coloring *n* colorante *m*; **food** — colorante alimentario *or* de alimentos
colorless *adj* incoloro, sin color
colostomy *n* (*pl* **-mies**) colostomía
colostrum *n* calostro

colposcopy *n* (*pl* **-pies**) colposcopia
coltsfoot *n* (*bot*) uña de caballo
column *n* columna; **spinal** *o* **vertebral** — columna vertebral, columna (*fam*)
coma *n* coma *m*
comatose *adj* comatoso, en coma
comb *vi* peine *m*; *vt* peinar; **to** — **one's hair** peinarse
combat *n* combate *m*; *vt* combatir; **to combat cancer**..combatir el cáncer
combative *adj* agresivo
combination *n* combinación *f*; **Smoking and diabetes are a bad combination** ..El hecho de fumar y ser diabético es una mala combinación.
come *vi* (*pret* **came**; *pp* **come**) venir; (*fam o vulg, to have an orgasm*) alcanzar el orgasmo, venirse (*fam or vulg*); **to** — **and go** ir y venir; **Does the pain come and go?**..El dolor, ¿va y viene?; **to** — **down** bajar(se); **Your sugar came down** ..(Se) Le bajó el azúcar; **to** — **down** (*fam, off a drug*) recuperarse de una intoxicación; **to** — **down with** (*a disease*) dar(*le*) (*a uno*), pegar(*le*) (*a uno*), coger* (*Esp*); **to** — **on** (*to begin*) empezar, comenzar; **Did the pain come on suddenly or gradually?**.. ¿Empezó (Comenzó) el dolor de repente o poco a poco?; **to** — **to** (*fam, regain consciousness*) volver en sí
**potentially offensive in Mexico and much of Central and South America*
comedo *n* (*pl* **comedones**) comedón *m*, espinilla (*fam*)
comfort *n* comodidad *f*, confort *m*; (*emotional*) consuelo; — **zone** zona de confort; *vt* consolar
comfortable *adj* cómodo
comfrey *n* (*bot*) consuelda
command *n* orden *f*; **Can she follow commands?**..¿Puede seguir órdenes?
comminuted *adj* (*fracture*) conminuta
commode *n* silla inodoro, silla con inodoro
common *adj* común; **a common problem**..un problema común; — **sense** sentido común
communicable *adj* transmisible, contagioso
communicate *vt, vi* comunicar(se)
communication *n* comunicación *f*
community *adj* comunitario; — **involve-**

ment participación comunitaria; *n* (*pl* **-ties**) comunidad *f*; **community-acquired** adquirido en la comunidad
comorbidity *n* comorbilidad
companion *n* compañero -ra *mf*, (*person accompanying*) acompañante *mf*
compartmentalization *n* (*psych*) compartimentalización *f*
compassion *n* compasión *f*
compassionate *adj* compasivo; — **use** (*pharm*) uso compasivo
compatible *adj* compatible
compensate *vi* compensar
compensation *n* (*psych, etc.*) compensación *f*
competency *n* (*to make medical decisions*) capacidad *f* (*para tomar decisiones médicas*)
competent *adj* capaz, competente
complain *vi* quejarse
complaint *n* queja; **chief** — motivo de consulta
complement *n* complemento
complementary *adj* complementario
complete *adj* completo
complex *n* complejo; **inferiority** — complejo de inferioridad; **Mycobacterium avium** — **(MAC)** complejo Mycobacterium avium; **Oedipus** — complejo de Edipo; **superiority** — complejo de superioridad
complexion *n* cutis *m*, tez *f*
compliance *n* cumplimiento, adherencia; — **with treatment** cumplimiento del tratamiento, adherencia al tratamiento
complication *n* complicación *f*
component *n* componente *m*
compound *n* compuesto
compress *n* compresa, paño; **cool** — compresa fría, paño frío; *vt* comprimir
compression *n* compresión *f*; **chest compressions** compresiones torácicas; **intermittent pneumatic** — compresión neumática intermitente; **spinal cord** — compresión medular (*form*), compresión de la médula espinal
compulsion *n* compulsión *f*
compulsive *adj* compulsivo
computer *n* computadora, ordenador *m*
concave *adj* cóncavo
conceive *vi* concebir
concentrate *n* concentrado; **factor VIII** — concentrado de factor VIII; *vt* con-

centrar; *vi* (*focus attention*) concentrarse

concentration *n* concentración *f*

concentrator *n* concentrador *m*; **oxygen** — concentrador de oxígeno

conception *n* (*obst*) concepción *f*

concern *n* inquietud *f*; **to address your concerns**..responder a sus inquietudes

concussion *n* conmoción *f* cerebral

condition *n* (*state*) estado, condición *f*; (*ailment*) afección *f*, condición *f*, enfermedad *f*; **critical** — estado crítico, condicion crítica; **preexisting** — condición preexistente

conditioned *adj* acondicionado

conditioner *n* (*for hair*) acondicionador *m* (*de cabello*)

conditioning *n* acondicionamiento; **physical** — acondicionamiento físico

condolence *n* condolencia; **Please accept my condolences**..Quiero dar mis condolencias

condom *n* condón *m*, preservativo

conduction *n* conducción *f*

conduit *n* conducto; **ileal** — conducto ileal

condyle *n* cóndilo

cone *n* (*anat, gyn, ophthalmology, etc.*) cono

confabulation *n* fabulación *f*, confabulación *f* (*Ang*), (el) suplir las lagunas de la memoria con hechos imaginarios o falsos recuerdos

confidence *n* confianza

confidential *adj* confidencial; **What you tell me is strictly confidential**..Lo que Ud. me dice es estrictamente confidencial.

confidentiality *n* intimidad *f*, confidencialidad *f*; **patient** — intimidad *or* confidencialidad del paciente

confirm *vt* confirmar

conflict *n* conflicto

confront *vt* enfrentar, afrontar, confrontar, hacer frente a; **to confront our fears**..enfrentar nuestros temores

confrontation *n* confrontación *f*

confrontational *adj* desafiante

confuse *vt* confundir

confused *adj* confundido; **to get** *o* **become** — confundirse

confusion *n* confusión *f*

congenital *adj* congénito

congested *adj* congestionado

congestion *n* congestión *f*; **nasal** — congestión nasal

congestive *adj* congestivo

congratulations *interj* (*obst, etc.*) ¡Felicidades! ¡Enhorabuena! (*esp. Esp*)

conization *n* conización *f*

conjugate *adj* conjugado; — **vaccine** vacuna conjugada

conjugated *adj* conjugado

conjunctiva *n* (*pl* -**vae**) conjuntiva

conjunctival *adj* conjuntival

conjunctivitis *n* conjuntivitis *f*

connect *vt* conectar; **Tendons connect muscles to bones**..Los tendones conectan los músculos con los huesos.

connection *n* conexión *f*, vínculo

consanguineous *adj* consanguíneo, que tiene antepasados en común

conscience *n* conciencia; **guilty** — cargo de conciencia, conciencia culpable

conscious *adj* consciente

consciousness *n* conciencia *or* consciencia, conocimiento; **altered level of** — alteración *f* del nivel de conciencia; **collective** — conciencia colectiva; **loss of** — pérdida del conocimiento *or* de la conciencia; **to lose** — perder el conocimiento *or* la conciencia; **to regain** — volver en sí; [*Note: conciencia is the more common spelling, but since it also means conscience, consciencia may be used to try to avoid confusion. According to the RAE consciencia should never mean conscience, but this distinction often goes unobserved.*]

consent *n* consentimiento, permiso; **informed** — consentimiento informado; *vi* consentir; **to** — consentir en

consequence *n* consecuencia

conservative *adj* (*measures, etc.*) conservador

conservator *n* tutor -ra *mf*, persona encargada de manejar los asuntos de otra que es incapaz de hacerlo por discapacidad mental

conserve *vt* conservar

conserving *adj* conservador; **breast-conserving surgery** cirugía conservadora de mama

consistency *n* (*pl* -**cies**) consistencia

console *vt* consolar

consolidation *n* consolidación *f*

constant *adj* constante
constipate *vt* estreñir
constipated *adj* estreñido; **to get** *o* **become** — estreñirse
constipation *n* estreñimiento
constituent *n* (*pharm*) componente *m*
constitution *n* constitución *f*, complexión *f*
constrict *vt* (*blood vessels, etc.*) contraer; (*blood flow*) restringir; *vi* (*blood vessels, etc.*) contraerse
constriction *n* constricción *f*
consult *n* consulta (*en el hospital*); **We need to get a renal consult**.. Tenemos que consultar con el equipo renal; *vt* consultar; **to consult a specialist**..consultar con *or* a un especialista
consultation *n* consulta
consumption *n* consumo; (*ant*) tuberculosis *f*
contact *n* contacto; **close** — contacto cercano; **eye** — contacto visual
contagious *adj* (*disease*) contagioso; (*fam, person*) contagioso (*fam*), que puede transmitir una enfermedad, que puede infectar a los demás; [*Note: properly, both* contagious *and* contagioso *apply to diseases, not people, though both are often applied to people in colloquial speech.*]
contain *vt* contener
container *n* contenedor *m*, recipiente *m*, envase *m*; **sharps** — contenedor de objetos punzantes
contaminant *n* contaminante *m*
contaminate *vt* contaminar
contaminated *adj* contaminado; **to become** — contaminarse
contamination *n* contaminación *f*
content *n* (*frec. pl*) contenido
continual *adj* continuo, habitual
continuous *adj* continuo
contour *n* contorno
contraception *n* anticoncepción *f*, contracepción *f*
contraceptive *adj* & *n* anticonceptivo; **oral** — anticonceptivo oral
contract *n* contrato, acuerdo; **pain management** — acuerdo entre el paciente y el médico sobre el uso de opiáceos; *vt* (*a disease*) contraer, dar(*le*) (*a uno*), pegar(*le*) (*a uno*), coger* (*Esp*); *vi* (*a muscle*) contraerse

potentially offensive in Mexico and much of Central and South America
contraction *n* contracción *f*; **Braxton-Hicks contractions** contracciones de Braxton-Hicks, falsos dolores de parto; **premature atrial** — (**PAC**) contracción auricular prematura (CAP); **premature ventricular** — (**PVC**) contracción ventricular prematura (CVP)
contracture *n* contractura; **Dupuytren's** — contractura de Dupuytren
contraindicated *adj* contraindicado
contraindication *n* contraindicación *f*
contrast *n* (*fam, contrast medium*) medio de contraste, contraste *m* (*fam*)
control *n* control *m*; **birth** — anticoncepción *f*; control de la natalidad; método anticonceptivo, anticonceptivo; **Do you use birth control?**..¿Usa Ud. algún método anticonceptivo?; — **freak** (*fam*) fanático -ca *mf* del control, persona que quiere controlar todo lo que hacen los demás; **in** — en control; **out of** — fuera de control; **tight** — (*of blood sugars*) control estricto (*de la glucemia*); **under** — bajo control; *vt* (*pret & pp* **-trolled**; *ger* **-trolling**) controlar
controlling *adj* (*person*) controlador
controversial *adj* controvertido
contusion *n* contusión *f*
convalescence *n* convalecencia
convalescent *adj* convaleciente
conventional *adj* convencional
conversion *n* (*psych, etc.*) conversión *f*
convex *adj* convexo
convulsion *n* convulsión *f*, ataque *m* (*fam*)
coo *vi* (*pret & pp* **cooed**) (*ped*) arrullar, hacer sonidos como una paloma
cook *n* cocinero -ra *mf*; *vt, vi* cocinar
cookie *n* galleta
cool *adj* fresco
cooperate *vi* colaborar, cooperar; **if he cooperates**..si él colabora
cooperative *adj* colaborador
coordination *n* coordinación *f*
copayment, copay (*fam*) *n* copago
COPD *abbr* **chronic obstructive pulmonary disease**. *V.* **disease**.
cope *vi* **to** — **with** afrontar, (*overcome*) superar, (*endure successfully*) sobrellevar, (*deal with*) lidiar con, (*face*) ha-

cer frente a

copious *adj* copioso

copper *n* cobre *m*; — **sulfate** sulfato de cobre

coral *n* coral *m*

cord *n* cordón *m*, cuerda; **spinal** — médula espinal; **umbilical** — cordón umbilical; **vocal** — cuerda vocal

corn *n* maíz *m*; (*foot lesion*) callo (*del pie*)

cornea *n* córnea

corneal *adj* corneal

cornstarch *n* maicena, almidón *m* de maíz

coronary *adj* coronario

coroner *n* forense *mf*, médico -ca *mf* forense, médico -ca *mf* legista (*esp. Mex*), oficial *mf* encargado de investigar casos de muerte

corporal *adj* corporal

corpse *n* cadáver *m*

corpus luteum *n* cuerpo lúteo

correct *adj* correcto; *vt* corregir

correction *n* corrección *f*

corrective *adj* corrector

correlation *n* correlación *f*

corrosive *adj* corrosivo

corset *n* (*ortho*) corsé *m*

cortex *n* (*pl* -**tices**) corteza

cortical *adj* cortical

cortices *pl de* **cortex**

corticosteroid *n* corticosteroide *or* corticoesteroide *m*

corticotropin *n* corticotropina, hormona adrenocorticotrópica

cortisol *n* cortisol *m*

cortisone *n* cortisona

cosmetic *adj* & *n* cosmético

cosmetologist *n* cosmetólogo -ga *mf*, esteticista *mf*

cost *n* costo, coste *m* (*Esp*); **cost-effective** costo-efectivo, coste-efectivo; **cost-effectiveness** costo-efectividad *m*, coste-efectividad *m*; **cost-saving** que ahorra costos *or* costes

costochondritis *n* costocondritis *f*

cotton *n* algodón *m*; — **ball** torunda (*form*); bola, bolita, mota, *or* copo de algodón; — **mouth** (*fam*) sequedad *f* de boca, boca seca

couch *n* (*psych*) diván *m*

couch potato (*fam*) persona sedentaria, persona que pasa mucho tiempo sentada en el sofá viendo la televisión

cough *n* tos *f*; **barking** — tos perruna; **dry** — tos seca; **hacking** — tos seca y fuerte; *vt* **to** — **up** expectorar (*form*); **Are you coughing up phlegm?**..Cuando tose, ¿hay flemas?...**Try to cough up phlegm from your lungs**..Trate de toser fuerte para sacar flemas de sus pulmones...**Are you coughing up blood?**..Cuando tose, ¿saca sangre?.. ¿Está tosiendo sangre?; *vi* toser; **Cough hard**..Tosa fuerte.

counseling *n* orientación *f*, consejería, consejo, asesoría, asesoramiento; **family** — orientación *or* consejería *or* asesoría familiar; **genetic** — asesoramiento *or* consejo genético; **marriage** — consejería *or* orientación *or* asesoría matrimonial

counselor *n* consejero -ra *mf*

count *n* recuento, número; **bacterial** *o* **bacteria** — recuento bacteriano *or* de bacterias; **complete blood** — (**CBC**) hemograma completo; **pill** — recuento *or* conteo de pastillas; **platelet** — recuento plaquetario *or* de plaquetas, número de plaquetas; **red blood cell** — número *or* recuento de glóbulos rojos *or* eritrocitos, número *or* recuento de hematíes (*esp. Esp*); **sperm** — recuento espermático *or* de espermatozoides; **white blood cell** — número *or* recuento de glóbulos blancos *or* leucocitos; *vt, vi* contar; **Count backwards from one hundred**..Cuente al revés a partir de cien; **to** — **calories** contar calorías

counteract *vt* contrarrestar

countertransference *n* (*psych*) contratransferencia

country *n* (*rural area*) campo

county *n* (*pl* -**ties**) (*US*) condado

couple *n* pareja

courage *n* valor *m*, coraje *m*

course *n* curso, transcurso, ciclo; — **of antibiotics** ciclo *or* curso de antibióticos; — **of a disease** curso *or* transcurso de una enfermedad; **to take its** — (*enfermedad, etc.*) seguir su curso; **It may be best to let nature take its course**..Puede ser mejor dejar las cosas seguir su curso natural.

cousin *n* primo -ma *mf*

cover *vt* cubrir, tapar; (*insurance*) cubrir, asegurar; **The wound should be covered**..La herida debe cubrirse...**Cover your right eye**..Cubra (Tape) su ojo derecho...**Your insurance covers this**..Su seguro cubre esto...**Your son is covered**..Su hijo está asegurado (cubierto).

coverage *n* (*insurance, etc.*) cobertura

CPAP *abbr* **continuous positive airway pressure**. *V.* **pressure**.

CPR *abbr* **cardiopulmonary resuscitation**. *V.* **resuscitation**.

crab (*fam*) **crab louse**. *V.* **louse**.

crack *n* (*bone, teeth*) fisura, (*skin*) grieta; (*cocaine*) crack *m*, forma de cocaína que se fuma; *vi* agrietarse, partirse

cracked *adj* agrietado, partido

cracker *n* galleta salada

cradle *n* cuna

cradle cap *n* costra láctea (*form*), inflamación escamosa del cuero cabelludo en lactantes

cramp *n* calambre *m*, (*en el abdomen*), retortijón *or* retorcijón *m* (*frec. pl*), cólico (*frec. pl*); **menstrual cramps** cólicos menstruales, dolores *mpl* menstruales (*fam*); **postpartum cramps** entuertos, contracciones bruscas y dolorosas del útero que ocurren en los días posteriores al parto; *vi* **My leg is cramping**..Tengo un calambre en la pierna...**I have cramping**..Tengo calambres (retortijones, retorcijones, cólicos).

cranberry *n* arándano (rojo); **— juice** jugo de arándano(s)

crania *pl de* **cranium**

cranial *adj* craneal, craneano

craniopharyngioma *n* craneofaringioma *m*

craniotomy *n* (*pl* -ties) craneotomía

cranium *n* (*pl* -nia) cráneo

crank *n* (*fam*) metanfetamina

crash cart *n* (*US*) carro de paro, carro de parada (*Esp*)

craving *n* ansia (*frec. pl*), deseo (*generalmente excesivo*), (*for food*) antojo (*frec. pl*); **craving for heroin**..ansias *or* deseo de heroína...**craving for sweets**..antojos de dulces

crawl *vi* (*ped*) gatear

crazy *adj* (*comp* -ier; *super* -iest) loco;

to drive (*someone*) — volver loco (*a alguien*); **His mother drove him crazy**..Su madre lo volvió loco; **to go** — volverse loco, perder la razón

cream *n* (*medicine, cosmetic*) crema, pomada; (*milk product*) nata, crema; **cleansing** — crema limpiadora; **cold** — crema fría, (tipo de) crema limpiadora; **hand** — crema para manos

crease *n* pliegue *m*; **palmar** — pliegue palmar

creatine *n* creatina

creatinine *n* creatinina

cretinism *n* cretinismo

crib *n* cuna

crib death *n* muerte *f* de cuna, síndrome *m* de muerte súbita infantil (*form*)

cricothyroid *adj* cricotiroideo

cried *pret & pp de* **cry**

cries *pl de* **cry**

cripple (*ant*) *n* discapacitado *mf*, lisiado -da *mf*; *vt* discapacitar, lisiar; [*Nota: cripple, como* lisiado, *puede ser ofensivo*.]

crisis *n* (*pl* -ses) crisis *f*; **blast** — crisis blástica; **identity** — crisis de identidad; **midlife** — crisis de la mediana edad

critical *adj* crítico

cromolyn sodium *n* cromoglicato de sodio, cromoglicato disódico (*esp. Esp*)

crooked *adj* torcido, chueco (*Mex*)

crop dusting *n* fumigación aérea

cross-eyed *adj* bizco

cross-match *n* prueba cruzada; *vt* realizar una prueba cruzada

cross-reactivity *n* reactividad cruzada

crotch *n* (*fam o vulg*) ingle *f*, entrepierna (*fam*)

croup *n* crup *m*; ronquera y dificultad para respirar producidas por irritación de la laringe o de la tráquea, generalmente debida a un virus

crowded *adj* (*dent*) apiñado; **— teeth** dientes apiñados

crown *n* (*dent, etc.*) corona; *vi* (*obst*) coronar

crowning *n* (*obst*) coronación *f*

crow's feet *npl* patas de gallo *or* gallina, arrugas al lado de los ojos

cruel *adj* cruel

cruelty *n* crueldad *f*

crush *vt* (*one's finger, hand, etc.*) aplastar, machucar; (*a tablet*) triturar (*form*), moler

crushing *adj* (*pain*) opresivo, aplastante

crust *n* costra

crutch *n* muleta

cry *n* (*pl* **cries**) llanto; (*shout*) grito; **baby's** — llanto del bebé; — **for help** grito de auxilio *or* socorro; *vi* (*pret & pp* **cried**) llorar; (*to call out*) gritar

cryoglobulin *n* crioglobulina

cryosurgery *n* criocirugía

cryotherapy *n* crioterapia

Cryptococcus *n* criptococo

cryptogenic *adj* criptogénico

cryptorchidism *n* criptorquidia

cryptosporidiosis *n* criptosporidiosis *f*

crystal *n* cristal *m*; (*fam, methamphetamine*) metanfetamina, cristal (*fam*)

crystalline *adj* cristalino

C-section *V.* **cesarean section**.

CSF *abbr* **cerebrospinal fluid**. *V.* **fluid**.

CT *abbr* **computed tomography**. *V.* **tomography** *y* **scan**.

cubic *adj* cúbico

cuddle *vt* abrazar, acariciar

cue *n* (*visual, auditory, etc.*) pista, señal *f*, clave *f* (*visual, auditiva, etc.*)

cuff *n* manguito; **blood pressure** — manguito del tensiómetro, manguito del dispositivo para medir la presión; **rotator** — manguito rotador

culdocentesis *n* (*pl* **-ses**) culdocentesis *f*

culture *n* cultura; (*micro*) cultivo; **blood** — hemocultivo (*form*), cultivo de sangre; — **of safety** (**excellence, etc.**) cultura de seguridad (excelencia, etc.); **stool** — coprocultivo (*form*), cultivo de heces (popó, etc.); **throat** — cultivo faríngeo (*form*), cultivo de garganta; **urine** — urocultivo (*form*), cultivo de orina; *vt* cultivar

cumulative *adj* acumulativo

cunnilingus *n* cunnilingus *m*, sexo oral (*practicado a una mujer*), estimulación *f* oral de la vulva y el clítoris

curable *adj* curable

curative *adj* curativo

curb *vt* (*appetite, craving, etc.*) suprimir (*form*), inhibir, frenar, disminuir

cure *n* cura, remedio; *vt* curar

curettage *n* curetaje *m*, legrado; **suction** — curetaje con succión

curette *n* cureta

curl *n* (*biceps*) curl *m*, flexión *f*

current *adj* actual; **his current condition**..su condición actual; *n* corriente *f*

curvature *n* curvatura

curve *n* curva; **growth** — curva de crecimiento; **learning** — curva de aprendizaje

cushion *n* cojín *m*; *vt* acojinar

cuspid *n* (*diente*) canino, colmillo

custom-fitted *adj* (hecho) a la medida

cut *n* cortada, herida; *vt* (*pret & pp* **cut**; *ger* **cutting**) cortar; **Did you cut your finger?**..¿Se cortó en el dedo?; **to** — **down (on)** (*fam*) usar *or* consumir menos, bajar(*le*) a; **You need to cut down on salt**..Tiene que consumir menos sal; **to** — **off** cortar, amputar; **to** — **oneself** cortarse; **Did you cut yourself?**.. ¿Se cortó?; **to** — **one's nails** cortarse las uñas; **to have one's hair** — cortarse el pelo

cutaneous *adj* cutáneo

cuticle *n* cutícula

cutoff point *n* punto de corte

cyanide *n* cianuro

cyanocobalamin *n* cianocobalamina, vitamina B_{12}

cyanosis *n* cianosis *f*

cyanotic *adj* cianótico, con la piel azulada

cyclamate *n* ciclamato

cycle *n* ciclo; **anovulatory** — ciclo anovulatorio; — **of chemotherapy** ciclo de quimioterapia; **life** — ciclo vital *or* biológico; **menstrual** — ciclo menstrual; **reproductive** — ciclo reproductivo *or* reproductor

cyclic, cyclical *adj* cíclico

cycling *n* (*sport*) ciclismo

cyclobenzaprine *n* ciclobenzaprina

cyclophosphamide *n* ciclofosfamida

cyclosporine, ciclosporin (*INN*) *n* ciclosporina

cylinder *n* cilindro

cyproheptadine *n* ciproheptadina

cyst *n* quiste *m*; **Baker** *o* **Baker's** — quiste de Baker, quiste poplíteo; — **passer** (*amebiasis*) portador -ra *mf* asintomático (*que expulsa quistes*); **dermoid** — quiste dermoide; **epidermal inclusion** — quiste epidermoide; **ganglion** — ganglión *m*, ganglio; **hydatid** — quiste hidatídico; **ovarian** —

quiste ovárico *or* de ovario; **pilonidal** — quiste pilonidal; **popliteal** — quiste poplíteo; **sebaceous** — (*fam*) quiste sebáceo (*fam*), quiste epidermoide **synovial** — quiste sinovial; **thyroglossal duct** — quiste del conducto tirogloso

cystectomy *n* (*pl* **-mies**) (*removal of bladder*) cistectomía; (*removal of cyst*) quistectomía

cysteine *n* cisteína

cystic *adj* quístico; (*related to bladder or gallbladder*) cístico

cysticercosis *n* cisticercosis *f*

cystic fibrosis *n* fibrosis quística

cystine *n* cistina

cystinuria *n* cistinuria

cystitis *n* cistitis *f*, infección *f* de la vejiga; **interstitial** — cistitis intersticial

cystocele *n* cistocele *m*

cystoscope *n* cistoscopio

cystoscopy *n* (*pl* **-pies**) cistoscopia

cytisine *n* citisina

cytology *n* citología, estudio microscópico de la célula

cytomegalovirus (CMV) *n* citomegalovirus *m* (CMV)

cytometry *n* citometría; **flow** — citometría de flujo

cytotoxic *adj* citotóxico

D

daclatasvir *n* daclatasvir *m*

dacryocystitis *n* dacriocistitis *f*

dad *n* papá *m*, padre *m*

daddy *n* (*pl* **-dies**) papi *m*, papito, padre *m*

daily *adj* diario; *adv* diariamente, cada día

dairy product *n* producto lácteo, producto derivado de la leche

damage *n* daño; **brain** — daño cerebral; *vt* dañar, hacer daño

damiana *n* (*bot*) damiana

damp *adj* húmedo, mojado

dampness *n* humedad *f*

danazol *n* danazol *m*

dandelion *n* (*bot*) diente *m* de león

dander *n* caspa (*de los animales*)

dandruff *n* caspa (*de los humanos*)

danger *n* peligro

dangerous *adj* peligroso

dapsone *n* dapsona

daptomycin *n* daptomicina

darbepoetin alfa *n* darbepoetina alfa

darifenacin *n* darifenacina

dark *adj* oscuro; (*complexion*) oscuro, moreno

darken *vt, vi* (*derm, etc.*) oscurecer(se)

darunavir *n* darunavir *m*

data *n o npl* datos, información *f*

date *n* fecha; — **of birth** *o* **birth** — fecha de nacimiento

daub *vt* untar

daughter *n* hija

daughter-in-law *n* (*pl* **daughters-in-law**) nuera

daunorubicin *n* daunorubicina

day *n* día *m*; **every** — todos los días; **every other** — en días alternos, cada dos días; **the** — **after** el día siguiente; **the** — **after tomorrow** pasado mañana; **the** — **before** el día anterior; **the** — **before yesterday** anteayer; **the following** — el día siguiente

daydream *vi* (*pret & pp* **-dreamed** *o* **-dreamt**) soñar despierto

daze *n* aturdimiento, mareo, estado de confusión o desorientación sin agitación; **in a** — aturdido, atarantado,

mareado; *vt* aturdir, atarantar
dazed *adj* aturdido, atarantado, mareado;
to become — aturdirse, atarantarse
D&C *abbr* dilatation and curettage. *V.*
dilatation.
DDS, D.D.S. *V.* Doctor of Dental Surgery.
DDT *V.* dichlorodiphenyltrichloroethane.
dead *adj* muerto
deadly *adj* mortal
deaf *adj* sordo; — **and mute** sordomudo;
— **person** sordo -da *mf*
deaf-and-dumb *adj* (*ant*) sordomudo
deafmute, deaf-mute *n* sordomudo -da
mf
deafmutism, deaf-mutism *n* sordomudez
f
deafness *n* sordera
death *n* muerte *f*, (*for statistics, etc.*) fallecimiento; **brain** — muerte cerebral;
— **wish** deseo de muerte, deseo inconsciente de morir; — **with dignity**
muerte digna; **natural** — muerte natural; **sudden** — muerte súbita
deathbed *n* lecho de muerte
debilitated *adj* debilitado
debilitating *adj* debilitante
debride *vt* desbridar
debridement *n* desbridamiento
decaffeinated *adj* descafeinado
decay *n* (*dent*) caries *f*
deceased *adj & n* difunto -ta *mf*
decibel *n* decibelio, decibel *m*
deciduous *adj* (*dent*) deciduo
deciliter *n* decilitro
decision *n* decisión *f*; **shared** — **making**
toma de decisiones compartidas; **surrogate** — **maker** sustituto -ta *mf* responsable de tomar decisiones
declaration *n* declaración *f*; **health care**
— *V.* **advance directive.**
decline *n* deterioro, (*in something measured*) descenso; *vt* no querer, rechazar
decompensation *n* (*psych*) descompensación *f*
decompression *n* descompresión *f*
deconditioned *adj* fuera de forma
decongestant *adj & n* descongestionante
m, descongestivo
decontaminate *vt* descontaminar
decrease *n* disminución *f*; *vt, vi* disminuir(se)

decubitus *n* decúbito; — **ulcer** úlcera de
decúbito
deductible *n* (*insurance*) deducible *m*,
franquicia (*esp. Esp*); **to reach your**
deductible..alcanzar el deducible (la
franquicia)
deep *adj* profundo, hondo
deep-fried *adj* frito (por sumergir en
aceite caliente)
DEET *n* (*repellent*) DEET *m*
defecate *vi* defecar
defecation *n* defecación *f*
defect *n* defecto; **atrial septal** — **(ASD)**
comunicación *f* interauricular (CIA);
birth — defecto congénito (*form*), defecto de nacimiento; **neural tube** —
defecto del tubo neural; **ventricular**
septal — **(VSD)** comunicación *f* interventricular (CIV)
defense *n* defensa
defibrillate *vt* desfibrilar
defibrillation *n* desfibrilación *f*
defibrillator *n* desfibrilador *m*; **automated external** — **(AED)** desfibrilador externo automático (DEA) (*V. también* **cardioverter-defibrillator.**)
deficiency *n* (*pl* -**cies**) deficiencia, carencia, falta
deficient *adj* deficiente; **to be** — **in** carecer de, faltar(*le*) (*a uno*)
deficit *n* déficit *m*, deficiencia, falta
definitive *adj* definitivo
deformed *adj* deforme
deformity *n* (*pl* -**ties**) deformidad *f*
degeneration *n* degeneración *f*; **age-related macular** — degeneración macular senil
degenerative *adj* degenerativo
degradation *n* degradación *f*
degree *n* grado; **37 degrees Centigrade**..
37 grados centígrados
dehiscence *n* dehiscencia; **wound** — dehiscencia de herida
dehumanizing *adj* deshumanizador, deshumanizante
dehumidifier *n* deshumidificador *m*
dehumidify *vt* (*pret & pp* -**fied**) deshumedecer
dehydrated *adj* deshidratado
dehydration *n* deshidratación *f*
dehydroepiandrosterone (DHEA) *n* dehidroepiandrosterona (DHEA)
déjà vu *n* déjà vu *m*, ya visto, sentimien-

to fuerte pero falso de haber vivido anteriormente una nueva situación

delavirdine *n* delavirdina

delay *n* retraso, retardo; **developmental** — desarrollo tardío, retraso en el desarrollo; *vt* retrasar, retardar

delayed *adj* retardado, tardío, retrasado; **developmentally** — con retraso en el desarrollo

deletion *n* deleción *f*

delicate *adj* delicado, frágil; (*subject*) delicado

delirious *adj* delirante; **to be** — tener delirio(s), estar delirando; **He's delirious** ..Tiene delirios..Está delirando.

delirium *n* delirio (*frec. pl*); — **tremens** delirium tremens *m*, delirios con temblor y alucinaciones (*debidos a la suspensión del alcohol*)

deliver (*obst*) *vt* (*mother as subject*) dar a luz; (*doctor or midwife as subject*) atender (*un parto*); **Mrs. Mata delivered a baby boy at two in the morning**..La señora Mata dio a luz a un niño a las dos de la madrugada..**Dr. Ford delivered Mrs. Mata**..El doctor Ford atendió el parto de la señora Mata...**Dr. Ford delivered the twins**..El Dr. Ford atendió el parto de los gemelos; *vi* dar a luz

delivery *n* (*pl* **-ries**) (*obst*) parto, alumbramiento; (*provision*) prestación *f*; **estimated date of** — fecha probable de parto; **health care** — prestación de servicios de salud

deltoid *n* deltoides *m*

delusion *n* delirio, falsa creencia patológica; **delusions of grandeur** delirios de grandeza

dementia *n* demencia; **Alzheimer's** — demencia de Alzheimer, demencia tipo Alzheimer; — **pugilistica** demencia pugilística; **multi-infarct** — (*ant*) demencia vascular, demencia multiinfarto (*ant*); **vascular** — demencia vascular

demonstrate *vt* demostrar

demyelinating *adj* desmielinizante

denatured *adj* desnaturalizado

denervation *n* denervación *f*

dengue *n* dengue *m*

denial *n* negación *f*, rechazo

dense *adj* denso

density *n* (*pl* **-ties**) densidad *f*; **bone mineral** — densidad mineral ósea

dental *adj* dental

dentin *n* dentina

dentist *n* odontólogo -ga *mf*, dentista *mf*

dentistry *n* odontología; **pediatric** — odontopediatra

denture *n* protesis *f* dental (*form*), dientes postizos, dentadura postiza

deodorant *adj* & *n* desodorante *m*

deoxyribonucleic acid (DNA) *n* ácido desoxirribonucleico (ADN)

department *n* departamento, unidad *f*; **Department of Motor Vehicles (DMV)** Departamento de Vehículos Motorizados, Departamento de Vehículos de Motor; **Department of Public Health, Public Health Department** Departamento de Salud Pública; **emergency** — **(ED)** unidad *or* departamento de urgencias; **fire** — cuerpo de bomberos

dependence *n* dependencia, hábito; **nicotine** — dependencia a la nicotina, hábito tabáquico

dependency *n* dependencia; **chemical** — drogodependencia, dependencia a sustancias

dependent *adj* dependiente; **You may become dependent on this medication**..Puede volverse dependiente de este medicamento; **oxygen-dependent, steroid-dependent, etc**. dependiente de oxígeno, dependiente de esteroides, etc.

depersonalization *n* (*psych*) despersonalización *f*

depigmentation *n* despigmentación *f*

depilatory *n* (*pl* **-ries**) depilatorio, producto para quitar el vello

deplete *vt* agotar

depletion *n* agotamiento

deposit *n* depósito, sedimento; *vt* depositar

depot *adj* (*pharm*) de depósito

depressant *adj* depresor

depressed *adj* deprimido; **to get** *o* **become** — deprimirse

depression *n* depresión *f*, tristeza profunda; **postpartum** — depresión posparto *or* postparto

depressive *adj* depresivo

deprivation *n* privación *f*; **androgen** —

privación de andrógenos; **sleep —** privación de(l) sueño

depth *n* profundidad *f*

derealization *n* (*psych*) desrealización *f*

derivative *n* derivado; **petroleum —** derivado del petróleo

dermoabrasion, dermabrasion *n* dermoabrasión *f*

dermal *adj* dérmico

dermatitis *n* dermatitis *f*; **atopic —** dermatitis atópica; **cercarial —** dermatitis por cercarias; **contact —** dermatitis de contacto; **— herpetiformis** dermatitis herpetiforme; **irritant —** dermatitis irritativa; **seborrheic —** dermatitis seborreica; **stasis —** dermatitis por estasis

dermatofibroma *n* dermatofibroma *m*

dermatological, dermatologic *adj* dermatológico

dermatologist *n* dermatólogo -ga *mf*, médico -ca *mf* especializado en la piel y sus enfermedades, especialista *mf* de la piel

dermatology *n* dermatología, rama de la medicina que se ocupa de la piel y sus enfermedades

dermatomyositis *n* dermatomiositis *f*

dermatophyte *n* dermatofito

dermatophytosis *n* dermatofitosis *f*

dermographism *n* dermografismo

dermopathy *n* dermopatía; **nephrogenic fibrosing —** fibrosis sistémica nefrogénica, dermopatía fibrosante nefrogénica

DES *V.* diethylstilbestrol.

descendant *n* descendiente *mf*

descending *adj* descendente

describe *vt* describir

desensitization *n* desensibilización *f*

desensitize *vt* desensibilizar

desipramine *n* desipramina

desire *n* deseo; *vt* desear

desloratadine *n* desloratadina

desmopressin *n* desmopresina

desogestrel *n* desogestrel *m*

despair *n* desesperación *f*, desesperanza

desperate *adj* desesperado; **to become —** desesperarse

desperation *n* desesperación *f*

despondent *adj* deprimido

dessert *n* postre *m*

destroy *vt* destruir

destructive *adj* destructivo

desvenlafaxine *n* desvenlafaxina

detached *adj* desprendido

detachment *n* desprendimiento; (*psych*) distanciamiento; **retinal —** desprendimiento de retina

detect *vt* detectar

detectable *adj* detectable

detection *n* detección *f*

detergent *n* detergente *m*

deteriorate *vi* (*condition of patient*) empeorar; (*substance*) deteriorarse

deterioration *n* deterioro

detoxification, detox (*fam*) *n* desintoxicación *f*

develop *vt* desarrollar; **to develop your muscles**..desarrollar los músculos; *vi* desarrollarse, aparecer(se), salir(se) (*fam*); **He is developing normally**.. Está desarrollándose normalmente... **When did this ulcer develop?**..¿Cuándo le apareció (salió) esta úlcera?

development *n* desarrollo; **language —** desarrollo del lenguaje; **physical —** desarrollo físico; **sexual —** desarrollo sexual; **speech —** desarrollo del habla

developmental *adj* del desarrollo; **— milestone** hito del desarrollo

deviated *adj* desviado

deviation *n* desviación *f*

device *n* dispositivo, aparato; **assistive —** dispositivo de ayuda; bastón *m*, andador *m*, u otro dispositivo para asistir con las actividades de la vida cotidiana; **assistive hearing —** dispositivo *or* aparato de ayuda auditiva; **intrauterine — (IUD)** dispositivo intrauterino (DIU), aparato (*fam*); **left ventricular assist —** dispositivo de asistencia ventricular izquierda; **safety —** dispositivo de seguridad

DEXA *V.* dual-energy X-ray absorptiometry.

dexamethasone *n* dexametasona

dexlansoprazole *n* dexlansoprazol *m*

dexterity *n* destreza

dextromethorphan *n* dextrometorfano

dextrose *n* dextrosa

DHEA *V.* dehydroepiandrosterone.

diabetes *n* diabetes *f*; **— insipidus** diabetes insípida; **(type 1, type 2) — mellitus** diabetes mellitus (tipo 1, tipo 2); **gestational —** diabetes gestacional

diabetic *adj & n* diabético -ca *mf;* — **foot** pie diabético

diabetologist *n* diabetólogo -ga *mf,* médico -ca *mf* especializado en diabetes, especialista *mf* en diabetes

diabetology *n* diabetología, rama de la medicina que se ocupa de la diabetes

diagnose *vt* diagnosticar

diagnosis *n (pl* -**ses**) diagnóstico; **differential** — diagnóstico diferencial; **fad** — diagnóstico *or* trastorno de moda; **pre-implantation genetic** — diagnóstico genético pre-implantacional *or* preimplantatorio

diagnostic *adj* diagnóstico

dialysis *n* diálisis *f;* **continuous ambulatory peritoneal** — **(CAPD)** diálisis peritoneal ambulatoria continua (DPAC)

dialyze *vt* dializar

diameter *n* diámetro

diaper *n* pañal *m;* **cloth** — pañal de tela; **disposable** — pañal desechable

diaphragm *n (anat, gyn)* diafragma *m*

diarrhea *n* diarrea; **traveler's** — diarrea del viajero

diarrheal *adj* diarreico

diary *n* diario

diastolic *adj* diastólico

diazepam *n* diazepam *m*

DIC *abbr* **disseminated intravascular coagulation.** *V.* **coagulation.**

dichlorodiphenyltrichloroethane (DDT) *n* diclorodifeniltricloroetano (DDT)

dick *n (vulg, penis)* pene *m*

diclofenac *n* diclofenaco

dicloxacillin *n* dicloxacilina

dicyclomine (*USAN*), **dicycloverine** (*INN*) *n* dicicloverina

didanosine *n* didanosina

die *vi (pret & pp* **died***; ger* **dying**) morir, fallecer

dieldrin *n* dieldrín *m*

diet *n* dieta, régimen *m,* alimentación *f (form);* **balanced** — alimentación equilibrada *or* balanceada, dieta equilibrada *or* balanceada; **cardiac** — dieta cardíaca; **clear liquid** — dieta líquida clara, dieta de líquidos claros; **consistent carbohydrate** — dieta diabética *or* para diabéticos, dieta en la que la cantidad de carbohidratos medida en calorías se mantiene constante; **diabetic** — dieta diabética *or* para diabéticos; **dysphagia** — dieta de *or* para disfagia; **full liquid** — dieta liquida completa; **high-fiber** — dieta rica *or* alta en fibra; **low-fat** — dieta baja en grasas; **mechanical soft** — dieta de fácil masticación; **Mediterranean** — dieta mediterránea; **nectar consistency** — dieta del néctar líquido; **puréed** — dieta puré; **renal** — dieta renal; **(sodium-, protein-, etc.) restricted** — dieta restringida (en sodio, en proteínas, etc.); **to be on a** — estar a dieta, seguir un régimen; **weight loss** — dieta para adelgazar, dieta de adelgazamiento, régimen adelgazante (*Esp*), dieta para bajar de peso; *vi* estar a dieta, seguir un régimen

dietary *adj* alimenticio, alimentario, dietético; — **needs** necesidades alimenticias *or* alimentarias

dietetic *adj* dietético; *npl* dietética

diethylene glycol *n* dietilenglicol *m*

diethylstilbestrol (DES) *n* dietilestilbestrol *m* (DES)

dietitian *n* dietista *mf,* dietista-nutricionista *mf* (*Esp*), especialista *mf* en alimentación

differentiated *adj* diferenciado; **partially** — parcialmente diferenciado; **poorly** — pobremente *or* poco diferenciado; **well** — bien diferenciado

difficulty *n* dificultad *f*

diffuse *adj* difuso

diffusion *n* difusión *f*

diflunisal *n* diflunisal *m*

digest *vt* digerir

digestible *adj* digerible, digestible

digestion *n* digestión *f*

digestive *adj* digestivo

digit *n (finger, toe)* dedo

digital *adj* digital

digitalis *n (pharm)* digital *f*

dignity *n* dignidad *f*

digoxin *n* digoxina

diiodohydroxyquinoline *n* diyodohidroxiquinoleína, diiodohidroxiquinoleína (*INN*), iodoquinol *m*

dilate *vt, vi* dilatar(se)

dilation, dilatation *n* dilatación *f;* — **and curettage (D&C)** dilatación y curetaje, dilatación y legrado

dilator *n* dilatador *m*
dildo *n* (*pl* **-dos**) consolador *m*, pene erecto artificial usado para gratificación sexual
diloxanide *n* diloxanida
diltiazem *n* diltiazem *m*
dilute *adj* diluido; *vt* diluir
dilution *n* dilución *f*
dilutional *adj* dilucional
dim *adj* (*comp* **dimmer**; *super* **dimmest**) oscuro, indistinto
dimenhydrinate *n* dimenhidrinato
dimension *n* dimensión *f*
dimethyl sulfoxide (DMSO) *n* dimetil sulfóxido
dimethyltryptamine (DMT) *n* dimetiltriptamina (DMT)
diminish *vt, vi* disminuir
dimple *n* hoyuelo
dinner *n* cena
diopter *n* dioptría
dioxide *n* dióxido
dioxin *n* dioxina
diphenhydramine *n* difenhidramina
diphenoxylate *n* difenoxilato
diphtheria *n* difteria
diplococcus *n* (*pl* **-ci**) diplococo
dipstick *n* (*for urine*) tira reactiva (*para orina*)
dipyridamole *n* dipiridamol *m*
direction *n* dirección *f*
directive *V.* **advance directive**.
Director of Nursing *n* director -ra *mf* de Enfermería
dirt *n* suciedad *f*
dirty *adj* (*comp* **-ier**; *super* **-iest**) sucio; **to get** — ensuciarse; **to get (something)** — ensuciar
disability *n* (*pl* **-ties**) discapacidad *f*, (*esp. with respect to work, possibly temporary*) incapacidad *f*, (*disorder*) trastorno; **developmental** — discapacidad del desarrollo; **intellectual** — discapacidad intelectual; **learning** — trastorno de aprendizaje; **physical** — discapacidad física
disabled *adj* discapacitado; (*esp. with respect to work, possibly temporarily*) incapacitado; **developmentally** — con discapacidad del desarrollo; — **person** discapacitado -da *mf*; **gravely** — severamente *or* gravemente discapacitado; **intellectually** — con discapacidad intelectual; **physically** — con discapacidad física

disabling *adj* incapacitante, discapacitante
disadvantage *n* inconveniente *m*, desventaja
disappear *vi* desaparecer
disaster *n* desastre *m*
disc *n* disco; **herniated** — hernia de disco; **intervertebral** — disco intervertebral; **optic** — disco óptico
discectomy *n* (*pl* **-mies**) discectomía
discharge *n* secreción *f*, (*vaginal*) flujo; (*from the hospital*) alta; — **before discharge**..antes del alta; — **summary** informe *m* de alta; *vt* dar de alta; **We are going to discharge you tomorrow**..Lo vamos a dar de alta mañana.
discipline *n* disciplina; *vt* disciplinar
discogram *n* discografía (*estudio*)
discography *n* discografía (*técnica*)
discoid *adj* discoide
discoloration *n* decoloración *f*
discomfort *n* molestia, (*euph*) dolor *m*; **You're going to feel a little discomfort**..Va a sentir un poco de dolor.
discontinue *vt* suspender, (*a catheter, monitor, etc.*) retirar
discouraged *adj* desalentado, desanimado; **to get** — desalentarse, desanimarse
discrepancy *n* discrepancia; **leg length** — discrepancia en la longitud de las piernas
disease *n* enfermedad *f*, mal *m*; **Addison's** —* enfermedad de Addison; **alcoholic liver** — enfermedad hepática alcohólica; **Alzheimer's** — enfermedad de Alzheimer; **benign breast** — enfermedad mamaria benigna, enfermedad fibroquística de la mama; **black lung** — enfermedad del pulmón negro; **calcium pyrophosphate deposition** — enfermedad por deposición de pirofosfatos de calcio; **cat-scratch** — enfermedad por arañazo de gato; **celiac** — enfermedad celíaca *or* celiaca, celiaquía; **Chagas** — enfermedad de Chagas; **chronic obstructive pulmonary** — (COPD) enfermedad pulmonar obstructiva crónica (EPOC); **connective tissue** — enfermedad del tejido conectivo *or* conjuntivo; **coronary artery** — enfermedad coronaria; **Creutz-**

feldt-Jakob — enfermedad de Creutzfeldt-Jakob; **Crohn's** — enfermedad de Crohn; **Cushing's** —* enfermedad de Cushing; **degenerative joint** — artrosis *f*, enfermedad articular degenerativa; **diverticular** — enfermedad diverticular; **fatty liver** — enfermedad de hígado graso; **fibrocystic breast** — enfermedad fibroquística de la mama, enfermedad mamaria benigna; **fifth** — eritema infeccioso, quinta enfermedad; **gastroesophageal reflux** — **(GERD)** enfermedad por reflujo gastroesofágico (ERGE); **Gaucher's** —*enfermedad de Gaucher; **graft-versus-host** — enfermedad de injerto contra el huésped; **Graves'** —* enfermedad de Graves; **hand, foot, and mouth** — enfermedad mano-pie-boca; **Hansen's** — enfermedad de Hansen, lepra; **heart** — enfermedad cardíaca *or* del corazón; **Hirschsprung's** —* enfermedad de Hirschsprung; **HIV** — enfermedad del *or* por VIH; **Hodgkin's** —* *(ant)* enfermedad *or* linfoma *m* de Hodgkin; **Huntington's** — enfermedad de Huntington; **hyaline membrane** — enfermedad de membrana hialina; **infectious** — enfermedad infecciosa; **inflammatory bowel** — enfermedad inflamatoria intestinal; **interstitial lung** — enfermedad intersticial pulmonar; **Kawasaki** — enfermedad de Kawasaki; **kidney** — enfermedad renal *(form)*, enfermedad del riñón; **Legionnaires'** — legionelosis *f*; **liver** — enfermedad hepática *(form)*, enfermedad del hígado; **Lyme** — enfermedad de Lyme; **mad cow** — *(fam)* encefalopatía espongiforme bovina, enfermedad de las vacas locas *(fam)*; **Ménière's** — enfermedad *f* de Ménière; **minimal change** — enfermedad de cambios mínimos; **mixed connective tissue** — enfermedad mixta del tejido conectivo *or* conjuntivo; **motor neuron** — enfermedad de neurona motora; **myeloproliferative** — enfermedad mieloproliferativa; **non-alcoholic fatty liver** — enfermedad hepática grasa no alcohólica; **Osler-Weber-Rendu** — enfermedad de Rendu-Osler-Weber; **Osgood-Schlatter** — enfermedad de Osgood-Schlat-

ter; **Paget's** — **(of bone)** enfermedad (ósea) de Paget; **Paget's** — **(of breast)** enfermedad de Paget (mamaria); **Parkinson's** —* enfermedad de Parkinson; **pelvic inflammatory** — **(PID)** enfermedad inflamatoria pélvica; **peripheral vascular** — enfermedad vascular periférica; **polycystic kidney** — poliquistosis *f* renal; **Pott's** —* mal *m* de Pott; **Raynaud's** — enfermedad de Raynaud; **rheumatic heart** — cardiopatía reumática; **sexually transmitted** — **(STD)** enfermedad de transmisión sexual (ETS); **sickle cell** — enfermedad de células falciformes, enfermedad drepanocítica *(esp. Esp)*; **venereal** — **(VD)** *(ant)* enfermedad de transmisión sexual (ETS), enfermedad venérea *(ant)*; **von Willebrand** — enfermedad de von Willebrand; **Whipple's** — enfermedad de Whipple; **Wilson's** —* enfermedad de Wilson

The non-possesive form is also used, especially in the medical literature: Addison disease, Cushing disease, etc.

disinfect *vt* desinfectar

disinfectant *adj & n* desinfectante *m*

disinhibition *n (psych)* desinhibición *f*

disk *V.* **disc.**

dislocate *vt* luxarse, dislocarse; **How did he dislocate his shoulder?**..¿Cómo se dislocó el hombro?

dislocation *n* luxación *f*, dislocación *f*

dislodge *vt* desalojar, desplazar

disorder *n* trastorno, alteración *f*; **adjustment** — trastorno de adaptación; **antisocial personality** — trastorno antisocial de la personalidad; **anxiety** — trastorno de ansiedad; **attention deficit hyperactivity** — **(ADHD)** trastorno por déficit de atención con hiperactividad (TDAH); **autism spectrum** — trastorno del espectro autista; **avoidant personality** — trastorno de la personalidad por evitación; **behavioral** — trastorno de (la) conducta; **binge eating** — trastorno por atracón; **bipolar** — trastorno bipolar; **body dysmorphic** — trastorno dismórfico corporal; **borderline personality** — trastorno límite de la personalidad; **cyclothymic** — trastorno ciclotímico; **dependent personality** — trastorno de la personalidad por dependencia; **eating** — trastorno alimentario; **female sexual arousal** — trastorno de la excitación sexual en la mujer; **histrionic personality** — trastorno histriónico de la personalidad; **language** — trastorno del lenguaje; **mood** — trastorno del estado de ánimo; **movement** — trastorno del movimiento; **myeloproliferative** — trastorno mieloproliferativo; **narcissistic personality** — trastorno narcisista de la personalidad; **obsessive compulsive** — trastorno obsesivo-compulsivo; **obsessive-compulsive personality** — trastorno obsesivo-compulsivo de la personalidad; **panic** — trastorno de pánico; **paranoid personality** — trastorno paranoide de la personalidad; **personality** — trastorno de la personalidad; **post-traumatic stress** — **(PTSD)** trastorno de estrés postraumático (TEPT); **schizoid personality** — trastorno esquizoide de la personalidad; **schizotypal personality** — trastorno esquizotípico de la personalidad; **seasonal affective** — trastorno afectivo estacional, depresión *f* invernal; **separation anxiety** — trastorno de ansiedad por separación; **sleep** — trastorno del sueño; **somatoform** — trastorno de somatización; **speech** — trastorno del habla

disoriented *adj* desorientado
dispense *vt* (*pharm*) dispensar
displaced *adj* desplazado
displacement *n* (*ortho, psych, etc.*) desplazamiento
disposable *adj* desechable
dissection *n* disección *f*; **aortic** — disección aórtica *or* de aorta; **lymph node** — disección ganglionar, (*complete*) vaciamiento ganglionar
disseminate *vi* diseminarse
dissemination *n* diseminación *f*
dissociation *n* (*psych*) disociación *f*
dissolve *vt, vi* disolver(se)
distal *adj* distal
distend *vt* distender; **to become distended** distender(se)
distention *n* distensión *f*
distilled *adj* destilado
distinguish *vt* distinguir
distracted *adj* distraído

distractible *adj* distraído, que se distrae fácilmente
distress *n* distrés *m*, aflicción *f*; **respiratory** — distrés respiratorio
district *n* distrito, área
disturbance *n* trastorno, alteración *f*
disulfiram *n* disulfiram *m*
diuresis *n* diuresis *f*
diuretic *adj & n* diurético
diversion *n* derivación *f*; — **program** (*US*) programa alterno, programa que ofrece una alternativa a una práctica dañina (como uso de drogas, prostitución, etc.) generalmente ordenadado por el tribunal; **drug** — desvío *or* desviación *f* de drogas; **urinary** — derivación urinaria
diverticulitis *n* diverticulitis *f*
diverticulosis *n* diverticulosis *f*
diverticulum *n* (*pl* -la) divertículo; **Meckel** *o* **Meckel's** — divertículo de Meckel
divide *vt* dividir
diving *n* (*sport*) buceo
divorce *n* divorcio; *vt* divorciarse de; **She divorced him**..Se divorció de él; *vi* divorciarse
dizziness *n* mareo
dizzy *adj* (*comp* -zier; *super* -ziest) mareado; **to make** (*one*) — dar(*le*) mareo
DMARD *abbr* **disease-modifying antirheumatic drug**. *V.* **drug**.
DMSO *V.* **dimethyl sulfoxide**.
DMT *V.* **dimethyltryptamine**.
DMV *abbr* **Department of Motor Vehicles**. *V.* **department**.
DNA *V.* **deoxyribonucleic acid**.
DNR *abbr* **Do Not Resuscitate**. *V.* **resuscitate**.
DO, D.O. *V.* **Doctor of Osteopathy**.
doctor, doc (*fam*) *n* médico -ca *mf*, doctor -ra *mf**; — **on call** médico de guardia; **family** — médico de cabecera, médico de la familia; **on-call** — médico de guardia; **primary care** — médico de atención primaria, médico de cabecera; **private** — médico privado (*V. también* **physician**.)
**abbreviated in front of surnames as* el Dr. *and* la Dra.
Doctor of Dental Surgery (DDS *o* **D.D.S.)** *n* odontólogo, ga *mf*, dentista *mf*, licenciado -da *mf* en odontología

Doctor of Medicine (MD o M.D.) n médico, doctor -ra mf, licenciado -da mf en medicina
Doctor of Osteopathy (DO o D.O.) n osteópata mf, licenciado -da mf en osteopatía
dog n perro; **guide —, seeing eye —** perro guía
domestic adj doméstico, casero
dominant adj dominante; **— gene (hand, hemisphere, etc.)** gen (mano, hemisferio, etc.) dominante
donate vt donar
donation n donación f; **blood (organ, etc.) —** donación de sangre (órganos, etc.)
donepezil n donepezilo
donor adj de donante; n donante mf; **living —** donante vivo; **organ —** donante de órganos; **universal —** donante universal
dopamine n dopamina
dope n (fam o vulg) narcóticos, drogas
dopey, doped up adj (fam) drogado
doping n (sports) dopaje m
Doppler V. ultrasound.
dorsal adj dorsal
dosage n dosificación f; (dose) dosis f
dose n dosis f; **high-dose*** a or en dosis altas; **low-dose*** a or en dosis bajas, (birth control) de baja dosis; **test —** dosis de prueba
*There are at least 12 possible translations of this term using the prepositions a, en, or de; using singular or plural; and inverting the order of the adjective and noun. Using de implies a fundamental quality of the medication under discussion. All permutations are seen; the two listed the most common.
dosing n dosificación f
double adj & adv doble; **— vision** visión f doble; **to see —** ver doble; vt doblar
double-jointed adj (person) que tiene doble articulación, que puede doblar las articulaciones más de lo normal
doubt n duda; vt dudar; **I doubt that's going to help.**.Dudo que vaya a ayudar.
douche n lavado or ducha vaginal; vi darse un lavado or una ducha vaginal
doula n doula mf, persona sin titulación que asiste a las embarazadas

down adj (fam, depressed) triste, deprimido; **Are you feeling down?**.¿Se siente triste?; adv hacia abajo; **Look down.**.Mire hacia abajo.
downer n (fam) sedante m
doxazocin n doxazocina
doxorubicin n doxorubicina
doxycycline n doxiciclina
doze vi dormitar
Dr. V. doctor.
drag n (of a cigarette) calada; **Not a single drag!**.¡Ni siquiera una calada!
drain n drenaje m; **surgical —** drenaje quirúrgico; vt drenar; **to drain an abscess**..drenar un absceso; vi salir(le), drenar; **Is the wound still draining pus?**.¿Todavía le sale pus de la herida?
drainage n (procedure) drenaje m; (material drained) drenaje, líquido drenado, secreciones fpl
drank pret de drink
drape n paño; **surgical —** paño quirúrgico
draw n extracción f; **blood —** extracción de sangre; **You need to go to the laboratory for a blood draw**..Tiene que ir al laboratorio para que le saquen sangre; vt (pret drew; pp drawn) **to — blood** sacar sangre, extraer sangre (form)
dream n sueño; vt, vi (pret & pp dreamed o dreamt) soñar; **to — of o about** soñar con
dress n vestido; vt vestir; (a wound) vendar; vi (también **to get dressed**) vestirse
dressing n venda, apósito (form), cura, (after application) vendaje m; **compression —** vendaje compresivo; **occlusive —** vendaje or apósito oclusivo, cura oclusiva (esp. Esp); **pressure —** vendaje compresivo
drew pret de draw
dried pret & pp de dry
drill (dent) n torno, taladro; vt perforar
drink n bebida; **energy —** bebida energizante or energética; **protein —** bebida proteínica; vt, vi (pret drank; pp drunk) beber, tomar; **Do you drink alcohol much?**.¿Bebe (Toma) Ud. alcohol con frecuencia?
drip n goteo; **postnasal —** goteo pos-

nasal *or* postnasal, goteo retronasal; *vi*
(*pret & pp* **dripped**; *ger* **dripping**) gotear

drive *n* impulso; **sex —** impulso sexual,
libido *f*; *vt, vi* (*pret* **drove**; *pp* **driven**)
(*a vehicle*) conducir, manejar; **driving
under the influence (DUI)**..conducir
bajo los efectos del alcohol

driver *n* conductor -ra *mf*; **designated —**
conductor designado, persona de un
grupo a la que le ha tocado no beber
para conducir

dronedarone *n* dronedarona

drool *n* baba; *vi* babear

drooling *n* babeo

droop *vi* (*eyelids, etc.*) caerse (*los párpados, etc.*)

drop *n* gota; (*in level of something being
measured*) descenso, disminución *f*,
baja; **cough —** pastilla para la tos; **ear
drops** gotas óticas (*form*), gotas para
los oídos; **eye drops** colirio, gotas oftálmicas (*form*), gotas para los ojos;
foot — pie caído; **ophthalmic drops**
gotas oftálmicas, colirio; **otic drops**
gotas óticas; **wrist —** muñeca caída; *vi*
(*pret & pp* **dropped**; *ger* **dropping**)
bajar(se); **His sugar dropped**..(Se) Le
bajó el azúcar.

droplet *n* gotícula, gota chica (*de esputo
que puede flotar en el aire y transmitir
infección*)

drospirenone *n* drospirenona

drove *pret de* **drive**

drown *vt, vi* ahogar(se)

drowsy *adj* (*comp* **-sier**; *super* **-siest**)
somnoliento (*form*), que tiene sueño; **to
be —** tener sueño

drug *n* droga, medicamento; **antiepileptic —** antiepiléptico; **designer —** droga de diseño; **disease-modifying antirheumatic — (DMARD)** fármaco antirreumático modificador de la enfermedad (FARME); **— holiday** descanso
del medicamento; **hard —** droga dura;
**nonsteroidal antiinflammatory —
(NSAID)** antiinflamatorio no esteroideo (AINE); **orphan —** medicamento
huérfano; **prescription —** medicamento recetado, medicina recetada, medicamento de venta con receta médica;
soft — droga blanda; *vt* (*pret & pp*
drugged; *ger* **drugging**) drogar

druggist *n* (*ant*) farmacéutico -ca *mf*, boticario -ria *mf*

drugstore *n* farmacia, botica

drunk (*pp de* **drink**) *adj* borracho; **to get
—** emborracharse; *n* (*person*) borracho
-cha *mf*

dry *adj* seco; **— heaves** (*fam*) arcadas
(*form*), vómitos secos, intento de vomitar sin nada que expulsar; **— mouth**
sequedad *f* de boca, boca seca; **to get
—** secarse; *vt* (*pret & pp* **dried**) secar;
vi (*también* **to — out**) secarse

drying *adj* secante

dryness *n* sequedad *f*, resequedad *f*

DTP *abbr* **diphtheria, tetanus, and pertussis**. *V.* **vaccine**.

DTs, the (*fam*) *V.* **delirium tremens**.

**dual-energy X-ray absorptiometry
(DEXA)** *n* absorciometría de rayos X
de energía dual

duct *n* conducto, vía; **bile —** conducto
biliar; **common bile —** conducto colédoco, colédoco (*fam*), conducto biliar
común; **cystic —** conducto cístico; **left
hepatic —** conducto hepático izquierdo; **lacrimal —** conducto lagrimal;
pancreatic — conducto pancreático;
right hepatic — conducto hepático
derecho; **tear —** conducto lagrimal

ductal *adj* ductal

ductus arteriosus *n* conducto arterioso;
patent — — conducto arterioso persistente

due *adj* **— date** (*obst*) fecha probable de
parto; **to be —** (*obst*) esperar dar a luz;
When are you due?.. ¿Cuándo espera
dar a luz?...¿Cuál es la fecha del parto?;
prep **— to** debido a, como consecuencia de; **ascites due to liver failure**..
ascitis debida a insuficiencia hepática

DUI *abbr* **driving under the influence**.
V. **drive**.

dull *adj* (*pain*) sordo; (*object*) romo; *vt*
(*pain*) calmar (*dolor*)

duloxetine *n* duloxetina

dumb *adj* (*ant, mute*) mudo

duodenal *adj* duodenal; **— switch** cruce
m duodenal

duodenitis *n* duodenitis *f*

duodenum *n* duodeno

durable *adj* duradero

duration *n* duración *f*

dust *n* polvo; **house —** polvo doméstico

or casero, polvo de la casa
dutasteride *n* dutasterida
DVT *abbr* **deep venous thrombosis**. *V.*
  thrombosis.
dwarf *n* enano -na *mf*
dwarfism *n* enanismo
dye *n* tinte *m*, tintura, colorante *m*
dying *ger de* **die**
dysarthria *n* disartria
dyscrasia *n* discrasia
dysentery *n* disentería
dysfunction *n* disfunción *f*; **diastolic —**
  disfunción diastólica; **erectile — (ED)**
  disfunción eréctil; **temporomandibu-**
  lar joint — disfunción temporomandibular, disfunción de la articulación
  temporomandibular

dysfunctional *adj* disfuncional
dyskinesia *n* discinesia; **tardive —** discinesia tardía
dyslexia *n* dislexia
dyslipidemia *n* dislipidemia
dyspepsia *n* (*form*) dispepsia, indigestión *f*
dysphasia *n* disfasia, dificultad *f* para
  comunicarse debida a un problema del
  cerebro
dysplasia *n* displasia, desorden *f* de crecimiento en un tejido
dysplastic *adj* displásico
dystrophy *n* distrofia; **reflex sympathe-**
  tic — (*ant*) síndrome *m* de dolor regional complejo, distrofia simpática refleja (*ant*)

E

ear *n* oreja, (*organ of hearing*) oído; **ex-**
  ternal — oído externo; **glue —** (*fam*)
  otitis media con derrame, otitis media
  serosa; **inner —** oído interno; **middle**
  — oído medio; **outer —** oído externo;
  swimmer's — (*fam*) otitis externa,
  oído de nadador (*fam*)
ear ache *n* dolor *m* de oído
ear candle *n* vela de oído
eardrum, ear drum *n* tímpano
earlier *adj & adv* (*comp de* **early**) más
  temprano; **to go to bed earlier**..acos-
  tarse más temprano
earliest *adj & adv* (*super de* **early**) **the**
  — possible appointment la cita lo
  más pronto posible
ear lobe, earlobe *n* lóbulo de la oreja
early *adj* (*comp* **earlier**; *super* **ear-liest**)
  temprano, (*development*) precoz; **—**
  puberty pubertad precoz; **— during ear-**
  ly pregnancy..durante el principio del
  embarazo; *adv* temprano
earmuffs, ear muffs *n* orejeras

ear, nose, and throat (ENT) *n* otorrinolaringología (*form*); oídos, nariz y garganta
earplug *n* tapón auditivo *or* de oído
earring *n* arete *m*
earthquake *n* terremoto, (*light*) temblor
  m (de tierra)
earwax *n* cerumen *m* (*form*), cera de los
  oídos
eat *vt, vi* (*pret* **ate**; *pp* **eaten**) comer
EBV *abbr* **Epstein-Barr virus**. *V.* **virus**.
ECG *V.* **electrocardiogram**.
Echinacea (*bot*) Echinacea
echinococcosis *n* equinococosis *f*
Echinococcus *n* equinococo
echocardiogram, echo (*fam*) *n* ecocardiografía, ecocardiograma *m* (*esp.*
  Amer)
echocardiography *n* ecocardiografía;
  stress — ecocardiografía de estrés *or*
  esfuerzo; **transesophageal —** ecocardiografía transesofágica; **transthora-**
  cic — ecocardiografía transtorácica

eclampsia *n* eclampsia

ecstasy *n* (*fam*) metilendioximetanfetamina (MDMA), éxtasis *m* (*fam*); liquid — gammahidroxibutirato, éxtasis líquido

ECT *abbr* electroconvulsive therapy. *V.* therapy.

ecthyma *n* ectima *m*

ectopic *adj* ectópico

ectropion *n* ectropión *m*, inversión *f* hacia fuera del párpado inferior

eczema *n* eccema *or* eczema *m*

ED *abbr* emergency department. *V.* department.

ED *abbr* erectile dysfunction. *V.* dysfunction.

edema *n* edema *m*, hinchazón *f*; pulmonary — edema pulmonar

edge *n* borde *m*, margen *m*; cutting — (*of a blade*) borde cortante; cutting — technology tecnología (de) punta; to be on — (*fam*) estar nervioso, estar irritable; to take the — off (*fam*) calmar un poco (*dolor, ansiedad, etc.*)

edoxaban *n* edoxabán *m*

educate *vt* educar

education *n* educación *f*; diabetic — educación diabetológica (*form*), educación en diabetes; sex — educación sexual

EEG *V.* electroencephalogram *y* electroencephalography.

efavirenz *n* efavirenz *m*

effect *n* efecto; adverse — efecto adverso; cumulative — efecto acumulativo; side — efecto secundario; to take — hacer efecto

effective *adj* eficaz, efectivo; (*clinical research*) eficaz bajo condiciones normales (*See note under* efficacy.)

effectiveness *n* eficacia, efectividad *f*; (*clinical research*) eficacia bajo condiciones normales (*See note under* efficacy.)

effeminate *adj* afeminado

efficacious *adj* eficaz, efectivo; (*clinical research*) eficaz bajo condiciones controladas (*See note under* efficacy.)

efficacy *n* eficacia, efectividad *f*; (*clinical research*) eficacia bajo condiciones controladas; [*Note: While English-speaking health professionals often distinguish between* efficacy *and* effec-

tiveness, *most Spanish-speaking health professionals use* eficacia *and* efectividad *interchangeably.*]

effort *n* esfuerzo

effusion *n* derrame *m*; pericardial — derrame pericárdico; pleural — derrame pleural

EGD *V.* esophagogastroduodenoscopy.

egg *n* huevo; (*fam, ovum*) óvulo, huevo (*fam*); — white clara de huevo; — yolk yema de huevo

ego *n* (*pl* egos) (*psych*) yo; (*lay sense*) ego *m*

egocentric *adj* egocéntrico

egoism *n* egoísmo

egoist *n* egoísta *mf*

egoistic *adj* egoísta

egotism *n* egotismo

egotist *n* egotista *mf*

egotistic *adj* egotista

ejaculate *n* eyaculado; *vi* eyacular

ejaculation *n* eyaculación *f*; premature — eyaculación precoz

EKG (*ant*) *V.* electrocardiogram.

elastic *adj* elástico

elbow *n* codo

elderly *adj* de edad avanzada, mayor

elective *adj* (*surg*) programado, electivo

electric, electrical *adj* eléctrico

electrocardiogram (ECG) *n* electrocardiograma *m* (ECG)

electrocardiography (ECG) *n* electrocardiografía (ECG)

electrocute *vt* electrocutar

electrocution *n* electrocución *f*

electrode *n* electrodo

electroencephalogram (EEG) *n* electroencefalograma *m* (EEG)

electroencephalography (EEG) *n* electroencefalografía (EEG)

electrolysis *n* electrólisis *f*

electrolyte *adj* electrolítico; *n* electrolito *or* electrólito

electromyography (EMG) *n* electromiografía (EMG)

electrophoresis *n* electroforesis *f*

electrophysiologic, electrophysiological *adj* electrofisiológico

electrophysiology (EP) *n* electrofisiología (EF)

element *n* elemento; trace — oligoelemento

elephantiasis *n* elefantiasis *f*

eletriptan *n* eletriptán *m*
elevate *vt* elevar; **Keep your legs elevated**..Mantenga las piernas elevadas.
elevation *n* elevación *f*
eliminate *vt* eliminar
elimination *n* eliminación *f*
elixir *n* elíxir *or* elixir *m*
elute *vt* liberar; **drug-eluting** liberador de fármacos
emaciated *adj* severamente enflaquecido, demacrado
emasculate *vt* emascular
embarrass *vt* **to feel embarrassed**..sentirse avergonzado, sentir vergüenza
embarrassment *n* vergüenza
embolectomy *n* (*pl* **-mies**) embolectomía
embolism *n* embolia; **pulmonary** — embolia pulmonar
embolization *n* embolización *f*; **uterine artery** — embolización de las arterias uterinas
embolus *n* (*pl* **-li**) émbolo
embrace *n* abrazo; *vt* abrazar
embryo *n* (*pl* **-os**) embrión *m*
embryology *n* embriología
embryonal *adj* embrionario; — **carcinoma** carcinoma embrionario
embryonic *adj* embrionario; — **stem cell** célula madre embrionaria
emergency *n* (*pl* **-cies**) (*medical*) urgencia, emergencia, (*non-medical*) emergencia; — **C-section** cesarea de emergencia; — **department (ED)** unidad de urgencias; — **room (ER)** sala de urgencias *or* emergencias
emerging *adj* emergente; — **disease** enfermedad *f* emergente
emesis *n* emesis *f*
emetic *adj* emético; *n* vomitivo, emético
EMG *V.* **electromyography**.
emollient *adj* & *n* emoliente *m*
emotion *n* emoción *f*
emotional *adj* emocional, afectivo, emotivo
empathy *n* empatía
emphysema *n* enfisema *m*
empirical *adj* empírico
employ *vt* emplear
employer *n* empleador -ra *mf*, patrón -trona *mf* (*fam*)
employment *n* empleo
empower *vt* (*psych*) apoyar, dar confianza, facilitar, ayudar, permitir; (*sociopo-litical*) capacitar (*V. también la nota bajo* **enable**.)
empty *adj* vacío; **on an** — **stomach** en ayunas; *vt* (*pret* & *pp* **-tied**) vaciar; **to empty one's bladder**..vaciar la vejiga
emptying *n* vaciamiento
empyema *n* empiema *m*
emtricitabine *n* emtricitabina
enable *vt* (*psych*) facilitar, ayudar, permitir (*que alguien haga algo perjudicial*); **He enables her helplessness by doing everything for her**..El facilita su indefensión por hacer todo por ella; [*Nota: En el argot psiquiátrico inglés, cuando uno facilita que alguien haga algo perjudicial se habla de* to enable *y cuando uno facilita que alguien haga algo beneficioso, se habla de* to empower.]
enalapril *n* enalapril *m*
enamel *n* esmalte *m*
encephalitis *n* encefalitis *f*; **eastern equine** — encefalitis equina del este, encefalitis equina oriental (*Esp*); **Venezuelan equine** — encefalitis equina venezolana
encephalopathy *n* encefalopatía; **bovine spongiform** — encefalopatía espongiforme bovina, enfermedad *f* de las vacas locas (*fam*); **chronic traumatic** — encefalopatía traumática crónica; **hepatic** — encefalopatía hepática; **Wernicke's** — encefalopatía de Wernicke
end *n* fin *m*, final *m*; **end of life decisions**..decisiones al final de la vida; **end-stage** en fase *or* etapa terminal
endarterectomy *n* (*pl* **-mies**) endarterectomía; **carotid** — endarterectomía carotídea
endemic *adj* endémico
endocarditis *n* endocarditis *f*; **infectious** — endocarditis infecciosa
endocardium *n* (*pl* **-dia**) endocardio
endocervical *adj* endocervical
endocervix *n* (*pl* **-vices** *o* **-vixes**) endocérvix *m&f*
endocrine *adj* endocrino
endocrinologist *n* endocrinólogo -ga *mf*, médico -ca *mf* especializado en las hormonas y sus trastornos, especialista *mf* en hormonas
endocrinology *n* endocrinología, rama de la medicina que se ocupa de las hor-

monas y sus trastornos
endodontics *n* endodoncia
endodontist *n* endodoncista *mf*
endometriosis *n* endometriosis *f*
endometritis *n* endometritis *f*
endometrium *n* endometrio
endophthalmitis *n* endoftalmitis *f*
endorphin *n* endorfina
endoscope *n* endoscopio
endoscopic *adj* endoscópico; — **retrograde cholangiopancreatography (ERCP)** colangiopancreatografía retrógrada endoscópica (CPRE)
endoscopy *n* (*pl* **-pies**) endoscopia; **capsule** — endoscopia capsular; **upper** — endoscopia digestiva alta, esofagogastroduodenoscopia
endotracheal *adj* endotraqueal
endure *vt* aguantar, tolerar
enema *n* enema *m*, lavativa; **barium** — enema de bario, enema opaco; **retention** — enema de retención
energetic *adj* activo, con mucha energía
energy *n* energía
enfuvirtide *n* enfuvirtida
engineering *n* ingeniería; **genetic** — ingeniería genética
enlarge *vt*, *vi* agrandar(se); **enlarged heart** corazón agrandado
enlargement *n* agrandamiento, aumento de tamaño
enoxaparin sodium *n* enoxaparina de sodio
enrich *vt* enriquecer
enrollment *n* (*insurance, etc.*) inscripción *f*
ENT *V.* **ear, nose, and throat.**
entacapone *n* entacapona
entecavir *n* entecavir *m*
enteral *adj* enteral
enteric *adj* entérico; **enteric-coated** con cubierta entérica
enteritis *n* enteritis *f*; **eosinophilic** — enteritis eosinofílica; **regional** — enfermedad *f* de Crohn, enteritis regional
enterococcus *n* (*pl* **-ci**) enterococo; **vancomycin-resistant** — enterococo resistente a (la) vancomicina
enterocolitis *n* enterocolitis *f*
enteropathy *n* (*pl* **-thies**) enteropatía; **protein-losing** — enteropatía perdedora de proteínas
enterotoxin *n* enterotoxina

entrance *n* entrada
entrapment *n* compresión *f*, atrapamiento; **ulnar nerve** — compresión *or* atrapamiento del nervio cubital; **peripheral nerve** — compresión *or* atrapamiento de nervio periférico
entropion *n* entropión *m*, inversión *f* hacia dentro del párpado inferior
entry *n* entrada; **portal of** — puerta de entrada
enucleation *n* enucleación *f*
enuresis *n* enuresis *f*, (el) orinarse en la cama, (el) mojar la cama
envenomation *n* envenenamiento (*de origen animal*)
environment *n* (*in general*) medio ambiente; (*immediate surroundings*) entorno, ambiente *m*; **something in your environment**..algo en su entorno
environmental *adj* (*in general*) ambiental, del medio ambiente; (*immediate surroundings*) ambiental
enzyme *n* enzima *m&f*; [*Note: Masculine usage predominates in Spain, while feminine usage predominates in Latin America.*]
eosinophil *n* eosinófilo
eosinophilia *n* eosinofilia
EP *V.* **electrophysiology.**
ephedra *n* (*bot*) efedra
ephedrine *n* efedrina
epicondyle *n* (*of elbow*) (*lateral*) epicóndilo (lateral); (*medial*) epitróclea, epicóndilo medial (*esp. Amer*)
epicondylitis *n* (*lateral*) epicondilitis *f* (lateral); (*medial*) epitrocleítis *f*, epicondilitis *f* medial (*esp. Amer*)
epidemic *adj* epidémico; *n* epidemia
epidemiologist *n* epidemiólogo -ga *mf*, médico *mf* especializado en la propagación de enfermedades en poblaciones
epidemiology *n* epidemiología, estudio de la propagación de enfermedades en poblaciones
epididymis *n* (*pl* **-mides**) epidídimo
epididymitis *n* epididimitis *f*
epidural *adj* epidural
epigastric *adj* epigástrico
epiglottis *n* epiglotis *f*
epiglottitis *n* epiglotitis *f*
epilepsy *n* epilepsia
epileptic *adj* & *n* epiléptico -ca *mf*
epinephrine *n* epinefrina

epiphyseal *adj* epifisario
epiphysis *n* epífisis *f*
episiotomy *n* (*pl* -**mies**) episiotomía
episode *n* episodio
epispadias *n* epispadias *m*
eplerenone *n* eplerenona
epoetin alfa *n* epoetina alfa
EPS *abbr* **electrophysiology study.** *V.*
study.
epulis *n* épulis *m*
equilibrium *n* equilibrio
equipment *n* equipo; **durable medical**
— equipo médico duradero
equivalence *n* equivalencia
equivalent *adj & n* equivalente *m*
ER *abbr* **emergency room.** *V.* **room.**
eradicate *vt* erradicar
eradication *n* erradicación *f*
ERCP *V.* **endoscopic retrograde cho-**
langiopancreatography.
erect *adj* erecto
erectile *adj* eréctil
erection *n* erección *f*
ergocalciferol *n* ergocalciferol *m*
ergonomic *adj* ergonómico -ca
ergonomics *n* ergonomía
ergotamine *n* ergotamina
erode *vt* erosionar
erogenous *adj* erógeno
erosion *n* erosión *f*
erosive *adj* erosivo
erotic *adj* erótico
error *n* error *m*; **inborn** — **of metabo-**
lism error innato *or* congénito del metabolismo; **laboratory** — error de laboratorio; **medication** — error de medicación; **refractive** — error refractivo
ertapenem *n* ertapenem *m*
eruption *n* (*dent, derm, etc.*) erupción *f*;
fixed drug — erupción fija medicamentosa, erupción fija por medicamentos *or* drogas; **polymorphous light** —
erupción polimorfa lumínica
erysipelas *n* erisipela
erythema *n* eritema *m*; — **chronicum**
migrans eritema crónico migratorio;
— **infectiosum** eritema infeccioso; —
marginatum eritema marginado; —
multiforme eritema multiforme; —
nodosum eritema nodoso *or* nudoso
erythrocyte *n* eritrocito
erythromycin *n* eritromicina
erythropoietin *n* eritropoyetina

eschar *n* escara, costra
escitalopram *n* escitalopram *m*
esomeprazole *n* esomeprazol *m*
esophageal *adj* esofágico
esophagitis *n* esofagitis *f*; **erosive** —
esofagitis erosiva; **reflux** — esofagitis
por reflujo
esophagogastroduodenoscopy (EGD) *n*
esofagogastroduodenoscopia, endoscopia digestiva alta
esophagus *n* (*pl* -**gi**) esófago; **Barrett's**
o **Barrett** — esófago de Barrett
ESR *abbr* **erythrocyte sedimentation**
rate. *V.* **rate.**
essential *adj* esencial
estradiol *n* estradiol *m*
estriol *n* estriol *m*
estrogen *n* estrógeno; **conjugated estro-**
gens estrógenos conjugados
eszopiclone *n* eszopiclona
etanercept *n* etanercept *m*
ethambutol *n* etambutol *m*
ethanol *n* etanol *m*
ether *n* éter *m*
ethical *adj* ético
ethinyl estradiol (*USAN*), **ethinylestra-**
diol (*INN*) *n* etinilestradiol *m*
ethionamide *n* etionamida
ethmoid *adj* etmoidal; — **bone** hueso et-
moides; — **sinus** seno etmoidal
ethnic *adj* étnico
ethnicity *n* origen étnico, identidad étnica
ethosuximide *n* etosuximida
ethyl alcohol *n* etanol *m*
ethylene glycol *n* etilenglicol *m*
etoposide *n* etopósido
eucalyptus *n* (*bot*) eucalipto
eunuch *n* eunuco
euphoria *n* euforia
Eustachian tube *n* trompa de Eustaquio
euthanasia *n* eutanasia
evacuate *vt* evacuar
evacuation *n* evacuación *f*
evaluate *vt* evaluar, valorar
evaluation *n* evaluación *f*, valoración *f*
evening *n* (*early*) tarde *f*, (*after dark*) noche *f*
eventually *adv* con el tiempo; **Eventual-**
ly it will go away..Con el tiempo se le
va a quitar.
evidence *n* evidencia; **There is no evi-**
dence of tumor..No hay evidencia de

tumor
evil eye *n* mal *m* de ojo
evolution *n* evolución *f*
evolve *vi* evolucionar, desarrollarse
ex- *pref* ex; **ex-husband** ex marido, ex esposo; **ex-wife** ex esposa
exacerbation *n* exacerbación *f*, agudización *f*
exact *adj* exacto
examination, exam (*fam*) *n* exploración *f* (*form*), reconocimiento (*form*), examen *m*, revisión *f* (*fam*); **breast —** exploración mamaria, examen mamario *or* de mama *or* seno; **breast self-examination** (*form*) autoexploración mamaria, autoexamen mamario *or* de mama *or* seno, examen de los propios senos; **mini-mental state —** mini-examen *m* del estado mental; **pelvic —** examen pélvico, examen de las partes (íntimas) (*fam*); **physical —** exploración física, examen físico; **rectal —** tacto *or* examen rectal
examine *vt* explorar (*form*), reconocer (*form*), examinar, revisar (*fam*); **May I examine your leg?**...¿Puedo examinarle la pierna?
exanthem subitum *n* exantema súbito
excess *n* exceso
excessive *adj* excesivo
exchange *n* intercambio
excipient *n* excipiente *m*
excise *vt* extirpar, sacar (*fam*), quitar completamente con cirugía
excision *n* escisión *f*
excisional *adj* escisional
excite *vt* entusiasmar, emocionar; (*sexually*) excitar
excoriate *vt* excoriar
excoriation *n* excoriación *f*
excrement *n* excremento
excrete *vt* excretar
excretory *adj* excretor
excuse *n* excusa; **work —** excusa médica para el trabajo
exemestane *n* exemestano
exenatide *n* exenatida
exercise *n* ejercicio; **Kegel exercises** ejercicios de Kegel; **regular physical —** ejercicio físico regular; **stretching exercises** ejercicios de estiramiento; **warmup exercises** ejercicios de calentamiento; *vt* ejercitar; **to — muscles**

ejercitar los músculos; *vi* ejercitar(se), hacer ejercicio
exert *vt* **to — oneself** esforzarse, hacer esfuerzos
exertion *n* esfuerzo; **physical —** esfuerzo físico
exfoliation *n* exfoliación *f*
exfoliative *adj* exfoliativo
exhale *vt, vi* exhalar, sacar aire (*fam*)
exhaust *vt* agotar
exhausted *adj* agotado, exhausto; **to become —** agotarse
exhaust gases *npl* gases *mpl* de escape
exhausting *adj* agotador
exhaustion *n* agotamiento
exit *n* salida
expand *vt, vi* expandir(se)
expectant *adj* (*obst, fam*) embarazada, esperando bebé
expecting *adj* (*obst, fam*) embarazada, esperando bebé
expectorant *adj & n* expectorante *m*
experience *n* experiencia; *vt* (*to feel*) sentir, experimentar
experiment *n* experimento; *vi* experimentar
experimental *adj* experimental
expert *adj & n* experto -ta *mf*, especialista *mf*; **— opinion** opinión *f* de expertos
expiration *n* (*of a drug*) vencimiento, caducidad *f*; (*exhalation*) espiración *f*; **— date** fecha de vencimiento *or* caducidad
expiratory *adj* espiratorio
expire *vi* (*to die*) fallecer, morir
exploratory *adj* (*surg*) explorador
expose *vt* exponer
exposed *adj* expuesto, (*uncovered*) descubierto; **sun-exposed areas..** áreas expuestas al sol...**Have you been exposed to tuberculosis?**...¿Ha estado expuesto a la tuberculosis?
exposure *n* exposición *f*, contacto
express *vt* (*thoughts, ideas, etc.*) expresar; (*pus, etc.*) exprimir; **to — oneself** expresarse
expressive *adj* expresivo
expulsion *n* expulsión *f*
extend *vt, vi* extender(se)
extender *n* extensor *m*; **penis —** extensor de pene
extension *n* extensión *f*
extensive *adj* exhaustivo; **— testing**

pruebas exhaustivas
extensor *adj & n (anat)* extensor *m*
exterior *adj & n* exterior *m*
external *adj* externo
extra *adj* extra
extracorporeal *adj* extracorpóreo
extract *n (pharm)* extracto; **grape seed** — extracto de semilla de uva; **pine bark** — extracto de corteza de pino; *vt (to take out)* extraer, sacar
extraction *n (dent, etc.)* extracción *f*
extravasation *n* extravasación *f*
extremity *n (pl -ties)* extremidad *f*
extrovert *n* extrovertido -da *mf*
extroverted *adj* extrovertido
extubate *vt* extubar
extubation *n* extubación *f*
exudate *n* exudado
eye *n* ojo; **corner of the** — ángulo del ojo; — **shadow** sombras para ojos;

with the naked — a simple vista
eyeball *n* globo ocular *(form)*, globo del ojo
eyebright *n (bot)* eufrasia
eyebrow *n* ceja; **Raise your eyebrows..** Levante las cejas.
eyedropper *n* gotero, cuentagotas *m*
eyeglasses *npl* gafas, lentes *mpl*, anteojos, espejuelos *(esp. Carib)* (*V. también* **glasses.**)
eyeground *n* fondo de ojo
eyelash *n* pestaña
eyelid *n* párpado
eyesight *n* vista
eyestrain *n* cansancio *or* fatiga visual
eyewash *n* colirio, gotas para los ojos
eyewear *n* gafas, lentes *mpl*, anteojos, espejuelos *(esp. Carib)*; **protective** — gafas protectoras *or* de seguridad
ezetimibe *n* ezetimiba

F

face *n* cara, rostro; *vt (to confront)* enfrentar; *(to turn, facing)* voltearse hacia; **Face the wall, please..** Voltéese hacia la pared, por favor.
facedown *adv* boca abajo
facelift *n* ritidectomía *(form)*, estiramiento facial, lifting facial *(Ang)*, cirugía plástica para eliminar las arrugas de la cara
face mask *V.* **mask.**
face shield *n (medicine)* protector *m or* pantalla facial; *(sports)* protector facial
facet *n (anat)* faceta; — **joint injection** inyección facetaria *(form)*, inyección en la faceta articular
faceup *adv* boca arriba
facial *adj* facial; — **cleanser** limpiador facial, desmaquillador *m*; *n* tratamiento

facial, masaje *m* facial
facility *n (pl -ties)* centro, hospital *m*, asilo, residencia; **skilled nursing** — *(US)* centro de enfermería especializada, asilo *or* residencia para enfermos o discapacitados que requieren servicios de enfermería
factitious *adj* facticio, simulado, fingido
factor *n* factor *m*; **clotting** *o* **coagulation** — factor de coagulación; — **V Leiden** factor V de Leiden; **intrinsic** — factor intrínseco; **Rh** — factor Rh; **rheumatoid** — factor reumatoide *or* reumatoideo; **risk** — factor de riesgo; **sun protection** — **(SPF)** factor de protección solar (FPS)
facts of life *npl (ped, euph)* cómo se hacen los bebés

faculty *n* (*pl* **-ties**) facultad *f*
Fahrenheit *adj* Fahrenheit
fail *vi* fracasar, fallar
failure *n* insuficiencia, fallo, falla, fracaso; **adrenal —** insuficiencia suprarrenal; **congestive heart —** insuficiencia cardíaca congestiva; **— to thrive** desmedro; (*ped*) retraso del crecimiento, desmedro; **heart —** insuficiencia cardíaca, fallo cardíaco; **heart — with preserved ejection fraction** insuficiencia cardíaca con fracción de eyección preservada; **liver —** insuficiencia hepática, fallo hepático; **multisystem organ —** falla multiorgánica, fallo multiorgánico; **(acute, chronic) renal failure** insuficiencia renal (aguda, crónica); **respiratory —** insuficiencia respiratoria, fallo respiratorio, falla respiratoria; **treatment —** fracaso terapéutico *or* del tratamiento
faint *adj* **to feel —** sentir que se va a desmayar, sentirse mareado; **Do you feel faint?**..¿Siente que se va a desmayar?; *n* desmayo; *vi* desmayarse
fair *adj* (*complexion*) blanco, güero (*Mex*)
faith *n* (*religious*) fe *f*
fall *n* caída; (*in level of something being measured*) descenso, disminución *f*, baja; (*season*) otoño; **to prevent falls**.. prevenir las caídas; *vi* (*pret* **fell**; *pp* **fallen**) caerse; bajar(se); **to — down** caerse
fallen *pp de* **fall**
fallout *n* (*nuclear*) lluvia radiactiva
false *adj* falso, (*tooth, eye, etc.*) postizo; **— teeth** dientes postizos, dentadura postiza
famciclovir *n* famciclovir *m*
familial *adj* familiar
family *adj* familiar; *n* (*pl* **-lies**) familia; **dysfunctional —** familia disfuncional; **extended —** familia extendida; **— member** familiar *mf*; **— planning** planificación *f* familiar; **— practice** medicina familiar *or* de familia; **— tree** árbol genealógico *or* familiar
famotidine *n* famotidina
fang *n* colmillo
fantasize *vi* fantasear
fantasy *n* (*pl* **-sies**) fantasía
farmer *n* agricultor -ra *mf*, granjero -ra

mf
farsighted *adj* hipermétrope (*form*), que tiene dificultad para ver los objetos cercanos
farsightedness *n* hipermetropía (*form*), dificultad *f* para ver los objetos cercanos
fart (*vulg*) *n* flato (*form*), gas *m* (*expulsado del recto*), pedo (*vulg*); *vi* expulsar gases, tirarse pedos (*vulg*), tirarse un pedo (*vulg*)
fascia *n* (*pl* **-ciae**) fascia
fasciitis *n* fascitis *f*; **necrotizing —** fascitis necrotizante
fascioliasis *n* fascioliasis *f*
fasciotomy *n* (*pl* **-mies**) fasciotomía
fast *adj* rápido; **fast-acting** (*fam*) de acción rápida
fast *n* ayuno; *vi* ayunar, no comer nada
fasting *adj* en ayunas; **— blood glucose** glucemia en ayunas (*form*), azúcar en la sangre en ayunas; *n* ayuno, (el) ayunar; **Fasting for a day won't do you any harm**..Ayunar por un día no le hará ningún daño
fat *adj* (*comp* **fatter**; *super* **fattest**) gordo; **to get —** engordar(se); *n* grasa; **animal —** grasa animal; **milk —** grasa de leche; **saturated —** grasa saturada; **trans —** grasa trans; **unsaturated —** grasa insaturada
fatal *adj* mortal, fatal
fat burner *n* quemador *m* de grasa
father *n* padre *m*
fatherhood *n* paternidad *f*
father-in-law *n* (*pl* **fathers-in-law**) suegro
fatigue *n* fatiga, cansancio
fatty *adj* (*comp* **-tier**; *super* **-tiest**) (*tissue*) adiposo (*form*), graso; (*food*) graso, grasoso
fatty acid *n* ácido graso; **essential — —** ácido graso esencial; **monounsaturated — —** ácido graso monoinsaturado; **omega-3 — —** ácido graso omega-3; **polyunsaturated — —** ácido graso poliinsaturado; **saturated — —** ácido graso saturado; **trans — —** ácido graso trans; **unsaturated — —** ácido graso insaturado
favorable *adj* favorable
FDA *abbr* Food and Drug Administration. *V.* **administration.**

fear *n* miedo, temor *m*; **fear of needles**.. miedo a las agujas

features *npl* facciones *fpl*, rasgos

febrile *adj* febril

fecal *adj* fecal

feces *npl* heces *fpl*

fed *pret & pp de* feed

fee *n* (*doctor's*) honorarios

feeble *adj* débil

feed *vt* (*pret & pp* **fed**) alimentar (*form*), dar de comer; (*to breastfeed*) amamantar, lactar, dar el pecho, dar de mamar

feedback *n* retroalimentación *f*

feeding *n* alimentación *f*; **tube** — alimentación por sonda

feel *vt* (*pret & pp* **felt**) (*something external*) sentir; **Can you feel this?**..¿Puede sentir esto?...**Do you feel any pain?**.. ¿Siente algún dolor?; *vi* (*internally*) sentirse; **How do you feel?**..¿Cómo se siente?...**Do you feel sick?**..¿Se siente enfermo?...**I hope you feel better soon** ..Espero que se sienta mejor pronto; **to — bad** sentirse mal, (*spiritually or morally*) sentirse mal (con uno mismo); **I feel bad for having cheated on my husband**..Me siento mal (conmigo misma) por haber traicionado a mi esposo; **to — good about oneself** sentirse bien con uno mismo

feeling *n* (*sensation*) sensación *f*; (*emotion*) sentimiento, emoción *f*; (*sense of touch*) sensibilidad *f*; **feeling of warmth**..sensación de calor...**strong feelings** sentimientos fuertes...**Have you lost feeling in your feet?**..¿Ha perdido la sensibilidad en los pies?

feet *pl de* foot

fell *pret de* fall

fellatio *n* felación *f*, sexo oral (*practicado a un hombre*), estimulación *f* oral del pene

felodipine *n* felodipino, felodipina

felon *n* panadizo, infección de la punta de un dedo (*producida por el herpes en la mayoría de los casos*)

felt *pret & pp de* feel

female *adj* femenino; *n* mujer *f*, niña, chica

feminine *adj* femenino

feminization *n* feminización *f*

femoral *adj* femoral

femur *n* fémur *m*

fenofibrate *n* fenofibrato

fentanyl *n* fentanilo

ferric *adj* férrico

ferritin *n* ferritina

ferrous *adj* ferroso; **— sulfate** sulfato ferroso

fertile *adj* fértil

fertilization *n* fecundación *f*; **in vitro — (IVF)** fecundación in vitro (FIV)

fertilize *vt* fecundar

fetal *adj* fetal

fetish *n* fetiche *m*

fetus *n* feto

fever *n* fiebre *f*, calentura; **enteric —** fiebre entérica, fiebre tifoidea; **familial Mediterranean —** fiebre mediterránea familiar; **hay —** rinitis alérgica (*form*), fiebre de(l) heno, alergia al polen; **hemorrhagic —** fiebre hemorrágica; **Mediterranean spotted —** fiebre botonosa mediterránea; **Q —** fiebre Q; **relapsing —** fiebre recurrente; **rheumatic —** fiebre reumática; **Rocky Mountain spotted —** fiebre manchada *or* maculosa de las Montañas Rocosas; **scarlet —** escarlatina; **typhoid —** fiebre tifoidea; **valley —** (*fam*) coccidioidomicosis *f*; **yellow —** fiebre amarilla

fever blister *n* herpes *m* labial (*form*), fuego, calentura, erupción *f* en los labios (*debida al herpes*)

feverfew *n* (*bot*) matricaria

feverish *adj* con fiebre *or* calentura

few *adj* (*comp* less; *super* least) poco

fexofenadine *n* fexofenadina

fiancé *n* prometido, novio

fiancée *n* prometida, novia

fiber *n* fibra; **dietary —** fibra dietética *or* en la dieta; **insoluble —** fibra insoluble; **muscle —** fibra muscular; **nerve — ** fibra nerviosa; **soluble —** fibra soluble

fiberoptic *adj* de fibra óptica

fibrate *n* fibrato

fibrillation *n* fibrilación *f*; **atrial —** fibrilación auricular; **ventricular —** fibrilación ventricular

fibrin *n* fibrina

fibrinogen *n* fibrinógeno

fibrinolysis *n* fibrinolisis *f*, fibrinólisis *f*

fibrinolytic *adj & n* fibrinolítico

fibroadenoma *n* fibroadenoma *m*

fibrocystic *adj* fibroquístico

fibroid *n* (*gyn*) fibroma (uterino), mioma (uterino), tumor benigno del útero

fibroma *n* fibroma *m*

fibromyalgia *n* fibromialgia; síndrome crónico de dolor muscular, fatiga y otros malestares

fibrosis *n* fibrosis *f*; **idiopathic pulmonary** — fibrosis pulmonar idiopática; **nephrogenic systemic** — fibrosis sistémica nefrogénica

fibrotic *adj* fibrótico

fibula *n* peroné *m*, fíbula

fidget *vi* agitarse, moverse mucho (*con impaciencia o nerviosismo*), hacer movimientos inconscientes (*debido a impaciencia o nerviosismo*)

field *adj* de campaña; — **hospital** hospital *m* de campaña; *n* campo; — **of medicine** campo de la medicina; **visual**, — **of vision** campo visual *or* de visión

figure *n* (*of a person*) figura, línea

filariasis *n* filariasis *f*

file *n* lima; (*chart*) historia clínica, historial médico, expediente clínico *or* médico (*esp. Mex*); **nail** — lima de *or* para uñas; *vt* limar; **to** — **one's nails** limar(se) las uñas

filgrastim *n* filgrastim *m*

fill *vt* llenar; (*dent*) obturar (*form*), empastar, rellenar; **to** — **a cavity, to** — **a tooth** (*fam*) empastar *or* rellenar una muela *or* un diente; **to** — **a prescription** (*patient as subject*) presentar una receta para obtener un medicamento; (*pharmacist as subject*) surtir medicamento de acuerdo con una receta; **You can fill this prescription at any pharmacy**..Ud. puede presentar esta receta en cualquier farmacia para obtener el medicamento...**Any pharmacist can fill this prescription for you**..Cualquier farmacéutico puede surtirle su medicamento de acuerdo con esta receta; **to** — **out** (*a form, etc.*) llenar, rellenar, completar, cumplimentar (*Esp*) (*un formulario, etc.*)

filler *n* (*derm*) relleno

filling *n* (*dent*) obturación *f* (*form*), empaste *m*

film *n* película; (*fam, radiograph*) radiografía, placa (*fam*); **a thin film**..una fina película

filter *n* filtro; **inferior vena cava** — filtro de la vena cava inferior; *vt* filtrar

filtration *n* filtración *f*

finasteride *n* finasterida

finding *n* hallazgo

finger *n* dedo (de la mano); — **pad** pulpejo del dedo; **index** — dedo índice; **little** — dedo meñique (de la mano); **middle** — dedo medio, dedo corazón (*esp. Esp*); **ring** — dedo anular

fingernail *n* uña (de la mano)

fingerstick, finger stick *n* punción *f* digital (*form*), pinchazo en el dedo; — **glucose** glucemia capilar (*form*), medición *f* del azúcar a través de un pinchazo en el dedo

fingertip *n* punta del dedo

finish *vt* terminar

fire *n* fuego, incendio; — **department** cuerpo *or* departamento de bomberos; — **extinguisher** extintor *m* de incendios; **fire-resistant** ignífugo, resistente al fuego; — **retardant** retardante *m* de fuego

fire ant *n* hormiga de fuego, tipo de hormiga cuya picadura es muy dolorosa

firearm *n* arma de fuego

firefighter *n* bombero -ra *mf*

firm *adj* firme

first *adj* primero; — **aid** primeros auxilios; *adv* por primera vez; **When did you first feel chest pain?**..¿Cuándo le dolió el pecho por primera vez?

fish *n* (*pl* **fish** *o* **fishes**) pez *m*; (*after being caught, as food*) pescado

fishbone *n* espina

fishhook *n* anzuelo

fissure *n* fisura; **anal** — fisura anal

fist *n* puño; **Make a fist**..Cierre el puño.

fistula *n* (*pl* **-las** *o* **-lae**) fístula; **anal** — fístula anal; **arteriovenous** — fístula arteriovenosa; **mucous** — fístula mucosa

fit *adj* (*comp* **fitter**; *super* **fittest**) en forma, en buen estado físico; *n* (*attack*) ataque *m*, acceso, (*outburst*) arranque *m*, arrebato; — **of rage** arranque *or* arrebato de ira; *vt, vi* (*pret & pp* **fitted**; *ger* **fitting**) (*shoes, clothing*) quedar (bien); (*glasses, etc.*) ajustar; **You need shoes that fit (you) better**..Ud. necesita zapatos que le queden mejor.

fitness *n* acondicionamiento físico
fix *vt* arreglar, reparar
fixate *vt* (*ortho, form*) fijar; *vi* (*psych, etc.*) obsesionarse
fixation *n* (*ortho, psych, etc.*) fijación *f*
fixed *adj* fijo
flab *n* rollos (de grasa)
flabby *adj* (*comp* -**bier**; *super* -**biest**) fofo, flácido *or* fláccido, flojo
flaccid *adj* flácido *or* fláccido
flake (*skin*) *n* escama; *vi* descamarse (*form*), caerse en escamas
flaky *adj* (*comp* -**ier**; *super* -**iest**) escamoso
flame *n* llama; — **retardant** retardante *m* de fuego
flammable *adj* inflamable
flank *n* flanco, costado entre las costillas y la cadera
flap *n* (*surg*) colgajo
flare *n* empeoramiento súbito, ataque *m* (*fam*); *vi* (*también* to — **up**) empeorar súbitamente; [*Nota: El término* flare *se aplica mayormente al lupus y a las artritis inflamatorias.*]
flashback *n* flashback *m* (*Ang*), reviviscencia, recuerdo vivo hasta con alucinaciones de una experiencia traumática en el pasado; (*due to drugs*) recurrencia de alucinaciones producidas por una droga tomada en el pasado
flat *adj* (*comp* **flatter**; *super* **flattest**) plano
flat feet *n* pies planos; **She has flat feet** ..Ella tiene los pies planos.
flatline *n* asistolia, ausencia de actividad eléctrica (*indicada por un monitor cardíaco*)
flatulence *n* flatulencia
flatulent *adj* flatulento
flatus *n* flato, gas *m* (*expulsado del recto*)
flatworm *n* gusano plano
flavonoid *n* flavonoide *m*
flavor *n* sabor *m*; **cherry-flavored, lemon-flavored, etc.** con sabor a cereza, con sabor a limón, etc.
flaxseed *n* linaza, semilla de lino
flea *n* pulga
fleeting *adj* (*pain, etc.*) pasajero
flesh *n* carne *f*; **flesh-eating** devorador de carne
flex *vt* flexionar (*form*), doblar

flexibility *n* flexibilidad *f*
flexible *adj* flexible
flexion *n* flexión *f*
flexor *adj* & *n* flexor *m*
flies *pl de* **fly**
flight of ideas *n* (*psych*) fuga de ideas
flip *vt* (*pret* & *pp* **flipped**; *ger* **flipping**) **to — out** (*fam*) agitarse, trastornarse, reaccionar de una manera exagerada
floater *n* (*in the eye*) mosca volante, pequeños puntos o nubes que se mueven en el campo visual
flood *n* inundación *f*
floor *n* suelo, piso; — **of the mouth** suelo *or* piso de la boca; **pelvic** — suelo *or* piso pélvico *or* de la pelvis
flora *n* flora; **skin** — flora cutánea *or* de la piel
floss *n* (*dent*) seda *or* hilo dental; *vt, vi* limpiar (los dientes) con seda dental
flour *n* harina
flow *n* flujo; **blood** — flujo sanguíneo *or* de la sangre; **menstrual** — flujo menstrual; **peak** — (*spirometry*) flujo máximo; *vi* fluir
flu *n* influenza (*form*), gripe *f*; **Asian** — gripe asiática; **bird** — influenza *or* gripe aviar; **seasonal** — influenza *or* gripe estacional; **stomach** — (*fam*) gastroenteritis *f*, gripe estomacal (*fam*); **swine** — influenza *or* gripe porcina
fluconazole *n* fluconazol *m*
fluctuate *vi* fluctuar, oscilar, variar
fludrocortisone *n* fludrocortisona
fluid *n* líquido, fluido; **amniotic** — líquido amniótico; **body** — fluido *or* líquido corporal *or* del cuerpo; **cerebrospinal** — (**CSF**) líquido cefalorraquídeo (LCR); **pleural** — líquido pleural; **seminal** — líquido seminal; **synovial** — líquido sinovial
fluke *n* duela, (tipo de) gusano plano parásito; **liver** — duela del hígado
flumetasone *n* flumetasona
flunisolide *n* flunisolida
fluocinolone *n* fluocinolona
fluocinonide *n* fluocinónida
fluorescein *n* fluoresceína
fluorescent *adj* fluorescente
fluoridation *n* fluoración *f*, fluorización *f*
fluoride *n* fluoruro
fluorine *n* flúor *m*

fluoroquinolone *n* fluoroquinolona

fluoroscopy *n* (*pl* **-pies**) fluoroscopia

fluorouracil *n* fluorouracilo

fluoxetine *n* fluoxetina

fluphenazine *n* flufenazina

flurazepam *n* flurazepam *m*

flush *n* enrojecimiento (*de la piel*), rubefacción *f* (*form*), rubor *m*; (*due to menopause*) rubor *m*, sofoco, bochorno; *vi* ruborizarse, sonrojarse

flushing *n* enrojecimiento (*de la piel*), rubefacción *f* (*form*), rubor *m*

fluticasone *n* fluticasona

flutter *n* aleteo; **atrial** — aleteo auricular

fluvastatin *n* fluvastatina

fly *n* (*pl* **flies**) mosca

foam *n* espuma

foam rubber *n* gomaespuma, hule *m* espuma

foamy *adj* (*comp* **-ier**; *super* **-iest**) espumoso

focal *adj* focal

focus *n* (*pl* **foci** *o* **focuses**) foco; *vt* (*pret & pp* **focused** *o* **focussed**; *ger* **focusing** *o* **focussing**) enfocar; **to — on** centrarse en, enfocarse en; **We need to focus on your health**..Tenemos que centrarnos en su salud.

fold *n* pliegue *m*; **nail** — pliegue ungueal; **skin** — pliegue cutáneo; *vt* **to — one's arms** cruzar los brazos; **Fold your arms while I listen to your lungs**..Cruce los brazos mientras le escucho los pulmones.

folic acid *n* ácido fólico

folinic acid *n* ácido folínico

follicle *n* folículo; **hair** — folículo piloso; **ovarian** — folículo ovárico

folliculitis *n* foliculitis *f*

follow *vt* (*medically*) tratar, atender; **Who follows you for your diabetes?** ..¿Quién le trata la diabetes?

follow-up *n* seguimiento, atención médica subsecuente

fondaparinux *n* fondaparinux *m*

fondle *vt* (*to caress*) acariciar, (*to molest*) molestar

fontanelle *n* fontanela, mollera

food *n* alimento(s), comida; **baby** — alimento(s) infantil(es), alimento(s) *or* comida para bebés; **canned** — alimento(s) enlatado(s), comida enlatada; **fast** — comida rápida; **health** — *o* **natural** — alimento(s) natural(es); **junk** — comida basura *or* chatarra; **processed** — alimento(s) procesado(s); [*Note:* comida *is a mass noun in this context, but* alimento *is not and therefore requires a plural form when referring to more than one type of food.*] [*Nota:* food, *como la palabra* comida, *es un nombre no contable y por eso* food *puede referirse a un alimento o varios alimentos, según el contexto. A pesar de que sea un nombre no contable, la forma plural,* foods, *es de uso común y siempre significa varios alimentos.*]

foodborne *adj* de transmisión alimentaria (*form*), transmitido por los alimentos

foot *n* (*pl* **feet**) pie *m*; (*unit of measure*) 0,3048 metros; **club** — pie zambo, malformación congénita del pie; **diabetic** — pie diabético

football *n* fútbol *or* futbol americano

footrest *n* reposapiés *m*

footwear *n* calzado (*zapatos, botas*)

foramen ovale *n* foramen *m* oval; **patent** — — foramen oval permeable

force *n* fuerza

forceps *n* (*pl* **-ceps**) (*obst, surg*) fórceps *m*

forearm *n* antebrazo

forefinger *n* dedo índice

forefoot *n* antepié *m*, parte *f* anterior del pie

forehead *n* frente *f*

foreign *adj* extraño; — **body** cuerpo extraño; — **proteins** proteínas extrañas

forensic *adj* forense

foreplay *n* preliminares *mpl*, caricias eróticas que preceden al acto sexual

foreskin *n* prepucio

forever *adv* para siempre; **Herpes is forever**..El herpes es para siempre.

forget *vt, vi* (*pret* **-got**; *pp* **-gotten**; *ger* **-getting**) olvidar

forgetful *adj* olvidadizo

forgetfulness *n* dificultad *f* para recordar, falta de memoria

forgive *vt* perdonar

form *n* forma; (*paper to fill out*) formulario (*cuestionario, etc.*); *vt, vi* formar(se)

formaldehyde *n* formaldehído; [*Note: The accent is not a misprint.*]

formalin *n* formol *m*
former *adj* ex; — **smoker** ex fumador -ra *mf*
formoterol *n* formoterol *m*
formula *n* (*pharm, math*) fórmula; (*ped*) fórmula, leche *f* artificial para lactantes
formulary *n* (*pl* -ries) formulario, lista de medicamentos disponibles
fortify *vt* (*pret & pp* -fied) (*food*) enriquecer
forward *adv* adelante, hacia adelante; **Lean forward**..Inclínese hacia adelante.
fosamprenavir *n* fosamprenavir *m*
fosinopril *n* fosinopril *m*
fossa *n* fosa
foster care *n* cuidado de crianza, crianza de huérfanos o niños abandonados por alguien que no es padre adoptivo y que recibe remuneración del gobierno
foul-smelling *adj* maloliente, que huele mal
fourth *n* cuarta parte, cuarto; **a fourth of the patients**..una cuarta parte de los pacientes
fraction *n* fracción *f*; **ejection** — fracción de eyección
fracture *n* fractura; **boxer's** — fractura del boxeador; **closed** — fractura cerrada; **comminuted** — fractura conminuta; **compound** — fractura abierta *or* expuesta; **green-stick** — fractura en tallo verde; **hairline** — fisura, grieta, fractura muy fina; **open** — fractura abierta; **pathologic** — fractura patológica; **skull** — fractura craneal *or* de cráneo; **spiral** — fractura espiroidea; **stress** — fractura por estrés; **vertebral compression** — aplastamiento vertebral, fractura por compresión de una vertebra; *vt, vi* fracturar(se), quebrar(se); **He fractured his femur**..Se fracturó (quebró) el fémur...**The bullet fractured his femur**..La bala le fracturó (quebró) el fémur.
fragile *adj* frágil, delicado, quebradizo
fragment *n* fragmento
frail *adj* frágil, débil
frames *npl* (*for eyeglasses*) monturas, armazones *mpl*, marcos
frantic *adj* frenético, agitado
fraternal *adj* fraterno
freak *n* (*vulg*) monstruo; *vi* **to — out**

(*fam*) agitarse, trastornarse, reaccionar de una manera exagerada
freckle *n* peca
free *adj* libre, suelto; (*no cost*) gratuito; **fat-free, sugar-free, etc**. sin grasa, sin azúcar, etc.; — **of pain** sin dolor; — **services** servicios gratuitos; **pain-free** sin dolor, (*method, procedure*) que no duele; *vt* soltar
free base *n* (*cocaine*) base *f* libre (*de cocaína*)
free-floating *adj* (*anxiety, etc.*) flotante
freeze *vt, vi* (*pret* froze; *pp* frozen) congelar(se)
freeze-dried *adj* liofilizado
frequency *n* (*pl* -cies) frecuencia
frequent *adj* frecuente
frequently *adv* frecuentemente, a menudo
fresh *adj* fresco
Freudian *adj* freudiano
friction *n* fricción *f*
fried (*pret & pp de* fry) *adj* frito
friend *n* amigo -ga *mf*
friendly *adj* amable
friendship *n* amistad *f*
fright *n* susto
frighten *vt* asustar
frigid *adj* (*ant*) con deseo sexual disminuido (*dicho de una mujer*), frígida (*ant*)
frigidity *n* (*ant*) deseo sexual disminuido (*en una mujer*), frigidez *f* (*ant*)
front *n* parte delantera, frente *m*; **the front of the knee**..la parte delantera de la rodilla; **in — of** frente a, delante de; **in front of a mirror**..frente a (delante de) un espejo
frontal *adj* frontal
frostbite *n* congelación *f*, daño a los tejidos producido por exposición al frío
frovatriptan *n* frovatriptán *m*
frown *vi* fruncir el ceño
froze *pret de* freeze
frozen *pp de* freeze
fructose *n* fructosa
fruit *n* (*pl* fruit *o* fruits) fruta; **citric** — fruta cítrica
frustrate *vt* frustrar
fry *vt* (*pret & pp* fried) freír
FSH *abbr* **follicle-stimulating hormone**. *V.* **hormone**.
full *adj* lleno; **to feel** — sentirse lleno

fulminant *adj* fulminante
fumes *npl* humo (*frec. pl*), vapores *mpl*
fumigate *vt* fumigar
fun *n* diversión *f;* **to have** — divertirse
function *n* función *f; vi* funcionar
fundus *n* (*gyn, ophth, etc.*) fondo
funeral home *n* funeraria
fungal *adj* fúngico, micótico
fungicide *n* fungicida *m*
fungus *n* (*pl* -**gi**) hongo
funny *adj* (*fam o vulg, unusual*) extraño,
raro; *adv* de una manera extraña *or*
rara; **She walks funny**..Camina de una
manera extraña (rara).
funny bone *n* (*fam*) codo
furious *adj* furioso
furosemide *n* furosemida
furuncle *n* forúnculo, infección *f* de un
folículo piloso
fuse *vt, vi* (*ortho*) fusionar(se)
fusion *n* fusión *f;* **lumbar** — fusión lumbar

G

gabapentin *n* gabapentina
gadolinium *n* gadolinio
gag *vt* (*pret & pp* **gagged**; *ger* **gagging**)
(*también* **to make** [*someone*] —) provocar el reflejo nauseoso (*p. ej., con un depresor*); **It gagged him**..It made him gag..Le provocó el reflejo nauseoso; *vi* tener el reflejo nauseoso; **She gagged**..Tuvo el reflejo nauseoso.
gain *n* aumento, ganancia; (*psych, etc.*) beneficio; **secondary** — beneficio secundario; **weight** — aumento de peso; *vt* **to** — **weight** subir *or* aumentar de peso
gait *n* marcha, forma de caminar
galactose *n* galactosa
galactosemia *n* galactosemia
galantamine *n* galantamina
gallbladder *n* vesícula (biliar)
gallium *n* galio
gallop *n* (*card*) galope *m*
gallstone *n* cálculo biliar (*form*), piedra en la vesícula
gambling *n* juego (*apostando*); — **addiction** (*fam*) adicción *f* al juego
gaming *n* (*euph*) juego (*apostando*)
gamma *n* gamma; — **knife** bisturí de rayos gamma

gamma-hydroxybutyrate, gamma-hydroxybutyric acid (GHB) *n* gammahidroxibutirato, ácido gamma hidroxibutírico, éxtasis líquido (*fam*)
gammopathy *n* gammapatía; **monoclonal** — **of undetermined significance** gammapatía monoclonal de significado incierto
ganciclovir *n* ganciclovir *m*
gang *n* pandilla
ganglion *n* (*pl* -**glia**) (*neuro*) ganglio; — **cyst** ganglión *m*
ganglioneuroma *n* ganglioneuroma *m*
gangrene *n* gangrena; **dry** — gangrena seca; **gas** — gangrena gaseosa
gap *n* espacio, brecha; (*in memory*) laguna mental; — **between your teeth** espacio entre los dientes; — **in coverage** brecha en cobertura
gargle *vi* hacer gárgaras
garlic *n* ajo
gas *n* gas *m;* (*US, fam*) gasolina; **natural** — gas natural; **nerve** — gas neurotóxico (*form*), gas nervioso; **tear** — gas lacrimógeno; **to have** — tener gases; **to pass** — expulsar gases; **Are you passing gas yet?**..¿Ya está expulsando gases?

gash *n* herida (*generalmente grande y producida por un objeto cortante*)

gasoline *n* (*US*) gasolina

gasp *vi* hacer esfuerzos para respirar, hacer esfuerzo marcado con cada respiración

gastrectomy *n* (*pl* -**mies**) gastrectomía; **sleeve** — gastrectomía en manga

gastric *adj* gástrico

gastrin *n* gastrina

gastrinoma *n* gastrinoma *m*

gastritis *n* gastritis *f*

gastrocnemius *n* gastrocnemio, músculo gemelo

gastroenteritis *n* gastroenteritis *f*

gastroenterologist *n* gastroenterólogo -ga *mf*, médico -ca *mf* especializado en el aparato digestivo y sus trastornos, médico del estómago (*fam*)

gastroenterology *n* gastroenterología, rama de la medicina que se ocupa del aparato digestivo y sus enfermedades

gastroesophageal *adj* gastroesofágico

gastrointestinal (GI) *adj* gastrointestinal (GI)

gastroparesis *n* gastroparesia

gastrostomy *n* (*pl* -**mies**) gastrostomía; **percutaneous endoscopic** — (**PEG**) gastrostomía endoscópica percutánea (GEP)

gauge *n* calibre *m*; **21** — **needle** aguja de calibre 21

gauze *n* gasa

gave *pret de* **give**

gay *adj & n* gay *mf*, homosexual *mf*, (*female*) lesbiana

gaze *n* mirada; — **palsy** parálisis *f* de la mirada

gel *n* gel *m*

gelatin *n* gelatina

gemfibrozil *n* gemfibrozilo

gender *n* género, sexo; — **identity** identidad *f* de género

gene *n* gen *m*

general *adj* general; **in** — por lo general

generalized *adj* generalizado

generation *n* generación *f*; **first (second, third, latest, etc.)** — primera (segunda, tercera, última, etc.) generación

generator *n* (*of a pacemaker, etc.*) generador *m*

generic *adj & n* (*pharm*) genérico

genetic *adj* genético

geneticist *n* genetista *mf*

genetics *n* genética

genital *adj* genital; *npl* genitales *mpl*

genius *n* genio

genome *n* genoma *m*; **human** — genoma humano

genotype *n* genotipo

gentamicin *n* gentamicina

gentian violet *n* violeta de genciana

gentle *adj* suave, ligero

genu valgum *n* genu valgo, rodillas pegadas (*fam*)

genu varum *n* genu varo, piernas arqueadas (*fam*)

GERD *abbr* **gastroesophageal reflux disease**. *V.* **disease**.

geriatric *adj* geriátrico

geriatrician *n* geriatra *mf*, médico -ca *mf* especializado en el envejecimiento y sus enfermedades

geriatrics *n* geriatría, rama de la medicina que se ocupa del envejecimiento y sus enfermedades

germ *n* germen *m*, microbio; (*of a seed*) germen *m*; **wheat** — germen de trigo

germinoma *n* germinoma *m*

gerontologist *n* gerontólogo -ga *mf*, especialista *mf* en envejecimiento

gerontology *n* gerontología, estudio del envejecimiento

gestation *n* gestación *f*

gestational *adj* gestacional

get *vt* (*pret* **got**; *pp* **gotten**; *ger* **getting**) (*to become*) ponerse, (*inflamed, sick, etc.*) inflamarse, enfermerse, etc.; (*a disease*) dar(le) (*a uno*), pegar(le) (*a uno*), coger* (*Esp*); **It got red**..Se puso rojo...**She got sick**..Se puso enferma..Se enfermó; **to** — **out of bed** levantarse de la cama; **to** — **over** (*an illness, etc.*) recuperarse; **to** — **up** levantarse

*potentially offensive in Mexico and much of Central and South America

GH *abbr* **growth hormone**. *V.* **hormone**.

GHB *V.* **gamma-hydroxybutyrate**.

GI *V.* **gastrointestinal**.

giant *adj* gigante

giardiasis *n* giardiasis *f*

giddy *adj* (*comp* -**dier**; *super* -**diest**) mareado

GIFT *abbr* **gamete intrafallopian**

transfer. *V.* transfer.

gifted *adj* superdotado

gigantism *n* gigantismo

Gila monster *n* monstruo de Gila

ginger *n* (*bot*) jengibre *m*

gingiva *n* (*pl* -vae) encía

gingivectomy *n* gingivectomía

gingivitis *n* gingivitis *f*; acute necrotizing ulcerative — gingivitis ulcerativa necrotizante aguda

Ginkgo biloba *n* (*bot*) Ginkgo biloba *m*

ginseng *n* (*bot*) ginseng *m*, mandrágora

girdle *n* cintura; pelvic — cintura pélvica; shoulder — cintura escapular

girl *n* niña, muchacha, chica

girlfriend *n* amiga, (*romantic*) novia

girth *n* perímetro

give *vt* (*pret* gave; *pp* given) dar; (*a disease*) contagiar (*form*), pegar, (*esp. STD*) pasar; to — out (*knee, etc.*) fallar(*le*); Your knee gave out?..¿Le falló la rodilla?; to — up (*smoking, etc.*) dejar de; You have to give up smoking..Tiene que dejar de fumar; to — up on (*diet, treatment, etc.*) abandonar, suspender

gland *n* glándula; (*fam, lymph node*) ganglio linfático; adrenal — glándula suprarrenal, suprarrenal *f* (*fam*); endocrine — glándula endocrina; lacrimal — glándula lagrimal; mammary — glándula mamaria; parathyroid — glándula paratiroides, paratiroides *f* (*fam*); parotid — glándula parótida, parótida (*fam*); pineal — glándula pineal; pituitary — glándula pituitaria, hipófisis *f*; prostate — glándula prostática, próstata (*fam*); salivary — glándula salival; sweat — glándula sudorípara; thyroid — glándula tiroides, tiroides *m&f* (*fam*)

glans *n* glande *m*

glass *n* (*material*) vidrio; (*tumbler*) vaso; a glass of milk..un vaso de leche

glasses *npl* gafas, lentes *mpl*, anteojos, espejuelos (*esp. Carib*); bifocal — lentes *or* gafas bifocales, bifocales *mpl or fpl* (*fam*); reading — gafas *or* lentes de lectura *or* para leer; safety — gafas protectoras *or* de seguridad

glaucoma *n* glaucoma *m*

glimepiride *n* glimepirida

glioblastoma *n* glioblastoma *m*; glio-

blastoma multiforme glioblastoma multiforme

glioma *n* glioma *m*

glipizide *n* glipizida

global *adj* global

globulin *n* globulina; gamma — gammaglobulina; immune — inmunoglobulina (*producto sanguíneo*)

glomerulonephritis *n* glomerulonefritis *f*

glossitis *n* glositis *f*

glottis *n* glotis *f*

glove *n* guante *m*

glucagon *n* glucagón *m*

glucagonoma *n* glucagonoma *m*

glucocorticoid *adj & n* glucocorticoide *m*

glucometer *n* (*fam*) medidor *m* de glucosa, glucómetro (*fam*)

glucosamine *n* glucosamina

glucose *n* glucosa

glue *n* (*as drug of abuse*) pegamento

glutamic acid *n* ácido glutámico

glutamine *n* glutamina

glutaraldehyde *n* glutaraldehído; [*Note: The accent is not a misprint.*]

gluteal *adj* glúteo

gluten *n* gluten *m*

gluteus *n* glúteo

glyburide (*USAN*), glibenclamide (*INN*) *n* gliburida, glibenclamida (*INN*)

glycerol, glycerin *n* glicerol *m*, glicerina

glycine *n* glicina

GMO *abbr* genetically modified organism. *V.* organism.

gnat *n* (*type that bite*) jején *m*, insecto parecido al mosquito pero más pequeño y que pica

gnawing *adj* (*pain*) sordo y persistente

GnRH *abbr* gonadotropin-releasing hormone. *V.* hormone.

go *vi* (*pret* went; *pp* gone) ir; to be going around (*a virus, etc.*) estar circulando; The flu is going around..La gripe está circulando; to — away (*pain, etc.*) quitarse, pasar; The pain should go away in a few days..El dolor debe quitarse (pasar) dentro de unos días; to — down (*temperature, blood glucose, etc.*) bajar(se); to — to the doctor ir *or* acudir al médico; to — up subir

goal *n* meta, objetivo; cholesterol —

meta *or* objetivo de colesterol; **goal-oriented** orientado al logro de objetivos, orientado a objetivos

God *n* Dios *m*

godfather *n* padrino

godmother *n* madrina

goggles *npl* gafas, gogles *mpl* (*Ang*); **safety** — gafas protectoras *or* de seguridad; **swimming** — gafas de natación *or* para nadar

goiter *n* bocio; **toxic multinodular** — bocio multinodular tóxico

gold *n* oro

goldenseal *n* (*bot*) sello de oro

golfer's elbow *n* (*fam*) epitrocleítis *f*, epicondilitis *f* medial (*esp. Amer*), codo de golfista (*fam*)

gonad *n* gónada

gonadorelin *n* gonadorelina

gonadotropin *n* gonadotropina, (*pharm*) gonadotrofina; **human chorionic** — **(HCG)** gonadotropina coriónica humana, (*pharm*) gonadotrofina coriónica humana

gonococcus *n* (*pl* -**ci**) gonococo

gonorrhea *n* gonorrea

good *adj* (*comp* **better**; *super* **best**) bueno (**buen** *before masculine singular nouns*); **a good surgeon**..un buen cirujano; *n* bien *m*; **for your own** — por su propio bien

goosebumps *n* piel *f* de gallina

goserelin *n* goserelina

got *pret de* **get**

gotten *pp de* **get**

gout *n* gota

gouty *adj* gotoso

gown *n* bata

grade *n* (*degree*) grado; **low-grade** (*fever, infection*) leve; (*tumor*) de bajo grado; **high-grade** (*tumor*) de alto grado

gradual *adj* gradual

gradually *adv* gradualmente, poco a poco

graduated *adj* graduado

graft *n* injerto; **bone** — injerto óseo *or* de hueso; **coronary artery bypass** — **(CABG)** injerto de derivación arterial coronaria (IDAC); **skin** — injerto cutáneo *or* de la piel; *vt* injertar, implantar un injerto

grain *n* (*pharm*) unidad *f* de peso equivalente a 0,0648 gramos; (*food*) grano, cereal *m*

gram *n* gramo

gramicidin *n* gramicidina

Gram-negative *adj* Gram negativo

Gram-positive *adj* Gram positivo

grandchild *n* (*pl* -**children**) nieto -ta *mf*; *npl* nietos

granddaughter *n* nieta

grandfather *n* abuelo

grandiose *adj* (*psych*) grandioso

grandiosity *n* (*psych*) grandiosidad *f*

grandmother *n* abuela

grandparent *n* abuelo -la *mf*; *npl* abuelos

grandson *n* nieto

granulation *n* granulación *f*

granule *n* gránulo

granulocyte *n* granulocito

granuloma *n* granuloma *m*; **pyogenic** — granuloma piógeno

granulomatosis *n* granulomatosis *f*; **with polyangiitis, Wegener's** — (*ant*) granulomatosis con poliangeítis, granulomatosis de Wegener (*ant*)

grapefruit *n* toronja, pomelo (*esp. Esp*)

graph *n* gráfico *or* gráfica

grasp *vt* agarrar

grass *n* hierba, césped *m*; (*fam, marijuana*) marihuana, mariguana (*Mex*), hierba (*fam*), mota (*Mex, CA; fam*); **allergic to grasses**..alérgico a la hierba *or* al césped

gratification *n* (*psych*) gratificación *f*

grave *adj* grave

gray *adj* gris; *n* (*rad*) gray *m*

grayish *adj* grisáceo

graze *vt* rozar

grease *n* grasa

greasy *adj* (*comp* -**ier**; *super* -**iest**) graso-so, graso, grasiento

greater *adj* mayor, más grande; **— than** superior a, por encima de, mayor de (*V. también* **higher**.)

great-grandchild *n* (*pl* -**children**) bisnieto -ta *mf*; *npl* bisnietos

great-granddaughter *n* bisnieta

great-grandfather *n* bisabuelo

great-grandmother *n* bisabuela

great-grandparent *n* bisabuelo -la *mf*; *npl* bisabuelos

great-grandson *n* bisnieto

green *adj* verde; (*fruit*) verde, no maduro

greenish *adj* verdoso

greens *npl* verduras

grew *pret de* **grow**

grief *n* duelo, dolor *m* emocional por una pérdida, *(due to death)* luto; **The five stages of grief in the Kübler-Ross model are denial, anger, bargaining, depression, and acceptance**..Las cinco etapas del duelo en el modelo de Kübler-Ross son la negación, ira, negociación, depresión y aceptación.

grill *vt* asar a la parrilla

grind *vt* (*pret & pp* **ground**) *(a pill, etc.)* triturar *(form)*, moler; *(one's teeth)* rechinar, apretar *(los dientes)*; **I think you're grinding your teeth in your sleep**..Creo que rechina (aprieta) los dientes durante el sueño.

grip *n* agarre *m*, prensión *f*; — **strength** fuerza de agarre *or* prensión; *vt* (*pret & pp* **gripped**; *ger* **gripping**) agarrar, apretar

griseofulvin *n* griseofulvina

groan *n* gemido; *vi* gemir

groggy *adj* mareado y débil *(debido a una droga, falta de sueño, etc.)*

groin *n* ingle *f*, entrepierna *(fam)*

ground *pret & pp de* **grind**

ground *n* suelo, tierra; *(electrical)* toma de tierra

group *n* grupo; **age** — grupo etario *(form)*, grupo de edad; **blood** — *(form)* grupo sanguíneo *(form)*, tipo de sangre; **peer** — grupo de iguales, grupo de personas de la misma edad y aproximadamente el mismo estatus social que comparten los mismos intereses y creencias y que influyen uno en el otro; **support** — grupo de apoyo

grow *vi* (*pret* **grew**; *pp* **grown**) crecer; **— old** envejecer; **to — out of** *(a habit)* quitarse(*le*) *(a uno)* con el tiempo, desaparecer con el tiempo *(un hábito)*; **She will grow out of it**..Se le quitará con el tiempo..Desaparecerá con el tiempo; **to — up** crecer, ser grande; **What are you going to be when you grow up?**..¿Qué vas a ser cuando seas grande?

growing pains *npl* dolores *mpl* de crecimiento, dolores de las piernas que ocurren en algunos niños durante el crecimiento

growl *vi* *(one's stomach)* rugir

grown *pp de* **grow**

grown-up *(fam)* *adj & n* adulto -ta *mf*

growth *n* crecimiento; *(on the body)* tumor *m*; — **spurt** estirón *m*, período de crecimiento rápido

grunt *n* gruñido; *vi* gruñir

G-tube *(fam)* **gastrostomy tube**. *V.* **tube**.

guaifenesin *n* guaifenesina

guanfacine *n* guanfacina

guard *n* protector *m*; **mouth** — protector bucal; **shin** — espinillera, canillera *(CA, SA)*

guardian *n* *(legal)* tutor -ra *mf*

guidance *n* orientación *f*, guía, consejo

guideline *n* guía, norma, pauta

guilt *n* culpa; **feelings of** — sentimientos de culpa

guinea pig *n* *(fig)* conejillo de Indias; **You're not a guinea pig**..Ud. no es un conejillo de Indias.

gulp *vt* **to — down** *(food)* engullir *(la comida)*

gum *n* goma; *(dent, frec. pl)* encía; **chewing** — chicle *m*, goma de mascar; **to chew** — mascar *or* masticar chicle; *vt (food)* masticar con las encías *(dicho de las personas que no tienen dientes)*

gumma *n* goma *m&f*

gun *n* arma de fuego, pistola

gurgle *n* *(stomach, etc.)* gorgoteo; *vi* gorgotear

gurney *n* camilla

gut *n* intestino, tripa *(fam, frec. pl)*

guttural *adj* gutural

gymnasium, gym *(fam)* *n* gimnasio

gymnastics *n* gimnasia

gynecological, gynecologic *adj* ginecológico

gynecologist *n* ginecólogo -ga *mf*, médico -ca *mf* cirujano especializado en el aparato reproductor femenino y sus enfermedades

gynecology *n* ginecología, rama de la medicina que se ocupa del aparato reproductor femenino y sus enfermedades

gynecomastia *n* ginecomastia

H

HAART *abbr* **highly active antiretroviral therapy.** *V.* **therapy.**
habit *n* hábito, costumbre *f*; **bad —** vicio, mal hábito; **eating habits** hábitos alimenticios, hábitos de comer
habit-forming *adj* que crea dependencia
habitual *adj* habitual
habituated *adj* habituado, (*used to*) acostumbrado, (*addicted*) adicto
habituation *n* habituación *f*
had *pret & pp de* **have**
hair *n* pelo, (*head*) cabello, (*body*) vello; **axillary —** vello axilar; **body —** vello (corporal); **facial —** vello facial; **gray —** cana; **— remover** depilatorio (*form*), crema *or* aerosol *m* para quitar el vello; **ingrown —** pelo encarnado; **pubic —** vello púbico
hairbrush *n* cepillo (para el pelo)
haircut *n* corte *m* de pelo; **to get a —** cortarse el pelo
haircutter *n* peluquero -ra *mf*, barbero
hairline *adj* (*fracture, etc.*) fina, muy delgada; *n* línea del cuero cabelludo; **receding —** entradas (*fam*)
hairspray *n* laca (*para el peinado, en aerosol*)
hairy *adj* peludo
half *adj* medio; **Take a half pill every morning..**Tome media pastilla todas las mañanas; **— brother** medio hermano; **— sister** media hermana; *adv* medio; **half asleep..**medio dormido; *n* (*pl* **halves**) mitad *f*
half-life *n* vida media
halfway house *n* (*US*) casa de rehabilitación (*esp. para drogadictos y alcohólicos después de tratamiento y antes de volver a la sociedad*)
halitosis *n* halitosis *f*, mal aliento (*fam*)
hallucination *n* alucinación *f*
hallucinogen *n* alucinógeno
hallux valgus *n* hallux valgus *m*, desviación *f* del dedo gordo hacia dentro
hallux varus *n* hallux varus *m*, desviación *f* del dedo gordo hacia afuera
halo *n* halo *m*
haloperidol *n* haloperidol *m*
halves *pl de* **half**

ham *n* jamón *m*
hamartoma *n* hamartoma *m*
hammer toe *n* dedo (*del pie*) en martillo
hamstring *n* tendón *m* de la corva
hand *n* mano *f*
handler *n* manipulador -ra *mf*; **food —** manipulador de alimentos
handgun *n* pistola
handheld *adj* de mano
handicap (*ant*) *V.* **disability.**
handicapped (*ant*) *V.* **disabled.**
hand lens *n* lupa
handout *n* folleto (*p. ej., con consejos médicos*)
hand sanitizer *n* desinfectante *m* de *or* para manos
handwriting *n* letra, escritura
hang *vt* (*pret & pp* **hanged** *o* **hung**) (*by the neck*) ahorcar; **to — oneself** ahorcarse; *vi* colgar
hangnail *n* padrastro (*en el dedo*)
hangover *n* resaca; **to have a —** tener una resaca
hantavirus *n* hantavirus *m*
happiness *n* felicidad *f*
happy *adj* feliz, contento
harassment *n* acoso; **sexual —** acoso sexual
hard *adj* duro; **— of hearing** que no oye bien, duro de oído
harden *vt, vi* endurecer(se); **hardened arteries** arterias ateroscleróticas (*form*), arterias endurecidas
hardening *n* endurecimiento; **— of the arteries** aterosclerosis *f* (*form*), endurecimiento de las arterias
hard hat *n* casco (protector)
hard-on *n* (*fam o vulg*) erección *f*
harelip *n* (*vulg*) labio hendido, labio leporino (*fam or vulg*)
harm *n* daño; *vt* dañar, hacer daño
harmful *adj* nocivo, dañino
harmless *adj* inofensivo, que no hace daño
harsh *adj* áspero
hashish *n* hachís *m*
hat *n* sombrero; **toilet —** sombrero (*fam*), recipiente *m* con forma de sombrero invertido que se coloca sobre el

inodoro para recolectar orina o heces
hate *n* odio; *vt* odiar
have *vt* (*pret & pp* **had**) tener; **You have herpes**..Ud. tiene herpes.
hawk *vt* **to — up** (*fam*) expectorar (*flemas*)
hawthorn *n* (*bot*) espino blanco
hay fever *n* rinitis alérgica (*form*), fiebre *f* del heno, alergia al polen
hazard *n* peligro, riesgo
hazardous *adj* peligroso, riesgoso
HBV *abbr* hepatitis B virus. *V.* virus.
HCG *abbr* **human chorionic gonadotropin.** *V.* **gonadotropin.**
HCV *abbr* **hepatitis C virus.** *V.* **virus.**
HDL *abbr* **high density lipoprotein.** *V.* **lipoprotein.**
head *n* cabeza; (*of an abscess*) parte blanca donde hay pus (*de un absceso*); (*of a bed*) cabecera; **I'm not saying it's all in your head**..No le estoy diciendo que todo está en su cabeza; **to come to a** — (*an abscess*) madurar (*un absceso*)
headache *n* cefalea (*form*), dolor *m* de cabeza; **cluster** — cefalea en racimos, dolores de cabeza que ocurren repetidivamente durante una o varias semanas; **migraine** — migraña, jaqueca; **tension** — cefalea tensional, dolor de cabeza por tensión
headrest *n* apoyacabezas *m*, reposacabezas *m*
heal *vt, vi* (*wound*) sanar, cicatrizar; (*in general*) curarse
healer *n* persona que cura; **faith** — curandero -ra *mf*, sanador -ra *mf*; **folk** *o* **traditional** — curandero -ra *mf* tradicional
healing *n* curación *f*; (*wound*) cicatrización *f*; **the art of healing**..el arte de curar...**Steroids can retard healing**..Los esteroides pueden retrasar la cicatrización; **faith** — curanderismo; **folk** — *o* **traditional** — medicina popular *or* tradicional, curanderismo
health *n* salud *f*, sanidad *f* (*esp. Esp*); — **care** *V.* **health care** *como artículo independiente*; — **enthusiast** naturista; **mental** — salud mental; **occupational** — salud ocupacional *or* laboral; **public** — sanidad *or* salud pública; **women's** — salud de la mujer

health care *n* atención *or* asistencia médica, atención *or* asistencia sanitaria (*esp.Esp*), servicios de salud *or* sanitarios *or* médicos, salud *f*; — — **directive** *V.* **advance directive**; — — **provider** profesional *mf* sanitario, proveedor -ra *mf* de salud; — — **system** sistema *m* de salud; **home** — — atención médica domiciliaria; **right to** — — derecho a atención *or* asistencia médica, derecho a servicios de salud; **to obtain** — — obtener atención *or* asistencia médica; **universal** — — sistema *m* de salud universal; [*Note:* health care *is a broad concept which admits many possible translations in Spanish. The above examples reflect current usage.*]
healthful *adj* saludable
Health Insurance Portability and Accountability Act (HIPPA) *n* Ley *f* de Portabilidad y Responsabilidad del Seguro Médico
healthy *adj* (*comp* -**ier**; *super* -**iest**) sano, saludable; [*Note:* sano *and* saludable *are often used interchangeably, but* sano *usually applies to people and connotes* sound *or* not ill, *while* saludable *applies to people and also things which promote health, and is more positive. An overweight man who smokes and eats junk food could be* sano, *but few would call him* saludable.]
hear *vt, vi* (*pret & pp* **heard**) oír; **to — of** oír hablar; **I haven't heard of that**..No he oído hablar de eso.
hearing *n* (*sense*) audición *f*, oído; **How is your hearing**..¿Cómo está su audición?..¿Cómo está oyendo?
heart *n* corazón *m*
heartbeat *n* latido del corazón
heartburn *n* acidez *f*, agruras (*esp. Mex*)
heart-healthy *adj* cardiosaludable
heat *n* calor *m*; **body** — calor corporal; *vt* (*también* **to — up**) calentar
heater *n* calefactor *m*
heating *n* calefacción *f*
heating pad *n* almohadilla térmica
heat rash *n* sudamina (*form*), miliaria (*form*), sarpullido *or* salpullido, erupción *f* que se manifiesta durante tiempos de calor

heatstroke *n* insolación *f*, golpe *m* de calor

heat wave *n* ola de calor

heaviness *n* pesadez *f*

heavy *adj* (*comp* **-ier**; *super* **-iest**) pesado; (*bleeding*) profuso; **— drinker** (**smoker, etc.**) persona que bebe (fuma, etc.) mucho

heavyset *adj* macizo, fornido

heel *n* (*of the foot or hand*) talón *m*; (*of the sole of a shoe*) tacón *m*; **— cup** talonera; **high-heeled** de tacón alto; **low-heeled** de tacón bajo

height *n* altura; (*of a person*) altura, talla, estatura

held *pret & pp de* **hold**

helical *adj* helicoidal

helium *n* helio

helix *n* hélice *f*; **double —** doble héli-ce

hellebore *n* (*bot*) eléboro

helmet *n* casco

help *interj* ¡Auxilio! ¡Socorro!; *n* ayuda, auxilio; *vt, vi* ayudar

helpless *adj* (*psych, etc.*) indefenso

helplessness *n* (*psych, etc.*) indefensión *f*; **learned —** indefensión aprendida

hemangioma *n* hemangioma *m*; **cavernous —** hemangioma cavernoso

hematocele *n* hematocele *m*

hematocrit *n* hematocrito

hematologist *n* hematólogo -ga *mf*, médico -ca *mf* especializado en la sangre y sus enfermedades, especialista *mf* de la sangre

hematology *n* hematología, rama de la medicina que se ocupa de la sangre y sus enfermedades

hematoma *n* hematoma *m*; **subdural —** hematoma subdural

hemiplegia *n* hemiplejía *or* hemiplejia

hemisphere *n* hemisferio

hemochromatosis *n* hemocromatosis *f*

hemodialysis *n* hemodiálisis *f*

hemoglobin *n* hemoglobina; **glycosylated** *o* **glycated —** hemoglobina glicosilada *or* glucosilada *or* glicada; **— A1c** hemoglobina A1c

hemoglobinuria *n* hemoglobinuria; **paroxysmal nocturnal —** hemoglobinuria paroxística nocturna

hemolysis *n* hemólisis *f*

hemolytic *adj* hemolítico

hemophilia *n* hemofilia

hemophiliac *n* hemofílico -ca *mf*

hemorrhage *n* hemorragia, sangrado (*fam*); **subarachnoid —** hemorragia subaracnoidea

hemorrhagic *adj* hemorrágico

hemorrhoid *n* hemorroide *f*, almorrana

hemorrhoidectomy *n* (*pl* **-mies**) hemorroidectomía

hemosiderosis *n* hemosiderosis *f*

henna *n* (*bot*) henna

heparin *n* heparina; **low-molecular-weight —** heparina de bajo peso molecular

hepatic *adj* hepático

hepatitis *n* hepatitis *f*; **— A (B, C, etc.)** hepatitis A (B, C, etc.)

hepatologist *n* hepatólogo -ga *mf*, médico -ca *mf* especializado en el hígado y sus enfermedades, especialista *mf* del hígado

hepatology *n* hepatología, rama de la medicina que se ocupa del hígado y sus enfermedades

hepatoma *n* hepatoma *m*

hepatorenal *adj* hepatorrenal

herb *n* (*medical*) planta medicinal, hierba *or* yerba

herbal *adj* herbal, herbario

herbalism *n* fitoterapia

herbalist *n* herbolario -ria *mf*, yerbatero -ra *mf*, yerbero -ra *mf*, herborista *mf*

herbicide *n* herbicida *m*

hereditary *adj* hereditario

heredity *n* herencia

heritable *adj* heredable

hermaphrodite *adj & n* hermafrodita *mf*

hermaphroditism *n* hermafroditismo

hernia *n* hernia; **femoral —** hernia femoral *or* crural; **hiatal —** hernia hiatal *or* de hiato; **incarcerated —** hernia incarcerada; **incisional —** eventración *f*, hernia incisional; **inguinal —** hernia inguinal; **reducible —** hernia reducible *or* reducible, hernia simple; **strangulated —** hernia estrangulada; **umbilical —** hernia umbilical

herniorrhaphy *n* (*pl* **-phies**) herniorrafia

heroin *n* heroína, chiva (*Mex, fam*); **black tar —** heroína marrón

herpangina *n* herpangina

herpes *n* herpes *m*; **— simplex** herpes simple, herpes simplex; **— zoster** herpes zóster, culebrilla (*fam*), zona *m*

(fam); **labial** — herpes labial, fuego *(fam)*, calentura *(fam)*, erupción en los labios *(debida al herpes)*
herpesvirus *n (pl* **-ruses)** herpesvirus *m*; **human** — **6 (8, etc.)** herpesvirus humano 6 (8, etc.)
herpetic *adj* herpético
heterosexual *adj & n* heterosexual *mf*
hiatal *adj* hiatal, de hiato
hiatus *n (anat)* hiato
hiccup *n* hipo; **to have the hiccups** tener hipo; *vi (pret & pp* **-cuped** *o* **-cupped;** *ger* **-cuping** *o* **-cupping)** hipar, tener hipo
hickey *n* chupetón *m*, chupón *m*, marca roja en la piel producida por un beso fuerte
hidradenitis suppurativa *n* hidradenitis supurativa, inflamación *f* e infección *f* de las glándulas sudoríporas de las axilas o de la ingle
high *adj* alto; *(something measured)* alto, elevado; *(fam, on drugs)* drogado; **Your cholesterol is high**..Su colesterol está alto (elevado); **high-dose** *V.* **dosis; high-fiber (high-protein, etc.)** alto *or* rico en fibra (proteínas, etc.); **high-pitched** agudo, de alta frecuencia
higher *(comp de* **high)** *adj (physically)* más alto, más arriba; *(numerically)* superior a, por encima de, mayor de; **higher on your back**..más arriba en su espalda; **It's higher than 200**..Es superior a 200..Está por encima de 200.. Es mayor de 200.
high-strung *adj (fam)* muy nervioso, muy intenso
hike *n* caminata; *vi* caminar *(en senderos campestres)*, hacer senderismo, hacer una caminata
hiking *n* senderismo
hip *n* cadera
hipbone *n* hueso de la cadera
HIPPA *V.* **Health Insurance Portability and Accountability Act.**
hippocampus *n* hipocampo
Hippocratic Oath *n* Juramento Hipocrático
hirsute *adj* hirsuto, velludo, peludo
hirsutism *n* hirsutismo
histamine *n* histamina
histidine *n* histidina
histiocytosis *n* histiocitosis *f*

histologic *adj* histológico
histology *n* histología
histoplasmosis *n* histoplasmosis *f*
history *n (pl* **-ries)** historia, historial *m*, antecedentes *mpl*; **family** — antecedentes familiares; — **and physical** historia clínica y examen físico; — **of** *(cancer, trauma, etc.)* antecedentes de *(cáncer, traumatismo, etc.)*; — **of the present illness** historia de la enfermedad actual; **medical** — historia clínica *or* médica, historial médico; **natural** — *(of a disease)* historia *or* evolución *f* natural *(de una enfermedad)*; **past medical** — antecedentes médicos *or* personales
histrionic *adj* histriónico
hit *vt (pret & pp* **hit;** *ger* **hitting)** golpear, pegar
HIV *abbr* **human immunodeficiency virus.** *V.* **virus.**
hives *npl* ronchas, urticaria *(form)*
HMO *abbr* **health maintenance organization.** *V.* **organization.**
hoarse *adj* ronco; **to be** — estar ronco, tener la voz ronca
hoarseness *n* ronquera
hobby *n (pl* **-bies)** pasatiempo
hold *vt (pret & pp* **held) to** — **one's breath** aguantar la respiración
hole *n* perforación *f*, hueco, agujero
holism *n* holismo
holistic *adj* holístico, integral
hollow *adj & n* hueco; — **of the hand** hueco de la mano
home *adj* domiciliario, casero; — **care** atención domiciliaria; — **remedy** remedio casero; *n* casa, hogar, domicilio; **You can go home**..Puede regresar a la casa; **at** — en casa; **convalescent** — *(ant)* casa de convalecencia *or* descanso, *(euph)* centro de enfermería especializada; **medical** — hogar médico; **nursing** — *(fam)* centro de enfermería especializada; **rest** — *(ant)* casa de reposo *or* descanso, *(euph)* centro de enfermería especializada
homebound *adj* incapaz de salir de la casa *(debido a debilidad)*
homeless *adj* sin hogar
homelessness *n* falta de vivienda *or* hogar
homemaker *n* ama de casa

homeopath *n* homeópata *mf*

homeopathic *adj* homeopático

homeopathy *n* homeopatía, sistema curativo en que se administra dosis pequeñas de sustancias que en dosis más grandes podrían causar o agravar la misma enfermedad que se pretende curar

homesick *adj* nostálgico (del hogar); **to be** — sentir nostalgia

homesickness *n* nostalgia (del hogar)

homophobia *n* homofobia

homophobic *adj* homofóbico

homosexual *adj & n* homosexual *mf*, gay *mf*, (*female*) lesbiana

honey *n* miel *f* (de abeja)

hooked *adj* (*fam, on drugs*) enganchado (*fam*), adicto; — **on heroin** enganchado a la heroína; **to get** — engancharse, volverse adicto

hookworm *n* uncinaria, anquilostoma *m*; [*Note: anquilostoma is in common usage despite the fact that the hookworm prevalent in Latin America is Necator americanus, not Ancylostoma duodenale.*]

hop *n* salto; *vi* (*pret & pp* **hopped**; *ger* **hopping**) saltar; **Hop on one foot.. Salte en un pie.**

hope *n* esperanza (*frec. pl*); **to lose** — desesperarse, perder la(s) esperanza(s); *vt, vi* esperar; **I hope you get well soon..**Espero que se recupere pronto; **to** — **for** esperar, tener esperanzas de

hopeless *adj* sin esperanza, desesperado

hops *n* (*bot*) lúpulo

horizontal *adj* horizontal

hormonal *adj* hormonal

hormone *n* hormona; **adrenocorticotropic** — (**ACTH**) corticotropina, hormona adrenocorticotrópica (HACT); **antidiuretic** — vasopresina, hormona antidiurética; **bovine growth** — hormona de crecimiento bovina; **follicle-stimulating** — (**FSH**) hormona folículo estimulante (HFE), folitropina; **gonadotropin-releasing** — (**GnRH**) hormona liberadora de gonadotropina(s); **(human) growth** — (**GH**) hormona de(l) crecimiento (humana); **luteinizing** — (**LH**) hormona luteinizante (HL); **parathyroid** — (**PTH**) hormona paratiroidea (HPT); **thyroid** — hormona tiroidea; **thyroid-stimulating** — (**TSH**) hormona estimulante del *or* de la tiroides, tirotropina

hornet *n* avispón *m*

horsefly *n* (*pl* **-flies**) tábano

horsetail *n* (*bot*) cola de caballo

hose *n* (*tube*) manguera

hose *npl* (*stockings*) medias; **support** — medias de compresión

hospice *V.* hospice care *bajo* care.

hospital *adj* hospitalario; *n* hospital *m*; **community** — hospital comunitario; **county** — (*US*) hospital del condado; **general** — hospital general; **mental** — hospital psiquiátrico *or* mental; **private** — hospital privado; **public** — hospital público; **teaching** — hospital de enseñanza, hospital universitario; **tertiary care** — hospital de tercer nivel, hospital terciario (*esp. Esp*); **university** — hospital universitario; **Veteran's Affairs (VA)** — (*US*) hospital de veteranos

hospitalist *n* médico -ca *mf* especializado en atender pacientes en el hospital

hospitalization *n* hospitalización *f*

hospitalize *vt* hospitalizar; **Have you ever been hospitalized before?..**¿Ha estado hospitalizado alguna vez?

host *n* (*parasitology*) huésped *m*, hospedador *m*

hostile *adj* hostil

hostility *n* hostilidad *f*

hot *adj* (*comp* **hotter**; *super* **hottest**) caliente; (*to the taste*) picante; **to be** — tener calor; (*the weather*) hacer calor; **to feel** — sentir calor; **Do you feel hot all the time?..**¿Siente calor todo el tiempo?

hot flash *n* sofoco, bochorno, calor *m*, fogaje *m* (*Carib*), sensación repentina de calor que suelen sufrir las mujeres durante la menopausia

hot sauce *n* salsa picante

hot springs *npl* aguas termales

hot tub *n* bañera caliente

hot-water bottle *n* bolsa de agua caliente

hour *n* hora; **office hours** horario(s) de consulta, horas de consulta; **visiting hours** horario(s) de visita, horas de visita

housebound *adj* incapaz de salir de la casa (*debido a debilidad*)

house call *n* visita domiciliaria *or* a domicilio, visita a la casa

housecleaner *n* limpiador -ra *mf* (de casas), doméstico -ca *mf*

housefly *n* (*pl* **-flies**) mosca doméstica

housewife *n* (*pl* **-wives**) ama de casa

HPV *abbr* **human papillomavirus**. *V.* **papillomavirus.**

HSV *abbr* **herpes simplex virus**. *V.* **virus.**

HTLV *abbr* **human T-lymphotrophic virus**. *V.* **virus.**

hug *n* abrazo; *vt* (*pret* & *pp* **hugged**; *ger* **hugging**) abrazar

human *adj* humano; — **being** ser humano; *n* humano

humanitarian *adj* humanitario

humeral *adj* humeral, del húmero

humerus *n* (*pl* **-ri**) húmero

humid *adj* húmedo

humidifier *n* humidificador *m*, aparato para aumentar la humedad del aire

humidify *vt* (*pret* & *pp* **-fied**) humedecer, humidificar

humidity *n* humedad *f*

humor *n* humor *m*; **You don't want to lose your sense of humor**..No deberías perder tu sentido del humor; **aqueous** — humor acuoso; **vitreous** — humor vítreo

hump *n* (*on the back*) joroba

humpback *n* (*fam o vulg*) joroba

humpbacked *adj* jorobado

hunchback *n* (*vulg*) jorobado -da *mf* (*fam o vulg*); (*hump*) joroba

hung *pret* & *pp* de **hang**

hunger *n* hambre *f*

hungover *adj* **to be** — tener una resaca

hungry *adj* **to be** — tener hambre

hurricane *n* huracán *m*

hurt *vt* (*pret* & *pp* **hurt**) (*to cause pain*) doler, hacer daño; (*to injure*) lesionar, lastimar; (*to harm*) hacer daño, dañar, lesionar, lastimar, hacer(*le*) mal; **This won't hurt you**.. Esto no le va a doler ...**I'm not going to hurt you**..No voy a hacerle daño...**Did you hurt your finger?**...¿Se lesionó el dedo?..¿Se lastimó el dedo?...**Eating seeds won't hurt you**..Comer semillas no le hará mal; **to get** — lesionarse, lastimarse; **to** — (*someone's*) **feelings** herir los sentimientos (*de alguien*); **She hurt his**

feelings..Ella hirió sus sentimientos; **to** — **oneself** lesionarse, lastimarse; **Did you hurt yourself?**..¿Se lesionó?..¿Se lastimó?; *vi* doler, sentir dolor; **Where does it hurt?**..¿Dónde le duele?...**Do you hurt all over?**..¿Le duele todo?... **Tell me if it hurts**..Dígame si le duele ..Dígame si siente dolor.

hurtful *adj* hiriente; **hurtful words**..palabras hirientes

husband *n* esposo, marido

hyaluronic acid *n* ácido hialurónico

hydatid *adj* hidatídico

hydatidiform *adj* (*obst*) hidatiforme

hydralazine *n* hidralazina

hydrangea *n* (*bot*) hortensia

hydrate *n* hidrato; *vt* hidratar

hydrocarbon *n* hidrocarburo

hydrocele *n* hidrocele *m*

hydrocephalus *n* hidrocefalia; **normal pressure** — hidrocefalia normotensiva

hydrochloric acid *n* ácido clorhídrico

hydrochloride *n* clorhidrato

hydrochlorothiazide *n* hidroclorotiazida

hydrocodone *n* hidrocodona

hydrocolloid *n* hidrocoloide *m*

hydrocortisone *n* hidrocortisona

hydrogel *n* hidrogel *m*

hydrogenated *adj* hidrogenado

hydrogen peroxide *n* peróxido de hidrógeno, agua oxigenada (*fam*)

hydromorphone *n* hidromorfona

hydronephrosis *n* hidronefrosis *f*

hydrophobia *n* hidrofobia, terror *m* al agua (*esp. en los rabiosos*)

hydroquinone *n* hidroquinona

hydrotherapy *n* hidroterapia, método curativo por medio del agua; **colon** — hidroterapia de colon

hydroxide *n* hidróxido

hydroxycarbamide *V.* **hydroxyurea.**

hydroxychloroquine *n* hidroxicloroquina

hydroxyurea *n* hidroxiurea, hidroxicarbamida (*INN*)

hydroxyzine *n* hidroxizina *or* hidroxicina

hygiene *n* higiene *f*, aseo; **oral** — higiene *or* aseo bucal

hygienic *adj* higiénico

hygienist *n* higienista *mf*; **dental** — higienista dental

hymen *n* himen *m*; **imperforate** — hi-

men imperforado
hyoid bone *n* hueso hioides
hyoscine *n* hioscina, escopolamina
hyoscyamine *n* hiosiamina
hyper (*fam*) hiperactivo, acelerado (*fam*)
hyperactive *adj* hiperactivo
hyperactivity *n* hiperactividad *f*
hyperalimentation *n* (*overfeeding*) hiperalimentación *f*; (*ant, TPN*) nutrición *f* parenteral total (NPT)
hyperbaric *adj* hiperbárico
hypercalcemia *n* hipercalcemia
hyperemesis gravidarum *n* (*obst*) hiperemesis gravídica, estado grave de náuseas y vómitos que aparece en etapas tempranas del embarazo
hyperfunctioning *adj* hiperfuncionante
hyperglycemia *n* hiperglucemia
hyperglycemic *adj* hiperglucémico
hyperhidrosis *n* hiperhidrosis *f*, sudoración excesiva principalmente de las manos y de los pies
hyperlipidemia *n* hiperlipidemia
hypermobile *adj* hipermóvil
hypernatremia *n* hipernatremia
hyperosmolar *adj* hiperosmolar
hyperparathyroid *adj* hiperparatiroideo
hyperparathyroidism *n* hiperparatiroidismo
hyperpigmentation *n* hiperpigmentación *f*
hyperplasia *n* hiperplasia; **benign prostatic** — hiperplasia prostática benigna; **congenital adrenal** — hiperplasia suprarrenal congénita
hyperplastic *adj* hiperplásico
hyperprolactinemia *n* hiperprolactinemia
hypersensitive *adj* hipersensible
hypersensitivity *n* hipersensibilidad *f*
hypertension *n* hipertensión *f*, presión alta (de la sangre) (*fam*); **benign intracranial** — hipertensión intracraneal benigna; **essential** — hipertensión esencial; **malignant** — hipertensión maligna; **portal** — hipertensión portal; **pulmonary** — hipertensión pulmonar; **renovascular** — hipertensión renovascular; **white-coat** — hipertensión de bata blanca
hypertensive *adj* (*crisis, disorder, state, etc.*) hipertensivo, (*effect*) hipertensor, (*patient*) hipertenso

hyperthermia *n* hipertermia
hyperthyroid *adj* hipertiroideo
hyperthyroidism *n* hipertiroidismo
hypertrophic *adj* hipertrófico
hypertrophy *n* hipertrofia
hyperuricemia *n* hiperuricemia
hyperventilate *vi* hiperventilar, respirar demasiado rápido
hyperventilation *n* hiperventilación *f*
hyphema *n* hipema *m*
hypnosis *n* hipnosis *f*
hypnotic *adj* & *n* hipnótico
hypnotism *n* hipnotismo
hypnotist *n* hipnotizador -ra *mf*
hypnotize *vt* hipnotizar
hypoallergenic *adj* hipoalergénico
hypocalcemia *n* hipocalcemia
hypochondriac *n* (*ant*) hipocondríaco *or* hipocondriaco -ca *mf*
hypochondriasis *n* (*ant*) hipocondría
hypodermic *adj* hipodérmico; *n* (*ant*) jeringa; inyección *f*
hypoglycemia *n* hipoglucemia
hypoglycemic *adj* (*pertaining to hypoglycemia*) hipoglucémico, (*causing hypoglycemia*) hipoglucemiante; — **coma** coma hipoglucémico; — **effect** efecto hipoglucemiante; **oral — agent** hipoglucemiante *m* oral
hypokalemia *n* hipopotasemia
hyponatremia *n* hiponatremia
hypoparathyroid *adj* hipoparatiroideo
hypoparathyroidism *n* hipoparatiroidismo
hypopigmentation *n* hipopigmentación *f*
hypopituitarism *n* hipopituitarismo
hypopnea *n* hipopnea
hypospadias *n* hipospadias *m*
hypotension *n* hipotensión *f*; **orthostatic** — hipotensión ortostática
hypotensive *adj* (*state, etc.*) hipotensivo, (*effect*) hipotensor, (*patient*) hipotenso
hypothalamus *n* hipotálamo
hypothermia *n* hipotermia
hypothyroid *adj* hipotiroideo
hypothyroidism *n* hipotiroidismo
hypovolemic *adj* hipovolémico
hysterectomy *n* (*pl* -**mies**) histerectomía; **total abdominal** — histerectomía abdominal total; **vaginal** — histerectomía vaginal
hysteria *n* (*ant*) crisis *f* de ansiedad, an-

siedad severa, histeria (*ant*)
hysterical *adj* (*ant*) severamente ansioso;

relativo a la ansiedad, histérico (*ant*)

I

ibandronate, ibandronate sodium (*USAN*), **ibandronic acid** (*INN*) *n* ibandronato, ibandronato sódico, ácido ibandrónico (*INN*)

ibuprofen *n* ibuprofeno

icaridin *n* icaridina, picaridina (*esp. Amer*)

ICD *abbr* **implantable cardioverter-defibrillator**. *V.* **defibrillator**.

ice *n* hielo; (*fam, methamphetamine*) metanfetamina; — **chips** trocitos *or* pedacitos de hielo; — **pack** bolsa *or* compresa de hielo; *vt* (*an injury*) aplicar hielo (*a una herida*)

ice cream *n* helado

ichthyosis *n* ictiosis *f*

ICU *abbr* **intensive care unit**. *V.* **unit**.

ID *V.* **identification**.

I&D *abbr* **incision and drainage**. *V.* **incision**.

id *n* (*psych*) ello *m*, id *m*, fuente *f* inconsciente de toda energía psíquica

idea *n* idea; **ideas of reference** (*psych*) ideas de referencia

ideal *adj* ideal

idealization *n* (*psych*) idealización *f*

identical *adj* idéntico

identification (ID) *n* identificación *f*

identify *vt* (*pret & pp* **-fied**) identificar; *vi* to — **with** identificarse con

identity *n* (*pl* **-ties**) identidad *f*; — **crisis** crisis *f* de identidad

idiopathic *adj* idiopático, sin causa conocida

ileal *adj* ileal

ileitis *n* ileítis *f*

ileostomy *n* (*pl* **-mies**) ileostomía

ileum *n* íleon *m*, tercera porción del intestino delgado

ileus *n* íleo

iliac *adj* ilíaco *or* iliaco

ilium *n* ilion *m*, hueso ilíaco *or* iliaco, hueso de la cadera

ill *adj* enfermo

illicit *adj* ilícito

illiteracy *n* analfabetismo

illiterate *adj* analfabeto

illness *n* enfermedad *f*, mal *m*; **mental** — enfermedad mental; **occupational** — enfermedad profesional *or* ocupacional; **present** — enfermedad actual

illusion *n* ilusión *f*

IM *V.* **intramuscular**.

image *n* imagen *f*; **body** — imagen corporal

imagery *n* imágenes *fpl*, visualización *f*; **guided** — visualización guiada

imaging *adj* imagenológico; *n* imaginología, uso de técnicas radiológicas para obtener imágenes del interior del cuerpo; **diagnostic** — diagnóstico por imagen *or* imágenes; — **study** estudio radiológico *or* imagenológico, estudio por imagen *or* imágenes, prueba de imagen; **magnetic resonance** — **(MRI)** (*technique*) imagen *or* imágenes por resonancia magnética (IRM); (*individual study*) resonancia magnética, IRM *f*; **an MRI of the brain**..una resonancia magnética del cerebro..una IRM del cerebro; **open MRI** resonancia magnética abierta

imbalance *n* desequilibrio; **chemical** — desequilibrio químico

imipenem *n* imipenem *m*
imipramine *n* imipramina
imiquimod *n* imiquimod *m*
immature *adj* inmaduro
immaturity *n* inmadurez *f*
immediate *adj* inmediato
immediately *adv* inmediatamente
immersion *n* inmersión *f*
immobile *adj* inmóvil
immobilization *n* inmovilización *f*
immobilize *vt* inmovilizar
immobilizer *n* inmovilizador *m*; **shoulder** — inmovilizador de hombro
immune *adj* inmune, inmunológico, inmunitario; — **reconstitution** reconstitución *f* inmune; — **response** respuesta inmunológica *or* inmunitaria; — **to** inmune a; — **tolerance** tolerancia inmunológica
immunity *n* inmunidad *f*; **immunity to..** inmunidad a *or* contra; **herd** — inmunidad colectiva *or* de grupo
immunization *n* inmunización *f*; (*vaccination*) vacunación *f*
immunize *vt* inmunizar, (*to vaccinate*) vacunar
immunizing *adj* inmunizador, inmunizante
immunocompetent *adj* inmunocompetente
immunocompromised *adj* inmunocomprometido
immunodeficiency *n* inmunodeficiencia; **common variable** — inmunodeficiencia variable común
immunodeficient *adj* inmunodeficiente
immunodepressed *adj* inmunodeprimido
immunodepression *n* inmunodepresión *f*
immunodepressive *adj* inmunodepresor
immunoglobulin *n* inmunoglobulina (*endógena*)
immunologic, immunological *adj* inmunológico
immunologist *n* inmunólogo -ga *mf*, médico -ca *mf* especializado en el sistema inmunológico y sus enfermedades
immunology *n* inmunología, rama de la medicina que se ocupa del sistema inmunológico y sus enfermedades
immunosuppressant *n* inmunosupresor *m*
immunosuppressed *adj* inmunosuprimido
immunosuppression *n* inmunosupresión *f*
immunosuppressive *adj* inmunosupresor
immunotherapy *n* inmunoterapia
impact *n* impacto
impacted *adj* impactado; (*dent*) impactado, retenido, incluido, que no ha podido salir por falta de espacio; (*with stool*) impactado (*con heces*)
impaction *n* impactación *f*; **cerumen** — tapón de cerumen; **dental** — inclusión dentaria; **fecal** — impactación fecal
impair *vt* dañar, perjudicar; **impaired physician** médico -ca *mf* a quien se le dificulta desempeñar su labor debido a enfermedad mental, alcoholismo o drogadicción
impairment *n* discapacidad *f*, trastorno, deficiencia, pérdida; **hearing** — discapacidad auditiva
impediment *n* **speech** — (*ant*) trastorno del habla
imperforate *adj* imperforado
impetigo *n* impétigo
impingement *n* (*of a nerve*) compresión *f* (*de un nervio*)
implant *n* implante *m*; **breast** — implante mamario; **cochlear** — implante coclear; **silicone** — implante de silicona; *vt* implantar
implantation *n* implantación *f*
impossible *adj* imposible
impotence *n* (*ant, sexual*) disfunción *f* eréctil, impotencia (*sexual*)
impotent *adj* (*ant*) con disfunción eréctil, impotente
impression *n* (*dent, etc.*) impresión *f*
improve *vt* mejorar; *vi* mejorarse, (*patient*) recuperarse
improvement *n* mejoría
impulse *n* impulso
impulsive *adj* impulsivo
impurity *n* (*pl* **-ties**) impureza
inability *n* incapacidad *f*
inactivated *adj* inactivado
inactive *adj* inactivo
inactivity *n* inactividad *f*
inadequate *adj* (*not suited*) inadecuado, (*insufficient*) insuficiente
inappropriate *adj* inadecuado, inapropiado, indebido
inbred *adj* endogámico (*form*), procrea-

do por uniones entre la misma familia extendida

inbreeding *n* endogamia (*form*), procreación *f* entre una familia extendida, procreación entre familiares

incapable *adj* incapaz

incapacitated *adj* incapacitado

incapacitating *adj* incapacitante

incarcerated *adj* incarcerado

incest *n* incesto

incestuous *adj* incestuoso

inch *n* pulgada, 2,54 centímetros

incidence *n* incidencia

incidentaloma *n* incidentaloma *m* (*Ang*), tumor detectado por casualidad en una prueba realizada por otro motivo

incision *n* incisión *f*, herida; **— and drainage (I&D)** incisión y drenaje

incisor *n* incisivo; **upper** *o* **maxillary central** — incisivo central superior; **lower** *o* **mandibular lateral** — incisivo lateral inferior

incoherent *adj* incoherente

income *n* ingresos; **low-income patients** pacientes de bajos recursos

incompatible *adj* incompatible

incompetence *n* incompetencia; **cervical** — incompetencia cervical

incompetent *adj* incompetente

incomplete *adj* incompleto

incontinence *n* incontinencia; **fecal** — incontinencia fecal, incapacidad *f* para retener las heces; **overflow** — incontinencia por rebosamiento; **stress** — incontinencia de esfuerzo; **urge** — incontinencia de urgencia; **urinary** — incontinencia urinaria, incapacidad *f* para retener la orina

incontinent *adj* incontinente, (*of urine*) incapaz de retener la orina, (*of stool*) incapaz de retener las heces

increase *n* aumento; *vt* aumentar, incrementar (*form*); **to increase the dose..** aumentar la dosis; *vi* aumentar

incubator *n* (*ped*) incubadora

incurable *adj* incurable

independent *adj* independiente

index *n* (*pl* **indexes** *o* **indices**) índice *m*; **ankle-brachial** — índice tobillo-brazo; **body mass** — **(BMI)** índice de masa corporal (IMC); **glycemic** — índice glucémico

indication *n* indicación *f*

indices *pl de* **index**

indifference *n* indiferencia

indigestion *n* indigestión *f*, dispepsia

indinavir *n* indinavir *m*

indistinct *adj* indistinto

individual *n* individuo (*inv*)

indomethacin *n* indometacina

induce *vt* inducir, provocar; **exercise-induced** inducido (provocado) por el ejercicio

induction *n* inducción *f*

indurated *adj* (*lesion*) indurado; (*skin*) endurecida

induration *n* (*lesion*) induración *f*, (*skin*) endurecimiento

indwelling *adj* permanente; **— catheter** catéter *or* sonda permanente

ineffective *adj* ineficaz

inert *adj* inerte

infancy *n* primer período de la vida (*aproximadamente el primer año*); [*Note:* infancia *refers to the period between birth and puberty and cannot be used to mean* infancy.]

infant *n* bebé *mf*, recién nacido -da *mf*, nene -na *mf* (*fam*)

infantile *adj* infantil, relativo a los bebés

infarct *n* infarto

infarction *n* infarto, acción *f* y efecto de un infarto; **acute myocardial** — infarto agudo de miocardio

infect *vt* infectar; **infected with** (*a disease*) infectado con; (*an agent of disease*) infectado con *or* por; **infected with TB**..infectado con TB; **infected with HIV**..infectado con *or* por VIH; **to become infected** infectarse

infection *n* infección *f*; **bacterial** — infección bacteriana *or* por bacterias; **bladder** — infección de vejiga; **fungal** — infección fúngica (*form*), infección micótica (*form*), infección de *or* por hongos; **upper respiratory tract** — infección de las vías respiratorias superiores *or* altas; **urinary tract** — **(UTI)** infección del tracto urinario (ITU), infección de orina (*fam*); **viral** — infección viral, infección de *or* por virus; **yeast** — candidiasis *f* (*form*), infección por hongos *or* levaduras

infectious *adj* infeccioso, contagioso (*fam*)

inferior *adj* (*anat*) inferior

infertile *adj* infértil, estéril
infertility *n* infertilidad *f*, esterilidad *f*
infest *vt* infestar; **infested with** infestado de; **to get** *o* **become infested with** infestarse de
infestation *n* infestación *f*; — **with** infestación de *or* por; **infestation of the scalp with lice**..infestación de piojos en la cabeza..infestación por piojos de la cabeza
infiltrate *vt, vi* infiltrar(se)
infiltrative, infiltrating *adj* infiltrante
infiltration *n* infiltración *f*
infirmary *n* (*pl* **-ries**) (*ant*) enfermería, local *m or* dependencia para enfermos o heridos
inflamed *adj* inflamado; **to become —** inflamarse
inflammable *adj* inflamable
inflammation *n* inflamación *f*
inflammatory *adj* inflamatorio
infliximab *n* infliximab *m*
influenza *n* (*form*) gripe *f*, influenza (*form*); **Asian —** gripe asiática; **avian —** gripe *or* influenza aviar; **seasonal —** influenza *or* gripe estacional; **swine —** gripe porcina
information *n* información *f*
infraorbital *adj* infraorbitario
infrared *adj* infrarrojo
infuse *vt* infundir
infusion *n* infusión *f*
ingest *vt* ingerir
ingestion *n* ingestión *f*
ingredient *n* ingrediente *m*; **active —** principio activo
ingrown *adj* encarnada, enterrada (*esp. Mex*)
inguinal *adj* inguinal
INH *V.* **isoniazid.**
inhalation *n* inhalación *f*; **smoke —** inhalación de humo
inhale *vt, vi* inhalar; **inhaled steroid** esteroide inhalado
inhaler *n* inhalador *m*; **dry powder —** inhalador de polvo seco; **metered-dose —** inhalador de dosis medida, inhalador dosificador (*esp. Esp*); **nasal —** inhalador nasal, atomizador *m* nasal (*esp. Mex*)
inherit *vt* heredar
inhibit *vt* inhibir
inhibited *adj* inhibido, cohibido

inhibition *n* inhibición *f*, cohibición *f*
inhibitor *n* inhibidor *m*; **angiotensin converting enzyme —** inhibidor de la enzima convertidora de angiotensina; **cholinesterase —** inhibidor de la colinesterasa; **fusion —** inhibidor de (la) fusión; **integrase —** inhibidor de la integrasa; **monoamine oxidase —** inhibidor de la monoaminooxidasa; **nonnucleoside reverse transcriptase — (NNRTI)** inhibidor no nucleósido de la transcriptasa inversa *or* reversa; **nucleoside reverse transcriptase — (NRTI)** inhibidor nucleósido de la transcriptasa inversa *or* reversa; **nucleotide reverse transcriptase — (NtRTI)** inhibidor nucleótido de la transcriptasa inversa *or* reversa; **protease —** inhibidor de la proteasa; **proton pump —** inhibidor de la bomba de protones; **selective serotonin reuptake —** inhibidor selectivo de la recaptación de serotonina
initial *adj* inicial, primero; *npl* iniciales *fpl*; *vt, vi* poner iniciales; **Initial here, please**..Ponga sus iniciales aquí, por favor.
inject *vt* inyectar, (*oneself*) inyectarse
injectable *adj* inyectable
injection *n* inyección *f*; **The nurse will give you an injection**..La enfermera le va a poner una inyección.
injure *vt* (*hurt, wound*) herir, lesionar; (*damage, harm*) lesionar, (*severely*) dañar; **The explosion injured 3 people**..La explosión hirió a 3 personas... **The bullet injured the nerve**..La bala lesionó el nervio; **to — oneself** lesionarse; **When did she injure herself?**.. ¿Cuándo se lesionó?; **to — one's knee (foot, etc.)** lesionarse la rodilla (pie, etc.)
injury *n* (*pl* **-ries**) herida, lesión *f*, traumatismo; **spinal cord —** lesión medular, lesión de la médula espinal; **sports —** lesión deportiva; **traumatic brain —** lesión cerebral traumática
inlay *n* (*dent*) incrustación *f* inlay, incrustación (*fam*)
inner *adj* interno, interior
inoculate *vt* inocular
inoculation *n* inoculación *f*
inoperable *adj* inoperable

inorganic *adj* inorgánico
inpatient *n* paciente hospitalizado
INR *abbr* **international normalized ratio.** *V.* **ratio.**
insane *adj* loco
insanity *n* locura
insect *n* insecto
insecticidal *adj* insecticida
insecticide *n* insecticida *m*
insecure *adj* inseguro
insecurity *n* inseguridad *f*
inseminate *vt* inseminar
insemination *n* inseminación *f*; **artificial** — inseminación artificial
insert *vt* introducir, insertar
inside *adj* interior, interno; *adv* dentro, adentro; *n* interior *m*, parte *f* de adentro; *prep* dentro de; **inside your body..** dentro de su cuerpo
insight *n* (*psych*) autoconocimiento, conocimiento de uno mismo
in situ, in situ, localizado
insole *n* plantilla (*del zapato*)
insoluble *adj* insoluble
insomnia *n* insomnio
instability *n* inestabilidad *f*
instep *n* empeine *m* (*del pie*)
instinct *n* instinto
institution *n* asilo, residencia, hospital *m*, establecimiento que ofrece cuidados prolongados (*esp. para pacientes psiquiátricos*); **mental** — hospital psiquiátrico *or* mental
institutionalized *adj* institucionalizado
instrument *n* instrumento
insufficiency *n* insuficiencia; **adrenal (aortic, venous, etc.)** — insuficiencia suprarrenal (aórtica, venosa, etc.)
insufficient *adj* insuficiente
insulin *n* insulina; **basal** — insulina basal; **human** — insulina humana; **analogue** análogo de la insulina; **aspart** insulina aspart, insulina asparta (*INN*); **detemir** insulina detemir; **glargine** insulina glargina; **glulisine** insulina glulisina; **lispro** insulina lispro; **intermediate-acting** — insulina de acción intermedia; **long-acting** — insulina de acción prolongada; **NPH** — insulina NPH; **pre-mixed** — insulina premezclada; **rapid-acting** — insulina de acción rápida; **rapid-acting** — **analogue** análogo de insulina de acción rápida; **recombinant** — insulina recombinante; **regular** — insulina regular; **to take** — inyectarse insulina
insulinoma *n* insulinoma *m*
insurance *n* seguro; **dental** — seguro dental; **health** — seguro sanitario *or* médico; **medical** — seguro médico; **private** — seguro privado
insured *adj* asegurado, que tiene seguro
intact *adj* intacto
intake *n* ingesta, consumo; **recommended daily** — ingesta diaria recomendada; **tolerable daily** — ingesta diaria admisible
integration *n* (*psych, etc.*) integración *f*
intellectual *adj* intelectual
intellectualize *vi* (*psych*) intelectualizar
intellectualization *n* (*psych*) intelectualización *f*
intelligence *n* inteligencia; — **quotient (IQ)** coeficiente *m or* cociente *m* intelectual (CI)
intelligent *adj* inteligente
intense *adj* intenso, fuerte
intensify *vt* (*pret & pp* -**fied**) intensificar
intensity *n* (*pl* -**ties**) intensidad *f*
intensive *adj* intensivo
intensivist *n* intensivista *mf*
interact *vi* interactuar
interaction *n* interacción *f*; **drug** — interacción medicamentosa (*form*), interacción de medicamentos
intercostal *adj* intercostal
intercourse *n* coito (*form*), relaciones *fpl* sexuales, relaciones (*fam*), el acto sexual; **unprotected** — relaciones sexuales sin protección; **When was the last time you had intercourse?..** ¿Cuándo fue la última vez que tuvo relaciones (sexuales)?...**during intercourse..** durante el acto sexual..durante las relaciones sexuales
interfere *vi* interferir
interferon *n* interferón *m*; **alpha (beta, etc.)** interferón alfa (beta, etc.); **pegylated** — interferón pegilado
interior *adj & n* interior *m*
intermediate *adj* intermedio; **intermediate-acting** de acción intermedia
intermittent *adj* intermitente
intern *n* interno -na *mf*
internal *adj* interno

internalize *vt* (*psych*) interiorizar
internet *n* internet *m&f*; **on the —** en el *or* la internet
internist *n* internista *mf*
interpersonal *adj* interpersonal
interpret *vt*, *vi* interpretar
interpreter *n* intérprete *mf*
interrogate *vt* (*a pacemaker*) interrogar (*un marcapasos*)
interruption *n* interrupción *f*
interstitial *adj* intersticial
intertrochanteric *adj* intertrocantérico, intertrocantéreo
interval *n* intervalo
intervention *n* intervención *f*; **percutaneous coronary — (PCI)** intervención coronaria percutánea (ICP)
interventional *adj* intervencionista
interventricular *adj* interventricular
intervertebral *adj* intervertebral
intestinal *adj* intestinal
intestine *n* intestino, tripa (*fam, frec. pl*); **large —** intestino grueso, colon *m*; **small —** intestino delgado
intimacy *n* intimidad *f*
intimate *adj* íntimo
intolerance *n* alergia, intolerancia; **cold —** intolerancia al frío; **lactose —** intolerancia a la lactosa; [*Note: In Spanish* alergia *is used much more often than* intolerancia *when referring to medications.*]
intolerant *adj* (*of medication, etc.*) alérgico, intolerante; [*Note:* intolerante *is not used much in this context save for the phrases* intolerante a la lactosa *and* intolerante al gluten.]
intoxication *n* intoxicación *f*
intraabdominal, **intra-abdominal** *adj* intraabdominal *or* intra-abdominal
intraaortic *adj* intraaórtico
intraarticular, **intra-articular** *adj* intraarticular *or* intra-articular
intracranial *adj* intracraneal, endocraneal, intracraneano
intractable *adj* resistente al tratamiento
intradermal *adj* intradérmico
intramuscular (IM) *adj* intramuscular (IM)
intranasal *adj* intranasal
intraocular *adj* intraocular
intraoperative *adj* intraoperatorio
intraosseous *adj* intraóseo

intrauterine *adj* intrauterino
intravenous (IV) *adj* intravenoso (IV), endovenoso (EV)
intrinsic *adj* intrínseco
introspection *n* introspección *f*
introversion *n* (*psych, etc.*) introversión *f*
introvert *n* introvertido -da *mf*
introverted *adj* introvertido
intubate *vt* intubar
intubation *n* intubación *f*
intussusception *n* invaginación *f* intestinal
in utero, en el útero
invade *vt* invadir
invalid (*ant*) **disabled person.** V. **disabled.**
invasive *adj* invasivo, invasor; **minimally —** mínimamente invasivo
investigational *adj* (*medication, etc.*) en investigación
invisible *adj* invisible
in vitro, in vitro, en el laboratorio
involuntary *adj* involuntario
involvement *n* participación *f*; (*path*) compromiso; **involvement in the community**..participación en la comunidad; **lymph node —** compromiso de los ganglios linfáticos
iodide *n* yoduro
iodine *n* yodo
iodized *adj* yodado
iodoquinol *n* iodoquinol *m*, diyodohidroxiquinoleína, diiodohidroxiquinolina (*INN*)
ion *n* ion *or* ión *m*
iontophoresis *n* iontoforesis *f*
ipecac *n* ipecacuana; **syrup of —** jarabe *m* de ipecacuana
ipratropium bromide *n* bromuro de ipratropio
IQ *abbr* **intelligence quotient.** V. **intelligence.**
irbesartan *n* irbesartán *m*
iris *n* (*pl* irides *o* irises) iris *m*
iritis *n* iritis *f*
iron *n* hierro
irradiate *vt* irradiar, tratar con radiación
irradiation *n* irradiación *f*; **food —** irradiación de alimentos
irregular *adj* irregular
irreversible *adj* irreversible
irrigate *vt* irrigar

irrigation *n* irrigación *f*; **colonic —** hidroterapia de colon
irritability *n* irritabilidad *f*
irritable *adj* irritable
irritant *n* irritante *m*, agente *m* irritante
irritate *vt* irritar; **to become irritated** irritarse
irritating *adj* (*person, event, etc.*) molesto; (*substance*) irritante
irritation *n* irritación *f*
ischemia *n* isquemia
ischemic *adj* isquémico
ischium *n* isquion *m*
islet *n* islote *m*; **pancreatic islets** islotes pancreáticos
isolate *vt* aislar; **to — oneself** aislarse
isolation *n* aislamiento; **protective —** aislamiento protector; **respiratory —** aislamiento respiratorio; **reverse —** aislamiento inverso
isoleucine *n* isoleucina
isometric *adj* isométrico
isoniazid (INH) *n* isoniazida
isopropyl alcohol *n* alcohol isopropílico
isosorbide dinitrate *n* dinitrato de isosorbida

isotope *n* isótopo
isotretinoin *n* isotretinoína
isradipine *n* isradipino, isradipina
itch *n* picazón *f*, comezón *f*; *vi* picar, sentir *or* tener picazón *or* comezón; **Where does it itch?**..¿Dónde le pica?.. ¿Dónde siente picazón (comezón)?... **Does your arm itch?**..¿Le pica el brazo?...**Do you itch?**..¿Siente picazón (comezón)?..¿Tiene picazón (comezón)?; **to have an —** tener picazón *or* comezón (*localizada*)
itching, itchiness *n* picazón *f*, comezón *f*; **to relieve the itching**..aliviar la picazón (comezón)
ITP *abbr* **immune thrombocytopenia.** *V.* **thrombocytopenia.**
ITP *abbr* (*ant*) **idiopathic thrombocytopenic purpura.** *V.* **purpura.**
itraconazole *n* itraconazol *m*
IUD *abbr* **intrauterine device.** *V.* **device.**
IV *V.* **intravenous.**
ivermectin *n* ivermectina
IVF *abbr* **in vitro fertilization.** *V.* **fertilization.**

J

jabbing *adj* (*pain*) punzante
jacket *n* chaqueta, chamarra (*esp. Mex*)
jack off, to (*vulg*) masturbarse, hacerse la paja (*vulg*)
jaundice *n* ictericia (*form*), coloración amarilla de la piel y los ojos
jaw *n* mandíbula, quijada; **lower —** mandíbula inferior, mandíbula (*fam*); **upper —** mandíbula *or* maxilar *m* superior, maxilar (*fam*)
jawbone *n* mandíbula inferior (*form*), mandíbula, quijada
jealous *adj* celoso; **to be —** ser celoso;

My husband is very jealous..Mi esposo es muy celoso; **to be — (of someone)** estar celoso (*de alguien*), tener celos (*de alguien*); **She is jealous of her sister**..Está celosa de su hermana.. Tiene celos de su hermana.
Jehovah's Witness *n* Testigo de Jehová
jejunal *adj* yeyunal
jejunum *n* yeyuno
jellyfish *n* (*pl* **-fish** *o* **-fishes**) medusa, aguamala
jerk off, to (*vulg*) masturbarse, hacerse la paja (*vulg*)

jet lag *n* desfase horario, desequilibrio del ritmo circadiano producido por viajar en avión a través de los husos horarios
job *n* trabajo, empleo
jock itch *n* (*fam o vulg*) tiña inguinal, infección *f* por hongos de la ingle
jockstrap *n* (*fam*) suspensorio
jog *vi* (*pret & pp* **jogged**; *ger* **jogging**) correr, trotar
jogging *n* jogging *m* (*Ang*), footing (*Ang*), (el) correr, (el) trotar
join (*two objects*) *vt* unir, juntar; *vi* unirse
joint *adj* articular; — **pain** dolor *m* articular *or* de las articulaciones; *n* articulación *f*, coyuntura (*fam*); (*fam, marijuana cigarette*) cigarrillo de marihuana, porro (*fam*); **knee (ankle, etc.)** — articulación de la rodilla (tobillo, etc.)
judgmental *adj* crítico, reprobador
judo *n* judo
jugular *adj* yugular
juice *n* jugo, zumo (*esp. Esp*); **grapefruit** — jugo de toronja, zumo de pomelo (*esp. Esp*)
junk food *n* comida chatarra, comida basura (*esp. Esp*)
junkie *n* (*vulg*) adicto -ta *mf* a la heroína
justice *n* justicia
just in case, por si acaso
juvenile *adj* juvenil

K

karate *n* karate *m*
karyotype *n* cariotipo
kava *n* (*bot*) kava *m&f*
keloid *n* queloide *m*
kelp *n* kelp *m*, tipo de alga marina
keratectomy *n* (*pl* **-mies**) queratectomía; **photorefractive** — (**PRK**); queratectomía fotorrefractiva
keratin *n* queratina
keratitis *n* queratitis *f*
keratomileusis *n* queratomileusis *f*; **laser-assisted in situ** — (**LASIK**) queratomileusis in situ asistida por láser
keratosis *n* queratosis *f*; **actinic** — queratosis actínica; **seborrheic** — queratosis seborreica
keratotomy *n* (*pl* **-mies**) queratotomía; **radial** — queratotomía radial
kernicterus *n* kernicterus *m*
ketamine *n* ketamina
ketoacidosis *n* cetoacidosis *f*
ketoconazole *n* ketoconazol *m*
ketone *n* cetona

ketoprofen *n* ketoprofeno
ketorolac *n* ketorolaco
ketotic *adj* cetónico
ketotifen *n* ketotifeno
kick *n* patada; *vt, vi* patear, dar una patada, dar patadas; (*fam, a habit*) dejar (*un vicio*); **Can you feel your baby kicking?**..¿Siente las patadas de su bebé?; **to** — **the bucket** (*fam*) morir
kid *n* (*fam*) niño -ña *mf*
kidney *n* riñón *m*; **horseshoe** — riñón en herradura
kill *vt* matar
kilogram, kilo (*fam*) *n* kilogramo, kilo (*fam*)
kin *n* parientes *mf*, familia; **next of** — parientes más cercanos
kind *adj* amable
kinesiology *n* kinesiología, quinesiología (*RAE*)
kinetic *adj* cinético
kiss *n* beso; *vt* besar
kissing bug *n* chinche *f*, chinche besuco-

na (*Mex*), chinche picuda (*Guat, El Salv*), pito (*Col*), chipo (*Ven*), chirimacha (*Perú*), vinchuca (*Arg, Bol, Chile, Ur*)

kit *n* estuche *m*, botiquín *m*; **epinephrine —** estuche de epinefrina; **first-aid —** botiquín de primeros auxilios

kleptomania *n* cleptomanía

knee *n* rodilla; **back of the —** corva

kneecap *n* rótula

kneepad *n* rodillera

knife *n* (*pl* **knives**) cuchillo

knife-like *adj* (*pain*) punzante

knit *vi* (*pret & pp* **knitted**; *ger* **knitting**) (*ortho*) soldar(se)

knives *pl de* **knife**

knock knees *n* (*fam*) genu valgo, rodillas pegadas (*fam*)

knot *n* nudo; **knot in my back**..nudo en mi espalda

knuckle *n* nudillo

kwashiorkor *n* kwashiorkor *m*

kyphoscoliosis *n* cifoescoliosis *f*

kyphosis *n* cifosis *f*

L

lab *n* (*fam*) laboratorio; (*result*) resultado de laboratorio; **Your labs were normal**..Sus resultados de laboratorio son normales*; **cath —** laboratorio de cateterismo

**The present tense is more appropriate for this sentence in Spanish.*

label *n* etiqueta

labetalol *n* labetalol *m*

labia *pl de* **labium**

labial *adj* labial

labile *adj* lábil

labium *n* (*pl* **labia**) labio (genital)

labor *n* trabajo de parto; **— and delivery** trabajo de parto y parto; **Labor and Delivery** sala de partos; **labor pains** dolores *mpl* de(l) parto; **to be in —** estar de parto, estar en trabajo de parto; **to go into —** ponerse de parto, entrar en trabajo de parto

laboratory *n* (*pl* **-ries**) laboratorio; **catheterization —** laboratorio de cateterismo

labral *adj* del labrum, relativo al labrum

labrum *n* labrum *m*

labyrinth *n* (*anat*) laberinto

labyrinthitis *n* laberintitis *f*

lace *vt* adulterar; **laced with**..adulterado con

lacerate *vt* lacerar, desgarrar, herir con un golpe cortante

laceration *n* laceración *f*, desgarro, herida producida por un golpe cortante

lack *n* falta, carencia

lacrimal *adj* lagrimal

lactase *n* lactasa

lactate *n* lactato; *vi* producir y secretar leche

lactation *n* producción *f* y secreción *f* de leche; (*period of milk production*) lactancia

lactic *adj* láctico; **— acid** ácido láctico; **— dehydrogenase** deshidrogenasa láctica

lactobacillus *n* lactobacilo

lactose *n* lactosa

lactulose *n* lactulosa

lag *n* retraso, intervalo; *vi* (*pret & pp* **lagged**; *ger* **lagging**) retrasarse

laid up, (*fam*) incapacitado temporalmente

lain *pp de* **lie**

lamb *n* (*meat*) carne *f* de cordero, cordero; **lamb's wool** lana de oveja

lame *adj* cojo
laminaria *n* laminaria
laminectomy *n* (*pl* **-mies**) laminectomía
lamivudine *n* lamivudina
lamotrigine *n* lamotrigina
lamp *n* lámpara; **heat** — lámpara de calor; **slit** — lámpara de hendidura; **sun** — lámpara solar; **ultraviolet** — lámpara ultravioleta; **Wood's** — lámpara de Wood
lance *vt* (*an abscess*) abrir con bisturí (*un absceso*)
lancet *n* lanceta; **diabetic** — lanceta para diabéticos; — **device** lancetero
language *n* (*referring to structure and development*) lenguaje *m*; **body** — lenguaje corporal
lanolin *n* lanolina
lansoprazole *n* lansoprazol *m*
lanugo *n* lanugo, vello de los bebés
lap *n* (*of a person*) regazo
laparoscope *n* laparoscopio
laparoscopic *adj* laparoscópico
laparoscopy *n* (*pl* **-pies**) laparoscopia
laparotomy *n* (*pl* **-mies**) laparotomía; **exploratory** — laparotomía exploradora
lapse *n* lapso, lapsus *m*; — **of memory** laguna mental, lapsus de memoria
lard *n* manteca (de cerdo)
large *adj* grande
larva migrans *n* larva migrans *f*; **cutaneous** — — larva migrans cutánea; **visceral** — — larva migrans visceral
laryngeal *adj* laríngeo
laryngectomy *n* (*pl* **-mies**) laringectomía
larynges *pl de* **larynx**
laryngitis *n* laringitis *f*
laryngoplasty *n* (*pl* **-ties**) laringoplastia
laryngoscope *n* laringoscopio
laryngoscopy *n* (*pl* **-pies**) laringoscopia
larynx *n* (*pl* **larynges** *o* **larynxes**) laringe *f*
laser *n* láser *m*
LASIK *abbr* **laser-assisted in situ keratomileusis**. *V.* **keratomileusis**.
last *adj* último; **your last period**..su último período..su última menstruación; *vi* durar, alcanzar; **How long did the pain last?**..¿Cuánto tiempo le duró el dolor?...**These pills should last a month**..Estas pastillas deberían alcanzarle por un mes.

last rites *npl* últimos ritos
latanoprost *n* latanoprost *m*
late *adj* (*development, etc.*) tardío; *adv* tarde
latent *adj* latente
later *adv* más tarde
lateral *adj* (*anat*) externo, lateral; **lateral aspect of the leg**..cara externa de la pierna
latex *n* látex *m*
latrine *n* letrina
laugh *n* risa; *vi* reír(se)
laughing gas *n* gas *m* hilarante
lavage *n* lavado; **bronchoalveolar** — lavado broncoalveolar; **gastric** — lavado gástrico; **peritoneal** — lavado peritoneal
lawsuit *n* demanda
lax *adj* laxo, flojo
laxity *n* laxitud *f*
laxative *adj & n* laxante *m*; **bulk** — laxante que aumenta el volumen de la materia fecal
lay *adj* lego (*Esp, form*), no profesional; — **opinion** opinión lega *or* no profesional
lay *pret de* **lie**
layer *n* capa; **layers of the skin**..capas de la piel
layperson *n* persona sin formación médica
lazy eye *n* ambliopía, ojo perezoso *or* vago (*fam*), disminución *f* de la agudeza visual sin lesión orgánica del ojo
lb *V.* **pound**.
L-carnitine *n* L-carnitina
LDL *abbr* **low density lipoprotein**. *V.* **lipoprotein**.
lead *n* (*ECG*) derivación *f*; *vi* llevar a, terminar en; **This can lead to amputation if you don't treat it**..Esto puede llevar a una amputación si no se trata.
lead *n* (*metal*) plomo
lean *adj* (*person*) flaco, delgado; (*meat*) magro, sin grasa; *vi* inclinarse; **Lean forward**..Inclínese hacia adelante.
learn *vt, vi* aprender (a); **to learn to read**..aprender a leer
learner *n* aprendiz -za *mf*; **slow** — (*ped*) niño -ña *mf* con dificultad para aprender
learning *n* aprendizaje *m*
least (*super de* **little** *and* **few**) *adj* menor;

the least harm..el menor daño; *adv* menos; **the least invasive option**..la opción menos invasiva
leathers *npl (fam, for physical restraint)* correas
lecithin *n* lecitina
leech *n* sanguijuela
LEEP *abbr* **loop electrosurgical excision procedure**. *V*. **procedure**.
leflunomide *n* leflunomida
left *adj* izquierdo; *n (left-hand side)* izquierda
left-handed *adj* zurdo
leg *n* pierna
legume *n* legumbre *f*
leiomyoma *n* leiomioma *m*; **uterine —** leiomioma uterino
leiomyosarcoma *n* leiomiosarcoma *m*
leishmaniasis *n* leishmaniasis *f*; **cutaneous —** leishmaniasis cutánea; **mucocutaneous —** leishmaniasis mucocutánea, espundia; **visceral —** leishmaniasis visceral
leisure *n* ocio
lemon *n* limón *m*
lemon flower *n (bot)* azahar *m*
length *n* longitud *f*, largo
lens *n* lente *m&f*; *(of the eye)* cristalino; **bifocal —** lente bifocal; **(hard, soft) contact —** lente de contacto (rígido, blando); **progressive —** lente progresivo; **trifocal —** lente trifocal
lentigo *n* lentigo
lepromatous *adj* lepromatoso
leprosy *n* lepra, enfermedad *f* de Hansen; **borderline —** lepra dimorfa; **lepromatous —** lepra lepromatosa; **tuberculoid —** lepra tuberculoide
leptospirosis *n* leptospirosis *f*
lesbian *adj* lesbiana; *n* lesbiana, mujer *f* homosexual; **—, gay, bisexual, and transgender (LGBT)** lesbianas, gays, transexuales y bisexuales; lesbianas, gays, bisexuales y transgéneros; [*Note: The first translation is not a literal translation, since* transexual *is not synonymous with* transgénero, *but it is the more common translation and can be found in the title of various organizations.*]
lesion *n* lesión *f*
less *(comp de* **little** *o* **few)** *adj* menos; **less pills**..menos pastillas; **— than** me-

nos de; **less than there was before**.. menos de lo que había antes; *adv* menos; **— than** menos que; **to eat less than usual**..comer menos que de costumbre
letdown *n (obst)* reflejo de eyección de la leche *(form)*, bajada de la leche
lethal *adj* letal
lethargic *adj* letárgico
lethargy *n* letargo, somnolencia
letter *n* carta; *(of eye chart, etc.)* letra; **Do you want me to write a letter for you?**..¿Quiere que le escriba una carta?
leucine *n* leucina
leucovorin *n* leucovorina, ácido folínico
leukemia *n* leucemia; **acute lymphoblastic** *o* **lymphocytic —** leucemia linfoblástica *or* linfocítica aguda; **acute myeloid —** leucemia mieloide aguda; **chronic lymphocytic —** leucemia linfocítica crónica; **chronic myeloid —** leucemia mieloide crónica
leukocyte *n* leucocito, glóbulo blanco
leukoencephalopathy *n* leucoencefalopatía; **progressive multifocal —** leucoencefalopatía multifocal progresiva
leukoplakia *n* leucoplasia, manchas blancas en la boca o lengua; **oral hairy —** leucoplasia vellosa oral
leuprorelin, leuprolide *n* leuprorelina, leuprolida
levamisole *n* levamisol *m*
level *adj (terreno)* llano; **How far can you walk on level ground before you get short of breath?**..¿Qué distancia puede caminar por terreno llano antes de que le falte el aire?; *n* nivel *m*, concentración *f*; **blood sugar —** nivel de azúcar en la sangre; **— of consciousness** nivel de conciencia *or* consciencia; **socioeconomic —** nivel socioeconómico; **therapeutic —** nivel terapéutico
levetiracetam *n* levetiracetam *m*
levodopa *n* levodopa
levofloxacin *n* levofloxacino, levofloxacina
levonorgestrel *n* levonorgestrel *m*
levothyroxine *n* levotiroxina
LGBT *abbr* **lesbian, gay, bisexual, and transgender**. *V*. **lesbian**.
LGV *V*. **lymphogranuloma venereum**.
LH *abbr* **luteinizing hormone**. *V*. **hor-**

mone.

LHRH *abbr* **luteinizing hormone-releasing hormone.** *V.* **hormone.**

libido *n* libido *f*, deseo sexual

lice *pl de* **louse**

lichen planus *n* liquen plano

lichen simplex chronicus *n* liquen simple crónico

lick *vt* lamer

licorice *n* regaliz *m*

lid *V.* **eyelid.**

lidocaine *n* lidocaína; **viscous** — lidocaína viscosa

lie *vi* (*pret* **lay**; *pp* **lain**; *ger* **lying**) **to — down** acostarse; Lie down, please.. Acuéstese, por favor.

life *n* vida; **for** — de por vida; **for the rest of your** — por el resto de su vida; **— expectancy** expectativa *or* esperanza de vida; **life-saving** que salva vidas, que puede salvar la vida; **life-threatening** potencialmente mortal, que pone en peligro la vida; **sex** — vida sexual; **social** — vida social

lifelong *adj* de por vida

lifestyle *n* estilo de vida

lifetime *n* vida, toda una vida, período de tiempo vivido

lift *n* grúa; **bladder** — reparación *f* de cistocele; **heel** — talonera, cojín *m* que se coloca en el calzado para levantar el talón; **patient** — grúa para levantar pacientes; *vt* levantar; **Avoid heavy lifting.**.Evite levantar objetos pesados; **to — weights** levantar pesas

ligament *n* ligamento; **anterior cruciate** — ligamento cruzado anterior

ligamentum flavum *n* ligamento amarillo

ligation *n* (*surg*) ligadura; **tubal** — ligadura de trompas, ligadura tubárica (*esp. Esp*)

light *adj* (*case of disease*) leve; (*touch*) suave, ligero; (*weight*) ligero, liviano; **— sleeper** persona de sueño ligero; *n* luz *f*

lightening *n* (*obst*) encajamiento, descenso del feto al final del embarazo

lightheaded *adj* mareado; **to be** *o* **feel** — sentir que se va a desmayar, estar *or* sentirse mareado

lightheadedness *n* sensación *f* de desmayo, mareo

lightning *n* relámpago

limb *n* extremidad *f* (*form*), miembro; **residual** — (*form*) muñón *m*

limber *adj* flexible

lime *n* (*fruit*) lima

limit *n* límite *m*; **above normal limits**.. por encima de los límites normales... **below normal limits.**.por debajo de los límites normales...**within normal limits.**.dentro de los límites normales; **lower — of normal** límite inferior normal; **upper — of normal** límite superior normal; **Your sugar is over twice the upper limit of normal.**.Su azúcar está dos veces por encima del límite superior normal; *vt* limitar

limp *adj* flácido *or* fláccido, relajado; *n* cojera; **to have a** — cojear; *vi* cojear

lindane *n* lindano

line *n* línea; (*catheter*) catéter *m*; **arterial** — catéter arterial; **central** — catéter venoso central; **first (second, etc.)** — de primera (segunda, etc.) línea; **gum** — línea de la encía; *vt* (*the intestine, etc.*) recubrir, revestir; **Mucus lines the walls of the stomach.**.El moco recubre las paredes del estómago; **to — up** alinear; *vi* **to — up** alinearse

lineage *n* estirpe *f*; **myeloid (lymphoid, B, T, etc.)** — estirpe mieloide (linfoide, B, T, etc.)

linezolid *n* linezolid *m*

liniment *n* linimento

lining *n* (*of the stomach, etc.*) revestimiento

linked *adj* ligado, asociado; **— to cancer** asociado con (el) cáncer; **sex-linked** ligado al sexo; **X-linked** ligado al cromosoma X

linoleic acid *n* ácido linoleico

liothyronine *n* liotironina

lip *n* labio; **cleft** — labio hendido; **lower** — labio inferior; **upper** — labio superior

lipase *n* lipasa

lipid *n* lípido

lipodystrophy *n* lipodistrofia

lipoma *n* lipoma *m*

lipoprotein *n* lipoproteína; **high density — (HDL)** lipoproteína de alta densidad; **low density — (LDL)** lipoproteína de baja densidad; **very low density — (VLDL)** lipoproteína de muy baja

densidad
liposarcoma *n* liposarcoma *m*
liposuction *n* liposucción *f*
lip-read *vi* (*pret & pp* -**read**) leer los labios
lip reading *n* lectura de los labios
lipstick *n* lápiz *m* labial, labial *m* (*fam*)
liquid *adj & n* líquido; — **nitrogen** nitrógeno líquido
liraglutide *n* liraglutida
lisdexamfetamine *n* lisdexanfetamina
lisinopril *n* lisinopril *m*
lisp *n* ceceo; *vi* cecear
listen *vi* escuchar; **I'm going to listen to your lungs**..Voy a escucharle los pulmones.
listeriosis *n* listeriosis *f*
listless *adj* apático (*debido a cansancio, enfermedad, etc.*)
liter *n* litro
lithium *n* litio
lithotripsy *n* litotricia; **extracorporeal shock wave** — litotricia extracorpórea por ondas de choque
litter *n* (*stretcher*) camilla
little *adj* (*comp* **less**; *super* **least**) (*size*) pequeño, chico; (*quantity, degree*) poco; **a little tumor**..un tumor pequeño... **a little milk**..un poco de leche...**little time**..poco tiempo; — **brother** (*fam*) hermano menor; — **sister** (*fam*) hermana menor; *adv* poco; **a little sunburned**..un poco quemado...**She eats little**.. Ella come poco; *n* poco; — **by** — poco a poco
live *adj* (*vaccine, etc.*) vivo; *vi* vivir; **to** — **with** vivir con, convivir con; **to live with diabetes**..vivir con diabetes...**to live with smokers**..convivir con fumadores...**Who do you live with?**..¿Con quién vive Ud.?
liver *n* hígado; **fatty** — hígado graso
liver spot *n* lentigo solar, mancha parduzca en la piel que suele aparecer en la vejez
lives *pl de* **life**
living will *n* testamento vital
load *n* carga; **viral** — carga viral
lobar *adj* lobar
lobe *n* lóbulo
lobectomy *n* (*pl* -**mies**) lobectomía
lobelia *n* (*bot*) lobelia
lobotomy *n* (*pl* -**mies**) lobotomía

lobular *adj* lobular
local *adj* local
localization *n* localización *f*
localized *adj* localizado
lochia *n* loquios, líquido que sale del útero después del parto
lockjaw *n* (*fam, ant*) tétanos
lodge *vi* alojarse; **The bullet lodged near the aorta**..La bala se alojó cerca de la aorta.
log *n* libreta, cuaderno, diario; **glucose** — libreta de autocontrol (*del diabético*), libreta donde se anotan los niveles del azúcar
log$_{10}$ *n* log$_{10}$ *m*; **6 log$_{10}$ copies/ml**..6 log$_{10}$ copias/ml
loner *n* (*fam*) solitario -ria *mf*
long *adj* largo; *adv* **How long have you had diabetes?**..¿Hace cuánto que tiene diabetes?...**How long were you unconscious?**..¿Por cuánto tiempo estuvo inconsciente?; **long-acting** de acción prolongada
longevity *n* longevidad *f*
long-term *adj* a largo plazo
look *vi* mirar; **Look upward**..Mire hacia arriba; **to** — **like** verse, parecerse; **What did this sore look like when you first noticed it?**..¿Cómo se veía esta herida cuando la vió por primera vez?...**She looks like her mother**..Se parece a su madre.
loop *n* (*IUD*) lazo; (*of bowel*) asa (*intestinal*)
loose *adj* suelto, flojo
loosen *vt* soltar, aflojar; **Loosen your belt, please**..Suelte (Afloje) el cinturón, por favor.
loperamide *n* loperamida
lopinavir *n* lopinavir *m*
loratadine *n* loratadina
lorazepam *n* lorazepam *m*
lordosis *n* lordosis *f*
losartan *n* losartán *m*
lose *vt* (*pret & pp* **lost**) perder; **to** — **consciousness** perder el conocimiento *or* la conciencia; **to** — **one's voice** perder la voz; **to** — **weight** perder peso
loss *n* pérdida; **I'm sorry for your loss**.. Le doy mi más sentido pésame..Lamento mucho su pérdida; **hair** — caída del cabello; **hearing** — pérdida de audición; **weight** — pérdida de peso

lost *pret & pp de* **lose**

lot *n* (*pharm*) lote *m*; **a — (*fam*) mucho; Do you sleep a lot?..¿Duerme mucho?; a — of** (*fam*) mucho(s); **a lot of milk**..mucha leche...**a lot of pimples**.. muchos granos

lotion *n* loción *f*; **hand — loción para manos; tanning** *o* **suntan — (*to increase tanning*) bronceador *m*; (*sunscreen*) filtro solar, protector *m* solar

louse *n* (*pl* **lice**) piojo; **body — piojo del cuerpo; crab — ladilla; head — piojo de la cabeza; pubic — ladilla, piojo del pubis *or* púbico**

lovastatin *n* lovastatina

love *n* amor *m*; **in — with** enamorado de; **to fall in — with** enamorarse de; **to make — hacer el amor; *vt, vi* querer, amar; loved one** ser querido *or* amado

loving *adj* cariñoso, afectuoso

low *adj* bajo; **low in calories**..bajo en calorías...**Your calcium is low**.. Su calcio está bajo; **low-dose** *V.* **dosis; low-fat (low-sodium, etc.)** bajo en grasa (sodio, etc.); **low-pitched** grave, de baja frecuencia

lower (*comp de* **low**) *adj* más bajo; (*anat*) inferior (*form*), bajo, de abajo; **— than** más bajo que; (*a number*) inferior a, por debajo de; **lower than before**..más bajo que antes...**lower than 140**..inferior a 140..por debajo de 140; **the — part** la parte baja *or* de abajo; *vt* bajar; **You need to lower your cholesterol**..Ud. necesita bajar el colesterol...**Lower your arm**..Baje el brazo.

lozenge *n* pastilla para chupar

LSD *V.* **lysergic acid diethylamide.**

lubricant *adj & n* lubricante *m*

lubricate *vt* lubricar

lubrication *n* lubricación *f*

Ludwig's angina *n* angina de Ludwig

lukewarm *adj* tibio

lumbar *adj* lumbar

lump *n* bulto, nódulo (*form*), bola, (*due to trauma, esp. about the head*) chichón *m*; **breast — bulto en la mama *or* el pecho *or* el seno**

lumpectomy *n* (*pl* -**mies**) lumpectomía

lumpy *adj* (*comp* -**ier**; *super* -**iest**) nodular (*form*), que tiene bolitas; **— breasts** senos grumosos, senos que tienen bolitas

lunch *n* almuerzo, comida (*esp. Mex*), comida del mediodía; **to have — almorzar, comer (*esp. Mex*), tomar la comida del mediodía**

lung *n* pulmón *m*

lupus *n* lupus *m*; **discoid — lupus discoide; systemic — erythematosus (SLE)** lupus eritematoso sistémico (LES)

luteal *adj* lúteo

lye *n* lejía

lying (*ger de* **lie**) *adj* (*también* — **down**) acostado

lymph *n* linfa

lymphadenitis *n* linfadenitis *f*

lymphangitis *n* linfangitis *f*

lymphatic *adj* linfático

lymphedema *n* linfedema *m*

lymphocyte *n* linfocito; **B (T, CD4, etc.) — linfocito B (T, CD4, etc.)**

lymphogranuloma venereum (LGV) *n* linfogranuloma venéreo (LGV)

lymphoid *adj* linfoide

lymphoma *n* linfoma *m*; **B cell — linfoma de células B; Hodgkin's — linfoma (de) Hodgkin; mucosa-associated lymphoid tissue (MALT) — linfoma MALT, linfoma de tejido linfoide asociado a mucosas; non-Hodgkin's — linfoma no Hodgkin; T cell — linfoma de células T**

lyophilized *adj* liofilizado

lysergic acid diethylamide (LSD) *n* dietilamida del ácido lisérgico (LSD)

lysine *n* lisina

lysis *n* lisis *f*; **— of adhesions** lisis de adherencias

M

MAC *V.* **Mycobacterium avium complex.**
macerate *vt* macerar; *vi* macerarse; **macerated tissue**..tejido macerado
macrobiotic *adj* macrobiótico
macular degeneration *n* degeneración *f* macular
mad *adj* (*comp* **madder**; *super* **maddest**) enojado, enfadado; (*crazy*) loco; **to get** — enojarse, enfadarse
made *pret & pp de* **make**
maggot *n* cresa, larva de mosca
magnesium *n* magnesio; — **sulfate** sulfato de magnesio
magnifying glass *n* lupa
maintain *vt* mantener
maintenance *n* mantenimiento; **methadone** — mantenimiento con metadona
major *adj* (*anat, surgery*) mayor
makeup *n* maquillaje *m*, cosméticos
malabsorption *n* malabsorción *f*
malaise *n* malestar *m* general, sensación *f* de estar enfermo
malaria *n* malaria, paludismo
malathion *n* malatión *m*
male *adj* masculino; *n* varón *m*, hombre *m*, macho
malformation *n* malformación *f*, deformidad *f*; **arteriovenous** — malformación arteriovenosa
malignancy *n* malignidad *f*, cáncer *m*
malignant *adj* maligno
malinger *vi* hacerse el enfermo (*para evitar el trabajo, obtener compensación, etc.*)
malleolus *n* maléolo; **lateral** — maléolo externo; **medial** — maléolo interno
malnourished *adj* desnutrido, malnutrido
malnutrition *n* malnutrición *f*, desnutrición *f*
malocclusion *n* maloclusión *f*
malpractice *n* mala praxis *f*
maltodextrin *n* maltodextrina
maltreatment *n* (*form*) maltrato, abuso; **child** — maltrato infantil, maltrato a (los) niños; **elder** — maltrato a (las) personas mayores, maltrato a (los) adultos mayores (*Amer*); **physical** — maltrato físico; **psychological** — maltrato psicológico; **sexual** — maltrato sexual
mammaplasty *V.* **mammoplasty.**
mammary *adj* mamario
mammogram *n* mamografía (*estudio*)
mammography *n* mamografía (*técnica*); **digital** — mamografía digital
mammoplasty *n* (*pl* **-ties**) mamoplastia; **augmentation** — mamoplastia de aumento, cirugía para aumentar el tamaño de los senos; **reduction** — mamoplastia de reducción, cirugía para reducir el tamaño de los senos
man *n* (*pl* **men**) hombre *m*
manage *vt* manejar, gestionar, administrar
managed care *n* (*US*) atención (médica) administrada, atención médica gestionada con fines de contener costos
management *n* manejo; **pain** — manejo del dolor
mandible *n* mandíbula inferior, mandíbula (*fam*)
maneuver *n* maniobra; **Heimlich** — maniobra de Heimlich; *vt, vi* maniobrar
manganese *n* manganeso
manhood *n* edad *f* viril; masculinidad *f*, virilidad *f*
mania *n* manía
manic *adj* maníaco *or* maniaco
manic-depressive *adj* (*ant*) bipolar, maníaco-depresivo *or* maniaco-depresivo
manicure *n* manicura
manifestation *n* manifestación *f*
manipulate *vt* manipular
manipulation *n* manipulación *f*; **high-velocity** — manipulación de alta velocidad; **spinal** — manipulación espinal *or* de la columna
manipulative *adj* manipulador
manometry *n* manometría
manual *adj* manual
manubrium *n* manubrio
many *adj* (*comp* **more**; *super* **most**) muchos; **many times**..muchas veces
maraviroc *n* maraviroc *m*

margarine *n* margarina
margin *n* margen *m*
marijuana *n* mariguana, marihuana (*esp. Mex*), hierba (*fam*), mota (*Mex, CA; fam*); **medical** — marihuana medicinal
marital *adj* matrimonial; — **problems** problemas matrimoniales
mark *n* marca
marker *n* marcador *m*
married *adj* casado; **Are you married?** ..¿Está casado?
marrow *n* médula; **bone** — médula ósea
marshmallow *n* (*bot*) malvavisco
martial arts *npl* artes *mpl&fpl* marciales; [*Note: Feminine usage is more common.*]
mascara *n* rímel *m*
masculine *adj* masculino
masculinity *n* masculinidad *f*
mash *n* (*crushing injury*) machucón *m*; *vt* machucar, aplastar, pillar (*Esp*)
mask *n* máscara, mascarilla, careta; **gas** — máscara antigás, máscara de gas; **oxygen** — máscara *or* mascarilla de oxígeno; **surgical** — cubrebocas *m*, barbijo, mascarilla *or* máscara quirúrgica; **welding** — careta para soldar; *vt* (*signs, symptoms*) enmascarar, ocultar
masochism *n* masoquismo
masochist *n* masoquista *mf*
masochistic *adj* masoquista
mass *n* masa; (*tumor*) masa, tumor *m*; **a suspicious mass**..una masa sospechosa; **bone** — masa ósea; **muscle** — masa muscular
massage *n* masaje *m*; **cardiac** — masaje cardíaco; **to give a** — dar (un) masaje; *vt* masajear
masseur *n* masajista *m*
masseuse *n* masajista *f*
massive *adj* masivo
MAST *V.* **military anti-shock trousers.**
mastectomy *n* (*pl* -**mies**) mastectomía; **modified radical** — mastectomía radical modificada
mastitis *n* mastitis *f*
mastocytosis *n* mastocitosis *f*
mastoid *adj* mastoideo
mastoidectomy *n* (*pl* -**mies**) mastoidectomía
mastoiditis *n* mastoiditis *f*
masturbate *vt, vi* masturbar(se)
masturbation *n* masturbación *f*

match *vt* (*blood, tissue*) ser (enteramente) compatible con; **Your sister's tissue type matches your own**..El tipo de tejido de su hermana es (enteramente) compatible con el suyo.
material *n* material *m*
maternal *adj* materno; (*motherly*) maternal; — **grandfather** abuelo materno; — **instinct** instinto maternal
maternity *n* maternidad *f*
matrix *n* matriz *f*; **nail** — matriz ungueal
matter *n* (*anat*) sustancia; **gray** — sustancia gris; **white** — sustancia blanca
mattress *n* colchón *m*
mature *adj* maduro; *vi* madurar
maturity *n* madurez *f*
maxilla *n* (*pl* -**lae**) maxilar *m* superior
maxillary *adj* maxilar
maxillofacial *adj* maxilofacial
maximal *adj* máximo
maximize *vt* maximizar
maximum *adj & n* (*pl* -**mums**) máximo
MD, M.D. *V.* **Doctor of Medicine.**
MDA *V.* **methylene dioxyamphetamine.**
MDMA *V.* **methylene dioxymethamphetamine.**
meal *n* comida; **Meals on Wheels** programa *m* para repartir comidas a domicilio a gente de edad avanzada
mean *adj* (*math*) medio; (*cruel*) cruel; *n* media, promedio
measles *n* sarampión *m*; **German** *o* **three-day** — rubéola *or* rubeola (*form*), sarampión alemán
measure *n* medida; **heroic measures** medidas heroicas; *vt* medir
measurement *n* (*act*) medición *f*, (*value obtained*) valor *m*, medida; **Blood glucose measurement is easy**..La medición de la glucosa en sangre es fácil.
measuring tape *n* cinta métrica
meat *n* carne *f*; **dark** — carne oscura; **organ meats** vísceras; **red** — carne roja; **white** — carne blanca
meatus *n* (*pl* **meatus**) meato
mebendazole *n* mebendazol *m*
mechanism *n* mecanismo; **coping** — mecanismo de afrontamiento; **defense** — mecanismo de defensa
meclizine, meclozine (*INN*) *n* meclizina, meclozina (*INN*)
meconium *n* meconio

med (*fam, often pl*) *V.* **medication**.
medial *adj* (*anat*) interno, medial; — **thigh** muslo interno
median *adj* (*nerve*) mediano; (*stat*) relativo a la mediana; **the — age** la mediana de edad; *n* (*stat*) mediana
mediastinal *adj* mediastínico
mediastinoscopy *n* (*pl* **-pies**) mediastinoscopia
mediastinum *n* mediastino
medic *n* miembro de un cuerpo militar de sanidad
medical *adj* médico; — **savings account** (*US*) cuenta de ahorro dedicada a los gastos médicos
medicate *vt* medicar; **medicated shampoo**..champú medicado
medication *n* medicamento
medicinal *adj* medicinal
medicine *n* (*field*) medicina; (*medication*) medicina, medicamento; **addiction** — medicina de la adicción; **allergy (ulcer, etc.)** — medicina antialérgica (antiulcerosa, etc.); **complementary and alternative** — medicina complementaria y alternativa; **evidence-based** — medicina basada en la evidencia; **family** — medicina familiar *or* de familia; **folk** — medicina tradicional *or* popular, curanderismo; **herbal** — fitoterapia; **holistic** — medicina holística *or* integral; **integrative** — medicina integrativa; **internal** — medicina interna; **nuclear** — medicina nuclear; **numbing** — (*fam*) anestésico (local); **occupational** — medicina laboral *or* ocupacional; **physical** — **and rehabilitation** medicina física y rehabilitación; **preventive** — medicina preventiva; **regenerative** — medicina regenerativa; **socialized** — medicina socializada; **sports** — medicina deportiva; **traditional** — medicina tradicional *or* popular; **veterinary** — veterinaria; **Western** — medicina occidental
medicine cabinet *n* botiquín *m*
medicine dropper *n* gotero, cuentagotas *m* (*esp. Esp*)
medicolegal *adj* medicolegal
meditate *vi* meditar
meditation *n* meditación *f*
medium *adj* mediano; *n* medio; **contrast** — medio de contraste, contraste *m*

(*fam*)
medroxyprogesterone *n* medroxiprogesterona
medulla *n* (*pl* **-lae**) (*of the brainstem*) bulbo raquídeo, médula oblonga; **adrenal** — médula suprarrenal *or* adrenal
medullary *adj* medular
mefloquine *n* mefloquina
megacolon *n* megacolon *m*
megadose *n* megadosis *f*
megestrol *n* megestrol *m*
melancholy *n* melancolía, tristeza
melanin *n* melanina
melanoma *n* melanoma *m*
melarsoprol *n* melarsoprol *m*
melasma *n* cloasma *m*, melasma *m*, paño (*fam*), manchas en la cara que aparecen durante el embarazo
melatonin *n* melatonina
meloxicam *n* meloxicam *m*
melphalan *n* melfalán *m*
memantine *n* memantina
member *n* miembro; (*limb*) extremidad *f* (*form*), miembro; **family** — miembro de la familia, familiar *mf*
membrane *n* membrana; **mucous** — membrana mucosa; **tympanic** — membrana timpánica
memory *n* (*pl* **-ries**) memoria; **long-term** — memoria a largo plazo; **short-term** — memoria a corto plazo
men *pl de* **man**
menarche *n* menarquia, menarca, primera menstruación
meninges *pl de* **meninx**
meningioma *n* meningioma *m*
meningitis *n* meningitis *f*
meningocele *n* meningocele *m*
meningococcal *adj* meningocócico
meningococcus *n* (*pl* **-ci**) meningococo
meninx *n* (*pl* **meninges**) (*frec. pl*) meninge *f*
meniscal *adj* meniscal
meniscectomy *n* (*pl* **-mies**) meniscectomía
meniscus *n* (*pl* **-ci**) menisco; **torn** — menisco roto
menopausal *adj* menopáusico
menopause *n* menopausia
men's room *n* baño de hombres
menstrual *adj* menstrual
menstruate *vi* menstruar
menstruation *n* menstruación *f*

mental *adj* mental; (*pertaining to chin*) mentoniano
menthol *n* mentol *m*
meperidine *n* meperidina, petidina (*INN*)
meralgia paresthetica *n* meralgia parestésica
mercury *n* mercurio
mercy killing *n* eutanasia, muerte piadosa
meropenem *n* meropenem *m*
mesalamine (*USAN*), **mesalazine** (*INN*) *n* mesalamina, mesalazina (*INN*)
mescal *n* mezcal *m*
mescaline *n* mescalina *or* mezcalina
mesenteric *adj* mesentérico
mesentery *n* mesenterio
mesh *n* (*surg*) malla
mesothelioma *n* mesotelioma *m*
mesotherapy *n* mesoterapia
metabolic *adj* metabólico
metabolism *n* metabolismo; **basal —** metabolismo basal
metacarpal *adj* & *n* metacarpiano
metal *n* metal *m*; **heavy —** metal pesado
metallic *adj* metálico
metastasis *n* (*pl* **-ses**) metástasis *f*
metastasize *vi* metastatizar, diseminarse
metastatic *adj* metastásico
metatarsal *adj* & *n* metatarsiano
metaxalone *n* metaxalona
meter *n* (*measuring device*) medidor *m*; (*unit of length*) metro; **blood glucose —** medidor de glucosa en sangre, aparato para medir el azúcar en la sangre; **square —** metro cuadrado
metformin *n* metformina
meth (*fam*) *V.* **methamphetamine**.
methacholine *n* metacolina
methadone *n* metadona
methamphetamine, metamphetamine (*INN*) *n* metanfetamina
methane *n* metano
methanol *n* metanol *m*
methaqualone *n* metacualona
methicillin *n* meticilina
methimazole *n* metimazol *m*, tiamazol *m* (*INN*)
methionine *n* metionina
methocarbamol *n* metocarbamol *m*
method *n* método; **Lamaze —** método Lamaze; **rhythm —** método del ritmo
methotrexate *n* metotrexato, metotrexate *m*

methyl alcohol *n* metanol *m*
methylcellulose *n* metilcelulosa
methyldopa *n* metildopa
methylene blue *n* azul *m* de metileno
methylene dioxyamphetamine (MDA) *n* metilendioxianfetamina (MDA), droga del amor (*fam*)
methylene dioxymethamphetamine (MDMA) *n* metilendioximetanfetamina (MDMA), éxtasis *m* (*fam*)
methylphenidate *n* metilfenidato
methylprednisolone *n* metilprednisolona
meticillin (*INN*) *n* meticilina
metoclopramide *n* metoclopramida
metolazone *n* metolazona
metoprolol *n* metoprolol *m*
metric system *n* sistema métrico
metronidazole *n* metronidazol *m*
mice *pl de* **mouse**
miconazole *n* miconazol *m*
microalbuminuria *n* microalbuminuria
microbe *n* microbio
microbial *adj* microbiano
microbicide *n* microbicida *m*
microbiology *n* microbiología, estudio de los microbios
microdermabrasion *n* microdermoabrasión *f*
microdiscectomy *n* (*pl* **-mies**) microdiscectomía
microflora *n* microflora
microgram *n* microgramo
micrometastasis *n* (*pl* **-ses**) micrometástasis *f*
micronized *adj* (*pharm*) micronizado
micronutrient *n* micronutriente *m*
microorganism *n* microorganismo, microbio
microscope *n* microscopio; **electron —** microscopio electrónico; **light —** microscopio de luz
microscopic *adj* microscópico
microscopy *n* microscopia *or* microscopía
microsurgery *n* microcirugía
microvascular *adj* microvascular
microwave *n* (*rad*) microonda; (*fam, oven*) microondas *m*
mid *adj* medio; **mid-cycle** medio ciclo
midazolam *n* midazolam *m*
midbrain *n* mesencéfalo (*form*), cerebro medio
middle *adj* (*finger*) medio; *n* medio,

(*length*) mitad *f*; **in the middle of your hand**..en medio de la mano...**the middle of your arm**..la mitad del brazo... **in the middle of the night**..en medio de la noche

midget *n* (*ant*) enano -na *mf*

midlife *adj* de mediana edad; *n* mediana edad

midline *n* (*of the body*) eje *m* (central), línea media (*del cuerpo*)

midodrine *n* midodrina

midstream urine orina de la mitad del chorro, orina del chorro medio, orina recogida a mitad del chorro

midwife *n* (*pl* -**wives**) partera, comadrona; **male** — partero, comadrón *m*

mifepristone *n* mifepristona

migraine (*fam*) **migraine headache**. *V.* **headache**.

migrate *vi* (*within the body, e.g., parasites*) migrar

mild *adj* (*soap, etc.*) suave; (*illness*) leve

mildew *n* moho

milestone *n* hito; **developmental** — hito del desarrollo

milia *n* milia, puntitos blanquecinos que tienden a ocurrir en la cara

miliaria *n* sudamina (*form*), miliaria (*form*), sarpullido *or* salpullido, erupción *f* que se manifiesta durante tiempos de calor

miliary *adj* miliar

milk *n* leche *f*; **breast** — leche materna; **cow's** — leche de vaca; **lactose-free** — leche deslactosada *or* sin lactosa; **low-fat** — leche baja en grasa; — **product** producto lácteo *or* de la leche; **non-fat** — leche descremada *or* desnatada; **pasteurized** — leche pasteurizada; **raw** — leche cruda, leche bronca (*Mex*); **skim** — leche descremada *or* desnatada; **soy** — leche de soya *or* soja; **unpasteurized** — leche sin pasteurizar, leche no pasteurizada; **whole** — leche entera

milk of magnesia *n* leche *f* de magnesia

milk thistle *n* (*bot*) cardo mariano

milligram *n* miligramo

milliliter *n* mililitro

millimeter *n* milímetro

millirem *n* (*rad, ant*) milirem *m*

millisecond *n* milisegundo

millisievert *n* (*rad*) milisievert *m*

mimic *vt* (*pret & pp* -**icked**; *ger* -**icking**) imitar

mind *n* mente *f*; **to lose one's** — volverse loco, perder la razón; *vt* (*to obey*) obedecer, hacer caso; **He doesn't mind me**..No me obedece..No me hace caso.

mindful *adj* consciente, atento

mindfulness *n* atención plena; una técnica de meditación que enfatiza reconocimiento y aceptación de los sentimientos, pensamientos y sensaciones corporales propias

miner *n* minero -ra *mf*

mineral *adj & n* mineral *m*

minimal *adj* mínimo

minimize *vt* minimizar

minimum *adj & n* (*pl* -**mums**) mínimo

minocycline *n* minociclina

minor *adj* (*anat, surgery*) menor; *n* menor *mf* (de edad); **emancipated** — menor emancipado

minoxidil *n* minoxidil *m*

mint *n* (*bot*) menta

minute *n* minuto

miracle *n* milagro

mirror *n* espejo

mirtazapine *n* mirtazapina

miscarriage *n* aborto espontáneo

miscarry *vi* (*pret & pp* -**ried**) abortar (*sin intención*), sufrir un aborto

mischievous *adj* travieso

misery *n* miseria

misoprostol *n* misoprostol *m*

miss *vt* (*work, an appointment, etc.*) faltar (a); (*dose of medication*) no tomar, dejar de tomar; (*a loved one, etc.*) extrañar; **Did you miss work?**..¿Faltó al trabajo?...**Ten pills are missing**..Faltan diez pastillas...**Try not to miss this appointment**..Trate de no faltar a esta cita...**Don't miss a single dose of this medicine**..No deje de tomar una sola dosis de esta medicina...**Have you missed a period recently?**..¿Le ha faltado el período últimamente?..**Do you miss your husband?**..¿Extraña a su esposo?

missing *adj* ausente; — **tooth** diente ausente

mistreat *vt* maltratar

mistreatment *n* maltrato

mite *n* ácaro; **dust** — ácaro del polvo; **harvest** — ácaro de la cosecha, ácaro

rojo, larva roja de ciertos ácaros
mitral *adj* mitral
mittelschmerz *n* dolor *m* de ovulación, dolores pélvicos que aparecen con la ovulación
mix *vt* mezclar
mixed *adj* mezclado; (*in medical nomenclature*) mixto; — **connective tissue disease** enfermedad mixta del tejido conectivo
mixture *n* mezcla
moan *n* gemido; *vi* gemir
mobile *adj* móvil; **mobile MRI unit**.. unidad *f* móvil de resonancia magnética
mobility *n* movilidad *f*
mobilization *n* movilización *f*; **passive** — movilización pasiva
mobilize *vt* movilizar
modafinil *n* modafinilo
moderate *adj* moderado
moderation *n* moderación *f*
modification *n* modificación *f*; **behavior** — modificación de la conducta
modifier *n* modificador *m*; **biologic response** — modificador de la respuesta biológica
modify *vt* (*pret & pp* -**fied**) modificar
modulator *n* modulador *m*; **immune** — inmunomodulador *m*; **selective estrogen receptor** — modulador selectivo de los receptores estrogénicos
moist *adj* húmedo
moisten *vt* humedecer, mojar un poco
moisture *n* humedad *f*
moisturize *vt* humedecer, (*skin*) hidratar
moisturizer *n* hidratante *m&f**, humectante *m*
*The RAE lists hidratante *as feminine, but masculine usage is at least as common.*
moisturizing *adj* hidratante, humectante
molar *adj* (*dent, obst*) molar; *n* molar *m* (*form*), muela; **third** — tercer molar, muela del juicio (*fam*)
mold *n* (*dent*) molde *m*; (*fungus*) moho; *vt* moldear
mole *n* (*derm*) lunar *m*; (*obst*) mola; **hidatidiform** — mola hidatiforme
molecular *adj* molecular
molecule *n* molécula
molest *vt* acosar, abusar (*sexualmente*)
molluscum contagiosum *n* molusco contagioso
mom *n* mamá, madre *f*
mommy *n* (*pl* -**mies**) mami *f*, mamita, madre *f*
mometasone *n* mometasona
monitor *n* monitor *m*; **blood pressure** — tensiómetro, baumanómetro (*Mex*), aparato para medir la presión de la sangre; **cardiac** — monitor cardíaco; **event** — monitor de eventos; **fetal heart** — monitor fetal, cardiotocógrafo; **blood glucose** — medidor *m* de glucosa en sangre, aparato para medir el azúcar en la sangre; **Holter** — monitor Holter, monitor cardíaco ambulatorio continuo de 24 horas; *vt* monitorizar, monitorear, seguir
monitoring *n* monitorización *f*, monitoreo, seguimiento; **ambulatory ECG** — monitorización electrocardiográfica ambulatoria, monitoreo electrocardiográfico ambulatorio
mono (*fam*) *V.* **mononucleosis**.
monoclonal *adj* monoclonal
monogamous *adj* monógamo
monogamy *n* monogamia
mononucleosis *n* mononucleosis *f*
monophasic *adj* (*pharm*) monofásico
monosodium glutamate (MSG) *n* glutamato monosódico (GMS)
monounsaturated *adj* monoinsaturado
mons pubis *n* pubis *m*, parte *f* inferior del vientre, (*in women*) monte *m* de Venus
monster *n* monstruo
mons veneris *n* monte *m* de Venus
montelukast *n* montelukast *m*
month *n* mes *m*
monthly *adj* mensual
mood *n* estado de ánimo, humor *m*; **mood swings** oscilaciones *fpl* de humor, cambios repentinos del estado de ánimo; **to be in a bad** — estar de mal humor; **to be in a good** — estar de buen humor
morale *n* moral *f*
moral *adj* moral; — **support** apoyo moral
morbid *adj* (*path*) mórbido, patológico; — **obesity** obesidad mórbida
morbidity *n* morbilidad *f*
more *adj* más; **a few more days**..unos días más; *adv* más; **more difficult**..

más difícil; *n* más; — **than** más que, (*a number*) más de; **more than usual..** más que de costumbre...**more than 200..**más de 200

morgue *n* morgue *f*, depósito de cadáveres

morning *adj* matutino, matinal, en la mañana; — **sickness** náuseas matutinas (*form*), náuseas *or* vómitos del embarazo; — **stiffness** rigidez matutina (*form*), rigidez en la mañana; *n* mañana

morphea *n* morfea, una forma de esclerodermia localizada

morphine *n* morfina

morphology *n* morfología

mortal *adj* mortal, fatal

mortality *n* mortalidad *f*; **infant** — mortalidad infantil

mortuary *n* (*pl* **-ries**) (*funeral home*) funeraria; (*morgue*) morgue *f*, depósito de cadáveres

mosquito *n* (*pl* **-toes** *o* **-tos**) mosquito

most *adj* mayoría de; **in most cases..**en la mayoría de los casos; *adv* más; **the most effective drug..**el medicamento más eficaz

mother *n* madre *f*; **surrogate** — madre sustituta *or* portadora

motherhood *n* maternidad *f*

mother-in-law *n* (*pl* **mothers-in-law**) suegra

motility *n* movilidad *f*, motilidad *f*; **sperm** — movilidad *or* motilidad espermática *or* de los espermatozoides

motion *n* movimiento; — **sickness** mareo por movimiento; **range of** — rango de movimiento

motivate *vt* motivar

motivation *n* motivación *f*

motor *adj* (*nerve, etc.*) motor

motorcycle *n* motocicleta, moto *f* (*fam*)

mountain *n* montaña

mountaineering *n* alpinismo, montañismo

mourn *vt, vi* lamentar, llevar luto (*por alguien*)

mouse *n* (*pl* **mice**) ratón *m*

moustache *n* bigote *m*

mouth *n* boca; **by** — por vía oral (*form*), por la boca; **mouth-to-mouth** boca a boca

mouthful *n* (*pl* **-fuls**) bocado

mouthpiece *n* boquilla

mouthwash *n* enjuague *m* bucal, colutorio

move *vt* mover, (*a patient*) trasladar; **We have to move you to another room..** Tenemos que trasladarlo a otro cuarto; **to** — **one's bowels** defecar (*form*), ir al baño, hacer del baño (*Mex*), dar del cuerpo (*Carib*), hacer popó (*fam*), hacer caca (*esp. ped, fam or vulg*); *vi* moverse; **Don't move..**No se mueva.

movement *n* movimiento; **bowel** — *V.* **bowel**; **rapid eye** — **(REM)** movimientos oculares rápidos (MOR)

moxibustion *n* moxibustión *f*

moxifloxacin *n* moxifloxacino, moxifloxacina

MR *abbr* **magnetic resonance**. *V.* **resonance.**

MRI *n* IRM *f* (*V.* también **magnetic resonance imaging** *bajo* **imaging**.)

MRSA *abbr* **methicillin-resistant Staphylococcus aureus**. *V.* **Staphylococcus aureus.**

MSG *V.* **monosodium glutamate.**

much *adj & adv* mucho

mucinous *adj* mucinoso

mucocele *n* mucocele *m*

mucocutaneous *adj* mucocutáneo

mucolytic *adj & n* mucolítico

mucormycosis *n* mucormicosis *f*

mucosa *n* mucosa

mucous *adj* mucoso

mucus *n* mucosidad *f*, moco

mullein *n* (*bot*) gordolobo

multidisciplinary *adj* multidisciplinario, multidisciplinar

multifactorial *adj* multifactorial

multifocal *adj* multifocal

multinodular *adj* multinodular

multiple *adj* múltiple

multiply *vt, vi* (*pret & pp* **-plied**) multiplicar(se)

multivitamin *adj* multivitamínico; *n* multivitamínico, polivitamínico (*Esp*)

mumps *n o npl* parotiditis *f* (*form*), paperas; [*Nota:* mumps *se usa con verbos singulares más que con verbos plurales.*]

mupirocin *n* mupirocina

murmur *n* (*card*) soplo; **heart** — soplo cardíaco

muscle *n* músculo; **biceps** — músculo bíceps, bíceps *m*; **deltoid** — músculo deltoides, deltoides *m*; **gastrocnemius** — músculo gastrocnemio, gastrocnemio; **gluteus** — músculo glúteo, glúteo; **pectoral** — músculo pectoral, pectoral *m*; **psoas** — músculo psoas, psoas *m*; **quadriceps** — músculo cuádriceps, cuádriceps *m*; **skeletal** — músculo esquelético; **smooth** — músculo liso; **soleus** — músculo sóleo, sóleo; **trapezius** — músculo trapecio, trapecio; **triceps** — músculo tríceps, tríceps *m*

muscular *adj* muscular; (*person*) musculoso; — **dystrophy** distrofia muscular

musculoskeletal *adj* musculoesquelético

mushroom *n* (*wild*) hongo, seta; **poisonous** — hongo venenoso, seta venenosa

musician *n* músico -ca *mf*

mutant *adj* & *n* mutante *m*

mutation *n* mutación *f*; **BRCA** — mutación BRCA

mute *adj* & *n* mudo -da *mf*

mutilate *vt* mutilar

mutilation *n* mutilación *f*

mutism *n* mutismo, mudez *f*; **selective** — mutismo selectivo

myalgia *n* mialgia

myasthenia gravis *n* miastenia grave *or* gravis

mycophenolate mofetil *n* micofenolato de mofetilo

mycosis fungoides *n* micosis *f* fungoide

mycotic *adj* micótico

myelin *n* mielina

myelitis *n* mielitis *f*; **transverse** — mielitis transversa

myelodysplasia *n* mielodisplasia

myelodysplastic *adj* mielodisplásico

myelofibrosis *n* mielofibrosis; **primary** — mielofibrosis primaria

myelogram *n* mielografía (*estudio*)

myelography *n* mielografía (*técnica*)

myeloma *n* mieloma *m*; **multiple** — mieloma múltiple

myelomeningocele *n* mielomeningocele *m*

myeloproliferative *adj* mieloproliferativo

myocardial *adj* miocárdico

myocarditis *n* miocarditis *f*

myocardium *n* miocardio

myofascial *adj* miofascial

myoglobin *n* mioglobina

myoma *n* mioma *m*; **uterine** — mioma uterino

myopathy *n* miopatía

myopia *n* miopía, vista corta, dificultad *f* para ver los objetos lejanos

myopic *adj* miope, corto de vista, que tiene dificultad para ver los objetos lejanos

myositis *n* miositis *f*

myringitis *n* miringitis *f*

myringoplasty *n* (*pl* -**ties**) miringoplastia

myth *n* mito

myxedema *n* mixedema *m*

myxoma *n* mixoma *m*

N

nabumetone *n* nabumetona

nafcillin *n* nafcilina

nagging *adj* (*pain*) persistente

nail *n* (*anat*) uña; (*carpentry*) clavo; **ingrown** — uña encarnada, uña enterrada (*esp. Mex*); — **clippers** cortauñas *m*; — **file** lima de *or* para uñas; — **polish** esmalte *m* de *or* para uñas; — **scissors** tijeras de *or* para uñas

nailbed *n* lecho ungueal

naked *adj* desnudo

nalidixic acid *n* ácido nalidíxico

naloxone *n* naloxona
naltrexone *n* naltrexona
name *n* nombre *m*; **first** — nombre, nombre de pila; **last** — apellido; **middle** — segundo nombre; [*Note: Native Spanish speakers may or may not have a middle name. Almost all have two last names, a paternal surname followed by a maternal surname. See also* **surname**.]
nap *n* siesta; **to take a** — tomar una siesta; *vi* (*pret & pp* **napped**; *ger* **napping**) tomar una siesta
napalm *n* napalm *m*
naphazoline *n* nafazolina
napkin *V.* **sanitary.**
naproxen *n* naproxeno
naratriptan *n* naratriptán *m*
narcissism *n* narcisismo
narcissist *n* narcisista *mf*
narcissistic *adj* narcisista
narcolepsy *n* narcolepsia
narcotic *adj & n* narcótico
narrow *adj* estrecho
narrowing *n* estenosis *f* (*form*), estrechamiento
nasal *adj* nasal; — **passages** conductos *or* vías nasales; — **voice** voz nasal *or* gangosa
nasogastric *adj* nasogástrico
nasopharynx *n* nasofaringe *f*
natural *adj* natural
nature *n* naturaleza
naturopath *n* naturista *mf*, naturópata *mf*
naturopathic *adj* naturista, naturopático
naturopathy *n* medicina naturista, naturopatía
nausea *n* náusea (*frec. pl*); — **and vomiting** náusea(s) y vómito(s)
nauseate *vt* causar náusea(s)
nauseated *adj* con náusea(s); **to be** *o* **feel** — tener náusea(s); **Do you feel nauseated?**..¿Tiene náusea(s)?
nauseating *adj* asqueroso, nauseabundo, que causa náusea(s)
nauseous *adj* con náusea(s); (*nauseating*) asqueroso, nauseabundo, que causa náusea(s)
navel *n* ombligo
near *prep* cerca de
nearsighted *adj* miope (*form*), corto de vista, que tiene dificultad para ver los objetos lejanos

nearsightedness *n* miopía (*form*), vista corta, dificultad *f* para ver los objetos lejanos
nebivolol *n* nebivolol *m*
nebulization *n* nebulización *f*
nebulizer *n* nebulizador *m*; **handheld** — nebulizador de mano
neck *n* cuello; **back of the** — nuca
necrobiosis lipoidica diabeticorum *n* necrobiosis lipoídica diabeticorum
necrolysis *n* necrólisis *f*; **toxic epidermal** — necrólisis epidérmica tóxica
necrophilia *n* necrofilia
necrophobia *n* necrofobia
necrosis *n* necrosis *f*
necrotic *adj* necrótico
necrotizing *adj* necrotizante, necrosante
need *n* necesidad *f*; **special needs** necesidades especiales; *vt* necesitar, hacer(*le*) falta (*a uno*); **You need iron**..Necesita hierro..Le hace falta hierro.
needle *n* aguja; **butterfly** — aguja mariposa; — **exchange** intercambio de agujas
needlestick *n* pinchazo de aguja; — **injury** lesión *f* por pinchazo (de aguja)
needy *adj* (*psych, fam*) necesitado emocionalmente, que requiere mucha atención
negative *adj & n* negativo; **false** — falso negativo; **true** — verdadero negativo
negativism *n* (*psych, etc.*) negativismo
neglect *n* negligencia, descuido; *vt* descuidar, desatender
negligence *n* negligencia
negligent *adj* negligente
neighbor *n* vecino -na *mf*
neighborhood *n* barrio, vecindario, vecindad *f*
nelfinavir *n* nelfinavir *m*
neoadjuvant *adj* neoadyuvante
neomycin *n* neomicina
neonatal *adj* neonatal
neonate *n* neonato -ta *mf*, recién nacido -da *mf*
neonatologist *n* neonatólogo -ga *mf*, médico -ca *mf* especializado en recién nacidos
neonatology *n* neonatología, rama de la pediatría que se ocupa de los recién nacidos
neoplasia *n* neoplasia (*proceso*)
neoplasm *n* neoplasia (*tumor*)

neoplastic *adj* neoplásico
neostigmine *n* neostigmina
nephew *n* sobrino
nephrectomy *n* (*pl* -mies) nefrectomía
nephritic *adj* nefrítico
nephritis *n* nefritis *f*
nephrogenic *adj* nefrogénico, nefrógeno
nephrolithiasis *n* nefrolitiasis *f*
nephrologist *n* nefrólogo -ga *mf*, médico -ca *mf* especializado en el riñón y sus enfermedades, especialista *mf* del riñón
nephrology *n* nefrología, rama de la medicina que se ocupa del riñón y sus enfermedades
nephropathy *n* nefropatía; diabetic — nefropatía diabética
nephrosis *n* nefrosis *f*
nephrostomy *n* (*pl* -mies) nefrostomía
nephrotic *adj* nefrótico
nerve *n* nervio; acoustic — nervio auditivo; cranial — par *m* craneal facial — nervio facial; femoral — nervio crural *or* femoral; median — nervio mediano; optic — nervio óptico; phrenic — nervio frénico; pinched — (*fam*) nervio comprimido *or* atrapado; radial — nervio radial; sciatic — nervio ciático; spinal — nervio espinal; trigeminal — nervio trigémino; ulnar — nervio cubital; vagus — nervio vago
nervous *adj* nervioso; to be — estar nervioso
nervousness *n* nerviosismo
nettle *n* (*bot*) ortiga
network *n* red *f*; network of hospitals.. red de hospitales
neural *adj* neural
neuralgia *n* neuralgia; postherpetic — neuralgia postherpética; trigeminal — neuralgia del trigémino
neuritis *n* neuritis *f*; optical — neuritis óptica
neuroanatomy *n* neuroanatomía
neuroblastoma *n* neuroblastoma *m*
neurofibroma *n* neurofibroma *m*
neurofibromatosis *n* neurofibromatosis *f*
neurogenic *adj* neurogénico, neurógeno
neuroleptic *adj* & *n* neuroléptico
neurological, neurologic *adj* neurológico
neurologist *n* neurólogo -ga *mf*, médico

-ca *mf* especializado en el sistema nervioso y sus enfermedades
neurology *n* neurología, rama de la medicina que se ocupa del sistema nervioso y sus enfermedades
neuroma *n* neurinoma *m*; neuroma *m*; acoustic — (*vestibular schwannoma*) schwannoma *m* vestibular, neurinoma del acústico; Morton's — neuroma de Morton
neuromuscular *adj* neuromuscular
neuron *n* neurona
neuroophthalmology, neuro-ophthalmology *n* neurooftalmología *or* neuro-oftalmología
neuropathy *n* neuropatía *f*; diabetic — neuropatía diabética; peripheral — neuropatía periférica; sensory — neuropatía sensitiva *or* sensorial
neurophysiology *n* neurofisiología
neurosis *n* (*pl* -ses) (*ant*) trastorno de ansiedad, neurosis *f* (*ant*)
neurosurgeon *n* neurocirujano -na *mf*
neurosurgery *n* (*pl* -ries) neurocirugía
neurosyphilis *n* neurosífilis *f*
neurotic *adj* (*ant*) crónica y excesivamente ansioso, neurótico -ca *mf* (*ant*)
neurotoxic *adj* neurotóxico
neutral *adj* (*chem, etc.*) neutro
neutralize *vt* neutralizar
neutropenia *n* neutropenia
neutrophil *n* neutrófilo
never *adv* nunca
nevi *pl* de nevus
nevirapine *n* nevirapina
nevus *n* (*pl* nevi) nevo; dysplastic — nevo displásico
newborn *n* recién nacido -da *mf*; premature — recién nacido prematuro, prematuro -ra *mf* (*fam*)
next *adj* próximo, siguiente; Next!...¡Él que sigue!; the — injection la próxima inyección
niacin *n* niacina
nick *n* cortada pequeña, (*during surgery*) perforación *f*; *vt* cortar levemente, perforar (*sin querer*)
nickel *n* níquel *m*
niclosamide *n* niclosamida
nicotine *n* nicotina
nicotinic acid *n* ácido nicotínico
niece *n* sobrina
nifedipine *n* nifedipino, nifedipina

nifurtimox *n* nifurtimox *m*
night *adj* nocturno; — **terrors** terrores nocturnos; *n* noche *f*; **at** — en *or* por *or* durante la noche; **last** — anoche
nightlight *n* luz nocturna
nightmare *n* pesadilla
nighttime *n* noche *f*
nipple *n* (*female*) pezón *m*; (*male*) tetilla; (*of a baby bottle*) tetina; — **shield** pezonera
nit *n* liendre *f*
nitrate *n* nitrato
nitric acid *n* ácido nítrico
nitrite *n* nitrito
nitro (*fam*) *V*. nitroglycerin.
nitrofurantoin *n* nitrofurantoína
nitrogen *n* nitrógeno; — **dioxide** dióxido de nitrógeno
nitroglycerin *n* nitroglicerina
nitrous oxide *n* óxido nitroso
nizatidine *n* nizatidina
NNRTI *abbr* **non-nucleoside reverse transcriptase inhibitor**. *V*. **inhibitor**.
nocardiosis *n* nocardiosis *f*
nocturnal *adj* nocturno; — **emission** emisión nocturna, sueño húmedo (*fam*)
nocturnist *n* médico de guardia durante la noche, médico que atiende a los pacientes de un hospital durante la noche
nod *vt, vi* (*pret & pp* **nodded**; *ger* **nodding**) mover (la cabeza) arriba y abajo; **Nod your head up and down to say yes.**.Mueva la cabeza arriba y abajo para decir sí; **to** — **out** (*fam, as on heroin*) cabecear, inclinar la cabeza hacia el pecho
node *n* (*card*) nódulo *or* nodo; (*lymph*) ganglio; **atrioventricular** — nódulo *or* nodo auriculoventricular; **lymph** — ganglio linfático; **sentinel** — ganglio centinela; **sinus** *o* **sinoatrial** — nódulo *or* nodo sinusal *or* sinoauricular
nodular *adj* nodular
nodule *n* nódulo
noise *n* ruido
nonabsorbable *adj* no absorbible, no reabsorbible (*esp. Esp*)
nonflammable *adj* no inflamable, incombustible, que no se quema
noninvasive *adj* no invasivo, no invasor; — **procedure** procedimiento no invasivo
nonketotic *adj* no cetósico; [*Note: The* s

is correct even though ketotic *translates as* cetónico *with an* n.]
non-prescription *adj* (*pharm*) de venta libre, que se vende sin receta
nonprofit, non-profit *adj* sin ánimo de lucro, sin fines de lucro
nonspecific *adj* inespecífico
nonsteroidal *adj* no esteroideo
non-stick *adj* (*dressing*) no adherente (*venda*)
nontoxic *adj* no tóxico
nonunion *adj* (*ortho*) no consolidado; — **fracture** pseudoartrosis *or* seudoartrosis *f* (*form*), fractura no consolidada, fractura que no ha sanado
noon *n* mediodía *m*
norepinephrine *n* noradrenalina, norepinefrina (*INN*)
norethindrone (*USAN*), **norethisterone** (*INN*) *n* noretindrona, noretisterona (*INN*)
norfloxacin *n* norfloxacino, norfloxacina
norgestimate *n* norgestimato
norgestrel *n* norgestrel *m*
norm *n* norma
normal *adj* normal
normalize *vt* normalizar
normally *adv* normalmente
nortriptyline *n* nortriptilina
nose *n* nariz *f*; **to blow one's** — sonarse la nariz, soplarse la nariz (*Carib*); **to pick one's** — hurgarse la nariz, sacarse los mocos
nosebleed *n* hemorragia nasal (*form*), sangrado nasal *or* por la nariz
no-see-um *n* (*fam*) jején *m*
nostril *n* fosa *or* orificio nasal
notalgia paresthetica *n* notalgia parestésica
notice *vt* notar, darse cuenta; **When did you notice there was blood in your stool?**..¿Cuándo notó (se dio cuenta) que había sangre en las heces?
noticeable *adj* evidente, visible; **It won't be noticeable**..No se notará.
notification *n* notificación *f*
nourish *vt* nutrir, alimentar
nourishing *adj* nutritivo, alimenticio
nourishment *n* nutrición *f*, alimentación *f*
Novocaine (*marca*) *V*. procaine.
NPH *V*. insulin.
NRTI *abbr* **nucleoside reverse tran-**

scriptase inhibitor. *V.* **inhibitor.**
NSAID *abbr* **nonsteroidal antiinflammatory drug.** *V.* **drug.**
NtRTI *abbr* **nucleotide reverse transcriptase inhibitor.** *V.* **inhibitor.**
nuclear *adj* nuclear
numb *adj* dormido; **to get** *o* **become —** dormirse; **Do your hands get numb?..** ¿Se le duermen las manos?; *vt* (*también* **to — up**) anestesiar, dormir; **I'm going to numb up your finger..** Le voy a anestesiar (dormir) el dedo.
number *n* número, cifra; **— one** (*euph, urination*) (el) orinar; **— two** (*euph, defecation*) (el) defecar; **to do — one** orinar, hacer del uno (*euph*); **to do — two** defecar, hacer del dos (*euph*)
numbness *n* entumecimiento, adormecimiento, pérdida de sensibilidad
nurse *n* enfermero -ra *mf*; **charge —** enfermero jefe (de sala *or* de turno); **home health —** enfermero domiciliario, enfermero que hace visitas a la casa; **licensed vocational —** enfermero vocacional con licencia; **— supervisor** enfermero supervisor; **registered —** enfermero registrado; *vt* (*to breastfeed*) amamantar, lactar, dar el pecho, dar de mamar; (*to care for patients*)

cuidar; *vi* (*to suckle*) mamar
nurse practitioner *n* (*US*) enfermero -ra *mf* que tiene entrenamiento adicional para diagnosticar y tratar enfermedades comunes
nursery *n* (*pl* **-ries**) (*también* **nursery school**) guardería *or* escuela infantil, jardín *m* de infancia, jardín de niños (*Mex*); **newborn —** unidad *f* de neonatología (*form*), sala de recién nacidos
nursing *n* enfermería; **— home** (*fam*) centro de enfermería especializada
nurture *vt* nutrir, criar, apoyar
nutrient *n* nutriente *m*
nutrition *n* nutrición *f*; **enteral —** nutrición enteral; **peripheral parenteral —** nutrición parenteral periférica; **total parenteral — (TPN)** nutrición parenteral total (NPT)
nutritional *adj* nutricional; (*providing nutrition*) nutritivo; **— state** estado nutricional; **— value** valor nutritivo *or* nutricional
nutritionist *n* nutricionista *mf*
nutritious *adj* nutritivo
nylon *n* nailon *m*
nystagmus *n* nistagmo
nystatin *n* nistatina

O

oatmeal *n* avena
OB (*fam*) *V.* **obstetrics.**
obese *adj* obeso
obesity *n* obesidad *f*; **central —** obesidad central; **morbid —** obesidad mórbida
obey *vt* obedecer
object *n* objeto
objective *n* objetivo

oblique *adj* (*rad, etc.*) oblicuo
oblong *adj* (*pharm, etc.*) oblongo
observation *n* observación *f*
obsession *n* obsesión *f*
obsessive-compulsive *adj* obsesivo-compulsivo
obstetrical, obstetric *adj* obstétrico
obstetrician *n* obstetra *mf*, tocólogo -ga *mf*

obstetrics (OB) *n* obstetricia; tocología; rama de la medicina que se ocupa del embarazo, parto y puerperio

obstruct *vt* obstruir, bloquear

obstruction *n* obstrucción *f*; **partial small bowel** — obstrucción intestinal parcial, obstrucción parcial del intestino delgado; **upper airway** — obstrucción de la(s) vía(s) aérea(s) superior(es)

obstructive *adj* obstructivo

occasionally *adv* de vez en cuando, a veces

occipital *adj* occipital

occlusion *n* oclusión *f*

occlusive *adj* oclusivo

occupation *n* ocupación *f*, trabajo

occupational *adj* ocupacional, laboral; — **health** salud *f* laboral *or* ocupacional; — **therapy** terapia ocupacional

occurrence *n* ocurrencia

ochronosis *n* ocronosis *f*

octogenarian *n* octogenario -ria *mf*

ocular *adj* ocular

oculist *n* (*optometrist*) optómetra *mf*, oculista *mf*; (*ophthalmologist*) oftalmólogo -ga *mf*, oculista *mf*

odor *n* olor *m*; **body** — olor corporal; **foot** — olor de pies

odorless *adj* inodoro, sin olor

off *prep* (*drugs, a medication, etc.*) (ya) no usando, (ya) no tomando; **How long have you been off heroin?**..¿Hace cuánto que no usa heroína? ...**Are you off prednisone?**..¿Ya no toma prednisona?

office *n* oficina, (*of a doctor*) consultorio

ofloxacin *n* ofloxacino, ofloxacina

often *adv* a menudo, frecuentemente; **How often do you have chest pain?**.. ¿Con qué frecuencia le duele el pecho? ..¿Cada cuánto le duele el pecho?

oil *n* aceite *m*; **castor** — aceite de ricino; **citronella** — aceite de citronela; **coconut** — aceite de coco; **cod-liver** — aceite de hígado de bacalao; **corn** — aceite de maíz; **essential** — aceite esencial; **evening primrose** — aceite de onagra; **fish** — aceite de pescado; **geranium** — aceite de geranio; **lemon eucalyptus** — aceite de eucalipto de limón; **lemon** — aceite de limón; **min-**

eral — aceite mineral; **olive** — aceite de oliva; **palm** — aceite de palma; **peanut** — aceite de maní *or* cacahuete *or* cacahuate; **rape-seed** — aceite de colza; **safflower** — aceite de cártamo; **tea tree** — aceite del árbol del té; **vegetable** — aceite vegetal

oily *adj* graso, grasoso; — **complexion** cutis graso; — **hair** cabello graso; — **skin** piel grasa *or* grasosa

ointment *n* pomada, ungüento

olanzapine *n* olanzapina

old *adj* viejo, de edad avanzada; **How old are you?**..¿Cuántos años tiene Ud.?; — **man** hombre *m* de edad avanzada, viejo, anciano; — **woman** mujer *f* de edad avanzada, vieja, anciana; **to grow** — envejecer; [*Note: The terms* viejo *and* anciano *when applied to people can be off-putting to some Spanish speakers.*]

older (*comp de* old) *adj* más viejo, mayor; — **sister** hermana mayor

olecranon *n* olécranon *m*

olfactory *adj* olfativo

olmesartan *n* olmesartán *m*

olsalazine *n* olsalazina

ombudsman *n* ombudsman *mf*, empleado -da *mf* del hospital que maneja disputas entre pacientes y personal

omentum *n* omento, epiplón *m*

omeprazole *n* omeprazol *m*

on *prep* (*drugs, a medication, etc.*) usando, tomando, bajo el efecto de; **Are you on lithium?**..¿Está tomando litio?...**Were you on PCP when you kicked the policeman?**..¿Estaba bajo el efecto de la fenciclidina cuando le dio una patada al policía?

onchocerciasis *n* oncocercosis *f*

oncologist *n* oncólogo -ga *mf*, médico -ca *mf* especializado en tumores; **radiation** — oncólogo radioterapeuta, oncólogo radioterápico (*Esp*), médico que trata el cáncer con radiación ionizante

oncology *n* oncología, rama de la medicina que se ocupa de los tumores; **radiation** — oncología radioterápica, radiooncología

ondansetron *n* ondansetrón *m*

one-armed *adj* manco

one-eyed *adj* tuerto

one-legged *adj* con una sola pierna

onion n cebolla

online adv en línea

only adj solo, único; **progestin-only** de progestina sola; adv sólo, solamente; **Take this only for severe pain**..Tome esto sólo (solamente) para dolor severo

onset n inicio, comienzo; **age at —** edad f de inicio or comienzo; **early-onset** de inicio or comienzo precoz; **juvenile-onset** de inicio or comienzo juvenil; **late-onset** de inicio or comienzo tardío

onychomycosis n onicomicosis f

oophorectomy n (pl -mies) ovariectomía

opacity n (pl -ties) opacidad f

opaque adj opaco

open vt, vi abrir(se); **Open your mouth**.. Abra la boca.

opening n abertura

operable adj operable, que se puede corregir con cirugía

operate vt, vi operar; **to operate machinery**..operar maquinaria...**We need to operate on your leg**..Tenemos que operarle (de) la pierna.

operation n operación f; **to have an —** operarse, tener una operación

operative adj operatorio

operatory n (dent) gabinete m, habitación f donde el dentista trata a los pacientes

ophthalmic adj oftálmico

ophthalmologist n oftalmólogo -ga mf, médico -ca mf especializado en los ojos y sus enfermedades, médico de los ojos (fam)

ophthalmology n oftalmología, rama de la medicina que se ocupa de los ojos y sus enfermedades

ophthalmoscope n oftalmoscopio

opiate adj & n opiáceo

opinion n opinión f; **second —** segunda opinión

opioid adj & n opioide m

opium n opio

opportunistic adj oportunista

optical, optic adj óptico

optician n óptico -ca mf

optics n óptica

optimal adj óptimo

optimism n optimismo

optimistic adj optimista

optimize vt optimizar

optimum adj óptimo

option n opción f; **treatment options** opciones de tratamiento

optometrist n optómetra mf, optometrista mf (Ang)

optometry n optometría

OR abbr **operating room**. V. room.

oral adj oral, bucal

orange adj naranja, anaranjado; n (color) naranja m; (fruit) naranja

orbit n (anat) órbita

orbital adj orbitario

orchiectomy, orchidectomy n (pl -mies) orquiectomía or orquidectomía

orchitis n orquitis f

order n (sequence) orden m; (command) orden f; (medical) indicación f (form), orden f; **birth —** orden de nacimiento; **standing —** orden permanente; vt indicar (form), ordenar; **just what the doctor ordered**..justo lo que el médico ordenó

orderly n (pl -lies) (ant) camillero, auxiliar mf de enfermería

orf n ectima contagioso

organ n órgano, víscera; **hollow —** órgano hueco, víscera hueca; **solid —** órgano sólido; **vital —** órgano vital

organic adj orgánico; **— food** alimento orgánico (frec. pl)

organism n organismo; **genetically modified — (GMO)** organismo genéticamente modificado (OGM) or modificado genéticamente (OMG)

organization n organización f; **health maintenance — (HMO)** (US) plan m de salud que procura reducir costos al contratar médicos de acuerdo al número de pacientes que atienden; **World Health Organization (WHO)** Organización Mundial de la Salud (OMS)

organochlorate n organoclorado

organophosphate n organofosforado

orgasm n orgasmo

orientation n orientación f; **sexual —** orientación sexual

orifice n orificio

orlistat n orlistat m

oropharynx n (pl -rynges o -rynxes) orofaringe f

orphan n huérfano -na mf

orphanage n orfanato, orfelinato, orfanatorio

orthodontia (ant) **orthodontics**. V. orthodontic.

orthodontic *adj* ortodóntico *or* ortodóncico; *npl* ortodoncia, rama de la odontología que se ocupa de trastornos de la alineación de la dentadura y su tratamiento

orthodontist *n* ortodoncista *mf*

orthomolecular *adj* ortomolecular

orthopedic, orthopaedic *adj* ortopédico

orthopedics, orthopaedics *n* ortopedia

orthopedist, orthopaedist *n* ortopedista *mf*, médico de los huesos (*fam*); (*surgeon*) cirujano -na *mf* ortopédico, cirujano de los huesos (*fam*)

orthopod (*fam*) *V.* **orthopedist.**

orthosis *n* (*pl* **-ses**) ortesis *f*; **ankle foot** — ortesis de tobillo-pie

orthotic *adj* ortésico, relativo a una ortesis; *n* (*orthotic device*) ortesis *f*

orthotist *n* ortesista *mf*, técnico ortopédico (*esp. Esp*), especialista *mf* en ortesis; [*Note:* técnica ortopédica *means* orthopedic technique *and is not generally used to refer to a female orthotist.*]

oseltamivir *n* oseltamivir *m*

osmosis *n* ósmosis *f*

osseous *adj* óseo

ossicle *n* (*of the ear*) huesecillo (*del oído*)

osteitis *n* osteítis *f*; — **fibrosa cystica** osteítis fibrosa quística

osteoarthritis *n* artrosis *f*, osteoartritis *f* (*Ang*)

osteochondritis dissecans *n* osteocondritis *f* disecante

osteogenesis imperfecta *n* osteogénesis imperfecta

osteoma *n* osteoma *m*

osteomalacia *n* osteomalacia

osteomyelitis *n* osteomielitis *f*

osteonecrosis *n* osteonecrosis *f*

osteopath *n* osteópata *mf*, médico -ca *mf* especializado en osteopatía

osteopathic *adj* osteopático

osteopathy *n* osteopatía, rama de la medicina que enfatiza holismo y emplea manipulación de los huesos y músculos para curar

osteopenia *n* osteopenia

osteophyte *n* osteofito

osteoporosis *n* osteoporosis *f*

osteosarcoma *n* osteosarcoma *m*

ostomy *n* (*pl* **-mies**) ostomía

otic *adj* ótico

otitis *n* otitis *f*; — **externa** otitis externa; — **media** otitis media; — **media with effusion** otitis media con derrame; **secretory** — **media** otitis media serosa

otolaryngologist *n* otorrinolaringólogo -ga *mf*; médico -ca *mf* cirujano especializado en el oído, nariz y garganta y sus enfermedades

otolaryngology *n* otorrinolaringología; rama de la medicina que se ocupa del oído, nariz y garganta y sus enfermedades

otosclerosis *n* otosclerosis *f*

otoscope *n* otoscopio

ouch *interj* ¡Ay!

ounce (oz.) *n* onza (onz.)

out *adv* (*none left*) sin; **out of medication**..sin medicamentos; **Are you all out?**...¿No le queda ninguno?

outbreak *n* brote *m*; (*derm*) erupción *f*

outburst *n* (*emotional*) estallido, arrebato

outcome *n* resultado, desenlace *m*; **outcomes research** investigación *f* de resultados

outdated, out of date *adj* (*pharm, etc.*) caducado, vencido

outdoors *n* aire *m* libre

outer *adj* externo, exterior

outgoing *adj* extrovertido

outgrow *vt* (*pret* **-grew**; *pp* **-grown**) (*a habit*) quitarse(*le*) (*a uno*) con el tiempo, desaparecer con el tiempo (*un hábito*); **He will outgrow it.**.Se le quitará con el tiempo..Desaparecerá con el tiempo.

outlet *n* (*anat*) salida; (*psych*) válvula de escape, desahogo; (*electrical*) tomacorriente *m*; **bladder** — salida de la vejiga

outpatient *adj* ambulatorio, de consulta externa, externo; — **clinic** clínica ambulatoria; — **procedure** procedimiento ambulatorio; — **services** servicios ambulatorios *or* de consulta externa; *n* paciente *mf* ambulatorio *or* externo

output *n* gasto; **urine** — gasto urinario

outreach *n* divulgación *f*, extensión *f*, extensión de servicios y educación a gente necesitada; — **program** programa *m* de divulgación *or* extensión

outside *adj* exterior, externo; *n* exterior *m*; *prep* (*también* — **of**) fuera de

ova *pl de* **ovum**

oval *adj* (*pharm, etc.*) oval

ovarian *adj* ovárico

ovary *n* (*pl* **-ries**) ovario

over *adv* (*greater than*) superior a, por encima de, mayor de (*V. también* **higher**); (*older than*) mayor de; **people over 50 (years old)**..personas mayores de cincuenta años; *prep* sobre; **Your blood pressure is 150 over 80**..Su presión (arterial) es de 150 sobre 80

overactive *adj* hiperactivo, demasiado activo

overate *pret de* **overeat**

overbite *n* sobremordida

overcome *vt* (*pret* **-came**; *pp* **-come**) superar, vencer; **to overcome fears**..superar (vencer) miedos

overcompensate *vi* sobrecompensar

overcompensation *n* (*psych, etc.*) sobrecompensación *f*

overcrowding *n* hacinamiento

overdo *vt* (*pret* **-did**; *pp* **-done**) **to — it** (*fam*) excederse; **Don't overdo it**..No se exceda

overdose *n* sobredosis *f*, dosis excesiva

overdue *adj* **You are overdue for your mammogram**..Ya ha pasado la fecha para su mamograma.

overeat *vi* (*pret* **-ate**; *pp* **-eaten**) comer en exceso

overexcite *vt* sobreexcitar; **to become overexcited** sobreexcitarse

overexert *vt* **to — oneself** esforzarse demasiado

overexertion *n* esfuerzo excesivo

overgrowth *n* sobrecrecimiento

overload *n* sobrecarga; **iron —** sobrecarga de hierro; *vt* sobrecargar

overnight *adv* durante la noche, toda la noche

overproduction *n* sobreproducción *f*

overreact *vi* reaccionar exageradamente

over-the-counter *adj* (*pharm*) de venta libre, que se vende sin receta

overuse *n* sobreuso; **— injury** lesión *f* por sobreuso

overutilization *n* sobreutilización *f*

overweight *adj* pasado de peso, que tiene sobrepeso

overwhelm *vt* agobiar

ovulate *vi* ovular

ovulation *n* ovulación *f*

ovum *n* (*pl* **ova**) óvulo, huevo (*fam*)

owie *n* (*ped, fam*) herida

oxalate *n* oxalato

oxcarbazepine *n* oxcarbazepina

oxidant *n* oxidante *m*

oxide *n* óxido

oximeter *n* oxímetro

oximetry *n* oximetría; **pulse —** pulsioximetría, oximetría de pulso

oxybutynin *n* oxibutinina

oxycodone *n* oxicodona

oxygen *n* oxígeno; **home —** oxígeno domiciliario, oxígeno en la casa; **hyperbaric —** oxígeno hiperbárico

oxymorphone *n* oximorfona

oxytocin *n* oxitocina

oz. *V.* **ounce**.

ozone *n* ozono

P

PABA *V.* **paraaminobenzoic acid**.

PAC *abbr* **premature atrial contrac-**tion. *V.* **contraction**.

pacemaker *n* marcapasos *m*

pacifier *n* chupete *m*, chupón *m*

pack *n* (*compress*) compresa; (*of cigarettes*) cajetilla, paquete *m*; **ice** — bolsa de hielo; **packs per day** cajetillas diarias, paquetes diarios

package insert *n* (*pharm*) prospecto (*del envase*), hoja de información (*que acompaña un medicamento*)

packing *n* (*act*) taponamiento; (*material*) gasa u otro material usado para llenar una cavidad, (*once packed*) taponamiento, tapón *m*; **nasal** — taponamiento nasal

paclitaxel *n* paclitaxel *m*

pad *n* (*cushion*) cojín *m*, almohadilla; (*of the finger*) yema (*del dedo*); **alcohol** — gasa *or* toallita con alcohol; **heating** — almohadilla térmica; **sanitary** — toalla sanitaria *or* femenina; *vt* (*pret & pp* **padded**; *ger* **padding**) acolchar, acojinar

padded *adj* acolchado, acojinado

padding *n* acolchado, material usado para acolchar

page *n* (*overhead*) llamada por altavoz; (*by pager*) llamada por buscapersonas; *vt* perifonear (*form*), llamar por altavoz; llamar por buscapersonas

pager *n* buscapersonas *m*

pain *n* dolor *m*; **a pain in the back**..un dolor en la espalda; **back** — dolor de espalda; **breakthrough** — dolor irruptivo; **dull** — dolor sordo; **growing pains** dolores de(l) crecimiento; **joint** — dolor de las articulaciones; **labor pains** dolores de(l) parto; **low back** — dolor lumbar, dolor de la espalda baja; **nagging** — dolor persistente; **phantom** — dolor fantasma; — **reliever,** — **pill** (*fam*) analgésico (*form*), calmante *m*, pastilla para el dolor; **sharp** — dolor agudo; **stabbing** — dolor punzante; **to be in** — tener dolor

painful *adj* doloroso; — **procedure** procedimiento doloroso

painkiller *n* (*fam*) analgésico (*form*), calmante *m*, pastilla para el dolor

painless *adj* indoloro (*form*), sin dolor, que no causa dolor

paint *n* pintura; **lead-based** — pintura a base de plomo

palatable *adj* de sabor aceptable, que no sabe mal

palate *n* paladar *m*; **cleft** — paladar hendido; **hard** — paladar duro; **soft** — paladar blando

pale *adj* pálido

palladium *n* paladio

palliation *n* paliación *f*

palliative *adj* paliativo

pallidotomy *n* (*pl* **-mies**) palidotomía

pallor *n* palidez *f*

palm *n* (*anat, bot*) palma

palmar *adj* palmar, de la palma

palpate *vt* palpar

palpitate *vi* palpitar

palpitation *n* palpitación *f*, latido rápido o fuerte del corazón

palsy *n* (*pl* **-sies**) parálisis *f*; **Bell's** — parálisis de Bell; **cerebral** — parálisis cerebral; **facial** — parálisis facial

pamper *vt* consentir, mimar

pamphlet *n* folleto

pancreas *n* (*pl* **-creases**) páncreas *m*

pancreatectomy *n* (*pl* **-mies**) pancreatectomía

pancreatic *adj* pancreático

pancreatitis *n* pancreatitis *f*

pancrelipase *n* pancrelipasa

pandemic *n* pandemia

pang *n* punzada, dolor breve y agudo; **hunger** — punzada de hambre

panhypopituitarism *n* panhipopituitarismo

panic *n* pánico

panoramic *adj* (*rad*) panorámico

pant *vi* jadear

panties *npl* calzones *mpl*, bragas, pantaletas

pantoprazole *n* pantoprazol *m*

pants *npl* pantalones *mpl*

pantyhose *npl* pantimedias

paper *n* papel *m*

papilla *n* papila

papillary *adj* papilar

papillomavirus *n* virus *m* del papiloma papilomavirus *m*; **human** — (HPV) virus *m* del papiloma humano (VPH), papilomavirus humano (PVH)

Pap smear *V.* **smear**.

paraaminobenzoic acid, para-aminobenzoic acid (PABA) *n* ácido para-aminobenzoico *or* para-aminobenzoico (PABA)

paracentesis *n* (*pl* **-ses**) paracentesis *f*

paracetamol *n* paracetamol *m*, acetami-

nofén *m*, acetaminofeno
paracoccidioidomycosis *n* paracocci-dioidomicosis *f*
paradoxical *adj* paradójico
paragonimiasis *n* paragonimiasis *f*
parainfluenza *n* parainfluenza
paralysis *n* parálisis *f*; **sleep —** parálisis del sueño
paralyze *vt* paralizar
paralyzing *adj* paralizante
paramedic *n* paramédico -ca *mf*, persona con entrenamiento médico básico encargada de llevar heridos y enfermos al hospital
paranasal *adj* paranasal
paranoia *n* paranoia
paranoid *adj* paranoico, paranoide
paraparesis *n* paraparesia; **tropical spastic —** paraparesia espástica tropical
paraphilia *n* parafilia
paraphimosis *n* parafimosis *f*
paraplegia *n* paraplejia *or* paraplejía
paraplegic *adj & n* parapléjico -ca *mf*
paraquat *n* paraquat *m*
parasite *n* parásito
parasitic *adj* parasitario
parasitology *n* parasitología, estudio de los parásitos y sus efectos en el organismo
paraspinal *adj* paraespinal
parasympathetic *adj* parasimpático
parathion *n* paratión *m*
parathyroid *adj* paratiroideo; *n* (*fam*) glándula paratiroidea, paratiroides *f* (*fam*)
parathyroidectomy *n* (*pl* -mies) paratiroidectomía
paratyphoid *adj* paratifoidea; **— fever** paratifoidea; *n* paratifoidea
paregoric *n* paregórico, tintura de opio alcanforada
parent *n* padre *m*, madre *f*; *npl* padres *mpl*; **adoptive parents** padres adoptivos; **biologic parents** padres biológicos
parental *adj* parental
parenteral *adj* parenteral
parenthood *n* paternidad *f*, maternidad *f*, (el) tener hijos
parenting *n* crianza de los niños; **— education** educación *f* parental, educación para padres (y madres); **— skills**

habilidades *fpl* parentales; **— workshop** taller *m* para padres (y madres)
paresis *n* paresia
paresthesia *n* parestesia
parietal *adj* parietal
parkinsonism *n* parkinsonismo
paromomycin *n* paromomicina
paronychia *n* paroniquia
parotid *adj* parotídeo; *n* (*fam*) glándula parótida, parótida (*fam*)
parotitis *n* parotiditis *f*
paroxetine *n* paroxetina
paroxysm *n* paroxismo
paroxysmal *adj* paroxístico
part *n* parte *f*; **parts per billion** partes por mil millones; **parts per million** partes por millón
partial *adj* parcial
participation *n* participación *f*
particle *n* partícula
partner *n* (*professional*) socio -cia *mf*; (*life partner*) pareja, compañero -ra *or* pareja sentimental
parvovirus *n* parvovirus *m*
pass *vt* (*parasites, a stone, etc.*) eliminar, expulsar, botar (*esp. Carib, fam*); **Have you ever passed a stone?**..¿Ha eliminado (expulsado, botado) alguna vez una piedra (al orinar)?; **to — (away)** (*euph*) morir, fallecer; **to — gas** expulsar gases; *vi* **to — out** perder el conocimiento *or* la conciencia, (*to faint*) desmayarse
passage *n* conducto, vía; **nasal passages** conductos *or* vías nasales
passenger *n* pasajero -ra *mf*
passing *n* (*euph, death*) partida (*euph*), muerte *f*
passion flower *n* (*bot*) pasiflora, pasionaria
passive *adj* pasivo
passive-aggressive *adj* pasivo-agresivo
paste *n* pasta
pasteurized *adj* pasteurizado
pastime *n* pasatiempo
pat *n* palmadita, golpecito; *vt* (*pret & pp* **patted**; *ger* **patting**) dar palmaditas *or* golpecitos
patch *n* parche *m*; **nicotine —** parche de nicotina
patella *n* (*pl* -lae) rótula
paternal *adj* paterno; (*fatherly*) paternal
paternity *n* paternidad *f*

path (*fam*) *V.* **pathology**.
pathogen *n* patógeno, agente patógeno
pathological, pathologic *adj* patológico
pathological liar *n* mentiroso -sa *mf* compulsivo
pathologist *n* patólogo -ga *mf*, médico -ca *mf* que estudia tejidos y líquidos corporales con fines diagnósticos; **anatomic** — anatomopatólogo -ga *mf*; **speech language** — (*form*), **speech** — logopeda *mf* (*form*), fonoaudiólogo -ga *mf*, terapeuta *mf* del lenguaje
pathology *n* patología, estudio de los tejidos y líquidos corporales con fines diagnósticos; **anatomic** — anatomía patológica; **speech language** — (*form*), **speech** — logopedia (*form*), fonoaudiología, terapia del lenguaje, terapia del habla (*esp. Mex*)
patient *adj* paciente; *n* paciente *mf*, enfermo -ma *mf*; **patient-centered** centrado en el paciente
pattern *n* patrón *m*
paunch *n* barriga, panza, panzón *m*
pavillion *n* pabellón *m*
PCB *V.* **polychlorinated biphenyl**.
PCI *abbr* **percutaneous coronary intervention**. *V.* **intervention**.
PCP *V.* **phencyclidine**.
PCR *abbr* **polymerase chain reaction**. *V.* **reaction**.
peace *n* paz *f*; — **of mind** tranquilidad *f* (*mental*)
peak *n* valor máximo, máximo, pico; — **expiratory flow** flujo espiratorio máximo; *vi* alcanzar un máximo *or* pico
peanut *n* maní *m*, cacahuete *or* cacahuate *m*; — **butter** mantequilla de maní *or* cacahuete *or* cacahuate
pectoral *adj* & *n* pectoral *m*
pediatric *adj* pediátrico
pediatrician *n* pediatra *mf*
pediatrics *n* pediatría
pediculosis *n* pediculosis *f*, infestación *f* de piojos (*esp. en la cabeza*)
pedicure *n* pedicura
pedophilia *n* pedofilia *or* paidofilia
pee *n* (*fam*) orina, pipí *m* (*esp. ped, fam*); *vi* orinar, hacer pipí (*esp. ped, fam*)
peel *n* (*derm, procedure*) exfoliación *f*; **chemical** — exfoliación química; *vi* (*skin*) descamarse (*form*), pelarse, despellejarse (*fam*)

peeling *n* (*derm*) exfoliación *f* (*form*), descamación *f* (*form*), (el) pelarse; (*treatment*) exfoliación química
pee pee *n* (*ped, fam*) (*urine*) orina, pipí *m* (*ped, fam*); (*penis*) pene *m*, pipí *m* (*ped, fam*); **to go** — orinar, hacer pipí
peer *n* igual *mf*, par *mf*; (*V. también* **group** *y* **pressure**.)
PEG *abbr* **percutaneous endoscopic gastrostomy**. *V.* **gastrostomy**.
PEG *abbr* **polyethylene glycol** *V.* **polyethylene**.
pegfilgrastim *n* pegfilgrastim *m*
peginterferon *n* peginterferón *m*
pegylated *adj* pegilado
pellagra *n* pelagra
pelvic *adj* pélvico, pelviano
pelvis *n* pelvis *f*
pemphigoid *n* penfigoide *m*
pemphigus *n* pénfigo
pen *n* pluma; **insulin** — pluma de insulina, dispositivo tipo pluma para la inyección de insulina
penciclovir *n* penciclovir *m*
pending *adj* pendiente
penetrate *vt* penetrar
penetrating *adj* penetrante
penetration *n* penetración *f*
penicillin *n* penicilina
penile *adj* peneano, peniano (*RAE*)
penis *n* pene *m*, miembro (*fam*)
pentachlorophenol *n* pentaclorofenol *m*
pentoxifylline *n* pentoxifilina
people *n* personas, gente *f*; **little** — (*euph, dwarfs*) enanos -nas *mfpl*
pep *n* (*fam*) energía, vigor *m*
pepper *n* pimienta
peppermint *n* (*bot*) hierbabuena
pepsin *n* pepsina
peptic *adj* péptico
per *prep* por; **beats** — **minute** latidos por minuto
percent *n* por ciento
percentage *n* porcentaje *m*
perception *n* percepción *f*; **depth** — percepción de la profundidad
perchlorate *n* perclorato
percutaneous *adj* percutáneo
perfectionism *n* perfeccionismo
perfectionist *adj* & *n* perfeccionista *mf*
perforate *vt* perforar
perforation *n* perforación *f*
performance *n* rendimiento, desempeño;

performance-enhancing drugs drogas para mejorar el rendimiento

perfume *n* perfume *m*

perfusion *n* perfusión *f*

perianal *adj* perianal

pericardial *adj* pericárdico

pericarditis *n* pericarditis *f*; **constrictive** — pericarditis constrictiva

pericardium *n* pericardio

perinatal *adj* perinatal

perineal *adj* perineal

perinephric *adj* perirrenal

period *n* período *or* periodo; *(menstrual)* período *or* periodo, menstruación *f*, regla; **Do you still have periods?**..¿Sigue menstruando?..¿Todavía menstrua? ...**Are you on your period?**..¿Está menstruando hoy?...**When was your last period?**..¿Cuándo fue su último período (última menstruación)?; **incubation** — período de incubación

periodic *adj* periódico

periodontal *adj* periodontal

periodontics *n* periodoncia

periodontist *n* periodoncista *mf*

perioral *adj* perioral

periorbital *adj* periorbitario

peripheral *adj* periférico

periphery *n* periferia

peristalsis *n* peristaltismo, peristalsis *f*

peritoneal *adj* peritoneal

peritoneum *n* peritoneo

peritonitis *n* peritonitis *f*

periungual *adj* periungueal

perleche *n* queilitis *f* angular, boquera *(frec. pl)*, agrietamiento e inflamación en los ángulos de la boca

permanent *adj* permanente

permanganate *n* permanganato

permethrin *n* permetrina

permission *n* permiso

peroneal *adj* peroneo

peroxide *n* peróxido

perphenazine *n* perfenazina

persist *vi* persistir

persistent *adj* persistente

person *n* persona, individuo; **blind** — ciego -ga *mf*; **deaf** — sordo -da *mf*; **disabled** — discapacitado -da *mf*; **from — to** — de persona a persona; **little** — *(euph, dwarf)* enano -na *mf*; **old** — persona de edad avanzada; — **with HIV** persona con VIH; **sick** —

enfermo -ma *mf*; **wounded** — herido -da *mf*; **young** — joven *mf*

personal *adj* personal

personality *n* (*pl* **-ties**) personalidad *f*; **type A** — personalidad tipo A

personnel *n* personal *m*; **health** — personal sanitario *or* de salud

perspiration *n* transpiración *f*, sudoración *f*

perspire *vi* transpirar, sudar

pertussis *n* tos ferina, tos convulsiva *or* convulsa, coqueluche *m&f* (*fam*)

pessary *n* (*pl* **-ries**) pesario, dispositivo que se coloca en la vagina para corregir el descenso del útero

pessimism *n* pesimismo

pessimistic *adj* pesimista

pesticide *n* pesticida *m*, plaguicida *m*

pet *n* mascota

PET *abbr* positron emission tomography. (*V.* **tomography** *y* **scan**.)

PET-CT *abbr* positron emission tomography-computed tomography. (*V.* **tomography** *y* **scan**.)

pethidine *n* petidina, meperidina

petrolatum *n* vaselina, petrolato

petroleum *n* petróleo; — **jelly** vaselina, petrolato

pewterwort *n* (*bot*) cola de caballo

peyote *n* peyote *m*

pH *n* pH *m*

phallic *adj* fálico

phalloplasty *n* faloplastia

phallus *n* falo

phantom pain *n* dolor *m* fantasma

pharmaceutical *adj* farmacéutico; *n* fármaco

pharmacist *n* farmacéutico -ca *mf*, boticario -ria *mf*

pharmacologic, pharmacological *adj* farmacológico

pharmacologist *n* farmacólogo -ga *mf*, especialista *mf* en medicamentos

pharmacology *n* farmacología, estudio de los medicamentos

pharmacopoeia *n* farmacopea

pharmacy *n* (*pl* **-cies**) farmacia, botica

pharyngeal *adj* faríngeo

pharynges *pl de* **pharynx**

pharyngitis *n* faringitis *f*

pharynx *n* (*pl* **-rynges** *o* **-rynxes**) faringe *f*

phase *n* fase *f*

phenazopyridine *n* fenazopiridina
phencyclidine (PCP) *n* fenciclidina
phenobarbital *n* fenobarbital *m*
phenol *n* fenol *m*
phenomenon *n* fenómeno; **Raynaud's** — fenómeno de Raynaud
phenothiazine *n* fenotiazina
phenotype *n* fenotipo
phentermine *n* fentermina
phenylalanine *n* fenilalanina
phenylephrine *n* fenilefrina
phenylketonuria (PKU) *n* fenilcetonuria
phenylpropanolamine *n* fenilpropanolamina
phenytoin *n* fenitoína
pheochromocytoma *n* feocromocitoma *m*
phimosis *n* (*pl* -ses) fimosis *f*
phlebitis *n* flebitis *f*
phlebotomist *n* flebotomista *mf*, persona capacitada para extraer sangre
phlebotomy *n* flebotomía, extracción *f* de sangre de una vena; **therapeutic** — flebotomía *or* sangría terapéutica
phlegm *n* flema (*frec. pl*)
phlegmon *n* flemón *m*
phobia *n* fobia, temor morboso y obsesivo; **— of the dark, — of dogs, etc.** fobia a la oscuridad, fobia a los perros, etc.; **social** — fobia social
phone *n* (*fam*) teléfono; **cellular** —, **cell** — (*fam*) teléfono celular, celular *m* (*fam*)
phonophoresis *n* fonoforesis *f*
phosphate *n* fosfato
phosphorus *n* fósforo
photoallergy *n* (*pl* -gies) fotoalergia
photocoagulation *n* fotocoagulación *f*
photorejuvenation *n* fotorrejuvenecimiento
photosensitive *adj* fotosensible
photosensitivity *n* fotosensibilidad *f*
phototherapy *n* fototerapia
phototoxic *adj* fototóxico
phrenic *adj* frénico
physiatrist *n* fisiatra *mf*, médico -ca *mf* especializado en medicina física y rehabilitación
physiatry *n* fisiatría, medicina física y rehabilitación
physical *adj* físico; *n* (*fam*) examen físico
physician *n* médico -ca *mf*, doctor -ra *mf*;

attending — médico tratante, médico jefe de residentes y estudiantes en un hospital de enseñanza; **family** — médico de cabecera, médico de la familia; **family practice** — médico familiar *or* de familia; **on-call** —, **— on call** médico de turno *or* guardia; **osteopathic** — osteópata *mf*, médico -ca *mf* especializado en osteopatía; **personal** — médico personal *or* de cabecera; **primary care** — médico de atención primaria; **private** — médico privado; **treating** — médico tratante
physiological, physiologic *adj* fisiológico
physiologist *n* fisiólogo -ga *mf*
physiology *n* fisiología
physiotherapist *n* fisioterapeuta *mf*
physiotherapy *n* fisioterapia
physique *n* físico
physostigmine *n* fisostigmina
phytoestrogen *n* fitoestrógeno
picaridin *n* picaridina (*esp. Amer*), icaridina (*INN*)
PICC *abbr* **peripherally-inserted central catheter.** *V.* **catheter.**
pick *vt* (*a scab, etc.*) rascarse, quitarse; **to — one's nose** sacarse los mocos, meterse el dedo en la nariz (para sacarse los mocos), hurgarse la nariz; **to — pimples** espichar los granos *or* barros, reventarse los granos
PID *abbr* **pelvic inflammatory disease.** *V.* **disease.**
piddle *vi* (*fam*) orinar
pierce *vt* perforar
piercing *adj* (*pain*) punzante (*dolor*); *n* piercing *m* (*Ang*), pirsin *m* (*Ang*), perforación *f* de partes del cuerpo para insertar aretes o pendientes
pig *n* cerdo, puerco
pigeon-toed *adj* con los pies torcidos hacia dentro
pigment *n* pigmento
pigmentation *n* pigmentación *f*
pigmented *adj* pigmentado
pilar *adj* pilar
piles *npl* (*ant*) hemorroides *fpl*, almorranas
pill *n* pastilla, píldora; **birth control** — píldora anticonceptiva; **morning after** — píldora del día después; **pain** — analgésico (*form*), calmante *m*, pastilla

para el dolor; — **cutter** cortador *m* de pastillas, cortapastillas *m* (*esp. Mex*), aparato para cortar pastillas; — **organizer** organizador *m* de pastillas, caja dividida en secciones para organizar pastillas de acuerdo con el día y la hora de tomarlas; **sleeping** — somnífero (*form*), pastilla para dormir; **the** — (*fam, oral contraceptive*) la píldora anticonceptiva, la píldora (*fam*); **water** — (*fam*) diurético, pastilla para eliminar el agua

pillow *n* almohada

pilocarpine *n* pilocarpina

pilonidal *adj* pilonidal

pimple *n* grano, barro

pin *n* alfiler *m*; (*ortho*) clavo

pinch *vt, vi* (*to bind*) apretar; (*a nerve*) comprimir, atrapar

pindolol *n* pindolol *m*

pineal *adj* pineal

pineapple *n* piña

pinguecula *n* pinguécula

pink *adj* rosado

pinkeye *n* (*fam*) conjuntivitis *f*, ojo rojo (*fam*)

pins and needles *npl* (*sensation*) hormigueo

pinta *n* pinta, infección *f* tropical que causa manchas en la piel

pinworm *n* oxiuro, pequeña lombriz blanca que afecta en particular a los niños

pioglitazone *n* pioglitazona

pipe *n* (*for smoking*) pipa

piss (*vulg*) *n* orina, pis *m* (*fam or vulg*); *vi* orinar, hacer pis (*fam or vulg*)

pitch *n* (*sound*) frecuencia (*form*), tono

pitcher *n* jarra

pituitary *adj* pituitario, hipofisario; *n* (*fam*) glándula pituitaria, hipófisis *f*

pityriasis *n* pitiriasis *f*; — **alba** pitiriasis alba; — **rosea** pitiriasis rosada; — **versicolor** pitiriasis versicolor

PKU *V.* **phenylketonuria.**

place *n* sitio, lugar *m*; *vt* colocar, poner, ubicar; (*a patient*) trasladar, mover, poner, arreglar dónde va a vivir (*se aplica al paciente demasiado debilitado para quedarse en casa o para regresar a la casa tras una hospitalización*); **Place your hands on your hips**..Coloque (Ponga) las manos en la

cintura...**Have you thought about placing your mother in a skilled nursing facility?**..¿Ha pensado en poner a su mamá en un centro de enfermería especializada?

placebo *n* (*pl* **-bos** *o* **-boes**) placebo

placement *n* colocación *f*; (*of a patient*) traslado, arreglo de dónde va a vivir (*se aplica al paciente demasiado debilitado para quedarse en casa o para regresar a la casa tras una hospitalización*); **Your father is going to be discharged soon and we need to decide about placement**..Le van a dar de alta pronto a su papá y tenemos que decidir a dónde va a ir...**Placement is going to be difficult because he requires round-the-clock care**..Arreglar (Decidir) dónde va a vivir será difícil porque requiere atención a todas horas.

placenta *n* (*pl* **-tas** *o* **-tae**) placenta; — **previa** placenta previa

placental *adj* placentario; — **abruption** desprendimiento prematuro de placenta

plague *n* peste *f*; **bubonic** — peste bubónica

plan *n* plan *m*; **group insurance** — plan de seguro colectivo *or* de grupo; **written action** — plan de acción escrito, plan escrito para el paciente con el manejo de diferentes situaciones relacionadas a su enfermedad

plane *n* plano

planned parenthood *n* planificación *f* familiar

plant *n* (*bot*) planta

plantar *adj* plantar

plaque *n* placa; **atherosclerotic** — placa aterosclerótica; **bacterial** — placa bacteriana; **dental** — placa dental

plasma *n* *adj* plasmático; — **potassium** potasio plasmático; *n* plasma *m*; **fresh frozen** — plasma fresco congelado

plasmapheresis *n* plasmaféresis *f*

plaster *n* (*for a cast*) yeso; (*medicinal*) emplasto, cataplasma

plastic *n* plástico

plate *n* (*dent*) prótesis *f* dental (*form*), dientes postizos, dentadura postiza; (*surg*) placa

platelet *n* plaqueta

platinum *n* platino

pleasure *n* placer *m*, gusto

pledget *n* torunda, trozo de algodón o gasa usado para limpiar heridas o para detener hemorrhagia

plethysmography *n* pletismografía

pleura *n* (*pl* -**rae**) pleura

pleural *adj* pleural

pleurisy *n* pleuresía

pleuritic *adj* pleurítico

pleuritis *n* pleuritis *f*

plexus *n* (*pl* -**xi** *o* -**xuses**) plexo; **brachial** — plexo braquial

plug *n* tapón *m*

plunger *n* (*of a syringe*) émbolo

PMS *abbr* **premenstrual syndrome.** *V.* **syndrome.**

pneumococcal *adj* neumocócico

pneumococcus *n* (*pl* -**ci**) neumococo

pneumoconiosis *n* (*pl* -**ses**) neumoconiosis *f*

pneumonectomy *n* (*pl* -**mies**) neumonectomía

pneumonia *n* neumonía, pulmonía (*fam*); **aspiration** — neumonía por aspiración; **community-acquired** — neumonía adquirida en la comunidad; **cryptogenic organizing** — neumonía organizada criptogénica

pneumonitis *n* neumonitis *f*; **hypersensitivity** — neumonitis por hipersensibilidad

pneumothorax *n* neumotórax *m*

pockmark *n* cacaraña, hoyo en el rostro producido por la viruela

podagra *n* podagra *m*, ataque *m* de gota en el dedo gordo del pie

podiatrist *n* podólogo -ga *mf*

podiatry *n* podología

podophyllotoxin, podofilox *n* podofilotoxina

point *n* (*anat*) punto; — **of care testing** pruebas en el lugar de atención, pruebas a la cabecera del paciente

poison *n* veneno; **ant** — hormiguicida *m*, veneno para hormigas; **rat** — raticida *m*, veneno para ratas; *vt* envenenar

poisoning *n* envenenamiento, intoxicación *f*; **food** — intoxicación alimentaria (*form*), intoxicación por alimentos, intoxicación por productos bacterianos en la comida

poison ivy *n* (*bot*) hiedra venenosa

poison oak *n* (*bot*) roble venenoso

poisonous *adj* venenoso

poison sumac *n* (*bot*) zumaque venenoso

policy *n* (*pl* -**cies**) póliza; política; **insurance** — póliza de seguro; **It's not our policy to give confidential information over the telephone.**.No estamos autorizados a proporcionar información confidencial por teléfono.

poliomyelitis, polio (*fam*) *n* poliomielitis *f*, polio *f* (*fam*)

polish *vt* (*dent, etc.*) pulir

pollen *n* polen *m*

polluted *adj* contaminado

pollution *n* contaminación *f*; **air** — contaminación atmosférica (*form*), contaminación del aire; **water** — contaminación del agua

polyangiitis *n* poliangeítis *f*; **microscopic** — poliangeítis microscópica

polyarteritis nodosa *n* poliarteritis nodosa

polycarbophil *n* policarbófilo *or* policarbofilo

polychlorinated biphenyl (PCB) *n* bifenilo policlorado (BPC), policlorobifenilo

polyclonal *adj* policlonal

polycystic *adj* poliquístico

polycythemia *n* policitemia; — **vera** policitemia vera

polyethylene *n* polietileno; — **glycol (PEG)** polietilenglicol *m* (PEG)

polymyalgia rheumatica *n* polimialgia reumática

polymyositis *n* polimiositis *f*

polymyxin B *n* polimixina B

polyneuropathy *n* polineuropatía

polyp *n* pólipo; **adenomatous** — pólipo adenomatoso; **hyperplastic** — pólipo hiperplásico; **juvenile** — pólipo juvenil; **nasal** — pólipo nasal

polypectomy *n* (*pl* -**mies**) polipectomía

polypharmacy *n* polifarmacia

polyposis *n* poliposis *f*; **familial adenomatous** — poliposis adenomatosa familiar

polypropylene *n* polipropileno

polysaccharide *adj* polisacarídico; *n* polisacárido

polysomnography *n* polisomnografía

polyunsaturated *adj* poliinsaturado

polyurethane *n* poliuretano

polyvalent *adj* polivalente

polyvinyl chloride *n* cloruro de polivini-

lo
pons *n* puente (troncoencefálico), protuberancia (anular)
pool *n* (*genetics*) acervo; **gene** — acervo genético; *vi* (*blood, etc.*) acumularse, estancarse (*la sangre*)
pooling *n* acumulación *f*, estancamiento
poop *n* (*fam*) heces *fpl* (*form*), popó (*fam*), caca (*esp. ped, fam or vulg*)
pooped *adj* (*fam, exhausted*) agotado, exhausto
poo poo *n* (*ped, fam*) heces *fpl* (*form*), popó (*fam*), caca (*esp. ped, fam or vulg*); **to go** — — defecar (*form*), hacer popó *or* caca
poorly *adv* mal
pop *n* estallido; **Did you hear a pop?..** ¿Escuchó un estallido?; *vt, vi* (*fam*) reventar(se); **to — a pimple** (*fam o vulg*) reventarse un grano
popliteal *adj* poplíteo
population *n* población *f*
porcelain *n* porcelana
porcine *adj* porcino
pore *n* poro
pork *n* carne *f* de cerdo
porphyria *n* porfiria; **— cutanea tarda** porfiria cutánea tarda
portable *adj* portátil
portal *adj* portal; (*vein*) porta
portal *n* portal *m*; **patient** — portal del paciente; **— of entry** portal de entrada
portion *n* porción *f*
Portuguese man-of-war *n* fragata *or* carabela portuguesa, agua mala (*fam*)
port-wine stain *n* mancha en vino de Oporto
position *n* posición *f*; **fetal** — posición fetal; **missionary** — posición misionera; *vt* poner en posición, colocar
positive *adj & n* positivo; **false** — falso positivo; **true** — verdadero positivo
possibility *n* posibilidad *f*
possible.. *adj* posible; **as much as possible..** lo más posible
post- *pref* post- *or* pos-; [*Note: When applying the Spanish prefix post-, the RAE recommends dropping the* t *when it is followed by a consonant, although in practice the* t *is often included. The translations that follow reflect current usage.*]
posterior *adj* posterior

postexposure *adj* postexposición
postictal *adj* postictal
postmenopausal *adj* posmenopáusico
post-mortem *adj & adv* post mórtem
post mortem *n* autopsia, necropsia
postnasal *adj* posnasal *or* postnasal; **— drip** goteo posnasal *or* postnasal, goteo retronasal
postnatal *adj* posnatal *or* postnatal
postoperative *adj* postoperatorio
postpartum *adj & adv* posparto *or* postparto (*inv*); **the second week postpartum..** la segunda semana posparto
postpone *vt* posponer, retrasar
postprandial *adj* posprandial, después de las comidas
post-traumatic *adj* postraumático
postural *adj* postural
posture *n* postura
pot (*fam*) marihuana, mariguana (*Mex*), hierba (*fam*), mota (*Mex, CA; fam*)
potable *adj* potable, que se puede beber
potassium *n* potasio; **— chloride** cloruro potásico *or* de potasio; **— hydroxide** hidróxido potásico *or* de potasio
potato *n* (*pl* **-toes**) papa, patata (*esp. Esp*)
potbelly *n* barriga, panza, panzón *m*
potency *n* (*pl* **-cies**) potencia
potent *adj* potente
potential *adj & n* potencial *m*; **evoked** — potencial evocado
potty *n* (*pl* **-ties**) (*ped, fam*) inodoro, inodoro para niños; **to go** — usar el inodoro
pouch *n* (*surg*) reservorio; **ileal** — reservorio ileal
poultice *n* emplasto, cataplasma
poultry *n* aves *fpl* de corral
pound (lb) *n* libra (lb)
poverty *n* pobreza
povidone iodine *n* povidona yodada, iodopovidona
powder *n* polvo; **dry inhalation** — polvo seco para inhalación
powdered *adj* en polvo
power *n* poder *m*; **durable** — **of attorney for health care** (*US*) poder notarial duradero para atención médica; **— of attorney** poder notarial
powerful *adj* (*medication, etc.*) potente, fuerte
PPD *V.* **purified protein derivative.**

practice *n* práctica; *(doctor's)* consultorio, consulta, negocio; **Dr. Lee has a large practice.**.El doctor Lee tiene muchos pacientes; **clinical** — práctica clínica; *vt* practicar, *(medicine, dentistry, etc.)* ejercer, practicar *(la medicina, la odontología, etc.)*; *vi* practicar

practitioner *n* practicante *mf*; *(physician)* clínico -ca *mf*; **general** — médico -ca *mf* generalista *or* general

pramipexole *n* pramipexol *m*

pramlintide *n* pramlintida

prasugrel *n* prasugrel *m*

pravastatin *n* pravastatina

pray *vi* rezar, orar

prayer *n* oración *f*

praziquantel *n* praziquantel *m*, praziquantel *m* *(INN)*

prazosin *n* prazosina

prebiotic *n* prebiótico

precancerous *adj* precanceroso

precaution *n* precaución *f*; **as a precaution.**.por *or* como precaución; **airborne precautions** precauciones de transmisión aérea, precauciones aéreas *(fam)*; **contact precautions** precauciones de contacto; **droplet precautions** precauciones de transmisión por gotas, precauciones por gotas *(fam)*; **standard precautions** precauciones estándar; **universal precautions** *(ant)* precauciones universales *(ant)*

precise *adj* preciso

precision *n* precisión *f*

precocious *adj* precoz

precordial *adj* precordial

precursor *n* precursor *m*

predict *vt* predecir, pronosticar; **I can't predict how long she will live.**.No puedo predecir cuánto tiempo va a vivir.

predispose *vt* predisponer

predisposed *adj* predispuesto, propenso

predisposing *adj* predisponente

predisposition *n* predisposición *f*

prednisolone *n* prednisolona

prednisone *n* prednisona

preeclampsia *n* preeclampsia

preemie *n* *(fam)* recién nacido -da *mf* prematuro, prematuro -ra *mf* *(fam)*

preexisting *adj* preexistente

prefilled *adj* prellenado; — **syringe** jeringa prellenada

pregabalin *n* pregabalina

pregnancy *n* *(pl* -**cies)** embarazo; **ectopic** — embarazo ectópico; **tubal** — embarazo tubárico; **unwanted** — embarazo no deseado

pregnant *adj* embarazada, encinta *(fam)*; **You are three months pregnant.**.Ud. tiene tres meses de embarazo; **to get** *o* **become** — embarazarse, quedarse embarazada

prehypertension *n* prehipertensión *f*

pre-implantation *adj* preimplantacional, preimplantatorio

preliminary *adj* preliminar

premalignant *adj* premaligno

premature *adj* prematuro, precoz

premedication *n* premedicación *f*

premenopausal *adj* premenopáusico

premenstrual *adj* premenstrual

premolar *adj & n* premolar *m*

prenatal *adj* prenatal

preoperative *adj* preoperatorio

prep *n* *(fam)* preparación quirúrgica, preparación del paciente para un procedimiento o una cirugía

preparation *n* preparación *f*; *(pharm)* preparado

prepare *vt* preparar

prepubertal *adj* prepuberal

presbycusis *n* presbiacusia

presbyopia *n* presbicia, vista cansada *(fam)*

presbyopic *adj* présbita *or* présbite

preschool *n* guardería *or* escuela infantil, jardín *m* de infancia, jardín de niños *(Mex)*

prescribe *vt* recetar, prescribir

prescription *n* receta (médica)

presence *n* presencia

presentation *n* presentación *f*; **breech** — presentación pelviana *or* de nalgas, presentación pélvica *(Mex)*

preservative *n* conservante *m*, conservador *m* *(Mex)*

preserve *vt* preservar; **to preserve cognitive function.**.preservar la función cognitiva

press *vt* presionar; *(a button)* presionar, pulsar, oprimir; **Does it hurt when I press here?**..¿Le duele cuando presiono aquí?

pressure *n* presión *f*, opresión *f*, tensión *f*; **like a pressure over your chest.**.

como una opresión (presión) en el pecho; **bilevel positive airway** — presión positiva con dos niveles de la vía aérea; **blood** — tensión *or* presión arterial (*form*), presión sanguínea (*form*), presión de la sangre (*fam*); **continuous positive airway** — (CPAP) presión positiva continua de la vía aérea; **diastolic** — presión diastólica; **high blood** — hipertensión *f* (*form*), presión alta (*fam*); **You have high blood pressure**..Ud. tiene hipertensión (presión alta); **peer** — presión social *or* de grupo; **social** — presión social; **systolic** — presión sistólica

pressure point *n* punto de presión

preterm *adj* pretérmino (*inv*); — **contractions** contracciones *fpl* pretérmino

prevalent *adj* prevalente

prevalence *n* prevalencia

prevent *vt* (*disease, etc.*) prevenir, evitar; **to prevent cavities**..prevenir (evitar) la caries

preventable *adj* prevenible; — **disease** enfermedad *f* prevenible

prevention *n* prevención *f*; **HIV** — prevención del VIH

preventive *adj* preventivo

previous *adj* anterior, previo; **your previous doctor**..su médico -ca *mf* anterior

priapism *n* priapismo

prick *n* pinchazo, piquete *m*; (*vulg, penis*) pene *m*; *vt* pinchar; **to** — **oneself** pincharse

prickle *vi* hormiguear, picar

prickly heat *n* sudamina (*form*), miliaria (*form*), sarpullido *or* salpullido, erupción *f* que se manifiesta durante tiempos de calor

pride *n* orgullo

priest *n* sacerdote *m*, cura *m*

primaquine *n* primaquina

primary *adj* primario

primidone *n* primidona

primitive *adj* primitivo

principle *n* principio; **pleasure** — principio del placer

prion *n* prion *or* prión *m*

prison *n* prisión *f*, cárcel *f*

privacy *n* intimidad *f*, privacidad *f*; **the right to privacy**..el derecho a la intimidad *or* privacidad

private *adj* privado, íntimo; — **doctor** médico -ca *mf* privado; — **parts** (*fam*) genitales *mpl*, partes íntimas (*fam*)

PRK *abbr* photorefractive keratectomy. *V.* **keratectomy.**

probability *n* (*pl* -ties) probabilidad *f*

probably *adv* probablemente

probenecid *n* probenecid *m*

probiotic *n* probiótico

problem *n* problema *m*

probucol *n* probucol *m*

procainamide *n* procainamida

procaine *n* procaína, novocaína

procarbazine *n* procarbazina

procedure *n* procedimiento; **loop electrosurgical excision** — (LEEP) procedimiento de escisión electroquirúrgica con asa

process *n* proceso; (*anat*) apófisis *f*; **mastoid** — apófisis mastoides; **xiphoid** — apófisis xifoides

processed *adj* (*food*) procesado

pro-choice *adj* pro-elección, a favor de la legalización del aborto voluntario

proctitis *n* proctitis *f*

prodrome *n* pródromo, malestar *m* que precede a una enfermedad

produce *vt* producir

product *n* producto

professional *adj* profesional; — **courtesy** prestación gratuita de servicios a colegas; *n* profesional *mf*; **health** — profesional de la salud, profesional sanitario

profile *n* perfil *m*

progeria *n* progeria

progesterone *n* progesterona

prognosis *n* (*pl* -ses) pronóstico

prognostic *adj* pronóstico

program *n* programa *m*

progress *n* progreso; *vi* progresar

progression *n* progresión *f*

progressive *adj* progresivo

proguanil *n* proguanil *m*

projectile *n* proyectil *m*; — **vomiting** vómito(s) en proyectil, vómito(s) fuertes

projection *n* (*psych, etc.*) proyección *f*

prolactin *n* prolactina

prolactinoma *n* prolactinoma *m*

prolapse *n* prolapso; **mitral-valve** — prolapso de la válvula mitral; **rectal** — prolapso rectal *or* del recto; **uterine** — prolapso uterino *or* del útero

pro-life *adj* pro-vida, en contra de la legalización del aborto voluntario
proliferate *vi* proliferar
proliferation *n* proliferación *f*
proliferative *adj* proliferativo
proline *n* prolina
prolong *vt* prolongar; **to prolong death..** prolongar la muerte
prolotherapy *n* proloterapia
promethazine *n* prometazina
prominence *n* prominencia; **bony —** prominencia ósea
pronation *n* pronación *f*
prone *adj* (*facedown*) prono (*form, inv*), boca abajo; (*predisposed*) propenso, predispuesto; **with the patient in the prone position..**con el paciente en posición prono..con el paciente boca abajo; **accident-prone** propenso a los accidentes
prong *n* **four-pronged cane** bastón *m* de cuatro patas *or* apoyos *or* puntos; **nasal prongs** cánula nasal, puntas nasales (*Mex*)
proper *adj* adecuado, apropiado
prophylactic *adj* profiláctico; *n* (*ant*) condón *m*, preservativo
prophylaxis *n* profilaxis *f*; **postexposure —** profilaxis postexposición
proportion *n* proporción *f*
propranolol *n* propranolol *m*
proprioception *n* propiocepción *f*
proprioceptive *adj* propioceptivo
proptosis *n* proptosis *f*
propylene glycol *n* propilenglicol *m*
propylthiouracil *n* propiltiouracilo
prostaglandin *n* prostaglandina
prostate *n* (*fam*) glándula prostática, próstata (*fam*)
prostatectomy *n* (*pl* -mies) prostatectomía
prostatic *adj* prostático
prostatism *n* prostatismo
prostatitis *n* prostatitis *f*
prosthesis *n* (*pl* -ses) prótesis *f*
prosthetic *adj* protésico, postizo
prosthetist *n* técnico ortopédico, especialista *mf* en prótesis; [*Note:* técnica ortopédica *means* orthopedic technique *and is not generally used to refer to a female prosthetist.*]
prostitute *n* prostituto -ta *mf*
protease *n* proteasa

protect *vt* proteger; **to — against** proteger contra; **to — from** proteger de; **to — oneself** protegerse
protection *n* protección *f*
protective *adj* protector
protector *n* protector *m*; **hearing —** protector auditivo
protein *adj* proteico (*form*); *n* proteína (*frec. pl*); **— supplement** suplemento proteico, suplemento de proteína(s)
protocol *n* protocolo
protozoan *adj* protozoario; *n* protozoo, protozoario
protozoon *n* (*pl* -zoa) protozoo, protozoario; [*Nota:* protozoan *y* protozoon *se usan intercambiablemente para decir* protozoo, *pero para decir el plural, no se usa mucho* protozoans, *sino* protozoa.]
protrude *vi* protruir, sobresalir, proyectar hacia adelante
protuberance *n* protuberancia
proud *adj* orgulloso
provide *vt* proveer, proporcionar
provider *n* proveedor -ra *mf*; **health care —** profesional *mf* sanitario, proveedor -ra *mf* de salud
provoke *vt* provocar
proximal *adj* próximo
proxy *n* apoderado -da *mf*, representante *mf*; **health care —** apoderado (para tomar decisiones médicas)
prune *n* ciruela pasa
pruritus *n* prurito, picazón *f*, comezón *f*
PSA *abbr* **prostate-specific antigen.** *V.* **antigen.**
pseudo- *pref* pseudo-, seudo- (*RAE*)
pseudoaneurysm *n* pseudoaneurisma *or* seudoaneurisma *m*
pseudoarthrosis *n* (*ortho*) pseudoartrosis *or* seudoartrosis *f*
pseudocyesis *n* pseudociesis *f*
pseudocyst *n* pseudoquiste *or* seudoquiste *m*; **pancreatic —** pseudoquiste *or* seudoquiste pancreático
pseudoephedrine *n* pseudoefedrina, seudoefedrina
pseudogout *n* pseudogota *or* seudogota
pseudohypoparathyroidism *n* pseudohipoparatiroidismo *or* seudohipoparatiroidismo
pseudotumor *n* pseudotumor *or* seudotumor *m*; **— cerebri** pseudotumor *or*

seudotumor cerebral
psilocybin *n* psilocibina
psittacosis *n* psitacosis *f*
psoas *n* psoas *m*
psoralen *n* psoraleno; — **plus ultraviolet A (PUVA)** psoraleno más luz ultravioleta A
psoriasis *n* psoriasis *f*
psoriatic *adj* psoriásico
PSR *abbr* **patient service representative.** *V.* **representative.**
psyche *n* (*psych*) psique *f*, psiquis *f*;
(*soul*) alma
psych out *vt* (*fam*) intimidar, hacer que
(*alguien*) pierda la confianza; **to get
psyched out** sentirse intimidado, perder la confianza
psychiatric *adj* psiquiátrico
psychiatrist *n* psiquiatra *mf*
psychiatry *n* psiquiatría; **child** — paidopsiquiatría (*form*), psiquiatría infantil
or de niños
psychic *adj* psíquico *or* síquico
psychoactive *adj* psicoactivo
psychoanalysis *n* psicoanálisis *m*, análisis *m* (*fam*)
psychoanalyst *n* psicoanalista *mf*, analista *mf* (*fam*)
psychoanalyze *vt* psicoanalizar
psychodynamic *adj* psicodinámico; *npl*
(*psychodynamic therapy*) psicodinámi-
ca
psychogenic *adj* psicógeno, psicogénico
psychological *adj* psicológico
psychologist *n* psicólogo -ga *mf*
psychology *n* psicología
psychomotor *adj* psicomotor
psychopath *n* psicópata *mf*
psychosis *n* (*pl* **-ses**) psicosis *f*
psychosocial *adj* psicosocial
psychosomatic *adj* psicosomático
psychotherapist *n* psicoterapeuta *mf*
psychotherapy *n* psicoterapia
psychotic *adj* & *n* psicótico -ca *mf*
psychotropic *adj* psicotrópico
psyllium *n* psyllium
PT *abbr* **prothrombin time.** *V.* **time.**
PTCA *abbr* **percutaneous transluminal
coronary angioplasty.** *V.* **angioplasty.**
pterygium *n* pterigión *m*, carnosidad *f* en
el ojo
PTH *abbr* **parathyroid hormone.** *V.*

hormone.
ptomaine *n* tomaína
ptosis *n* ptosis *f*
PTSD *abbr* **post-traumatic stress disorder.** *V.* **disorder.**
PTT *abbr* **partial thromboplastin time.**
V. **time.**
pubertal *adj* puberal
puberty *n* pubertad *f*; **precocious** — pubertad precoz
pubescent *adj* pubescente
pubic *adj* púbico, pubiano; — **area** pubis *m* (*form*), parte *f* inferior del vientre, (*in women*) monte *m* de Venus
pubis *n* pubis *m*, hueso que forma la parte anterior de la pélvis
public *adj* público
pudendal *adj* pudendo
puerperal *adj* puerperal
puerperium *n* puerperio
puff *n* (*fam, of an inhaler*) inhalación *f*
puffer (*fam*) *V.* **inhaler.**
puffy *adj* (*comp* **-fier**; *super* **-fiest**) hinchado
puke (*fam o vulg*) *V.* **vomit.**
pull *vt* **to — a muscle** sufrir una distensión (muscular), sufrir un tirón (muscular); **He pulled a calf muscle**..Sufrió
una distensión (un tirón) en la pantorrilla; **pulled muscle** distensión *f* (muscular), tirón *m* (muscular)
pulmonary *adj* pulmonar
pulmonic *adj* pulmonar
pulmonologist *n* neumólogo -ga *mf*, médico -ca *mf* especializado en los pulmones y sus enfermedades, especialista
mf de los pulmones
pulmonology *n* neumología, rama de la
medicina que se ocupa de los pulmones
y sus enfermedades
pulp *n* (*dent*) pulpa
pulpectomy *n* (*dent*) pulpectomía
pulsation *n* pulsación *f*
pulse *n* pulso; **I'm going to take your
pulse**..Voy a tomarle el pulso..**pulse of
steroids**..pulso de esteroides; **carotid
(radial, etc.)** — pulso carotídeo (radial, etc.)
pumice stone *n* piedra pómez
pump *n* bomba; **breast** — sacaleches *m*,
extractor *m* de leche; **insulin** — bomba
de insulina; **intraaortic balloon** —
balón *m* de contrapulsación aórtica; *vt*

(*blood*) bombear, impulsar (*la sangre*)

puncture *n* punción *f*, pinchazo, piquete *m*; **lumbar —** punción lumbar; *vt* puncionar, punzar, pinchar, picar

pupil *n* (*of the eye*) pupila (*del ojo*)

pure *adj* puro

purée *n* puré *m*

purgative (*ant*) *adj* purgante; *n* purgante *m*, purga

purge *n* (*ant*) purga

purification *n* purificación *f*

purified protein derivative (PPD) derivado proteico purificado, PPD *m&f*

purifier *n* purificador *m*

purify *vt* (*pret & pp* **-fied**) purificar

purine *n* purina

purple *adj* morado

purpura *n* púrpura; **Henoch-Schönlein —** púrpura de Henoch-Schönlein; **idiopathic thrombocytopenic — (ITP)** (*ant*) trombocitopenia inmune (TPI), púrpura trombocitopénica idiopática (PTI) (*ant*); **thrombotic thrombocytopenic — (TTP)** púrpura trombocitopénica trombótica (PTT)

purse *vt* (*one's lips*) fruncir (*los labios*)

pus *n* pus *m*

push *vi* (*obst*) pujar, empujar; **Take a deep breath and push!**..¡Respire profundo y puje!

pushup, push-up *n* flexión *f* (de brazos), lagartija (*esp. Mex*)

pustule *n* pústula

put *vt* (*pret & pp* **put**; *ger* **putting**) **to — on** (*clothing, etc.*) ponerse (*ropa, etc.*); **Put on this gown so that it opens over your back**..Póngase esta bata con la abertura hacia atrás; **to — on lipstick** pintarse los labios; **to — on makeup** maquillarse; **to — on nail polish** pintarse las uñas

PUVA *abbr* **psoralen plus ultraviolet A**. *V*. **psoralen**.

PVC *abbr* **premature ventricular contraction**. *V*. **contraction**.

pyelogram *n* urografía (*estudio*), pielograma *m*; **intravenous —** urografía intravenosa

pyelography *n* urografía (*técnica*)

pyelonephritis *n* pielonefritis *f*

pyloric *adj* pilórico

pyloroplasty *n* (*pl* **-ties**) piloroplastia

pylorus *n* píloro

pyoderma gangrenosum *n* pioderma gangrenoso

pyogenic *adj* piógeno, piogénico

pyorrhea *n* piorrea

pyrantel *n* pirantel *m*

pyrazinamide *n* pirazinamida

pyrethrin *n* piretrina

pyridoxine *n* piridoxina

pyrimethamine *n* pirimetamina

pyromania *n* piromanía

Q

quack *n* (*fam*) matasanos *mf*, charlatán -tana *mf*

quadrant *n* cuadrante *m*; **left lower —** cuadrante inferior izquierdo **right upper —** cuadrante superior derecho

quadriceps *n* cuádriceps *m*

quadriplegia *n* tetraplejía, cuadriplejía

quadriplegic *adj & n* tetrapléjico -ca *mf*, cuadripléjico -ca *mf*

quadruplet *n* cuatrillizo -za *mf*

quality *n* (*pl* **-ties**) calidad *f*; **— of life** calidad de vida

quantity *n* cantidad *f*

quarantine *n* cuarentena; *vt* poner en

cuarentena
quart *n* cuarto (de galón)
quarter *n* cuarta parte, cuarto; **a quarter of a tablet**..la cuarta parte de una tableta
queasy *adj* (*comp* **-ier**; *super* **-iest**) con un poco de náusea(s), que tiene náusea(s); **I feel queasy**..Siento un poco de náusea(s).
quetiapine *n* quetiapina
quickening *n* (*obst*) primeros movimientos fetales percibidos por la embaraza-

da
quiet *n* silencio; *vi* **to — down** tranquilizarse, calmarse
quinacrine *n* quinacrina, mepacrina (*INN*)
quinapril *n* quinapril *m*
quinine *n* quinina
quintuplet *n* quintillizo -za *mf*
quit *vt* (*pret & pp* **quit**; *ger* **quitting**) dejar de, (*to discontinue*) suspender; **You need to quit smoking**..Tiene que dejar de fumar.

R

rabeprazole *n* rabeprazol *m*
rabid *adj* rabioso, que padece rabia
rabies *n* rabia
raccoon *n* mapache *m*
race *n* (*of people*) raza; *vi* (*one's heart*) latir rápido (*el corazón*)
radial *adj* (*anat*) radial
radiate *vi* (*pain*) irradiar(se)
radiation *n* radiación *f*; **ionizing —** radiación ionizante
radical *adj* radical
radiculopathy *n* radiculopatía; **cervical —** radiculopatía cervical
radii *pl de* **radius**
radioactive *adj* radiactivo
radioactivity *n* radiactividad *f*
radiofrequency *n* radiofrecuencia
radiography *n* radiografía
radioiodine *n* radioyodo
radioisotope *n* radioisótopo
radiologist *n* radiólogo -ga *mf*, médico -ca *mf* especializado en imágenes diagnósticas y su uso para guiar intervenciones

radiology *n* radiología, rama de la medicina que se ocupa de las imágenes diagnósticas y su uso para guiar intervenciones
radionuclide *n* radionúclido
radiosurgery *n* radiocirugía
radium *n* radio (*elemento*)
radius *n* (*pl* **radii**) radio
radon *n* radón *m*
rage *n* ira, rabia, furia, cólera; **road —** conducción agresiva, violencia vial
ragweed *n* (*bot*) ambrosía
rail *n* bed *o* side **—** barandilla, baranda
raise *vt* levantar, elevar; (*a child*) criar; **Raise your leg**..Levante su pierna... **This medicine may raise your sugar**.. Esta medicina puede elevarle el azúcar.
raloxifene *n* raloxifeno
raltegravir *n* raltegravir *m*
ramipril *n* ramipril *m*
ran *pret de* **run**
random *adj* aleatorio; **in random fashion**..en forma aleatoria; **at —** al azar
range *n* rango; **in normal —** en rango

normal; — **of motion** rango de movimiento; — **of values** rango de valores
ranitidine *n* ranitidina
rape *n* violación *f* (*sexual*); **date** — violación en una cita; *vt* violar
rapid *adj* rápido; **rapid-acting** de acción rápida
rare *adj* raro, poco común; (*meat*) poco hecho, poco cocido *or* cocinado
rarely *adv* raras veces
rasburicase *n* rasburicasa
rash *n* erupción cutánea *or* de la piel, (*esp. due to heat or chafing*) sarpullido *or* salpullido; **diaper** — dermatitis *f* del pañal
RAST *abbr* **radioallergosorbent test**. *V.* test.
rat *n* rata
rate *n* tasa, frecuencia; **basal metabolic** — tasa metabólica basal; **birth** — tasa de natalidad, natalidad *f*; **death** — tasa de mortalidad, mortalidad *f*; **erythrocyte sedimentation rate** — **(ESR)** velocidad *f* de sedimentación globular (VSG); **heart** — frecuencia cardíaca; **infant mortality** — tasa de mortalidad infantil; **respiratory** — frecuencia respiratoria; **success** — tasa *or* índice *m* de éxito
ratio *n* (*math*) razón *f*; **international normalized** — **(INR)** razón normalizada internacional
ration *n* ración *f*
rationalization *n* (*psych*) racionalización *f*
rationalize *vt, vi* (*psych*) racionalizar
rattlesnake *n* serpiente *f* de cascabel
raw *adj* (*food*) crudo; (*skin, mucous membrane*) excoriado (*form*), pelado, en carne viva
ray *n* rayo; **the sun's rays**..los rayos solares..los rayos del sol
razor *n* maquinilla *or* máquina de afeitar; **electric** — máquina de afeitar (*eléctrica*), afeitadora; **safety** *o* **manual** — maquinilla de afeitar, maquinilla (*fam*), rastrillo, máquina de afeitar (*manual*)
RDA *abbr* **recommended daily allowance** *V.* allowance.
RDI *abbr* **recommended daily intake**. *V.* intake.
reach *n* alcance *m*; **out of reach of children**..fuera del alcance de los niños; *vt, vi* alcanzar
react *vi* responder, reaccionar; **The body can react to stress in different ways..** El cuerpo puede responder al estrés de distintas maneras.
reaction *n* reacción *f*; **adverse** — reacción adversa; **allergic** — reacción alérgica; **conversion** — trastorno de conversión; **cross** — reacción cruzada; **delayed** — reacción tardía; **grief** — reacción de duelo; **id** — reacción ide, autoeccematización *or* autoeczematización *f*, dermatitis *f* por autosensibilización; **polymerase chain** — **(PCR)** reacción en cadena de la polimerasa; **transfusion** — reacción transfusional
reactivate *vt* reactivar
reactivation *n* reactivación *f*
reactive *adj* reactivo
reactivity *n* reactividad *f*
read *vt, vi* (*pret & pp* **read**) leer; **to** — **lips** leer los labios
reading *n* (*of an instrument*) lectura
reagent *n* reactivo
reality *n* (*pl* **-ties**) realidad *f*; — **testing** (*psych*) prueba de realidad
realize *vt* darse cuenta; **When did you realize she was sick?..**¿Cuándo se dio cuenta que estaba enferma?
rear end *n* (*fam*) nalgas, trasero (*fam*)
reason *n* razón *f*, motivo
reassignment *n* reasignación *f*; **gender** — reasignación de género *or* sexo, cambio de sexo (*fam*)
reattach *vt* reconectar, recolocar
rebound *n* rebote *m*; — **hypertension** hipertensión *f* de rebote
recall *n* recuperación *f* (*form*), recuerdo, memoria a corto plazo, capacidad *f* para recordar; (*of a defective product*) retirada (*de un producto defectuoso*); *vt* recordar; (*a defective product*) retirar
receding hairline *n* entradas
recently *adv* recientemente, últimamente
receptionist *n* recepcionista *mf*
receptive *adj* receptivo
receptor *n* receptor *m*; **estrogen receptor-positive** positivo para receptores de estrógeno
recessive *adj* recesivo
recipient *n* (*of a transfusion, transplant, etc.*) receptor -ra *mf* (*de una transfu-*

sión, un trasplante, etc.)
recliner *n* silla reclinable
reclining *adj* reclinable
recognition *n* reconocimiento
recognize *vt* reconocer
recombinant *adj* recombinante
recommend *vt* recomendar
recommendation *n* recomendación *f*
reconnect *vt* reconectar
reconstitution *n* reconstitución *f*; **immune — reconstitución inmune
reconstruct *vt* reconstruir
reconstruction *n* reconstrucción *f*
reconstructive *adj* reconstructivo
record *n* registro; **electronic health —, electronic medical —** historia clínica electrónica; **medical —** historia clínica, historial médico, expediente clínico (*esp. Mex*); **personal health —** historia clínica personal; *vt* registrar; **Record your sugars in this booklet.**. Registre sus niveles de azúcar en esta libreta; [*Nota:* electronic medical record *viene siendo reemplazado por* electronic health record. *Teóricamente el último es un término más amplio que incluye más información del paciente como persona, aunque la mayoría de las personas intercambian los dos términos. De modo paralelo,* personal health record *viene reemplazando a* medical record.]
recorder *V.* **monitor.**
recourse *n* recurso
recover *vt, vi* recuperar; **How long will it take for him to recover?**. ¿Cuánto tardará en recuperarse?
recovery *n* recuperación *f*
recreation *n* recreación *f*, (*esp. during school*) recreo
recreational *adj* recreativo; **recreational use of drugs**..uso recreativo de drogas
recta *pl de* **rectum**
rectal *adj* rectal; *n* (*fam*) tacto *or* examen *m* rectal
rectocele *n* rectocele *m*
rectum *n* (*pl* **-ta** *o* **-tums**) recto
recumbent *adj* (*form*) decúbito (*form, inv*), acostado
recuperate *vi* recuperarse
recuperation *n* recuperación *f*
recur *vi* (*pret & pp* **recurred**; *ger* **recurring**) recurrir

recurrence *n* recurrencia
recurrent *adj* recurrente
recycle *vt* reciclar
recycling *n* reciclaje *m*
red *adj* (*comp* **redder**; *super* **reddest**) rojo; **— flag** llamado *or* llamada de atención, señal *f* de alerta, signo de algún problema
red clover *n* (*bot*) trébol rojo
Red Crescent *n* Media Luna Roja
Red Cross *n* Cruz Roja
reddening *n* enrojecimiento
reddish *adj* rojizo
redness *n* rubor *m* (*form*), rojez *f*
reduce *vt* reducir, disminuir, bajar; (*ortho*) reducir; *vi* (*fam, to lose weight*) bajar de peso
reducible *adj* (*hernia*) reductible *or* reducible
reduction *n* reducción *f*; **breast —** reducción mamaria *or* de senos; **open — and internal fixation** reducción abierta y fijación interna
reevaluate *vt* revalorar, revaluar, volver a evaluar
refeeding *n* realimentación *f*
refer *vt* (*pret & pp* **referred**; *ger* **referring**) (*a patient*) remitir, mandar a ver; **I'm going to refer you to an allergist** ..Le voy a remitir a un alergólogo.
reference *n* referencia
referral *n* remisión *f*, derivación *f* (*esp. Esp*)
referred *adj* (*pain*) referido
refill *n* (*of a medication*) nuevo surtido, surtido adicional (*autorizado previamente en la receta médica*), relleno (*Ang*), refill *m* (*Ang*); autorización *f* para surtidos adicionales (*en el futuro*); **Why didn't you get a refill?**..¿Por qué no obtuvo un nuevo surtido (*autorizado previamente en la receta médica*)? **...It says here on the bottle you have three refills left**..Dice aquí en el frasco que le quedan tres surtidos...**I'm giving you five refills so you won't have to see me for a while**..Le estoy dando autorización para cinco surtidos adicionales para que no necesite visitarme por un rato...**We don't give early refills of narcotics**..No surtimos de nuevo los narcóticos antes de la fecha acordada; *vt* (*patient as subject*) obte-

ner un nuevo surtido (*de un medicamento en la farmacia, de acuerdo con una receta hecha previamente*), conseguir un relleno *or* refill; (*pharmacist as subject*) surtir(*le*) de nuevo (*un medicamento de acuerdo con una receta hecha previamente*), rellenar (*Ang*), refill (*Ang*); (*physician as subject*) recetar de nuevo, dar(*le*) una nueva receta para, rellenar (*Ang*), refill (*Ang*) (*V. también* **renew**); **You need to refill your medications before they run out**..Tiene que obtener nuevos surtidos de sus medicamentos antes de que se le acaben...**The pharmacist can refill your digoxin without your having to see me**..El farmacéutico puede surtirle de nuevo su digoxina sin que me tenga que visitar...**Dr. Lee can refill your glipizide**..El doctor Lee puede recetarle de nuevo su glipizida; [*Note: The practice of authorizing future refills of medication is uncommon in countries where Spanish is spoken and often requires considerable explanation. Eventually the terms* refill, relleno, *and* rellenar *will likely be used commonly by Spanish-speaking persons living in the US.*]

reflex *n* reflejo; **conditioned** — reflejo condicionado; **gag** — reflejo nauseoso; **patellar** — reflejo rotuliano; — **hammer** martillo de reflejos; **startle** — reflejo de sobresalto

reflexology *n* reflexología

reflux *n* reflujo; **acid** — reflujo ácido; **gastroesophageal** — reflujo gastroesofágico

refraction *n* refracción *f*

refractive *adj* refractivo

refractory *adj* resistente al tratamiento

refrigerate *vt* refrigerar

refrigeration *n* refrigeración *f*

refrigerator *n* refrigerador *m*

refuse *vt* rechazar; **to refuse a transfusion**..rechazar una transfusión

regain *vt* recuperar, recobrar; **to regain use of your leg**..recuperar (recobrar) el uso de su pierna; **to** — **consciousness** volver en sí; **to** — **weight** recuperar peso

regenerate *vi* regenerarse

regeneration *n* regeneración *f*

regenerative *adj* regenerativo

regimen *n* régimen *m*

region *n* región *f*

regional *adj* regional

registry *n* registro; **tumor** — registro de tumores

regression *n* (*psych, oncology, etc.*) regresión *f*

regular *adj* regular; — **physical activity** actividad física regular

regurgitate *vt* regurgitar, vomitar sin esfuerzo

regurgitation *n* regurgitación *f*; **aortic (mitral etc.)** — regurgitación aórtica (mitral, etc.)

rehab (*fam*) *V.* **rehabilitation**.

rehabilitate *vt* rehabilitar; **to become rehabilitated** rehabilitarse

rehabilitation *n* rehabilitación *f*

rehydrate *vt* rehidratar

rehydration *n* rehidratación *f*

reinfect *vt, vi* reinfectar(se)

reinfection *n* reinfección *f*

reinforce *vt* reforzar

reinforcement *n* (*psych, etc.*) refuerzo

reject *vt* rechazar

rejection *n* rechazo; **to tolerate rejection**..tolerar el rechazo

rejuvenate *vt* rejuvenecer; **to become rejuvenated** rejuvenecerse

relapse *n* recaída; *vi* recaer

relate *vi* **to** — **to** (*fam*) entenderse bien con

related *adj* emparentado; (*associated*) relacionado; **She is related to me**..Es pariente mía...**cancer-related complications**..complicaciones relacionadas con el cáncer; — **donor** donante emparentado, donante que es familiar de uno

relation *n* relación *f*

relationship *n* relación *f*; **doctor-patient** — relación médico-paciente

relative *n* familiar *mf*, pariente *mf*; **blood** — pariente consanguíneo (*form*), pariente que tiene antepasados en común (*con uno*); [*Note: The RAE lists* familiar *as masculine only, but feminine usage when referring to females is the norm.*]

relax *vt* relajar, aflojar; **Relax your leg**..Relaje (Afloje) la pierna; *vi* relajarse; **Relax**..Relájese.

relaxant *n* relajante *m*; **muscle** — rela-

jante muscular
relaxation *n* relajación *f*; **— techniques** técnicas de relajación
relaxing *adj* relajante
release *n* liberación *f*; **carpal tunnel —** liberación del túnel carpiano; **controlled-release** de liberación controlada; **extended-release** de liberación prolongada; **slow-release** de liberación lenta; **sustained-release** de liberación sostenida; **timed-release** de liberación controlada; *vt* liberar; **copper-releasing, hormone-releasing, etc.** liberador de cobre, liberador de hormona, etc.
reliability *n* (*device*) fiabilidad *f*
reliable *adj* (*device*) fiable
relief *n* alivio; (*aid*) ayuda, auxilio, socorro
relieve *vt* aliviar
religion *n* religión *f*; **What is your religion?**..¿Cuál es su religión?
rem *n* (*rad, ant*) rem *m* (*ant*)
REM *abbr* **rapid eye movement.** *V.* **movement.**
remedy *n* (*pl* **-dies**) remedio; **cough —** remedio para la tos; **home —** remedio casero
remember *vt* recordar, acordarse (de); **Remember these three objects**..Recuerde estos tres objetos...**I remember her**..Me acuerdo de ella...**I remember you**..Lo recuerdo a Ud...Me acuerdo de ti.
reminder *n* recordatorio
remission *n* remisión *f*; **complete —** remisión completa; **partial —** remisión parcial; **spontaneous —** remisión espontánea; **to go into —** entrar en remisión
remodeling *n* remodelación *f*; **bone —** remodelación ósea; **cardiac —** remodelación cardíaca
remorse *n* remordimiento, arrepentimiento
removable *adj* removible, extraíble, que se puede quitar
removal *n* extracción *f*, eliminación *f*, remoción *f*, (*sonda, catéter, etc.*) retirada, retiro (*Amer*); **tattoo —** eliminación *or* remoción de tatuajes
remove *vt* extraer (*form*), remover, quitar, sacar, (*a catheter, monitor, stitches, etc.*) retirar, quitar

renal *adj* renal
renew *vt* (*a medication*) recetar de nuevo, dar una nueva receta para (*un medicamento*) **Any of my partners can renew your medication if I'm not here**..Cualquiera de mis colegas puede recetarle de nuevo (darle una nueva receta para) sus medicamentos si no estoy aquí.
renovascular *adj* renovascular
repaglinide *n* repaglinida
repair *n* reparación *f*; *vt* reparar, arreglar (*fam*)
repeat *vt* repetir
repellent *n* repelente *m*; **insect —** repelente de insectos
reperfusion *n* reperfusión *f*
repetition *n* repetición *f*
repetitive *adj* repetitivo
replace *vt* reemplazar, sustituir (*V. también* **substitute.**)
replacement *n* reemplazo, sustitución *f* (*esp. Esp*); **aortic (mitral, etc.) valve —** reemplazo valvular aórtico (mitral, etc.), sustitución valvular aórtica (mitral, etc.), reemplazo *or* sustitución de válvula aórtica (mitral, etc.); **catheter —** cambio de catéter; **joint —** artroplastia (*form*), reemplazo *or* sustitución articular; **total hip (knee) —** artroplastia total de cadera (rodilla), reemplazo total de cadera (rodilla); [*Note: The definite article can be added to the translations above to personalize a statement*: Ud. necesita un reemplazo de la válvula aórtica..You need replacement of your aortic valve.]
replicate *vi* (*viruses*) replicarse
report *n* informe *m*, declaración *f*; **operative —** informe quirúrgico; *vt* reportar, declarar; **The law requires me to report your condition to the Public Health Department**..La ley me exige reportar su enfermedad al Departamento de Salud Pública.
reportable *adj* (*disease*) de declaración obligatoria; **— disease** enfermedad de declaración obligatoria
representative *n* representante *mf*; **patient service — (PSR)** representante de servicio(s) al paciente
repress *vt* (*psych*) reprimir
repression *n* (*psych*) represión *f*

reproduce *vt, vi* reproducir(se)
reproduction *n* reproducción *f*; **assisted —** reproducción asistida
reproductive *adj* reproductor, reproductivo
reschedule *vt* (*an appointment*) reprogramar, cambiar para otra fecha (*una cita*)
rescue *n* rescate *m*, salvamento; **air —** rescate aéreo; **— inhaler** inhalador *m* de rescate; *vt* rescatar, salvar
rescuer *n* socorrista *mf*, rescatador -ra *mf*
research *n* investigación *f*; **cancer —** investigación sobre el cáncer, investigación del cáncer
resect *vt* resecar, extirpar
resectable *adj* resecable, extirpable
resection *n* resección *f*; **transurethral — of the prostate (TURP)** resección transuretral de próstata (RTU)
reserpine *n* reserpina
reserve *n* reserva
reservoir *n* reservorio
resident *n* residente *mf*; (*physician*) médico -ca *mf* residente, residente *mf*; **family practice —** residente de medicina familiar; **medical —** residente de medicina interna; **surgical —** residente de cirugía
residual *adj* residual
residue *n* residuo
resin *n* (*dent, etc.*) resina
resist *vt* resistir
resistance *n* (*micro, psych, etc.*) resistencia; **cross-resistance** resistencia cruzada; **insulin —** resistencia a la insulina
resistant *adj* resistente; **methicillin-resistant** resistente a (la) meticilina; **multidrug-resistant** multirresistente, resistente a múltiples fármacos *or* drogas
resolution *n* resolución *f*; **conflict —** resolución de conflictos; **high —** alta resolución
resolve *vi* resolverse
resonance *n* resonancia; **magnetic — (MR)** resonancia magnética (RM); **nuclear magnetic — (NMR)** (*ant*) resonancia magnética, resonancia magnética nuclear (RMN) (*ant*)
resorb *vt* reabsorber; **to get resorbed** reabsorberse
resorption *n* reabsorción *f*
resort *n* recurso; (*spa*) balneario, spa *m*;

last — último recurso
resource *n* recurso
respect *n* respeto; *vt* respetar
respiration *n* respiración *f*
respirator *n* (*mask*) respirador *m*, máscara *or* mascarilla con filtro; (*ventilator*) ventilador *m*, respirador *m*, aparato para suministrar respiración artificial
respiratory *adj* respiratorio
respire *vt, vi* respirar
respite *n* relevo, respiro, descanso; (*V. también* **respite care** *bajo* **care.**)
respond *vi* responder
responder *n* respondiente *mf*; **emergency —** miembro de un equipo de emergencias; **first —** primer respondiente
response *n* respuesta; **complete —** respuesta completa; **immune —** respuesta inmunológica *or* inmunitaria; **partial —** respuesta parcial; **sustained —** respuesta sostenida
rest *n* descanso, reposo; (*remaining portion*) demás, resto; **the rest of the pills** ..las demás pastillas..el resto de las pastillas; **at —** en reposo; **bed —** reposo en cama; **bowel —** descanso *or* reposo del intestino; *vt* apoyar; **Rest your arm here**..Apoye su brazo aquí; *vi* descansar, reposar
restenosis *n* reestenosis *f*
resting *adj* en reposo; **— heart rate** frecuencia cardíaca en reposo
restless *adj* inquieto, intranquilo
restlessness *n* inquietud *f*, agitación *f*
restoration *n* (*dent, surg*) restauración *f*
restorative *adj* (*dent, surg, etc.*) restaurador, restaurativo; (*sleep*) reparador
restore *vt* restablecer; (*dent, surg*) restaurar
restrain *vt* (*a patient*) sujetar, inmovilizar, contener (*a un paciente*), restringir la libertad de movimiento (*de un paciente, para que no se haga daño a sí mismo o a los demás*)
restraint *n* (*of a patient*) contención *f*, sujeción *f*; **chemical —** contención *or* sujeción química; **mechanical —** contención *or* sujeción mecánica; **physical restraints** correas, ataduras, cintas para limitar los movimientos de un paciente agitado
restrict *vt* restringir, limitar
restriction *n* restricción *f*, limitación *f*;

intrauterine growth — restricción del crecimiento intrauterino, crecimiento intrauterino retardado; **(medical) work** — restricción de trabajo (por indicaciones médicas)

restroom n (*US*) baño, servicios

result n resultado; **laboratory** —, **lab** — (*fam*) resultado de laboratorio

resurfacing n (*derm*) rejuvenecimiento; **laser** — rejuvenecimiento (con) láser

resuscitate vt reanimar; **Do Not Resuscitate (DNR)** no reanimar (NR); **Do Not Resuscitate order, DNR order** (*fam*) orden f de no reanimar (ONR)

resuscitation n reanimación f; **cardiopulmonary** — **(CPR)** reanimación cardiopulmonar (RCP)

resynchronization n resincronización f; **cardiac** — resincronización cardíaca

retain vt retener; **to** — **water** retener agua

retainer n (*orthodontics*) retenedor m

retardation n retraso, retardo; **intrauterine growth** — (*ant*) V. **intrauterine growth restriction** bajo **restriction**; **mental** —* discapacidad intelectual, retraso mental[†]

potencialmente ofensivo [†]potentially offensive

retarded* adj retrasado; **mentally** —* con discapacidad intelectual, retrasado mental[†]

potencialmente ofensivo, [†]potentially offensive

retch vi tener arcadas (*form*), vomitar sin nada que expulsar

retching n arcadas (*form*), acción f de vomitar sin nada que expulsar

retention n retención f; **urinary** — retención urinaria

reticulocyte n reticulocito

retina n (*pl* **-nas** o **-nae**) retina; **detached** — desprendimiento de retina

retinal adj retiniano, de retina

retinitis n retinitis f; — **pigmentosa** retinitis pigmentosa

retinoblastoma n retinoblastoma m

retinoic acid n ácido retinoico

retinoid n retinoide m

retinol n retinol m

retinopathy n retinopatía; **diabetic** — retinopatía diabética

retraining n reentrenamiento

retrograde adj retrógrado

retroperitoneal adj retroperitoneal

retroviral adj retroviral

retrovirus n retrovirus m

reusable adj reutilizable

revaccination n revacunación f

revascularization n revascularización f

reversal n reversión f; **vasectomy** — reversión de vasectomía

reversible adj reversible

review of systems n revisión f por sistemas

revision n revisión f

revitalize vt revitalizar

revitalizing adj revitalizador

revive vt reanimar

rhabdomyolysis n rabdomiolisis or rabdomiólisis f

rhabdomyoma n rabdomioma m

rhabdomyosarcoma n rabdomiosarcoma m

rheumatic adj reumático

rheumatism n (*ant*) reumatismo, reuma or reúma m&f; **palindromic** — reumatismo palindrómico

rheumatoid adj reumatoide

rheumatologist n reumatólogo -ga mf, médico -ca mf especializado en las articulaciones y las enfermedades que las afectan

rheumatology n reumatología, rama de la medicina que se ocupa de las las articulaciones y las enfermedades que las afectan

rhinitis n rinitis f; **allergic** — rinitis alérgica

rhinophyma n rinofima m&f

rhinoplasty n (*pl* **-ties**) rinoplastia

rhinovirus n rinovirus m

rhythm n ritmo

rhytidectomy n ritidectomía, estiramiento facial, lifting m facial (*Ang*)

rib n costilla; — **cage** caja torácica

ribavirin n ribavirina

riboflavin n riboflavina

ribonucleic acid (RNA) n ácido ribonucleico (ARN)

rice n arroz m; **red yeast** — arroz de levadura roja

rich adj (*abundant*) rico; — **in protein** rico en proteínas

ricin n ricina

rickets n raquitismo

rifabutin *n* rifabutina
rifampin (*USAN*), **rifampicin** (*INN*) *n* rifampicina, rifampina
rifamycin *n* rifamicina
rifaximin *n* rifaximina
right *adj* derecho; *n* (*right-hand side*) derecha; (*legal, moral*) derecho
right-handed *adj* diestro (*form*), que escribe con la mano derecha; **Are you right-handed or left-handed?**..¿Escribe Ud. con la mano derecha o la izquierda?
rigid *adj* rígido
rigidity *n* rigidez *f*
rigor mortis *n* rigor mortis, rígor mortis *m* (*RAE*)
rilpivirine *n* rilpivirina
rimantadine *n* rimantadina
ring *n* anillo; **vaginal —** anillo vaginal
ringing *n* (*in the ear*) zumbido
ringworm *n* tinea corporis (*form*), tiña corporal *or* del cuerpo
rinse *n* enjuague *m*; *vt* enjuagar
ripe *adj* (*fruit*) maduro
rise *n* aumento, elevación *f*; *vi* (*pret* **rose**; *pp* **risen**) subir(se)
risedronate, risedronate sodium (*USAN*), **risedronic acid** (*INN*) *n* risedronato, risedronato sódico, ácido risedrónico (*INN*)
risk *n* riesgo; **at —** de *or* en riesgo; **at — for** en riesgo de; **calculated —** riesgo calculado; **high-risk** de alto riesgo; **low-risk** de bajo riesgo; **risks and benefits** riesgos y beneficios; **to run the — of** correr el riesgo de; **to take a —** arriesgarse, tomar un riesgo; *vt* arriesgar
risky *adj* (*comp* **-ier**; *super* **-iest**) riesgoso
risperidone *n* risperidona
ritonavir *n* ritonavir *m*
ritual *n* ritual *m*
rituximab *n* rituximab *m*
rivalry *n* rivalidad *f*; **sibling —** rivalidad entre hermanos, rivalidad fraterna
rivaroxaban *n* rivaroxabán *m*
rivastigmine *n* rivastigmina
rizatriptan *n* rizatriptán *m*
RNA *V.* **ribonucleic acid**.
roast *vt* asar
robotic *adj* robótico
rock climbing *n* escalada

rod *n* (*bacteria*) bacilo; (*of the eye*) bastón *m*; (*ortho*) barra; **Harrington —** barra de Harrington
rodent *n* roedor *m*
rodenticide *n* rodenticida *m*
roflumilast *n* roflumilast *m*
role *n* papel *m*; **— model** modelo de conducta; **— playing** *o* **play** juegos de rol
roll *vi* **to — over** voltearse, darse vuelta; **Now roll over**..Ahora voltéese (dese vuelta); **to — up** (*one's sleeve, pants leg, etc.*) arremangarse, subirse la manga; **Roll up your sleeve**..Arremánguese..Súbase la manga.
roof of the mouth *n* paladar *m*
room *n* habitación *f*, sala, cuarto; **the patient's room**..la habitación del paciente; **delivery —** sala de partos; **emergency — (ER)** sala de urgencias *or* emergencias; **operating — (OR)** quirófano, sala de operaciones; **recovery —** sala de reanimación *or* recuperación; **waiting —** sala de espera
root *n* raíz *f*; **hair —** raíz del pelo *or* cabello; **nerve —** raíz nerviosa; **— canal** (*fam, root canal therapy*) endodoncia, tratamiento de conducto; **tooth — o — of a tooth** raíz dental, raíz de un diente
ropinirole *n* ropinirol *m*
rosacea *n* (*fam*) acné *m&f* rosácea, rosácea (*fam*) (*V. también* **acne**.)
rose *pret de* **rise**
rosemary *n* (*bot*) romero
roseola, roseola infantum (*form*) *n* roseola, roséola (*RAE*), exantema súbito
rosiglitazone *n* rosiglitazona
rosuvastatin *n* rosuvastatina
rot *vt, vi* (*pret & pp* **rotted**; *ger* **rotting**) pudrir(se)
rotator cuff *n* manguito rotador
rotten *adj* podrido
rough *adj* (*skin, etc.*) áspero
roughage *n* fibra
roughness *n* aspereza
round *adj* redondo; *vi* (*to visit patients*) pasar visita, visitar diariamente a los pacientes hospitalizados
rounds *npl* (*by doctors*) pase *m* de visita, rondas (*Ang*); **to make —** pasar visita, visitar diariamente a los pacientes hospitalizados
round-the-clock *adj & adv* a todas horas, las 24 horas del día

roundworm *n* nemátodo, nematodo (*RAE*), filo de gusanos que incluye algunos que pueden infestar a los seres humanos

rouse *vt* despertar

route *n* vía; — **of administration** vía de administración

routine *adj* rutinario; *n* rutina; **daily —** rutina diaria *or* cotidiana

Roux-en-Y, Y de Roux; **Roux-en-Y gastric bypass** bypass gástrico en Y de Roux, derivación gástrica en Y de Roux

rub *vt* (*pret & pp* **rubbed**; *ger* **rubbing**) frotar; (*to massage*) masajear; (*to chafe*) rozar; *vi* rozar

rubber *n* goma, caucho, hule *m*; (*fam, condom*) condón *m*, preservativo

rubella *n* rubéola *or* rubeola, sarampión *m* alemán

rubeola *n* (*form*) sarampión *m*

rule *n* regla; *vt* **to — out** descartar; **Cancer was ruled out**..Se descartó el cáncer.

rum *n* ron *m*

rumination *n* (*psych*) rumiación *f*

run *vi* (*pret* **ran**; *pp* **run**; *ger* **running**) correr; **My nose is running**..Tengo mucosidad..Tengo flujo nasal..Tengo escurrimiento nasal (*esp. Mex*); **to — in one's family** venir de familia; **to — out** acabarse; **When did your medicine run out?**..¿Cuándo se le acabó la medicina?; **to — over** atropellar, arrollar

runaway *n* niño -ña *mf* que ha abandonado el hogar

run-down *adj* debilitado, decaído, agotado

runny *adj* (*comp* **-nier**; *super* **-niest**) líquido, de consistencia líquida; **to have a — nose** tener mucosidad, tener secreción nasal (*form*), tener flujo nasal, tener escurrimiento nasal (*esp. Mex*)

runs, the (*fam*) diarrea

rupture *n* ruptura, rotura; **premature — of membranes** ruptura *or* rotura prematura de membranas; *vt, vi* reventar(se); **ruptured appendix** apéndice perforado

rural *adj* rural

rusty *adj* oxidado; — **nail** clavo oxidado

rutin *n* (*bot*) rutina

Rx *n* receta

S

sac *n* (*anat*) saco

saccharin *n* sacarina

sacra *pl de* **sacrum**

sacral *adj* sacro

sacroiliac *adj* sacroilíaco *or* sacroiliaco

sacrum *n* (*pl* **-cra**) sacro

sad *adj* (*comp* **sadder**; *super* **saddest**) triste

sadism *n* sadismo

sadist *n* sádico -ca *mf*

sadistic *adj* sádico

sadness *n* tristeza

sadomasochism *n* sadomasoquismo

sadomasochist *n* sadomasoquista *mf*

sadomasochistic *adj* sadomasoquista

safe *adj* seguro, sin riesgo

safety *n* seguridad *f*

safety pin imperdible *m*

sag *vi* (*pret & pp* **sagged**; *ger* **sagging**) caerse; **sagging breasts** pechos *or* senos caídos

sage *n* (*bot*) salvia

salad *n* ensalada
salbutamol *n* salbutamol *m*
salicylate *n* salicilato
salicylic acid *n* ácido salicílico
saline *adj* salino
saliva *n* saliva
salivary *adj* salival
salivate *vi* salivar
salivation *n* salivación *f*
salmeterol *n* salmeterol *m*
salmonellosis *n* salmonelosis *f*
salpingitis *n* salpingitis *f*
salpingo-oophorectomy *n* (*pl* -mies) salpingooforectomía *or* salpingo-ooforectomía
salsalate *n* salsalato
salt *n* sal *f*; **Epsom —** sal de Epsom; **iodized —** sal yodada; **oral rehydration salts** sales de rehidratación oral; **— substitute** sustituto de (la) sal; **smelling salts** carbonato de amonio, carbonato amónico (*esp. Esp*) (*que se utiliza para reanimar a un desmayado*)
salted *adj* salado, que tiene sal
saltine *n* galleta salada
salty *adj* salado
salvage *adj* de rescate; **— therapy** terapia *or* tratamiento de rescate; *n* rescate *m*, salvamento; *vt* rescatar, salvar
salve *n* ungüento, pomada
sample *n* muestra
sanatorium *n* (*ant*) sanatorio (*ant*)
sandfly *n* (*pl* -flies) flebótomo, tipo de jején cuya picadura puede transmitir el protozoo que causa leishmaniasis
sane *adj* cuerdo
sanitary *adj* (*clean, hygienic*) higiénico; (*pertaining to sanitation*) sanitario; **— pad** *o* **napkin** toalla sanitaria *or* femenina
sanitation *n* saneamiento (ambiental), sanidad *f*, medidas sanitarias
sanitizer *n* desinfectante *m*; **hand —** desinfectante para manos
sanity *n* cordura
saphenous *adj* safeno
saquinavir *n* saquinavir *m*
sarcoidosis *n* sarcoidosis *f*
sarcoma *n* sarcoma *m*; **Ewing —** sarcoma de Ewing; **Kaposi —** sarcoma de Kaposi
sarin *n* sarín *m*
SARS *abbr* **severe acute respiratory**

syndrome. *V.* **syndrome.**
sarsaparilla *n* (*bot*) zarzaparrilla
sassafras *n* (*bot*) sasafrás *m*
sat *pret & pp de* **sit**
satiety *n* saciedad *f*; **early —** saciedad precoz *or* temprana
saturate *vt* saturar
saturation *n* saturación *f*; **oxygen —** saturación de oxígeno
sauna *n* sauna *m&f*; [*Note: The RAE lists* sauna *as feminine, but masculine usage is common.*]
save *vt* salvar; **We want to save your leg** ..Queremos salvar su pierna.
saw *pret de* **see**
saw palmetto *n* (*bot*) palma enana americana
saxagliptin *n* saxagliptina
scab *n* costra
scabies *n* sarna, escabiosis *f* (*form*); **Norwegian —** sarna noruega
scald *n* escaldadura; *vt* escaldar; **to — oneself** escaldarse
scale *n* escala; (*for weighing*) balanza, báscula; (*piece of skin*) escama; **pain —** escala del dolor; **sliding —** (*payment, insulin*) escala móvil (*honorarios, insulina*); *vt* (*dent*) limpiar (*los dientes*) quitando el sarro
scaling *n* (*derm*) descamación *f*; (*dent*) limpieza, eliminación *f* del sarro
scalp *n* cuero cabelludo
scalpel *n* bisturí *m*, escalpelo
scaly *adj* (*comp* -ier; *super* -iest) escamoso
scan *n* estudio por imagen utilizando diversas técnicas como la tomografía, la resonancia magnética y la gammagrafía; **bone —** gammagrafía ósea; **CT** *o* **CAT —** tomografía computarizada, TC *m&f*, TAC *m&f*; **gallium —** gammagrafía con galio; **nuclear —** gammagrafía; **PET —** tomografía por emisión de positrones, PET *m&f*; **PET-CT — PET-CT** *m*; **thallium —** gammagrafía con talio; *vt* (*pret & pp* **scanned**; *ger* **scanning**) escanear (*Ang*); realizar un estudio por imagen utilizando tomografía, resonancia magnética o gammagrafía; [*Note: Because* tomografía *is feminine,* TAC, TC, PET, *and* PET-CT *should be feminine also, but they are often treated as masculine, in particu-*

lar PET-CT, *which is almost always treated as masculine.*]

scanner *n* escáner *m* (*Ang*), aparato que obtiene imágenes del cuerpo utilizando ondas electromagnéticas; **CT** — tomógrafo; **MRI** — resonador magnético

scapula *n* (*pl* **-lae**) omóplato *or* omoplato, escápula

scar *n* cicatriz *f*; **to leave a** — dejar cicatriz

scare *n* susto

scarlatina *n* escarlatina

scarring *adj* que deja cicatriz; *n* cicatrización *f*, cicatrices *fpl*

schedule *n* horario; **vaccination** — esquema *m or* calendario de vacunación, calendario vacunal (*esp. Esp*); *vt* (*an appointment, surgery, etc.*) programar (*una cita, una cirugía, etc.*)

schistosomiasis *n* esquistosomiasis *f*

schizoaffective *adj* esquizoafectivo

schizophrenia *n* esquizofrenia; **paranoid** — esquizofrenia paranoide

schizophrenic *adj & n* esquizofrénico -ca *mf*

school *n* escuela; **medical** — facultad *f or* escuela de medicina

schwannoma *n* schwannoma *m*; **vestibular** — schwannoma vestibular

sciatic *adj* ciático

sciatica *n* ciática

scientific *adj* científico

scientist *n* científico -ca *mf*

scissors *npl* tijeras; **a pair of scissors..** unas tijeras; **bandage** — tijeras para vendajes; **nail** — tijeras de *or* para uñas

sclera *n* (*pl* **-rae**) esclerótica

scleritis *n* escleritis *f*

scleroderma *n* esclerodermia, esclerosis sistémica progresiva; **localized** — esclerodermia localizada

sclerosing *adj* esclerosante

sclerosis *n* esclerosis *f*; **amyotrophic lateral** — esclerosis lateral amiotrófica; **multiple** — esclerosis múltiple; **progressive systemic** — esclerosis sistémica progresiva; **tuberous** — esclerosis tuberosa

sclerotherapy *n* escleroterapia

sclerotic *adj* esclerótico

scoliosis *n* escoliosis *f*

scooter *n* scooter *m*; **mobility** — scooter

para discapacitados

scopolamine *n* escopolamina, hyoscina (*INN*)

score *n* puntuación *f*, puntaje *m*, índice *m*; **Apgar** — puntaje de Apgar, índice de Apgar (*esp. Esp*); **coronary artery calcium** — puntaje de calcio arterial coronario, puntuación de calcio en arterias coronarias; **Gleason** — puntuación *or* puntaje de Gleason; **T-score** puntuación T; **Z-score** puntuación Z

scored *adj* (*pharm*) ranurado

scorpion *n* alacrán *m* (*esp. Amer*), escorpión *m*

scrape *n* (*fam*) abrasión *f*, raspadura; *vt* raspar

scratch *n* rasguño, (*by claws*) arañazo; *vt* rasguñar, arañar; (*an itch, etc.*) rascarse; **You have to quit scratching..**Tiene que dejar de rascarse.

screen *n* (*screening test*) prueba de detección; *vt, vi* realizar pruebas de detección, realizar exámenes en personas que no tienen síntomas para detectar enfermedades ocultas; **We need to screen everyone over 50 for colon cancer..**Tenemos que realizar pruebas de detección para cáncer de colon a todos los pacientes mayores de 50 años.

screening *n* cribado (*form*), tamizaje *m* (*form*), realización *f* de exámenes de detección; **cancer** — cribado *or* tamizaje del cáncer, detección *f* del cáncer (*en personas sin síntomas, usando examenes*)

screw *n* (*ortho*) tornillo

script (*fam*) *V.* **prescription.**

scrofula *n* escrófula

scrotal *adj* escrotal

scrotum *n* escroto

scurvy *n* escorbuto

seal *vt* (*dent, etc.*) sellar

sealant *n* (*dent, etc.*) sellador *m*

seasickness *n* mareo (en barco), mal *m* de mar

season *n* (*winter, spring, etc.*) estación *f*; (*for a disease, etc.*) temporada; **flu** — temporada gripal *or* de la gripe

seasonal *adj* estacional

seat *n* asiento, silla; **Have a seat..**Siéntese..Tome asiento; **child car** — asiento de seguridad infantil (*para vehículo*), silla de coche para niño (*Esp*); — **belt**

cinturón *m* de seguridad, cinturón (*fam*); **shower** — silla *or* asiento de ducha

sea urchin *n* erizo de mar

sebaceous *adj* sebáceo

seborrhea *n* seborrea

seborrheic *adj* seborreico

sebum *n* sebo

second *adj* segundo; *n* segundo

secondary *adj* secundario

secretary *n* (*pl* **-ries**) secretario -ria *mf*

secrete *vt* secretar, segregar (*form*)

secretion *n* secreción *f*

secretory *adj* secretorio

section *n* sección *f*; **frozen** — biopsia por congelación

sedate *vt* sedar, tranquilizar

sedation *n* sedación *f*; **conscious** — sedación consciente

sedative *adj* & *n* sedante *m*

sedentary *adj* sedentario

sediment *n* sedimento

see *vt*, *vi* (*pret* **saw**; *pp* **seen**) ver; **to see a doctor**..consultar a un médico; **When was the last time you saw an eye doctor?**..¿Cuándo fue la última vez que consultó a un médico de los ojos?

seek *vt* buscar; **to seek medical attention**..buscar atención médica..acudir al médico

seen *pp de* **see**

segment *n* segmento

seize *vi* convulsionar, tener una convulsión, tener convulsiones

seizure *n* crisis (epiléptica), convulsión *f*, ataque (epiléptico); **absence** — crisis de ausencia; **complex partial** — crisis parcial compleja; **febrile** — convulsión febril; **focal** — (*ant*) crisis parcial; **generalized** — crisis generalizada; **gran mal** — (*ant*) crisis *or* convulsión tónico-clónica; **partial** — crisis parcial; **petit mal** — (*ant*) crisis de ausencia; **psychomotor** *o* **temporal lobe** — (*ant*) crisis parcial compleja; **tonic-clonic** — crisis *or* convulsión tónico-clónica

selective *adj* selectivo

selegiline *n* selegilina

selenium *n* selenio

self-absorbed *adj* ensimismado, absorto en uno mismo

self-awareness *n* autoconocimiento, autoconsciencia, autoconciencia

self-catheterization *n* autosondaje *m*, colocación *f* de una sonda en la vejiga por uno mismo, uso por uno mismo de una sonda para vaciar la vejiga

self-centered *adj* egocéntrico

self-confidence *n* autoconfianza, confianza en uno mismo

self-conscious *adj* cohibido, preocupado por lo que los demás puedan pensar de uno

self-control *n* autocontrol *m*, control *m* de los propios impulsos y reacciones

self-destructive *adj* autodestructivo

self-discipline *n* autodisciplina

self-esteem *n* autoestima

self-examination *n* autoexploración *f* (*form*), autoexamen *m*

self-fulfilling prophecy *n* profecía autocumplida

self-help *n* autoayuda

self-image *n* autoimagen *f*

self-inflicted *adj* autoinfligido, causado por uno mismo

self-limited *adj* (*disease*) autolimitado, que se resuelve solo

self-medicate *vi* automedicarse, tomar un medicamento sin indicación por un médico

self-prescribe *vt* autorrecetarse, automedicarse

self-realization *n* autorrealización *f*

self-respect *n* autorrespeto, respeto hacia uno mismo

self-treatment *n* autotratamiento

semen *n* semen *m*, esperma *m&f*

semicircular canal *n* canal *m or* conducto semicircular

seminal *adj* seminal

seminoma *n* seminoma *m*

semi-rigid *adj* semirrígido

senile *adj* senil

senior citizen *n* (*US*) persona de edad avanzada, persona que recibe ciertos derechos debido a su edad mayor

senna *n* (*bot*) sen *m*

sensation *n* sensación *f*, sensibilidad *f*; **light touch** — sensibilidad táctil; — **of pain** sensación de dolor

sense *n* sentido; — **of balance** sentido de(l) equilibrio; — **of hearing** sentido del oído *or* de la audición; — **of hu-**

mor sentido del humor; — **of sight** sentido de la vista; — **of smell** sentido del olfato; — **of taste** sentido del gusto; — **of touch** sentido del tacto

sensitive *adj* sensible; *(person, empathetic)* sensible; *(person, easily hurt)* susceptible; *(subject, delicate)* delicado; **a test sensitive for**..una prueba sensible para...**sensitive to her needs**.. sensible a sus necesidades...**He's so sensitive**..Es tan susceptible...**a sensitive subject**..un tema delicado

sensitivity *n* *(pl* **-ties)** sensibilidad *f*

sensitize *vt* sensibilizar; **to become sensitized** sensibilizarse

sensory *adj* sensitivo, sensorial

sentinel *adj (node, event, etc.)* centinela

separate *adj* separado; *vt* separar

separation *n* separación *f*; *(couple)* separación, ruptura

sepsis *n* sepsis *f*

septa *pl de* **septum**

septic *adj* séptico

septicemia *n* septicemia

septoplasty *n* *(pl* **-ties)** septoplastia

septum *n* *(pl* **-ta)** tabique *m*; **deviated —** tabique desviado; **interatrial —** tabique interauricular; **interventricular —** tabique interventricular; **nasal —** tabique nasal

sera *pl de* **serum**

serial *adj* seriado

series *n* *(pl* **series)** serie *f*

serine *n* serina

serious *adj (illness, condition)* grave, serio; *(person)* serio

seroconversion *n* seroconversión *f*

serologic, serological *adj* serológico

serology *n* *(pl* **-gies)** serología

seronegative *adj* seronegativo

seropositive *adj* seropositivo

serotonin *n* serotonina

serotype *n* serotipo

sertaconazole *n* sertaconazol *m*

sertraline *n* sertralina

serum *adj* sérico; — **sodium** sodio sérico; *n* *(pl* **sera)** suero

service *n* *(frec. pl)* servicio *(frec. pl)*; **emergency services** servicios de emergencia; **medical services** servicios médicos; **social services** servicios sociales

serving *n* porción *f*, ración *f*; **amount per —** cantidad *f* por porción; **servings per container** porciones por envase; — **size** tamaño de porción

set *vt (pret & pp* **set**; *ger* **setting)** *(a fracture)* reducir *(una fractura)*

setting *n* contexto; **in the setting of renal insufficiency**..en el contexto de insuficiencia renal

sevelamer *n* sevelámero

sever *vt* cortar completamente *(p. ej., una arteria)*

severe *adj* severo

severity *n* severidad *f*, gravedad *f*, *(pain)* intensidad *f*

sew *vt (pp* **sewn)** *(fam, to suture)* suturar, coser *(fam)*

sewage *n* aguas negras, *(wastewater)* aguas residuales

sex *n* sexo, relaciones *fpl* sexuales; **oral —** sexo oral; **safe —** sexo seguro, sexo sin riesgo de infección; **to have —** tener relaciones (sexuales), tener sexo

sexology *n* sexología

sexual *adj* sexual

sexuality *n* sexualidad *f*

shaft *n (hair, penis)* tallo

shake *vt (pret* **shook**; *pp* **shaken)** agitar, sacudir; **Shake well before using**.. Agíte(se) bien antes de usar...**You shouldn't shake your child**..No debe sacudir a su niño...**Shake your head to say no**..Mueva la cabeza de lado a lado para decir no; *vi (to tremble)* temblar

shakes, the *(fam)* temblores *mpl*

shaky *adj (fam)* tembloroso

shaman *n* chamán -mana *mf*, brujo -ja *mf*

shame *n* vergüenza

shampoo *n* *(pl* **-poos)** champú *m*; *vt, vi (pret & pp* **-pooed)** lavarse (el pelo)

shape *n* forma; *(condition)* condición *f*, estado; **in —** en forma; **to keep in —** mantenerse en forma

shaping *n (psych)* moldeamiento

share *n* parte *f*; — **of cost** *(US)* parte del costo *(que tiene que pagar el paciente)*; *vt* compartir; **shared decision making**..toma de decisiones compartida; **to — needles** compartir agujas

shark *n* tiburón *m*

sharp *adj (pain)* agudo; *(object)* punzante; **Sharp or dull?** *(neuro exam)*.. ¿Agudo o sordo?..¿Pincha o no?; — **object** objeto punzante; *n (fam)* objeto

punzante; **sharps container** contenedor *m* de objetos punzantes
shave *vt, vi* afeitar(se)
shaver *n* (*también* **electric —**) *V.* **electric razor** *bajo* **razor.**
shaving cream *n* crema *or* espuma de afeitar
sheath *n* vaina; **nerve —** vaina nerviosa *or* del nervio
shed *vt* (*pret & pp* **shed**; *ger* **shedding**) (*viruses, parasites, etc.*) excretar, secretar, liberar, esparcir
sheepskin *n* piel *f* de cordero *or* oveja
sheet *n* (*bed*) sábana
shellfish *n* (*pl* **-fish** *o* **-fishes**) marisco
shell shock *n* (*ant*) trastorno de estrés postraumático (TEPT), neurosis *f* de guerra (*ant*)
shelter *n* refugio, albergue *m*, centro de acogida (*Esp*); **battered women's —** refugio *or* albergue para mujeres maltratadas; **homeless —** refugio *or* albergue para personas sin hogar; **women's —** refugio *or* albergue para mujeres
shigellosis *n* shigelosis *f*
shin *n* espinilla; **— splints** síndrome *m* de estrés de la tibia medial, dolor *m* de espinilla debido a ejercicio excesivo
shinbone *n* tibia (*form*), espinilla, canilla
shingles *n* herpes zóster, culebrilla (*fam*), zona *m* (*fam*)
shirt *n* camisa
shiver *n* escalofrío; *vi* tiritar, temblar (*de frío o miedo*)
shock *n* choque *m*, shock *m* (*Ang*); **anaphylactic —** choque *or* shock anafiláctico; **cardiogenic —** choque *or* shock cardiogénico; **electric —** descarga eléctrica, choque *or* shock eléctrico; **hypovolemic —** choque *or* shock hipovolémico; **neurogenic —** choque *or* shock neurogénico; **septic —** choque *or* shock séptico
shoe *n* zapato; **orthopedic shoes** zapatos ortopédicos
shook *pret de* **shake**
shoot *vt* (*pret & pp* **shot**) (*a gun*) disparar; **to be shot**..recibir un disparo *or* balazo; **He was shot in the leg**..Recibió un disparo (balazo) en la pierna; **to — up** (*fam*) inyectarse (*drogas*)
shooting *adj* (*pain*) punzante
short *adj* (*stature*) bajo; (*dimension*)

corto; (*time*) breve, corto; **short-acting** de acción corta; **to be — of breath** *V.* **breath.**
shortness *V.* **breath.**
short-term *adj* a *or* de corto plazo
shot *n* (*fam*) inyección *f*
shot *pret & pp de* **shoot**
shoulder *n* hombro; **frozen —** hombro congelado; **— blade** (*fam*) omóplato *or* omoplato, escápula
show *vt* mostrar, enseñar; **Show me your feet**..Muéstreme sus pies.
shower *n* ducha; **to take a —** ducharse, darse *or* tomar una ducha
shrank *pret de* **shrink**
shrapnel *n* metralla
shrimp *n* camarón *m*
shrink *n* (*fam*) psiquiatra *mf*; *vt, vi* (*pret* **shrank**; *pp* **shrunk**) (*tumor, etc.*) encoger(se), achicar(se)
shrug *vt* (*pret & pp* **shrugged**; *ger* **shrugging**) **to — one's shoulders** (*part of neuro exam*) elevar los hombros
shrunk *pp de* **shrink**
shunt *n* (*physio*) cortocircuito; (*surg*) derivación *f*; **arteriovenous —** cortocircuito arteriovenoso; **portacaval —** derivación portocava; **transjugular intrahepatic portosystemic — (TIPS)** derivación portosistémica percutánea intrahepática, derivación intrahepática portosistémica transyugular; **ventriculoperitoneal —** derivación ventriculoperitoneal
shut-in *n* persona que no puede salir del hogar (*por enfermedad o discapacidad*)
shy *adj* tímido
shyness *n* timidez *f*, retraimiento
sialoadenitis *n* sialoadenitis *f*
sibling *n* hermano -na *mf*; *npl* hermanos
sibutramine *n* sibutramina
sick *adj* enfermo; **— person** enfermo -ma *mf*; **to get —** enfermarse
sickbed *n* lecho (de enfermo)
sickly *adj* (*comp* **-lier**; *super* **-liest**) enfermizo
sickness *n* enfermedad *f*, mal *m*; **altitude —** mal de altura, mal de montaña, soroche *m* (*SA*); **decompression —** enfermedad por descompresión; **morning —** náuseas matutinas (*form*), náuseas

or vómitos del embarazo; **motion —** mareo (producido por el movimiento); **radiation —** enfermedad por radiación; **serum —** enfermedad del suero; **sleeping —** enfermedad del sueño

side *n* lado, (*anat*) costado; **on your father's side**..por el lado de su padre; **to sleep on one's —** dormir de lado *or* costado

siderail *n* (*of a bed*) barandilla, baranda

SIDS *abbr* **sudden infant death syndrome.** *V.* **syndrome.**

sieve *n* (*for urine*) colador *m*

sievert *n* (*rad*) sievert *m*

sigh *n* suspiro; *vi* suspirar

sight *n* vista

sighted *adj* que puede ver

sigmoid *adj* sigmoide *or* sigmoideo

sigmoidoscope *n* sigmoidoscopio

sigmoidoscopy *n* (*pl* -**pies**) sigmoidoscopia; **flexible —** sigmoidoscopia flexible

sign *n* (*of an illness*) signo; **— language** lenguaje *m* *or* lengua de señas *or* signos; **vital signs** constantes *fpl or* signos vitales; **warning —** señal *f* de advertencia *or* alerta; *vt, vi* (*one's name*) firmar; (*deaf language*) comunicarse mediante el lenguaje de señas (lengua de señas, etc.)

signature *n* firma

significance *n* significado

significant *adj* significativo; **— other** (*ant*) pareja, compañero -ra *mf or* pareja sentimental

sildenafil *n* sildenafil *m*, sildenafilo (*INN*)

silica *n* sílice *m*

silicone *n* silicona

silicosis *n* silicosis *f*

silk *n* seda

silodosin *n* silodosina

silver *n* plata; **— nitrate** nitrato de plata; **— sulfadiazine** sulfadiazina de plata

silymarin *n* silimarina

simeprevir *n* simeprevir *m*

simethicone, simeticone (*INN*) *n* simeticona

simvastatin *n* simvastatina

since *adv* desde; **since you were injured** ..desde que se lesionó; *prep* desde; **since your last visit**..desde su última visita

single *adj* (*unmarried*) soltero

sinoatrial *adj* sinoauricular

sinus *n* (*paranasal*) seno; (*pilonidal*); seno *or* sinus *m*; **ethmoid —** seno etmoidal; **frontal —** seno frontal; **maxillary —** seno maxilar; **paranasal —** seno paranasal; **pilonidal —** seno *or* sinus pilonidal; **sphenoid —** seno esfenoidal; **— tract** tracto sinusal

sinusitis *n* sinusitis *f*

sip *n* sorbo; **sip of water**..sorbo de agua; *vt* (*pret & pp* **sipped;** *ger* **sipping**) sorber

sirolimus *n* sirolimus *m*, sirolimús *m* (*INN*)

sister *n* hermana

sister-in-law *n* (*pl* **sisters-in-law**) cuñada

sit *vi* (*pret & pp* **sat;** *ger* **sitting**) sentarse; (*to remain seated*) quedarse sentado; **You shouldn't sit for long periods of time**..No debe quedarse sentado por períodos prolongados; **to — down** sentarse; **to — up** (*from a supine position*) sentarse, incorporarse (*de una posición supina*)

sitagliptin *n* sitagliptina

site *n* sitio; **surgical —** sitio quirúrgico

sit-up *n* ejercicio abdominal, abdominal *m* (*fam*)

size *n* tamaño

skeletal *adj* esquelético

skeleton *n* esqueleto

skiing *n* esquí *m*, (el) esquiar

skill *n* habilidad *f*, destreza; **communication skills** habilidades comunicativas *or* de comunicación; **coping skills** habilidades de afrontamiento; **social skills** habilidades sociales

skin *adj* dérmico; *n* piel *f*; (*of the face*) cutis *m*, tez *f*; (*of fruit*) piel; *vt* (*pret & pp* **skinned;** *ger* **skinning**) (*to scrape*) raspar; **How did you skin your knee?** ..¿Cómo se raspó la rodilla?

skin popping *n* (*fam*) inyección subcutánea (*form*), inyección bajo la piel (*de drogas*)

skin tag *n* (*derm*) acrocordón *m* (*form*), pequeño tumor benigno de la piel que tiende a ocurrir en el cuello y en las axilas

skip *vt* (*pret & pp* **skipped;** *ger* **skipping**) saltarse; **to — a beat** saltarse un latido; **My heart skipped a beat**..Mi corazón se saltó un latido; **to — a meal** saltarse una comida; **Don't skip breakfast**..No se salte el desayuno.

skirt *n* falda

skull *n* cráneo

skullcap *n* (*bot*) escutelaria

skunk *n* zorrillo, mofeta (*esp. Esp*)

slam *vt* (*pret & pp* **slammed**; *ger* **slamming**) (*fam, drugs*) inyectarse (*drogas*)

slash *vt* cortar; **to slash one's wrists**.. cortarse las venas

SLE *abbr* **systemic lupus erythematosus.** *V.* **lupus.**

sleep *n* sueño; (*eye secretions*) legaña, lagaña (*Amer*); — **apnea** apnea del sueño; **to go to** — dormirse, quedarse dormido; **Do you have trouble going to sleep?**..¿Tiene dificultad para dormirse (quedarse dormido)?...**Does your arm go to sleep?**..¿Se le duerme el brazo?; **to go without** — ir sin dormir, trasnochar, desvelarse; **to put to** — (*to anesthetize*) anestesiar (*form*), dormir; **We will put you to sleep for the operation**..Lo vamos a anestesiar (dormir) para la operación; *vi* (*pret & pp* **slept**) dormir

sleeper (*fam*) *V.* **sleeping pill.**

sleepiness *n* somnolencia

sleeping pill *n* somnífero (*form*), pastilla para dormir

sleepwalk *vi* caminar dormido

sleepwalking *n* sonambulismo (*form*), (el) caminar dormido

sleepy *adj* (*comp* **-ier**; *super* **-iest**) que tiene sueño, somnoliento (*form*); **to be** — tener sueño; **to make** — dar sueño; **This medicine may make you sleepy**.. Este medicamento le puede dar sueño.

sleeve *n* manga; **long-sleeve shirt**..camisa de manga larga

slept *pret & pp de* **sleep**

sliding *adj* (*hernia*) deslizante; — **scale** (*payment, insulin*) escala móvil (*honorarios, insulina*)

slight *adj* leve, ligero

sling *n* cabestrillo

slip *n* resbalón *m*; **Freudian** — lapsus freudiano; *vi* (*pret & pp* **slipped**; *ger* **slipping**) resbalar(se)

slippery elm *n* (*bot*) olmo americano

sliver *n* astilla

slouch *vi* sentarse o pararse con mala postura

slough *vi* (*también* **to — off**) desprenderse, caerse

slow *adj* lento

slur *vt* (*pret & pp* **slurred**; *ger* **slurring**) **to — one's words** *o* **speech** arrastrar las palabras, tener dificultad para articular palabras

small *adj* pequeño, chico; **to get smaller** (*tumor, etc.*) encogerse, achicarse; *n* — **of the back** parte baja de la espalda

smallpox *n* viruela

smart *adj* inteligente, listo; *vi* doler, arder

smarting *n* dolor *m*, ardor *m*, quemazón *f*, escozor *m*

smear *n* (*micro*) frotis *m*; **blood** — frotis de sangre; **Papanicolaou** — (*form*), **Pap** — citología cervical *or* exfoliativa (*form*), citología (*fam*), prueba de Papanicolaou, prueba que se hace durante el examen pélvico con el fin de detectar cáncer cervical

smegma *n* esmegma *m*

smell *n* olor *m*; *vt* oler; **Can you smell this?**..¿Puede oler esto?; *vi* oler; **to — bad** oler mal; **to — like** oler a

smile *n* sonrisa; *vi* sonreír(se)

smog *n* esmog *m*, niebla tóxica

smoke *n* humo; **secondhand tobacco** — humo ambiental del tabaco, humo de tabaco de segunda mano; *vt, vi* fumar

smoke detector *n* detector *m* de humo

smoker *n* fumador -ra *mf*

smoking *n* tabaquismo, (el) fumar; **passive** — tabaquismo pasivo; **No smoking**..Prohibido fumar

smooth *adj* (*surface*) liso; (*skin, etc.*) suave, terso, liso; (*hair*) liso, suave; **to make (something)** — alisar (*algo*); *vt* (*dent, etc.*) alisar

smother *vt, vi* asfixiar(se) (*form*), ahogar(se)

snack *n* bocadillo, refrigerio, botana (*Mex*), algo que se come entre comidas; *vi* comer entre comidas, comer bocadillos

snail *n* caracol *m*

snake *n* serpiente *f*

sneeze *n* estornudo; *vi* estornudar; **You should sneeze into your elbow**..Debe estornudar en el codo.

sniff vt (*glue, etc.*) inhalar, esnifar (*Ang*) (*pegamento, etc.*); vi aspirar por la nariz

sniffle n acto de sorber(se) los mocos; **to have the sniffles** (*fam*) tener mucosidad, tener secreción nasal (*form*), tener flujo nasal, tener escurrimiento nasal (*esp. Mex*); vi sorber(se) los mocos

snore vi roncar

snoring n ronquido (*frec. pl*), (el) roncar

snort vt (*cocaine, etc.*) inhalar, esnifar (*Ang*), aspirar (*cocaína, etc.*)

snot n (*vulg*) mucosidad f (*form*), mocos

snuff n (*tobacco*) rapé m, tabaco para inhalar

soak n remojar, sumergir en agua (*por un período prolongado*)

soap n jabón m

sober adj sobrio; vi **to — up** (*from an intoxication*) recuperar la sobriedad; (*lifestyle change*) dejar el alcohol, dejar de tomar; vt **to sober (one) up** bajar(le) la borrachera

sobriety n sobriedad f

soccer n fútbol or futbol m

social adj social

socioeconomic adj socioeconómico

sock n calcetín m

socket n (*dent*) alvéolo or alveolo; (*ortho*) cavidad f de un hueso en que encaja otro; **eye —** cuenca ocular or del ojo; **hip —** acetábulo

sodium n sodio; **— benzoate** benzoato sódico or de sodio; **— bicarbonate** bicarbonato sódico or de sodio; **— chloride** cloruro sódico or de sodio; **— fluoride** fluoruro sódico or de sodio; **— hydroxide** hidróxido sódico or de sodio; **— lauryl sulfate** lauril sulfato de sodio; **— stibogluconate** estibogluconato de sodio

sodomize vt sodomizar

sodomy n sodomía

sofosbuvir n sofosbuvir m

soft adj (*not hard*) blando, (*not rough*) suave; **— water** agua blanda

soft drink n refresco

soften vt (*make less hard*) ablandar, (*make smoother*) suavizar

softening adj (*lotion, etc.*) suavizante

soil vt ensuciar; **to — oneself** ensuciarse

solar adj solar

soldier n soldado mf

sole n (*of the foot*) planta; (*of a shoe*) suela

soleus n sóleo

solid adj & n sólido

solifenacin n solifenacina

soluble adj soluble

solution n solución f; **buffer —** solución tampón, solución amortiguadora; **electrolyte —** suero fisiológico, solución electrolítica; **normal saline —** solución salina normal, suero (*fam*); **oral rehydration —** solución or suero de rehidratación oral

solvent n solvente m, disolvente m (*Esp*)

somatic adj somático

somatization n somatización f

somatotropin n somatotropina

somatropin n somatropina

somnolence n somnolencia

somnolent adj somnoliento, que tiene sueño

son n hijo

son-in-law n (*pl* sons-in-law) yerno

sonogram n sonograma m, sonografía (*estudio*)

sonography V. ultrasonography.

soon adv pronto

soothe vt aliviar, calmar

sorbitol n sorbitol m

sore adj dolorido, adolorido (*Amer*); **— throat** dolor m de garganta; n llaga, herida, úlcera; **pressure —** úlcera de decúbito (*form*), úlcera por presión, llaga debida a permanecer mucho tiempo sentado o encamado sin cambiar de posición

sorry adj **to be —** sentir, lamentar; **I'm sorry you had to wait so long**..Lamento (Siento) que haya tenido que esperar tanto tiempo...**I'm sorry**..Lo siento.

sotalol n sotalol m

soul n alma

sound n sonido, ruido; **bowel sounds** ruidos or sonidos intestinales; **heart sounds** ruidos or sonidos cardíacos

soup n sopa, (*broth-based, without cream*) caldo

sour adj agrio

source n fuente f, origen m; **— of infection** fuente de infección; **— of protein** fuente de proteínas

soy n soja or soya

spa *n* spa *m*, balneario; **medical —, med — (***fam***)** spa médico

space *n* espacio; **web —** espacio entre los dedos

spaced out *adj* (*fam*) ido, distraído, drogado

spacer *n* (*for metered-dose inhaler*) cámara espaciadora

spacey *adj* (*fam*) distraído, olvidadizo

span *n* (*distance*) envergadura; (*time*) período *or* periodo; **arm —** envergadura de brazos; **attention —** período de atención

spare *vt* conservar, preservar; **limb-sparing** conservador del miembro; **nerve-sparing** conservador de nervios; **valve-sparing** conservador de la válvula

spasm *n* espasmo

spasmodic *adj* espasmódico

spastic *adj* espástico

spasticity *n* espasticidad *f*

spat *pret & pp de* **spit**

spatial *adj* espacial

speak *vt, vi* (*pret* **spoke**; *pp* **spoken**) hablar

spearmint *n* (*bot*) hierbabuena, menta verde

specialist *n* especialista *mf*; **heart (liver, etc.) —** especialista del corazón (hígado, etc.); **infectious disease —** infectólogo -ga *mf*, especialista *mf* en enfermedades infecciosas; **— in allergies (immunology, etc.)** especialista en alergias (inmunología, etc.)

specialty *n* (*pl* **-ties**) especialidad *f*

species *n* (*pl* **-cies**) especie *f*

specific *adj* específico; **a test specific for..**una prueba específica para

specimen *n* espécimen *m*, muestra

spectinomycin *n* espectinomicina

spectrum *n* (*pl* **-tra**) espectro

speculum *n* (*pl* **-la** *o* **-lums**) espéculo

speech *n* habla; **esophageal —** habla esofágica; **— development** desarrollo del habla; **pressured —** habla apresurada, presión *f* del habla

speed *n* (*fam*) metanfetamina

spell *n* episodio, ataque *m*, acceso

spell *vt* deletrear; **Can you spell the word 'world' backwards?..**¿Puede deletrear la palabra 'mundo' al revés?

sperm *n* (*individual spermatozoon*) espermatozoide *m*; (*semen*) semen *m*, esperma *m&f*

spermatocele *n* espermatocele *m*

spermatozoon (*pl* **-zoa**) *n* espermatozoide *m*

spermicidal *adj* espermicida

spermicide *n* espermicida *m*

SPF *abbr* **sun protection factor**. *V.* **factor**.

sphenoid *adj* esfenoidal

spherocytosis *n* esferocitosis *f*; **hereditary —** esferocitosis hereditaria

sphincter *n* esfínter *m*

sphincterotomy *n* (*pl* **-mies**) esfinterotomía

spice *n* especia, condimento

spicy *adj* (*comp* **-ier**; *super* **-iest**) condimentado, (*hot*) picante

spider *n* araña; (*derm, fam*) araña vascular; **brown recluse —** araña reclusa, araña violinista (*esp. Mex*)

spider angioma *n* araña vascular

spin *vi* (*pret & pp* **spun**; *ger* **spinning**) dar vueltas, girar; **Do you feel as though everything is spinning?..** ¿Siente que todo le da vueltas?

spina bifida *n* espina bífida

spinach *n* espinaca (*frec. pl*)

spinal *adj* espinal, raquídeo

spine *n* columna (vertebral); (*thorn*) espina; **cervical —** columna cervical; **lumbar —** columna lumbar; **lumbosacral —** columna lumbosacra; **thoracic —** columna dorsal *or* torácica

spinosad *n* spinosad *m*

spirits *n* (*morale*) ánimo, humor *m*

spiritual *adj* espiritual

spirochete *n* espiroqueta

spirometer *n* espirómetro; **incentive —** espirómetro incentivado

spirometry *n* espirometría; **incentive —** espirometría incentivada

spironolactone *n* espironolactona

spit *n* saliva; *vt, vi* (*pret & pp* **spat**; *ger* **spitting**) escupir; **to — (***something***) out** escupir (*algo*); **to — up** (*ped, fam*) regurgitar, devolverse(*le*) (*a uno*) la comida (*fam*)

spleen *n* bazo; **accessory —** bazo accesorio

splenectomy *n* (*pl* **-mies**) esplenectomía

splenic *adj* esplénico

splint *n* (*basic*) tablilla, (*manufactured, with straps, etc.*) férula; **cock-up —**

férula cock-up; **inflatable air** — férula inflable, férula hinchable (*esp. Esp*); **neutral wrist** — férula de muñeca en posición neutra; **spica** — espica de yeso; *vt* entablillar, colocar una tablilla en

splinter *n* astilla

split *adj* partido, agrietado; *n* grieta, hendidura; *vt, vi* (*pret & pp* **split**; *ger* **splitting**) partir(se), agrietar(se)

splitting *n* (*psych*) división *f*

spoil *vt* (*a child*) consentir, mimar; *vi* (*food, etc.*) echarse a perder

spoke *pret de* **speak**

spoken *pp de* **speak**

spokesperson *n* representante *mf*, vocero -ra *mf*; **We would like one family member to serve as spokesperson.**. Quisiéramos que un solo familiar haga de representante (vocero).

spondylolysis *n* espondilolisis *f*

spondylolysthesis *n* espondilolistesis *f*

spondylosis *n* espondilosis *f*

sponge *n* esponja

sponsor *n* (*AA, etc.*) patrocinador -ra *mf*

spontaneous *adj* espontáneo

spoonful *n* (*tablespoonful*) cucharada sopera *or* grande, cucharada, 15 ml; (*teaspoonful*) cucharadita, 5 ml

sporadic *adj* esporádico

spore *n* espora

sporotrichosis *n* esporotricosis *f*

sport *n* deporte *m*; **contact** — deporte de contacto; **to play sports** practicar *or* realizar deporte(s)

spot *n* mancha

spotting *n* (*gyn*) manchado, sangrado uterino leve (*que deja manchas en la ropa interior*)

spouse *n* esposo -sa *mf*

sprain *n* esguince *m* (*form*), torcedura; *vt* torcerse; **Did you sprain your ankle?** ..¿Se torció el tobillo?

spray *n* aerosol *m*, spray *m*, espray *m* (*RAE*), atomizador *m*; (*of an inhaler*) inhalación *f*, disparo; **hair** — laca (*para el peinado, en aerosol*); **nasal** — aerosol *or* spray nasal; **pepper** — aerosol *or* spray de pimienta, gas pimienta

spread *n* propagación *f*; (*from person to person*) transmisión *f*; (*within the body*) propagación, extensión *f*, diseminación *f*; *vt* (*pret & pp* **spread**) propagar; **to spread disease**..propagar en-

fermedades; *vi* propagarse; (*from person to person*) transmitirse; (*within the body*) propagarse, extenderse, diseminarse

spring *n* primavera

sprue *n* esprue *m*; **nontropical** *o* **celiac** — enfermedad celíaca *or* celiaca, celiaquía, esprue celíaco; **tropical** — esprue tropical

spun *pret & pp de* **spin**

spur *n* (*ortho*) espolón *m*; **bone** — espolón óseo; **calcaneal** — (*form*), **heel** — espolón calcáneo (*form*), espolón en el talón

spurt *V.* **growth**.

sputum *n* esputo, flema

squamous *adj* escamoso

square *adj* cuadrado; — **meter** metro cuadrado

squat *n* (*exercise*) sentadilla; *vi* (*pret & pp* **squatted**; *ger* **squatting**) ponerse en cuclillas

squeeze *vt* apretar; **Squeeze my fingers as hard as you can**..Apriete mis dedos lo más fuerte que pueda.

squint *vt, vi* entrecerrar, entornar (*los ojos*)

squirt *n* inhalación *f*, disparo; **one squirt in each nostril**..una inhalación (un disparo) en cada fosa nasal

stab *vt* acuchillar, apuñalar

stabbing *adj* (*pain*) punzante

stability *n* estabilidad *f*

stabilization *n* estabilización *f*

stabilize *vt, vi* estabilizar(se)

stabilizer *n* estabilizador *m*; **mood** — estabilizador del ánimo

stable *adj* estable

staff *n* personal *m*; **hospital** — personal del hospital

stage *n* (*disease, etc.*) estadio, etapa; (*cancer*) estadio; (*sleep*) etapa; (*puberty*) estadio

stagger *vi* tambalear(se)

staging *n* (*tumor*) estadificación *f*

stain *n* mancha; (*micro*) tinción *f*, coloración *f*; **Gram** — tinción *or* coloración de Gram; **port-wine** — hemangioma plano (*form*), mancha en vino de Oporto; *vt* manchar; **Smoking stains your teeth**..Fumar mancha los dientes.

stamina *n* resistencia

stammer *vi* tartamudear

stand (*pret & pp* **stood**) *vt* (*to endure*) aguantar, tolerar; *vi* (*to be standing*) estar de pie, estar parado; (*to stand up*) levantarse, pararse, ponerse de pie; **Avoid standing for long periods of time**..Evite estar de pie por períodos largos...**Now stand (up)**.. Ahora levántese.

standard *adj & n* estándar *m*, norma; **gold** — estándar de oro (*Ang*), prueba diagnóstica definitiva; — **of care** estándar *or* norma de atención *or* cuidado

standing *adj* de pie, parado; — **order** orden *f* permanente

stapedectomy *n* (*pl* -**mies**) estapedectomía

Staphylococcus aureus, staph (*fam*), Staphylococcus aureus, estafilococo; **methicillin-resistant** — — (**MRSA**) Staphylococcus aureus resistente a (la) meticilina (SARM)

staple *n* (*surg*) grapa

starch *n* almidón *m*

stare *vi* fijar la vista; **Stare at that point on the wall**..Fije la vista en ese punto en la pared.

starvation *n* inanición *f* (*form*), hambre *f*; **to die of starvation**..morir de hambre

starve *vi* pasar hambre; morir de hambre; *vt* privar de comida

stasis *n* estasis *f*, estancamiento; **venous** — estasis venosa, insuficiencia venosa; [*Note: estasis is often treated as masculine, but the feminine form is consistent with its etymological roots and is the only form accepted by the RAE.*]

state *n* estado, condición *f*; **hypercoagulable** — estado de hipercoagulabilidad; **state-of-the-art** de última generación, (*technology*) (de) punta; **steady** — estado estacionario

statin *n* estatina

station *n* estación *f*, control *m*, central *f*; **nursing** — control de enfermería (*esp. Esp*), estación de enfermería, central *f* de enfermería (*Mex*)

statistic *n* estadística (*cifra*); *npl* estadística (*campo de las matemáticas*)

status *n* estado; **axillary lymph node** — estado de los ganglios linfáticos axilares; **marital** — estado civil; **mental** — estado mental; — **asthmaticus** estado asmático; — **epilepticus** estado epiléptico

stavudine *n* estavudina

stay *n* estancia, estadía; **hospital** — estancia *or* estadía hospitalaria *or* en el hospital; *vi* **to** — **in bed** guardar cama

STD *abbr* **sexually transmitted disease**. *V.* **disease.**

steak *n* bistec *m*

steam *n* vapor *m*; *vt* (*to cook by steaming*) cocer al vapor

steatohepatitis *n* esteatohepatitis *f*; **non-alcoholic** — esteatohepatitis no alcohólica

steel *n* acero; **stainless** — acero inoxidable

stenosis *n* (*pl* -**ses**) estenosis *f*; **aortic** (**mitral, etc.**) — estenosis aórtica (mitral, etc.); **hypertrophic pyloric** — estenosis hipertrófica de píloro

stenotic *adj* estenótico

stent *n* stent *m*; malla cilíndrica para mantener abierto un conducto, una arteria o una vena; **bare-metal** — stent de metal desnudo; **drug-eluting** — stent liberador de fármaco(s)

step *n* paso; **the next** — el próximo paso; **the best next** — el mejor paso a seguir; **to take a** — dar un paso; **twelve-step program** programa *m* de doce pasos; *vi* (*pret & pp* **stepped**; *ger* **stepping**) dar un paso

stepbrother *n* hermanastro

stepchild *n* (*pl* -**children**) hijastro -tra *mf*

stepdaughter *n* hijastra

stepfather *n* padrastro

stepmother *n* madrastra

stepsister *n* hermanastra

stepson *n* hijastro

stereotactic *adj* estereotáxico

sterile *adj* estéril, aséptico; (*persona*) infértil, estéril

sterility *n* esterilidad *f*

sterilization *n* esterilización *f*

sterilize *vt* esterilizar

sterna *pl de* **sternum**

sternal *adj* esternal

sternum *n* (*pl* -**na**) esternón *m*

steroid *adj* esteroideo; *n* esteroide *m*; **anabolic** — esteroide anabolizante *or* anabólico

stethoscope *n* estetoscopio, fonendoscopio

stevia *n* (*bot*) estevia

stick *n* (*prick*) pinchazo, piquete *m*; **You are going to feel a stick.**.Va a sentir un pinchazo (piquete); *vt* (*pret & pp* **stuck**) pinchar; **to — oneself** pincharse; **to — out one's tongue** (*también* **to stick one's — out**) sacar la lengua; **Stick out your tongue.**.Saque la lengua; *vi* **to — out** sobresalir, proyectar hacia adelante

sticker *n* (*bot*) espina

sticky *adj* (*comp* **-ier**; *super* **-iest**) pegajoso

sties *pl de* **sty**

stiff *adj* rígido, tieso; **Do your hands feel stiff?**.¿Siente las manos rígidas (tiesas)?

stiffness *n* rigidez *f*; **morning —** rigidez matutina (*form*), rigidez en la mañana

stillbirth *n* mortinato, parto de un feto muerto después de 28 semanas de embarazo

stillborn *adj* mortinato (*form*), nacido muerto

stimulant *adj & n* estimulante *m*

stimulate *vt* estimular

stimulating *adj* estimulante

stimulation *n* estimulación *f*; **digital —** estimulación digital; **transcutaneous electrical nerve — (TENS)** estimulación nerviosa eléctrica transcutánea (ENET)

stimulus *n* (*pl* **-li**) estímulo

sting *n* (*pain*) dolor *m*, dolor agudo y repentino; (*of an insect*) picadura; **bee —** picadura de abeja; *vt* (*pret & pp* **stung**) picar; *vi* doler; **The numbing medication will sting a little bit.**.El anestésico le va a doler un poco.

stinger *n* aguijón *m*

stinging *n* dolor *m*, ardor *m*, picor *m* (*esp. Esp*)

stinging nettle *n* (*bot*) ortiga

stingray *n* raya (*pez*)

stirrup *n* (*anat, gyn, etc.*) estribo

stitch *n* punto (de sutura); (*pain in side*) dolor *m* de costado; *vt* (*también* **to — up**) (*fam*) suturar, coser (*fam*)

St. John's wort *n* (*bot*) hipérico, hierba de San Juan

stocking *n* media; **compression stockings** medias de compresión, medias

compresivas (*esp. Esp*)

stocky *adj* robusto, fornido

stoic *adj* (*referring to patients*) con alta tolerancia al dolor, que no se queja mucho

stoma *n* estoma *m*, abertura artificial entre un órgano y el exterior del cuerpo

stomach *adj* estomacal; *n* estómago; (*fam, abdomen*) abdomen *m*, barriga, estómago (*fam*); **on an empty —** en ayunas; **to be sick to one's —** (*fam*) tener náusea(s)

stomachache *n* dolor *m* de estómago

stomatitis *n* estomatitis *f*

stone *n* cálculo (*form*), piedra; **kidney —** cálculo renal, piedra del *or* en el riñón

stood *pret & pp de* **stand**

stool *n* heces *fpl* (*form*), popó (*fam*), caca (*esp. ped, fam or vulg*), deposición *f* (*Esp, SA*), evacuación *f*, excremento; **loose stools** heces pastosas *or* líquidas; **— softener** ablandador *m* de heces, ablandador fecal

stool *n* banco, taburete *m*; **shower —** silla *or* asiento de ducha

stoop *vi* (*también* **to — over**) agacharse, doblarse

stooped *adj* encorvado; **to become —** encorvarse

stop *vt* (*pret & pp* **stopped**; *ger* **stopping**) (*a habit, etc.*) dejar de; (*a medication, etc.*) suspender; *vi* **to — up** taparse; **My nose stops up.**.Se me tapa la nariz.

store *n* reserva; **the body's store of iron .**.la reserva de hierro del organismo; *vt* almacenar

strabismus *n* estrabismo

straight *adj* recto, derecho

straighten *vt, vi* enderezar(se); **Straighten your leg.**.Enderece la pierna.

strain *n* (*stress*) estrés *m*, presión *f*; (*of bacteria, etc.*) cepa; (*muscle, tendon*) distensión *f* (muscular), tirón *m* (muscular), desgarro parcial de un músculo o tendón debido a uso excesivo o incorrecto; *vt* (*a muscle or tendon*) sufrir una distensión (muscular), sufrir un tirón (muscular), lastimar por uso excesivo o incorrecto (*un músculo o un tendón*); (*one's eyes, one's voice*) forzar (*la vista, la voz*); (*urine for stones*) colar (*la orina para piedras*); *vi* es-

forzarse, hacer un gran esfuerzo; (*at stool*) pujar (*para defecar*)
straitjacket *n* camisa de fuerza
strangle *vt, vi* estrangular(se)
strangulated *adj* estrangulado
strangulation *n* estrangulación *f*
strap *n* correa, tira
strawberry *n* (*pl* -ries) fresa
streak *n* raya, línea, (*stria*) estría
stream *n* chorro; **urinary** — chorro miccional (*form*), chorro de la orina
strength *n* fuerza; **the strength in your hand**..la fuerza de su mano...**to recover your strength**..recuperar su(s) fuerza(s); **double-strength** de doble fuerza, de doble dosis; **extra-strength** de fuerza extra; **physical** — fuerza física
strengthen *vt* (*muscles, bones, etc.*) fortalecer, reforzar
strenuous *adj* extenuante, intenso, vigoroso; — **activity** actividades *fpl* extenuantes
strep *n* (*fam*) estreptococo; — **throat** faringitis producida por el estreptococo
streptokinase *n* estreptoquinasa
streptomycin *n* estreptomicina
stress *n* estrés *m*; **Are you under a lot of stress?**..¿Está bajo mucho estrés?; **job** — estrés laboral *or* en el trabajo; *vt* **to** — (*someone*) **out, to put** — **on** (*someone*) estresar; *vi* **to** — **out** estresarse
stressed *adj* estresado
stressful *adj* estresante
stressor *n* estresor *m*
stretch *vt, vi* estirar(se)
stretcher *n* (*litter*) camilla
stretching *n* estiramiento
stretch mark *n* (*fam*) estría
stria *n* (*pl* -ae) estría
strict *adj* estricto
stricture *n* estenosis *f*, estrechez *f*; **esophageal** — estenosis esofágica
strike *vt* (*pret & pp* **struck**) pegar, golpear
strip *n* tira; **test** — tira reactiva (*para sangre*)
stripping *V.* **vein stripping.**
stroke *n* (*blow*) golpe *m*; (*cerebrovascular event*) (*all types*) ictus (apopléjico) (*form*), apoplejía (*form*), accidente *m* cerebrovascular (*form*), ataque *m* (cerebral), embolia (*fam*), derrame *m* (*fam*);

(*embolic*) embolia cerebral; (*hemorrhagic*) derrame *or* hemorragia cerebral; (*ischemic*) accidente cerebrovascular isquémico, infarto cerebral
strong *adj* fuerte
strongyloidiasis *n* estrongiloidiasis *f*
struck *pret & pp de* **strike**
structural *adj* estructural
structured *adj* estructurado; **a more structured environment**..un ambiente más estructurado
strung out *adj* (*fam, on drugs*) adicto; **strung out on heroin**..adicto a la heroína
strychnine *n* estricnina
stub *vt* (*pret & pp* **stubbed**; *ger* **stubbing**) **to** — **one's foot (against)** tropezar (con)
stuck *pret & pp de* **stick**
student *n* estudiante *mf*; **medical** — estudiante *mf* de medicina
study *n* (*pl* -dies) estudio; **double-blind** — estudio doble ciego; **electrophysiology** — (**EPS**) estudio electrofisiológico (EEF); **sleep** — estudio del sueño
stuffed up, stuffy *adj* (*fam*) (*person*) con congestión nasal (*form*), con la nariz tapada (*fam*); (*nose*) tapada; **I'm stuffed up**..**My nose is stuffed up**..Tengo la nariz tapada
stumble *vi* tropezar, dar un traspié
stump *n* (*anat*) muñón *m*
stun *vt* (*pret & pp* **stunned**; *ger* **stunning**) aturdir, dejar brevemente incapacitado; **to become stunned** aturdirse, quedar brevemente incapacitado
stung *pret & pp de* **sting**
stun gun *n* pistola *or* arma paralizante, paralizador *m*
stunt *vt* (*growth, development*) impedir (*el crecimiento, el desarrollo*)
stupor *n* estupor *m*
stutter *vi* tartamudear
sty, stye *n* (*pl* **styes**) orzuelo, perrilla (*Mex, fam*)
subacromial *adj* subacromial
subacute *adj* subagudo
subarachnoid *adj* subaracnoideo
subclavian *adj* subclavio
subclinical *adj* subclínico
subconjunctival *adj* subconjuntival
subconscious *adj* subconsciente; *n* subconsciencia *or* subconciencia

subcutaneous adj subcutáneo
subdural adj subdural
sublethal adj subletal
sublimation n (psych) sublimación f
sublingual adj sublingual
subluxation n subluxación f
submandibular adj submandibular
submental adj submentoniano
subnormal adj debajo de lo normal; [Note: The Spanish term subnormal is similar in meaning and usage to the English term retarded and is best avoided in medical conversations.]
subspecialist n subespecialista mf
subspecialty n (pl -ties) subespecialidad f
substance n sustancia
substitute n sustituto, (person) sustituto -ta mf; **salt** — sustituto de (la) sal; vt sustituir; **You can substitute tortillas for bread**..Puede sustituir el pan por las tortillas; [Note: The order of the two objects tortillas and bread is reversed when translating to Spanish. It may be helpful to think of sustituir as a synonym for the English verb to replace. The sentence above would then read: You can replace bread with tortillas..Puede sustituir el pan por las tortillas.]
substitution n (psych, etc.) sustitución f
subtotal adj subtotal
subtract vt, vi (arith) restar; **Subtract 7 from 100**..Reste 7 a 100.
subungual adj subungueal
suck vt, vi chupar, (at mother's breast) mamar; **to — one's thumb** chuparse el dedo
suckle vt amamantar, lactar, dar el pecho, dar de mamar; vi mamar
sucralfate n sucralfato
sucralose n sucralosa
sucrose n sacarosa
suction n succión f
sudden adj súbito
suddenly adv de repente; **Did it happen suddenly?**..¿Ocurrió de repente?
sue vt, vi demandar
sufentanil n sufentanilo
suffer vi sufrir; **to — from** padecer; **She suffers from arthritis**..Ella padece artritis.
sufferer n persona que padece; **asthma**

— persona que padece asma
suffering n sufrimiento; **to prevent suffering**..evitar or prevenir el sufrimiento
sufficient adj suficiente
suffocate vt, vi asfixiar(se) (form), ahogar(se)
suffocation n asfixia
sugar n azúcar m&f
sugarless adj sin azúcar
suggestibility n sugestionabilidad f
suggestion n sugerencia, (psych) sugestión f; **power of** — poder m de la sugestión
suicidal adj suicida, con tendencias suicidas, que piensa en suicidarse
suicide n suicidio; **assisted** — suicidio asistido; **physician-assisted** — suicidio asistido por un médico; **— attempt** intento suicida or de suicidio; **— gesture** gesto suicida; **to commit** — suicidarse
suitable adj adecuado, apropiado, idóneo; **a suitable donor**..un donante adecuado
suite n sala; **endoscopy** — sala de endoscopia
sulfacetamide n sulfacetamida
sulfadiazine n sulfadiazina
sulfa drugs n sulfas; [Note: The Spanish term sulfas is rarely used in the singular.]
sulfafurazole n sulfisoxazol m, sulfafurazol m (INN)
sulfamethoxazole n sulfametoxazol m
sulfasalazine n sulfasalazina
sulfate n sulfato
sulfisoxazole n sulfisoxazol m, sulfafurazol m (INN)
sulfite n sulfito
sulfonamide n sulfonamida
sulfonylurea n sulfonilurea
sulphur, sulfur n azufre m; **— dioxide** dióxido de azufre
sumatriptan n sumatriptán m
summer n verano
sun n sol m; **to get** — tomar el sol, asolearse
sunbath n baño de sol
sunbathe vi tomar baños de sol, tomar un baño de sol
sunblock n protector m or filtro or bloqueador m solar

sunburn *n* quemadura solar; *vi* (*también* **to get sunburned**) quemarse (con el sol); **Do you sunburn easily?..Do you get sunburned easily?**..¿Se quema fácilmente (con el sol)?

sundowning *n* síndrome vespertino

sunglasses *npl* anteojos *or* lentes oscuros, gafas *or* lentes de sol

sunlamp *n* lámpara solar

sunlight *n* luz *f* solar *or* del sol

sunscreen *n* protector *m or* filtro solar

sunstroke *n* insolación *f*

suntan *n* bronceado; **to get a —** broncearse

superego *n* (*pl* **-gos**) (*psych*) superyó, superego

superficial *adj* superficial

superior *adj* (*anat*) superior

supernumerary *adj* supernumerario

superstition *n* superstición *f*

supination *n* supinación *f*

supine *adj* supino, acostado boca arriba

supper *n* cena

supple *adj* flexible, ágil

supplement *n* suplemento, complemento; **dietary —** suplemento alimenticio *or* dietético

supplemental, supplementary *adj* suplementario; (*insurance*) complementario (*seguros*)

supply *n* (*pl* **-plies**) abastecimiento, surtido; **medical supplies** insumos *or* suministros médicos

support *n* (*physical*) soporte *m*; (*social*) apoyo; **advanced cardiac life — (ACLS)** soporte vital cardíaco avanzado; **arch —** plantilla; **basic life — (BLS)** soporte vital básico; **life —** soporte vital, uso de tecnología sofisticada para mantener vivo a un paciente crítico; **moral —** apoyo moral; **nutritional —** soporte nutricional; **group** grupo de apoyo; *vt* sostener, soportar; (*social sense*) apoyar

supportive *adj* que apoya

suppository *n* (*pl* **-ries**) supositorio; **vaginal —** óvulo, supositorio vaginal

suppress *vt* suprimir

suppressant *n* supresor *m*; **appetite —** supresor del apetito

suppression *n* (*psych, etc.*) supresión *f*

suppressive *adj* (*psych, etc.*) supresor

suppurate *vi* (*form*) supurar, salir(le) pus

suppuration *n* supuración *f*, secreción *f* de pus

suppurative *adj* supurativo

suramin *n* suramina

sure *adj* seguro; **to be —** to, **to make —** to asegurarse de; **Be sure to keep the wound clean**..Asegúrese de mantener limpia la herida.

surface *n* superficie *f*

surfactant *n* surfactante *m*

surgeon *n* cirujano -na *mf*; **general —** cirujano general; **oral —** cirujano oral *or* bucal; **orthopedic —** cirujano ortopédico, cirujano de los huesos (*fam*); **thoracic —** cirujano torácico; **vascular —** cirujano vascular

surgery *n* cirugía; **ambulatory —** cirugía ambulatoria; **bariatric —** cirugía bariátrica; **breast augmentation —** mamoplastia de aumento, cirugía para aumentar el tamaño de las mamas; **breast reduction —** mamoplastia de reducción, cirugía para reducir el tamaño de las mamas; **cosmetic —** cirugía estética *or* cosmética; **elective —** cirugía electiva *or* programada; **gender reassignment —** cirugía de reasignación de sexo *or* género; **general —** cirugía general; **laparoscopic —** cirugía laparoscópica; **major —** cirugía mayor; **maxillofacial —** cirugía maxilofacial; **minor —** cirugía menor; **open heart —** cirugía a corazón abierto; **open —** cirugía abierta; **oral —** cirugía oral *or* bucal; **orthopedic —** cirugía ortopédica; **outpatient —** cirugía ambulatoria, cirugía sin ingreso; **plastic —** cirugía plástica; **radical —** cirugía radical; **reconstructive —** cirugía reconstructiva; **robotic —** cirugía robótica; **sexual reassignment —** cirugía de reasignación de sexo; **thoracic —** cirugía torácica

surgical *adj* quirúrgico

surname *n* apellido; **maternal —** apellido materno; **paternal —** apellido paterno

surrogate *V.* **mother.**

surrounding *adj* (*area, tissue, etc.*) circundante

surveillance *n* vigilancia

survival *n* supervivencia

survive *vt, vi* sobrevivir

survivor *n* sobreviviente *mf*, superviviente *mf*; **cancer** — sobreviviente *or* superviviente del cáncer

susceptibility *n* susceptibilidad *f*

susceptible *adj* susceptible

suspend *vt* (*treatment, etc.*) suspender

suspension *n* suspensión *f*

suspicious *adj* sospechoso; **a suspicious mass**..una masa sospechosa

sustain *vt* sostener

suture *n* sutura; **absorbable** — sutura absorbible, sutura reabsorbible (*esp. Esp*); *vt* suturar, coser (*fam*)

swab *n* hisopo *or* bastoncillo de algodón, palillo con punta de algodón; *vt* frotar con hisopo (*para aplicar antiséptico, tomar una muestra, etc.*)

swaddle *vt* envolver con ropa apretada (*a un bebé*)

swallow *n* trago; **dry** — trago de saliva; *vt* tragar, pasar; *vi* (*dry swallow*) tragar *or* pasar saliva; **Swallow, please**..Trague (Pase) saliva, por favor.

swam *pret de* **swim**

sweat *n* sudor *m*; **night sweats** sudoración nocturna, sudores nocturnos; *vi* (*pret & pp* **sweat** *o* **sweated**) sudar

sweating *n* sudoración *f*, transpiración *f*

sweaty *adj* sudoroso

sweet *adj* dulce; **to have a — tooth** (*fam*) ser goloso, gustar(*le*) (*a uno*) los dulces; *npl* dulces *mpl*, caramelos

sweetener *n* edulcorante *m*; **artificial** — edulcorante artificial

swell *vi* (*pret* **swelled**; *pp* **swelled** *o* **swollen**) (*también* **to — up**) hincharse; **Do your feet swell (up)?**..¿Se le hinchan los pies?

swelling *n* hinchazón *f*

swim *vi* (*pret* **swam**; *pp* **swum**; *ger* **swimming**) nadar; **to go swimming** ir a bañarse, ir a nadar

swimmer's ear *n* (*fam*) otitis externa, oído de nadador (*fam*)

swimmer's itch *n* (*fam*) dermatitis *f* por cercarias

swimming *n* natación *f*, (el) nadar

swish *vt* enjuagar; **— and spit** enjuagar y escupir; **— and swallow** enjuagar y tragar

swollen (*pp de* **swell**) *adj* hinchado

swum *pp de* **swim**

symbiosis *n* (*psych, etc.*) simbiosis *f*

symmetrical *adj* simétrico

symmetry *n* simetría

sympathectomy *n* (*pl* **-mies**) simpatectomía

sympathetic *adj* compasivo, comprensivo; (*neuro*) simpático

sympathy *n* compasión *f*

symphysis *n* (*pl* **-ses**) sínfisis *f*

symptom *n* síntoma *m*

symptomatic *adj* sintomático

synapse *n* sinapsis *f*

synchronize *vt* sincronizar

syncope *n* síncope *m*

syndrome *n* síndrome *m*; **acquired immunodeficiency — (AIDS)** síndrome de inmunodeficiencia adquirida (SIDA *or* sida *m*); **adult respiratory distress — (ARDS)** síndrome de dificultad respiratoria del adulto (SDRA); **antiphospholipid** — síndrome antifosfolípido; **apical ballooning** — síndrome de discinesia apical (transitoria); **Asherman's** — síndrome de Asherman; **bacterial overgrowth** — sobrecrecimiento bacteriano intestinal; **battered child** — síndrome del niño maltratado; **blind loop** — síndrome de(l) asa ciega; **broken heart** — síndrome del corazón roto; **carcinoid** — síndrome carcinoide; **carpal tunnel** — síndrome del túnel carpiano; **chronic fatigue** — síndrome de fatiga crónica; **Churg-Strauss** — síndrome de Churg-Strauss; **compartmental** — síndrome compartimental; **complex regional pain** — síndrome de dolor regional complejo; **Cushing's** — síndrome de Cushing; **Down** — síndrome de Down; **Ehlers-Danlos** — síndrome de Ehlers-Danlos; **empty nest** — síndrome del nido vacío; **Felty's** — síndrome de Felty; **fetal alcohol** — síndrome alcohólico fetal; **Gilbert's** — síndrome de Gilbert; **Gilles de la Tourette** — síndrome de Gilles de la Tourette; **Guillain-Barré** — síndrome de Guillain-Barré; **hemolytic-uremic** — síndrome hemolítico-urémico; **hepatorenal** — síndrome hepatorrenal; **irritable bowel** — síndrome de(l) intestino irritable, síndrome de(l) colon irritable; **Klinefelter** — síndrome de Klinefelter; **Marfan** — síndrome de Marfán; **metabolic** — síndrome metabólico; **Munchausen** — síndrome de Munchausen; **myelodysplastic** — síndrome mielodisplásico; **nephrotic** — síndrome nefrótico; **neuroleptic malignant** — síndrome neuroléptico maligno; **obesity-hypoventilation** — síndrome de hipoventilación por obesidad; **Osler-Weber-Rendu** — síndrome de Osler-Weber-Rendu; **overactive bladder** — síndrome de vejiga hiperactiva; **overuse** — síndrome de sobrecarga, lesión *f* por sobrecarga (*esp. Esp*); **Peutz-Jeghers** — síndrome de Peutz-Jeghers; **Pickwickian** — (*ant*) síndrome de hipoventilación por obesidad, síndrome de Pickwick (*ant*); **polycystic ovary** — síndrome de ovario poliquístico; **postcon-cussion** — síndrome postconmocional; **post-polio** — síndrome post-polio; **premenstrual** — (PMS) síndrome premenstrual (SPM); **Reiter's** — (*ant*) artritis reactiva, síndrome de Reiter (*ant*); **restless legs** — síndrome de piernas inquietas; **Reye's** — síndrome de Reye; **severe acute respiratory** — (SARS) síndrome respiratorio agudo severo (SRAS); **Sheehan's** — síndrome de Sheehan; **short bowel** — síndrome de intestino corto; **Sjögren's** — síndrome de Sjögren; **staphylococcal scalded skin** — síndrome de la piel escaldada estafilocócica; **Stevens-Johnson** — síndrome de Stevens-Johnson; **sudden infant death** — (SIDS) síndrome de muerte súbita del lactante *or* infantil; **toxic shock** — síndrome de choque tóxico; **Turner** — síndrome de Turner; **wasting** — síndrome de desgaste; **Wernicke-Korsa-**

koff — síndrome de Wernicke-Korsakoff; **Wolff-Parkinson-White** — síndrome de Wolff-Parkinson-White
synergistic *adj* sinérgico
synergy *n* sinergia
synovial *adj* sinovial
synovitis *n* sinovitis *f*
synthesis *n* síntesis *f*
synthesize *vt* sintetizar
synthetic *adj* sintético
syphilis *n* sífilis *f*
syphilitic *adj* sifilítico
syringe *n* jeringa, jeringuilla (*Carib, Esp*); **bulb** — pera de goma
syringomyelia *n* siringomielia
syrup *n* jarabe *m*; **cough** — jarabe para la tos; **high-fructose corn** — jarabe de maíz de alta fructosa
system *n* sistema *m*; **autonomic nervous** — sistema nervioso autónomo; **cardiovascular** — sistema cardiovascular; **central nervous** — (CNS) sistema nervioso central (SNC); **digestive** — sistema digestivo; **endocrine** — sistema endocrino; **immune** — sistema inmunológico; **metric** — sistema métrico; **musculoskeletal** — sistema locomotor *or* musculoesquelético; **parasympathetic nervous** — sistema nervioso parasimpático; **peripheral nervous** — sistema nervioso periférico; **reproductive** — sistema reproductor *or* reproductivo; **respiratory** — sistema respiratorio; **skeletal** — sistema óseo *or* esquelético; **sympathetic nervous** — sistema nervioso simpático
systemic *adj* sistémico
systolic *adj* sistólico

tab 138 tea

T

table *n* mesa; **examination —, exam table** (*fam*) mesa de exploración (*form*), mesa (*fam*), camilla (*SA*); **operating** — mesa de operaciones *or* quirúrgica; **tilt** — mesa basculante *or* inclinada

tablespoonful *n* cucharada sopera *or* grande, cucharada, 15 ml

tablet *n* comprimido (*form*), tableta

taboo *adj* prohibido; *n* (*pl* **taboos**) tabú *m*

tachycardia *n* taquicardia; **paroxysmal supraventricular**—taquicardia paroxística supraventricular

tacrine *n* tacrina

tacrolimus *n* tacrolimus *m*, tacrolimús *m* (*INN*)

tactile *adj* táctil

tadalafil *n* tadalafilo

Taenia *n* tenia, solitaria

tailbone *n* (*fam*) cóccix *or* coxis *m*, colita (*Amer, fam*), rabadilla (*Amer, fam*)

tainted *adj* contaminado

take *vt* (*pret* **took**; *pp* **taken**) tomar; **to** — **off** (*clothing, etc.*) quitarse; **Take off your shirt.**.Quítese la camisa; **to** — **out** extraer (*form*), extirpar (*form*), sacar; **We have to take out your appendix.**.Tenemos que sacarle el apéndice.

talc *n* talco

talcum powder *n* talco, polvos de talco (*Esp*)

talk *vi* hablar

tall *adj* alto; **How tall are you?.**.¿Cuál es su altura?

talus *n* astrágalo

tamoxifen *n* tamoxifeno

tampon *n* tampón *m*

tamponade *n* taponamiento; **cardiac** — taponamiento cardíaco

tamsulosin *n* tamsulosina

tan *adj* & *n* bronceado; **to get a** — broncearse; *vi* (*pret* & *pp* **tanned**; *ger* **tanning**) broncearse

tangential *adj* (*psych*) tangencial

tangentiality *n* (*psych*) tangencialidad *f*

tank *n* (*for oxygen*) tanque *m*, tubo, cilindro (*para oxígeno*)

tannin *n* tanino

tantalum *n* tantalio

tantrum *n* berrinche *m*, rabieta, pataleta

tap *n* (*puncture*) punción *f*; **spinal** — punción lumbar; *vt* (*pret* & *pp* **tapped**; *ger* **tapping**) realizar una punción

tape *n* cinta, tela; **adhesive** — cinta adhesiva, esparadrapo; **dental** — cinta dental; — **measure** *o* **measuring** — cinta métrica

tapentadol *n* tapentadol *m*

taper *n* reducción *f or* disminución *f* gradual; *vt* reducir *or* disminuir gradualmente

tapeworm *n* tenia, solitaria

taping *n* vendaje *m* funcional

tar *n* (*cigarettes, shampoo, etc.*) alquitrán *m*

tarantula *n* tarántula

target *n* diana, blanco; — **organ** órgano blanco *or* diana; *vt* dirigirse a, atacar; (*to focus on*) centrarse en, enfocarse en; **to target cancer cells**..dirigirse a (atacar) las células cancerosas...**to target older male smokers**..centrarse (enfocarse) en los hombres fumadores mayores

tarsal *adj* (*ortho*) tarsiano, tarsal

tartar *n* (*dent*) cálculo (*form*), sarro (*dental*)

tartaric acid *n* ácido tartárico

task *n* tarea; **life** — tarea de la vida; **to stay on** — mantenerse enfocado en el trabajo

taste *n* gusto, sabor *m*; — **bud** papila gustativa; *vt* (*to try*) probar; **Taste it.**.Pruébelo...**Can you taste all right?.**.¿Distingue bien los sabores?; *vi* saber; **This medicine doesn't taste bad.**.Esta medicina no sabe mal; **to** — **like** saber a

tattoo *n* (*pl* **-toos**) tatuaje *m*

taught *pret* & *pp de* **teach**

taurine *n* taurina

tazarotene *n* tazaroteno

TB *V.* **tuberculosis.**

Td *abbr* **tetanus-diphtheria.** *V.* **vaccine.**

Tdap *abbr* **tetanus, diphtheria, and acellular pertussis.** *V.* **vaccine.**

tea *n* té *m*; (*medicinal*) infusión *f*; **green**

— té verde

teach *vt* (*pret & pp* **taught**) enseñar

teacher *n* maestro -tra *mf*, profesor -ra *mf*

team *n* equipo; **health care** — equipo sanitario *or* de salud; **sexual assault response** — equipo de respuesta al asalto sexual, equipo multidisciplinario entrenado para evaluar la víctima de una agresión sexual y a la vez recoger evidencia

tear *n* (*muscle, etc.*) desgarro, desgarre *m* (*esp. Mex*), rotura; **bucket handle** — rotura en asa de cubo; **meniscal** — rotura de menisco, rotura meniscal (*esp. Esp*); *vt, vi* (*pret* **tore**; *pp* **torn**) desgarrar(se), sufrir un desgarro; **I tore my calf muscle**..Me desgarré la pantorrilla.

tear *n* (*from crying*) lágrima; **artificial tears** lágrimas artificiales

tearful *adj* llorando, que está llorando

tease *vt* (*ped*) molestar, fastidiar

teaspoonful *n* (*pl* **-fuls**) cucharadita, 5 ml

teat *n* pezón *m*, teta; [*Note:* teta, *like* teat, *is a veterinary term that can be offensive when applied to people.*]

technetium *n* tecnecio

technician *n* técnico -ca *mf*; [*Note:* técnica *also means* technique, *which can cause confusion if the context is not clear.*]

technique *n* técnica; **aseptic** — técnica aséptica *or* estéril; **relaxation** — técnica de relajación; **sterile** — técnica estéril *or* aséptica

technology *n* (*pl* **-gies**) tecnología

teenage *adj* adolescente, de 13 a 19 años (de edad)

teenager *n* adolescente *mf*, joven *mf* de 13 a 19 años (de edad)

teens *npl* los años 13 a 19 (de edad)

teeth *pl de* tooth

teethe *vi* salir(*le*) (*a uno*) los dientes; **Is he teething yet?**..¿Ya le están saliendo los dientes?

teething *n* dentición *f* (*form*), erupción *f* dental (*form*), salida de los dientes

telangiectasia *n* telangiectasia; **hereditary hemorrhagic** — telangiectasia hemorrágica hereditaria

telaprevir *n* telaprevir *m*

telbivudine *n* telbivudina

telecoil *n* bobina telefónica, telebobina

telemedicine *n* telemedicina

telemetry *n* telemetría

telephone *n* teléfono; **cellular** — teléfono celular

telmisartan *n* telmisartán *m*

temazepam *n* temazepam *m*

temperament *n* temperamento

temperature *n* temperatura; (*fam, fever*) fiebre *f*, calentura; **axillary** — temperatura axilar; **oral** — temperatura oral; **rectal** — temperatura rectal; **room** — temperatura ambiente; **to take** (*someone's*) — tomar(*le*) la temperatura (*a alguien*); **to take one's** (*own*) — tomarse la temperatura; **Did you take your temperature at home?**..¿Se tomó la temperatura en casa?

temple *n* (*anat*) sien *f*

temporal *adj* temporal

temporary *adj* temporal; **This bandage is only temporary**..Este vendaje es solo temporal.

temporomandibular *adj* temporomandibular

tendency *n* (*pl* **-cies**) tendencia

tender *adj* (*sore*) dolorido, adolorido (*Amer*), que duele al tocar

tenderness *n* dolor *m* (al tocar)

tendinitis *n* tendinitis *f*; **calcific** — tendinitis calcificante

tendon *n* tendón *m*; **Achilles** — tendón de Aquiles

tendonitis *V.* tendinitis.

tenesmus *n* tenesmo, pujo

tennis *n* tenis *m*

tennis elbow *n* (*fam*) epicondilitis *f* (lateral), codo de tenista (*fam*)

tenofovir *n* tenofovir *m*

tenosynovitis *n* tenosinovitis *f*

TENS *abbr* transcutaneous electrical nerve stimulation. *V.* stimulation.

tense *adj* tenso; *vt* (*one's muscles*) tensar (*los músculos*); *vi* **to** — **up** ponerse tenso; **Try not to tense up**..Trate de no ponerse tenso.

tension *n* tensión *f*; **nervous** — tensión nerviosa

tent *n* tienda; **oxygen** — tienda de oxígeno

teratogenic *adj* teratogénico

teratogenicity *n* teratogenicidad *f*

teratoma *n* teratoma *m*

terazosin *n* terazosina

terbinafine *n* terbinafina
terconazole *n* terconazol *m*
terfenadine *n* terfenadina
term *n (obst, etc.)* término; **at** — a término; — **pregnancy** embarazo a término
terminal *adj* terminal
tertiary *adj* terciario, de tercer nivel *(esp. Mex)*
test *n* prueba, examen *m*, análisis *m*; **Your tests show**..Sus pruebas muestran; **blood** — análisis (prueba, examen) de sangre; **drug** — prueba de drogas; **eye** — examen oftalmológico *(form)*, examen de los ojos; **fecal occult blood** — prueba de sangre oculta en heces; **fertility** — prueba de fertilidad; **hearing** — examen auditivo, prueba de audición; **HIV** — prueba del VIH; **oral glucose tolerance** — prueba de tolerancia oral a la glucosa; **Pap** — *(fam)* citología cervical *or* exfoliativa *(form)*, citología *(fam)*, prueba de Papanicolaou; **patch** — prueba de(l) parche; **pregnancy** — prueba de embarazo; **pulmonary function** — prueba de función pulmonar; **radioallergosorbent** — **(RAST)** prueba radioalergosorbente *or* de radioalergoadsorción; **random drug** — prueba de drogas al azar; **screening** — prueba de detección; **skin** — prueba cutánea; **stool** — análisis de heces; **stool guaiac** — examen *or* prueba de guayacol en heces; **stress** — ergometría *(esp. Esp, form)* prueba de esfuerzo; **TB** — *(fam)* prueba de (la) tuberculosis; **tilt table** — prueba de inclinación, prueba de mesa basculante; **tuberculin skin** — **(TST)** prueba de (la) tuberculina; **urine** — análisis *or* examen *or* prueba de orina; *vt* analizar, hacer una prueba *or* examen *or* análisis, examinar; **I would like to test your urine for opiates**..Quisiera hacerle un análisis de la orina para detectar opiáceos.
testicle *n* testículo; **undescended** — testículo no descendido
testicular *adj* testicular
testing *n* evaluación *f*, valoración *f*, análisis *m*, realización *f* de pruebas para fines diagnósticos; **fecal occult blood** — (realización de) pruebas de sangre oculta en heces; **random drug** — (rea-

lización de) pruebas de drogas al azar; **urodynamic** — evaluación urodinámica, (realización de) pruebas urodinámicas
testosterone *n* testosterona
test strip *n* tira reactiva *(para sangre)*
test tube *n* tubo de ensayo
tetanus *n* tétanos *m*
tetracycline *n* tetraciclina
tetrahydrocannabinol (THC) *n* tetrahidrocannabinol *m* (THC)
tetralogy of Fallot *n* tetralogía de Fallot
tetraplegia *n* tetraplejía, cuadriplejía
thalamus *n* tálamo
thalassemia *n* talasemia
thalidomide *n* talidomida
thallium *n* talio
THC *V.* **tetrahydrocannabinol**.
theophylline *n* teofilina
theory *n (pl -ries)* teoría
therapeutic *adj* terapéutico
therapist *n* terapeuta *mf*; *(fam, psych)* psicoterapeuta *mf*; **behavioral** — terapeuta conductual; **cognitive behavioral** — terapeuta cognitivo conductual; **massage** — terapeuta masajista; **occupational** — terapeuta ocupacional; **physical** — fisioterapeuta *mf*, terapeuta físico; **respiratory** — terapeuta respiratorio; **speech** — logopeda *mf,* logoterapeuta *mf*, fonoaudiólogo -ga *mf*, terapeuta del lenguaje
therapy *n (pl -pies)* terapia, tratamiento; **antiretroviral** — **(ART)** terapia *or* tratamiento antirretroviral (TARV); **behavioral** — terapia conductual *or* de la conducta; **cardiac resynchronization** — terapia de resincronización cardíaca; **chelation** — terapia de quelación; **cognitive** — terapia cognitiva; **cognitive behavioral** — terapia cognitivo conductual*; **combination** — terapia combinada, tratamiento combinado; **consolidation** — tratamiento *or* terapia de consolidación; **diet** — dietoterapia; **directly observed** — tratamiento directamente observado; **electroconvulsive** — **(ECT)** terapia electroconvulsiva (TEC); **group** — terapia grupal *or* de grupo; **heat** — termoterapia, terapia de calor; **highly active antiretroviral** — **(HAART)** *(ant)* terapia *or* tratamiento antirretroviral (TARV),

terapia *or* tratamiento antirretroviral de gran actividad (TARGA) (*ant*); **hormone** *o* **hormonal** — hormonoterapia, terapia hormonal; **hormone-replacement** — terapia de reemplazo hormonal, terapia hormonal sustitutiva; **induction** — tratamiento *or* terapia de inducción; **language** — terapia del lenguaje; **maintenance** — (*oncology, addiction medicine, etc.*) terapia *or* tratamiento de mantenimiento; **massage** — terapia de masaje(s); **nicotine-replacement** — terapia de reemplazo de nicotina; **occupational** — terapia ocupacional; **photodynamic** — terapia fotodinámica; **physical** — fisioterapia, terapia física (*Amer*); **proton beam** —, **proton** — terapia con haz de protones, terapia de protones; **radiation** — radioterapia; **respiratory** — terapia respiratoria; **root canal** — (*form*) endodoncia (*form*), tratamiento de conducto; **salvage** — tratamiento *or* terapia de rescate; **speech** — logopedia, logoterapia, fonoaudiología, terapia del lenguaje, terapia del habla (*esp. Mex*); **ultrasound** — ultrasonoterapia, ultrasonido terapéutico; **whirlpool** — hidromasaje *m*
*cognitivo conductual *is considered a compound adjective and therefore the first word (cognitivo) is not required to agree in gender with the noun being modified.*
thermal *adj* térmico
thermocoagulation *n* termocoagulación *f*
thermometer *n* termómetro; **rectal** — termómetro rectal
thiabendazole *n* tiabendazol *m*
thiamazole *n* tiamazol *m*, metimazol *m*
thiamine *n* tiamina
thiazide *n* tiazida
thick *adj* (*dimension*) espeso, grueso; (*consistency*) espeso
thickness *n* (*dimension*) espesor *m*, grosor *m*; (*consistency*) espesor *m*, densidad *f*
thigh *n* muslo
thin *adj* (*comp* **thinner**; *super* **thinnest**) delgado, flaco (*fam*); (*hair*) escaso, ralo, delgado; (*liquid*) poco espeso; (*fam, blood*) anticoagulada; **to become** —

adelgazarse, (*esp. unintentionally*) enflaquecer(se); **to** — (*someone's*) **blood** tratar(le) (*a alguien*) con anticoagulante; **We need to thin your blood**..Necesitamos tratarlo con un anticoagulante.
think *vi* (*pret & pp* **thought**) pensar
thinking *n* pensamiento; **concrete** — pensamiento concreto; **magical** — pensamiento mágico
thiomersal, thimerosal *n* timerosal *m*, tiomersal *m* (*INN*)
third *n* tercio, tercera parte; **two thirds of a dose**..dos tercios de una dosis
thirst *n* sed *f*
thirsty *adj* **to be** — tener sed; **to make** — dar sed
thoracentesis *n* (*pl* -**ses**) toracocentesis *f*
thoraces *pl de* **thorax**
thoracic *adj* torácico
thoracoscopic *adj* toracoscópico
thoracoscopy *n* (*pl* -**pies**) toracoscopia; **video-assisted** — videotoracoscopia
thoracotomy *n* (*pl* -**mies**) toracotomía
thorax *n* (*pl* -**raxes** *o* -**races**) tórax *m*
thorn *n* espina
thought (*pret & pp de* **think**) *n* pensamiento
threat *n* amenaza
threaten *vt, vi* amenazar
threonine *n* treonina
threshold *n* umbral *m*; **auditory** — umbral de audición; **pain** — umbral de(l) dolor
threw *pret de* **throw**
throat *n* garganta; **sore** — dolor *m* de garganta
throb *vi* (*pret & pp* **throbbed**; *ger* **throbbing**) (*pain*) doler con cada latido del corazón
throbbing (*ger de* **throb**) *adj* (*pain*) pulsátil, que duele con cada latido del corazón
thrombectomy *n* (*pl* -**mies**) trombectomía
thrombi *pl de* **thrombus**
thromboangiitis obliterans *n* tromboangeítis *f* obliterante
thrombocytopenia *n* trombocitopenia; **immune** — (**ITP**) trombocitopenia inmune (TPI)
thrombocytosis *n* trombocitosis *f*; **essential** — trombocitosis esencial
thromboembolism *n* (*pl* -**li**) tromboem-

bolia
thrombolysis *n* trombolisis *f*
thrombolytic *adj* & *n* trombolítico
thrombophlebitis *n* tromboflebitis *f*
thrombosis *n* (*pl* **-ses**) trombosis *f*; **deep venous — (DVT)** trombosis venosa profunda (TVP)
thrombus *n* (*pl* **-bi**) trombo
throw *vt* (*pret* **threw**; *pp* **thrown**) **to — one's back out** (*fam*) lastimarse la espalda (*se refiere al concepto popular de que el dolor repentino de espalda se debe a una dislocación de una vertebra*); *vi* **to — up** (*fam*) V. **vomit**.
thrush *n* candidiasis *f* oral (*form*), algodoncillo (*Mex*), sapo (*PR, SD*), infección *f* por hongos en la boca
thumb *n* dedo pulgar (de la mano), pulgar *m* (de la mano)
thumbnail *n* uña del pulgar (de la mano)
thumb sucking *n* succión *f* del pulgar (*form*), (el) chuparse el pulgar
thump *n* golpe *m*; **precordial —** golpe precordial
thymectomy *n* (*pl* **-mies**) timectomía
thymi *pl de* **thymus**
thymol *n* timol *m*
thymoma *n* timoma *m*
thymus *n* (*pl* **-mi** *o* **-muses**) timo
thyroglobulin *n* tiroglobulina
thyroid *adj* tiroideo; **— storm** tormenta tiroidea, crisis tirotóxica; *n* (*fam*) glándula tiroides, tiroides *m&f* (*fam*)
thyroidectomy *n* (*pl* **-mies**) tiroidectomía
thyroiditis *n* tiroiditis *f*; **Hashimoto's —** tiroiditis de Hashimoto; **subacute —** tiroiditis subaguda
thyrotoxic *adj* tirotóxico
thyrotoxicosis *n* tirotoxicosis *f*
thyrotropin *n* tirotropina, hormona estimulante del *or* de la tiroides
thyroxine *n* tiroxina
TIA *abbr* **transient ischemic attack**. V. **attack**.
tiagabine *n* tiagabina
tibia *n* tibia
tic *n* tic *m*; **— douloureux** tic doloroso, neuralgia del trigémino
ticagrelor *n* ticagrelor *m*
tick *n* garrapata
ticker *n* (*fam, heart*) corazón *m*
tickle *n* cosquilleo, (*in the throat*) irrita-

ción *f*, picor *m* (*esp. Esp*); *vt* hacer(*le*) cosquillas; **I don't mean to be tickling you**..No es mi intención hacerle cosquillas.
tickling *n* cosquillas, cosquilleo
ticklish *adj* cosquilloso
tie *n* corbata; *npl* (*to restrain a patient*) ataduras, correas
tight *adj* apretado; (*control*) estricto; **— glucose control** control estricto de la glucosa
time *n* tiempo, vez *f*; (*by the clock*) hora; **all the time**..todo el tiempo...**a long time**..mucho tiempo...**a short time**..un rato, poco tiempo...**at times** a veces... **At what time?**..¿A qué hora?...**four times a day**..cuatro veces al día...**in order to save time**..para ahorrar tiempo...**Our time is up**.Se nos acabó el tiempo...**the first time**..la primera vez ...**the last time**..la última vez...**the next time**..la próxima vez...**three times as high**..tres veces más alto; **bleeding —** tiempo de sangrado, tiempo de sangría; **each — *o* every —** cada vez; **free —** tiempo libre; **from — to —** de vez en cuando; **in —** (*eventually*) con el tiempo; **leisure —** tiempo de ocio; **partial thromboplastin — (PTT)** tiempo parcial de tromboplastina (TPT); **prothrombin — (PT)** tiempo de protrombina (TP)
timid *adj* tímido
timolol *n* timolol *m*
tincture *n* tintura
tinea *n* tiña, tinea, infección *f* de la piel por hongos; **— capitis** tinea capitis (*form*), tiña del cuero cabelludo *or* de la cabeza; **— corporis** tinea corporis (*form*), tiña corporal *or* del cuerpo; **— cruris** tinea cruris (*form*), tiña inguinal; **— pedis** tinea pedis (*form*), pie *m* de atleta; **— versicolor** pitiriasis *f* versicolor
tingle *vi* hormiguear
tingling *n* hormigueo
tinidazole *n* tinidazol *m*
tinnitus *n* acúfeno (*frec. pl*), tinnitus *m* (*frec. pl*), zumbido de oídos
tiotropium bromide *n* bromuro de tiotropio
tip *n* (*of the tongue, finger, etc.*) punta (*de la lengua, del dedo, etc.*); (*recom-*

mendation) consejo
tipranavir *n* tipranavir *m*
TIPS *abbr* **transjugular intrahepatic portosystemic shunt**. *V.* **shunt**.
tiptoes *npl* **on** — de puntillas; **to walk on tiptoes**..caminar de puntillas
tire *vt, vi* (*también* **to** — **out**) cansarse; **Just walking to the bathroom tires him out**..Con sólo caminar al baño se cansa.
tired *adj* (*también* — **out**) cansado; **to get** — **(out)** cansarse
tiredness *n* cansancio
tiring *adj* fatigoso
tirosine *n* tirosina
tissue *n* tejido; (*facial*) pañuelo (de papel); **connective** — tejido conectivo *or* conjuntivo; **granulation** — tejido de granulación; **scar** — tejido cicatricial; **soft** — tejido blando
tissue plasminogen activator (tPA) *n* activador *m* tisular del plasminógeno, activador del plasminógeno tisular
titanium *n* titanio; — **oxide** óxido de titanio
titer *n* título
titrate *vt* titular
titration *n* titulación *f*
tizanidine *n* tizanidina
toast *n* pan tostado
tobacco *adj* tabáquico; *n* (*pl* **-cos**) tabaco; **chewing** — tabaco de mascar; **smokeless** — tabaco sin humo; — **use** tabaquismo
tocolysis *n* tocólisis *or* tocolisis *f*
tocolytic *adj* & *n* tocolítico
tocopherol *n* tocoferol *m*
today *adv* hoy
toe *n* dedo (del pie); **great** — (*form*), **big** — dedo gordo (del pie); **little** — dedo meñique *or* pequeño *or* chico (del pie)
toenail *n* uña (del pie)
tofu *n* tofu *m*
toilet *n* inodoro, retrete *m* (*esp. Esp*); — **bowl** taza del inodoro *or* retrete; — **paper** papel higiénico, papel sanitario (*Mex, CA, Carib*)
tolerance *n* tolerancia; **impaired glucose** — alteración *f* de la tolerancia a la glucosa; **(high, low) pain** — (alta, baja) tolerancia al dolor
tolerant *adj* tolerante
tolerate *vt* tolerar, soportar, aguantar

tolnaftate *n* tolnaftato
tolterodine *n* tolterodina
toluene *n* tolueno
tomato *n* (*pl* **-toes**) tomate *m*
tomogram *n* tomografía (*estudio*)
tomography *n* tomografía (*técnica*); **computed** — **(CT)** tomografía computarizada (TC); **computerized axial** — **(CAT)** tomografía axial computarizada (TAC); **positron emission** — **(PET)** tomografía por emisión de positrones; **positron emission tomography-computed tomography (PET-CT)** tomografía por emisión de positrones-tomografía computarizada; **spiral computed** — tomografía computarizada helicoidal
tomorrow *adv* mañana
tone *n* tono; **muscle** — tono muscular; *vt* (*one's muscles*) tonificar (*los músculos*)
toner *n* (*for skin*) tónico (para la piel)
tongue *n* lengua; — **depressor** *o* **blade** depresor *m* (de lengua), bajalenguas *m*, abatelenguas *m* (*Mex*), paleta (*fam*)
tonic *n* tónico, reconstituyente *m*
toning *n* tonificación *f*; — **exercises** ejercicios de tonificación
tonsil *n* amígdala, angina (*fam*)
tonsillectomy *n* (*pl* **-mies**) amigdalectomía
tonsillitis *n* amigdalitis *f*, tonsilitis *f*
took *pret de* **take**
tooth *n* (*pl* **teeth**) diente *m*, muela; **baby** — diente de leche; **back** — (*fam*) muela; **canine** — canino, colmillo; **deciduous** — diente deciduo *or* primario, diente de leche (*fam*); **false teeth** dentadura postiza, dientes postizos; **front** — incisivo; **milk** — diente de leche; **permanent** — diente permanente *or* definitivo; **primary** — diente primario *or* deciduo, diente de leche (*fam*); **set of teeth** dentadura; **temporary** — diente primario *or* deciduo, diente de leche (*fam*); **wisdom** — tercer molar (*form*), muela de(l) juicio
toothache *n* dolor *m* de muelas
toothbrush *n* cepillo de dientes *or* dental
toothpaste *n* pasta dental *or* de dientes, dentífrico
tophus *n* (*pl* **-phi**) tofo
topical *adj* tópico

topiramate *n* topiramato
tore *pret de* **tear**
torn *pp de* **tear**
torsemide (*USAN*), **torasemide** (*INN*) *n* torasemida (*INN*), torsemida
torsion *n* torsión *f*; **testicular** — torsión testicular
torso *n* torso
torticollis *n* tortícolis *f*
torture *n* tortura; *vt* torturar
torus *n* (*pl* **-ri** *o* **-ruses**) torus *m*; — **palatinus** torus palatino
total *adj & n* total *m*
touch *n* (*sense*) tacto; **therapeutic** — toque terapéutico; *vt* tocar
tough *adj* duro
tourniquet *n* torniquete *m*
towel *n* toalla
To Whom It May Concern A quien corresponda
toxemia *n* toxemia
toxemic *adj* toxémico
toxic *adj* tóxico
toxicity *n* toxicidad *f*
toxicologist *n* toxicólogo -ga *mf*, especialista *mf* en sustancias tóxicas
toxicology *n* toxicología, estudio de las sustancias tóxicas y sus efectos en el organismo
toxin *n* toxina
toxocariasis *n* toxocariasis *f*
toxoid *n* toxoide *m*; **diphtheria** — toxoide diftérico; **tetanus** — toxoide tetánico
toxoplasmosis *n* toxoplasmosis *f*
tPA *V.* **tissue plasminogen activator**.
TPN *abbr* **total parenteral nutrition**. *V.* **nutrition**.
trace *n* traza (*frec. pl*); **There is a trace of protein in your urine**..Hay trazas de proteínas en su orina.
tracer *n* trazador *m*
trachea *n* (*pl* **-cheae** *o* **-cheas**) tráquea
tracheitis *n* traqueítis *f*
tracheobronchitis *n* traqueobronquitis *f*
tracheostomy *n* (*pl* **-mies**) traqueostomía
tracheotomy *n* (*pl* **-mies**) traqueotomía
trachoma *n* tracoma *m*
tracing *n* (*ECG, etc.*) registro
tracks *npl* (*fam, from IV drug use*) marcas de pinchazos
tract *n* tracto, vía, aparato; **biliary** — vías biliares; **digestive** *o* **gastrointes-**

tinal — vía digestiva, tracto digestivo *or* gastrointestinal, aparato digestivo; **genital** — aparato *or* tracto genital; **genitourinary** — aparato *or* tracto genitourinario; **(upper, lower) respiratory** — vías respiratorias (superiores *or* altas, inferiores *or* bajas); **urinary** — aparato *or* tracto urinario
traction *n* tracción *f*
trade-off *n* situación *f* que requiere sacrificar una cosa para lograr otra; **You're facing a trade-off between putting up with the itching or having pain.**. Ud. tiene que escoger entre aguantar la comezón o padecer dolor.
tragus *n* trago
train *vi* entrenar
training *n* entrenamiento; **toilet** — (*ped*) entrenamiento para usar el baño
trait *n* rasgo; **sickle cell** — rasgo drepanocítico *or* falciforme; **thalassemia** — rasgo talasémico
tramadol *n* tramadol *m*
trance *n* trance *m*
tranquilize *vt* (*esp. vet*) sedar, tranquilizar (*esp. vet*)
tranquilizer *n* (*esp. vet*) sedante *m*, tranquilizante *m* (*esp. vet*)
transabdominal *adj* transabdominal
transaminase *n* transaminasa
transcatheter *adj* transcatéter
transcutaneous *adj* transcutáneo
transdermal *adj* transdérmico
trans fat (*fam*) **trans fatty acid**. *V.* **fatty acid**.
transfer *n* transferencia; (*of a patient*) traslado; **embryo** — transferencia embrionaria; **gamete intrafallopian** — **(GIFT)** transferencia intratubárica de gametos (TIG); *vt* (*pret & pp* **-ferred**; *ger* **-ferring**) transferir; (*a patient*) trasladar
transference *n* (*psych*) transferencia
transferrin *n* transferrina
transformation *n* transformación *f*
transfuse *vt* transfundir, hacer una transfusión, poner sangre (*fam*)
transfusion *n* transfusión *f*; **Have you ever had a transfusion before?**..¿Ha recibido alguna vez una transfusión?; **autologous blood** — autotransfusión *f*, transfusión de la propia sangre del paciente extraída previamente (*antes*

una cirugía, precedimiento, etc.); **exchange** — exanguinotransfusión *f*, reemplazo de la sangre (*del paciente*) con sangre donada; **to give a** — hacer una transfusión, poner sangre (*fam*); **I need to give you a transfusion**..Tengo que hacerle una transfusión..Tengo que ponerle sangre; — **of red blood cells (platelets, etc.)** transfusión de glóbulos rojos (plaquetas, etc.)

transgender *adj* transgénero (*inv*); **a — man** un transgénero; **a — person** un *or* una transgénero, una persona transgénero; **a — woman** una mujer transgénero, una transgénero

transgenderism *n* transgenerismo

transient *adj* transitorio, pasajero

transition *n* transición *f*

transitional *adj* transicional

translate *vt* traducir

translocation *n* translocación *f*

transmissible *adj* transmisible

transmission *n* transmisión *f*

transmit *vt* (*pret & pp* **-mitted**; *ger* **-mitting**) transmitir

transplant *n* trasplante *m*; **bone marrow** — trasplante de médula ósea; **hair** — trasplante capilar *or* de pelo; **heart** — trasplante cardíaco *or* de corazón; **kidney** — trasplante renal *or* de riñón; **liver** — trasplante hepático *or* de hígado; **lung** — trasplante pulmonar *or* de pulmón; **organ** — trasplante de órgano(s); **renal** — trasplante renal *or* de riñón; *vt* trasplantar

transport *n* transporte *m*; *vt* transportar

transposition *n* transposición *f*

transrectal *adj* transrectal

transsexual *adj & n* transexual *mf*

transurethral *adj* transuretral

transvaginal *adj* transvaginal

transvestism *n* travestismo

transvestite *n* travesti *mf*, travestido -da *mf* (*esp. Esp*)

trapeze *n* (*for a hospital bed*) trapecio (*para una cama hospitalaria*)

trapezius *n* trapecio

trauma *n* (*physical*) trauma *m*, traumatismo; (*psych*) trauma *m*

traumatic *adj* traumático

traumatize *vt* traumatizar

traumatologist *n* traumatólogo -ga *mf*

traumatology *n* traumatología

travel *n* (el) viajar, viajes *mpl*; **foreign** — viajes al extranjero

tray *n* bandeja, charola (*Mex*)

trazodone *n* trazodona

treadmill *n* caminadora (*Amer*), tapiz *m or* cinta rodante (*esp. Esp*)

treat *vt* tratar

treatable *adj* tratable, que se puede tratar

treatment *n* tratamiento; **breathing** — nebulización *f*; **maintenance** — (*oncology, addiction medicine, etc.*) tratamiento *or* terapia de mantenimiento

tremble *vi* temblar

tremor *n* temblor *m*; **Do you have a tremor?**..¿Le tiemblan las manos?; **essential** — temblor esencial

tremulous *adj* tembloroso

trench mouth *n* gingivitis ulcerativa necrotizante aguda

trend *n* tendencia

tretinoin *n* tretinoína

triage *n* triage *m*, evaluación *f* inicial de pacientes de urgencia para establecer prioridades

trial *n* ensayo, prueba; **clinical** — ensayo clínico; — **and error** ensayo y error, prueba y error

triamcinolone *n* triamcinolona

triamterene *n* triamtereno

triazolam *n* triazolam *m*

triceps *n* tríceps *m*

trichinosis, trichinellosis *n* triquinosis *f*, triquinelosis *f*

trichloroacetic acid *n* ácido tricloroacético

trichomoniasis *n* tricomoniasis *f*

trichotillomania *n* tricotilomanía, compulsión *f* a arrancarse el cabello

tricuspid *adj* tricúspide

tried *pret & pp de* **try**

tries *pl de* **try**

trifocal *adj* trifocal

trigeminal *adj* trigémino

trigger *n* gatillo; — **finger** dedo en gatillo; — **point** punto gatillo; *vt* provocar

triglyceride *n* triglicérido

trihexyphenidyl *n* trihexifenidilo

trimester *n* trimestre *m*

trimethoprim *n* trimetoprim *m*, trimetoprima (*INN*)

trip *vi* (*pret & pp* **tripped**; *ger* **tripping**) tropezar, dar un traspié

triphasic *adj* (*pharm*) trifásico

triplet *n* trillizo -za *mf*

trismus *n* trismo

trisomy *n* trisomía; **— 21** trisomía 21

trivalent *adj* trivalente

trochanter *n* trocánter *m*

trochanteric *adj* trocantérico, trocantéreo

troche *n* pastilla para chupar

tropical *adj* tropical

tropicamide *n* tropicamida

trospium chloride *n* cloruro de trospio

trouble *n* molestia (*frec. pl*); **Do you have trouble with your back?**.. Tiene molestia(s) en la espalda?

true *adj* verdadero

trunk *n* (*anat*) tronco

truss *n* braguero, faja para contener una hernia

trust *n* confianza; *vt* tener confianza en, confiar en

try *n* (*pl* **tries**) intento, prueba; *vt* (*pret & pp* **tried**) tratar de, intentar; (*a new medication, etc.*) probar; *vi* tratar, intentar

trypanosomiasis *n* tripanosomiasis *f*

trypsin *n* tripsina

tryptophan *n* triptófano

TSH *abbr* **thyroid-stimulating hormone**. *V.* **hormone.**

TST *abbr* **tuberculin skin test**. *V.* **test.**

TTP *abbr* **thrombotic thrombocytopenic purpura**. *V.* **purpura.**

tubal *adj* tubárico

tube *n* tubo, sonda, trompa, manguera; **chest —** tubo torácico *or* de tórax; **drainage —** tubo de drenaje; **endotracheal —** tubo endotraqueal; **Eustachian —** trompa de Eustaquio; **fallopian —** trompa uterina, trompa de Falopio (*ant*); **feeding —** sonda de alimentación; **gastrostomy —, G-tube** (*fam*) sonda de gastrostomía; **nasogastric —** sonda nasogástrica

tuberculin *n* tuberculina

tuberculoid *adj* tuberculoide

tuberculosis (TB) *n* tuberculosis *f* (TB); **latent — infection** infección tuberculosa latente

tuberculous *adj* tuberculoso

tuberous *adj* tuberoso

tubing *n* tubería

tubo-ovarian *adj* tubo-ovárico

tubular *adj* tubular

tubule *n* túbulo

tularemia *n* tularemia

tummy *n* (*pl* **-mies**) (*ped*) barriga, panza; **— tuck** (*fam*) *V.* **abdominoplasty.**

tumor *adj* tumoral; *n* tumor *m*; **benign — tumor** benigno; **brain —** tumor cerebral; **desmoid —** tumor desmoide; **malignant —** tumor maligno; **Wilms' —** tumor de Wilms

tuna *n* atún *m*

tuning fork *n* diapasón *m*

tunnel *n* túnel *m*; **carpal —** túnel carpiano; **tarsal —** túnel tarsiano

turbinate *n* cornete *m*

turistas, the (*fam*) diarrea del viajero

turn *n* vuelta; *vt* (*a patient in bed*) cambiar de posición, voltear (*a un encamado*); *vi* darse vuelta; **to — around** darse media vuelta; **to — red (blue, etc.)** ponerse colorado (azul, etc.); **to — out** resultar; **The tests turned out negative**..Las pruebas resultaron negativas; **to — over** (*on the exam table*) voltearse, darse vuelta

TURP *abbr* **transurethral resection of the prostate**. *V.* **resection.**

turpentine *n* trementina

tweak *vt* (*fam*) usar metanfetamina

tweaker *n* (*fam*) persona que usa metanfetamina

tweezers *npl* pinzas, tenaza(s)

twice *adv* dos veces; **— daily, — a day** dos veces al día

twin *adj & n* gemelo -la *mf*, mellizo -za *mf*; **conjoined —** gemelo unido, hermano -na *mf* siamés, gemelo siamés; **fraternal —** mellizo, gemelo que no se parece a su hermano; **identical —** gemelo idéntico; **Siamese —** (*ant*) hermano -na *mf* siamés, gemelo siamés, gemelo unido

twinge *n* (*of pain*) punzada, dolor agudo y repentino

twist *vt, vi* (*one's ankle, etc.*) torcerse, doblarse; **Did you twist your ankle?**.. ¿Se torció el tobillo?

twitch *n* tic *m*, sacudida (muscular), contracción breve e involuntaria de un músculo

tympanic *adj* timpánico

tympanoplasty *n* (*pl* **-ties**) timpanoplastia

type *n* tipo; **blood —** grupo sanguíneo (*form*), tipo de sangre; **tissue —** tipo

de tejido; **this type of problem.**.este tipo de problemas (*plural required*)
typhoid *adj* tifoideo; *n* (*fam*) fiebre tifoidea, tifoidea (*fam*)

typhus *n* tifus *m*
typical *adj* típico
tyramine *n* tiramina
tyrosine *n* tirosina

U

ugly *adj* feo
ulcer *n* úlcera, llaga; **aphthous —** afta; **decubitus —** úlcera de decúbito (*form*), úlcera por presión, llaga debida a permanecer mucho tiempo sentado o encamado sin cambiar de posición; **duodenal —** úlcera duodenal *or* del duodeno; **gastric —** úlcera gástrica *or* del estómago; **peptic —** úlcera péptica; **stress —** úlcera de estrés
ulcerated *adj* ulcerado
ulceration *n* ulceración *f*
ulipristal *n* ulipristal *m*
ulna *n* cúbito
ulnar *adj* cubital
ultrafiltration *n* ultrafiltración *f*
ultrasonography *n* ecografía (*técnica*); **Doppler —** ecografía Doppler; **duplex —** ecografía dúplex
ultrasound *adj* ultrasónico; *n* ultrasonido; (*fam, imaging study*) ecografía
ultraviolet *adj* ultravioleta
umbilical *adj* umbilical
umbilicus *n* (*pl* **-ci**) ombligo
unable *adj* incapaz
unaffected *adj* no afectado
unavoidable *adj* inevitable
unaware *adj* inconsciente, ignorante
unbearable *adj* insoportable, intolerable
unbuckle *vt* desabrochar(se)
unburdening *n* desahogo
unbutton *vt* desabrochar(se), desabotonar(se); **Can you unbutton your shirt?**..¿Puede desabrocharse la camisa?

uncertainty *n* incertidumbre *f*
uncle *n* tío
uncomfortable *adj* incómodo
uncommon *adj* poco común
uncomplicated *adj* sin complicaciones
unconscious *adj* inconsciente; **unconscious patient**..paciente inconsciente... **unconscious thoughts**..pensamientos inconscientes; *n* (*fam, unconscious mind*) mente *f* inconsciente, inconsciente *m* (*fam*)
uncooperative *adj* no colaborador
uncovered *adj* descubierto
underachiever *n* persona que no alcanza su potencial
underarm *n* axila
undercooked *adj* poco cocido *or* cocinado
undergo *vt* (*pret* **-went**; *pp* **-gone**) someterse a; **I hope you don't have to undergo another surgery**..Espero que no tenga que someterse a otra cirugía.
underlying *adj* subyacente
undernourished *adj* desnutrido, malnutrido, subalimentado
undernourishment *n* malnutrición *f*, desnutrición *f*, subalimentación *f*
underpants *npl* (*men's*) calzoncillos; (*women's*) calzón *m* (*frec. pl*), pantaletas (*esp. Mex*), bloomer *m* (*esp. CA, frec. pl*), panties *mpl* (*esp. Carib*), bragas (*esp. Esp*)
undershirt *n* camiseta

underwater *adj* submarino
underwear *n* ropa interior
underweight *adj* con bajo peso, por debajo del peso normal
underwent *pret de* **undergo**
undesirable *adj* indeseable
undetectable *adj* indetectable
undifferentiated *adj* indiferenciado
undigested *adj* no digerido
unequal *adj* desigual
unexpected *adj* inesperado
unfavorable *adj* desfavorable
ungual *adj* ungueal
unhappy *adj* infeliz, descontento
unhealthy *adj* poco *or* no saludable, (*conditions*) insalubre
uniform *adj* uniforme; *n* uniforme *m*
unilateral *adj* unilateral
uninsured *adj* sin seguro, no asegurado
unintended *adj* no planeado, no deseado, accidental; — **pregnancy** embarazo no planeado *or* planificado, embarazo no deseado
union *n* (*ortho, etc.*) unión *f*
unit *n* unidad *f*; **coronary care** — unidad coronaria; **intensive care** — **(ICU)** unidad de cuidados intensivos (UCI), unidad de terapia intensiva (UTI) (*SA*); **international** — unidad internacional; — **of blood** unidad de sangre
unite *vt, vi* unir(se)
universal *adj* universal
unmarried *adj* soltero
Unna boot *n* bota de Unna
unpleasant *adj* desagradable
unrelated *adj* (*not connected*) no asociado; (*not family*) no emparentado
unresectable *adj* irresecable
unresponsive *adj* que no responde
unsanitary *adj* antihigiénico
unsaturated *adj* insaturado
unstable *adj* inestable
unsteady *adj* (*on one's feet*) de marcha inestable, propenso a caerse
unsuitable *adj* inadecuado
untreated *adj* no tratado
unusual *adj* inusual, raro, extraño
unvaccinated *adj* no vacunado, sin vacunar
unwanted *adj* no deseado, indeseado
up *adv* hacia arriba, para arriba; (*high*) alto, elevado; **Look up**..Mire hacia arriba...**from the waist up**..de la cintura para arriba...**Your sugar is up**..Su azúcar está alto (elevado).
uphill *adv* cuesta arriba
upper *adj* (*anat*) superior (*form*), alto, de arriba
upright *adj* erguido
upset *adj* molesto, trastornado; **to get o become** — molestarse, trastornarse; **to have an** — **stomach** tener dolor de estómago, sentirse mal del estómago; *vt* (*pret & pp* **upset**; *ger* **upsetting**) molestar, trastornar
uptake *n* captación *f*
upward *adv* hacia arriba
uranium *n* uranio
urban *adj* urbano
urea *n* urea
uremia *n* uremia
uremic *adj* urémico
ureter *n* uréter *m*
ureteral *adj* ureteral
urethra *n* uretra
urethral *adj* uretral
urethritis *n* uretritis *f*; **non-gonococcal** — uretritis no gonocócica
urge *n* deseo, necesidad *f*; **the urge to urinate**..la necesidad de orinar
urgent *adj* urgente
uric acid *n* ácido úrico
urinal *n* (*hand-held*) orinal *m*, pato (*Amer*)
urinalysis *n* (*pl* -**ses**) análisis *m* de orina
urinary *adj* urinario
urinate *vi* orinar, hacer pipí (*esp. ped, fam*)
urine *n* orina
urodynamics *n* urodinámica
urogenital *adj* urogenital
urogram *n* urografía (*estudio*), urograma *m*
urography *n* urografía (*técnica*); **excretory** — urografía excretora
urokinase *n* uroquinasa (*INN*), urokinasa *or* urocinasa
urologist *n* urólogo -ga *mf*, médico -ca *mf* cirujano especializado en el aparato urinario
urology *n* urología, rama de la medicina que se ocupa del aparato urinario
urosepsis *n* urosepsis *f*
urticaria *n* urticaria
use *n* uso, empleo; **use of her leg**..uso de

su pierna; **excessive** — uso excesivo; *vt* usar, utilizar, emplear; **to get used to** acostumbrarse a; **as you get used to** ..a medida que se acostumbra a; **to —up** usar todo; **Have you used up all your codeine?**..¿Ha usado toda su codeína?; **used up** agotado

useless *adj* inútil

user *n* usuario -ria *mf*, consumidor -ra *mf*

usual *adj* usual, habitual; **your usual dose**..su dosis habitual; **as —** como de costumbre, como siempre; **Keep taking your medications as usual**..Siga tomando sus medicamentos como de costumbre; **than —** que de costumbre;

Are you drinking more liquids than usual?..¿Está tomando más líquidos que de costumbre?

usually *adv* normalmente, en la mayoría de casos

uteri *pl de* **uterus**

uterine *adj* uterino

uterus *n* (*pl* **-ri**) útero, matriz *f*

UTI *abbr* **urinary tract infection**. *V.* **infection**.

utilize *vt* utilizar

uvea *n* úvea

uveitis *n* uveítis *f*

uvula *n* (*pl* **-las** *o* **-lae**) úvula, campanilla (*fam*)

V

VA *V.* **Veterans Affairs**.

vaccinate *vt* vacunar; **Have you been vaccinated against tetanus?**..¿Ha sido vacunado contra el tétano?

vaccination *n* vacunación *f*

vaccine *n* vacuna; **attenuated** — vacuna atenuada; **BCG** — vacuna BCG; **conjugated** — vacuna conjugada; **diphtheria, tetanus, and pertussis (DTP)** — vacuna contra (la) difteria, (el) tétanos y (la) tos ferina, vacuna DTP; **flu** — vacuna antigripal (*form*), vacuna contra la influenza *or* gripe; **Haemophilus influenzae type b** — vacuna contra (el) Haemophilus influenzae tipo b; **hepatitis B** — vacuna contra la hepatitis B; **inactivated** — vacuna inactivada; **influenza** — *V.* **flu** — *arriba*; **live** — vacuna viva; **meningococcal** — vacuna meningocócica, vacuna contra la meningitis meningocócica; **measles, mumps, and rubella (MMR)** — vacuna triple viral; vacuna contra el sarampión, las paperas y la rubéola;

oral polio — vacuna antipoliomielítica oral, vacuna oral contra la polio; **pneumococcal** — vacuna neumocócica, vacuna contra la neumonía; **rabies** — vacuna contra la rabia; **Sabin** — vacuna Sabin; **Salk** — vacuna Salk; **smallpox** — vacuna contra la viruela; **tetanus-diphtheria (Td)** — vacuna contra (el) tétanos y (la) difteria, vacuna Td; **tetanus, diphtheria, and acellular pertussis (Tdap)** — vacuna contra (la) difteria, (el) tétanos y (la) tos ferina (DTP), vacuna contra el tétanos, la difteria y la tos ferina (*Ang*), vacuna Tdap (*Ang*) (*el componente contra la tos ferina siendo acelular en las traducciones antecedentes*); **varicella** — vacuna contra la varicela

vaccinee *n* vacunado -da *mf*

vaccinia *n* vacuna

vagal *adj* vagal

vagina *n* vagina

vaginal *adj* vaginal

vaginitis *n* vaginitis *f*

vaginosis n vaginosis f; **bacterial —** vaginosis bacteriana

vagotomy n (pl -mies) vagotomía; **selective —** vagotomía selectiva

vagus n vago

valacyclovir n valaciclovir m

valdecoxib n valdecoxib m

valerian n (bot) valeriana

valgus adj valgo, desviado hacia afuera (refiriéndose a una extremidad o parte de ella en relación con el eje del cuerpo)

valid adj válido

validation n (psych, etc.) validación f

validity n validez f

valine n valina

vallecula n vallécula

valproic acid, valproate sodium (USAN), **valproate** n ácido valproico, valproato sódico or de sodio, valproato

valsartan n valsartán m

value n valor m; **nutritional —** valor nutritivo; **the patient's values**..los valores del paciente

valve n válvula; **aortic —** válvula aórtica; **mitral —** válvula mitral; **pulmonic —** válvula pulmonar; **pyloric —** válvula pilórica; **tricuspid —** válvula tricúspide

valvotomy n (pl -mies) valvulotomía, valvuloplastia

valvuloplasty n (pl -ties) valvuloplastia

vancomycin n vancomicina

vapor n vapor m

vaporization n vaporización f

vaporizer n vaporizador m

vardenafil n vardenafil m, vardenafilo

varenicline n vareniclina

variable adj & n variable f

variant adj & n variante f; **lupus —** variante de lupus

variation n variación f

varicella n varicela

varices pl de **varix**

varicocele n varicocele m

varicose adj varicoso; **— vein** vena varicosa

varix n (pl -ices) (frec. pl) várice or varice f, variz f (Esp)

varus adj varo, desviado hacia dentro (refiriéndose a una extremidad o parte de ella en relación con el eje del cuerpo)

vary vi (pret & pp -ried) variar, oscilar

vascular adj vascular

vasculitis n vasculitis f; **hypersensitivity —** vasculitis por hipersensibilidad; **leukocytoclastic —** vasculitis leucocitoclástica; **necrotizing —** vasculitis necrotizante

vas deferens n conducto deferente

vasectomy n (pl -mies) vasectomía

Vaseline (marca) V. **petroleum jelly** bajo **petroleum.**

vasoconstriction n vasoconstricción f

vasoconstrictor n vasoconstrictor m

vasodilation n vasodilatación f

vasodilator n vasodilatador m

vasopressin n vasopresina, hormona antidiurética

vasospasm n vasoespasmo

vasovagal adj vasovagal

VD abbr **venereal disease.** V. **disease.**

vector n vector m

vegan adj & n vegano -na mf

veganism n veganismo

vegetable adj vegetal; n vegetal m, verdura, hortaliza; **to live as a vegetable** (fam)..vivir en estado vegetativo; **leafy green —** verdura de hoja verde

vegetarian adj & n vegetariano -na mf

vegetarianism n vegetarianismo

vegetation n vegetación f

vegetative adj vegetativo; **persistent — state** estado vegetativo persistente

veggie (fam) V. **vegetable.**

vehicle n vehículo; (pharm) excipiente m

vein n vena; **antecubital —** vena antecubital; **external jugular —** vena yugular externa; **femoral —** vena femoral; **great saphenous —** vena safena interna; **internal jugular —** vena yugular interna; **portal —** vena porta; **saphenous —** vena safena; **subclavian —** vena subclavia

vein stripping n cirugía de várices, fleboextracción f (form)

vena cava n vena cava; **inferior — —** vena cava inferior; **superior — —** vena cava superior

veneer n (dent) carilla; **porcelain —** carilla de porcelana

venereal adj (ant) de transmisión sexual, venéreo (ant)

venipuncture n venopunción f, punción venosa, punción f de una vena para

sacar sangre o inyectar algo
venlafaxine *n* venlafaxina
venogram *n* flebografía, venografía (*estudio*)
venography *n* flebografía, venografía (*técnica*)
venom *n* veneno
venomous *adj* venenoso
venous *adj* venoso
ventilation *n* ventilación *f*; **mechanical** — ventilación mecánica; **noninvasive positive pressure** — ventilación no invasiva con presión positiva
ventilator *n* ventilador *m*, respirador *m*, aparato para suministrar respiración artificial
ventral *adj* ventral
ventricle *n* ventrículo
ventricular *adj* ventricular
venule *n* vénula
verapamil *n* verapamilo, verapamil *m*
vertebra *n* (*pl* -brae) vértebra
vertebral *adj* vertebral
vertebroplasty *n* (*pl* -ties) vertebroplastia
vertex *n* (*anat*) coronilla, vértice *m*, parte *f* superior de la cabeza
vertical *adj* vertical
vertigo *n* vértigo
vesicle *n* vesícula, ampolla
vessel *n* vaso; **blood** — vaso sanguíneo
vestibular *adj* vestibular
vestibule *n* vestíbulo
veteran *n* veterano -na *mf*
Veterans Affairs (VA) *n* Asuntos de Veteranos
veterinarian *n* veterinario -ria *mf*
veterinary *adj* veterinario
viable *adj* viable
vial *n* frasco, vial *m*
vibration *n* vibración *f*
vibrator *n* vibrador *m*
victim *n* víctima; **I'm not a victim, I'm a survivor!**..No soy víctima, !Soy sobreviviente!
vidarabine *n* vidarabina
video *n* video, vídeo *m* (*RAE*)
view *n* (*radiografía, etc.*) vista; **oblique** — vista oblicua
vigabatrin *n* vigabatrina
vigor *n* vigor *m*
vigorous *adj* vigoroso
vinblastine *n* vinblastina

vincristine *n* vincristina
vinegar *n* vinagre *m*
violence *n* violencia; **domestic** — violencia doméstica; **gun** — violencia con armas de fuego
violent *adj* violento
violin spider *V.* **brown recluse spider** *bajo* **spider**.
viper *n* víbora
viral *adj* viral, vírico
viremia *n* viremia
virgin *n* virgen *mf*
virginity *n* virginidad *f*
virility *n* virilidad *f*
virilization *n* virilización *f*
virologic, virological *adj* virológico
virology *n* virología, estudio de los virus
virtual *adj* virtual
virulence *n* virulencia
virulent *adj* virulento
virus *n* (*pl* **viruses**) virus *m*; **attenuated** — virus atenuado; **Epstein-Barr** — **(EBV)** virus Epstein-Barr (VEB); **flu** — virus gripal *or* de la gripe; **hepatitis B** — **(HBV), hepatitis C** — **(HCV),** etc. virus de la hepatitis B (VHB), virus de la hepatitis C (VHC), etc.; **herpes simplex** — **(HSV)** virus herpes simple (VHS); **human immunodeficiency** — **(HIV)** virus de (la) inmunodeficiencia humana (VIH); **human T-lymphotrophic** — virus linfotrópico humano de células T; **influenza** — virus de (la) influenza; **live** — virus vivo; **Norwalk** — virus Norwalk; **respiratory syncytial** — virus respiratorio sincitial; **varicella-zoster** — virus varicela-zóster; **West Nile** — virus del Nilo Occidental
visceral *adj* visceral
viscosity *n* (*pl* -ties) viscosidad *f*
viscous *adj* viscoso
visible *adj* visible
vision *n* visión *f*, vista; **blurred** — visión nublada *or* borrosa; **double** — visión doble; **far** — visión lejana; **near** — visión cercana; **night** — visión nocturna; **peripheral** — visión periférica; **tunnel** — visión de túnel
visit *n* consulta, visita; **doctor's** — consulta *or* visita médica, consulta con el médico, visita al médico; **unscheduled** — consulta sin cita, consulta *or* visita

no programada; *vt* visitar
visitor *n* visitante *mf*
visual *adj* visual
visualization *n* visualización *f*
visualize *vt* visualizar
vital *adj* vital
vitality *n* vitalidad *f*
vitamin *adj* vitamínico; *n* vitamina; **fat-soluble** — vitamina liposoluble; — **A (B₁₂, etc.)** vitamina A (B₁₂, etc.); — **B complex** complejo vitamínico B; **water-soluble** — vitamina hidrosoluble
vitiligo *n* vitíligo *or* vitiligo
vitreous *adj* vítreo
VLDL *abbr* **very low density lipoprotein.** *V.* **lipoprotein.**
vocal *adj* vocal
voice *n* voz *f*; **to hear voices** (*psych*) oír *or* escuchar voces

void *vi* vaciar la vejiga, orinar
volt *n* voltio
volume *n* volumen *m*; **tidal** — volumen corriente
voluntary *adj* voluntario
volunteer *n* voluntario -ria *mf*
volvulus *n* vólvulo
vomit *n* vómito (*frec. pl*); *vt, vi* vomitar, arrojar (*fam*), devolver (*fam*), deponer (*Mex, fam*); **Did you vomit blood?**.. ¿Vomitó sangre?
vomiting *n* vómito (*frec. pl*), (el) vomitar
voodoo *n* vudú *m*
voriconazole *n* voriconazol *m*
voyeurism *n* voyeurismo
VSD *abbr* **ventricular septal defect.** *V.* **defect.**
vulnerable *adj* vulnerable
vulva *n* (*pl* -vae) vulva

W

wafer *n* (*pharm*) tableta dispersable, comprimido dispersable (*esp. Esp*)
waist *n* cintura
waistline *n* parte más estrecha de la cintura, circunferencia de la cintura
wait *vi* esperar; **to** — **for** esperar; **Other patients are waiting for me**..Otros pacientes me esperan.
waiting list *n* lista de espera
wake *vt, vi* (*pret* woke; *pp* woke *o* waked) (*también* **to** — **up**) despertar(se)
wake-up call *n* (*fam*) llamada *or* llamado de atención
walk *vi* caminar, andar; **Walk over here** ..Camine hacia acá..**Let me see how you walk**..Déjeme ver como camina; **to** — **in one's sleep** caminar dormido
walker *n* andador *m*, andadera (*Mex*), aparato que se usa como soporte al caminar; **front-wheeled** — andador con

ruedas delanteras
walking *n* (el) caminar; **Walking is good for you**..Caminar es bueno para Ud.
wall *n* pared *f*; **abdominal** — pared abdominal; **chest** — pared torácica
wall-eyed *adj* (*fam*) con un ojo despistado, con un ojo desviado hacia afuera
war *n* guerra; **nuclear** — guerra nuclear
ward *n* (*of a hospital*) sala; **maternity** — sala de maternidad; **observation** — sala de observación
ward clerk (*ant*) *V.* **patient service representative** *bajo* **representative.**
warfarin *n* warfarina
warm *adj* tibio, un poco caliente; **to be** *o* **feel** — tener *or* sentir calor; — **water** (*very warm*) agua caliente, (*not very warm*) agua tibia; *vt* (*también* **to** — **up**) calentar; *vi* **to** — **up** calentarse; (*sports*) hacer (el) calentamiento, hacer

ejercicios de calentamiento
warmth *n* calor *m*
warmup *n* (ejercicios de) calentamiento
warning *n* advertencia, aviso, alerta; — **sign** señal *f* de advertencia *or* alerta
wart *n* verruga; **genital** — verruga genital; **plantar** — verruga plantar
wash *vt* lavar; **to** — **one's hair (face, hands, etc.)** lavarse el pelo (la cara, las manos, etc.)
washcloth *n* toallita *or* toalla facial, paño
wasp *n* avispa
waste *n* desechos, residuos; **hazardous** — desechos *or* residuos peligrosos; **medical** — desechos *or* residuos médicos; **metabolic** — desechos *or* residuos metabólicos; *vt* desperdiciar; (*money*) malgastar; **We don't want to waste health care dollars**..No queremos malgastar recursos sanitarios.
wastewater *n* aguas residuales
wasting *n* desgaste *m*; **muscle** — desgaste muscular
watchful waiting *n* espera vigilante
water *n* agua; **distilled** — agua destilada; **drinking** — agua potable; **fresh** — agua dulce; **hard** — agua dura, agua con alto contenido de sales; **mineral** — agua mineral; **purified** — agua purificada; **running** — agua corriente; **salt** — agua salada; **soft** — agua blanda, agua con bajo contenido de sales; **tap** — agua del grifo, agua de la llave, agua de la canilla (*esp. SA*)
waterborne *adj* transmitido por el agua
waterbrash *n* salivación *f* refleja que precede al vómito
watery *adj* acuoso; — **discharge** secreción acuosa
wave *n* ola; (*sound, light, etc.*) onda; **brain** — onda cerebral; **heat** — ola de calor; **shock** — onda de choque
wavelength *n* longitud *f* de onda
wax *n* cera; **ear** — cerumen *m* (*form*), cera de los oídos
weak *adj* débil
weaken *vt, vi* debilitar(se)
weakening *n* debilitamiento, decaimiento
weakness *n* debilidad *f*
wean *vt* destetar
weaning *n* destete *m*; — **from the ventilator** destete del respirador *or* ventila-

dor
weapon *n* arma; **biologic** — arma biológica; **chemical** — arma química
wear *vt* (*pret* **wore**; *pp* **worn**) usar, llevar; **You should wear a hat**..Debe usar sombrero...**You need to wear this brace**..Tiene que usar este aparato ortopédico...**Wear light-colored clothing when you are around ticks**..Use ropa de colores claros cuando haya garrapatas; *vi* **to** — **off** pasar; **The numbness will wear off in a couple of hours**..El entumecimiento se le pasará en un par de horas; **to** — **out** gastar(se); **This prosthesis will wear out in 10 or 15 years**..Esta prótesis se gastará en 10 ó 15 años..Esta prótesis durará 10 ó 15 años.
weather *n* tiempo; **under the** — (*fam*) (un poco) enfermo
web *n* membrana; **esophageal** — membrana esofágica
webbed *adj* alado; — **neck** cuello alado
weed (*fam*) marihuana, mariguana (*Mex*), hierba (*fam*), mota (*Mex, CA; fam*)
week *n* semana
weekend *n* fin *m* de semana; — **warrior** guerrero -ra *mf* de fin de semana
weep *vi* (*pret & pp* **wept**) llorar; (*lesion*) secretar líquido
Wegener's granulomatosis *n* (*ant*) granulomatosis con poliangeítis, granulomatosis *f* de Wegener (*ant*)
weigh *vt, vi* pesar; **The nurse will weigh you**..La enfermera lo va a pesar...**How much do you weigh?**..¿Cuánto pesa?
weight *n* peso; (*sports*) pesa; **excess** — sobrepeso; **ideal body** — peso corporal ideal; **lean body** — peso corporal magro; **to lift weights** levantar pesas
weightlifting *n* levantamiento de pesas, (el) levantar pesas, (*in competition*) halterofilia; — **belt** cinturón de levantamiento
welfare *n* bienestar *m*; (*US, governmental assistance*) asistencia social
well *adj & adv* (*comp* **better**; *super* **best**) bien; **to get** — recuperarse, mejorarse, curarse
wellbeing, well-being *n* bienestar *m*
wellness *n* bienestar *m*, sanidad *f*
welt *n* verdugo
went *pret de* **go**

wept *pret & pp de* **weep**

wet *adj* (*comp* **wetter**; *super* **wettest**) mojado; **to get —** mojarse; *vt* (*pret & pp* **wet** *o* **wetted**; *ger* **wetting**) mojar; **to — the bed** orinarse en la cama, mojar la cama

wet dream *n* emisión nocturna (*form*), sueño húmedo

wet nurse *n* nodriza

wheal *n* (*hive*) roncha, habón *m* (*esp. Esp*); (*welt*) verdugo

wheat *n* trigo

wheelchair *n* silla de ruedas; **electric —** silla de ruedas eléctrica; **folding —** silla de ruedas plegable; **manual —** silla de ruedas manual; **motorized —** silla de ruedas motorizada

wheeze *n* sibilancia (*form*), silbido (en el pecho); *vi* tener sibilancias, tener silbidos (en el pecho); **Have you been wheezing?**..¿Ha tenido sibilancias al respirar?..¿Ha tenido silbidos en el pecho?

wheezing *n* sibilancias (*form*), silbidos (en el pecho)

whenever *adv* (*doesn't matter when*) cuando quiera, a la hora que sea; (*every time that*) cada vez que; **whenever you have pain**..cada vez que tenga dolor

whey *n* suero de leche

whiplash *n* latigazo (cervical)

whipworm *n* tricocéfalo

whirlpool *n* bañera de hidromasaje, tina de hidromasaje (*esp. Mex*)

whisper *vt* susurrar, decir en voz baja; **I'm going to whisper a word to see if you can hear me**..Voy a susurrar una palabra para ver si me puede esuchar; *vi* susurrar, hablar en voz baja

white *adj* blanco; *n* (*of an egg*) clara

whitehead *n* (*derm*) punto blanco

whitener *n* blanqueador *m*; **teeth** *o* **tooth —** blanqueador dental

whitening *n* (*dent*) blanqueamiento (dental)

white noise *n* ruido blanco

whitish *adj* blanquecino

whitlow *n* panadizo (herpético), infección de la punta de un dedo (*producida por el herpes en la mayoría de los casos*)

WHO *abbr* **World Health Organiza-** tion. *V.* **organization**.

whole *adj* integral, entero, total, todo el; **— blood** sangre total; **whole-grain cereals** cereales integrales; **— milk** leche entera; **— wheat** trigo integral; **the whole tumor**..todo el tumor

whooping cough *n* tos ferina, coqueluche *m&f* (*fam*)

wick *n* mecha

wide *adj* ancho

widen *vt* ensanchar, hacer más ancho

widow *n* viuda

widowed *adj* viudo

widower *n* viudo

width *n* anchura, ancho

wife *n* (*pl* **wives**) esposa

wig *n* peluca

wiggle *vt, vi* mover(se); **Wiggle your toes**..Mueva sus dedos del pie.

wild *adj* (*animal*) salvaje, (*plant*) silvestre

will *n* voluntad *f*; **against your —** contra su voluntad; **of one's own free —** por voluntad propia; **— power** fuerza de voluntad, autodisciplina; **— to live** ganas de vivir

wind *n* viento; (*fam, stamina*) resistencia, capacidad *f* para esforzarse sin quedarse sin aliento

windburn *n* sequedad *f* y ardor de la piel producidos por el viento

winded *adj* (*fam*) sin aliento *or* aire

windpipe *n* (*fam*) tráquea

wine *n* vino; **red —** vino tinto; **white —** vino blanco

wing *n* (*of a hospital*) ala

winged scapula *n* escápula alada

winter *n* invierno; **— itch** sequedad *f* de la piel con comezón que ocurre generalmente en el invierno

wipe *vt* enjugar; **to — oneself** (*after moving bowels*) limpiarse

wire *n* alambre *m*

wired *adj* (*fam*) acelerado

wishful thinking *n* (el) creer que algo es verdadero porque se desea intensamente

witchcraft *n* brujería

witch hazel *n* agua de hamamelis

withdrawal *n* síndrome *m* de abstinencia (*form*), síntomas sufridos por el adicto o alcohólico al suspender drogas o alcohol

withdrawn *adj* retraído
wives *pl de* **wife**
woke *pret de* **wake**
woman *n* (*pl* **women**) mujer *f*
womb *n* útero, matriz *f*, vientre *m* (*fam*)
women *pl de* **woman**
women's room *n* baño de mujeres *or* damas
wool *n* lana
woozy *adj* (*fam*) mareado, drogado
word *n* palabra; — **finding difficulty** dificultad *f* para encontrar palabras
wore *pret de* **wear**
work *adj* laboral, del trabajo; *n* trabajo; **social** — trabajo social; *vi* trabajar; (*to function*) funcionar, trabajar; **Your kidneys have stopped working**.. Sus riñones han dejado de funcionar; **to — out** (*to exercise*) hacer ejercicio (*esp. del tipo que se hace en un gimnasio*)
worker *n* obrero -ra *mf*, trabajador -ra *mf*; **social** — trabajador social, asistente *mf* social
worker's compensation *n* compensación *f* laboral, programa *m* de seguro para compensar heridas relacionadas al trabajo
workout *n* sesión *f* de ejercicio (*esp. del tipo que se hace en un gimnasio*)
workplace *n* lugar *m* de(l) trabajo
workshop *n* taller *m*; **parenting** — taller de padres
workup *n* conjunto de exámenes que se realiza para determinar la causa de un síntoma o signo
worm *n* gusano; (*intestinal*) lombriz *f*, gusano
worn *pp de* **wear**
worry *n* (*pl* **-ries**) preocupación *f*, inquietud *f*; *vi* (*pret & pp* **-ried**) preocuparse; **You worry too much**..Se preocupa demasiado.
worse (*comp de* **bad** y **badly**) *adj & adv* peor; **to get** — empeorar, agravarse; **to make** — agravar, empeorar; **Is there anything that makes the pain worse?** ..¿Hay algo que le agrave el dolor?
worsening *n* empeoramiento, agravamiento
wound *n* herida; **entrance** — orificio de entrada; **exit** — orificio de salida; **flesh** — herida superficial (*que no afecta ningún órgano*); **gunshot** — herida de bala, balazo (*fam*); **knife** — cuchillada; **penetrating** — herida penetrante; **puncture** — herida punzante; **stab** — puñalada, cuchillada; *vt* herir
wounded *adj* herido; **the** — los heridos
wrap *n* (*bandage material*) venda; **self-adherent elastic** — venda elástica autoadherente (*Amer*), venda elástica cohesiva (*Esp*); *vt* (*pret & pp* **wrapped**; *ger* **wrapping**) envolver
wrench *vt* **to** — **one's back** (*fam*) lastimarse la espalda
wrinkle *n* arruga; **Smoking causes wrinkles**..Fumar causa arrugas; *vt, vi* arrugar(se)
wrist *n* muñeca
writer's cramp *n* calambre *m* del escribiente *or* escritor
writhe *vi* retorcerse

X

xanthoma *n* xantoma *m*
x-ray *adj* de rayos X; — **department** unidad *f* de rayos equis; *n* rayo X; (*film*) radiografía, placa (*fam*); **chest**

— radiografía de tórax; *vt* hacer una radiografía de, radiografiar (*esp. Esp, form*); **We need to x-ray your foot.**.

Tenemos que hacer una radiografía de su pie (radiografiar su pie).

Y

yarrow *n* (*bot*) milenrama
yawn *n* bostezo; *vi* bostezar
yaws *n* pian *m*, frambesia
year *n* año
yearly *adj* anual; *adv* anualmente
yeast *n* levadura; **brewer's** — levadura de cerveza; — **infection** candidiasis *f* (*form*), infección por levaduras *or* hongos
yellow *adj* amarillo
yellowish *adj* amarillento
yellow jacket *n* avispa amarilla, (tipo de) avispa
yesterday *adv* ayer
yoga *n* yoga *m*
yogurt *n* yogur *m*
yohimbine *n* yohimbina
yolk *n* yema; **egg** — yema de huevo; — **sac** saco vitelino
young *adj* joven; — **person** joven *mf*
younger (*comp of* **young**) *adj* más joven, menor; — **brother** hermano menor
youth *n* juventud *f*
yucca *n* (*bot*) yuca

Z

zafirlukast *n* zafirlukast *m*
zalcitabine *n* zalcitabina
zaleplon *n* zaleplón *m*, zaleplon *m*
zanamivir *n* zanamivir *m*
zen *adj* & *n* zen *m*
zidovudine *n* zidovudina
zinc *n* zinc *m*; — **oxide** óxido de zinc
zip code *n* código postal
zipper *n* cierre *m*, cremallera (*esp. Esp*)
ziprasidone *n* ziprasidona
zit *n* (*fam o vulg*) grano, barro
zoledronic acid, zoledronate *n* ácido zoledrónico, zoledronato (*esp. Esp*)
zolmitriptan *n* zolmitriptán *m*
zolpidem *n* zolpidem *m*
zombie *n* zombi *or* zombie *m*; **to feel like a** — sentirse como un zombi
zone *n* zona; **comfort** — zona de confort
zoophilia *n* zoofilia
zoster (*fam*) V. **herpes zoster**.
zygomycosis *n* zigomicosis *f*
zygote *n* cigoto

ESPAÑOL-INGLÉS

SPANISH-ENGLISH

A

AA *See* **Alcohólicos Anónimos**.

AAN *abbr* **anticuerpo antinuclear.** *See* **anticuerpo.**

abacavir *m* abacavir

abajo *adv* below; **de —** lower; **la parte de abajo**..the lower part; **hacia —** downward, down

abandonar *vt (una dieta, un tratamiento, etc.)* to give up on, to stop

abandono *m* cessation; **— del tabaco** smoking cessation

abastecimiento *m* supply

abatelenguas *m (pl* **-guas)** *(Mex)* tongue depressor *o* blade

abdomen *m* abdomen, belly, stomach *(fam)*

abdominal *adj* abdominal; *m (ejercicio)* sit-up

abdominoplastia *f* abdominoplasty

abeja *f* bee; **— africanizada** *or* **asesina** Africanized *o* killer bee

abertura *f* opening

abierto -ta *(pp of* **abrir)** *adj* open

ablación *f* ablation; **— con yodo radiactivo** radioactive iodine ablation; **— por radiofrecuencia** radiofrequency ablation

ablandador *m* softener; **— de heces, — fecal** stool softener

ablandar *vt* to soften

abombamiento *m (abultamiento)* bulging, bulge

abordaje *m* approach; **— quirúrgico** surgical approach

abortar *vt* to abort; *vi (con intención)* to have an abortion; *(sin intención)* to miscarry, to have a miscarriage

abortivo *adj & m* abortifacient

aborto *m* abortion, miscarriage; **— de repetición** habitual abortion; **— espontáneo** spontaneous abortion, miscarriage; **— habitual** habitual abortion; **— incompleto** incomplete abortion; **— por nacimiento parcial** partial birth abortion; **— terapéutico** therapeutic abortion; **amenaza de —**

threatened abortion; **sufrir un —** to miscarry; **tener un —** to have an abortion; *(espontáneo)* to miscarry

abotonar *vt, vr* to button (up)

abrasión *f (form)* abrasion

abrasivo -va *adj & m* abrasive

abrazar *vt* to embrace, hug

abrazo *m* embrace, hug

abrigo *m* coat

abrir *vt, vr (pp* **abierto)** to open

abrochar *vt, vr* to buckle, to button (up)

absceso *m* abscess

absentismo *m* absenteeism

absorbente *adj* absorbent

absorber *vt* to absorb

absorbible *adj (sutura, etc.)* absorbable; **no —** nonabsorbable

absorciometría de rayos X de energía dual *f* dual-energy X-ray absorptiometry (DEXA)

absorción *f* absorption

abstenerse *vr* to abstain; **— del alcohol** to abstain from drinking alcohol

abstinencia *f* abstinence; **— periódica** rhythm method

abuelo -la *m* grandfather, grandparent; *f* grandmother

abultamiento *m* bulging, bulge

abultar *vi* to bulge, to bulge out

aburrido -da *adj* bored

aburrir *vt* to bore; *vr* to become bored

abusador -ra *mf* abuser

abusar *vi* to abuse; *(sexualmente)* to abuse, molest *(sexually)*

abusivo -va *adj* abusive

abuso *m* maltreatment *(form)*, abuse; **— de (los) adultos mayores** *(esp. Mex)* elder maltreatment *o* abuse; **— de drogas** drug abuse; **— de (los) niños** child maltreatment *o* abuse; **— de (las) personas mayores** elder maltreatment *o* abuse; **— de sustancias** substance abuse; **— físico** physical maltreatment *o* abuse; **— infantil** child maltreatment *o* abuse; **— psicológico** psychological maltreatment *o* abuse; **— sexual** sexual maltreatment *o* abuse

acabar *vi* (*medicina, etc.*) to run out; **Se me acabaron las pastillas**..I ran out of pills..My pills ran out.

acalasia *f* achalasia

acalculoso -sa *adj* acalculous

acantosis nigricans *f* acanthosis nigricans

acarbosa *f* acarbose

acariciar *vt* to caress, to fondle

ácaro *m* mite; (*garrapata*) tick; — **de la cosecha** harvest mite, chigger; — **del polvo** dust mite; — **rojo** harvest mite, chigger

acaso *adv* **por si** — just in case

acatarrarse *vr* to catch a cold

acatisia *f* akathisia

accesible *adj* accessible; — **para silla(s) de ruedas** wheelchair accessible

acceso *m* access; (*ataque*) fit, spell; — **a la atención médica** access to medical care; — **para silla(s) de ruedas** wheelchair access; — **venoso** venous access

accesorio -ria *adj* accessory

accidentado -da *adj* injured (*in an accident*); *mf* accident victim

accidental *adj* accidental, unintended; **muerte** *f* — accidental death

accidentarse *vr* to have an accident

accidente *m* accident; — **cerebrovascular** cerebrovascular accident, stroke; — **cerebrovascular isquémico** ischemic stroke; — **de trabajo** work-related accident; — **de tráfico** *or* **tránsito** traffic accident; — **isquémico transitorio (AIT)** transient ischemic attack (TIA); — **laboral** work-related accident

acción *f* action; **de** — **corta** short-acting; **de** — **intermedia** intermediate-acting; **de** — **prolongada** long-acting; **de** — **rápida** rapid-acting, fast-acting

aceite *m* oil; — **de cacahuete** *or* **cacahuate** peanut oil; — **de cártamo** safflower oil; — **de citronela** citronella oil; — **de coco** coconut oil; — **de colza** rapeseed oil; — **de eucalipto de limón** lemon eucalyptus oil; — **de geranio** geranium oil; — **de hígado de bacalao** cod-liver oil; — **del árbol del té** tea tree oil; — **de limón** lemon oil; — **de maíz** corn oil; — **de maní** peanut oil; — **de oliva** olive oil; — **de onagra** evening primrose oil; — **de palma** palm oil; — **de pescado** fish oil; — **de ricino** castor oil; — **esencial** essential oil; — **mineral** mineral oil; — **vegetal** vegetable oil

acelerado -da *adj* (*fam*) hyperactive, nervously energetic, wired (*fam*)

acelular *adj* acellular

aceptación *f* (*etapa del duelo, etc.*) acceptance

acero *m* steel; — **inoxidable** stainless steel

acervo genético *m* gene pool

acetábulo *m* acetabulum

acetaminofén, acetaminofeno *m* acetaminophen, paracetamol (*INN*)

acetato *m* acetate

acetazolamida *f* acetazolamide

acético -ca *adj* acetic

acetilcisteína *f* acetylcysteine

acetona *f* acetone

achacoso -sa *adj* sickly, having many ailments, complaining of many ailments

achaque *m* mild illness, ailment, affliction, complaint

acíbar *m* (*bot*) aloe

aciclovir *m* acyclovir

acidez *f* acidity; (*estomacal*) heartburn, acid stomach (*fam*)

ácido -da *adj & m* acid; — **acético** acetic acid; — **acetilsalicílico** acetylsalicylic acid; — **alendrónico** alendronic acid, alendronate; **ácidos alfa hidróxidos** alpha hydroxy acids; — **ascórbico** ascorbic acid; — **azelaico** azelaic acid; — **bórico** boric acid; — **clorhídrico** hydrochloric acid; — **del estómago** stomach acid; — **desoxirribonucleico (ADN)** deoxyribonucleic acid (DNA); — **fólico** folic acid, folate; — **folínico** folinic acid, leucovorin (*USAN*); — **gamma hidroxibutírico** gamma-hydroxybutyrate *o* gamma-hydroxybutyric acid (GHB), liquid ecstasy (*fam*); — **gástrico** gastric acid; — **glutámico** glutamic acid; — **graso** *See* **ácido graso** *as a separate entry*; — **hialurónico** hyaluronic acid; — **ibandrónico** ibandronic acid, ibandronate; — **láctico** lactic acid; — **linoleico** linoleic acid; — **nalidíxico** nalidixic acid; — **nicotínico** nicotinic acid, niacin; — **nítrico**

nitric acid; — **paraaminobenzoico** *or* **para-aminobenzoico** paraaminobenzoic *o* para-aminobenzoic acid (PABA); — **retinoico** retinoic acid; — **ribonucleico (ARN)** ribonucleic acid (RNA); — **risedrónico** risedronic acid, risedronate; — **salicílico** salicylic acid; — **tartárico** tartaric acid; — **tricloroacético** trichloroacetic acid; — **úrico** uric acid; — **valproico** valproic acid, valproate; — **zoledrónico** zoledronic acid, zoledronate

ácido graso *m* fatty acid; — — **esencial** essential fatty acid; — — **insaturado** unsaturated fatty acid; — — **monoinsaturado** monounsaturated fatty acid; — — **omega-3** omega-3 fatty acid; — **poliinsaturado** polyunsaturated fatty acid; — — **saturado** saturated fatty acid; — — **trans** trans fatty acid

acidophilus *m* acidophilus

aclarar *vt* (*la voz o la garganta*) to clear (*one's throat*)

aclimatarse *vr* to become acclimated

acné *m&f* acne; — **quístico** cystic acne; — **rosácea** acne rosacea, rosacea (*fam*)

acojinado -da *adj* padded

acojinar *vt* to pad, cushion

acolchado -da *adj* padded; *m* padding

acolchar *vt* to pad, cushion

acompañante *mf* companion, person accompanying

acondicionador *m* conditioner; — **de cabello** *or* **pelo**, — **capilar** (*esp. Esp*) hair conditioner

acondicionamiento *m* conditioning; — **físico** physical conditioning, fitness

acondroplasia *f* achondroplasia

acongojar *vt* to upset, worry, concern

aconsejar *vt* to advise

acontecimiento *m* occurrence, event, development

acordarse *vr* to remember, to recall; **Me acuerdo de eso**..I remember that.

acortar *vt* to shorten

acosar *vt* to harass, (*ped*) to bully

acoso *m* harassment, (*ped*) bullying; — **sexual** sexual harassment

acostarse *vr* to lie down; (*en la cama, para dormir*) to go to bed

acostumbrarse *vr* to get used to

acrilamida *f* acrylamide

acrílico -ca *adj & m* acrylic

acrocordón *m* (*derm*) acrochordon, skin tag

acrofobia *f* acrophobia

acromegalia *f* acromegaly

acta *f* certificate; — **de nacimiento** birth certificate

actínico -ca *adj* actinic

actinomicosis *f* actinomycosis

actitud *f* attitude

activador *m* activator; — **tisular del plasminógeno**, — **del plasminógeno tisular** tissue plasminogen activator (tPA)

activar *vt* to activate

actividad *f* activity; **actividades cotidianas** activities of daily living

activo -va *adj* active, energetic; **sexualmente** — sexually active

acto *m* act; — **sexual** sexual intercourse, intercourse; **durante el acto sexual**.. during sexual intercourse

ACTP *abbr* angioplastia coronaria transluminal percutánea. *See* angioplastia.

actual *adj* current

actualización *f* (*psych*) actualization

actuar *vi* (*droga, etc.*) to act

acuchillar *vt* to stab

acudir *vi* to seek, to go; — **al médico** to go to the doctor, to seek medical attention

acúfeno *m* (*frec. pl*) tinnitus

acumulación *f* accumulation, buildup

acumular *vt* to accumulate; *vr* to accumulate, build up

acumulativo -va *adj* cumulative; **efecto** — cumulative effect

acuoso -sa *adj* aqueous, watery; **secreción acuosa** watery discharge

acupresión *f* acupressure

acupuntura *f* acupuncture

acústico -ca *adj* acoustic

adalimumab *m* adalimumab

adapaleno *m* adapalene

adaptación *f* adaptation

adaptar *vt, vr* to adapt, to adjust; **bien adaptado** well-adjusted

adecuado -da *adj* appropriate, suitable; (*suficiente*) adequate, sufficient

adefovir *m* adefovir

adelante *adv* **hacia** — forward

adelgazarse *vr* to get *o* become thin, to lose weight

adenitis *f* adenitis
adenocarcinoma *m* adenocarcinoma
adenoidectomía *f* adenoidectomy
adenoides *fpl* adenoids
adenoiditis *f* adenoiditis
adenoma *m* adenoma; — velloso villous adenoma
adenomatoso -sa *adj* adenomatous
adenomiosis *f* adenomyosis
adenosina *f* adenosine
adenovirus *m* (*pl* -rus) adenovirus
adentro *adv* inside
adherencia *f* adherence; (*brida*) adhesion; — al tratamiento adherence to treatment
adherido -da *adj* adherent, attached
adhesivo -va *adj & m* adhesive
adicción *f* addiction; — a la heroína heroin addiction
adictivo -va *adj* addictive
adicto -ta *adj* addicted; volverse — to get *o* become addicted; *mf* addict; — a la heroína heroin addict
adiposo -sa *adj* fatty; tejido — fatty tissue
aditivo -va *adj & m* additive
administración *f* administration; Administración de Alimentos y Drogas (*US*) Food and Drug Administration (FDA)
administrador -ra *mf* administrator; — de casos case manager
administrar *vt* (*una droga, etc.*) to administer; (*un hospital, etc.*) to administrate
admisión *f* (*Ang, al hospital*) admission
admitir *vt* (*Ang, al hospital*) to admit
ADN *abbr* ácido desoxirribonucleico. See ácido.
adolescencia *f* adolescence
adolescente *adj & mf* adolescent
adolorido -da (*Amer*) See dolorido.
adopción *f* adoption
adoptar *vt* to adopt
adoptivo -va *adj* adoptive; padres adoptivos adoptive parents
adormecer *vt* (*con anestesia local*) to anesthetize, to numb up; *vr* (*entumecerse*) to become numb, to go to sleep (*fam*), to fall asleep (*fam*)
adormecido -da *adj* numb, asleep (*fam*)
adormecimiento *m* numbness
adormilado -da *adj* drowsy

adquirido -da *adj* acquired; — en la comunidad community-acquired
adquirir *vt* to acquire
adrenal *adj* adrenal; *f* adrenal gland
adrenalectomía *f* adrenalectomy
adrenalina *f* adrenaline
adsorbente *adj* adsorbent
adulterar *vt* to adulterate
adulto -ta *adj & mf* adult, grown-up (*fam*)
adverso -sa *adj* adverse
advertencia *f* warning
adyuvante *adj* adjuvant
aeróbic *m* aerobics; — de bajo impacto low impact aerobics
aeróbico -ca *adj* (*metabolismo*) aerobic; *mpl* (*esp. SA*) aerobics
aeróbics *mpl* (*esp. Mex*) aerobics
aerobio -bia *adj* (*micro*) aerobic
aerosol *m* aerosol, spray; inhaler; — de pimienta pepper spray; — dosificador metered-dose inhaler; — nasal nasal inhaler *o* spray; en — aerosolized
afasia *f* aphasia; — expresiva expressive aphasia; — receptiva receptive aphasia
afección *f* (*cariño*) affection; (*enfermedad*) disease, condition, affliction
afectar *vt* to affect; afectado por..affected by; no afectado unaffected
afectivo -va *adj* emotional
afecto *m* affection; (*psych*) affect; — aplanado flat affect; — embotado blunted affect
afectuoso -sa *adj* affectionate
afeitadora *f* (electric) shaver
afeitar *vt, vr* to shave
afeminado -da *adj* effeminate
aféresis *f* apheresis
afilado -da *adj* sharp
afinidad *f* affinity
aflatoxina *f* aflatoxin
aflicción *f* distress; affliction
afligir *vt* to afflict; (*apenar*) to upset, disturb; to hurt
aflojar *vt* to loosen; (*relajar*) to relax; Afloje el brazo..Relax your arm.
afónico -ca *adj* hoarse, having lost one's voice; estar — to be hoarse, to have lost one's voice
afrecho *m* bran
afrodisíaco, afrodisiaco *adj & m* aphrodisiac

afrontar *vt* to face, confront, (*lidiar con*) to cope with

afta *f* aphthous ulcer (*form*), canker sore; (*candidiasis oral*) thrush

agachar *vt* (*la cabeza*) to bend down (*one's head*); **Agache la cabeza**..Bend your head down; *vr* to bend over, bend down, stoop

agammaglobulinemia *f* agammaglobulinemia

agarradera *f* (*barra*) grab bar

agarrar *vt* to grasp, grip; (*fam, una enfermedad*) to catch (*a disease*)

agarre *m* grip

agencia *f* agency

agente *m* (*pharm, etc.*) agent; — **naranja** Agent Orange; — **patógeno** pathogen

ágil *adj* agile

agitación *f* agitation, restlessness

agitado -da *adj* agitated, upset

agitar *vt* to agitate, to upset; to shake; **Agítese bien antes de usarse**..Shake well before using; *vr* to become agitated, to become upset; to fidget

agobiar *vt* overwhelm

agonía *f* suffering preceding death, period preceding death; agony, intense pain, intense suffering

agónico -ca *adj* agonal

agorafobia *f* agoraphobia

agotado -da *adj* exhausted, run-down; used up

agotador -ra *adj* exhausting, tiring

agotamiento *m* extreme fatigue, exhaustion; (*profesional*) burnout

agotar *vt* to exhaust, to tire out; to deplete; *vr* to become exhausted, to tire out; to become depleted

agrandamiento *m* enlargement

agrandar *vt* to enlarge, make bigger; *vr* to get *o* become bigger

agravamiento *m* worsening, deterioration

agravar *vt* to aggravate, make worse; *vi, vr* to get worse; **Se agravó**..He got worse.

agregar *vt* to add; **No agregue sal**.. Don't add salt.

agresión *f* aggression; (*asalto*) assault; — **sexual** sexual assault

agresivo -va *adj* aggressive, combative

agrícola *adj* agricultural

agricultor -ra *mf* farmer

agrietado -da *adj* cracked, split, (*labios, piel*) chapped

agrietarse *vr* to crack, to split, (*labios, piel*) to chap, get chapped

agrio -gria *adj* sour

agrupación *f* cluster; — **de casos** cluster of cases

agruras *fpl* heartburn

agua *f* water; — **corriente** running water; — **de hamamelis** witch hazel; — **del grifo**, — **de la llave** tap water; — **destilada** distilled water; — **dulce** fresh water; — **dura** hard water; — **en el pulmón (la rodilla, etc.)** water on the lung (the knee, etc.); — **hirviendo** boiling water; — **mala** (*carabela portuguesa*) Portuguese man-of-war, stinging jellyfish; — **mineral** mineral water; **aguas negras** sewage, domestic wastewater; — **oxigenada** hydrogen peroxide; — **potable** potable water, drinking water; — **purificada** purified water; **aguas residuales** wastewater; — **salada** salt water; **aguas termales** hot springs

aguacate *m* avocado

aguamala *See* **agua mala** *under* **agua**.

aguantar *vt* to tolerate, endure, stand, bear; — **la respiración** (*fam*) to hold one's breath; **Aguante la respiración** ..Hold your breath.

agudeza *f* acuity; — **visual** visual acuity

agudización *f* (*form*) exacerbation, flare

agudo -da *adj* (*enfermedad*) acute; (*dolor*) sharp; (*tono*) high-pitched

aguijón *m* stinger

aguja *f* needle; — **hipodérmica** hypodermic needle; — **mariposa** butterfly needle

agujero *m* hole

ahogar *vt* to drown; (*asfixiar*) to suffocate, smother; *vr* to drown; to suffocate, smother, to choke (*due to fumes, lack of air, etc.*), to feel short of breath; **Siento que me ahogo**..I feel short of breath.

ahogo *m* choking sensation, shortness of breath

ahorcar *vt* to hang (*by the neck*); *vr* to hang oneself

AINE *abbr* antiinflamatorio no esteroideo. *See* **antiinflamatorio**.

airbag *m* airbag

aire *m* air; — **acondicionado** air conditioning; — **ambiente** *or* **ambiental** room air; — **contaminado** air pollution, smog; — **del ambiente** room air; **al** — **libre** outdoors; **tener** — (*esp. Mex, fam; en el pecho, abdomen, etc.*) to have air (*in one's chest, abdomen, etc.*) (*refers to a popular belief that pain in the chest or abdomen may be due to trapped air*)

aislado -da *adj* isolated; (*emocionalmente*) isolated, alienated

aislamiento *m* isolation; — **inverso** reverse isolation; — **protector** protective isolation; — **respiratorio** respiratory isolation

aislar *vt* to isolate; *vr* to isolate oneself

AIT *abbr* **accidente isquémico transitorio**. *See* **accidente**.

ajo *m* garlic

ajustable *adj* adjustable

ajustador *m* (*Carib*) brassiere

ajustar *vt* to adjust, to fit

ajuste *m* adjustment

ala *f* (*de un hospital*) wing (*of a hospital*)

alacrán *m* scorpion

alado -da *adj* webbed, winged; **cuello** — webbed neck; **escápula** — winged scapula

alambre *m* wire; — **de púas** barbed wire

alanina *f* alanine

alarma *f* alarm; — **de cama** bed alarm

albendazol *m* albendazole

albergue *m* shelter; — **para mujeres** women's shelter; — **para mujeres maltratadas** battered women's shelter; — **para personas sin hogar** homeless shelter

albinismo *m* albinism

albino -na *adj* & *mf* albino

albúmina *f* albumin

albuminuria *f* albuminuria

albuterol *m* albuterol

alcalino -na *adj* alkaline

alcalosis *f* alkalosis

alcance *m* reach; **fuera del** — **de los niños** out of reach of children

alcanfor *m* camphor

alcanzar *vt, vi* to reach; (*durar*) to last; **Las pastillas sólo me alcanzaron dos semanas**..The pills only lasted me two weeks.

alcaptonuria *f* alkaptonuria

alcohol *m* alcohol, liquor; — **bencílico** benzyl alcohol; — **desnaturalizado** denatured alcohol; — **isopropílico** isopropyl alcohol; — **para fricciones** *or* **para frotar** rubbing alcohol

alcohólico -ca *adj* & *mf* alcoholic; — **en recuperación** recovering alcoholic

Alcohólicos Anónimos (AA) *mpl* Alcoholics Anonymous (AA)

alcoholismo *m* alcoholism

aldosterona *f* aldosterone

aldosteronismo *m* aldosteronism

aleatorio -ria *adj* random; **pruebas aleatorias** random testing

alegre *adj* cheerful

alendronato, alendronato sódico, ácido alendrónico (*INN*) *m* alendronate, alendronate sodium (*USAN*), alendronic acid (*INN*)

alérgeno, alergeno *m* allergen

alergia *f* allergy; — **al polen** allergy to pollen, hay fever; **alergias estacionales** seasonal allergies

alérgico -ca *adj* allergic; **¿Es Ud. alérgico a la penicilina?**..Are you allergic to penicillin?

alergista *mf* allergist

alergología *f* study of allergies

alergólogo -ga *mf* allergist

alerta *adj* alert; *f* alert; — **sanitaria** health alert

aleteo *m* flutter; — **auricular** atrial flutter

alfa *f* alpha; — **fetoproteína** alpha fetoprotein; — **galactosidasa** alpha galactosidase; — **metildopa** alpha methyldopa

alfalfa *f* (*bot*) alfalfa

alfiler *m* pin

alfuzosina *f* alfuzosin

alga *f* alga; — **verdeazulada** blue-green algae; [*Nota: En inglés se usa casi siempre la forma plural:* algae.]

alginato *m* alginate

algodón *m* cotton

algodoncillo *m* (*Mex*) thrush

alheña *f* (*bot*) henna

alienado -da *adj* alienated

aliento *m* breath; **mal** — bad breath

alimentación *f* feeding, nourishment, diet; — **equilibrada** *or* **balanceada** balanced diet; — **por sonda** tube feed-

ing
alimentar *vt* to feed
alimentario -ria *adj* alimentary; (*dieté-tico*) dietary
alimenticio -cia *adj* (*nutricional*) nutritional; (*dietético*) dietary
alimento *m* food; **alimentos enlatados** canned food(s); **alimentos infantiles** baby food(s); **alimentos naturales** health *o* natural food(s); **alimentos para bebés** baby food(s); **alimentos procesados** processed food(s); [*Nota: La traducción de* alimento *es siempre* food, *pero la traducción de* alimentos *puede ser equivalentemente* food *o* foods.]
alineación *f* alignment
alineamiento *m* alignment
alinear *vt* to align; *vr* to line up
alisar *vt* (*dent, etc.*) to make smooth, to smooth
alitiásico -ca *adj* acalculous
aliviar *vt* to alleviate, soothe, relieve; *vr* (*síntoma*) to resolve, to get better; (*Mex, fam, dar a luz*) to give birth, deliver
alivio *m* relief
alma *f* soul
almacén *m* store, reserve
almacenar *vt* to store, to reserve
almidón *m* starch; — **de maíz** cornstarch
almohada *f* pillow, cushion
almohadilla *f* small pillow, cushion, pad; — **térmica** *or* **eléctrica** heating pad
almorrana *f* hemorrhoid
almorzar *vi* to have lunch, to have a morning meal (*often social*)
almotriptán *m* almotriptan
almuerzo *m* lunch, morning meal (*often social*)
aloe, **áloe** *m* (*bot*) aloe
aloinjerto *m* allograft
alojarse *vr* to lodge
alópata *mf* allopath
alopatía *f* allopathy
alopático -ca *adj* allopathic
alopecia *f* alopecia
alopurinol *m* allopurinol
alpinismo *m* mountaineering
alprazolam *m* alprazolam
alquitrán *m* tar; — **de hulla** coal tar
alrededor *adv* around; — **del brazo** around your arm

alsine *m* (*bot*) chickweed
alta *f* (*del hospital*) discharge; **dar de —** to discharge
alteplasa *f* alteplase
alteración *f* disturbance; — **del nivel de conciencia** altered level of consciousness
alterado -da *adj* (*molesto*) upset
alterar *vt* to upset; *vr* to get *o* become upset
alternar *vt, vi* to alternate
alternativa *f* alternative
alterno -na *adj* alternate; **días alternos** alternate days
altitud *f* altitude; **en —** at high altitude; **gran —** high altitude
alto -ta *adj* high, tall; upper; **Su glucosa está muy alta**..Your glucose is very high...**¿Es muy alto su papá?**..Is your father very tall?; **vías respiratorias altas** upper respiratory tract
altura *f* height; altitude, elevation; **¿Cuál es su altura?**..How tall are you?; **en —** at high altitude; **gran —** high altitude
alubias *fpl* beans
alucinación *f* hallucination
alumbramiento *m* childbirth, moment of delivery; delivery of the placenta and fetal membranes
alumbre *m* alum
aluminio *m* aluminum
alvéolo, **alveolo** *m* (*dent*) alveolus, socket; (*lung*) alveolus
amable *adj* friendly, kind
ama de casa *f* homemaker, housewife
amalgama *f* (*dent*) amalgam
amamantamiento *m* breastfeeding
amamantar *vt* to breastfeed, to feed, to nurse
amantadina *f* amantadine
amar *vt, vi* to love
amargo -ga *adj* bitter
amargón *m* (*bot*) dandelion
amarillento -ta *adj* yellowish
amarillo -lla *adj* yellow
ambidiestro, **ambidextro -tra** *adj* ambidextrous
ambiental *adj* environmental
ambiente *m* surroundings, environment
ambivalencia *f* ambivalence
ambliopía *f* amblyopia, lazy eye (*fam*)
ambrosía *f* (*bot*) ragweed
ambulación *f* ambulation

ambulancia *f* ambulance
ambulatorio -ria *adj* ambulatory, outpatient; **cirugía —** outpatient surgery; **paciente** *mf* — outpatient; **procedimiento —** outpatient procedure
ameba *f* ameba
amebiano -na *adj* amebic
amebiasis *f* amebiasis
amenaza *f* threat
amenazar *vt, vi* to threaten
amenorrea *f* amenorrhea
amianto *m* asbestos
amiba *f* ameba
amibiano -na *adj* amebic
amibiasis *f* amebiasis
amígdala *f* tonsil; (*cerebral*) amigdala
amigdalectomía *f* tonsillectomy
amigdalitis *f* tonsillitis
amigo -ga *mf* friend
amilasa *f* amylase
amiloidosis *f* amyloidosis
amilorida *f* amiloride
aminoácido *m* amino acid
aminoglucósido *m* aminoglycoside
amiodarona *f* amiodarone
amiotrófico -ca *adj* amyotrophic
amistad *f* friendship; *fpl* friends
amitriptilina *f* amitriptyline
amlodipina *f* amlodipine
amlodipino *m* amlodipine
amnesia *f* amnesia
amniocentesis *f* (*pl* -sis) amniocentesis
amnionitis *f* amnionitis
amniótico -ca *adj* amniotic
amoniaco, amoníaco *m* ammonia
amonio *m* ammonium
amor *m* love; **hacer el —** to make love
amortiguado -da *adj* buffered
amoxicilina *f* amoxicillin
ampicilina *f* ampicillin
ampolla *f* blister; **— de sangre** blood blister; **— de Vater** ampulla of Vater
ampolloso -sa *adj* bullous
amprenavir *m* amprenavir
ámpula *f* (*Mex, Cuba*) ampule
amputación *f* amputation; **— por debajo de la rodilla** below-the-knee amputation; **— por encima de la rodilla** above-the-knee amputation
amputado -da *mf* amputee
amputar *vt* to amputate, to cut off (*fam*)
anabólico -ca *adj* anabolic
anabolizante *adj* anabolic

anacardo *m* cashew
anaeróbico -ca *adj* anaerobic (*esp. metabolism*)
anaerobio -bia *adj* (*micro*) anaerobic
anafiláctico -ca *adj* anaphylactic
anafilactoide *adj* anaphylactoid
anafilaxia, anafilaxis *f* anaphylaxis
anal *adj* anal
analfabetismo *m* illiteracy
analfabeto -ta *adj* illiterate
analgesia *f* analgesia; **— controlada por el paciente** patient-controlled analgesia
analgésico -ca *adj & m* analgesic
análisis *m* (*pl* -sis) analysis, test, assay, testing; (*psych, fam*) psychoanalysis, analysis (*fam*); **— de heces** stool test; **— de orina** urinalysis (*form*), urine test; **— de sangre** blood test; **— de semen** semen analysis
analista *mf* (*psych, fam*) psychoanalyst, analyst (*fam*)
analizador *m* analyzer
analizar *vt* to analyze
análogo *m* analogue
anaranjado -da *adj* orange
anastomosis *f* anastomosis
anastrozol *m* anastrozole
anatomía *f* anatomy; **— patológica** anatomic pathology
anatómico -ca *adj* anatomical
anatomopatólogo -ga *mf* anatomic pathologist
ancho -cha *adj* wide; *m* width
anchura *f* width
anciano -na *adj* old, elderly; *m* old man, old person; *f* old woman
andadera *f* (*Mex*) walker
andador *m* walker; **— con ruedas delanteras** front-wheeled walker
andar *vi* to walk
andrógeno *m* androgen
androginia *f* androgyny
andropausia *f* andropause
anemia *f* anemia; **— aplásica** aplastic anemia; **— de células falciformes, — drepanocítica, — falciforme** sickle cell anemia; **— ferropénica** (*form*) iron deficiency anemia; **— hemolítica** hemolytic anemia; **— perniciosa** pernicious anemia; **— por deficiencia de hierro** iron deficiency anemia; **— sideroblástica** sideroblastic anemia

anémico -ca *adj* anemic
anencefalia *f* anencephaly
anergia *f* anergy
anestesia *f* anesthesia; — **epidural** epidural anesthesia; — **espinal** spinal anesthesia; — **general** general anesthesia; — **local** local anesthesia; — **raquídea** spinal anesthesia; — **regional** regional anesthesia
anestesiar *vt* (*local*) to anesthetize, to numb up (*fam*); (*general*) to anesthetize, to put to sleep (*fam*)
anestésico -ca *adj & m* anesthetic; — **general** general anesthetic; — **local** local anesthetic, numbing medicine (*fam*)
anestesiología *f* anesthesiology
anestesiólogo -ga *mf* anesthesiologist
anestesista *mf* anesthesiologist; anesthetist
aneurisma *m* aneurysm; — **aórtico abdominal,** — **de aorta abdominal** abdominal aortic aneurysm; — **disecante** dissecting aneurysm; — **micótico** mycotic aneurysm
anexial *adj* adnexal
anfetamina *f* amphetamine
anfotericina B *f* amphotericin B
angeítis *f* angiitis
angélica *f* (*bot*) angelica
angiitis *f* (*Ang*) angiitis
angina *f* (*de pecho*) angina; (*amígdala*) tonsil; — **de Prinzmetal** Prinzmetal angina, variant angina; — **de Vincent** Vincent's angina; — **inestable** unstable angina; **tener anginas** (*Mex, fam*) to have tonsillitis; — **variante** *or* **vasoespástica** variant *o* vasospastic angina
anginoso -sa *adj* anginal
angiodisplasia *f* angiodysplasia
angioedema *m* angioedema
angiografía *f* (*técnica*) angiography; (*estudio*) angiogram; — **por tomografía computarizada** computed tomographic (CT) angiography
angiograma *m* angiogram
angioma *m* angioma; — **aracniforme** spider angioma, spider (*fam*)
angiomatosis *f* angiomatosis; — **bacilar** bacillary angiomatosis
angioplastia *f* angioplasty; — **coronaria transluminal percutánea (ACTP)** percutaneous transluminal coronary

angioplasty (PTCA)
angiosarcoma *m* angiosarcoma
ángulo *m* angle, bend; — **del ojo** angle *o* corner of the eye
angustia *f* anxiety, anguish
anhedonia *f* (*psych*) anhedonia
anilina *f* aniline
anillo *m* ring; — **vaginal** vaginal ring
animal *adj & m* animal; — **de compañía** companion animal; — **de servicio** service animal
animalito *m* (*esp. Mex, fam*) bug, insect; parasite
ánimo *m* spirits, mood, energy; **estado de** — mood; **oscilaciones** *fpl* **del** — mood swings
ano *m* anus
anoche *adv* last night
anomalía *f* anomaly, malformation, abnormality; — **congénita** congenital anomaly, birth defect
anomia *f* (*psych*) anomie
anorexia *f* anorexia; — **nerviosa** anorexia nervosa
anorexígeno -na *adj & m* anorexiant
anormal *adj* abnormal
anormalidad *f* abnormality
anotar *vt* (*valores del azúcar, etc.*) to record (*sugar values, etc.*)
anovulación *f* anovulation
anovulatorio -ria *adj* anovulatory
anquilosis *f* ankylosis
anquilostoma *m* hookworm
anquilostomiasis *f* ancylostomiasis
ansia *f* (*frec. pl*) craving, desire; anxiety; — **de nicotina** craving for nicotine
ansiedad *f* anxiety; — **de ejecución** *or* **desempeño** *or* **rendimiento** performance anxiety
ansiolítico -ca *adj* anxiolitic, antianxiety; *m* anxiolitic
ansioso -sa *adj* anxious
antagonista *m* antagonist; — **del calcio** calcium antagonist, calcium channel blocker; — **del CCR5** CCR5 antagonist; — **del receptor de angiotensina** angiotensin receptor blocker
anteanoche *adv* the night before last
anteayer *adv* the day before yesterday
antebrazo *m* forearm
antecedentes *mpl* history; — **de cáncer (traumatismo, etc.)** history of cancer (trauma, etc.); — **familiares** family

history; — **médicos, patológicos** *or* **personales** past medical history
anteojos *mpl* glasses, eyeglasses; — **oscuros** sunglasses
antepasado *m* ancestor
antepié *m* forefoot
anterior *adj* anterior; (*previo*) previous
antes *adv* before; **No tenía dolor antes..**I didn't have pain before; — **de** before; **antes de las comidas..** before meals; — **de que** before; **antes de que se vaya..**before you go
antiácido -da *adj & m* antacid
antialérgico -ca *adj* preventing or treating allergies; *m* allergy medicine
antianginoso -sa *adj & m* antianginal
antiarrítmico -ca *adj & m* antiarrhythmic
antiasmático -ca *adj & m* antiasthmatic
antibacteriano -na *adj* antibacterial
antibiótico -ca *adj & m* antibiotic; — **de amplio espectro** broad-spectrum antibiotic
anticanceroso -sa *adj* anti-cancer
anticoagulante *adj* anticoagulant; *m* anticoagulant, blood thinner (*fam*); — **lúpico** lupus anticoagulant
anticoagular *vt* (*Ang*) to anticoagulate
anticolinérgico -ca *adj & m* anticholinergic
anticoncepción *f* contraception, birth control
anticonceptivo -va *adj & m* contraceptive; — **oral** oral contraceptive, birth control pill
anticongelante *m* antifreeze
anticonvulsivante *adj* anticonvulsant; *m* antiepileptic
anticonvulsivo -va *adj* anticonvulsant; *m* antiepileptic
anticuerpo *m* antibody; **anticuerpos contra su propio organismo..**antibodies against your own body; **anticuerpo antifosfolípido** antiphospholipid antibody; **anticuerpo antimitocondrial** antimitochondrial antibody; **anticuerpo antinuclear (AAN)** antinuclear antibody (ANA)
antidepresivo -va *adj & m* antidepressant; — **tricíclico** tricyclic antidepressant
antidiarreico -ca *adj & m* antidiarrheal
antídoto *m* antidote

antidroga *adj* antidrug
antiemético -ca *adj & m* antiemetic
antiepiléptico -ca *adj* anticonvulsant; *m* antiepileptic drug, antiepileptic (*fam*)
antier *See* **anteayer**.
antiespasmódico -ca *adj & m* antispasmodic
antiespástico -ca *adj & m* antispasmodic
antifúngico -ca *adj & m* antifungal
antigás *adj* (*contra los gases*) antigas
antígeno *m* antigen; — **carcinoembrionario** carcinoembryonic antigen; — **prostático específico (APE)** prostate-specific antigen (PSA)
antigripal *adj* anti-flu
antihelmíntico -ca *adj & m* anthelmintic
antihigiénico -ca *adj* unsanitary
antihipertensivo -va *adj & m* antihypertensive
antihistamínico -ca *adj & m* antihistamine
antiinflamatorio -ria *adj* antiinflammatory; *m* antiinflammatory agent, antiinflammatory (*fam*); — **no esteroideo (AINE)** non-steroidal antiinflammatory drug (NSAID)
antimicótico -ca *adj & m* antifungal
antimicrobiano -na *adj & m* antimicrobial
antimonial *m* antimonial
antineoplásico -ca *adj* anti-cancer
antioxidante *adj & m* antioxidant
antipalúdico -ca *adj & m* antimalarial
antiparasitario -ria *adj* antiparasitic
antipático -ca *adj* unfriendly
antipirético -ca *adj & m* antipyretic
antipsicótico -ca *adj & m* antipsychotic
antirreflujo *adj* antireflux
antirretroviral *adj & m* antiretroviral
antiséptico -ca *adj & m* antiseptic
antisocial *adj* antisocial
antisuero *m* antiserum
antitabaco *adj* antismoking
antitérmico -ca *adj & m* antipyretic
antitoxina *f* antitoxin
antitranspirante *adj & m* antiperspirant
antitrombótico -ca *adj & m* antithrombotic
antiulceroso -sa *adj* preventing or treating ulcers; **medicamento** — ulcer medicine; *m* ulcer medicine
antiveneno *m* antivenin, antivenom

antiviral *adj & m* antiviral
antojo *m* craving; (*derm, fam*) birthmark
ántrax *m* carbuncle; (*Ang, carbunco*) anthrax
anual *adj* annual, yearly
anualmente *adv* yearly
anular *adj* annular
anzuelo *m* fishhook
añadir *vt* to add
año *m* year; **Tengo tres años..**I'm three (years old); **años reproductivos** childbearing years
añoso -sa *adj* older
aorta *f* aorta
aórtico -ca *adj* aortic
apachurrar *vt* to mash, press down
aparato *m* apparatus, device; (*dent*) appliance; (*digestivo, etc.*) tract, system; (*obst, fam, DIU*) intrauterine device (IUD); — **de ayuda auditiva** assistive hearing device; — **de ortodoncia** braces; — **digestivo** digestive *o* gastrointestinal tract, digestive system; — **extraoral** (*orthodontics*) headgear; — **genital** genital tract; — **genitourinario** genitourinary tract; — **locomotor** musculoskeletal system; — **ortopédico** brace; — **reproductor** *or* **reproductivo** reproductive system; — **respiratorio** respiratory tract *o* system; — **urinario** urinary tract
aparecer *vi* to appear, to develop
apariencia *f* appearance
apatía *f* apathy
apático -ca *adj* apathetic, listless
APE *abbr* **antígeno prostático específico.** *V.* **antígeno.**
apellido *m* last name, surname; — **materno** maternal surname; — **paterno** paternal surname
apenar *vt* to pain, sadden, distress; *vr* to become sad *o* pained *o* distressed; (*Amer, sentir vergüenza*) to feel embarrassed
apéndice *m* appendix
apendicectomía *f* appendectomy
apendicitis *f* appendicitis
apetito *m* appetite
Apgar *m* (*fam*) Apgar score
apiñado -da *adj* (*dent*) crowded; **dientes apiñados** crowded teeth
apio *m* celery
apixabán *m* apixaban

aplásico -ca *adj* aplastic
aplastamiento *m* crushing; — **vertebral** vertebral compression fracture
aplastante *adj* (*dolor, etc.*) crushing
aplastar *vt* to crush
aplicación *f* application
aplicador *m* applicator, swab; — **de algodón** cotton applicator *o* swab
aplicar *vt* to apply
apnea *f* apnea; — **obstructiva del sueño** obstructive sleep apnea
apoderado -da *mf* (*para tomar decisiones médicas*) health care proxy *o* agent
apófisis *f* (*pl* -sis) (*anat*) process; — **mastoides** mastoid process; — **xifoides** xiphoid process
apósito *m* dressing; — **oclusivo** occlusive dressing
apoyacabezas *m* headrest
apoyar *vt* to support, to rest; **Debemos apoyar las decisiones de nuestros hijos..**We should support our children's decisions...**Apoye el brazo en un cojín..**Rest your arm on a cushion.
apoyo *m* support; — **moral** moral support
apraxia *f* apraxia
aprender *vt, vi* to learn; **aprender a caminar..**to learn to walk
aprendizaje *m* learning
apretado -da *adj* tight
apretar *vt* to squeeze, to constrict, to grip; (*ropa, calzado*) to pinch, to be too tight; — **los dientes** to bite down, (*como hábito*) to grind one's teeth; **¿Aprieta los dientes cuando se siente estresada?..**Do you grind your teeth when you feel stressed?; *vi* (*ropa, calzado*) to bind, to be too tight
apropiado -da *adj* appropriate, suitable
aproximadamente *adv* approximately
aptitud *f* aptitude
apuñalar *vt* to stab
A quien corresponda, To Whom It May Concern
arador de la sarna *m* scabies mite
araña *f* spider; — **capulina** black widow (spider); — **reclusa,** — **parda,** — **marrón** brown recluse (spider); — **vascular** spider angioma, spider (*fam*); — **violinista** (*esp. Mex*) brown recluse (spider)
arañar *vt* to scratch, to claw

arañazo *m* scratch (*esp. by claws*)
arandanera *f* (*bot*) bilberry
arándano *m* (*bot*) cranberry; (*mirtilo*) bilberry; — **rojo** cranberry
árbol genealógico, árbol familiar *m* family tree
arcada *f* (*frec. pl*) retching, dry heaves (*fam*)
arco *m* arch; — **caído** fallen arch; — **del pie** arch of the foot
arder *vi* to burn, to sting; **Esto le va a arder un poco**..This will burn (sting) a little bit.
ardiente *adj* burning
ardilla *f* squirrel
ardor *m* (*sensación*) burning, burning sensation; **Siento ardor en los pies**..I feel burning in my feet.
área *f* area, district
arete *m* earring
argatroban *m* argatroban
arginina *f* arginine
argón *m* argon
aripiprazol *m* aripiprazole
arma *f* weapon; — **biológica** biologic weapon; — **de fuego** firearm; — **paralizante** stun gun; — **química** chemical weapon
armadillo *m* armadillo
armazones *mpl* (*para lentes*) frames (*for eyeglasses*)
ARN *abbr* **ácido ribonucleico**. See **ácido**.
árnica *f* (*bot*) arnica
aromaterapia *f* aromatherapy
arquear *vt* to arch; — **la espalda** to arch one's back
arrastrar *vt* — **las palabras** to slur one's words *o* speech, to slur
arrebato *m* (*emocional*) (emotional) outburst
arreglar *vt* (*fam*) to repair, fix
arremangarse *vr* to roll up one's sleeve or pant leg
arrepentimiento *m* remorse
arriba *adv* above; — **de 100** (*Amer*) above 100, higher than 100; **de** — upper; **hacia** — upward, up
arriesgar *vt* to risk; *vr* to take a risk, to risk oneself
arritmia *f* arrhythmia
arrojar *vt* (*fam, vomitar*) to vomit, to throw up (*fam*)

arrollar *vt* (*atropellar*) to run over
arroz *m* rice
arruga *f* wrinkle; **arrugas del fumador**.. smoker's wrinkles
arrugar *vt, vr* to wrinkle
arrullar *vi* (*ped*) to coo
arsenal terapéutico *m* armamentarium
arsénico *m* arsenic; **trióxido de** — arsenic trioxide
artemisinina *f* artemisinin
arteria *f* artery; — **braquial** brachial artery; — **carótida (común)** (common) carotid artery; — **(coronaria) circunfleja** circumflex (coronary) artery; — **coronaria (derecha)** (right) coronary artery; — **coronaria (principal) izquierda** left (main) coronary artery; — **(coronaria) descendente anterior izquierda** left anterior descending (coronary) artery; **arterias endurecidas** (*fam*) hardened arteries (*fam*); — **femoral** femoral artery; — **humeral** brachial artery; — **ilíaca** *or* **iliaca** iliac artery; — **mesentérica (superior, inferior)** (superior, inferior) mesenteric artery; — **poplítea** popliteal artery; — **radial** radial artery; — **subclavia** subclavian artery
arterial *adj* arterial
arteriografía *f* (*técnica*) angiography; (*estudio*) angiogram
arteriosclerosis, arterioesclerosis *f* arteriosclerosis
arteriovenoso -sa *adj* arteriovenous
arteritis *f* arteritis; — **de células gigantes** giant cell arteritis; — **de Takayasu** Takayasu's arteritis; — **temporal** temporal arteritis
artes marciales *mpl&fpl* martial arts
articulación *f* joint; — **de la rodilla (tobillo, etc.)** knee (ankle, etc.) joint
articular *adj* articular; **dolor** — joint pain
artificial *adj* artificial
artrítico -ca *adj* arthritic
artritis *f* arthritis; — **juvenil** juvenile arthritis; — **reactiva** reactive arthritis; — **reumatoide** rheumatoid arthritis
artrografía *f* (*técnica*) arthrography; (*estudio*) arthrogram
artroplastia *f* arthroplasty; — **total de cadera** total hip replacement; — **total de rodilla** total knee replacement

artroscopia, artroscopía f arthroscopy
artroscópico -ca adj arthroscopic
artrosis f osteoarthritis, degenerative joint disease
asa f (intestinal) loop (of bowel)
asado -da adj roasted, grilled; **— a la parrilla** grilled, broiled, barbecued
asaltar vt to assault
asalto m assault
asar vt to roast, to grill; **— a la parrilla** to grill, broil, to barbecue
asbesto m asbestos
asbestosis f asbestosis
ascariasis, ascaridiasis f ascariasis
áscaris m (pl -ris) roundworm
ascendente adj ascending
ascitis f ascites
asco m (náusea) nausea
ascórbico -ca adj ascorbic
asegurado -da adj insured; **no —** uninsured
aseguranza f (Mex) insurance
asegurarse vr to check, to make sure, to be sure; **Me aseguré de mantenerlo limpio..**I made sure to keep it clean.
asentaderas fpl (fam) buttocks, bottom (fam)
aseo m hygiene; **— bucal** oral hygiene
aséptico -ca adj aseptic, sterile
asequible adj affordable; **cuidado de la salud —** affordable health care
asertividad f assertiveness
asesor -ra mf (consejero) counselor
asesoramiento m counseling; **— genético** genetic counseling
asesoría f counseling; **— familiar** family counseling; **— matrimonial** marriage counseling
asfixia f asphyxia, suffocation
asfixiar vt, vr to asphyxiate, suffocate
asiento m seat; **— de ducha** shower stool o seat; **— de seguridad infantil** (para vehículo); child car seat
asilo m asylum, institution, home; **— de ancianos** skilled nursing facility, nursing home (fam), board and care
asimilación f (psych) assimilation
asintomático -ca adj asymptomatic
asistencia f assistance; **— domiciliaria** home care; **— médica** health care; **— pública** governmental assistance, welfare ; **— sanitaria** (Esp, SA) health care; **— social** governmental assistance, welfare

asistente mf assistant, aide; **— médico** medical assistant
asistir vt to assist, aid; (una clínica, clase, etc.) to attend; **asistido por computadora, asistido por vacío, etc.** computer-assisted, vacuum-assisted, etc.
asistivo -va adj (Ang) assistive
asistolia f asystole, flatline (fam)
asma f asthma
asmático -ca adj & mf asthmatic
asociación f association; **— libre** free association
asociado -da adj associated, linked; **— con** associated with, linked to; **no —** unrelated
asolearse vr to get sun
asparagina f asparagine
aspartame, aspartamo m aspartame
aspecto m appearance
aspereza f roughness
aspergilosis f aspergillosis
áspero -ra adj (piel, etc.) rough
aspiración f aspiration; **— articular** joint aspiration; **— con aguja fina** fine needle aspiration
aspirar vt (inhalar) to inhale, breathe in; (por la nariz) to sniff; (con jeringa) to aspirate
aspirina f aspirin
asqueroso -sa adj (nauseabundo) nauseating
astenia f weakness, lack of energy, asthenia (ant)
astigmatismo m astigmatism
astilla f sliver, splinter, chip, fragment
astillar vt, vr to chip
astrágalo m talus
astringente adj & m astringent
Asuntos de Veteranos mpl Veterans Affairs (VA)
asustar vt to frighten
atacar vt to attack
ataduras fpl ties, (para limitar los movimientos de un paciente agitado) restraints, (de cuero) leathers (fam)
ataque m attack, bout, spell, fit; (fam, crisis epiléptica) seizure, convulsion; **— cardíaco** or **al corazón** heart attack; **— cerebral** stroke; **— de asma** asthma attack; **— de nervios** (fam) anxiety attack, panic attack; **— de pánico** panic attack; **— isquémico tran-**

sitorio **(AIT)** transient ischemic attack (TIA)

atarantado -da *adj* dazed, in a daze, stunned

atarantar *vt* to daze, stun; *vr* to become dazed *o* stunned

ataxia *f* ataxia

atáxico -ca *adj* ataxic

atazanavir *m* atazanavir

atención *f* attention, care; — **administrada** managed care; — **a largo plazo** long-term care; — **crítica** critical care; — **de enfermería** nursing care; — **de la salud** (*esp. Esp*) health care; — **de tercer nivel** (*esp. Mex*) tertiary care; — **domiciliaria** home care; — **médica** medical attention, health care; — **médica administrada** managed care; — **médica domiciliaria** home health care; — **prenatal** prenatal care; — **primaria** primary care; — **sanitaria** (*esp. Esp*) health care; — **terciaria** tertiary care

atender *vt* (*a un paciente*) to take care of, to care for, to treat, to attend; (*un parto*) to deliver; **La Dra. Gomez atendió tres partos anoche.**.Dr. Gomez delivered three babies last night... **Atendió a la señora Reid**..She delivered Mrs. Reid...**Atendió a los gemelos**..She delivered the twins.

atenolol *m* atenolol

atento -ta *adj* attentive, mindful

atenuado -da *adj* attenuated

ateroesclerosis *f* atherosclerosis

ateroma *m* atheroma

aterosclerosis *f* atherosclerosis

atípico -ca *adj* atypical

atleta *mf* athlete

atlético -ca *adj* athletic

atmósfera *f* atmosphere

atomizador nasal *m* nasal inhaler (*esp. Mex*)

atomoxetina *f* atomoxetine

atópico -ca *adj* atopic

atorvastatina *f* atorvastatin

atovacuona *f* atovaquone

atracón *m* (*de comida*) food binge

atragantamiento *m* choking (*on food*)

atragantarse *vr* to choke; — **con** to choke on

atrapamiento *m* entrapment; — **del nervio cubital** ulnar nerve entrapment; —

de nervio nerve entrapment, entrapped nerve, pinched nerve (*fam*); — **de nervio periférico** peripheral nerve entrapment

atrás *adv* back; ago, earlier; **tres días atrás**..three days ago..three days earlier; **hacia** — backward, back; **la parte de** — the back part

atrasado -da *adj* behind, delayed

atrofia *f* atrophy

atrofiar *vt* to cause to atrophy; *vr* to atrophy, to become atrophied

atropellar *vt* to run over

atropina *f* atropine

atún *m* tuna

aturdido -da *adj* dazed, in a daze, stunned

aturdimiento *m* daze

aturdir *vt* to stun, daze, make dizzy; *vr* to become stunned *o* dazed *o* dizzy

audición *f* sense of hearing, hearing

audífono *m* hearing aid

audiograma *m* audiogram

audiología *f* audiology

audiólogo -ga *mf* audiologist

audiometría *f* audiometry

audiométrico -ca *adj* audiometric

audiómetro *m* audiometer

audioprotesista *mf* (*esp. Esp*) specialist in hearing aids

auditivo -va *adj* auditory

aumentar *vt* to increase, (*de tamaño*) to make bigger, enlarge; *vi* to increase, to get bigger

aumento *m* increase, gain, rise, augmentation; — **mamario** *or* **de senos** breast augmentation

aura *f* aura

aurícula *f* (*del corazón*) atrium

auricular *adj* atrial

auriculoventricular *adj* atrioventricular

ausencia *f* absence

ausente *adj* absent, missing

ausentismo *m* (*esp. Amer*) absenteeism

autismo *m* autism

autista *adj* autistic; *mf* autistic person, person with autism

autístico -ca *adj* autistic

autoafirmación *f* self-confidence, assertiveness

autoayuda *f* self-help

autoclave *f* autoclave

autoconciencia *f* self-awareness

autoconfianza *f* self-confidence
autoconocimiento *m* self-awareness
autoconsciencia *f* self-awareness
autocontrol *m* self-control
autodestructivo -va *adj* self-destructive
autodisciplina *f* self-discipline, will power
autoeccematización, autoeczematización *f* autoeczematization, id reaction
autoestima *f* self-esteem
autoevaluación *f* self-examination
autoexamen *m* self-examination; — **mamario** *or* **de mama** *or* **seno** breast self-examination
autoexploración *f* (*form*) self-examination; — **mamaria** breast self-examination
autoimagen *f* self-image
autoinfligido -da *adj* self-inflicted
autoinmune *adj* autoimmune
autoinmunidad *f* autoimmunity
autoinyector *m* autoinjector; — **de epinefrina** epinephrine autoinjector
autolimitado -da *adj* self-limited
autólogo -ga *adj* autologous
automedicarse *vr* to self-medicate
automóvil *m* automobile, car
autonomía *f* autonomy; — **del paciente** patient autonomy
autopsia *f* autopsy
autorrealización *f* self-realization
autorrecetarse *vr* to self-prescribe
autorrespeto *m* self-respect
autosómico -ca *adj* autosomal
autosondaje *m* self-catheterization (*of the bladder*)
autotransfusión *f* autologous blood transfusion
autotratamiento *m* self-treatment
auxiliar *adj* auxiliary, ancillary; *mf* assistant, aide; — **de enfermería certificado** certified nursing assistant
auxilio *interj* Help!; *m* help, assistance;

(*después de un desastre*) aid, relief; **primeros auxilios** first aid
AV *See* **auriculoventricular**.
avanzado -da *adj* advanced
ave *f* bird; **aves de corral** poultry, fowl
avena *f* oatmeal
avergonzado -a *adj* ashamed, embarrassed
aversión *f* aversion
avisar *vt* to notify
aviso *m* warning, advisory; — **sanitario** (public) health advisory
avispa *f* wasp; — **amarilla** yellow jacket
avispón *m* hornet
axila *f* axilla, armpit (*fam*); **Tengo un grano en la axila.**.I have a pimple under my arm.
axilar *adj* axillary
ay *interj* Ouch!
ayer *adv* yesterday
ayuda *f* help, assistance, aid, relief
ayudante *mf* assistant, aide
ayudar *vt, vi* to help, assist, aid
ayunar *vi* to fast
ayunas, en fasting; **glucosa en ayunas.**. fasting glucose
ayuno *m* fast, fasting; **glucosa en ayuno** ..fasting glucose
azahar *m* (*bot*) lemon flower
azar *m* **al** — at random
azarcón *m* lead oxide (*toxic Mexican folk remedy*)
azatioprina *f* azathioprine
azelastina *f* azelastine
azitromicina *f* azithromycin
AZT *m&f* AZT
azúcar *m&f* sugar; **sin** — sugarless
azucarado -da *adj* sugar-coated
azufre *m* sulphur *o* sulfur
azul *adj* blue; — **de metileno** methylene blue
azulado -da *adj* bluish

B

baba f drool
babear vi to drool
babeo m drooling
babero m bib
babesiosis f babesiosis
bacilo m bacillus, rod; — **de Calmette-Guérin (BCG)** bacille Calmette-Guérin (BCG)
bacinica, bacinilla f bedpan
bacitracina f bacitracin
baclofeno m baclofen
bacteria f bacterium; [*Nota: En inglés se usa casi siempre el plural:* bacteria.]
bacteriano -na adj bacterial
bactericida adj bactericidal
bacteriemia f bacteremia
baja f fall, drop
bajada f drop; — **de la leche** (obst) letdown
bajalenguas m (pl -guas) tongue depressor o blade
bajar vt to lower, to reduce; vi, vr to go down, fall, drop; **Le bajó el potasio**..Your potassium went down; — **de peso** to lose weight; **bajar(le) (a uno) la regla** (fam) to have one's period, to start one's period; **Me bajó la regla ayer**..My period started yesterday.
bajo -ja adj low; (anat) lower; (de estatura) short; **Su sodio está bajo**..Your sodium is low...**una dieta baja en fibra**..a low-fiber diet...**la parte baja**..the lower part; **espalda** — lower back; **más** — **que** lower than; **más** — **que antes**..lower than before; **parte** — **del abdomen (de la espalda, etc.)** lower abdomen (back, etc.)
bala f bullet; — **de oxígeno** oxygen tank
balanceado -da adj (comida, etc.) balanced
balanitis f balanitis
balanza f balance scale, scale
balazo m shot; (herida) gunshot wound; **Recibió un balazo en el hombro**..He was shot in the shoulder.
balbucear vi (ped) to babble
balbuceo m (ped) babble
balneario m health resort o spa (with therapeutic baths)

balneoterapia f water therapy, therapeutic bathing
balón m (deportes) ball; (de un catéter) balloon; — **de contrapulsación intraaórtico** intraaortic balloon counterpulsation
baloncesto m basketball
bálsamo m balm, salve; — **labial** lip balm
banana f (Arg, Ecu, Esp) banana
banano m (Col) banana
banco m bank; (taburete) stool; — **de alimentos** food bank; — **de órganos** organ bank; — **de sangre** blood bank
banda f (ortodoncia, etc.) band; (gástrica) band, banding; — **gástrica ajustable por laparoscopía** or **laparoscópica** laparoscopic adjustable gastric banding
bandeja f tray
bañadera f (Cuba, tina) bathtub
bañar vt to wash, bathe; vr to wash oneself, bathe, take a bath; (nadar) to go swimming
bañera f bathtub; — **de hidromasaje** whirlpool
baño m bath; bathroom, restroom; — **de asiento** sitz bath; — **de damas** women's room; — **de esponja** sponge bath; — **de hombres** men's room; — **de mujeres** women's room; — **de regadera** (esp. Mex) shower; — **de sol** sunbath; — **de vapor** steam bath; **hacer del** — (Mex) to have a bowel movement; **ir al** — (euph, defecar) to have a bowel movement, to go to the bathroom (euph)
barandilla, baranda f bedrail o bed rail, siderail o side rail
barba f beard, whiskers
barbero m barber
barbijo m surgical mask
barbilla f chin
barbitúrico m barbiturate
bardana f (bot) burdock
bariátrico -ca adj bariatric
bario m barium
barotrauma m barotrauma
barra f bar, (ortho) rod; — **de Harring-**

ton Harrington rod; — **de seguridad** grab bar

barrera *f* barrier; — **placentaria** placental barrier

barriga *f* belly, stomach (*fam*), tummy (*ped, fam*)

barrigón -na *adj* potbellied

barriguita *f* (*ped*) tummy

barrio *m* neighborhood

barro *m* blackhead, pimple

basal *adj* baseline, basal; **valor** — baseline value

báscula *f* scale (*for weighing*)

base *f* base; **a** — **de aceite, a** — **de agua, etc.** oil-based, water-based, etc.; — **de datos** data base; — **libre** (*cocaína*) free base (*cocaine*)

básico -ca *adj* basic

basquetbol *m* basketball

bastón *m* cane; (*del ojo*) rod; — **de cuatro patas** *or* **apoyos** *or* **puntos** four-pronged cane

bastoncillo de algodón *m* (*Esp*) cotton swab

bata *f* gown

baumanómetro *m* (*Mex*) blood pressure monitor

bazo *m* spleen; — **accesorio** accesory spleen

BCG *abbr* **bacilo de Calmette-Guérin**. *See* **bacilo.**

bebé *mf* (*pl* **bebés**) baby

beber *vt, vi* to drink

bebida *f* drink

beclometasona *f* beclomethasone, beclomethasone dipropionate (*USAN*), beclometasone (*INN*)

béisbol *m* baseball

belladona *f* (*bot*) belladonna

benazepril *m* benazepril

bencedrina *f* benzedrine

benceno *m* benzene

beneficencia *f* beneficence

beneficio *m* benefit; (*psych, etc.*) gain; **para su** — for your benefit; — **secundario** secondary gain

beneficioso -sa *adj* beneficial

benigno -na *adj* benign

benzatropina *f* benzatropine

benzoato *m* benzoate; — **sódico** *or* **de sodio** sodium benzoate

benzodiazepina, benzodiacepina *f* benzodiazepine

benzoína *f* benzoin

benzonatato *m* benzonatate

benztropina, benzatropina (*INN*) *f* benztropine, benzatropine (*INN*)

beriberi *m* beriberi

berrinche *m* tantrum

besar *vt* to kiss

beso *m* kiss

bestialidad *f* bestiality

beta *f* beta; **beta-bloqueador, beta-bloqueante** *m* beta blocker; **beta-hemolítico** beta-hemolytic

betabloqueador, betabloqueante *m* beta blocker

betacaroteno *m* beta carotene

betametasona *f* betamethasone

bezoar *m* bezoar

biberón *m* baby bottle

bicarbonato *m* bicarbonate; — **sódico** *or* **de sodio** sodium bicarbonate

bíceps *m* (*pl* **bíceps**) biceps

bicho *m* bug, tiny animal

bicicleta *f* bicycle; — **estática** stationary bicycle; **ir** *or* **montar en** — to ride a bicycle

bicúspide *adj & m* bicuspid

bien *adj & adv* well, all right; **Estoy bien** ..I'm well...**Estoy comiendo bien**..I'm eating well; *m* good, benefit, welfare; **por su** — for your benefit; **por su propio** — for your own good

bienestar *m* wellbeing, welfare; wellness

bifásico -ca *adj* (*pharm*) biphasic

bifenilo policlorado (BPC) *m* polychlorinated biphenyl (PCB)

bifocal *adj* bifocal; *mpl o fpl* (*fam*) bifocal glasses *o* eyeglasses, bifocals (*fam*)

bigote *m* moustache

bilateral *adj* bilateral

biliar *adj* biliary

bilirrubina *f* bilirubin

bilis *f* bile

bioactivo -va *adj* bioactive

biodegradable *adj* biodegradable

bioequivalencia *f* bioequivalence

bioequivalente *adj* bioequivalent

bioestadística *f* biostatistics

bioética *f* bioethics

biofármaco *m* (*pharm*) biologic, biopharmaceutical

bioidéntico -ca *adj* bioidentical

bioingeniería *f* bioengineering

biología *f* biology

biológico -ca *adj* biologic *o* biological; *m* (*pharm*) biologic
biomecánica *f* biomechanics
biomédico -ca *adj* biomedical
biometría hemática completa *f* complete blood count
bioprostésico -ca *adj* bioprosthetic
bioprótesis *f* (*pl* -sis) bioprosthesis
biopsia *f* biopsy; — **cutánea** skin biopsy; — **de hígado** liver biopsy; — **de mama** breast biopsy; — **de médula ósea** bone marrow biopsy; — **de piel** skin biopsy; — **de próstata** prostate biopsy; — **de riñón** renal *o* kidney biopsy; — **estereotáxica** stereotactic biopsy; — **escisional** excisional biopsy; — **incisional** incisional biopsy; — **por congelación** frozen section
bioquímico -ca *adj* biochemical; *f* biochemistry
biorretroalimentación *f* biofeedback
biotecnología *f* biotechnology
bioterrorismo *m* bioterrorism
bióxido *See* **dióxido.**
bíper *m* (*Amer*) beeper, pager
bipolar *adj* bipolar
bisabuelo -la *m* great-grandfather, great-grandparent; *f* great-grandmother
bisacodilo *m* bisacodyl
bisel *m* (*de un aguja*) bevel (*of a needle*)
bisexual *adj* bisexual
bisfenol A *m* bisphenol A
bisfosfonato *m* bisphosphonate
bisinosis *f* byssinosis
bismuto *m* bismuth
bisnieto -ta *m* great-grandson, great-grandchild; *f* great-granddaughter
bisoprolol *m* bisoprolol
bistec *m* steak, beefsteak
bisturí *m* (*pl* -ríes *or* -rís) scalpel; — **de rayos gamma** gamma knife
bizco -ca *adj* cross-eyed; *mf* cross-eyed person
blanco -ca *adj* white, (*tez*) fair; *m* target; **órgano** — target organ
blando -da *adj* soft; (*comida*) bland
blanqueador *m* bleach; (*dent*) whitener
blanqueamiento *m* (*dent*) whitening
blanquecino -na *adj* whitish
blanquillo *m* (*Mex*) egg
blastomicosis *f* blastomycosis
blefaritis *f* blepharitis
blefaroplastia *f* blepharoplasty

bleomicina *f* bleomycin
blister *m* (*fam, envase*) blister pack
bloomer *m* (*esp. CA, frec. pl*) (women's) underpants, panties
bloque de mordida *m* (*dent*) bite block
bloqueado -da *adj* blocked
bloqueador *m* (*pharm*) blocker; — **beta** beta blocker; — **de los canales del calcio** calcium channel blocker; — **del receptor de angiotensina** angiotensin receptor blocker; — **H₂** H₂ blocker; — **neuromuscular** neuromuscular blocker; — **solar** sunscreen, sunblock
bloqueante *m* blocker; — **de los canales del calcio** calcium channel blocker; — **neuromuscular** neuromuscular blocker
bloquear *vt* (*pharm, physio, etc.*) to block
bloqueo *m* block; obstruction, blockage; (*psych*) blocking; — **cardíaco** heart block; — **de rama** bundle branch block; — **nervioso** nerve block
blot *m* (*pl* blots) blot; **Western (Southern, etc.)** — Western (Southern, etc.) blot
blusa *f* blouse
bobina telefónica *f* telecoil
boca *f* mouth; — **abajo** prone (*form*), facedown; — **a** — mouth-to-mouth; — **arriba** faceup; **por la** — by mouth
bocadillo *m* snack
bocado *m* mouthful, bite (*of food*)
boceprevir *m* boceprevir
bochorno *m* (*esp. Mex*) hot flash
bocio *m* goiter; — **multinodular tóxico** toxic multinodular goiter
bola *f* lump; ball; — **de algodón** cotton ball
bolita *f* small lump; small ball; — **de algodón** cotton ball
bolo *m* bolus
bolsa *f* bursa; bag; — **de agua caliente** hot-water bottle; — **de aire** airbag; — **de colostomía** colostomy bag; — **de hielo** ice pack; — **de las aguas** bag of waters
bomba *f* pump; (*arma*) bomb; — **atómica** atomic bomb; — **de insulina** insulin pump; — **de relojería** *or* **de tiempo** time bomb
bombear *vt* (*sangre*) to pump (blood)
bombero -ra *mf* fireman

bombona de oxígeno *f* oxygen tank
boqueras *fpl* (*fam*) cheilitis
boquilla *f* mouthpiece
borde *m* border, edge, margin; **— cortante** cutting edge (*of a knife, etc.*)
bórico -ca *adj* boric
borrachera *f* drunken spree, binge; **bajar(le) la borrachera** to sober (*one*) up
borracho -cha *adj & mf* drunk
borrarse *vr* (*la vista*) to blur, to become blurred *o* blurry
borreliosis *f* borreliosis; **— de Lyme** Lyme borreliosis
borroso -sa *adj* blurred, blurry; **visión borrosa** blurred vision
bostezar *vi* to yawn
bostezo *m* yawn
bota *f* boot; **— de Unna** Unna boot
botana *f* (*Mex*) snack
botánico -ca *adj* botanical
botar *vt* (*esp. Carib, fam*) to eliminate, expel, pass; **— aire** to breathe out; **— una piedra** (*al orinar*) to pass a stone
botella *f* bottle
botica *f* pharmacy, drugstore
boticario -ria *mf* pharmacist
botiquín *m* medicine cabinet; **— de primeros auxilios** first-aid kit
botón *m* button; **— de llamada** call button
botulismo *m* botulism
bóveda palatina *f* (*form*) hard palate
bovino -va *adj* bovine
BPC *See* **bifenilo policlorado**.
brackets *mpl* (*orthodontics*) brackets, (*fam, aparato de ortodoncia*) braces
bradicardia *f* bradycardia
bragas *fpl* (*esp. Esp*) (women's) underpants, panties
braguero *m* truss
braille *m* Braille
braquial *adj* brachial
braquiterapia *f* brachytherapy
brazalete *m* bracelet; **— de alerta médica** medic alert bracelet; **— de identificación** ID bracelet
brazo *m* arm
brécol *m* broccoli
breve *adj* (*tiempo*) brief, short
brida *f* (*adherencia*) adhesion
brócoli, bróculi *m* broccoli
bromo *m* bromine

bromocriptina *f* bromocriptine
bromuro *m* bromide; **— de aclidinio** aclidinium bromide; **— de ipratropio** ipratropium bromide
bronceado -da *adj* tan; *m* tan, suntan
bronceador *m* tanning *o* suntan lotion (*to increase tanning*)
broncearse *vr* to tan, to get a tan
broncoalveolar *adj* bronchoalveolar
broncoconstricción *f* bronchoconstriction
broncodilatador *m* bronchodilator
broncoespasmo *m* bronchospasm
broncogénico -ca *adj* bronchogenic
broncógeno -na *adj* bronchogenic
bronconeumonía *f* bronchopneumonia
broncoscopia, broncoscopía *f* bronchoscopy
broncoscopio *m* bronchoscope
bronquial *adj* bronchial
bronquiectasia *f* bronchiectasis
bronquio *m* bronchus
bronquiolitis *f* bronchiolitis; **— obliterante** bronchiolitis obliterans
bronquiolo *m* bronchiole
bronquitis *f* bronchitis; **— crónica** chronic bronchitis
brote *m* outbreak
brucelosis *f* brucellosis
brujería *f* witchcraft
brujo *m* (*chamán*) shaman
bruxismo *m* bruxism
bubón *m* bubo
bubónico -ca *adj* bubonic
bucal *adj* oral
buceo *m* (*deporte*) diving
budesonida, budesónida (*INN*) *f* budesonide
bueno -na *adj* (**buen** before masculine singular nouns) good; **un buen médico**..a good doctor
bulbar *adj* bulbar
bulbo *m* bulb; **— raquídeo** medulla (*of the brainstem*)
bulimia *f* bulimia
bulímico -ca *adj* bulimic
bulloso -sa *adj* bullous
bulto *m* lump, swelling; **— en la mama** *or* **el pecho** *or* **el seno** breast lump
bumetanida *f* bumetanide
buprenorfina *f* buprenorphin
bupropión *m* bupropion
burbuja *f* bubble

burnout *m* (*Ang*) burnout
bursitis *f* bursitis; — **anserina** anserine bursitis; — **olecraneana** olecranon bursitis; — **prepatelar, — prerrotuliana** (*Esp*) prepatellar bursitis; — **subacromial** subacromial bursitis; — **trocantérica** (*Amer*), — **trocantérea** (*Esp*) trochanteric bursitis
buscapersonas *m* (*pl* -**nas**) pager, beeper

buspirona *f* buspirone
busto *m* bust, female breast
busulfán, busulfano (*INN*) *m* busulfan
butalbital *m* butalbital
bypass *m* (*Ang*) bypass; — **femoro-poplíteo** femoropopliteal bypass; — **gástrico** gastric bypass; — **triple (cuádruple, etc.)** triple (quadruple, etc.) bypass

C

cabecear *vi* (*como hacen los adictos a la heroína*) to nod out (*fam*)
cabecera *f* head (*of a bed*); **a la —** at the bedside; **de —** bedside
cabello *m* (scalp) hair
cabestrillo *m* sling
cabeza *f* head; — **del húmero** head of the humerus
cabra *f* goat
caca *f* (*esp. ped, fam or vulg*) stool (*form*), bowel movement, poo poo (*ped, fam*); **hacer —** to have a bowel movement, to go poo poo (*ped, fam*)
cacahuete, cacahuate *m* peanut
cacaraña *f* pockmark
cactus, cacto *m* (*pl* -**tus**, -**tos**) cactus
cadáver *m* cadaver, corpse
cadavérico -ca *adj* cadaveric
cadena *f* chain; — **de custodia** chain of custody; — **de frío** chain of cold; — **de supervivencia** chain of survival; — **ligera** light chain; — **pesada** heavy chain; **de — larga** long-chain; **de — media** medium-chain; **de — ramificada** branched-chain
cadera *f* hip
cadmio *m* cadmium
caducado -da *adj* (*medicamento, etc.*) outdated, out of date
caducidad *f* (*de un medicamento, etc.*)

expiration; **fecha de —** expiration date
caer *vi* **caer(le) bien** (*a uno*) to agree with; **No me cae bien**..It doesn't agree with me; *vr* to fall, fall down, collapse; (*los párpados, etc.*) to droop, sag; (*una costra, etc.*) to slough
café *m* coffee; **de color —** brown
cafeína *f* caffeine
caído -da *adj* fallen; *f* fall, collapse, loss; — **del cabello** hair loss; — **de mollera** sunken fontanel; (*Mex, CA*) pediatric folk illness manifest by a sunken fontanel and other signs of dehydration and believed to be caused by improper handling of the infant
caja *f* (*de cigarillos*) pack; **cajas diarias** packs per day; — **torácica** rib cage
cajetilla *f* (*de cigarillos*) pack; **cajetillas diarias** packs per day
calada *f* (*de un cigarillo*) drag
calambre *m* cramp; — **del escribiente** *or* **escritor** writer's cramp
calamina *f* calamine
calcetín *m* sock
calcificarse *vr* to calcify
calcifilaxis, calcifilaxia (*esp. Esp*) *f* calciphylaxis
calcinosis *f* calcinosis
calcio *m* calcium
calcipotrieno *m* calcipotriene

calcitonina *f* calcitonin
calcitriol *m* calcitriol
cálculo *m* calculus, stone (*fam*); (*dent*) calculus, tartar; — **biliar** gallstone; — **renal** renal calculus, kidney stone
caldo *m* broth, broth-based soup without cream
calefacción *f* heating
calendario *m* (*horario*) schedule; — **de vacunación**, — **vacunal** (*esp. Esp*) vaccination schedule
calentamiento *m* warmup; **hacer ejercicios de** —, **hacer (el)** — to warm up (*before exercise*)
calentar *vt*, *vr* to warm (up), to heat (up)
calentura *f* fever; (*en los labios*) fever blister, cold sore
calibrar *vt* to calibrate
calibre *m* gauge; **aguja de** — **21** 21 gauge needle
calidad *f* quality; **atención médica de** — quality health care; — **de vida** quality of life
caliente *adj* warm, hot
calistenia *f* calisthenics
callo *m* callus; (*en el pie*) corn (*on the foot*)
callosidad *f* callus, hardened skin
calma *f* calm
calmante *adj* calming; *m* analgesic (*form*), painkiller (*fam*), pain pill (*fam*)
calmar *vt* to calm, soothe; *vr* to calm down, quiet down
calor *m* heat, warmth; — **corporal** body heat; **tener** *or* **sentir** — to be *o* feel hot; **Tengo mucho calor**..I'm very hot.
caloría *f* calorie
calostro *m* colostrum
calvicie *f* baldness; — **del vértice** vertex baldness; — **frontal** frontal baldness
calvo -va *adj* bald
calzado *m* footwear; — **ortopédico** orthopedic shoes
calzón *m* (*frec. pl*) (women's) underpants, panties
calzoncillos *mpl* (men's) underpants
cama *f* bed; — **de hospital** hospital bed; **guardar** — to stay in bed; **reposo en** — bed rest
cámara *f* chamber; — **espaciadora** spacer (*for metered-dose inhaler*); — **hiperbárica** hyperbaric chamber
camarón *m* shrimp

cambiar *vt*, *vi* to change
cambio *m* change, adjustment; — **de catéter** catheter change *o* replacement; **cambios de humor** (*psych*) mood swings; — **de sexo** (*fam*) gender reassignment, sex change (*fam*); — **de vendaje** bandage change
camilla *f* stretcher, litter, gurney; (*SA, mesa*) exam table
caminadora *f* treadmill
caminar *vi* to walk
caminata *f* long walk, hike
camisa *f* shirt; — **de fuerza** strait-jacket
camiseta *f* undershirt
campanilla *f* uvula
campaña *f* campaign; field; — **contra el tabaco** anti-smoking campaign; — **de vacunación** vaccination campaign; **hospital de** — field hospital
campo *m* field; rural area, country; — **de la enfermería** field of nursing; — **visual** *or* **de visión** visual field
cana *f* gray hair
canadillo *m* (*bot*) ephedra
canal *m* canal; — **del parto** birth canal
cancelar *vt* to cancel
cáncer *m* cancer, malignancy; — **cervical** cervical cancer; — **colorrectal** colorectal cancer; — **cutáneo** skin cancer; — **de cabeza y cuello** head and neck cancer; — **de células renales** renal cell cancer, kidney cancer (*fam*); — **de cérvix** cervical cancer; — **de colon** colon cancer; — **de cuello uterino** cervical cancer; — **de esófago** esophageal cancer, cancer of the esophagus; — **de estómago** gastric cancer, stomach cancer; — **de hígado** liver cancer; — **de hueso** bone cancer; — **de laringe** laryngeal cancer, cancer of the larynx; — **de mama** breast cancer; — **de ovario** ovarian cancer; — **de páncreas** pancreatic cancer; — **de pecho** breast cancer; — **de piel** skin cancer; — **de próstata** prostate cancer; — **de pulmón de células no pequeñas** non-small-cell lung cancer; — **de pulmón de células pequeñas** small-cell lung cancer; — **de recto** rectal cancer, cancer of the rectum; — **de riñón** renal cell cancer, kidney cancer (*fam*); — **de tiroides** thyroid cancer; — **de útero** uterine cancer, cancer of the uterus; —

de vejiga bladder cancer; — **gástrico** gastric cancer, stomach cancer; — **laríngeo** laryngeal cancer; — **óseo** bone cancer; — **pulmonar** lung cancer; — **rectal** rectal cancer; — **renal** renal cell cancer, kidney cancer (*fam*); — **uterino** uterine cancer; — **vesical** (*form*) bladder cancer

cancerígeno -na *adj* carcinogenic, cancer-causing; *m* carcinogen

cancerología *f* (*esp. Mex*) oncology

canceroso -sa *adj* cancerous, having cancer, pertaining to cancer

candesartán *m* candesartan

candidato -ta *mf* candidate; **candidato a trasplante hepático**..candidate for a liver transplant

candidiasis *f* candidiasis

canguro *mf* (*Esp, niñera*) baby-sitter

canilla *f* leg, shin

canillera *f* (*CA, SA*) shin guard

canino *m* (*diente*) cuspid, canine tooth

cannabidiol (CBD) *m* cannabidiol (CBD)

cannabinoide *adj & m* cannabinoid; — **sintético** synthetic cannabinoid

cannabis *m* cannabis

cansado -da *adj* tired

cansancio *m* tiredness, fatigue; — **visual** eyestrain

cansar *vt* to tire (out), to make tired; *vr* to tire (out), to get tired

cantidad *f* quantity, amount; — **por porción** amount per serving

canto negro *m* (*PR, fam*) bruise

cánula *f* cannula; — **nasal** nasal cannula, nasal prongs

CAP *abbr* **conducto arterioso persistente**. *See* **conducto**.

capa *f* coating, layer; **capas de la piel**.. layers of the skin

capacidad *f* ability, capacity; — **para manejar** ability to drive; — **vital forzada** forced vital capacity

capacitar *vt* to train, to empower

capaz *adj* capable, competent

capecitabina *f* capecitabine

capilar *adj* capillary; (*relativo al cabello*) pertaining to hair; **trasplante** *m* **capilar** hair transplant; *m* capillary

capitación *f* (*seguros*) capitation

capsaicina *f* capsaicin

cápsula *f* capsule, pill

capsulitis *f* capsulitis; — **adhesiva** adhesive capsulitis

captación *f* uptake

captopril *m* captopril

capuchón *m* (*de aguja, etc.*) cap; — **cervical** cervical cap

cara *f* face; aspect; **la cara interna del muslo**..the medial aspect of the thigh

carabela portuguesa *f* (*Esp*) Portuguese man-of-war, type of jellyfish that stings

caracol *m* snail

carácter *m* characteristic; — **sexual secundario** secondary sex characteristic

característico -ca *adj & f* characteristic

caramelo *m* (*dulce*) candy, piece of candy; *mpl* candy, sweets

carbamazepina *f* carbamazepine

carbapenem *m* carbapenem

carbidopa *f* carbidopa

carbohidrato *m* carbohydrate

carbón *m* coal, charcoal; — **activado** activated charcoal

carbonatado -da *adj* carbonated

carbonato *m* carbonate; — **amónico** (*esp. Esp*), — **de amonio** ammonium carbonate, (*que se utiliza para reanimar a un desmayado*) smelling salts; — **cálcico** *or* **de calcio** calcium carbonate

carbono *m* carbon (*element*)

carboximetilcelulosa *f* carboxymethylcellulose

carbunco *m* anthrax

cárcel *f* jail; prison

carcinogénico -ca *adj* carcinogenic, cancer-causing

carcinógeno -na *adj* carcinogenic, cancer-causing; *m* carcinogen

carcinoide *adj & m* carcinoid; **tumor** *m* — carcinoid tumor

carcinoma *m* carcinoma; — **basocelular** basal cell carcinoma; — **broncogénico** bronchogenic carcinoma; — **de células escamosas** squamous cell carcinoma; — **de células no pequeñas** non-small-cell carcinoma; — **de células pequeñas** small-cell carcinoma; — **de células renales** renal cell carcinoma; — **de células transicionales** transitional cell carcinoma; — **ductal in situ** ductal carcinoma in situ; — **escamocelular** *or* **escamoso** squamous cell carcinoma; — **hepatocelular** hepatocellular carci-

noma; — **lobulillar** *or* **lobular** lobular carcinoma; — **renal** renal cell carcinoma
carcinomatosis *f* carcinomatosis
cardenal *m* (*Esp*) bruise
cardíaco, cardiaco -ca *adj* cardiac
cardiogénico -ca *adj* cardiogenic
cardiógeno -na *adj* cardiogenic
cardiología *f* cardiology
cardiólogo -ga *mf* cardiologist
cardiomiopatía *f* cardiomyopathy; — **de takotsubo** takotsubo cardiomyopathy; — **dilatada** dilated cardiomyopathy; — **hipertrófica** hypertrophic cardiomyopathy; — **por estrés** stress-induced cardiomyopathy; — **restrictiva** restrictive cardiomyopathy
cardiopatía *f* cardiopathy; — **isquémica** ischemic cardiomyopathy; — **reumática** rheumatic heart disease
cardiopulmonar *adj* cardiopulmonary
cardiorrespiratorio -ria *adj* cardiorespiratory
cardiosaludable *adj* heart-healthy
cardiotocógrafo *m* fetal (heart) monitor
cardiovascular *adj* cardiovascular
cardioversión *f* cardioversion; — **eléctrica sincronizada** synchronized electrical cardioversion
cardioversor *m* cardioverter; — **desfibrilador implantable** implantable cardioverter-defibrillator (ICD)
carditis *f* carditis
cardo *m* thistle; — **mariano** (*bot*) milk thistle
carecer *vi* — **de** to lack, to be deficient in
carencia *f* lack, deficiency
careta *f* mask (*esp. protective*); — **para soldar** welding mask
carga *f* burden, load; — **tumoral** tumor burden; — **viral** viral load
cargo de conciencia *m* guilty conscience
caries *f* (*dent*) caries, tooth decay
carilla *f* (*dent*) veneer; — **de porcelana** porcelain veneer
cariño *m* affection
cariñoso -sa *adj* affectionate
cariotipo *m* karyotype
carisoprodol *m* carisoprodol
carne *f* flesh; meat; — **blanca** white meat; — **de cerdo** pork; — **de cordero** lamb; — **de vaca** *or* **de res** beef; —

oscura dark meat; **en** — **viva** excoriated (*form*), raw
carnitina *f* carnitine
carnosidad *f* (*en el ojo*) pterygium (*form*), benign growth on the eye
caroteno *m* carotene; **beta-caroteno** beta-carotene
carotídeo -a *adj* carotid
carótido -da *adj* carotid
carpiano -na *adj* carpal
carraspear *vi* to clear one's throat
carraspera *f* irritation of the throat, phlegm in the throat
carrito de emergencia *m* (*Mex*) crash cart
carro *m* cart; car, automobile; — **de paro**, — **de parada** (*Esp*), — **de emergencia** crash cart
carta *f* letter; **una carta de su médico**..a letter from your doctor; — **de Snellen** eye chart
cartílago *m* cartilage
carvedilol *m* carvedilol
casa *f* home; — **de cuna** (*Mex*) orphanage; — **de reposo** *or* **descanso** convalescent home; **en** — at home
casado -da *adj* married
cáscara sagrada *f* (*bot*) cascara sagrada
casco *m* helmet; — **de seguridad** hard hat
cascorvo -va *adj* (*CA, SA*) bowlegged
casero -ra *adj* made in the home; **remedio** — home remedy
caso *m* case; **en 9 de 10 casos**..in 9 out of 10 cases
caspa *f* dandruff; (*de animales*) dander
castaño -ña *adj* brown
castración *f* castration
castrar *vt* to castrate
casualidad *f* chance; **por** — by chance
catabólico -ca *adj* catabolic
catalepsia *f* catalepsy
cataplasma *f* medicinal plaster, poultice
cataplexia *f* cataplexy
catarata *f* cataract
catarro *m* cold, runny nose; **tener** — to have a cold
catarsis *f* (*pl* -**sis**) (*psych*) catharsis
catártico -ca *adj* (*psych*) cathartic
catástrofe *f* catastrophe
catatonia *f* catatonia
catatónico -ca *adj* catatonic
catéter *m* catheter, line; — **central de**

inserción periférica peripherally-inserted central catheter (PICC); **— de arteria pulmonar** pulmonary artery catheter; **— de Hickman** Hickman catheter; **— de Swan-Ganz** pulmonary artery *o* Swan-Ganz catheter; **— epidural** epidural catheter; **— implantable** implantable catheter; **— venoso central** central venous catheter, central line; **— vesical** urinary catheter

cateterismo *m* catheterization; **— cardíaco** cardiac catheterization

cateterización *f* catheterization

cateterizar *vt* to catheterize

catgut *m* catgut

caucho *m* (*esp. Esp*) rubber

causa *f* cause

causalgia *f* causalgia

causar *vt* to cause

cáustico -ca *adj* caustic

cauterio *m* cautery

cauterización *f* cauterization

cauterizar *vt* to cauterize

cavidad *f* cavity

CBD *See* **cannabidiol.**

cc *abbr* **centímetro cúbico.** *See* **centímetro.**

cebolla *f* onion

cecear *vi* to lisp

ceceo *m* lisp

cedazo *m* sieve

cefaclor *m* cefaclor

cefalea *f* (*form*) headache; **— en racimos** cluster headache; **— tensional** tension headache

cefalexina *f* cephalexin

cefálico -ca *adj* cephalic

cefalorraquídeo -a *adj* cerebrospinal

cefalosporina *f* cephalosporin

cefazolina *f* cefazolin

cefdinir *m* cefdinir

cefepima *f* cefepime

cefoperazona *f* cefoperazone

cefotaxima *f* cefotaxime

cefoxitina *f* cefoxitin

ceftazidima *f* ceftazidime

ceftriaxona *f* ceftriaxone

cefuroxima *f* cefuroxime

ceguera *f* blindness; **— nocturna** night blindness

ceja *f* eyebrow, brow

celecoxib *m* celecoxib

celíaco, celiaco -ca *adj* celiac

celiaquía *f* celiac disease

célibe *adj* celibate

celos *mpl* **tener — de** to be jealous of; **Tiene celos de su hermano..**He is jealous of his brother.

celoso -sa *adj* jealous; **Ella es muy celosa..**She is very jealous.

Celsius *adj* Celsius; **100 grados Celsius** ..100 degrees Celsius

célula *f* cell; **— asesina natural** natural killer cell; **— B** B cell; **— CD4** CD4 cell; **— cerebral** brain cell; **células escamosas atípicas de significado indeterminado** atypical squamous cells of undetermined significance (ASCUS); **— madre** stem cell; **— plasmática** plasma cell; **— T auxiliar** *or* **ayudante** helper T cell; **— T citotóxica** cytotoxic T cell; **— T colaboradora** helper T cell; **— transicional** transitional cell; **— T supresora** suppressor T cell

celular *adj* cellular; *m* (*fam, teléfono*) cellular telephone, cell phone (*fam*)

celulitis *f* cellulitis; (*depósitos de grasa*) cellulite

cena *f* dinner, supper

centígrado -da *adj* Centigrade; **40 grados centígrados..**40 degrees Centigrade

centímetro (cm) *m* centimeter (cm); **— cúbico (cc)** cubic centimeter (cc)

centinela *adj* (* gánglio, evento, etc.*) sentinel

centrado -da *adj* centered; (*emocionalmente*) centered, relaxed and with a clear mind; **— en el paciente** patient-centered

central *adj* central; *f* station; **— de enfermería** (*Mex*) nursing station

centrarse *vr* to focus on

centro *m* center; **— ambulatorio** clinic; **— de acogida** (*Esp*) shelter; **— de acondicionamiento físico** fitness center; **— de cirugía** surgery center; **— de Control de Envenenamientos e Intoxicaciones** (*US*) Poison Control Center; **— de día** day center; **— de enfermería especializada** skilled nursing facility; **— de salud rural** rural health center; **— de urgencias** urgent care center; **— diurno** day center; **— médico** medical center; **Centros para el**

Control y la Prevención de Enfermedades (*US*) Centers for Disease Control and Prevention (CDC); — **quirúrgico** surgery center; — **sanitario** medical center; — **sociosanitario** assisted
living facility *o* center; — **terciario**
tertiary care center

cepa *f* (*de una bacteria, etc.*) strain (*of a
bacteria, etc.*)

cepillado *m* brushing

cepillar *vt* to brush; *vr* — **el pelo** to
brush one's hair; — **los dientes** to
brush one's teeth

cepillo *m* brush, (*para el pelo*) hairbrush;
— **de dientes** *or* **dental** toothbrush

cera *f* wax; — **de los oídos** earwax

cerámica *adj* (*dent, etc.*) ceramic

cerca *adv* near, close; — **de** near, close
to

cercano -na *adj* close; **amigo -ga** *mf* —
close friend

cerclaje *m* cerclage

cerda *f* bristle; **de** — **dura** stiff-bristle *o*
hard-bristle; **de** — **suave** soft-bristle

cerdo *m* pig

cereal *m* cereal, grain

cerebelo *m* cerebellum

cerebral *adj* cerebral

cerebro *m* brain; — **medio** midbrain

cerebrovascular *adj* cerebrovascular

cerrado -da *adj* (*traumatismo, etc.*)
closed

cerrar *vt* to close; **cuando cierro los
ojos**..when I close my eyes; — **la
mano** to make a fist; *vi, vr* to close

certificado -da *adj* certified; *m* certificate; — **(médico) de defunción** death
certificate; — **de nacimiento** birth certificate

cerumen *m* cerumen, earwax (*fam*)

cerveza *f* beer

cervical *adj* (*obst, ortho*) cervical

cervicitis *f* cervicitis

cervix *m&f* (*pl* -**vix**) cervix

cerviz *f* (*pl* -**vices**) back of the neck

cesárea *f* cesarean section

cetirizina, cetiricina (*esp. Esp*) *f* cetirizine

cetoacidosis *f* ketoacidosis

cetona *f* ketone

cetónico -ca *adj* ketotic

cetósico -ca *adj* **no** — nonketotic

chalazión *m* chalazion

chamaco -ca *m* boy, child; *f* girl

chamán -mana *mf* shaman

chamarra *f* (*Mex*) jacket

chamorro *m* (*Mex, fam*) calf (*of leg*)

champú *m* (*pl* -**pús**) shampoo

chancro *m* chancre; — **blando** soft
chancre

chancroide *m* chancroid

chaparro -ra *adj* short and stocky

chaqueta *f* jacket; (*Mex, vulg*) masturbation

charola *f* (*Mex*) tray

chasquido *m* (*card*) click

chata *f* bedpan

chequear *vt* to check

chequeo *m* (*médico*) checkup

chichón *m* lump, bump (*due to trauma,
esp. about the head*)

chichote *m* (*Nic, fam*) lump, bump (*due
to trauma, esp. about the head*)

chicle *m* chewing gum

chico -ca *adj* little, small; *m* boy, child; *f*
girl

chile *m* chili pepper

chimpinilla *f* (*CA, fam*) shin

chinche *f* bedbug; (*vector de la enfermedad de Chagas*) kissing bug; — **besu-
cona** (*Mex*), — **picuda** (*Guat, ES*)
kissing bug

chindondo *m* (*El Salv, fam*) lump, bump
(*due to trauma, esp. about the head*)

chipo *m* (*Ven*) kissing bug

chipote *m* (*Mex, fam*) lump, bump (*due
to trauma, esp. about the head*)

chirimacha *f* (*Perú*) kissing bug

chiva *f* (*Mex, fam*) heroin; (*PR*) jaw

chivola *f* (*El Salv*) lump

chocolate *m* chocolate

choque *m* shock; (*fam, accidente de
tránsito*) traffic accident, motor vehicle
accident; — **anafiláctico** anaphylactic
shock; — **cardiogénico** cardiogenic
shock; — **hipovolémico** hypovolemic
shock; — **neurogénico** neurogenic
shock; — **séptico** septic shock

choquezuela *f* (*fam*) kneecap

chorro *m* (*de la orina*) stream (*of urine*);
— **miccional** (*form*) urinary stream;
orina del — **medio** midstream urine

chucho *m* (*Amer*) chill (*esp. due to malaria*)

chueco -ca *adj* (*Mex*) crooked

chupar *vt* to suck; *vr* — **el pulgar** to

suck one's thumb
chupete *m* pacifier
chupetón *m* (*marca producida por un beso*) hickey
chupón *m* pacifier; (*marca producida por un beso*) hickey
churro *m* (*Mex*) diarrhea
CIA *abbr* **comunicación interauricular.** *See* **comunicación.**
cianocobalamina *f* cyanocobalamin, vitamin B₁₂
cianosis *f* cyanosis
cianótico -ca *adj* cyanotic
cianuro *m* cyanide
ciático -ca *adj* sciatic; *f* sciatica
cicatriz *f* (*pl* -**trices**) scar; **dejar** — to leave a scar
cicatrización *f* healing; scarring
cicatrizar *vt, vr* to heal (*a wound*)
ciclamato *m* cyclamate
cíclico -ca *adj* cyclic
ciclismo *m* cycling (*sport*)
ciclo *m* cycle; — **anovulatorio** anovulatory cycle; — **biológico** life cycle; — **de antibióticos** course of antibiotics; — **de quimioterapia** cycle of chemotherapy; — **menstrual** menstrual cycle; — **ovulatorio** ovulatory cycle; — **reproductivo** *or* **reproductor** reproductive cycle; — **vital** life cycle
ciclobenzaprina *f* cyclobenzaprine
ciclofosfamida *f* cyclophosphamide
ciclopirox *m* ciclopirox
ciclosporina *f* cyclosporine, ciclosporin (*INN*)
cidofovir *m* cidofovir
ciego -ga *adj* blind; *mf* blind person; *m* (*anat*) cecum
científico -ca *adj* scientific; *mf* scientist
cierre *m* zipper; (*psych, surg, etc.*) closure
cifoescoliosis *f* kyphoscoliosis
cifosis *f* kyphosis
cifra *f* number
cigarrillo *m* cigarette
cigarro *m* (*puro*) cigar; (*cigarillo*) cigarette
cigoto *m* zygote
cilindro *m* cylinder; — **de oxígeno** oxygen tank
cilostazol *m* cilostazol
cimicífuga *f* (*bot*) black cohosh
cinc *See* **zinc.**

cinético -ca *adj* kinetic
cinta *f* band, tape; — **adhesiva** adhesive tape; — **de medir** tape measure *o* measuring tape; — **dental** dental tape; — **métrica** tape measure *o* measuring tape; — **rodante** (*esp. Esp*) treadmill
cinto *m* belt
cintura *f* waist, waistline; (*anat*) girdle; (*fam, espalda baja*) lower back; **de la cintura hacia arriba..** from the waist up; — **escapular** shoulder girdle; — **pélvica** *or* **pelviana** pelvic girdle
cinturón *m* belt; — **de levantamiento** weightlifting belt; — **de seguridad** seat belt, safety belt
ciprofloxacina *f* ciprofloxacin
ciprofloxacino *m* ciprofloxacin
ciproheptadina *f* cyproheptadine
circadiano -na *adj* circadian
circulación *f* circulation, blood flow; — **colateral** collateral circulation; — **extracorpórea** extracorporeal circulation; — **fetal** fetal circulation; — **pulmonar** pulmonary circulation; — **sistémica** systemic circulation
circular *vi* to circulate, to flow; **estar circulando** (*un virus, etc.*) to be going around
circulatorio -ria *adj* circulatory
círculo *m* circle; — **vicioso** vicious circle
circuncidar *vt* (*pp* -**ciso**) to circumcise
circuncisión *f* circumcision
circunciso -sa (*pp of* **circuncidar**) *adj* circumcised
circundante *adj* surrounding
circunscrito -ta *adj* localized
cirrosis *f* cirrhosis; — **biliar primaria** primary biliary cirrhosis
cirrótico -ca *adj & mf* cirrhotic
cirugía *f* surgery; — **abierta** open surgery; — **a corazón abierto** open heart surgery; — **ambulatoria** ambulatory *o* outpatient surgery; — **bariátrica** bariatric surgery; — **bucal** oral surgery; — **cosmética** cosmetic surgery; — **de reasignación de sexo** *or* **género** sexual *o* gender reassignment surgery; — **de revascularización coronaria** coronary artery bypass surgery; — **de várices** vein stripping; — **electiva** elective surgery; — **estética** cosmetic surgery; — **general** general surgery; — **laparoscópica** laparoscopic surgery;

— **maxilofacial** maxillofacial surgery; — **mayor** major surgery; — **menor** minor surgery; — **oral** oral surgery; — **ortopédica** orthopedic surgery; — **plástica** plastic surgery; — **radical** radical surgery; — **reconstructiva** reconstructive surgery; — **robótica** robotic surgery; — **torácica** thoracic surgery

cirujano -na *mf* surgeon; — **bucal** oral surgeon; — **dentista** (*esp. Mex*) dentist; — **general** general surgeon; — **oral** oral surgeon; — **ortopédico** orthopedic surgeon; — **torácico** thoracic surgeon; — **vascular** vascular surgeon

cisplatino *m* cisplatin

cistectomía *f* cystectomy, removal of the bladder

cisteína *f* cysteine

cisticercosis *f* cysticercosis

cístico -ca *adj* cystic (*related to bladder or gallbladder*)

cistinuria *f* cystinuria

cistitis *f* cystitis; — **intersticial** interstitial cystitis

cistocele *m* cystocele

cistoscopia, cistoscopía *f* cystoscopy

cistoscopio *m* cystoscope

cita *f* appointment

citalopram *m* citalopram

citisina *f* cytisine

citología *f* cytology; (*fam*) Papanicolaou smear, Pap smear (*fam*); — **cervical** *or* **exfoliativa** Papanicolaou smear, Pap smear (*fam*)

citomegalovirus (CMV) *m* cytomegalovirus (CMV)

citometría *f* cytometry; — **de flujo** flow cytometry

citotóxico -ca *adj* cytotoxic

citrato *m* citrate

cítrico -ca *adj* citric; *mpl* citrus fruits

CIV *abbr* **comunicación interventricular.** *See* **comunicación.**

clamidia *f* chlamydia

clara de huevo *f* egg white

claritromicina *f* clarithromycin

claro -ra *adj* clear

clase *f* class

clásico -ca *adj* classic

claudicación *f* claudication; — **intermitente** intermittent claudication

claustrofobia *f* claustrophobia

clavícula *f* clavicle, collar bone (*fam*)

clavo *m* nail; (*ortho*) pin

cleptomanía *f* kleptomania

clima *m* climate

climaterio *m* climacteric

clímax *m* (*pl* **-max**) (*orgasmo*) climax, orgasm

clindamicina *f* clindamycin

clínico -ca *adj* clinical; *mf* clinician, practitioner; *f* clinic; — **de consulta externa** *or* **ambulatoria** outpatient clinic; — **de urgencias** urgent care clinic; — **gratuita** free clinic

clip *m* clip

clipar *vt* (*surg*) to clip

clítoris *m* clitoris

cloasma *m* melasma

clobetasol *m* clobetasol

clofazimina *f* clofazimine

clofibrato *m* clofibrate

clomifeno *m* clomifene, clomiphene

clon *m* clone

clonazepam *m* clonazepam

clónico -ca *adj* clonic

clonidina *f* clonidine

clonus *m* clonus

clopidogrel *m* clopidogrel

cloración *f* chlorination

clorado -da *adj* chlorinated

clorambucilo *m* chlorambucil

cloranfenicol *m* chloramphenicol

clordano *m* chlordane

clorfeniramina, clorfenamina (*INN*) *f* chlorpheniramine (*USAN*), chlorphenamine (*INN*)

clorhexidina *f* chlorhexidine

clorhidrato *m* hydrochloride

clorhídrico -ca *adj* hydrochloric

cloro *m* chlorine

cloroformo *m* chloroform

cloroquina *f* chloroquine

clortalidona *f* chlorthalidone

cloruro *m* chloride; — **de aluminio** aluminum chloride; — **de polivinilo** polyvinyl chloride; — **de potasio** potassium chloride; — **de sodio** sodium chloride; — **de trospio** trospium chloride; — **potásico** potassium chloride; — **sódico** sodium chloride

clostridio *m* Clostridium

clotrimazol *m* clotrimazole

clozapina *f* clozapine

club *m* club; — **de salud** health club

cm *See* **centímetro.**
CMV *See* **citomegalovirus.**
coagulación *f* coagulation; — **intravascular diseminada** disseminated intravascular coagulation (DIC)
coagular *vt* to cause to coagulate *o* clot; *vr* to coagulate, to clot
coágulo *m* clot
coagulopatía *f* coagulopathy
coartación *f* coarctation
cobalto *m* cobalt
cobaya *m&f* guinea pig (*lab animal*)
cobertura *f* (*seguros, etc.*) coverage
cobija *f* (*esp. Mex*) blanket
cobrar *vt, vi* to charge
cobre *m* copper
cobro *m* bill, charge
coca *f* (*bot*) coca; (*fam cocaína*) cocaine, coke (*fam*)
cocaína *f* cocaine, coke (*fam*)
cocainómano -na *mf* cocaine user, cocaine addict
coccidioidomicosis *f* coccidioidomycosis
cóccix *m* coccyx, tailbone (*fam*)
cocer *vt* (*carne, etc.*) to boil; — **al horno** to bake; — **al vapor** to steam
coche *m* automobile, car
cocido -da *adj* boiled; — **al horno** baked; — **al vapor** steamed; **poco** — undercooked
cociente *m* quotient; — **intelectual (CI)** intelligence quotient (IQ); — **internacional normalizado** international normalized ratio (INR)
cocinar *vt, vi* to cook; **poco cocinado** undercooked
cocinero -ra *mf* cook
cóclea *f* cochlea
coclear *adj* cochlear
coco *m* (*bacteria*) coccus; (*nuez*) coconut
cóctel, coctel *m* cocktail; (*de medicamentos*) cocktail (*of medications*)
codeína *f* codeine
codependencia *f* codependency
código azul *m* (*Ang*) Code Blue
código postal *m* zip code
codo *m* elbow; — **de golfista** golfer's elbow; — **de tenista** tennis elbow
coeficiente intelectual (CI) *m* intelligence quotient (IQ)
coenzima Q *m&f* coenzyme Q
coger *vt* (*esp. Esp, una enfermedad*) to contract, to catch (*a disease*)
cognitivo -va *adj* cognitive
cohibición *f* inhibition
cohibido -da *adj* inhibited
coinfección, co-infección *f* coinfection
coito *m* coitus; — **interrumpido** coitus interruptus; — **sin protección** unprotected intercourse, unprotected sex (*fam*)
coitus interruptus *m* coitus interruptus
cojear *vi* to limp
cojera *f* limp
cojín *m* cushion, pad; — **eléctrico** heating pad
cojo -ja *adj* lame, crippled; *mf* lame *o* crippled person
cojón *m* (*vulg*) testicle, ball (*fam o vulg*)
cola *f* (*pegamento*) glue
colaborador -ra *adj* cooperative; **no** — uncooperative
cola de caballo *f* (*bot*) horsetail, pewterwort
colador *m* (*para orina*) sieve
colágeno *m* collagen
colangiocarcinoma *m* cholangiocarcinoma
colangiografía *f* (*técnica*) cholangiography; (*estudio*) cholangiogram; — **transhepática percutánea** percutaneous transhepatic cholangiography; percutaneous transhepatic cholangiogram
colangiopancreatografía retrógrada endoscópica (CPRE) *f* endoscopic retrograde cholangiopancreatography (ERCP)
colangitis *f* cholangitis
colapsarse *vr* (*un pulmón, etc.*) to collapse
colapso *m* collapse; (*crisis*) breakdown; — **nervioso** nervous breakdown
colar *vt* (*la orina para piedras*) to strain (*urine for stones*)
colateral *adj* collateral
colchicina *f* colchicine
colchón *m* mattress
colección *f* (*de sangre, etc.*) collection (*of blood, etc.*)
colecistectomía *f* cholecystectomy
colecistitis *f* cholecystitis; — **alitiásica** *or* **acalculosa** acalculous cholecystitis
colectomía *f* colectomy
colédoco -ca *adj* choledochal; *m* (*fam*) common bile duct

colega *mf* colleague
colelitiasis *f* cholelithiasis
cólera *m* cholera; *f* anger, rage
colesevelam *m* colesevelam
colestasis *f* cholestasis; — **intrahepática del embarazo** intrahepatic cholestasis of pregnancy
colesteatoma *m* cholesteatoma
colesterol *m* cholesterol; — **LDL (HDL, etc.)** LDL (HDL, etc.) cholesterol; — **total** total cholesterol
colestipol *m* colestipol
colestiramina *f* cholestyramine
colgajo *m* (*surg*) flap
cólico *m* (*ped, frec. pl*) colic; (*surg, etc.; frec. pl*) colic (*form*), abdominal cramp(s), abdominal cramping; — **menstrual** (*frec. pl*) menstrual cramp(s), menstrual cramping
coliflor *f* cauliflower
coliforme *adj & m* coliform
colirio *m* eyewash, eye drops
colita *f* (*Amer, fam*) coccyx, tailbone (*fam*)
colitis *f* colitis; — **isquémica** ischemic colitis; — **microscópica** microscopic colitis; — **seudomembranosa** pseudomembranous colitis; — **ulcerosa** ulcerative colitis
collar, collarín *m* (*ortho*) collar; — **cervical (rígido, blando)** (hard, soft) cervical collar
colmillo *m* cuspid, canine tooth; (*de un animal*) fang
colocación *f* placement; — **de un catéter** catheterization, placement of a catheter
colocar *vt* to position, to place
coloide *m* colloid
colon *m* colon, large bowel; — **ascendente** ascending colon; — **derecho** right colon; — **descendente** descending colon; — **espástico** (*ant*) irritable bowel syndrome, spastic colon (*ant*); — **izquierdo** left colon; — **sigmoide** *or* **sigmoideo** sigmoid colon; — **transverso** transverse colon
colonización *f* colonization
colonoscopia, colonoscopía *f* colonoscopy; — **virtual** virtual colonoscopy
colonoscopio *m* colonoscope
color *m* color
coloración *f* (*micro*) stain; — **de Gram** Gram's stain

colorado -da *adj* red
colorante *m* dye, coloring; — **alimentario** *or* **de alimentos** food coloring, food dye
colorrectal *adj* colorectal
colostomía *f* colostomy; **bolsa de** *or* **para** — colostomy bag
colposcopia, colposcopía *f* colposcopy
columna *f* column; (*fam, espina*) spinal column, spine, backbone; — **cervical** cervical spine; — **dorsal** thoracic spine; — **lumbar** lumbar spine; — **lumbosacra** lumbosacral spine; — **torácica** thoracic spine; — **vertebral** spinal column, spine, backbone
colutorio *m* mouthwash
coma *m* coma; **en** — in a coma, comatose
comadrón *m* male midwife
comadrona *f* midwife
comatoso -sa *adj* comatose
combate *m* combat
combatir *vt* to combat
combinación *f* combination
comenzar *vt, vi* to begin
comer *vt, vi* to eat; (*esp. Mex*) to have lunch; **dar de** — to feed; *vr* — **las uñas** to bite *o* chew one's nails
comezón *f* itch, itching, itchiness; **sentir** *or* **tener** — to itch, to have an itch, to have itching
comida *f* food, meal; (*esp. Mex*) lunch; — **balanceada** (*Amer*) balanced meal; — **basura** *or* **chatarra** junk food; — **enlatada** canned food; — **equilibrada** (*Esp*) balanced meal; — **para bebés** baby food; — **procesada** processed food; — **rápida** fast food
comienzo *m* onset, beginning; **de** — **juvenil** juvenile-onset; **de** — **precoz** early-onset; **de** — **tardío** late-onset; **edad** *f* **de** — age at onset
comodidad *f* comfort
cómodo -da *adj* comfortable; *m* (*Mex, bacinilla*) bedpan
comorbilidad *f* comorbidity
compañero -ra *mf* companion; — **sentimental** (life) partner
compartimentalización *f* (*psych*) compartmentalization
compartir *vt* to share; — **agujas** *or* **jeringas** to share needles
compasión *f* compassion, sympathy

compasivo -va *adj* compassionate, sympathetic; **uso —** (*pharm*) compassionate use

compatible *adj* compatible

compensación *f* (*psych, etc.*) compensation; **— laboral** worker's compensation

compensar *vi* to compensate

competente *adj* competent

complejo *m* complex; **— de Edipo** Oedipus complex; **— de inferioridad** inferiority complex; **— de superioridad** superiority complex; **— Mycobacterium avium** Mycobacterium avium complex (MAC); **— vitamínico B** vitamin B complex

complementario -ria *adj* complementary; (*seguros*) supplemental

complemento *m* complement; (*suplemento*) supplement

completo -ta *adj* complete

complexión *f* build, constitution

complicación *f* complication

cumplimentar *vt* (*Esp, un formulario*) to fill out, to complete (*a form*)

componente *m* component; (*pharm*) constituent

componer *vt* (*pp* -puesto) to fix; *vr* (*fam, recuperarse*) to get well

comportamiento *m* behavior

comportarse *vr* to behave, act

comprensivo -va *adj* sympathetic

compresa *f* compress, pack; **— de hielo** ice pack

compresión *f* compression; (*de un nervio*) entrapment; **— de la médula espinal** spinal cord compression; **— del nervio cubital** ulnar nerve entrapment; **— de nervio** nerve entrapment, entrapped nerve, pinched nerve (*fam*); **— de nervio periférico** peripheral nerve entrapment; **— medular** spinal cord compression; **— torácica** chest compression

comprimido *m* (*form*) tablet; **— dispersable** (*esp. Esp, pharm*) wafer

comprimir *vt* to compress

comprometer *vt* to compromise

compuesto (*pp of* componer) *m* compound

compulsión *f* compulsion

compulsivo -va *adj* compulsive

computadora *f* computer

común *adj* common; **un problema común**..a common problem; **poco —** uncommon

comunicación *f* communication; **— interauricular (CIA)** atrial septal defect (ASD); **— interventricular (CIV)** ventricular septal defect (VSD)

comunicar *vt, vr* to communicate

comunidad *f* community

comunitario -ria *adj* pertaining to the community; **participación —** community involvement

cóncavo -va *adj* concave

concebir *vi* to conceive

concentración *f* concentration

concentrado -da *adj* concentrated; *m* (*pharm, etc.*) concentrate; **concentrado de factores de coagulación** coagulation factor concentrate; **— de hematíes** unit of packed red blood cells

concentrador *m* concentrator; **— de oxígeno** oxygen concentrator

concentrar *vt, vr* to concentrate

concepción *f* (*obst, etc.*) conception

conciencia *f* conscience; (*conocimiento*) consciousness, awareness; **cargo de —** guilty conscience; **— colectiva** collective consciousness; **— culpable** guilty conscience; **perder la —** to lose consciousness; **pérdida de —** loss of consciousness

concientización *f* awareness; **— del cáncer de mama** breast cancer awareness

conclusión *f* (*psych*) closure

concusión *f* concussion

condado *m* county (*US*)

condición *f* condition, state; **— crítica** critical condition; **— preexistente** preexisting condition

condicionado -da *adj* conditioned

condicionamiento *m* conditioning; **— físico** physical conditioning, fitness

cóndilo *m* condyle

condimentado -da *adj* spicy

condimento *m* spice

condolencia *f* condolence; **Mis condolencias a**..My condolences to

condón *m* condom, rubber (*fam*)

condrocalcinosis *f* chondrocalcinosis

condrosarcoma *m* chondrosarcoma

conducción *f* conduction; driving; **— agresiva** aggressive driving, road rage (*fam*)

conducir vt (*un vehículo*) to drive
conducta f behavior
conducto m duct, canal, conduit; — **arterioso persistente** or **permeable (CAP)** patent ductus arteriosus (PDA); — **auditivo** auditory canal; — **biliar** bile duct; — **cístico** cystic duct; — **colédoco** common bile duct; — **de Eustaquio** Eustachian tube; — **deferente** vas deferens; — **hepático (derecho, izquierdo)** (right, left) hepatic duct; — **ileal** ileal conduit; — **lagrimal** lacrimal duct, tear duct (*fam*); **conductos nasales** nasal passages; — **pancreático** pancreatic duct; — **semicircular** semicircular canal
conductor -ra mf driver; — **designado** designated driver
conectar vt to connect, attach
conectivopatía f connective tissue disease
conejillo de Indias m guinea pig (*esp. figuratively*)
conexión f connection
confabulación f (*Ang*) confabulation
confianza f confidence, trust; — **en uno mismo** self-confidence; **tener — (en)** to trust
confiar vi to trust; **Confío en mis hijos** ..I trust my children.
confidencial adj confidential
confidencialidad f confidentiality
confirmar vt to confirm
conflicto m conflict
confort m comfort
confortar vt to comfort
confrontación f confrontation
confrontar vt to confront
confrontativo -va, confrontacional adj confrontational
confundido -da adj confused
confundir vt to confuse; vr to get o become confused
confusión f confusion
congelación f (*daño a los tejidos por el frío*) frostbite
congelar vt, vr to freeze
congénito -ta adj congenital
congestión f congestion; — **nasal** nasal congestion
congestionado -da adj congested
congestivo -va adj congestive
conización f conization; — **con asa dia-**

térmica loop electrosurgical excision procedure (LEEP)
conjugado -da adj (*bilirrubina, estrógenos*) conjugated; (*vacuna*) conjugate
conjuntiva f conjunctiva
conjuntival adj conjunctival
conjuntivitis f conjunctivitis, pinkeye (*fam*)
conminuta adj (*fractura*) comminuted
conmoción cerebral f concussion
cono m (*anat, gyn, ophthalmology, etc.*) cone
conocimiento m (*consciencia*) consciousness; — **de uno mismo** insight; **perder el —** to lose consciousness, to black out; **pérdida de —** loss of consciousness, blackout
consanguíneo -a adj consanguineous, having a common ancestor, related by blood (*fam*)
consciencia f consciousness, awareness; — **colectiva** collective consciousness; **perder la —** to lose consciousness; **pérdida de —** loss of consciousness
consciente adj conscious, aware; (*atento*) mindful, attentive
consecuencia f consequence; **como — de** as a consequence of, due to
consecutivo -va adj consecutive
consejería f counseling; — **familiar** family counseling; — **matrimonial** marriage counseling
consejero -ra mf counselor
consejo m advice, counseling; (*recomendación*) recommendation, tip; — **genético** genetic counseling; **en contra del consejo médico**..against medical advice
consentimiento m consent; — **informado** informed consent
consentir vt to pamper, spoil; vi to consent; — **en** to consent to
conservador -ra adj conservative, conserving; — **de mama** breast-conserving; m (*Mex, conservante*) preservative
conservante m preservative
conservar vt to conserve
consistencia f consistency
consolador m (*juego sexual*) dildo
consolar vt to console, to comfort
consolidación f consolidation
constante adj constant; fpl — **vitales** vital signs

constipación *f* (*catarro, congestión*) cold, nasal congestion; (*estreñimiento*) constipation

constipado -da *adj* (*congestionado*) having a cold, congested, having nasal congestion; (*estreñido*) constipated; *m* cold, nasal congestion

constiparse *vr* to catch a cold, to become congested; (*estreñirse*) to become constipated

constitución *f* constitution

constituyente *m* (*pharm*) constituent

constricción *f* constriction

consuelda *f* (*bot*) comfrey

consulta *f* visit, doctor's visit; (*con un especialista*) consultation, (*en el hospital*) consult; (*consultorio*) office, doctor's office; — **externa** outpatient services; — **médica** doctor's visit; — **no programada** *or* **sin cita** unscheduled visit, drop-in (*fam*); **de** — **externa** outpatient; **horas de** — office hours; **pasar** — (*Esp*) to round, to visit patients

consultar *vt, vi* to consult; — **con** *or* **a un especialista** to consult a specialist

consultorio *m* (doctor's) office

consumidor -ra *mf* user

consumo *m* consumption, intake; — **diario recomendado** recommended daily intake

contacto *m* contact, exposure; — **cercano** close contact; — **visual** eye contact

contagiar *vt* to infect, to give (*fam*) (*a disease*); *vr* to become infected, to catch (*a disease*)

contagioso -sa *adj* (*una enfermedad*) communicable (*form*), contagious, infectious, catching (*fam*); (*fam, una persona*) capable of infecting others, contagious (*fam*); [*Nota: En principio contagioso y* contagious *se aplican a las enfermedades y no a las personas aún cuando ambos son aplicados a personas en lenguaje familiar.*]

contaminación *f* contamination, (*el ambiente*) pollution; — **ambiental** pollution (*of the environment in general*); — **atmosférica** (*form*) air pollution, smog (*fam*); — **del agua** water pollution; — **del aire** air pollution, smog (*fam*)

contaminado -da *adj* contaminated, (*el ambiente*) polluted

contaminar *vt* to contaminate, (*el ambiente*) to pollute; *vr* to become contaminated, to become polluted

contar *vt, vi* to count; — **calorías** to count calories

contención *f* (*sujeción*) restraint; — **mecánica** mechanical restraint; — **química** chemical restraint

contenedor *m* container; — **de objetos punzantes** sharps container

contener *vt* to contain; (*a un paciente*) to restrain; — **la respiración** to hold one's breath

contenido *m* content (*frec. pl*)

contento -ta *adj* happy

conteo *m* count; — **de bacterias** bacterial count; — **de glóbulos rojos (leucocitos, etc.)** red blood cell (leukocyte, etc.) count; — **de pastillas** pill count; — **sanguíneo completo (CSC)** complete blood count (CBC)

contexto *m* setting; **en el contexto de daño hepático**..in the setting of liver damage

contextura *f* build

continuo -nua *adj* continuous; (*habitual*) continual

contorno *m* contour

contracción *f* contraction; — **auricular prematura (CAP)** premature atrial contraction (PAC); **contracciones de Braxton-Hicks** Braxton-Hicks contractions; — **ventricular prematura (CVP)** premature ventricular contraction (PVC)

contracepción *f* contraception

contraceptivo -va *adj & m* contraceptive

contractura *f* contracture; — **de Dupuytren** Dupuytren's contracture

contraer *vt* (*una enfermedad*) to contract, to catch (*fam*); (*vasos sanguíneos*) to constrict; *vr* (*un músculo*) to contract; (*vasos sanguíneos*) to constrict

contraindicación *f* contraindication

contraindicado -da *adj* contraindicated

contrarrestar *vt* to counteract

contraste *m* (*fam, medio de contraste*) contrast medium, contrast (*fam*)

contrato *m* contract

contratransferencia *f* (*psych*) countertransference

control *m* control; (*estación*) station; **bajo** — under control; — **de enfermería** nursing station; — **de la ira** anger management; — **de la natalidad** birth control; — **del enojo** anger management; — **de uno mismo** self-control; — **estricto** (*de la glucemia*) tight control (*of blood sugars*); **en** — in control; **fuera de** — out of control

controlador -ra *adj* (*persona*) controlling

controlar *vt* to control

controvertido -da *adj* controversial

contusión *f* contusion

convalecencia *f* convalescence

convalecerse *vr* to convalesce

convaleciente *adj* convalescent

convencional *adj* conventional

conversión *f* conversion

convexo -xa *adj* convex

convivir *vi* to live together; **convivir con drogadictos**..to live with drug addicts

convulsión *f* convulsion, seizure; — **febril** febrile seizure; — **tónico-clónica** tonic-clonic seizure

convulsionar *vi* to have a seizure, to seize

cónyuge *mf* spouse

cooperar *vi* to cooperate

coordinación *f* coordination

copago *m* copayment, copay (*fam*)

copioso -sa *adj* copious

copo *m* (*de algodón*) cotton ball

coprocultivo *m* stool culture

coqueluche *m&f* (*fam*) pertussis (*form*), whooping cough

coraje *m* (*valor*) courage, (*rabia*) rage

coral *m* coral

corazón *m* heart

corazoncillo *m* (*bot*) St. John's wort

corbata *f* tie (*article of clothing*)

cordal *See* **muela cordal**.

cordero *m* lamb

cordón *m* cord; — **umbilical** umbilical cord

cordura *f* sanity

corea *m&f* chorea; — **de Huntington** Huntington's chorea

coriocarcinoma *m* choriocarcinoma

coriorretinitis *f* chorioretinitis

córnea *f* cornea

corneal *adj* corneal

cornete *m* turbinate

corona *f* (*anat, dent*) crown

coronación *f* (*obst*) crowning

coronar *vi* (*obst*) to crown

coronario -ria *adj* coronary

coronilla *f* (*de la cabeza*) vertex (*of the head*), top part of the head

corporal *adj* corporal, pertaining to the body

corpúsculo *m* corpuscle

correas *fpl* (*fam, para sujetar a un paciente*) leather restraints, leathers (*fam*)

corrección *f* correction, adjustment

correctivo -va *adj* corrective

correcto -ta *adj* correct

corrector -ra *adj* corrective

corregir *vt* to correct

correlación *f* correlation

correr *vi* to run, to flow

corriente *f* current

corrosivo -va *adj* corrosive

corsé *m* (*pl* -sés) (*ortho*) corset, truss

cortado -da *adj* cut; (*labios, piel*) chapped; *f* cut

cortador de pastillas *m* pill cutter

cortadura *f* cut

cortapastillas *m* (*esp. Mex*) pill cutter

cortar *vt* to cut, (*amputar*) to cut off; *vr* to cut oneself; **Me corté**..I cut myself; — **el pelo** to get a haircut; — **las uñas** to cut one's nails

cortaúñas *m* nail clippers, clippers (*fam*)

corte *m* (*surg*) incision; — **de pelo** haircut

corteza *f* bark; (*anat*) cortex

cortical *adj* cortical

corticosteroide, corticoesteroide *m* corticosteroid

corticotropina *f* corticotropin, adrenocorticotropic hormone (ACTH)

cortisol *m* cortisol

cortisona *f* cortisone

corto -ta *adj* short; **a** — **plazo** short-term; — **de vista** nearsighted

cortocircuito arteriovenoso *m* arteriovenous shunt

corva *f* back of the knee; **tendón** *m* **de la** — hamstring

coser *vt* (*una herida*) to suture, to sew, to stitch (up) (*fam*)

cosmético -ca *adj* & *m* cosmetic; *mpl* cosmetics, makeup

cosmetólogo -ga *mf* cosmetologist

cosquillas *fpl* tickling

cosquilleo *m* tickling
cosquilloso -sa *adj* ticklish
costado *m* (*anat*) side
coste *m* (*Esp*) charge, cost; **que ahorra costes** cost-saving
costeable *adj* (*Ang*) affordable
coste-efectividad *m* (*Esp*) cost-effectiveness
coste-efectivo -va *adj* (*Esp*) cost-effective
costilla *f* rib
costo *m* charge, cost; **que ahorra costos** cost-saving
costocondritis *f* costochondritis
costo-efectividad *m* cost-effectiveness
costo-efectivo -va *adj* cost-effective
costra *f* eschar (*form*), scab, crust; **— láctea** cradle cap
costumbre *f* habit; **como de —** as usual; **¿Está comiendo tanto como de costumbre?**..Are you eating as much as usual; **mala —** bad habit; **que de —** than usual; **¿Está orinando más que de costumbre?**..Are you urinating more than usual?
cotidiano -na *adj* daily
cotilo *m* acetabulum
Cotonete (*trademark*) *See* **hisopo.**
coxis *m* coccyx, tailbone (*fam*)
coyuntura *f* (*fam*) joint
CPRE *See* **colangiopancreatografía retrógrada endoscópica.**
crack *m* (*Ang*) crack cocaine, crack (*fam*)
craneal *adj* cranial
craneano -na *adj* cranial
cráneo *m* cranium (*form*), skull
craneofaringioma *m* craniopharyngioma
craneotomía *f* craniotomy
creatina *f* creatine
creatinina *f* creatinine
crecer *vi* to grow, to get bigger
crecimiento *m* growth; **— intrauterino retardado** (*Esp*) intrauterine growth retardation
creencia *f* belief
crema *f* cream, balm; **— bronceadora** tanning *o* suntan lotion (*to increase tanning*); **— de afeitar** shaving cream; **— dental** toothpaste; **— fría** cold cream; **— limpiadora** cleansing cream; **— para manos** hand cream
cremallera *f* (*Esp*) zipper
cresa *f* maggot

cretinismo *m* cretinism
cretino -na *mf* cretin
criar *vt* (*a un niño*) to raise (*a child*); (*amamantar*) to breastfeed, to feed, to nurse
criatura *f* (*fam*) infant, baby
cribado *m* (*form*) screening; **— del cáncer** cancer screening
cricotiroideo -a *adj* cricothyroid
crioconservación *f* cryoconservation
crioglobulina *f* cryoglobulin
crioterapia *f* cryotherapy
criptogénico -ca *adj* cryptogenic
criptorquidia *f* cryptorchidism
criptosporidiosis *f* cryptosporidiosis
crisis *f* (*pl* **-sis**) crisis; breakdown; exacerbation, attack (*fam*); (*epiléptica*) seizure; **— asmática** asthma exacerbation, asthma attack (*fam*); **— blástica** blast crisis; **— convulsiva** (epileptic) seizure; **— de angustia** *or* **ansiedad** anxiety attack; **— de asma** asthma exacerbation, asthma attack (*fam*); **— de ausencia** absence seizure; **— de identidad** identity crisis; **— de la mediana edad** midlife crisis; **— del lóbulo temporal** (*ant*) complex partial seizure, temporal lobe seizure (*ant*); **— de pánico** panic attack; **— epiléptica** (epileptic) seizure; **— generalizada** generalized seizure; **— nerviosa** nervous breakdown; **— parcial (compleja)** (complex) partial seizure; **— tirotóxica** thyroid storm; **— tónico-clónica** tonic-clonic seizure
cristal *m* crystal; (*fam, metanfetamina*) methamphetamine, crystal (*fam*)
cristalino -na *adj* crystalline; *m* lens (*of the eye*)
crítico -ca *adj* critical
cromato *m* chromate
cromo *m* chromium
cromoglicato de sodio, cromoglicato disódico (*esp. Esp*) *m* cromolyn sodium
cromomicosis *f* chromomycosis
cromosoma *m* chromosome
cromosómico -ca *adj* chromosomal
crónicamente *adv* chronically
crónico -ca *adj* chronic
cruce duodenal *m* (*surg*) duodenal switch
crudo -da *adj* raw; **andar —** (*Mex*) to

have a hangover, to be hungover

cruel *adj* cruel

crueldad *f* cruelty

crup *m* croup

cruzar *vt* — **los brazos** to fold one's arms

Cruz Roja *f* Red Cross

CSC *abbr* **conteo sanguíneo completo.** *See* **conteo.**

cuadrado -da *adj* square; **metro —** square meter

cuadrante *m* quadrant; — **inferior derecho** right lower quadrant; — **superior inzquierdo** left upper quadrant

cuadriceps *m* (*pl* **-ceps**) quadriceps

cuadril *m* hip bone, hip

cuadrillizo -za *mf* quadruplet

cuadriparesia *f* quadriplegia, tetraplegia

cuadriplejía *f* quadriplegia, tetraplegia

cuadripléjico -ca *adj & mf* quadriplegic, tetraplegic

cuanto *adv* ¿**Cada cuánto (tiempo)?**.. How often?..¿**Cada cuánto (tiempo) se puede donar sangre?**..How often can you donate blood?

cuarentena *f* quarantine; (*Mex, CA; obst*) forty days following childbirth; **poner en —** to quarantine

cuarto *m* fourth, quarter; (*habitación*) room, bedroom; (*de galón*) quart; — **de baño** bathroom

cuatrillizo -za *mf* quadruplet

cubierta *f* (*de una pastilla*) coating (*of a pill*)

cubierto *pp of* **cubrir**

cubital *adj* ulnar

cúbito *m* ulna

cubrebocas *m* surgical mask

cubrir *vt* (*pp* **cubierto**) to cover, to coat; (*seguros*) to cover; **Su seguro cubre**.. Your insurance covers

cucaracha *f* cockroach

cucharada *f* spoonful, tablespoonful; — **grande** *or* **sopera** tablespoonful

cucharadita *f* spoonful, teaspoonful

cuchilla *f* (*de afeitar*) razor blade

cuchillada *f* knife wound

cuchillo *m* knife

cuclillas *fpl* **ponerse en —** to squat

cuello *m* neck; collar; — **uterino** *or* **de la matriz** cervix

cuenca *f* (*del ojo*) eye socket

cuenta *f* (*factura*) bill

cuentagotas *m* (*esp. Esp*) eyedropper, medicine dropper

cuerda *f* cord; — **vocal** vocal cord

cuerdo -da *adj* sane

cuero cabelludo *m* scalp

cuerpo *m* body; — **de bomberos** fire department; — **extraño** foreign body; — **lúteo** corpus luteum; **dar del —** (*Carib*) to have a bowel movement

cuesta arriba *adv* uphill

cuestionario *m* questionnaire

cuidado *m* (*frec. pl*) care; **cuidado(s) a largo plazo** long-term care; **cuidado(s) crítico(s)** critical care; **cuidado(s) de enfermería** nursing care; — **del pie (de la piel, de la herida, etc.)** foot care, skin care, wound care, etc.; — **de relevo** *or* **respiro** respite care; **cuidado(s) en el hogar** home care; **cuidado(s) intensivo(s)** intensive care; **cuidado(s) prenatal(es)** prenatal care; **cuidado(s) prolongado(s)** long-term care; **tener —** to be careful; **Tenga cuidado**..Be careful.

cuidador -ra *mf* caregiver

cuidadoso -sa *adj* careful

cuidar *vt* to take care of, care for; **Yo lo cuido solo**..I take care of him by myself; *vr* to take care of oneself; (*fam, usar anticonceptivo*) to use birth control

culdocentesis *f* (*pl* **-sis**) culdocentesis

culebra *f* snake

culebrilla *f* (*esp. Carib*) shingles

culo (*vulg*) *m* buttocks; (*ano*) anus

culpa *f* guilt; **sentimientos de —** feelings of guilt

cultivar *vt* (*micro*) to culture

cultivo *m* (*micro*) culture; — **de garganta** throat culture; — **de heces** stool culture; — **de orina** urine culture; — **de sangre** blood culture; — **faríngeo** (*form*) throat culture

cultura *f* culture; — **de seguridad (excelencia, etc.)** culture of safety (excellence, etc.)

culturismo *m* bodybuilding

culturista *mf* bodybuilder

cumpleaños *m* (*pl* **-años**) birthday; ¡**Feliz cumpleaños!**..Happy birthday!

cumplimiento *m* compliance; — **del tratamiento** compliance with treatment

cuna *f* cradle, crib; — **portátil** bassinet

cunnilingus *m* cunnilingus, oral sex (*performed on a female*)

cuña *f* (*chata*) bedpan

cuñado -da *m* brother-in-law; *f* sister-in-law

cura *m* priest; *f* cure; (*vendaje*) bandage, dressing (*often adhesive*); — **oclusiva** (*esp. Esp*) occlusive dressing

curable *adj* curable

curación *f* healing, recovery; (*de una herida*) treatment (*cleaning and bandaging, etc.*)

curandería *f* traditional *o* folk medicine; faith healing

curanderismo *m* traditional *o* folk medicine; faith healing

curandero -ra *mf* traditional *o* folk healer; faith healer

curar *vt* to cure, heal; (*una herida*) to treat (*a wound, by cleaning and bandaging, etc.*); *vr* to be cured, get well, to heal

curativo -va *adj* curative

cureta *f* curette

curetaje *m* curettage; — **con succión** suction curettage

curita *f* (*Amer*) small adhesive bandage

curl *m* curl (*biceps*)

curso *m* course

curva *f* curve, bend; — **de aprendizaje** learning curve; — **de crecimiento** growth curve

curvatura *f* curvature

cutáneo -a *adj* cutaneous

cutícula *f* cuticle

cutis *m* complexion, skin (*of the face*)

D

daclatasvir *m* daclatasvir

dacriocistitis *f* dacryocystitis

daltoniano -na *adj* (*form*) color-blind

daltónico -ca *adj* (*form*) color-blind

daltonismo *m* color blindness

damiana *f* (*bot*) damiana

danazol *m* danazol

dañar *vt* to damage, harm

dañino -na *adj* harmful

daño *m* damage, harm; — **cerebral** brain damage; **hacer** — to hurt, harm, to damage; to be bad for (*one*), to make (*one*) sick; **La caída no le hizo ningún daño**..The fall didn't hurt her at all ...¿**Le hace daño la medicina?**..Is the medicine making you sick?

dapsona *f* dapsone

daptomicina *f* daptomycin

dar *vt* to give; *vi* **dar(le)** (**a uno**) (*una enfermedad*) to catch, get; **Me dio un catarro**..I caught a cold; — **a luz** to give birth to; **La señora Ruiz dio a luz a una niña ayer**..Mrs. Ruiz gave birth to a baby girl yesterday; — **de alta** (*del hospital*) to discharge (*from the hospital*); — **de comer** to feed; — **del cuerpo** (*Carib*) to have a bowel movement; — **de mamar**, — **pecho** to breastfeed, to feed, to nurse; ¿**Le va a dar de mamar?**.. Are you going to breastfeed him?; — **un traspié** to trip; *vr* — **cuenta** to notice, to realize; — **vuelta** to turn; (*voltearse*) to turn over, roll over

darbepoetina alfa *f* darbepoetin alfa

darifenacina *f* darifenacin

darunavir *m* darunavir

datos *mpl* data

daunorubicina *f* daunorubicin

DCI *abbr* desfibrilador cardioversor implantable. *See* desfibrilador.

DDT *See* diclorodifeniltricloroetano.

DEA *abbr* **desfibrilador externo automático**. *See* **desfibrilador**.

deambulación *f* ambulation (*form*), walking

deambular *vi* to ambulate (*form*), to walk

debajo *adv* below; **(por) — de** below, lower than; **(por) debajo de 40**..below 40..lower than 40...**(por) debajo de la rodilla**..below the knee

debido -a a, due to

débil *adj* weak

debilidad *f* weakness

debilitado -da *adj* debilitated, run-down

debilitamiento *m* weakening

debilitante *adj* debilitating

debilitar *vt* to weaken, make weak; *vr* to weaken, become weak

decaer *vi* to weaken, to get worse; (*deprimirse*) to become depressed

decaído -da *adj* weak, run-down; (*deprimido*) depressed

decaimiento *m* decline, weakening, weakness; (*depresión*) depression

decibelio, decibel *m* decibel

decidir *vt*, *vr* to decide

decilitro *m* deciliter

decisión *f* decision; **toma de decisiones compartida** shared decision making

declaración *f* declaration; **enfermedad de — obligatoria** reportable disease

declarar *vt* to report

decoloración *f* discoloration

decúbito *m* decubitus; **úlcera de —** decubitus ulcer

dedo *m* digit, (*de la mano*) finger; (*del pie*) toe; **— anular** ring finger; **— chico (del pie)** little toe; **— corazón** (*esp. Esp*) middle finger; **— en gatillo** trigger finger; **— (del pie) en martillo** hammer toe; **dedos en palillo de tambor** clubbing, clubbed digits; **— en resorte** trigger finger; **— gordo (de la mano)** thumb; **— gordo (del pie)** great toe (*form*), big toe; **— índice** index finger, forefinger; **— medio** middle finger; **— meñique (de la mano)** little finger; **— meñique (del pie)** little toe; **— pequeño (de la mano)** (*Esp*) little finger; **— pequeño (del pie)** little toe; **— pulgar (de la mano)** thumb; **— pulgar (del pie)** great toe (*form*), big toe

deducible *m* (*seguros*) deductible

DEET *m* (*repelente*) DEET

defecación *f* defecation, bowel movement; **— dolorosa** painful bowel movement

defecar *vi* to defecate, to have a bowel movement

defecto *m* defect; **— congénito** congenital defect; **— del tubo neural** neural tube defect; **— de nacimiento** birth defect

defensa *f* defense

defensor -ra *mf* advocate; **— del paciente** *or* **de pacientes** patient advocate; **— del pueblo** ombudsman

deficiencia *f* deficiency, deficit

deficiente *adj* deficient

déficit *m* (*pl* **-cits**) deficit

definitivo -va *adj* definitive

deforme *adj* deformed

deformidad *f* deformity, malformation

defunción *f* death

degeneración *f* degeneration; **— macular senil, — macular relacionada con la edad** (*Mex*) age-related macular degeneration

degenerar *vi* to degenerate

degenerativo -va *adj* degenerative

degradación *f* degradation

dehidroepiandrosterona (DHEA) *f* dehydroepiandrosterone (DHEA)

dehiscencia *f* dehiscence; **— de herida** wound dehiscence

dejar *vi* **— de** to quit, stop, give up; ¿**Cuándo dejó de comer?**..When did you quit eating?...**Debe dejar de fumar**..You should give up smoking.

déjà vu *m* déjà vu

delantal *m* apron; **— de plomo** lead apron

delante *adv* in front; **delante del corazón**..in front of your heart

delantero -ra *adj* front; **la parte delantera de**..the front of

delavirdina *f* delavirdine

deleción *f* deletion

deletrear *vt* to spell

delgado -da *adj* thin, lean

delicado -da *adj* frail, fragile; (*tema*) sensitive, delicate

delirante *adj* delirious

delirar *vi* to be delirious; **Está delirando**..He's delirious.

delirio *m* delirium; delusion; **delirios de grandeza** delusions of grandeur; **tener delirio(s)** to be delirious

delirium tremens *m* delirium tremens, the d.t.'s (*fam*)

deltoides *m* (*pl* **-des**) deltoid

demacrado -da *adj* emaciated

demanda *f* (*legal*) lawsuit

demandar *vt* (*legal*) to sue

demás *adj* rest of the; **las demás lesiones** ..the rest of the lesions

demencia *f* dementia; — **de Alzheimer** Alzheimer's dementia; — **multiinfarto** (*ant*) vascular dementia, multi-infarct dementia (*ant*); — **pugilística** dementia pugilistica; — **tipo Alzheimer** Alzheimer's dementia; — **vascular** vascular dementia

demostrar *vt* to demonstrate

denervación *f* denervation

dengue *m* dengue

densidad *f* density; — **mineral ósea** bone mineral density

denso -sa *adj* dense

dentadura *f* teeth, set of teeth; — **postiza** denture, false teeth (*fam*)

dental *adj* dental

dentario -ria *adj* dental

dentición *f* (*form, erupción*) teething

dentífrico *m* toothpaste

dentina *f* dentin

dentista *mf* dentist, Doctor of Dental Surgery (DDS *o* D.D.S.)

dentistería *f* (*Amer*) dentistry; dental office, dental clinic

dentro *adv* inside; **dentro de su boca**.. inside your mouth

departamento *m* department; — **de urgencias** emergency department (ED), emergency room (ER); **Departamento de Vehículos Motorizados, Departamento de Vehículos de Motor** Department of Motor Vehicles (DMV)

dependencia *f* dependence, dependency; — **a** *or* **de la heroína (nicotina, etc.)** heroin (nicotine, etc.) dependence; — **a** *or* **de sustancias** chemical dependency; **que crea** — habit-forming, addicting; [*Nota: No hay mucha diferencia entre* dependence *y* dependency; *los ejemplos mencionados representan el uso actual.*]

dependiente *adj* dependent; — **de oxíge-** no **(esteroides, etc.)** oxygen-dependent, steroid-dependent, etc.

depilatorio *m* depilatory, hair remover

deponer *vt, vi* (*pp* **depuesto**) (*Mex, fam*) to vomit, to throw up (*fam*)

deporte *m* sport; — **de contacto** contact sport; **hacer** *or* **realizar deporte(s)** to play sports

deposición *f* (*Esp, SA*) bowel movement

depositar *vt* to deposit

depósito *m* deposit, buildup; **de** — (*pharm*) depot; — **de cadáveres** morgue

depresión *f* depression; — **posparto** postpartum depression; — **invernal** seasonal affective disorder

depresivo -va *adj* depressive

depresor -ra *adj* (*pharm, physio*) depressant; *m* (*de lengua*) tongue depressor *o* blade

deprimido -da *adj* depressed, despondent

deprimirse *vr* to get *o* become depressed

depuesto *pp of* **deponer**

depuración *f* purification

depurador *m* purifier

depurar *vt* to purify

derecho -cha *adj* right; (*recto*) straight; *m* right (*legal, moral*); — **a atención médica** right to health care; *f* right, right-hand side

derivación *f* (*surg*) shunt, bypass, diversion; (*esp. Esp, interconsulta*) referral; — **cardiopulmonar** cardiopulmonary bypass; — **gástrica** gastric bypass; — **intrahepática portosistémica transyugular** transjugular intrahepatic portosystemic shunt (TIPS); — **portocava** portacaval shunt; — **portosistémica percutánea intrahepática** transjugular intrahepatic portosystemic shunt (TIPS); — **urinaria** urinary diversion; — **ventriculoperitoneal** ventriculoperitoneal shunt

derivado *m* derivative; — **del petróleo** petroleum derivative; — **proteico purificado** purified protein derivative (PPD)

dermatitis *f* dermatitis; — **atópica** atopic dermatitis; — **del pañal** diaper rash; — **herpetiforme** dermatitis herpetiformis; — **irritativa** irritant dermatitis; — **por autosensibilización** id reaction, autoeczematization; — **por cercarias** cercarial dermatitis, swimmer's itch (*fam*); — **por contacto** contact dermatitis; — **por estasis** stasis dermatitis; — **seborreica** seborrheic dermatitis

dermatofibroma *m* dermatofibroma
dermatofito *m* dermatophyte
dermatofitosis *f* dermatophytosis
dermatología *f* dermatology
dermatológico -ca *adj* dermatological
dermatólogo -ga *mf* dermatologist, skin doctor (*fam*)
dermatomiositis *f* dermatomyositis
dérmico -ca *adj* dermal, pertaining to the skin
dermoabrasión *f* dermabrasion, peeling
dermografismo *m* dermographism
derrame *m* effusion; (*hemorragia*) hemorrhage, bleed; (*fam, ictus*) stroke; — **cerebral** cerebral hemorrhage, hemorrhagic stroke; — **pericárdico** pericardial effusion; — **pleural** pleural effusion
DES *See* dietilestilbestrol.
desabotonar *vt, vr* to unbutton
desabrochar *vt, vr* to unbutton
desafiante *adj* confrontational
desafío *m* challenge
desagradable *adj* unpleasant
desahogo *m* (*psych*) unburdening; (*válvula de escape*) outlet
desahuciado -da *adj* terminal, without hope of survival
desalentado -da *adj* discouraged
desalojar *vt* to dislodge
desanimado -da *adj* discouraged
desaparecer *vi* to disappear
desarrollar *vt* to develop; *vr* to develop, to evolve
desarrollo *m* development; — **físico** **(sexual, etc.)** physical (sexual, etc.) development; — **tardío** developmental delay
desastre *m* disaster
desatender *vt* to neglect
desayunar *vi, vr* to have breakfast
desayuno *m* breakfast
desbalance *m* imbalance
desbridamiento *m* debridement
desbridar *vt* to debride
descafeinado -da *adj* decaffeinated
descalzo -za *adj* barefoot

descamación *f* (*derm, form*) peeling, scaling
descamarse *vr* (*derm, form*) to peel, to flake
descansar *vt, vi* to rest
descanso *m* rest, relaxation; — **del intestino** bowel rest; — **del medicamento** drug holiday
descarga eléctrica *f* electric shock
descartable *adj* disposable
descartar *vt* to rule out; **Tenemos que descartar cáncer..**We need to rule out cancer.
descendente *adj* descending
descendiente *mf* descendant
descenso *m* fall, decline
descompensación *f* (*psych, etc.*) decompensation
descompresión *f* decompression
descongestionante *adj & m* decongestant
descongestivo -va *adj & m* decongestant
descontaminar *vt* to decontaminate
descontento -ta *adj* unhappy
descontinuar *vt* to discontinue
describir *vt* to describe
descubierto -ta *adj* uncovered, bare
descuidado -da *adj* careless
descuidar *vt* to neglect
descuido *m* neglect, carelessness
desde *adv* since; **desde que empezó a vomitar..**since you began vomiting; *prep* since; **desde la niñez..** since childhood
desear *vt* to desire; **no deseado** unwanted, unintended
desechable *adj* disposable
desecho *m* (*secreción*) discharge; *mpl* (*residuos*) waste; — **médicos** medical waste; — **metabólicos** metabolic waste; — **peligrosos** hazardous waste
desempeño *m* performance
desenlace *m* outcome
desensibilización *f* desensitization
desensibilizar *vt* to desensitize
deseo *m* desire, urge; — **sexual** sexual desire, libido
desequilibrio *m* imbalance
desesperación *f* desperation, despair
desesperado -da *adj* hopeless, desperate
desesperanza *f* despair
desesperarse *vr* to lose hope; to become desperate, to become agitated
desfase horario *m* jet lag

desfavorable *adj* unfavorable
desfibrilación *f* defibrillation
desfibrilador *m* defibrillator; — **cardioversor implantable (DCI)** implantable cardioverter-defibrillator (ICD); — **externo automático** *or* **automatizado (DEA)** automated external defibrillator (AED)
desfibrilar *vt* to defibrillate
desgarrar *vt* to tear, to lacerate; (*fam, expectorar*) to cough up
desgarre *m* (*esp. Mex*) *See* **desgarro**.
desgarro *m* laceration, tear; (*muscular*) torn muscle, pulled muscle
desgaste *m* wasting; (*profesional*) burnout; — **muscular** muscle wasting
desguanzado -da *adj* (*Mex, fam*) rundown, tired
deshabituación *f* cessation (*of a habit*), detoxification; — **tabáquica** smoking cessation
deshidratación *f* dehydration
deshidratado -da *adj* dehydrated
deshidrogenasa láctica *f* lactic dehydrogenase
deshumanizador -ra *adj* dehumanizing
deshumanizante *adj* dehumanizing
deshumedecer *vt* to dehumidify
deshumidificador *m* dehumidifier
desigual *adj* unequal
desinfectante *adj & m* disinfectant; — **de** *or* **para manos** hand sanitizer
desinfectar *vt* to disinfect
desinhibición *f* (*psych*) disinhibition
desintoxicación *f* detoxification
desipramina *f* desipramine
desloratadina *f* desloratadine
desmayarse *vr* to faint, pass out, to black out
desmayo *m* faint, blackout
desmedro *m* decline, deterioration; weakness, emaciation; failure to thrive
desmielinizante *adj* demyelinating
desmopresina *f* desmopressin
desmoralizar *vt* to demoralize; *vr* to become demoralized
desnaturalizado -da *adj* denatured
desnudo -da *adj* naked, bare
desnutrición *f* malnutrition
desnutrido -da *adj* malnourished, undernourished
desodorante *m* deodorant
desogestrel *m* desogestrel

desorden *m* disorder
desorientado -da *adj* disoriented
despellejarse *vr* (*fam*) to peel
despersonalización *f* (*psych*) depersonalization
despertar *vt* (*pp* **-tado** *or* **-pierto**) to wake up, rouse; *vr* to wake up
despierto -ta (*pp of* **despertar**) *adj* awake
despigmentación *f* depigmentation; **agente de** — depigmenting agent
despistado -da *adj* absent-minded, distracted, forgetful
despistaje *m* (*esp. Esp*) screening; — **del cáncer** cancer screening
desplazamiento *m* (*ortho, psych, etc.*) displacement
desplazar *vt* to displace
desplomarse *vr* to collapse
desprenderse *vr* to slough (off), to become detached
desprendido -da *adj* detached
desprendimiento *m* detachment; — **prematuro de placenta** placental abruption, abruptio placentae (*form*); — **de retina** retinal detachment, detached retina
después *adv* after; — **de comer** after eating; *prep* — **de** after; **después de dos días**..after two days
desrealización *f* (*psych*) derealization
destetar *vt* to wean
destete *m* weaning
destilado -da *adj* distilled
destreza *f* dexterity, skill
destructivo -va *adj* destructive
destruir *vt* to destroy
desvanecerse *vr* to faint
desvelarse *vr* to go without sleep
desvenlafaxina *f* desvenlafaxine
desventaja *f* disadvantage
desviación *f* deviation; diversion; — **de drogas** drug diversion; — **septal** septal deviation
desviado -da *adj* deviated
desvío *m* diversion; — **de drogas** drug diversion
detección *f* detection, screening; **examen** *m* **de** — screening test, screen
detectable *adj* detectable
detectar *vt* to detect
detector de humo *m* smoke detector
detergente *m* detergent

deteriorarse *vr* to deteriorate
deterioro *m* deterioration, decline
detrás de *prep* behind
devolver *vt, vi* (*pp* devuelto) (*fam*) to vomit, to throw up (*fam*); (*ped, fam*) to regurgitate, to spit up (*fam*)
dexametasona *f* dexamethasone
dexlansoprazol *m* dexlansoprazole
dextrometorfano *m* dextromethorphan
dextrosa *f* dextrose
DHEA *See* dehidroepiandrosterona.
día *m* day; cada dos días every other day; el — anterior the day before; el — siguiente the day after, the following day; en días alternos every other day; todos los días every day
diabetes *f* diabetes; — gestacional gestational diabetes; — insípida diabetes insipidus; — mellitus (tipo 1, tipo 2) (type 1, type 2) diabetes mellitus
diabético -ca *adj & mf* diabetic
diabetología *f* diabetology, study of diabetes
diabetológico -ca *adj* (*form*) diabetic
diabetólogo -ga *mf* diabetologist, specialist in diabetes
diafragma *m* (*anat, gyn*) diaphragm
diagnosticar *vt* to diagnose
diagnóstico -ca *adj* diagnostic; *m* diagnosis; — diferencial differential diagnosis; — genético genetic testing; — preimplantacional *or* preimplantatorio pre-implantation genetic diagnosis; — por imagen *or* imágenes diagnostic imaging
diagrama *m* diagram
diálisis *f* dialysis; — peritoneal ambulatoria continua (DPAC) continuous ambulatory peritoneal dialysis (CAPD)
dializar *vt* to dialyze
diámetro *m* diameter
diana *f* target; órgano — target organ
diapasón *m* tuning fork
diario -ria *adj* daily; a — daily, every day; *m* log, diary
diarrea *f* diarrhea; — del viajero traveler's diarrhea
diarreico -ca *adj* diarrheal
diastólico -ca *adj* diastolic
diazepam *m* diazepam
dicicloverina *f* dicyclomine (*USAN*), dicycloverine (*INN*)
diclofenaco *m* diclofenac

diclorodifeniltricloroetano (DDT) *m* dichlorodiphenyltrichloroethane (DDT)
dicloxacilina *f* dicloxacillin
didanosina *f* didanosine
dieldrín *m* dieldrin
diente *m* tooth, front tooth; — deciduo deciduous *o* primary tooth, baby tooth (*fam*); — de conejo (*fam*) bucktooth; — definitivo permanent tooth; — de leche primary tooth, baby tooth; — impactado impacted tooth, dental impaction; — incisivo incisor, front tooth; — incluido (*Esp*) impacted tooth, dental impaction; — permanente permanent tooth; dientes postizos false teeth; — primario primary tooth, baby tooth (*fam*); — retenido impacted tooth, dental impaction; — salido bucktooth
diente de león *m* (*bot*) dandelion
diestro -tra *adj* right-handed
dieta *f* diet; — alta en fibra high-fiber diet; — baja en grasa low-fat diet; — balanceada balanced diet; — cardíaca cardiac diet; — con restricción de sodio (proteínas, etc.) sodium-restricted diet, protein-restricted diet, etc.; — de adelgazamiento weight loss diet; — de disfagia dysphagia diet; — de fácil masticación mechanical soft diet; — de líquidos claros clear liquid diet; — del néctar líquido nectar consistency diet; — diabética diabetic diet, consistent carbohydrate diet; — equilibrada balanced diet; — líquida clara clear liquid diet; — líquida completa full liquid diet; — mediterránea Mediterranean diet; — para adelgazar *or* bajar de peso weight loss diet; — para diabéticos diabetic diet, consistent carbohydrate diet; — para disfagia dysphagia diet; — puré puréed diet; — renal renal diet; — restringida en sodio (proteínas, etc.) sodium-restricted diet, protein-restricted diet, etc.; — rica en fibra high-fiber diet; estar a — to be on a diet, to diet
dietético -ca *adj* dietary, dietetic; *f* dietetics
dietilamida del ácido lisérgico *f* lysergic acid diethylamide (LSD)
dietilestilbestrol (DES) *m* diethylstilbestrol (DES)

dietista *mf* dietitian
dietista-nutricionista *mf* (*Esp*) dietitian
dietoterapia *f* diet therapy
difenhidramina *f* diphenhydramine
difenilhidantoína *f* phenytoin
diferenciado -da *adj* differentiated; **bien** — well differentiated; **parcialmente** — partially differentiated; **pobremente** *or* **poco** — poorly differentiated
dificultad *f* difficulty; — **para recordar** difficulty remembering, forgetfulness; — **para respirar** difficulty breathing, shortness of breath
diflunisal *m* diflunisal
difteria *f* diphtheria
difunto -ta *adj & mf* deceased
difusión *f* diffusion
difuso -sa *adj* diffuse
digerible *adj* digestible
digerir *vt* to digest
digestible *adj* (*Ang*) digestible
digestión *f* digestion
digestivo -va *adj* digestive
digital *adj* digital; *f* (*pharm*) digitalis
dignidad *f* dignity
digoxina *f* digoxin
diiodohidroxiquinoleína *f* diiodohydroxyquinoline, iodoquinol
dilatación *f* dilation *o* dilatation, enlargement; — **y curetaje** *or* **legrado** dilatation (dilation) and curettage (D&C); [*Nota: Algunas autoridades distinguen entre* dilation *y* dilatation, *pero la mayoría de los profesionales médicos los usan intercambiablemente.* Dilatation *se encuentra más que todo en la literatura médica o para referirse a procedimientos, p. ej.,* esophageal dilatation.]
dilatador *m* dilator
dilatar *vt, vr* to dilate
diloxanida *f* diloxanide
diltiazem *m* diltiazem
dilución *f* dilution
dilucional *adj* dilutional
diluido -da *adj* dilute
diluir *vt* to dilute
dimenhidrinato *m* dimenhydrinate
dimensión *f* dimension
dimetil sulfóxido (DMSO) *m* dimethyl sulfoxide (DMSO)
dimetiltriptamina (DMT) *f* dimethyltryptamine (DMT)

dimorfa *adj* (*lepra*) borderline
dinitrato de isosorbida *m* isosorbide dinitrate
dioptría *f* diopter
Dios *m* God
dióxido *m* dioxide; — **de azufre** sulfur dioxide; — **de carbono** carbon dioxide
dioxina *f* dioxin
dipiridamol *m* dipyridamole
diplococo *m* diplococcus
dirección *f* direction; (*domicilio*) address; — **de correo electrónico** e-mail address
director -ra *mf* director; — **de Enfermería** Director of Nursing
directriz anticipada *f* advance directive
disartria *f* dysarthria
discapacidad *f* disability, impairment; **con** — **del desarrollo** developmentally disabled; **con** — **física** physically disabled; **con** — **intelectual** intellectually disabled; — **del desarrollo** developmental disability; — **física** physical disability; — **intelectual** intellectual disability
discapacitado -da *adj* disabled; — **del desarrollo** (*Amer*) developmentally disabled; — **intelectualmente** intellectually disabled; *mf* disabled person
discapacitante *adj* disabling
discectomía *f* discectomy
discinesia tardía *f* tardive dyskinesia
disciplina *f* discipline
disciplinar *vt* to discipline
disco *m* disc; — **abultado** bulging disc; — **intervertebral** intervertebral disc; — **óptico** optic disc; **hernia de** — herniated disc
discografía *f* discography
discoide *adj* discoid
discrasia *f* dyscrasia
discrepancia *f* discrepancy; — **en la longitud de las piernas** leg length discrepancy
disección *f* dissection; — **aórtica** *or* **de aorta** aortic dissection; — **ganglionar** lymph node dissection
diseminación *f* dissemination, spread
diseminar *vt* to spread; *vr* to disseminate, spread, (*cáncer*) to metastasize
disentería *f* dysentery
disfasia *f* dysphasia
disfunción *f* dysfunction; — **de la arti-**

culación temporomandibular temporomandibular joint dysfunction; — **diastólica** diastolic dysfunction; — **eréctil** erectile dysfunction (ED); — **orgánica múltiple** multisystem organ failure

disfuncional *adj* dysfunctional; **familia** — dysfunctional family; **hemorragia uterina** — dysfunctional uterine bleeding

dislexia *f* dyslexia

dislipidemia *f* dyslipidemia

dislocación *f* dislocation

dislocar *vt* to dislocate; *vr* to become dislocated

disminución *f* reduction, decrease, drop (*in level of something being measured*); — **gradual** (*de la dosis de un medicamento, etc.*) taper

disminuir *vt* to reduce, decrease; — **gradualmente** (*la dosis de un medicamento, etc.*) to taper; *vi, vr* to diminish, decrease

disociación *f* (*psych*) dissociation

disolvente *m* solvent

disolver *vt, vr* (*pp* **disuelto**) to dissolve

disparar *vt* to shoot

disparo *m* (*de un arma*) shot; (*de un inhalador*) spray, puff

dispensar *vt* (*pharm*) to dispense

dispepsia *f* dyspepsia (*form*), indigestion

displasia *f* dysplasia

displásico -ca *adj* dysplastic

disponible *adj* available

dispositivo *m* device; — **de asistencia ventricular izquierda** left ventricular assist device; — **de ayuda** assistive device; — **de ayuda auditiva** assistive hearing device; — **de seguridad** safety device; — **intrauterino (DIU)** intrauterine device (IUD)

distal *adj* distal

distanciamiento *m* (*psych*) detachment

distender *vt* to distend; *vi, vr* to become distended

distendido -da *adj* distended, (*estómago*) bloated

distensión *f* distention; (*muscular*) pulled muscle, strain; — **abdominal** abdominal distention, bloating

distinguir *vt* to distinguish

distraído -da *adj* absent-minded, distracted; distractible

distrés *m* distress; — **respiratorio** respiratory distress

distrito *m* district

distrofia *f* dystrophy; — **muscular** muscular dystrophy; — **simpática refleja** (*ant*) complex regional pain syndrome, reflex sympathetic dystrophy (*ant*)

disuelto *pp of* **disolver**

disulfiram *m* disulfiram

DIU *abbr* **dispositivo intrauterino**. *See* **dispositivo**.

diuresis *f* diuresis

diurético -ca *adj* diuretic; *m* diuretic, water pill (*fam*)

diván *m* (*psych*) couch

diversión *f* (*entretenimiento*) fun

diverticulitis *f* diverticulitis

divertículo *m* diverticulum; — **de Meckel** Meckel diverticulum

diverticulosis *f* diverticulosis

divertirse *vr* to have fun

dividir *vt* to divide

divieso *m* (*esp. Esp*) abscess, boil

división *f* (*psych, de la personalidad*) splitting

divorciarse *vr* to divorce

divorcio *m* divorce

divulgación *f* outreach; **programa de** — outreach program

diyodohidroxiquinoleína *f* diiodohydroxyquinoline, iodoquinol

DMSO *See* **dimetil sulfóxido**.

DMT *See* **dimetiltriptamina**.

doblar *vt* to bend, flex; to double; **Doble el brazo**..Bend your arm; *vr* to bend, bend over, bend down; (*torcerse*) to twist, to sprain; **Dóblese**..Bend over... **Me doblé el tobillo**..I twisted my ankle.

doble *adj* double; **visión** — double vision; *adv* double; **ver** — to see double

doctor -ra *mf* doctor*, physician, Doctor of Medicine (MD *o* M.D.) *antes de los apellidos se abrevia como* Dr.

documento *m* document; — **de voluntad anticipada** (*Amer*), — **de voluntades anticipadas** (*Esp*) advance directive

dolencia *f* illness, ailment

doler *vt, vi* to hurt; ¿**Le duele?**..Does it hurt?...¿**Le duele el pie?**..Does your foot hurt?...¿**Dónde le duele?**..Where does it hurt?

dolor *m* pain, ache; — **agudo** sharp pain; — **articular** joint pain; — **de barriga** bellyache, stomachache *o* stomach ache; — **de caballo** (*Mex, fam*) sideache; — **de cabeza** headache; — **de cabeza en racimos** cluster headache; — **de cabeza tensional** tension headache; **dolores de(l) crecimiento** growing pains; — **de espalda** backache; — **de estómago** stomachache *o* stomach ache; — **de garganta** sore throat; — **de las articulaciones** joint pain; — **de la espalda baja** low back pain; — **de muelas** toothache; — **de oído** ear ache; **dolores de(l) parto** labor pains; — **fantasma** phantom pain; — **irruptivo** breakthrough pain; — **lumbar** low back pain; — **menstrual** menstrual cramp, menstrual pain; — **punzante** sharp *o* jabbing pain; — **sordo** dull pain; **sin** — painless

dolorido -da *adj* sore, tender, painful

doloroso -sa *adj* painful; **muerte** — painful death

doméstico -ca *adj* domestic; *mf* housecleaner, person who helps in the home

domiciliario -ria *adj* pertaining to the home, at home; **fisioterapia** — home physical therapy, physical therapy at home

domicilio *m* home; (*dirección*) address

dominante *adj* dominant; **mano** *f* — dominant hand

donación *f* donation; — **de órganos (sangre, etc.)** organ (blood, etc.) donation

donador -ra *mf* donor

donante *mf* donor; — **de órganos** organ donor; — **universal** universal donor; — **vivo** living donor; **semen** *m* **de** — donor semen

donar *vt* to donate

donepezilo *m* donepezil

dopaje *m* doping

dopamina *f* dopamine

Doppler *m* Doppler

dormido -da *adj* asleep; (*entumecido*) numb, asleep (*fam*); **Tengo dormido el brazo**..My arm is numb (asleep); **permanecer** — to stay asleep; **quedarse** — to fall asleep, to go to sleep

dormir *vt* (*a un niño, etc.*) to put to sleep; (*fam, anestesiar*) to anesthetize, (*con anestesia general*) to put under anesthesia, to put to sleep (*fam*); (*con anestesia local*) to numb up; *vi* to sleep; *vr* to go to sleep, to fall asleep; (*entumecerse*) to get *o* become numb, to go to sleep (*fam*), to fall asleep (*fam*); **Se me duerme el brazo**..My arm gets numb (goes to sleep, falls asleep).

dormitar *vi* to doze

dormitorio *m* bedroom

dorsal *adj* dorsal

dorso *m* (*de la mano*) back (*of the hand*)

dos *m* **hacer del** — (*euph, defecar*) to defecate (*form*), to have a bowel movement, to do number two (*euph*)

dosificación *f* dosage, dosing

dosis *f* (*pl* **dosis**) dose, dosage; **a** *or* **en** — **altas** high-dose; **a** *or* **en** — **bajas, de baja** — low-dose

doula *mf* doula

doxazocina *f* doxazocin

doxiciclina *f* doxycycline

doxorubicina *f* doxorubicin

DPAC *abbr* **diálisis peritoneal ambulatoria continua.** See **diálisis.**

Dr. *abbr* **doctor.** See **doctor.**

Dra. *abbr* **doctora.** See **doctor.**

drenaje *m* (*procedimiento, líquido drenado*) drainage; (*utensilio*) drain; — **Penrose** Penrose drain

drenar *vt* to drain

droga *f* drug; — **blanda** soft drug; — **de abuso** drug of abuse; — **de diseño** designer drug; — **del amor** (*fam*) methylene dioxyamphetamine (MDA); — **diseñada** designer drug; — **dura** hard drug

drogadicción *f* drug addiction

drogadicto -ta *mf* drug abuser, drug addict

drogado -da *adj* drugged, high (*fam*)

drogar *vt* to drug; *vr* to take drugs, to get high (*fam*)

drogodependencia *f* chemical dependency, dependency on drugs

dronedarona *f* dronedarone

drospirenona *f* drospirenone

DTP *abbr* **difteria, tétanos y tos ferina.** See **vacuna.**

ducha *f* shower; **darse una** — to take a shower, to shower (*vaginal*) to douche; **tomar una** — to take a shower, to

shower
ducharse *vr* to take a shower, to shower
ductal *adj* ductal
duda *f* doubt
dudar *vt* to doubt; **Lo dudo**..I doubt it.
duela *f* (*parásito*) fluke; — **del hígado** liver fluke
duelo *m* (*pena*) grief
dulce *adj* sweet; *m* piece of candy; *mpl* candy, sweets

duloxetina *f* duloxetine
duodenal *adj* duodenal
duodenitis *f* duodenitis
duodeno *m* duodenum
duración *f* duration
duradero -ra *adj* durable
durar *vi* to last; **El dolor me duró toda la noche**..The pain lasted all night.
duro -ra *adj* hard, tough; stiff; — **de oído** hard of hearing

E

eccema *m* eczema
ECG *See* **electrocardiograma** *and* **electrocardiografía**.
echar *vt* — **aire** (*Esp*) to breathe out; — **de menos** to miss; **¿Echa de menos a su hija?**..Do you miss your daughter?; *vr* — **a perder** to spoil (*food, etc.*)
Echinacea (*bot*) Echinacea
eclampsia *f* eclampsia
ecocardiografía *f* (*técnica*) echocardiography; (*estudio*) echocardiogram, echo (*fam*); — **de estrés** *or* **esfuerzo** stress echocardiography; stress echocardiogram, stress echo; — **transesofágica** transesophageal echocardiography; transesophageal echocardiogram; — **transtorácica** transthoracic echocardiography; transthoracic echocardiogram
ecocardiograma *m* (*esp. Amer*) echocardiogram, echo (*fam*)
ecografía *f* (*técnica*) ultrasonography, ultrasound; (*estudio*) ultrasound, sonogram (*form*); — **cardíaca** (*Esp*) echocardiography; — **Doppler** Doppler ultrasonography; Doppler ultrasound
ectima *m* ecthyma; — **contagioso** orf
ectópico -ca *adj* ectopic
ectropión *f* ectropion, outward droop of

the lower eyelid
eczema *m* eczema
edad *f* age; **de — avanzada** elderly; — **fértil** child-bearing age; — **gestacional** gestational age; — **ósea** bone age; **mediana —** middle age, midlife; **tercera —** old age
edema *m* edema; — **pulmonar** pulmonary edema
edoxabán *m* edoxaban
educación *f* education; — **sexual** sex education
educar *vt* to educate
edulcorante *m* sweetener; — **artificial** artificial sweetener
EEF *abbr* estudio electrofisiológico. *See* **estudio**.
EEG *See* **electroencefalografía**.
EF *See* **electrofisiología**.
efavirenz *m* efavirenz
efectividad *f* effectiveness
efectivo -va *adj* effective
efecto *m* effect; — **adverso** adverse effect; — **secundario** side effect; **hacer** *or* **surtir —** to take effect, to have an effect
efedra *f* (*bot*) ephedra
efedrina *f* ephedrine
eficacia *f* effectiveness, efficacy (*form*)

eficaz *adj* effective, efficacious (*form*)

eficiente *adj* efficient

ego *m* ego (*lay sense*)

egocéntrico -ca *adj* egocentric, self-centered

egoísmo *m* egoism

egoísta *adj* egoistic; *mf* egoist

egotismo *m* egotism

egotista *adj* egotistic; *mf* egotist

EIP *abbr* **enfermedad inflamatoria pélvica**. *See* **enfermedad**.

eje *m* axis; — **(central)** (*del cuerpo*) midline (*of the body*)

ejercer *vt* (*la medicina, la odontología, etc.*) to practice (*medicine, dentistry, etc.*)

ejercicio *m* exercise; — **abdominal** situp; **ejercicios de Kegel** Kegel exercises; **hacer** — to exercise

ejercitar *vt, vr* to exercise; — **la mente** to exercise one's mind, to do mental exercises

EKG (*ant*) *See* **electrocardiograma** *and* **electrocardiografía**.

elástico -ca *adj* elastic

eléboro *m* (*bot*) hellebore

elección *f* choice; **medicamento de** — drug of choice; **medicamento de primera (segunda, etc.)** — drug of first (second, etc.) choice

electivo -va *adj* (*surg*) elective

eléctrico -ca *adj* electric, electrical

electrocardiografía (ECG) *f* electrocardiography (ECG)

electrocardiograma (ECG) *m* electrocardiogram (ECG)

electrocución *f* electrocution

electrocutar *vt* to electrocute

electrodo *m* electrode

electroencefalografía (EEG) *f* electroencephalography (EEG)

electroencefalograma (EEG) *m* electroencephalogram (EEG)

electrofisiología (EF) *f* electrophysiology (EP)

electrofisiológico -ca *adj* electrophysiologic *o* electrophysiological

electroforesis *f* electrophoresis

electrolítico -ca *adj* pertaining to electrolytes; **desequilibrio** — electrolyte imbalance

electrolito, electrólito *m* electrolyte

electromiografía (EMG) *f* electromyography (EMG)

elefantiasis *f* elephantiasis

elegible *adj* eligible

elemento *m* element; **elementos traza** trace elements

eletriptán *m* eletriptan

elevación *f* elevation, rise

elevar *vt* to elevate, raise

eliminación *f* elimination, removal; — **de tatuajes** tattoo removal

eliminar *vt* to eliminate, to pass

elíxir, elixir *m* elixir

ello *m* (*psych*) id

emascular *vt* to emasculate

embarazada *adj* pregnant; **quedarse** — (*esp. Esp*) to get *o* become pregnant; *f* pregnant woman

embarazarse *vr* to get *o* become pregnant

embarazo *m* pregnancy; **Tengo cuatro meses de embarazo**..I'm four months pregnant; — **ectópico** ectopic pregnancy; — **no deseado** unwanted pregnancy; — **tubárico** tubal pregnancy

embolectomía *f* embolectomy

embolia *f* embolism; (*fam*) stroke; — **cerebral** cerebral embolism, embolic stroke; — **pulmonar** pulmonary embolism

embolización *f* embolization; — **de las arterias uterinas** uterine artery embolization

émbolo *m* embolus; (*de una jeringa*) plunger (*of a syringe*)

emborracharse *vr* to get drunk

embriagarse *vr* to get drunk

embriología *f* embryology

embrión *m* embryo

embrionario -ria *adj* embryonic, embryonal; **carcinoma** — embryonal carcinoma; **desarrollo** — embryonic development; [*Nota: No hay mucha diferencia entre* embryonic *y* embryonal; *los ejemplos mencionados representan el uso actual.*]

emergencia *f* emergency; **cirugía de** — emergency surgery

emergente *adj* emerging; **enfermedad** — emerging disease

emesis *f* emesis

emético -ca *adj & m* emetic

EMG *See* **electromiografía**.

emoción *f* emotion, feeling

emocional *adj* emotional

emocionar *vt* to excite

emoliente *adj & m* emollient

emotivo -va *adj* (*persona*) emotional, moody; (*tema*) emotional, moving

empacho *m* (*fam*) indigestion, (*Mex*) folk illness manifest by abdominal bloating and other gastrointestinal complaints believed to be due to food obstructing the intestine

empañado -da *adj* blurred; **vista —** blurred vision

empañarse *vr* (*la vista*) to blur, to become blurred *o* blurry; **Se me empaña la vista**..My vision blurs..My vision gets blurred (blurry).

emparentado -da *adj* related; **donante no —** unrelated donor

empastar *vt* (*dent*) to fill (*a cavity*)

empaste *m* (*dent*) filling

empatía *f* empathy

empeine *m* instep, top of foot; (*ingle*) pubic area; (*tiña*) ringworm

empeoramiento *m* worsening, deterioration

empeorar *vt* to make worse; *vi, vr* to get worse, to deteriorate

empezar *vt, vi* to begin

empiema *m* empyema

empírico -ca *adj* empirical

emplasto *m* (*medicinal*) plaster

empleador -ra *mf* employer

emplear *vt* to employ; (*utilizar*) to use, utilize

empleo *m* employment, job; (*uso*) use

emtricitabina *f* emtricitabine

enalapril *m* enalapril

enamorarse *vr* to fall in love; **enamorado de** in love with

enanismo *m* dwarfism

enano -na *mf* dwarf, little person (*euph*)

encajamiento *m* (*obst*) lightening, dropping of the fetus in late pregnancy

encamado -da *adj* bedridden, in bed, in a bed

encarnado -da *adj* (*uña, etc.*) ingrown

encefalitis *f* encephalitis; **— equina del este, — equina oriental** (*Esp*) eastern equine encephalitis; **— equina venezolana** Venezuelan equine encephalitis

encefalopatía *f* encephalopathy; **— de Wernicke** Wernicke's encephalopathy; **— espongiforme bovina** bovine spongiform encephalopathy, mad cow disease (*fam*); **— traumática crónica** chronic traumatic encephalopathy

enchufe *m* electrical outlet

encía *f* gingiva (*form*), gum

encima *adv* above; **— de** above; **encima de su corazón**..above your heart; **por — de** above, over; **por encima de 140** ..above 140..over 140

encinta *adj* (*fam*) pregnant

encogerse *vr* **— de hombros** to shrug one's shoulders

encorvado -da *adj* stooped, bent over

encorvamiento *m* kyphosis (*form*), stooped posture, hunched back

encorvarse *vr* to become stooped (*as with age*)

endarterectomía *f* endarterectomy; **— carotídea** carotid endarterectomy

endémico -ca *adj* endemic

enderezar *vt, vi, vr* to straighten

endocardio *m* endocardium

endocarditis *f* endocarditis; **— infecciosa** infectious endocarditis

endocervical *adj* endocervical

endocérvix *m&f* (*pl* **-vix**) endocervix

endocraneal *adj* intracranial

endocraneano -na *adj* intracranial

endocrino -na *adj* endocrine

endocrinología *f* endocrinology

endocrinólogo -ga *mf* endocrinologist

endodoncia *f* (*campo de odontología*) endodontics; (*tratamiento*) root canal therapy (*form*), root canal (*fam*)

endodoncista *mf* endodontist

endogamia *f* inbreeding

endogámico *adj* inbred

endometrio *m* endometrium

endometriosis *f* endometriosis

endometritis *f* endometritis

endorfina *f* endorphin

endoscopia, endoscopía *f* endoscopy; **— capsular** capsule endoscopy; **— digestiva alta** esophagogastroduodenoscopy (EGD), upper endoscopy

endoscópico -ca *adj* endoscopic

endoscopio *m* endoscope

endotraqueal *adj* endotracheal

endovenoso -sa (EV) *adj* intravenous (IV)

endurecer *vt* to harden, make hard; *vr* to harden, become hard

endurecimiento *m* hardening

enema *m* enema; — **de bario** barium enema; — **de retención** retention enema; — **opaco** barium enema

energía *f* energy

ENET *abbr* **estimulación nerviosa eléctrica transcutánea.** *See* **estimulación.**

enfadarse *vr* to get *o* become angry, to get mad

enfermarse *vr* to become ill, to get sick

enfermedad *f* disease, sickness, illness; — **actual** present illness; — **articular degenerativa** degenerative joint disease, osteoarthritis; — **cardíaca** heart disease; — **celíaca** *or* **celiaca** celiac disease; — **coronaria** coronary artery disease; — **de Addison** Addison's disease*; — **de Alzheimer** Alzheimer's disease; — **de cambios mínimos** minimal change disease; — **de células falciformes** sickle cell disease; — **de Chagas** Chagas disease; — **de Creutzfeldt-Jakob** Creutzfeldt-Jakob disease; — **de Crohn** Crohn's disease, regional enteritis; — **de Cushing** Cushing's disease*; — **de descompresión** decompression sickness, the bends (*fam*); — **de Gaucher** Gaucher's disease*; — **de Graves** Graves' disease*; — **de Hansen** Hansen's disease, leprosy; — **de hígado graso** fatty liver disease; — **de Hirschsprung** Hirschsprung's disease*; — **de Hodgkin** Hodgkin's disease*; — **de Huntington** Huntington's disease; — **de injerto contra huésped** graft-versus-host disease; — **de Kawasaki** Kawasaki disease; — **de las vacas locas** mad cow disease; — **del corazón** heart disease; — **del hígado** liver disease; — **del legionario** Legionnaires' disease; — **del riñón** kidney disease; — **del sueño** sleeping sickness; — **del suero** serum sickness; — **del tejido conectivo** *or* **conjuntivo** connective tissue disease; — **del VIH** HIV disease; — **de Lyme** Lyme disease; — **de membrana hialina** hyaline membrane disease; — **de Ménière** Ménière's disease; — **de neurona motora** motor neuron disease; — **de Osgood-Schlatter** Osgood-Schlatter disease; — **de Paget mamaria** Paget's disease of breast; — **de Parkinson** Parkinson's disease*; — **del pulmón**

negro black lung disease; — **de Pott** Pott's disease*; — **de Raynaud** Raynaud's disease; — **de Rendu-Osler-Weber** Osler-Weber-Rendu disease; — **de transmisión sexual (ETS)** sexually transmitted disease (STD); — **de von Willebrand** von Willebrand disease; — **de Whipple** Whipple's disease; — **de Wilson** Wilson's disease*; — **diverticular** diverticular disease; — **drepanocítica** (*esp. Esp*) sickle cell disease; — **fibroquística de la mama** fibrocystic breast disease, benign breast disease; — **hepática alcohólica** alcoholic liver disease; — **hepática grasa** fatty liver disease; — **hepática grasa no alcohólica** non-alcoholic fatty liver disease; — **inflamatoria intestinal** inflammatory bowel disease; — **inflamatoria pélvica (EIP)** pelvic inflammatory disease (PID); — **intersticial pulmonar** interstitial lung disease; — **laboral** occupational illness; — **mamaria benigna** benign breast disease, fibrocystic breast disease; — **mano-pie-boca** hand, foot, and mouth disease; — **mental** mental illness; — **mieloproliferativa** myeloproliferative disease; — **mixta del tejido conectivo** *or* **conjuntivo** mixed connective tissue disease; — **ocupacional** occupational illness; — **ósea de Paget** Paget's disease of bone; — **por arañazo de gato** cat-scratch disease; — **por deposición de pirofosfatos de calcio** calcium pyrophosphate deposition disease; — **por descompresión** decompression sickness, the bends (*fam*); — **por radiación** radiation sickness; — **por reflujo gastroesofágico (ERGE)** gastroesophageal reflux disease (GERD); — **por VIH** HIV disease; — **profesional** occupational illness; — **pulmonar obstructiva crónica (EPOC)** chronic obstructive pulmonary disease (COPD); — **renal** kidney disease; — **vascular periférica** peripheral vascular disease; — **venérea** (*ant*) sexually transmitted disease (STD), venereal disease (VD) (*ant*); **quinta** — fifth disease

*La forma no posesiva también se usa, sobre todo en la literatura médica:

Addison disease, Cushing disease, etc.

enfermería *f* nursing; (*local para enfermos*) infirmary

enfermero -ra *mf* nurse; — **domiciliario** home health nurse; — **jefe (de sala** or **de turno)** charge nurse; — **registrado** registered nurse; — **supervisor** nurse supervisor; — **vocacional con licencia** licensed vocational nurse

enfermizo -za *adj* sickly

enfermo -ma *adj* sick, ill; *mf* sick person, patient

enfisema *m* emphysema

enflaquecer *vi, vr* to become thin

enfocar *vt* to focus; *vr* — **en** to focus on

enfrentar *vt* to confront, face

enfrente *adv* de — front; **la parte de enfrente de**..the front of

enfuvirtida *f* enfuvirtide

engancharse *vr* to get hooked, to become addicted; — **a la heroína** to get hooked on heroin

engordar *vi, vr* to gain weight, to get fat (*fam*)

engrosamiento *m* enlargement, thickening

engullir *vt* (*la comida*) to gulp down (*food*)

enhorabuena *interj* (*Esp; obst; etc.*) Congratulations!

enjuagar *vt* to rinse, to swish; — **y escupir** swish and spit; — **y tragar** swish and swallow

enjuage *m* rinse; — **bucal** mouthwash

enjugar *vt* to wipe

enlace *m* (*obst, psych*) bond

enloquecerse *vr* to go crazy

enmascarar *vt* (*signos, síntomas*) to mask

enojado -da *adj* angry, mad

enojarse *vr* to become angry, to get mad

enojo *m* rage, anger

enoxaparina de sodio *f* enoxaparin sodium

enriquecer *vt* to enrich, fortify

enrojecimiento *m* reddening, flush, flushing

ensalada *f* salad

ensayo *m* trial; (*prueba*) assay; — **clínico** clinical trial; — **de laboratorio** laboratory assay; — **de liberación de interferón gamma** interferon gamma release assay; — **y error** trial and error

enseñar *vt* to teach; to show

ensimismado -da *adj* self-absorbed, lost in thought

ensordecimiento *m* hearing loss

ensuciar *vt* to soil, to get (*something*) dirty; *vr* to soil oneself, to get dirty

entablillar *vt* to splint

entacapona *f* entacapone

entecavir *m* entecavir

enteral *adj* enteral

entérico -ca *adj* enteric; **con cubierta** — enteric-coated

enteritis *f* enteritis; — **eosinofílica** eosinophilic enteritis; — **regional** regional enteritis, Crohn's disease

entero -ra *adj* whole

enterococo *m* enterococcus; — **resistente a (la) vancomicina** vancomycin-resistant enterococcus

enterocolitis *f* enterocolitis

enteropatía *f* enteropathy; — **perdedora de proteínas** protein-losing enteropathy

enterotoxina *f* enterotoxin

enterrado -da *adj* (*esp. Mex; uña, etc.*) ingrown

entornar *vt, vi* (*los ojos*) to squint (*one's eyes*)

entorno *m* environment, immediate surroundings; — **estructurado** structured environment; — **familiar** family *o* home environment

entrada *f* entry; **portal** *m* de — portal of entry; *fpl* receding hairline

entre *prep* between; — **sus dientes** between your teeth

entrecejo *m* space between one's eyebrows

entrecerrar *vt, vi* (*los ojos*) to squint (*one's eyes*)

entrenamiento *m* training; — **para usar el baño** (*ped*) toilet training

entrenar *vt, vi* to train

entrepierna *f* (*frec. pl*) groin, pubic area

entristecerse *vr* to become sad

entropión *m* entropion, inward droop of the lower eyelid

entuertos *mpl* (*fam*) postpartum cramps

entumecerse *vr* to become numb, to go to sleep (*fam*), to fall asleep (*fam*)

entumecido -da *adj* numb, asleep (*fam*)

entumecimiento *m* numbness

entumido -da *adj* numb, asleep (*fam*)

entumirse *vr* to become numb, to go to sleep (*fam*), to fall asleep (*fam*)
enucleación *f* enucleation
enuresis *f* enuresis, bed wetting
envase *m* container; — **blister** blister pack
envejecer *vi* to grow old
envejecimiento *m* aging
envenenamiento *m* poisoning
envenenar *vt* to poison
envolver *vt* to wrap
enzima *m&f* enzyme; **enzimas pancreáticas** pancreatic enzymes
eosinofilia *f* eosinophilia
eosinófilo *m* eosinophil
epicondilitis *f* epicondylitis; — **lateral** lateral epicondylitis, tennis elbow (*fam*); — **medial** (*esp. Amer*) medial epicondylitis, golfer's elbow (*fam*)
epicóndilo *m* epicondyle; — **lateral** lateral epicondyle; — **medial** (*esp. Amer*) medial epicondyle
epidemia *f* epidemic
epidémico -ca *adj* epidemic
epidemiología *f* epidemiology
epididimitis *f* epididymitis
epidídimo *m* epididymis
epidural *adj* epidural
epifisario -ria *adj* epiphyseal
epífisis *f* (*pl* -sis) epiphysis
epigástrico -ca *adj* epigastric
epiglotis *f* epiglottis
epiglotitis *f* epiglottitis
epilepsia *f* epilepsy
epiléptico -ca *adj & mf* epileptic
epinefrina *f* epinephrine
epiplón *m* omentum
episiotomía *f* episiotomy
episodio *m* episode
epispadias *m* epispadias
epitróclea *f* (*del codo*) medial epicondyle (*of the elbow*)
epitrocleítis *f* medial epicondylitis, golfer's elbow (*fam*)
eplerenona *f* eplerenone
EPOC *abbr* **enfermedad pulmonar obstructiva crónica**. *See* **enfermedad**.
epoetina alfa *f* epoetin alfa
épulis *m* (*pl* -lis) epulis
equilibrado -da *adj* balanced
equilibrio *m* equilibrium, balance
equinococosis *f* echinococcosis
equipo *m* equipment; (*grupo*) team; —

de salud health care team; — **médico duradero** durable medical equipment; — **sanitario** health care team
equivalente *adj & m* equivalent
erección *f* erection
eréctil *adj* erectile
erecto -ta *adj* erect
ergocalciferol *m* ergocalciferol
ergometría *f* (*form*) (*técnica*) exercise stress testing; (*esp. Esp, prueba*) exercise stress test
ergonomía *f* ergonomics
ergonómico -ca *adj* ergonomic
ergotamina *f* ergotamine
erguido *adj* upright
erisipela *f* erysipelas
eritema *m* erythema; — **crónico migratorio** erythema chronicum migrans; — **infeccioso** erythema infectiosum, fifth disease; — **marginado** erythema marginatum; — **multiforme** erythema multiforme; — **nodoso** *or* **nudoso** erythema nodosum
eritrocito *m* erythrocyte
eritromicina *f* erythromycin
eritropoyetina *f* erythropoietin, epoetin alfa
erizo de mar *m* sea urchin
erógeno -na *adj* erogenous
erosión *f* erosion
erosionar *vt, vr* to erode
erosivo -va *adj* erosive
erótico -ca *adj* erotic
erradicación *f* eradication
erradicar *vt* to eradicate
error *m* error; — **congénito del metabolismo** inborn error of metabolism; — **de laboratorio** laboratory error; — **de medicación** medication error; — **de refracción** refractive error; — **innato del metabolismo** inborn error of metabolism; — **refractivo** refractive error
ertapenem *m* ertapenem
eructar *vi* to burp, belch; **hacer** — (*a un bebé*) to burp (*a baby*)
erupción *f* (*derm*) eruption, rash, outbreak; (*dent, form*) teething; — **fija medicamentosa** fixed drug eruption; — **polimorfa lumínica** polymorphous light eruption
escabiasis *f* (*esp. Mex, form*) scabies
escabiosis *f* (*form*) scabies
escala *f* scale (*of measurement*); — **del**

dolor pain scale; — **móvil** (*honorarios, insulina*) sliding scale (*payment, insulin*)

escalada *f* rock climbing

escaldadura *f* scald

escaldar *vt* to scald; *vr* to scald oneself

escalofrío *m* chill

escalpelo *m* scalpel

escama *f* (*derm*) scale, flake

escamoso -sa *adj* squamous; (*descamativo*) scaly, flaky

escanear *vt* (*Ang*) to scan

escáner *m* (*Ang*) (*imagen*) scan; (*aparato*) scanner

escápula *f* scapula; — **alada** winged scapula

escara *f* eschar, scab, crust

escarlatina *f* scarlatina (*form*), scarlet fever

escaso -sa *adj* scarce, (*el pelo*) thin

escayola *f* (*ortho*) plaster; cast; — **desmontable** removable cast

escisión *f* excision

escisional *adj* excisional

escitalopram *m* escitalopram

esclera *f* (*Ang*) sclera

escleritis *f* scleritis

esclerodermia *f* scleroderma, progressive systemic sclerosis; — **localizada** localized scleroderma

esclerosante *adj* sclerosing

esclerosis *f* sclerosis; — **en placas** multiple sclerosis; — **lateral amiotrófica** amyotrophic lateral sclerosis; — **múltiple** multiple sclerosis; — **sistémica progresiva** progressive systemic sclerosis; — **tuberosa** tuberous sclerosis

escleroterapia *f* sclerotherapy

esclerótico -ca *adj* sclerotic; *f* sclera

escoliosis *f* scoliosis

escopolamina *f* scopolamine, hyoscine (*INN*)

escorbuto *m* scurvy

escorpión *m* (*esp. Esp*) scorpion

escotoma *m* scotoma, blind spot

escozor *m* burning, smarting

escritura *f* handwriting

escrófula *f* scrofula

escrotal *adj* scrotal

escroto *m* scrotum

escuchar *vt* to listen to, to hear; — **voces** (*psych*) to hear voices; *vi* to listen

escuela *f* school; — **de medicina** medical school

escupir *vt*, *vi* to spit, to spit out; **Escupió la pastilla**..He spit out the pill.

escurrimiento *m* (*esp. Mex*) secretion, drainage; — **nasal** nasal drainage; **tener** — **nasal** to have a runny nose

escutelaria *f* (*bot*) skullcap

esencial *adj* essential

esfenoidal *adj* sphenoid

esferocitosis *f* spherocytosis; — **hereditaria** hereditary spherocytosis

esfigmomanómetro *m* blood pressure monitor

esfínter *m* sphincter

esfinterotomía *f* sphincterotomy

esforzarse *vr* to exert oneself, to strain oneself; — **demasiado** to overexert oneself

esfuerzo *m* effort, exertion; — **físico** physical exertion; **hacer esfuerzos** to exert oneself

esguince *m* sprain

esmalte *m* enamel; — **de** *or* **para uñas** nail polish

esmegma *m* smegma

esmog *m* smog

esnifar *vt* (*Ang*) (*pegamento, gasolina*) to sniff, (*cocaína, heroína, anfetaminas*) to snort (*fam*), to sniff

esofágico -ca *adj* esophageal

esofagitis *f* esophagitis; — **erosiva** erosive esophagitis; — **por reflujo** reflux esophagitis

esófago *m* esophagus; — **de Barrett** Barrett's esophagus

esofagogastroduodenoscopia *f* esofagogastroduodenoscopy

esomeprazol *m* esomeprazole

espaciador *m* spacer

espacial *adj* spatial, space; **orientación** *f* — spatial orientation; **medicina** — space medicine

espacio *m* space, gap

espalda *f* back; — **baja** low back

esparadrapo *m* adhesive tape

espárrago *m* asparagus

espasmo *m* spasm

espasmódico -ca *adj* spasmodic

espasticidad *f* spasticity

espástico -ca *adj* spastic

especia *f* spice

especialidad *f* specialty

especialista *adj* & *mf* specialist, expert;

— del pulmón (riñón, etc.) lung (kidney, etc.) specialist; **— en alergias (enfermedades infecciosas, etc.)** specialist in allergies (infectious diseases, etc.)

especie f species

específico -ca adj specific; **una prueba específica para..**a test specific for

espécimen m (pl **-címenes**) specimen

espectinomicina f spectinomycin

espectro m spectrum

espéculo m speculum

espejo m mirror

espejuelos mpl (esp. Carib) glasses, eyeglasses

esperando adj (fam, embarazada) pregnant, expecting (fam)

esperanza f hope; **— de vida** life expectancy; **perder la —** to lose hope; **sin — ** hopeless; **tener esperanzas de** to hope for

esperar vt (desear) to hope for; (aguardar) to wait for; (contar con) to expect; vi to hope; to wait

espera vigilante f watchful waiting

esperma m&f sperm, semen

espermaticida adj spermicidal; m spermicide

espermatocele m spermatocele

espermatozoide m sperm, spermatozoon (form)

espermicida adj spermicidal; m spermicide

espeso -sa adj thick

espesor m thickness

espica de yeso f spica cast o splint

espichar vt (granos) to pick (pimples)

espina f (anat) spine; (de una planta) spine, thorn, sticker; (de un pescado) bone, fishbone; **— bífida** spina bifida; **— dorsal** spinal column, spine, backbone

espinaca f (frec. pl) spinach

espinal adj spinal

espinilla f (anat) shin; (derm) blackhead, pimple

espinillera f shin guard

espino blanco m (bot) hawthorn

espiración f expiration, exhalation

espirar vt, vi to expire, exhale

espiratorio -ria adj expiratory

espiritual adj spiritual

espirometría f spirometry; **— incentiva-** da incentive spirometry

espirómetro m spirometer; **— incentivado** incentive spirometer

espironolactona f spironolactone

espiroqueta f spirochete

esplenectomía f splenectomy

esplénico -ca adj splenic

espolón m (ortho) spur; **— calcáneo** (form), **— en el talón** heel spur; **— óseo** bone spur

espondilitis anquilosante f ankylosing spondylitis

espondilolisis f spondylolysis

espondilolistesis f spondylolysthesis

espondilosis f spondylosis

esponja f sponge

espontáneo -a adj spontaneous

espora f spore

esporádico -ca adj sporadic

esporotricosis f sporotrichosis

esposo -sa mf spouse; m husband; f wife

espray m spray

esprue, esprúe m sprue; **— celíaco** or **celiaco, — no tropical** celiac disease, nontropical o celiac sprue; **— tropical** tropical sprue

espuma f foam; **— de afeitar** shaving cream

espundia f mucocutaneous leishmaniasis

esputo m sputum

esquelético -ca adj skeletal

esqueleto m skeleton

esquema de vacunación m vaccination schedule

esquí m skiing

esquirla f sliver, shaving

esquistosomiasis f schistosomiasis

esquizoafectivo -va adj schizoaffective

esquizofrenia f schizophrenia; **— paranoide** paranoid schizophrenia

esquizofrénico -ca adj & mf schizophrenic

esquizoide adj schizoid

estabilidad f stability

estabilización f stabilization

estabilizador m stabilizer; **— del ánimo** or **humor** mood stabilizer

estabilizar vt, vr to stabilize

estable adj stable

estación f station; (del año) season; **— de enfermería** nursing station

estacional adj seasonal

estadía f stay; **— hospitalaria** or **en el**

hospital hospital stay

estadificación *f* (*de tumores*) staging

estadio *m* (*de enfermedad, del cáncer, de la pubertad, etc.*) stage

estadística *f* statistic; (*ciencia*) statistics

estado *m* status, state, condition, shape; **en buen estado físico**..in shape..fit; — **asmático** status asthmaticus; — **civil** marital status; — **crítico** critical condition; — **de ánimo** mood; — **de hipercoagulabilidad** hypercoagulable state; — **del arte** state of the art; — **epiléptico** status epilepticus; — **estacionario** steady state; — **mental** mental state; — **vegetativo** vegetative state

estafilococo *m* Staphylococcus

estallido *m* (*sonido*) pop; (*emocional*) outburst; **Escuché un estallido**..I heard a pop.

estancamiento *m* (*de sangre*) stasis (*form*), pooling

estancarse *vr* (*la sangre*) to pool

estancia *f* stay; — **hospitalaria** *or* **en el hospital** hospital stay

estándar *adj & m* standard; — **de atención** *or* **cuidado** standard of care

estapedectomía *f* stapedectomy

estasis *f* stasis; — **venosa** venous stasis *o* insufficiency

estatina *f* statin

estatura *f* (*de una persona*) height

estavudina *f* stavudine

esteatohepatitis *f* steatohepatitis; — **no alcohólica** non-alcoholic steatohepatitis

estenosis *f* (*pl* **-sis**) stenosis, stricture; — **aórtica** (**mitral, etc.**) aortic (mitral, etc.) stenosis; — **esofágica** esophageal stricture; — **hipertrófica de píloro** hypertrophic pyloric stenosis; — **ureteral** ureteral stricture

estenótico -ca *adj* stenotic

estereotáxico, estereotáctico -ca *adj* stereotactic

estereotipia *f* stereotypy

estéril *adj* sterile, aseptic; (*persona*) infertile, sterile

esterilidad *f* sterility; (*de las personas*) infertility, sterility

esterilización *f* sterilization

esterilizar *vt* to sterilize

esternal *adj* sternal

esternón *m* sternum, breast bone

esteroide *m* steroid; — **inhalado** inhaled steroid

esteroideo -a *adj* steroid

esteticista *mf* cosmetologist

estetoscopio *m* stethoscope

estevia *f* (*bot*) stevia

estibogluconato de sodio *m* sodium stibogluconate

estilo de vida *m* lifestyle

estimulación *f* stimulation; — **digital** digital stimulation; — **nerviosa eléctrica transcutánea (ENET)** transcutaneous electrical nerve stimulation (TENS)

estimulante *adj* stimulating, stimulant; *m* stimulant

estimular *vt* to stimulate

estímulo *m* stimulus

estiramiento *m* stretching; **ejercicios de** — stretching exercises; — **facial** rhytidectomy (*form*), facelift

estirar *vt, vr* to stretch

estirón *m* (*crecimiento rápido*) growth spurt

estirpe *f* lineage; — **mieloide (linfoide, B, T, etc.)** myeloid (lymphoid, B, T, etc.) lineage

estítico -ca *adj* (*esp. CA*) constipated

estoma *m* stoma

estomacal *adj* gastric, pertaining to the stomach

estómago *m* stomach; (*fam, abdomen*) abdomen, belly

estomaguito *m* (*ped*) tummy

estomatitis *f* stomatitis

estornudar *vi* to sneeze

estornudo *m* sneeze

estrabismo *m* strabismus

estradiol *m* estradiol

estrangulación *f* strangulation

estrangulado -da *adj* strangulated

estrangular *vt, vr* to strangle, choke

estrecho -cha *adj* narrow

estreñimiento *m* constipation

estreñir *vt* to constipate; *vr* to become constipated

estreptococo *m* Streptococcus

estreptomicina *f* streptomycin

estreptoquinasa, estreptocinasa, estreptokinasa *f* streptokinase

estrés *m* (*pl* **estreses**) stress; **bajo** — under stress; — **laboral** *or* **en el trabajo** job stress estresante *adj* stressful

estresar *vt* to stress, to put stress on; *vr* to become stressed, to stress out *(fam)*

estresor *m* stressor

estría *f* stria *(form)*, stretch mark

estribo *m (anat, gyn, etc.)* stirrup

estricnina *f* strychnine

estricto -ta *adj* strict; **control** — *(diabetes, etc.)* tight control

estriol *m* estriol

estrógeno *m* estrogen; **estrógenos conjugados** conjugated estrogens

estrongiloidiasis *f* strongyloidiasis

estructurado -da *adj* structured

estructural *adj* structural

estuche *m* kit; — **de epinefrina** epinephrine kit

estudiante *mf* student; — **de medicina** medical student

estudio *m* study; — **del sueño** sleep study; — **doble ciego** double-blind study; — **electrofisiológico (EEF)** electrophysiology study (EPS); — **radiológico** or **por imagen** or **imágenes** imaging study

estupor *m* stupor

eszopiclona *f* eszopiclone

etambutol *m* ethambutol

etanercept *m* etanercept

etanol *m* ethanol, ethyl alcohol

etapa *f (de una enfermedad, del sueño)* stage; **en** — **terminal** end-stage

éter *m* ether

ético -ca *adj* ethical

etilenglicol *m* ethylene glycol

etinilestradiol *m* ethinyl estradiol *(USAN)*, ethinylestradiol *(INN)*

etionamida *f* ethionamide

etiqueta *f* label

etmoidal *adj* ethmoid

étnico -ca *adj* ethnic

etopósido *m* etoposide

etosuximida *f* ethosuximide

ETS *abbr* **enfermedad de transmisión sexual.** *See* **enfermedad.**

eucalipto *m (bot)* eucalyptus

euforia *f* euphoria

eufrasia *f (bot)* eyebright

eunuco *m* eunuch

eutanasia *f* euthanasia, mercy killing

EV *See* **endovenoso.**

evacuación *f* evacuation; *(del intestino)* bowel movement; — **dolorosa** painful bowel movement

evacuar *vt* to evacuate; *(el intestino)* to have a bowel movement

evaluación *f* evaluation, assessment, testing; — **urodinámica** urodynamic testing

evaluar *vt* to evaluate

evaporarse *vr* to evaporate

eventración *f (hernia)* incisional hernia

evidencia *f* evidence; **basado en la** — evidence-based; — **científica** scientific evidence

evitación *f* avoidance

evitar *vt* to avoid, prevent; **Evite comidas grasas.** ..Avoid fatty foods.

evolución *f* evolution; — **natural** *(de una enfermedad)* natural history

evolucionar *vi* to evolve

ex *pref* former, ex-; — **esposa** former wife, ex-wife; — **esposo** former husband, ex-husband; — **fumador -ra** *mf* former smoker; **ex-marido** former husband, ex-husband

exacerbación *f* exacerbation

exactitud *f* accuracy

exacto -ta *adj* exact, accurate

examen *m* examination, exam *(fam)*; — **auditivo** hearing test; — **de detección** screening test, screen; — **de guayacol en heces** stool guaiac test; — **de los ojos** eye examination, eye exam; — **de mama** breast examination, breast exam; — **de orina** urinalysis *(form)*, urine test; — **de sangre** blood test; — **de seno** breast examination, breast exam; — **físico** physical examination, physical *(fam)*; — **mamario** breast examination, breast exam; — **oftalmológico** ophthalmologic examination, eye exam; — **pélvico** pelvic examination, pelvic *(fam)*; — **rectal** rectal examination, rectal exam

examinar *vt* to examine, to test

exantema súbito *m* roseola, roseola infantum *(form)*

excederse *vr* to overdo it; **Puede caminar, pero no se exceda.** ..You can walk, but don't overdo it.

excesivo -va *adj* excessive

exceso *m* excess

excipiente *m* excipient

excitación *f (sexual)* sexual arousal, sexual stimulation

excitar *vt* (*sexualmente*) to arouse (*sexually*); *vr* to become aroused (*sexually*)
excoriación *f* excoriation
excoriado -da *adj* excoriated, raw (*fam*)
excoriar *vt* to excoriate
excremento *m* excrement, stool
excretar *vt* to excrete
excretor -ra *adj* excretory
excusa *f* excuse
exemestano *m* exemestane
exenatida *f* exenatide
exfoliación *f* exfoliation; (*procedimiento*) peel; (*el concepto, la técnica*) peeling; — **química** chemical peel; chemical peeling
exfoliativo -va *adj* exfoliative
exhalar *vt, vi* to exhale
exhaustivo -va *adj* extensive
exhausto -ta *adj* exhausted, run-down
expandir *vt, vr* to expand
expectativa de vida *f* life expectancy
expectorante *adj & m* expectorant
expectorar *vt* (*form*) to cough up (and spit out)
expediente *m* (*esp. Mex*) chart, record; — **clínico** patient chart, medical record
expeler *vt* to expel
experiencia *f* experience
experimental *adj* experimental
experimentar *vi* to experiment; *vt* (*sentir*) to experience, to feel
experimento *m* experiment
experto -ta *adj & mf* expert
exploración *f* (*form, examen*) examination; — **física** physical examination, physical (*fam*); — **mamaria** breast examination, breast exam (*fam*)
explorador -ra *adj* (*surg*) exploratory
explorar *vt* (*form, examinar*) to examine; (*surg*) to explore
exponer *vt* (*pp* **expuesto**) to expose; *vr* to be exposed, to expose oneself; **No se exponga al humo**..Don't expose yourself to the smoke.
exposición *f* exposure
expresar *vt* to express; *vr* to express oneself
expresivo -va *adj* expressive
exprimir *vt* (*pus, etc.*) to express
expuesto -ta (*pp of* **exponer**) *adj* exposed; **Ella ha sido expuesta a él**..She has been exposed to him.
expulsar *vt* to expel, to pass

expulsión *f* expulsion, passing
éxtasis *m* (*fam*) methylene dioxymethamphetamine (MDMA), ecstacy (*fam*); — **líquido** (*fam*) gamma-hydroxybutyrate *o* gamma-hydroxybutyric acid (GHB), liquid ecstacy (*fam*)
extender *vt* (*anat*) to extend, to straighten; **Extienda la pierna**..Straighten your leg; *vr* to spread
extensión *f* (*anat*) extension; (*propagación*) spread; (*divulgación*) outreach; **programa de** — outreach program
extensor *adj* (*anat*) extensor; *m* extensor; extender; — **de pene** penis extender
extenuante *adj* exhausting, strenous
exterior *adj* outer, exterior, outside; *m* exterior, outside
externo -na *adj* external, outer, outside; (*anat*) lateral; **paciente** — outpatient
extintor de incendios *m* fire extinguisher
extirpable *adj* resectable
extirpar *vt* to resect, (*completamente*) to excise
extra *adj* extra
extracción *f* extraction, removal
extracorporal *adj* out-of-body; **experiencia** — out-of-body experience
extracorpóreo *adj* extracorporeal; out-of-body; **experiencia** — out-of-body experience
extracto *m* (*pharm*) extract; — **de corteza de pino** pine bark extract; — **de semilla de uva** grapeseed extract
extractor de leche *m* breast pump
extraer *vt* to extract, remove, take out
extraíble *adj* removable
extrañar *vt* to miss; **Extraño a mis hijos**..I miss my children.
extraño -ña *adj* unusual, foreign; **cuerpo** — foreign body
extravasación *f* extravasation
extravertido -da *See* **extrovertido**.
extremidad *f* extremity, limb
extrovertido -da *adj* extroverted, outgoing; *mf* extrovert
extubación *f* extubation
extubar *vt* to extubate
exudado *m* exudate
eyaculación *f* ejaculation; — **precoz** premature ejaculation
eyaculado *m* ejaculate
eyacular *vi* to ejaculate
ezetimiba *f* ezetimibe

F

fabulación *f* confabulation
facciones *fpl* features
facial *adj* facial
facticio -cia *adj* factitious
factor *m* factor; — **de coagulación** clotting *o* coagulation factor; — **V de Leiden** factor V Leiden; — **de protección solar (FPS)** sun protection factor (SPF); — **de riesgo** risk factor; — **intrínseco** intrinsic factor; — **reumatoide** *or* **reumatoideo** rheumatoid factor; — **Rh** Rh factor
factura *f (cuenta)* bill
facultad *f* faculty, ability; — **de medicina** medical school
Fahrenheit *adj* Fahrenheit
faja *f (para contener una hernia)* truss
falda *f* skirt
fálico -ca *adj* phallic
falla *f* failure; — **cardíaca** heart failure; — **multiorgánica** multisystem organ failure; — **respiratoria** respiratory failure
fallar *vi* to fail
fallecer *vi* to expire, die, pass (away) *(euph)*
fallecimiento *m* death
fallo *m* failure; — **cardíaco** heart failure; — **hepático** liver failure; — **multiorgánico** multisystem organ failure; — **respiratorio** respiratory failure
falo *m* phallus
falso -sa *adj* false
falta *f* lack, absence, deficit, deficiency; — **de aire** *or* **aliento** shortness of breath; — **de hogar** homelessness; — **de sueño** lack of sleep; — **de vivienda** homelessness; **hacer(le)** — **(a uno)** to need; **No le hace falta..**You don't need it.
faltar *vi* **faltar(le) (a uno)** to be low, to need, to lack; **Le falta potasio..**Your potassium is low..You need potassium; **faltar(le) el aire** *or* **aliento (a uno)** to be short of breath; **¿Le falta el aire?..** Are you short of breath?; — **a** *(una cita, el trabajo, etc.)* to miss *(an appointment, work, etc.)*

famciclovir *m* famciclovir
familia *f* family; — **extendida** extended family
familiar *adj* familial; *mf* relative, family member
famotidina *f* famotidine
fantasear *vi* to fantasize
fantasía *f* fantasy
farfallota *f (PR)* mumps
faringe *f* pharynx
faríngeo -a *adj* pharyngeal
faringitis *f* pharyngitis
farmacéutico -ca *adj* pharmaceutical; *mf* pharmacist
farmacia *f* pharmacy, drugstore
fármaco *m* pharmaceutical, medication; — **antirreumático modificador de la enfermedad (FARME)** disease-modifying antirheumatic drug (DMARD)
farmacodependencia *f* prescription drug dependency *o* dependence
farmacodependiente *mf* person dependent on prescription drugs
farmacología *f* pharmacology
farmacológico -ca *adj* pharmacologic *o* pharmacological
farmacólogo -ga *mf* pharmacologist
farmacopea *f* pharmacopoeia
FARME *abbr* **fármaco antirreumático modificador de la enfermedad.** *See* **fármaco.**
fascia *f* fascia
fascioliasis *f* fascioliasis
fasciotomía *f* fasciotomy
fascitis *f* fasciitis; — **necrotizante** *or* **necrosante** necrotizing fasciitis
fase *f* phase
fastidiar *vt (ped)* to tease
fastidioso -sa *adj* annoying, irritating
fatal *adj* fatal
fatiga *f* fatigue; — **visual** eyestrain
fatigar *vt* to tire (out); **Lo fatiga..**It tires him (out); *vr* to tire (out), get tired (out)
fatigoso -sa *adj* tiring
favorable *adj* favorable
fe *f (religiosa)* faith
febrícula *f* fever *(esp. low-grade and*

prolonged)
febril *adj* febrile
fecal *adj* fecal
fecha *f* date; — **de caducidad** expiration date; — **de nacimiento** birth date; — **de vencimiento** expiration date; — **probable de parto** estimated date of delivery, due date
fecundación *f* fertilization; — **in vitro (FIV)** in vitro fertilization (IVF)
fecundar *vt* (*obst*) to fertilize
felación *f* fellatio, oral sex (*performed on a male*)
felicidad *f* happiness; **¡Felicidades!** (*obst, etc.*) Congratulations!
feliz *adj* happy
felodipina *f* felodipine
felodipino *m* felodipine
femenino -na *adj* feminine, female
feminización *f* feminization
femoral *adj* femoral
fémur *m* femur
fenacetina *f* phenacetin
fenazopiridina *f* phenazopyridine
fenciclidina *f* phencyclidine (PCP)
fenilalanina *f* phenylalanine
fenilbutazona *f* phenylbutazone
fenilcetonuria *f* phenylketonuria (PKU)
fenilefrina *f* phenylephrine
fenilpropanolamina *f* phenylpropanolamine
fenitoína *f* phenytoin
fenobarbital *m* phenobarbital
fenofibrato *m* fenofibrate
fenol *m* phenol
fenómeno *m* phenomenon; — **de Raynaud** Raynaud's phenomenon
fenotiazina, fenotiacina (*esp. Esp*) *f* phenothiazine
fenotipo *m* phenotype
fentanilo *m* fentanyl
fentermina *f* phentermine
feo -a *adj* ugly; (*fam*) bad, awful; **Sabe feo.**.It tastes bad (awful).
feocromocitoma *m* pheochromocytoma
férrico -ca *adj* ferric
ferritina *f* ferritin
ferroso -sa *adj* ferrous
fértil *adj* fertile
fertilización *f* (*obst, Ang*) fertilization
fertilizar *vt* (*obst, Ang*) to fertilize
férula *f* (*form*) splint; — **cock-up** cock-up splint; — **de muñeca en posición**

neutra neutral wrist splint; — **inflable,** — **hinchable** (*esp. Esp*) inflatable air splint, air cast (*fam*)
fetal *adj* fetal
fetiche *m* fetish
fetichismo *m* fetishism
feto *m* fetus
fexofenadina *f* fexofenadine
fiabilidad *f* reliability
fiable *adj* reliable
fibra *f* fiber; — **dietética** dietary fiber; — **insoluble** insoluble fiber; — **muscular** muscle fiber; — **nerviosa** nerve fiber; — **soluble** soluble fiber
fibrato *m* fibrate
fibrilación *f* fibrillation; — **auricular** atrial fibrillation; — **ventricular** ventricular fibrillation
fibrina *f* fibrin
fibrinógeno *m* fibrinogen
fibrinolisis, fibrinólisis *f* fibrinolysis
fibrinolítico -ca *adj & m* fibrinolytic
fibroadenoma *m* fibroadenoma
fibroma *m* fibroma
fibromialgia *f* fibromyalgia
fibroquístico -ca *adj* fibrocystic
fibrosis *f* fibrosis; — **quística** cystic fibrosis
fibrótico -ca *adj* fibrotic
fíbula *f* fibula
fiebre *f* fever; — **amarilla** yellow fever; — **botonosa mediterránea** Mediterranean spotted fever; — **de(l) heno** allergic rhinitis (*form*), hay fever; — **entérica** enteric *o* typhoid fever; — **hemorrágica** hemorrhagic fever; — **manchada** *or* **maculosa de las Montañas Rocosas** Rocky Mountain spotted fever; — **mediterránea familiar** familial Mediterranean fever; — **Q** Q fever; — **recurrente** relapsing fever; — **reumática** rheumatic fever; — **tifoidea** typhoid fever
figura *f* (*de una persona*) figure
fijación *f* (*ortho, psych, etc.*) fixation
fijar *vt* (*ortho*) to fixate; — **la vista** to stare; *vr* — **en** to notice
fijo -ja *adj* fixed
filariasis *f* filariasis
filgrastim *m* filgrastim
filoso -sa *adj* sharp
filtración *f* filtration
filtrar *vt* to filter

filtro *m* filter; **cigarillo** *or* **cigarro con** — filter cigarette; — **de la vena cava inferior** inferior vena cava filter; — **solar** sunscreen

fimosis *f* phimosis

fin *m* end; — **de semana** weekend

final *adj* final

finasterida *f* finasteride

fingido -da *adj* factitious

firma *f* signature

firmar *vt, vi* to sign (*one's name*)

firme *adj* firm

fisiatra *mf* physiatrist, specialist in physical medicine and rehabilitation

fisiatría *f* physiatry, physical medicine and rehabilitation

físico -ca *adj* physical; *m* physique, build

fisicoculturismo *m* bodybuilding

fisicoculturista, fisiculturista *mf* bodybuilder

fisiología *f* physiology

fisiológico -ca *adj* physiological

fisiólogo -ga *mf* physiologist

fisioterapeuta *mf* physical therapist, physiotherapist

fisioterapia *f* physical therapy, physiotherapy

fisioterapista *mf* (*Ang*) physical therapist, physiotherapist

fisostigmina *f* physostigmine

fístula *f* fistula; — **anal** anal fistula; — **arteriovenosa** arteriovenous fistula; — **mucosa** mucous fistula

fisura *f* fissure, crack, split, hairline fracture; — **anal** anal fissure

fitoestrógeno *m* phytoestrogen

fitoterapia *f* herbal medicine, herbalism

flácido, fláccido -da *adj* flaccid, flabby, limp

flaco -ca *adj* (*fam*) thin, lean

flanco *m* flank

flato *m* flatus, gas (*expelled from rectum*)

flatulencia *f* flatulence

flatulento -ta *adj* flatulent

flavonoide *m* flavonoid

flebitis *f* phlebitis

fleboextracción *f* vein stripping

flebografía *f* (*técnica*) venography; (*estudio*) venogram

flebotomía *f* phlebotomy, blood drawing; — **terapéutica** therapeutic phlebotomy

flebotomiano -na *mf* phlebotomist

flebotomista *mf* phlebotomist

flebótomo *m* sandfly

flema *f* (*frec. pl*) phlegm, mucus

flemón *m* phlegmon

flexibilidad *f* flexibility

flexible *adj* flexible, supple, (*persona*) limber

flexión *f* flexion; (*de bíceps*) curl; (*de brazos*) pushup

flexionar *vt* (*form*) to flex

flexor -ra *adj & m* flexor

flictena *f* (*esp. Esp*) blister

flojo -ja *adj* (*suelto*) loose, lax; (*relajado*) relaxed, limp

flora *f* flora

flotante *adj* (*ansiedad, etc.*) free-floating

fluconazol *m* fluconazole

fluctuar *vi* to fluctuate

fludrocortisona *f* fludrocortisone

flufenazina, flufenacina (*esp. Esp*) *f* fluphenazine

fluido *m* fluid; — **corporal** *or* **del cuerpo** body fluid

fluir *vi* to flow, to run

flujo *m* flow, drainage, secretion, discharge; — **espiratorio máximo** peak expiratory flow; — **menstrual** menstrual flow; — **nasal** nasal drainage; **tener** — **nasal** to have a runny nose; — **sanguíneo** blood flow; — **vaginal** vaginal discharge

flumetasona *f* flumetasone

flunisolida *f* flunisolide

fluocinolona *f* fluocinolone

fluocinónida *f* fluocinonide

flúor *m* fluorine

fluoración *f* fluoridation

fluoresceina *f* fluorescein

fluorescente *adj* fluorescent

fluorización *f* fluoridation

fluoroquinolona *f* fluoroquinolone

fluoroscopia, fluoroscopía *f* fluoroscopy

fluorouracilo *m* fluorouracil

fluoruro *m* fluoride; — **sódico** *or* **de sodio** sodium fluoride

fluoxetina *f* fluoxetine

flurazepam *m* flurazepam

flúter *m* (*Ang*) flutter; — **auricular** atrial flutter

fluticasona *f* fluticasone

fluvastatina *f* fluvastatin

fobia *f* phobia; — **a alturas (arañas, etc.)** phobia of heights (spiders, etc.); — **social** social phobia

focal *adj* focal
foco *m* focus
fofo -fa *adj* flabby
fogaje *m* (*Carib, fam*) hot flash, flush
fogazo *m* (*Mex, fam*) herpes labialis (*form*), cold sore, fever blister
fólico -ca *adj* folic
foliculitis *f* folliculitis
folículo *m* follicle; — ovárico ovarian follicle; — piloso hair follicle
folitropina *f* follicle-stimulating hormone (FSH)
folleto *m* booklet, pamphlet, handout
fondaparinux *m* fondaparinux
fondillos *mpl* (*Carib, CA; fam*) buttocks
fondo *m* bottom; (*gyn, ophth, etc.*) fundus; (*de una úlcera*) base; — de ojo fundus of the eye, eyeground
fonendoscopio *m* stethescope
fonoaudiología *f* speech language pathology (*form*), speech pathology *o* therapy; speech pathology and audiology
fonoaudiólogo -ga *mf* speech language therapist (*form*), speech pathologist *o* therapist; specialist in speech therapy and audiology
fonoforesis *f* phonophoresis
fontanela *f* fontanelle; — abultada bulging fontanelle
footing *m* (*Ang*) jogging; hacer — to jog
foramen oval *m* foramen ovale; — — permeable patent foramen ovale
fórceps *m* (*pl* -ceps) (*obst, surg*) forceps
forense *adj* forensic; *mf* coroner
forma *f* form, shape; en — fit, in shape
formaldehído *m* formaldehyde
formalina *f* formalin
formar *vt, vr* to form
formol *m* formalin
formoterol *m* formoterol
fórmula *f* (*math, ped, pharm, etc.*) formula
formulario *m* (*pharm*) formulary; (*cuestionario, etc.*) form
fornido -da *adj* stocky, heavyset
fortalecer *vt* to strengthen, build up
fortificar *vt* to fortify
forúnculo *m* furuncle
forzar *vt* (*la vista, la voz*) to strain (*one's eyes, one's voice*)
fosa *f* fossa; — nasal nostril
fosamprenavir *m* fosamprenavir

fosfatasa alcalina *f* alkaline phosphatase
fosfato *m* phosphate
fósforo *m* phosphorus
fosinopril *m* fosinopril
fotoalergia *f* photoallergy
fotocoagulación *f* photocoagulation
fotorrejuvenecimiento *m* photorejuvenation
fotosensibilidad *f* photosensitivity
fotosensible *adj* photosensitive
fototerapia *f* phototherapy
fototóxico -ca *adj* phototoxic
FPS *abbr* factor de protección solar. See factor.
fracasar *vi* to fail
fracaso *m* failure; — terapéutico *or* del tratamiento treatment failure
fracción *f* fraction; — de eyección ejection fraction
fractura *f* fracture, break; — abierta open *o* compound fracture; — cerrada closed fracture; — compuesta compound *o* open fracture; — conminuta comminuted fracture; — craneal *or* de cráneo skull fracture; — del boxeador boxer's fracture; — en tallo verde greenstick fracture; — espiroidea spiral fracture; — expuesta open *o* compound fracture; — patológica pathologic fracture; — por estrés *or* sobrecarga stress fracture; — vertebral vertebral fracture
fracturar *vt, vr* to fracture, break
fragata portuguesa *f* Portuguese man-of-war
frágil *adj* fragile, brittle, frail, delicate
fragmento *m* fragment
frambesia *f* frambesia, yaws
franquicia *f* (*seguros, esp. Esp*) deductible
frasco *m* bottle, pill bottle, vial
fraterno -na *adj* fraternal
frazada *f* (*Amer*) blanket
frecuencia *f* frequency, rate; (*sonido*) frequency, pitch; ¿Con qué frecuencia?..How often?; — cardíaca heart rate; — respiratoria respiratory rate
frecuente *adj* frequent
frecuentemente *adv* frequently, often
freír *vt* to fry
frenético *adj* frantic
frénico -ca *adj* phrenic
frenos, frenillos *mpl* (*dent, fam*) braces

frente *f* forehead, brow; — **a** in front of, facing
fresa *f* strawberry
fresco -ca *adj* fresh; (*temperatura*) cool
fricción *f* friction
friccionar *vt* to rub; (*masajear*) to massage
frígida *adj* (*ant*) having low sexual desire, unresponsive sexually, frigid (*ant*)
frigidez *f* (*ant*) low sexual desire (*in a woman*), inability to respond sexually, frigidity (*ant*)
frigorífico *m* refrigerator
frijoles *mpl* beans
frío -a *adj* cold; *m* cold; **hacer** — to be cold (*the weather*); **Me duele más cuando hace frío**..It hurts more when the weather is cold; **tener** *or* **sentir** — to feel *o* feel cold; **Tengo frío**..I'm cold.
friolento -ta *adj* sensitive to cold
frito -ta *adj* fried
friza *f* (*PR, SD*) blanket
frontal *adj* frontal
frotar *vt* to rub
frotis *m* (*pl* **-tis**) (*micro*) smear; — **de Papanicolaou** Papanicolaou smear, Pap smear (*fam*); — **sanguineo** (*form*), — **de sangre** blood smear
frovatriptán *m* frovatriptan
fructosa *f* fructose
fruncir *vt* — **el ceño** *or* **entrecejo** to frown; — **los labios** to purse one's lips
fruta *f* fruit; — **cítrica** citrus fruit; — **seca** dried fruit

fuego *m* fire; (*fam, llaga en los labios*) cold sore, fever blister
fuente *f* source; (*obst*) bag of waters; — **de infección** source of infection; — **de proteína** source of protein
fuera *adv* — **de** outside, outside of; — **de sí** crazy, out of it (*fam*)
fuerte *adj* strong, powerful, severe
fuerza *f* force, strength; **de doble** — double-strength; **de** — **extra** extra-strength; — **de agarre** *or* **prensión** grip strength; — **de voluntad** will power
fuga de ideas *f* (*psych*) flight of ideas
fulminante *adj* fulminant
fumador -ra *mf* smoker
fumar *vt, vi* to smoke; **Prohibido fumar**..No smoking.
fumigación aérea *f* crop dusting
fumigar *vt* to fumigate
función *f* function
funcionamiento *m* performance
funcionar *vi* to function, to work, to act
funeraria *f* funeral home, mortuary
fúngico -ca *adj* fungal
furia *f* rage
furioso -sa *adj* furious
furosemida *f* furosemide
furúnculo *m* furuncle
fusil *m* rifle, gun
fusión *f* fusion
fusionar *vi, vr* (*ortho*) to fuse
fútbol *or* **futbol** *m* soccer; — **americano** football

G

gabapentina *f* gabapentin
gabinete *m* (*dent, form*) operatory (*form*), dental exam room
gadolinio *m* gadolinium
gafas *fpl* glasses, eyeglasses; goggles; —

bifocales bifocal glasses *o* eyeglasses, bifocals (*fam*); — **de lectura** reading glasses; — **de natación** swimming goggles; — **de seguridad** safety glasses *o* goggles; — **de sol** sunglasses; —

para nadar swimming goggles; — **protectoras** safety glasses *o* goggles

gago -ga *mf (fam)* stutterer, stammerer

gaguear *vi (fam)* to stutter, stammer

galactosa *f* galactose

galactosemia *f* galactosemia

galantamina *f* galantamine

galeno *m (fam)* doctor

galio *m* gallium

galleta *f* cookie, *(salada)* cracker

galope *m (card)* gallop

gamma *f* gamma

gammaglobulina *f* gamma globulin

gammagrafía *f (técnica)* nuclear scanning, nuclear medicine; *(estudio)* nuclear scan; — **con galio** gallium scanning; gallium scan; — **con talio** thallium scanning; thallium scan; — **ósea** bone scan

gammagrama *m (Mex)* nuclear scan

gammahidroxibutirato *m* gamma-hydroxybutyrate *o* gamma-hydroxybutyric acid (GHB), liquid ecstasy *(fam)*

gammapatía *f* gammopathy; — **monoclonal de significado incierto** monoclonal gammopathy of undetermined significance

ganancia *f* gain; — **de peso** weight gain

ganar *vt* to gain; — **peso** to gain weight

gancho *m (de pañal)* safety pin

ganciclovir *m* ganciclovir

ganglio *m* node; *(neuro)* ganglion; *(quiste)* ganglion cyst; **ganglios basales** basal ganglia; — **centinela** sentinel node; — **linfático** lymph node

ganglión *m (quiste)* ganglion cyst

ganglioneuroma *m* ganglioneuroma

gangoso -sa *adj (person)* having a nasal voice, *(voz)* nasal

gangrena *f* gangrene; — **gaseosa** gas gangrene; — **seca** dry gangrene

gargajear *vi (fam)* to cough up phlegm

gargajo *m (fam)* phlegm

garganta *f* throat

gárgaras *fpl* **hacer** — to gargle

garra *f* claw

garrapata *f* tick

gas *m* gas; **expulsar gases** to pass gas; **gases arteriales** arterial blood gas; **gases de escape** exhaust gases; — **de la risa** laughing gas; **gas hilarante** laughing gas; — **lacrimógeno** tear gas; — **natural** natural gas; — **neuro-**

tóxico *(form)*, — **nervioso** nerve gas; **tener gases** to have gas

gasa *f* gauze

gasolina *f* gasoline, gas *(fam)*

gasometría arterial *f* arterial blood gas

gastar *vi, vr* to wear out

gasto *m* output; — **cardíaco** cardiac output; — **energético de reposo** basal metabolic rate; — **urinario** urine output

gastrectomía *f* gastrectomy; — **en manga** sleeve gastrectomy

gástrico -ca *adj* gastric

gastrina *f* gastrin

gastrinoma *m* gastrinoma

gastritis *f* gastritis

gastrocnemio *m* gastrocnemius

gastroenteritis *f* gastroenteritis

gastroenterología *f* gastroenterology

gastroenterólogo -ga *mf* gastroenterologist

gastroesofágico -ca *adj* gastroesophageal

gastrointestinal (GI) *adj* gastrointestinal (GI)

gastroparesia *f* gastroparesis

gastrostomía *f* gastrostomy; — **endoscópica percutánea (GEP)** percutaneous endoscopic gastrostomy (PEG)

gatear *vi (ped)* to crawl

gatillo *m* trigger

gato *m* cat

gay *adj* gay

GCH *abbr* **gonadotropina coriónica humana**. *See* **gonadotropina**.

gel *m* gel

gelatina *f* gelatin, jelly

gemelo -la *adj & mf* twin; — **idéntico** identical twin; — **unido** *or* **siamés** conjoined twin

gemfibrozilo *m* gemfibrozil

gemido *m* moan, groan

gemir *vi* to moan, groan

gen *m* gene

generación *f* generation; **primera (segunda, tercera, última, etc.)** — first (second, third, latest, etc.) generation

generador *m (de un marcapasos, etc.)* generator

general *adj* general; **por lo** — in general

generalizado -da *adj* generalized

genérico -ca *adj & m (pharm)* generic

género *m* gender

genético -ca *adj* genetic; *f* genetics
genetista *mf* geneticist
genio *m* genius
genital *adj* genital; *mpl* genitals
genoma *m* genome; — **humano** human genome
genotipo *m* genotype
gentamicina *f* gentamicin
gente *f* people, persons
genu valgo *m* genu valgum
genu varo *m* genu varum
GEP *abbr* **gastrostomía endoscópica percutánea.** *See* **gastrostomía.**
geriatra *mf* geriatrician, physician who specializes in aging and associated conditions
geriatría *f* geriatrics, branch of medicine devoted to aging
geriátrico -ca *adj* geriatric; *m* home for the elderly, skilled nursing facility (*for the elderly*)
germen *m* (*pl* **gérmenes**) germ
germinoma *m* germinoma
gerontología *f* gerontology, study of aging
gerontólogo -ga *mf* gerontologist, specialist in aging
gestación *f* gestation
gestacional *adj* gestational
gestionar *vt* to manage
gesto *m* gesture; — **suicida** suicide gesture
gestor -ra *mf* manager; — **de casos** case manager
GI *See* **gastrointestinal.**
giardiasis *f* giardiasis
giba *f* humpback, hunchback, hump
gigante *adj* giant
gigantismo *m* gigantism
gimnasia *f* gymnastics
gimnasio *m* gymnasium, gym (*fam*), health club, fitness center
ginecología *f* gynecology
ginecológico -ca *adj* gynecological
ginecólogo -ga *mf* gynecologist
gingivectomía *f* gingivectomy
gingivitis *f* gingivitis; — **ulcerativa necrotizante aguda** acute necrotizing ulcerative gingivitis
ginkgo biloba *m* (*bot*) ginkgo biloba
ginseng *m* (*bot*) ginseng
glande *m* glans
glándula *f* gland; — **adrenal** (*Ang*) adrenal gland, adrenal (*fam*); — **endocrina** endocrine gland; — **hipofisaria** (*esp. Esp*) pituitary gland; — **lagrimal** or **lacrimal** lacrimal gland; — **mamaria** mammary gland; — **paratiroides** or **paratiroidea** parathyroid gland, parathyroid (*fam*); — **parótida** parotid gland, parotid (*fam*); — **pineal** pineal gland; — **pituitaria** pituitary gland, pituitary (*fam*); — **prostática** prostate gland, prostate (*fam*); — **salival** or **salivar** salivary gland; — **sudorípara** sweat gland; — **suprarrenal** adrenal gland, adrenal (*fam*); — **tiroides** or **tiroidea** thyroid gland, thyroid (*fam*)
glaucoma *m* glaucoma
gliburida, glibenclamida (*INN*) *f* glyburide (*USAN*), glibenclamide (*INN*)
glicerina *f* glycerol, glycerin
glicerol *m* glycerol, glycerin
glicina *f* glycine
glimepirida *f* glimepiride
glioblastoma *m* glioblastoma; — **multiforme** glioblastoma multiforme
glioma *m* glioma
glipizida *f* glipizide
global *adj* global
globo *m* — **ocular** or **del ojo** eyeball
globulina *f* globulin
glóbulo *m* — **blanco** leukocyte (*form*), white blood cell; — **rojo** erythrocyte (*form*), red blood cell
glomerulonefritis *f* glomerulonephritis
glositis *f* glossitis
glotis *f* glottis
glucagón *m* glucagon
glucagonoma *m* glucagonoma
glucemia capilar *f* (*form*) fingerstick glucose
glucocorticoide *adj & m* glucocorticoid
glucómetro *m* (*fam*) (blood) glucose monitor, glucometer (*fam*)
gluconato *m* gluconate; — **cálcico** or **de calcio** calcium gluconate
glucosa *f* glucose
glucosamina *f* glucosamine
glutamato monosódico (GMS) *m* monosodium glutamate (MSG)
glutámico -ca *adj* glutamic
glutamina *f* glutamine
glutaraldehído *m* glutaraldehyde
gluten *m* gluten
glúteo -a *adj* gluteal; *m* buttock

GMS *See* **glutamato monosódico.**

gogles *mpl* (*Mex*) goggles

golondrino *m* axillary hidradenitis suppurativa (*form*), boils under the arms

goloso -sa *adj* **ser** — to have a sweet tooth

golpe *m* blow, stroke; — **de calor** heat-stroke; — **precordial** precordial thump; — **psicológico** psychological blow

golpeado -da *adj* battered; **refugio para mujeres golpeadas** battered women's shelter

golpear *vt* to strike, hit; **Me golpeó aquí** ..It struck (hit) me here.

golpecito *m* pat; **dar golpecitos** to pat

goma *m&f* (*de la sífilis*) gumma; *f* gum; (*caucho*) rubber; — **de mascar** chewing gum; — **espuma** foam rubber

gomaespuma *f* foam rubber

gónada *f* gonad

gonadorelina *f* gonadorelin

gonadotropina, gonadotrofina (*INN*) *f* gonadotropin; — **coriónica humana (GCH)** human chorionic gonadotropin (HCG)

gonce *m* (*CA, fam, articulación*) joint

gonococo *m* gonococcus

gonorrea *f* gonorrhea

gordo -da *adj* fat

gordolobo *m* (*bot*) mullein

gorgotear *vi* (*estómago, etc.*) to gurgle

gorgoteo *m* (*estómago, etc.*) gurgle, gurgling

gorra *f* cap; — **de baño** shower cap

gorro *m* cap; — **de baño** *or* **ducha** shower cap; — **quirúrgico** scrub *o* surgical cap

goserelina *f* goserelin

gota *f* drop; (*enfermedad*) gout; **gotas oftálmicas** (*form*), **gotas para los ojos** ophthalmic drops (*form*), eye drops; **gotas óticas** (*form*), **gotas para los oídos** otic drops (*form*), ear drops

gotear *vi* to drip

goteo *m* drip; — **nasal** nasal drainage; **tener** — **nasal** to have a runny nose; — **posnasal** *or* **postnasal** postnasal drip

gotero *m* eyedropper, medicine dropper

gotoso -sa *adj* gouty

grado *m* grade; (*temperatura*) degree; **Está en el séptimo grado** ..She's in the seventh grade...**37 grados centígrados** ..37 degrees Centigrade; **de bajo** — low-grade; **de alto** — high-grade

graduable *adj* adjustable

graduado -da *adj* graduated

gradual *adj* gradual

gradualmente *adv* gradually

gráfica *f* graph

gráfico *m* graph

gragea *f* coated pill

gramicidina *f* gramicidin

Gram negativo -va *adj* Gram-negative

gramo *m* gram

Gram positivo -va *adj* Gram-positive

grande *adj* big, large; **ponerse más grande** ..to get bigger...**¿Qué tan grande era?** ..How big was it?... **cuando seas grande** ..when you grow up

grandiosidad *f* (*psych*) grandiosity

grandioso -sa *adj* (*psych*) grandiose

granjero -ra *mf* farmer

grano *m* grain, cereal; (*derm*) pimple; **de** — **entero** whole-grain

granulación *f* granulation

gránulo *m* granule

granulocito *m* granulocyte

granuloma *m* granuloma; — **piógeno** pyogenic granuloma

granulomatosis *f* granulomatosis; — **con poliangeítis,** — **de Wegener** (*ant*) granulomatosis with polyangiitis, Wegener's granulomatosis (*ant*)

grapa *f* (*surg*) staple, clip

grasiento -ta *adj* greasy, oily

graso -sa *adj* fatty, oily, greasy; **cabello** — oily hair; **comida** — greasy food; **cutis graso** oily skin *o* complexion; **hígado** — fatty liver; **piel grasa** oily skin; *f* fat, grease; — **animal** animal fat; — **de leche** milk fat; — **insaturada** unsaturated fat; — **saturada** saturated fat; — **trans** trans fat

grasoso -sa *adj* fatty, oily, greasy; **piel grasosa** oily skin

gratificación *f* (*psych, etc.*) gratification

gratuito -ta *adj* free; **atención médica** — free medical care, free health care

grave *adj* (*condición*) serious, grave; (*tono*) low-pitched; **¿Es grave?** ..Is it serious?

gravedad *f* severity

gray *m* (*rad*) gray

greta *f* toxic Mexican folk remedy con-

taining lead
grieta *f* crack, split
gripa (*Amer, fam*) *See* **gripe**.
gripal *adj* pertaining to influenza *o* flu;
— **temporada** — flu season
gripe *f* influenza (*form*), flu; — **asiática**
Asian influenza *o* flu; — **aviar** avian
influenza, bird flu; — **estacional** seasonal influenza *o* flu; — **estomacal**
gastroenteritis (*form*), stomach flu; —
porcina swine influenza *o* flu
gris *adj* gray
grisáceo -a *adj* grayish
griseofulvina *f* griseofulvin
gritar *vi* to cry, to call out
grito *m* cry; — **de auxilio** *or* **socorro** cry
for help
grosor *m* thickness
grúa *f* crane, lift; — **para levantar pacientes** patient lift
grueso -sa *adj* thick
gruñido *m* grunt
gruñir *vi* to grunt
grupo *m* group; — **de apoyo** support

group; — **de edad** age group; — **de
iguales**, — **de pares** (*Ang*) peer group;
— **etario** (*form*) age group; — **sanguíneo (A, B, etc.)** blood type (A, B, etc.)
guabucho *m* (*PR, SD; fam*) lump, bump
(*due to trauma*)
guaifenesina *f* guaifenesin
guanfacina *f* guanfacine
guante *m* glove
guardar cama *vt* to stay in bed
guardería infantil *f* nursery, day care
center
guardia *f* **de** — on call
güero -ra (*Mex*) *m* blond; *f* blond *o*
blonde
guerra *f* war; — **nuclear** nuclear war
guerrero -ra *mf* — **de fin de semana**
weekend warrior
guía *f* guideline; (*orientación*) guidance
guineo *m* (*Carib*) banana
gusano *m* worm; — **plano** flatworm; —
redondo roundworm
gusto *m* taste, flavor; (*placer*) pleasure
gutural *adj* guttural

H

habilidad *f* skill, ability; **habilidades
comunicativas** *or* **de comunicación**
communication skills; **habilidades de
afrontamiento** coping skills; **habilidades parentales** parenting skills; **habilidades sociales** social skills
habitación *f* room, bedroom
hábito *m* habit; **hábitos alimenticios**
eating habits; **mal** — bad habit
habituación *f* habituation
habituado -da *adj* habituated
habitual *adj* habitual, usual; (*continuo*)
continual; **la hora habitual**..the usual
time

habla *f* speech; **desarrollo del** — speech
development; — **apresurada** pres-
sured speech; — **esofágica** esophageal
speech
hablar *vt, vi* to speak, to talk
hacer *vt* hace tres años..three years ago.
..¿**Hace cuánto que tiene artritis?**..
How long have you had arthritis?; —
caca (*esp. ped, fam or vulg*) to have a
bowel movement; **hacer(le) caso** to
mind; — **daño** to hurt, to harm; —
efecto to take effect; — **frente a** to
face, confront, (*lidiar con*) to cope
with; — **pipí** (*ped, fam*) to urinate, to

go pee pee (*ped, fam*); — **pis** (*fam or vulg*) to urinate, to pee (*fam*); — **popó** *or* **pupú** (*fam*) to have a bowel movement, to go poo poo (*ped, fam*); *vi* — **del baño** (*Mex, fam*), — **del cuerpo** (*Carib*), — **de(l) vientre** (*Esp*) to have a bowel movement; *vr* — **una** *or* **la paja** (*vulg*) to masturbate, to jack off (*vulg*), to jerk off (*vulg*)

haces *pl of* **haz**

hachís *m* hashish

hacinamiento *m* overcrowding

HACT *abbr* **hormona adrenocorticotrópica.** *See* **hormona.**

halitosis *f* halitosis

hallazgo *m* finding

hallux valgus *m* hallux valgus

hallux varus *m* hallux varus

halo *m* halo

haloperidol *m* haloperidol

halotano *m* halothane

hamartoma *m* hamartoma

hambre *f* hunger; **tener** — to be hungry

hantavirus *m* (*pl* -**rus**) hantavirus

harina *f* flour

haz *m* (*pl* **haces**) (*luz, rayos X, etc.*) beam

hebilla *f* buckle

heces *fpl* feces,, stool(s), bowel movement(s)

hecho -cha *adj* **poco** — (*carne*) rare

helado -da *adj* frozen, cold; *m* ice cream

hélice *f* helix; **doble** — double helix

helicoidal *adj* helical

helio *m* helium

hemangioma *m* hemangioma; — **cavernoso** cavernous hemangioma; — **plano** port-wine stain

hematíe *m* (*form*) red blood cell

hematocele *m* hematocele

hematocrito *m* hematocrit

hematología *f* hematology

hematólogo -ga *mf* hematologist

hematoma *m* hematoma; — **subdural** subdural hematoma

hembra *adj & f* female

hemiplejía, hemiplejia *f* hemiplegia

hemisferio *m* hemisphere

hemocromatosis *f* hemochromatosis

hemocultivo *m* (*form*) blood culture

hemodiálisis *f* hemodialysis

hemofilia *f* hemophilia

hemofílico -ca *adj* pertaining to hemophilia; *mf* hemophiliac, person with hemophilia

hemoglobina *f* hemoglobin; — **A1c** hemoglobin A1c; — **glicosilada, glucosilada** *or* **glicada** glycosylated *o* glycated hemoglobin

hemoglobinuria *f* hemoglobinuria; — **paroxística nocturna** paroxysmal nocturnal hemoglobinuria

hemograma completo *m* complete blood count (CBC)

hemólisis *f* hemolysis

hemolítico -ca *adj* hemolytic

hemorragia *f* hemorrhage, bleeding, bleed; — **digestiva (alta, baja)** (upper, lower) GI bleed; — **nasal** nosebleed, bloody nose (*fam*); — **subaracnoidea** subarachnoid hemorrhage

hemorrágico -ca *adj* hemorrhagic

hemorroide *f* hemorrhoid

hemorroidectomía *f* hemorrhoidectomy

hemosiderosis *f* hemosiderosis

hendidura *f* crack, gap, split

henna *f* (*bot*) henna

heno *m* hay

heparina *f* heparin; — **de bajo peso molecular** low-molecular-weight heparin

hepático -ca *adj* hepatic

hepatitis *f* hepatitis; — **A (B, C, etc.)** hepatitis A (B, C, etc.)

hepatología *f* hepatology

hepatólogo -ga *mf* hepatologist

hepatoma *m* hepatoma

hepatorrenal *adj* hepatorenal

herbal *adj* herbal

herbario -ria *adj* herbal

herbicida *m* herbicide

herbolario -ria *mf* herbalist, person who sells or prescribes herbs

herborista *mf* herbalist, person who sells or prescribes herbs

heredable *adj* heritable

heredar *vt* to inherit

hereditario -ria *adj* hereditary

herencia *f* heredity

herido -da *adj* injured, wounded; *mf* wounded person; *f* injury, wound, cut, sore; — **de bala** gunshot wound; — **penetrante** penetrating wound; — **punzante** puncture wound

herir *vt* to injure, to wound

hermafrodita *adj & mf* hermaphrodite

hermafroditismo *m* hermaphroditism

hermanastro -tra *m* stepbrother; *f* stepsister

hermano -na *m* brother, sibling; *f* sister; — **siamés** conjoined twin

hernia *f* hernia; — **crural** femoral hernia; — **de hiato** hiatal hernia; — **estrangulada** strangulated hernia; — **femoral** femoral hernia; — **hiatal** hiatal hernia; — **incarcerada** incarcerated hernia; — **incisional** incisional hernia; — **inguinal** inguinal hernia; — **reductible** *or* **reducible** *or* **simple** reducible hernia; — **umbilical** umbilical hernia

herniorrafia *f* herniorrhaphy

heroína *f* heroin; — **marrón** black tar heroin

heroinómano -na *mf* heroin addict

herpangina *f* herpangina

herpes *m* herpes; — **labial** labial herpes, cold sore (*fam*), fever blister (*fam*); — **simple** herpes simplex; — **zóster** herpes zoster, shingles

herpesvirus *m* (*pl* **-rus**) herpesvirus; — **humano 6 (8, etc.)** human herpesvirus 6 (8, etc.)

herpético -ca *adj* herpetic

hervido -da *adj* boiled; **agua** — boiled water

hervir *vt* (*also* **hacer** —) to boil; *vi* to boil

heterosexual *adj* & *mf* heterosexual

HFE *abbr* **hormona folículo estimulante.** *See* **hormona.**

hiato *m* (*anat*) hiatus; **de** — hiatal

hidatídico -ca *adj* hydatid

hidatiforme, hidatidiforme *adj* (*obst*) hydatidiform

hidradenitis supurativa *f* hidradenitis suppurativa

hidralazina, hidralacina (*esp. Esp*) *f* hydralazine

hidratante *adj* moisturizing; *m&f* moisturizer

hidratar *vt* to hydrate, (*la piel*) to moisturize

hidrato *m* hydrate; — **de carbono** carbohydrate; — **de cloral** chloral hydrate

hidrocarburo, hidrocarbono *m* hydrocarbon

hidrocefalia *f* hydrocephalus; — **normotensiva** normal pressure hydrocephalus

hidrocele *m* hydrocele

hidroclorotiazida *f* hydrochlorothiazide

hidrocodona *f* hydrocodone

hidrocoloide *m* hydrocolloid

hidrocortisona *f* hydrocortisone

hidrofobia *f* hydrophobia

hidrogel *m* hydrogel

hidrogenado -da *adj* hydrogenated

hidromasaje *m* whirlpool therapy

hidromorfona *f* hydromorphone

hidronefrosis *f* hydronephrosis

hidroquinona *f* hydroquinone

hidroterapia *f* hydrotherapy; — **de colon** colon hydrotherapy, colonic irrigation, colonic (*fam*)

hidroxicarbamida *f* hydroxyurea, hydroxycarbamide (*INN*)

hidroxicina, hidroxizina (*INN*) *f* hydroxyzine

hidroxicloroquina *f* hydroxychloroquine

hidróxido *m* hydroxide; — **de aluminio** aluminum hydroxide; — **de potasio** potassium hydroxide; — **de sodio** sodium hydroxide; — **potásico** potassium hydroxide; — **sódico** sodium hydroxide

hidroxiurea *f* hydroxyurea, hydroxycarbamide (*INN*)

hiedra venenosa *f* (*bot*) poison ivy

hielo *m* ice; **pedacitos** *or* **trocitos de** — ice chips

hierba *f* grass; (*planta medicinal*) herb; (*fam, marihuana*) marijuana, pot (*fam*), grass (*fam*); — **de San Juan** St. John's wort

hierbabuena *f* (*bot*) spearmint, peppermint, mint

hierbatero -ra *mf* (*Amer*) herbalist, person who sells or prescribes herbs

hierbero -ra *mf* herbalist, person who sells or prescribes herbs

hierro *m* iron

hifema *See* **hipema.**

hígado *m* liver; — **graso** fatty liver

higiene *f* hygiene; — **bucal** oral hygiene

higiénico -ca *adj* hygienic, sanitary

higienista *mf* hygienist; — **dental** dental hygienist

hijastro -tra *m* stepson, stepchild; *f* stepdaughter

hijo -ja *m* son, child; — **de crianza** foster child; — **único** only child; *f* daughter

hilo dental *m* dental floss

himen *m* hymen; — **imperforado** imper-

forate hymen
hinchado -da *adj* swollen, puffy, bloated
hincharse *vr* to swell (up); (*estómago*) to get bloated
hinchazón *f* swelling; (*del estómago*) bloating
hioides *m* hyoid bone
hioscina *f* hyoscine
hipar *vi* to hiccup
hipema *m* hyphema
hiperactividad *f* hyperactivity
hiperactivo -va *adj* hyperactive, overactive
hiperalimentación *f* (*sobrealimentación*) hyperalimentation; (*ant, NPT*) total parenteral nutrition (TPN)
hiperbárico -ca *adj* hyperbaric
hipercalcemia *f* hypercalcemia
hiperemesis gravídica *f* (*obst*) hyperemesis gravidarum
hiperextensible *adj* double-jointed
hiperfuncionante *adj* hyperfunctioning
hiperglucemia See **hiperglucemia**.
hiperglicémico See **hiperglucémico**.
hiperglucemia *f* hyperglycemia
hiperglucémico -ca *adj* hyperglycemic
hiperhidrosis *f* hyperhidrosis
hipérico *m* (*bot*) St. John's wort
hiperlipidemia *f* hyperlipidemia
hipermétrope *adj* (*form*) farsighted
hipermetropía *f* (*form*) farsightedness
hipermóvil *adj* hypermobile
hipernatremia *f* hypernatremia
hiperosmolar *adj* hyperosmolar
hiperparatiroideo -a *adj* hyperparathyroid
hiperparatiroidismo *m* hyperparathyroidism
hiperpigmentación *f* hyperpigmentation
hiperplasia *f* hyperplasia; — **prostática benigna** benign prostatic hyperplasia; — **suprarrenal congénita** congenital adrenal hyperplasia
hiperplásico -ca *adj* hyperplastic
hiperprolactinemia *f* hyperprolactinemia
hipersensibilidad *f* hypersensitivity
hipersensible *adj* hypersensitive
hipertensión *f* (*arterial*) hypertension, high blood pressure (*fam*); — **de bata blanca** white-coat hypertension; — **intracraneal benigna** benign intracranial hypertension; — **esencial** essential

hypertension; — **maligna** malignant hypertension; — **portal** portal hypertension; — **pulmonar** pulmonary hypertension; — **renovascular** renovascular hypertension
hipertermia *f* hyperthermia
hipertiroideo -a *adj* hyperthyroid
hipertiroidismo *m* hyperthyroidism
hipertrofia *f* hypertrophy, enlargement
hipertrófico -ca *adj* hypertrophic
hiperuricemia *f* hyperuricemia
hiperventilación *f* hyperventilation
hiperventilar *vi* to hyperventilate
hipnosis *f* hypnosis
hipnótico -ca *adj & m* hypnotic
hipnotismo *m* hypnotism
hipnotista *mf* hypnotist
hipnotizador -ra *mf* hypnotist
hipnotizar *vt* to hypnotize
hipo *m* hiccup; **tener —** to have the hiccups, to hiccup
hipoalergénico -ca *adj* hypoallergenic
hipocalcemia *f* hypocalcemia
hipocaliemia *f* hypokalemia
hipocampo *m* hippocampus
hipocondría *f* somatiform disorder, hypochondriasis (*ant*)
hipocondríaco, hipocondriaco -ca *mf* person who worries excessively about his or her health, hypochondriac (*ant*)
hipocratismo digital *m* (*form*) clubbing
hipodérmico -ca *adj* hypodermic
hipofisario -ria *adj* pituitary
hipófisis *f* pituitary gland, pituitary (*fam*)
hipoglicemia See **hipoglucemia**.
hipoglicémico See **hipoglucémico**.
hipoglucemia *f* hypoglycemia
hipoglucemiante *adj* hypoglycemic (*causing hypoglycemia*); *m* hypoglycemic agent; — **oral** oral hypoglycemic agent
hipoglucémico -ca *adj* hypoglycemic (*pertaining to hypoglycemia*); **reacción hipoglucémica** hypoglycemic reaction
hiponatremia *f* hyponatremia
hipoparatiroideo -a *adj* hypoparathyroid
hipoparatiroidismo *m* hypoparathyroidism
hipopigmentación *f* hypopigmentation
hipopituitarismo *m* hypopituitarism
hipopnea *m* hypopnea

hipopotasemia *f* hypokalemia
hipospadias *m* hypospadias
hipotálamo *m* hypothalamus
hipotensión *f* hypotension; — **ortostática** orthostatic hypotension
hipotensor -ra *adj* hypotensive
hipotermia *f* hypothermia
hipotiroideo -a *adj* hypothyroid
hipotiroidismo *m* hypothyroidism
hipovolémico -ca *adj* hypovolemic
hirsutismo *m* hirsutism
hirsuto -ta *adj* hirsute
hirviendo -da *adj* boiling; **agua** — boiling water
hisopo *m* swab
histamina *f* histamine
histerectomía *f* hysterectomy; — **abdominal total** total abdominal hysterectomy; — **vaginal** vaginal hysterectomy
histeria *f* (*ant*) anxiety attack, severe anxiety, hysteria (*ant*)
histérico -ca *adj* severely anxious, anxiety-related, hysterical (*ant*)
histidina *f* histidine
histiocitosis *f* histiocytosis
histología *f* histology
histológico -ca *adj* histologic
histoplasmosis *f* histoplasmosis
historia *f* history; — **clínica** medical history; (*documento*) medical record, patient chart; — **clínica electrónica** electronic health record; — **clínica personal** personal health record; — **clínica y examen físico** history and physical; — **de la enfermedad actual** history of the present illness; — **natural** (*de una enfermedad*) natural history
historial médico *m* medical history; (*documento*) medical record, patient chart
histriónico -ca *adj* histrionic
hito del desarrollo *m* developmental milestone
HL *abbr* hormona luteinizante. *See* **hormona**.
hogar *m* home; — **de ancianos** skilled nursing facility, nursing home (*fam*), board and care; — **médico** medical home; **sin** — homeless
hoja *f* (*de cuchillo, etc.*) blade; — **de afeitar** razor blade
holismo *m* holism
holístico -ca *adj* holistic
hombre *m* man, male

hombro *m* shoulder; — **congelado** adhesive capsulitis (*form*), frozen shoulder
homeópata *mf* homeopath
homeopatía *f* homeopathy
homeopático -ca *adj* homeopathic
homofobia *f* homophobia
homofóbico -ca *adj* homophobic
homosexual *adj* homosexual, gay; *m* homosexual *o* gay man; *f* lesbian, homosexual *o* gay woman
hondo -da *adj* deep
hongo *m* fungus, yeast, mushroom; — **venenoso** poisonous mushroom; **infección** *f* **por hongos** fungal infection, yeast infection
honorarios *mpl* fee, bill
hora *f* hour, time; **¿A qué hora comió?..** What time did you eat?..When did you eat?; **horas de consulta** office hours; **horas de visita** visiting hours
horario *m* schedule; **horario(s) de consulta** office hours; **horario(s) de visita** visiting hours
horizontal *adj* horizontal
hormiga *f* ant; — **de fuego** fire ant
hormiguear *vi* to tingle
hormigueo *m* tingling
hormiguicida *m* ant poison
hormona *f* hormone; — **adrenocorticotrópica (HACT)** adrenocorticotropic hormone (ACTH), corticotropin; — **antidiurética** antidiuretic hormone, vasopressin; — **de crecimiento bovina** bovine growth hormone; — **de(l) crecimiento (humana)** (human) growth hormone (GH); — **estimulante del** *or* **de la tiroides** thyroid-stimulating hormone (TSH), thyrotropin; — **folículo estimulante (HFE)** follicle-stimulating hormone (FSH); — **liberadora de gonadotropina(s)** gonadotropin-releasing hormone (GnRH); — **luteinizante (HL)** luteinizing hormone (LH); — **paratiroidea (HPT)** parathyroid hormone (PTH); — **tiroidea** thyroid hormone
hormonal *adj* hormonal
hormonoterapia *f* hormone *o* hormonal therapy
horneado -da *adj* baked
hornear *vt* to bake
horno *m* **al** — baked
hortaliza *f* vegetable

hortensia *f* (*bot*) hydrangea

hospedador *m* (*parasitología*) host

hospital *m* hospital; — **comunitario** community hospital; — **de enseñanza** teaching hospital; — **del condado** county hospital; — **de tercer nivel** tertiary care hospital; — **de veteranos** Veterans Affairs (VA) hospital; — **general** general hospital; — **mental** psychiatric hospital, mental institution; — **privado** private hospital; — **psiquiátrico** psychiatric hospital, mental institution; — **público** public hospital; — **terciario** (*esp. Esp*) tertiary care hospital; — **universitario** university hospital, teaching hospital

hospitalario -ria *adj* pertaining to a hospital

hospitalizar *vt* to hospitalize

hostigamiento *m* (*ped*) bullying

hostigar *vt* (*ped*) to bully

hostil *adj* hostile

hostilidad *f* hostility

hoy *adv* today

hoyo *m* hole

hoyuelo *m* dimple

HPT *abbr* **hormona paratiroidea**. *See* **hormona**.

hueco -ca *adj* hollow; *m* hollow, hole; — **de la mano** hollow of the hand

huérfano -na *mf* orphan

huesecillo *m* (*del oído*) ossicle (*of the ear*)

huesero -ra *mf* (*esp. Mex, fam*) person who treats disorders of bones and joints

hueso *m* bone; — **de la cadera** hip bone; — **del pecho** breast bone; — **del tobillo** ankle bone; — **ilíaco** or **iliaco** ilium (*form*), hip bone; *mpl* (*Mex, CA; fam; articulaciones*) joints; **Se me hinchan los huesos**..My joints swell.

huésped *m* (*parasitología*) host

huevecillo *m* small egg (*of a parasite, etc.*)

huevo *m* egg; (*fam, óvulo*) ovum, egg (*fam*); (*esp. Mex, fam*) testicle, ball (*fam o vulg*)

hule *m* rubber; — **espuma** foam rubber

humanitario -ria *adj* humanitarian

humano -na *adj & m* human; **ser humano** human being

humectador *m* humidifier

humectante *adj* moisturizing

humedad *f* humidity, dampness, moisture

humedecer *vt* to humidify, moisturize, moisten

húmedo -da *adj* humid, damp, moist

humeral *adj* humeral, of the humerus

húmero *m* humerus

humidificador *m* humidifier

humidificar *vt* to humidify

humo *m* smoke, fumes; — **ambiental del tabaco**, — **de tabaco de segunda mano** secondhand tobacco smoke

humor *m* humor; (*psych*) mood, spirits; (*anat*) humor; **El humor es la mejor terapia**..Humor is the best therapy; **estar de buen** — to be in a good mood; **estar de mal** — to be in a bad mood; — **acuoso** aqueous humor; — **vítreo** vitreous humor; **oscilaciones** *fpl* **del** — mood swings

huracán *m* hurricane

hurgarse *vt* — **la nariz** to pick one's nose

I

ibandronato, ibandronato sódico *m* ibandronate, ibandronate sodium (*USAN*), ibandronic acid (*INN*)
ibuprofeno, ibuprofen *m* ibuprofen
icaridina *f* icaridin, picaridin
ICP *abbr* **intervención coronaria percutánea.** *See* **intervención.**
ictericia *f* (*form*) jaundice
ictiosis *f* ichthyosis
ictus *m* (*pl* **ictus**) (*form*) cerebrovascular accident, stroke
id *m* (*psych*) id
IDAC *abbr* **injerto de derivación arterial coronaria.** *See* **injerto.**
idea *f* idea; **ideas de referencia** (*psych*) ideas of reference
ideal *adj* ideal
idealización *f* (*psych*) idealization
idéntico -ca *adj* identical
identidad *f* identity; — **de género** gender identity; — **étnica** ethnicity
identificación *f* identification (ID)
identificar *vt* to identify; *vr* — **con** to identify with
idiopático -ca *adj* idiopathic
ido -da *adj* absent-minded, spacey (*fam*), spaced out (*fam*)
idóneo -a *adj* suitable
ignorante *adj* (*inconsciente*) unaware
ileal *adj* ileal
ileítis *f* ileitis
íleo *m* ileus
íleon *m* ileum, distal portion of the small intestine; (*ilion*) ilium, hip bone (*fam*)
ileostomía *f* ileostomy
ilíaco, iliaco -ca *adj* iliac; **hueso** — ilium (*form*), hip bone (*fam*)
ilion *m* ilium, hip bone (*fam*)
ilusión *f* illusion
IM *See* **intramuscular.**
imagen *f* (*pl* **imágenes**) image; (*frec. pl, imaginología*) imaging; — **corporal** body image; **diagnóstico por imagen** *or* **imágenes** diagnostic imaging; **estudio por imagen** *or* **imágenes** imaging study; **imagen** *or* **imágenes por resonancia magnética (IRM)** magnetic resonance imaging (MRI)
imagenología *f* imaging

imagenológico -ca *adj* pertaining to imaging
imaginología *f* imaging
imaginológico -ca *adj* pertaining to imaging
IMC *abbr* **índice de masa corporal.** *See* **índice.**
imipenem *m* imipenem
imipramina *f* imipramine
imiquimod *m* imiquimod
imitar *vt* to mimic
impactación *f* impaction; — **fecal** fecal impaction
impactado -da *adj* (*dent, etc.*) impacted
impacto *m* impact; **bajo** — low impact
impedimento *m* impediment
imperdible *m* safety pin
imperforado -da *adj* imperforate
impétigo *m* impetigo
implantación *f* implantation
implantar *vt* to implant
implante *m* implant; — **coclear** cochlear implant; — **de silicona** silicone implant; — **mamario** breast implant
imposible *adj* impossible
impotencia *f* (*sexual*) erectile dysfunction, impotence (*ant*)
impotente *adj* (*sexualmente*) having erectile dysfunction, impotent (*ant*)
impresión *f* (*dent, etc.*) impression
imprevisto -ta *adj* unexpected
impulsar *vt* (*sangre*) to pump (*blood*)
impulsivo -va *adj* impulsive
impulso *m* (*sexual, etc.*) drive
impureza *f* impurity
inactivado -da *adj* inactivated
inactividad *f* inactivity
inactivo -va *adj* inactive
inadecuado -da *adj* unsuitable, inappropriate
inafectado -da *adj* unaffected
inanición *f* starvation
inapropiado -da *adj* inappropriate
incapacidad *f* inability, disability
incapacitado -da *adj* incapacitated, (*discapacitado*) disabled
incapacitante *adj* incapacitating, disabling
incapaz *adj* incapable, unable

incarcerado -da *adj* incarcerated
incendio *m* fire
incertidumbre *f* uncertainty
incesto *m* incest
incestuoso -sa *adj* incestuous
incidencia *f* incidence
incidentaloma *m* (*Ang*) incidentaloma
incisión *f* incision; — **y drenaje** incision and drainage (I&D)
incisivo *m* incisor, front tooth; — **inferior central** lower *o* mandibular central incisor; — **superior lateral** upper *o* maxillary lateral incisor
inclinar *vt* — **la cabeza** to nod; *vr* to lean (forward); **Inclínese hacia adelante..Lean forward.**
incluido -da *adj* (*dent*) impacted
inclusión dentaria *f* (*Esp*) dental impaction
incoherente *adj* incoherent
incoloro -ra *adj* colorless
incombustible *adj* nonflammable
incómodo -da *adj* uncomfortable
incompatible *adj* incompatible
incompetencia *f* incompetence; — **cervical** cervical incompetence
incompetente *adj* incompetent
incompleto -ta *adj* incomplete
inconsciente, inconciente *adj* unconscious, unaware; (*psych*) unconscious; **mente** — unconscious mind, unconscious (*fam*); *m* (*fam, mente inconsciente*) unconscious mind, unconscious (*fam*)
incontinencia *f* incontinence; — **de esfuerzo** stress incontinence; — **de urgencia** urge incontinence; — **fecal** fecal incontinence; — **por rebosamiento** overflow incontinence; — **urinaria** urinary incontinence
incontinente *adj* incontinent
inconveniente *m* problem, disadvantage
incrementar *vt* to increase
incrustación inlay *f* (*dent*) inlay
incubadora *f* incubator
incurable *adj* incurable
indefensión *f* (*psych, etc.*) helplessness; — **aprendida** learned helplessness
indefenso -sa *adj* (*psych, etc.*) helpless
independiente *adj* independent
indeseable *adj* undesirable
indeseado -da *adj* unwanted, unintended
indetectable *adj* undetectable

indicación *f* indication; (*orden*) order
indicar *vt* (*ordenar*) to order
índice *m* index; — **de Apgar** (*esp. Esp*) Apgar score; — **de éxito** success rate; — **de masa corporal (IMC)** body mass index (BMI); — **glucémico** *or* **glicémico** glycemic index; — **tobillo-brazo** ankle-brachial index
indiferencia *f* indifference
indiferenciado -da *adj* undifferentiated
indigestión *f* indigestion
indinavir *m* indinavir
indistinto -ta *adj* indistinct
individuo *m* individual, person
indoloro -ra *adj* painless
indometacina *f* indomethacin
inducción *f* induction
inducido -da *adj* induced; — **por el ejercicio** exercise-induced
inducir *vt* to induce
induración *f* induration, hardening
indurado -da *adj* indurated, hardened
ineficaz *adj* ineffective
inerte *adj* inert
inespecífico -ca *adj* nonspecific
inesperado -da *adj* unexpected
inestabilidad *f* instability
inestable *adj* unstable
inevitable *adj* unavoidable
infancia *f* (early) childhood (*till puberty*); [*Nota:* infancy *se refiere a la primer etapa de vida, más o menos el primer año, y no quiere decir* infancia.]
infantil *adj* infantile
infarto *m* infarct, infarction; — **cerebral** (non-hemorrhagic) stroke; — **de miocardio** myocardial infarction, heart attack (*fam*)
infección *f* infection; — **del tracto urinario (ITU),** — **de orina** (*fam*) urinary tract infection (UTI); — **de transmisión sexual (ITS)** sexually transmitted disease (STD); — **de vejiga** bladder infection; — **fúngica** *or* **micótica** fungal infection; — **por hongos** fungal infection, (*levaduras*) yeast infection; — **de las vías respiratorias superiores** *or* **altas** upper respiratory tract infection
infeccioso -sa *adj* infectious; **enfermedad infecciosa** infectious disease
infectado -da *adj* infected; — **con** *or* **por** infected with

infectar *vt* to infect; *vr* to become infected

infectólogo -ga *mf* (*Amer*) infectious disease specialist

infeliz *adj* unhappy

inferior *adj* (*anat*) inferior, lower; — **a** lower than, below; **inferior a 70**..lower than (below) 70

infértil *adj* infertile

infertilidad *f* infertility

infestación *f* infestation; — **de** *or* **por** infestation with *o* of

infestado -da *adj* infested; — **de** infested with

infestar *vt* to infest; *vr* — **de** to become infested with

infiltración *f* infiltration

infiltrante *adj* infiltrative, infiltrating

infiltrar *vt, vr* to infiltrate

inflamable *adj* flammable, inflammable; **no** — nonflammable

inflamación *f* inflammation

inflamar *vt* to inflame; *vr* to become inflamed

inflamatorio -ria *adj* inflammatory

infliximab *m* infliximab

influenza *f* influenza, flu (*fam*); — **aviar** avian influenza, bird flu; — **estacional** seasonal influenza *o* flu; — **porcina** swine influenza *o* flu

información *f* information, data

informe *m* report; — **de alta**, — **clínico de alta** (*Esp*) discharge summary; — **quirúrgico** operative report

infraorbitario -ria *adj* infraorbital

infrarrojo -ja *adj* infrared

infundir *vt* to infuse

infusión *f* infusion; (*de hierbas*) infusion, herbal tea

ingeniería *f* engineering; — **genética** genetic engineering

ingerir *vt* to ingest

ingesta *f* intake; — **diaria admisible** tolerable daily intake; — **diaria recomendada** recommended daily intake

ingestión *f* ingestion

ingle *f* groin, pubic area

ingrediente *m* ingredient; — **activo** active ingredient

ingresar *vt* (*al hospital*) to admit (*to a hospital*)

ingreso *m* (*al hospital*) admission (*to a hospital*)

inguinal *adj* inguinal

inhalación *f* inhalation; — **de humo** smoke inhalation

inhalador *m* inhaler; — **de dosis medida** metered-dose inhaler; — **de polvo seco** dry powder inhaler; — **dosificador** (*esp. Esp*) metered-dose inhaler; — **nasal** nasal inhaler

inhalar *vt, vi* to inhale, breathe in; (*pegamento, gasolina*) to sniff, (*cocaína, heroína, anfetaminas*) to snort (*fam*), to sniff

inhibición *f* inhibition

inhibido -da *adj* inhibited

inhibidor -ra *adj* inhibiting; *m* inhibitor; — **de (la) fusión** fusion inhibitor; — **de la bomba de protones** proton pump inhibitor; — **de la colinesterasa** cholinesterase inhibitor; — **de la enzima convertidora de angiotensina** angiotensin converting enzyme inhibitor; — **de la integrasa** integrase inhibitor; — **de la monoaminooxidasa** monoamine oxidase inhibitor; — **del apetito** appetite suppressant; — **de la proteasa** protease inhibitor; — **no nucleósido de la transcriptasa inversa** non-nucleoside reverse transcriptase inhibitor (NNRTI); — **nucleósido de la transcriptasa inversa** *or* **reversa** nucleoside reverse transcriptase inhibitor (NRTI); — **nucleótido de la transcriptasa inversa** *or* **reversa** nucleotide reverse transcriptase inhibitor (NtRTI); — **selectivo de la recaptación de serotonina** selective serotonin reuptake inhibitor

inhibir *vt* to inhibit, (*el apetito, un deseo, etc.*) to curb

inicial *adj* initial; *fpl* initials

inicio *m* onset; **de** — **juvenil** juvenile-onset; **de** — **precoz** early-onset; **de** — **tardío** late-onset; **edad** *f* **de** — **age at** onset

injertar *vt* (*pp* **injertado** *or* **injerto**) to graft

injerto (*pp of* **injertar**) *m* graft ; — **cutáneo** skin graft; — **de derivación arterial coronaria (IDAC)** coronary artery bypass graft (CABG); — **de hueso** bone graft; — **de piel** skin graft

inmadurez *f* immaturity

inmaduro -ra *adj* immature; (*fruta*)

green, not yet ripe
inmediatamente *adv* immediately
inmediato -ta *adj* immediate
inmersión *f* immersion
inmóvil *adj* immobile
inmovilización *f* immobilization
inmovilizador *m* immobilizer; — **de hombro** shoulder immobilizer
inmovilizar *vt* to immobilize; (*contener*) to restrain
inmune *adj* immune; — **a** immune to
inmunidad *f* immunity; — **a** *or* **contra** immunity to; — **colectiva** *or* **de grupo** herd immunity
inmunitario -ria *adj* immune-related, immune
inmunización *f* immunization
inmunizador -ra *adj* immunizing
inmunizante *adj* immunizing
inmunizar *vt* to immunize
inmunocompetente *adj* immunocompetent
inmunocomprometido -da *adj* immunocompromised
inmunodeficiencia *f* immunodeficiency; — **variable común** common variable immunodeficiency
inmunodeficiente *adj* immunodeficient
inmunodepresión *f* immunodepression
inmunodepresor -ra *adj* immunodepressive
inmunodeprimido -da *adj* immunodepressed
inmunoglobulina *f* immunoglobulin; (*producto sanguíneo*) immune globulin
inmunología *f* immunology
inmunológico -ca *adj* immunological *o* immunologic, immune
inmunólogo -ga *mf* immunologist
inmunomodulador *m* immune modulator
inmunosupresión *f* immunosuppression
inmunosupresor *m* immunosuppressant
inmunosuprimido -da *adj* immunosuppressed
inmunoterapia *f* immunotherapy
inoculación *f* inoculation
inocular *vt* to inoculate
inodoro -ra *adj* odorless; *m* toilet, potty (*ped, fam*); **taza del** — toilet bowl
inofensivo -va *adj* (*que no hace daño*) harmless
inoperable *adj* inoperable

inorgánico -ca *adj* inorganic
inquieto -ta *adj* restless
inquietud *f* worry, anxiety, concern; restlessness; **responder a sus inquietudes** ..to address your concerns
insalubre *adj* unhealthy, unsanitary
insaturado -da *adj* unsaturated
inscripción *f* (*seguros, etc.*) enrollment
insecticida *adj* insecticidal; *m* insecticide
insecto *m* insect
inseguridad *f* insecurity
inseguro -ra *adj* insecure
inseminación *f* insemination; — **artificial** artificial insemination
inseminar *vt* to inseminate
insertar *vt* to insert, introduce
in situ, in situ
insolación *f* sunstroke, heatstroke
insoluble *adj* insoluble
insomnio *m* insomnia
insoportable *adj* unbearable
inspirar *vt, vi* to inhale, breathe in
instinto *m* instinct; — **maternal** maternal instinct
institucionalizado -da *adj* institutionalized
instrucción *f* instruction; *fpl* (*de un medicamento*) package insert
instrumento *m* instrument
insuficiencia *f* insufficiency, failure; (*valvular*) regurgitation; — **aórtica (mitral, etc.)** aortic (mitral, etc.) insufficiency *o* regurgitation; — **cardíaca con fracción de eyección preservada** heart failure with preserved ejection fraction; — **cardíaca congestiva** congestive heart failure; — **hepática** liver failure; — **renal (aguda, crónica)** (acute, chronic) renal insufficiency *o* failure; — **respiratoria** respiratory failure; — **suprarrenal** adrenal failure; — **venosa** venous insufficiency
insuficiente *adj* insufficient
insulina *f* insulin; **análogo de** — insulin analogue; — **aspart**, — **asparta** (*INN*) insulin aspart; — **basal** basal insulin; — **de acción intermedia** intermediate-acting insulin; — **de acción prolongada** long-acting insulin; — **de acción rápida** rapid-acting insulin; — **detemir** insulin detemir; — **glargina** insulin glargine; — **glulisina** insulin glulisine; — **humana** human insulin; —

lispro insulin lispro; — **NPH** NPH insulin; — **premezclada** pre-mixed insulin; — **recombinante** recombinant insulin; — **regular** regular insulin; **inyectarse** —, **ponerse** — (*fam*) to take insulin, to give oneself an insulin injection

insulinoma *m* insulinoma

insumos médicos *mpl* medical supplies

intacto -ta *adj* intact

integral *adj* (*holístico*) holistic; (*entero*) whole, whole-grain; **trigo** — whole wheat

intelecto *m* intellect

intelectual *adj* intellectual

intelectualizar *vi* (*psych*) to intellectualize

inteligencia *f* intelligence

inteligente *adj* intelligent

intensidad *f* intensity

intensificar *vt* to intensify

intensivista *mf* intensivist

intensivo -va *adj* intensive

intenso -sa *adj* intense, (*actividad*) strenuous

intentar *vt* to try

intento *m* try

interacción *f* interaction; — **medicamentosa** (*form*), — **de medicamentos** drug interaction

interactuar *vi* to interact

intercambio *m* exchange; — **de agujas** *or* **jeringas** needle exchange

interconsulta *f* (*form*) consult (*hospital setting usually*)

intercostal *adj* intercostal

interferir *vi* to interfere

interferón *m* interferon; — **alfa (beta, etc.)** alpha (beta, etc.) interferon; — **pegilado** pegylated interferon

interior *adj* inner, interior, inside; *m* interior, inside

interiorizar *vt* (*psych*) to internalize

intermedio -dia *adj* intermediate

intermitente *adj* intermittent

internar *vt* to admit (*to the hospital*), to hospitalize (*esp. psych*); *vr* to be admitted, to be hospitalized

internet *m&f* internet; **en el** *or* **la** — on the internet

internista *mf* internist

interno -na *adj* internal, inner, inside; (*anat*) medial; *mf* intern

interpersonal *adj* interpersonal

interpretar *vt, vi* to interpret

intérprete *mf* interpreter

interrupción *f* interruption; — **voluntaria del embarazo** (elective) abortion

intersticial *adj* interstitial

intertrocantéreo -a *adj* intertrochanteric

intertrocantérico -ca *adj* intertrochanteric

intervalo *m* interval

intervención *f* intervention; — **coronaria percutánea (ICP)** percutaneous coronary intervention (PCI)

intervencionista *adj* interventional

interventricular *adj* interventricular

intervertebral *adj* intervertebral

intestinal *adj* intestinal

intestino *m* intestine, bowel, gut; — **delgado** small intestine *o* bowel; — **grueso** large intestine *o* bowel, colon

intimidación *f* (*ped*) bullying

intimidad *f* intimacy; (*confidencialidad*) confidentiality, privacy

intimidar *vt* (*ped*) to bully

íntimo -ma *adj* intimate; (*confidencial*) confidential, private

intolerable *adj* intolerable, unbearable

intolerancia *f* intolerance; — **a la lactosa** lactose intolerance

intolerante *adj* (*a la lactosa, al gluten*) intolerant (of)

intoxicación *f* intoxication, poisoning; — **alimentaria** *or* **por alimentos** food poisoning

intraabdominal, intra-abdominal *adj* intraabdominal

intraaórtico -ca *adj* intraaortic

intraarticular, intra-articular *adj* intraarticular

intracraneal *adj* intracranial

intracraneano -na *adj* intracranial

intradérmico -ca *adj* intradermal

intramuscular (IM) *adj* intramuscular (IM)

intranasal *adj* intranasal

intranquilo -la *adj* restless, anxious, worried

intraocular *adj* intraocular

intraoperatorio -ria *adj* intraoperative

intraóseo -a *adj* intraosseous

intrauterino -na *adj* intrauterine

intravenoso -sa (IV) *adj* intravenous (IV)

introducir *vt* to introduce, insert
introspección *f* introspection
introvertido -da *adj* introverted; *mf* introvert
intubación *f* intubation
intubar *vt* to intubate
intususcepción *f* (*Ang, invaginación intestinal*) intussusception
inundación *f* flood
inusual *adj* unusual
inútil *adj* useless
invadir *vt* to invade
invaginación *f* (*intestinal*) intussusception
invalidante *adj* (*incapacitante*) disabling
invalidez *f* (*discapacidad*) disability
inválido -da *adj* (*discapacitado*) disabled; *mf* disabled person
invasivo -va *adj* invasive; **mínimamente** — minimally invasive; **no** — noninvasive
invasor -ra *adj* invasive
investigación *f* research; **en** — (*medicamento, etc.*) investigational
invierno *m* winter
invisible *adj* invisible
in vitro, in vitro
involuntario -ria *adj* involuntary
inyección *f* injection, shot (*fam*); **¿Me van a poner una inyección?**.. Are you going to give me an injection (a shot)?
inyectable *adj* injectable
inyectar *vt* to inject, to give (*someone*) an injection; *vr* to inject oneself, to give oneself an injection
iodopovidona *f* povidone iodine
iodoquinol *m* iodoquinol (*USAN*), diiodohydroxyquinoline (*INN*)
ion, ión *m* ion
iontoforesis *f* iontophoresis
ipecacuana *f* ipecac; **jarabe** *m* **de** — syrup of ipecac
ir *vi* to go; — **al baño** (*euph*) to have a bowel movement, to go to the bathroom (*euph*); — **al médico** to go to the doctor; — **y venir** to come and go; **El dolor va y viene.**.The pain comes and

goes.
ira *f* anger, rage
irbesartán *m* irbesartan
iris *m* (*pl* **iris**) iris
iritis *f* iritis
IRM *f* MRI; (*See also* **imagen por resonancia magnética** *under* **imagen.**)
irradiación *f* irradiation
irradiar *vt* (*un tumor, etc.*) to irradiate; *vi, vr* (*calor, dolor*) to radiate
irregular *adj* irregular
irresecable *adj* unresectable
irreversible *adj* irreversible
irrigación *f* irrigation
irrigar *vt* to irrigate
irritabilidad *f* irritability
irritable *adj* irritable
irritación *f* irritation
irritante *adj* irritating; **agente** *m* — irritant; *m* irritant
irritar *vt* to irritate; *vr* to become irritated
irrompible *adj* unbreakable
islote *m* islet; **islotes pancreáticos** pancreatic islets
isoleucina *f* isoleucine
isométrico -ca *adj* isometric
isoniazida, isoniacida *f* isoniazid (INH)
isosorbida *f* isosorbide
isótopo *m* isotope
isotretinoína *f* isotretinoin
isquemia *f* ischemia; — **cerebral transitoria** (*esp. Mex*) transient ischemic attack (TIA)
isquémico -ca *adj* ischemic
isquion *m* ischium
isradipina *f* isradipine
isradipino *m* isradipine
itraconazol *m* itraconazole
ITS *abbr* **infección de transmisión sexual.** *See* **infección.**
ITU *abbr* **infección del tracto urinario.** *See* **infección.**
IV *See* **intravenoso.**
ivermectina *f* ivermectin
izquierdo -da *adj* left; *f* left, left-hand side

J

jabón *m* soap
jadear *vi* to pant
jadeo *m* panting
jalea *f* (*medicinal*) jelly
jamón *m* ham
jaqueca *f* migraine headache, migraine (*fam*)
jarabe *m* syrup; — **de maíz de alta fructosa** high-fructose corn syrup; — **para la tos** cough syrup
jardín preescolar, jardín infantil, jardín de niños (*Mex*) *m* nursery school, preschool
jarra *f* pitcher
jefe -fa *mf* head, boss; — **de enfermeras** head nurse
jején *m* biting gnat, no-see-um (*fam*)
jelepate *m* (*CA*) bedbug
jengibre *m* (*bot*) ginger
jeringa *f* syringe; — **de goma** bulb syringe

jeringuilla *f* (*esp. Carib*) syringe
jimagua *mf* (*Cuba*) twin
jogging *m* (*Ang*) jogging; **hacer** — to jog
joroba *f* humpback, hunchback, hump
jorobado -da *adj* humpbacked; *mf* hunchback
joven *adj* young; *m* young man, young person; *f* young woman
juanete *m* bunion
judías *fpl* (*Esp*) beans
judo *m* judo
juego *m* (*apuestas*) gambling; **adicción** *f* **al** — gambling addiction; **juegos de rol(es)** role playing *o* play
jugo *m* juice; — **de fruta** fruit juice
juicio *m* sanity
juntar *vt* (*dos objetos*) to join
Juramento Hipocrático *m* Hippocratic Oath
juvenil *adj* juvenile
juventud *f* youth

K

karate *m* karate
kava *m&f* (*bot*) kava
kelp *m* kelp
kernicterus *m* kernicterus
ketamina *f* ketamine
ketoconazol *m* ketoconazole
ketoprofeno *m* ketoprofen

ketorolaco *m* ketorolac
ketotifeno *m* ketotifen
kilogramo, kilo (*fam*) *m* kilogram, kilo (*fam*)
kinesiología *f* kinesiology
kwashiorkor *m* kwashiorkor

L

laberintitis _f_ labyrinthitis
laberinto _m_ (_anat_) labyrinth
labetalol _m_ labetalol
labial _adj_ labial; _m_ (_fam_) lipstick
labio _m_ lip; (_genital_) labium (_form_), lip; — **inferior** lower lip; — **leporino** (_fam or vulg_) cleft lip; — **superior** upper lip
laboral _adj_ work-related, occupational
laboratorio _m_ laboratory; — **de cateterismo** catheterization laboratory, cath lab (_fam_)
labrum _m_ labrum; **desgarro del** — labral tear
laca _f_ (_para el cabello, en aerosol_) hair spray _o_ hairspray
laceración _f_ laceration
lacerar _vt_ to lacerate
lacrimal _adj_ lacrimal
lacrimógeno _m_ tear gas
lactancia _f_ lactation; (_amamantamiento_) breastfeeding; (_primer período de la vida_) infancy, period of breastfeeding; — **materna** breastfeeding
lactante _mf_ (_form_) infant, nursing infant
lactar _vt_ to breastfeed, to feed, to nurse; _vi_ to lactate
lactasa _f_ lactase
lácteo -a _adj_ pertaining to milk; **producto** — milk product
láctico -ca _adj_ lactic
lactobacilo _m_ lactobacillus
lactosa _f_ lactose
lactulosa _f_ lactulose
ladilla _f_ crab louse, pubic louse, crab (_fam_)
lado _m_ side; **por el lado de mi madre..** on my mother's side...**dormir de lado..** to sleep on one's side
lagaña _f_ (_Amer_) eye secretions, sleep (_fam_)
lagartija _f_ (_esp. Mex, flexión_) pushup
lágrima _f_ tear
lagrimal _adj_ lacrimal
laguna mental _f_ blackout, lapse of memory
lamentar _vt_ to be sorry (_about something_); **Lo lamento..**I'm sorry about that.

lamer _vt_ to lick
laminaria _f_ laminaria
laminectomía _f_ laminectomy
lamivudina _f_ lamivudine
lamotrigina _f_ lamotrigine
lámpara _f_ lamp; — **de calor** heat lamp; — **de hendidura** slit lamp; — **de Wood** Wood's lamp; — **solar** sunlamp; — **ultravioleta** ultraviolet lamp
lampazo _m_ (_bot_) burdock
lana _f_ wool; — **de oveja** lamb's wool
lanceta _f_ lancet
lancetero _m_ lancet device
lanolina _f_ lanolin
lansoprazol _m_ lansoprazole
lanugo _m_ lanugo
laparoscopia, laparoscopía _f_ laparoscopy
laparoscópico -ca _adj_ laparoscopic
laparoscopio _m_ laparoscope
laparotomía _f_ laparotomy; — **exploradora** exploratory laparotomy
lápiz labial _m_ lipstick
lapso _m_ lapse
lapsus _m_ lapse; — **de memoria** lapse of memory; — **freudiano** Freudian slip
largo -ga _adj_ long; **a** — **plazo** long-term; **hacer más** — to lengthen; _m_ length
laringe _f_ larynx
laringectomía _f_ laryngectomy
laríngeo -a _adj_ laryngeal
laringitis _f_ laryngitis
laringoplastia _f_ laryngoplasty
laringoscopia, laringoscopía _f_ laryngoscopy
laringoscopio _m_ laryngoscope
larva migrans _f_ larva migrans; — — **cutánea** cutaneous larva migrans; — — **visceral** visceral larva migrans
láser _m_ laser
lastimadura _f_ minor injury
lastimar _vt_ to hurt, injure; _vr_ to hurt _o_ injure oneself, to get hurt; **¿Se lastimó?..** Did you hurt yourself?...**¿Se lastimó la cabeza?**..Did you hurt your head?
latanoprost _m_ latanoprost
latente _adj_ latent
lateral _adj_ (_anat_) lateral

látex *m* latex

latido *m* beat; — **del corazón** heartbeat

latigazo cervical *m* whiplash

latir *vi* (*el corazón*) to beat

lauril sulfato de sodio *m* sodium lauryl sulfate

lavado *m* lavage; — **broncoalveolar** bronchoalveolar lavage; — **gástrico** gastric lavage; — **intestinal** enema, colon cleansing; — **peritoneal** peritoneal lavage; — **vaginal** douche; **darse un — vaginal** to douche

lavar *vt* to wash; *vr* to wash oneself; — **el pelo (la cara, las manos, etc.)** to wash one's hair (one's face, one's hands, etc.)

lavativa *f* enema

laxante *adj & m* laxative

laxitud *f* laxity

laxo -xa *adj* lax

lazo *m* bond; (*obst*) loop; — **afectivo** emotional bond

lb *See* libra.

L-carnitina *f* L-carnitine

leche *f* milk; — **baja en grasa** low-fat milk; — **bronca** (*Mex*), — **cruda** raw milk; — **descremada** non-fat *o* skim milk; — **deslactosada** lactose-free milk; — **desnatada** non-fat *o* skim milk; — **de soya** *or* **soja** soy milk; — **de vaca** cow's milk; — **entera** whole milk; — **materna** breast milk; — **no pasteurizada** unpasteurized milk; — **pasteurizada** pasteurized milk; — **sin lactosa** lactose-free milk; — **sin pasteurizar** unpasteurized milk

leche de magnesia *f* milk of magnesia

lecho *m* bed, sick bed; — **de enfermo** sick bed; — **de muerte** deathbed; — **ungueal** nail bed; — **vascular** vascular bed

lecitina *f* lecithin

lectura *f* (*de un instrumento*) reading; — **de los labios** lip reading

leer *vt, vi* to read; — **los labios** to lipread

leflunomida *f* leflunomide

legaña *f* eye secretions, sleep (*fam*)

lego -ga *adj* (*Esp, form; opinión, etc.*) lay; *mf* layperson

legra *f* curette

legrado *m* curettage; — **por succión** suction curettage

legumbre *f* legume

leiomioma *m* leiomyoma; — **uterino** uterine leiomyoma, fibroid (*fam*)

leiomiosarcoma *m* leiomyosarcoma

leishmaniasis, leishmaniosis *f* leishmaniasis; — **cutánea** cutaneous leishmaniasis; — **mucocutánea** mucocutaneous leishmaniasis; — **visceral** visceral leishmaniasis

lejía *f* lye

lengua *f* (*anat*) tongue; (*idioma*) language; — **de señas** *or* **signos** sign language; — **saburral** coated tongue; **sacar la** — to stick out one's tongue; **Saque la lengua**..Stick out your tongue.

lenguaje *m* language; — **corporal** body language; — **de señas** *or* **signos** sign language

lengüeta *f* (*de un anzuelo*) barb

lente *m&f* lens; — **bifocal** bifocal lens; — **de contacto (duro** *or* **rígido, blando)** (hard, soft) contact lens; — **progresivo** progressive lens; — **trifocal** trifocal lens; *mpl* glasses, eyeglasses; — **bifocales** bifocal glasses *o* eyeglasses, bifocals (*fam*); — **de lectura** reading glasses; — **de sol** *or* **oscuros** sunglasses

lentigo *m* lentigo

lento -ta *adj* slow

lepra *f* leprosy, Hansen's disease; — **dimorfa** borderline leprosy; — **lepromatosa** lepromatous leprosy; — **tuberculoide** tuberculoid leprosy

lepromatoso -sa *adj* lepromatous

leptospirosis *f* leptospirosis

LES *abbr* lupus eritematoso sistémico. *See* lupus.

lesbiana *adj* lesbian; *f* lesbian, gay woman

lesión *f* lesion, injury; — **de la médula espinal** spinal cord injury; — **deportiva** sports injury; — **por sobrecarga** (*esp. Esp*) overuse syndrome; — **traumática del cerebro** traumatic brain injury

lesionar *vt* to injure; *vr* to injure oneself, to get injured

letal *adj* lethal

letárgico -ca *adj* lethargic

letargo *m* lethargy

letra *f* (*de tabla de Snellen, etc.*) letter; (*escritura*) handwriting

letrina *f* latrine
leucemia *f* leukemia; — **linfoblástica** *or* **linfocítica aguda** acute lymphoblastic *o* lymphocytic leukemia; — **linfocítica crónica** chronic lymphocytic leukemia; — **mieloide aguda** acute myeloid leukemia; — **mieloide crónica** chronic myeloid leukemia
leucina *f* leucine
leucocito *m* leukocyte
leucoencefalopatía *f* leukoencephalopathy; — **multifocal progresiva** progressive multifocal leukoencephalopathy
leucoplasia *f* leukoplakia; — **vellosa oral** oral hairy leukoplakia
leucovorina *f* leucovorin (*USAN*), folinic acid (*INN*)
leuprorelina, leuprolida *f* leuprorelin, leuprolide
levadura *f* (*frec. pl*) yeast; **infección** *f* **por levaduras** yeast infection; — **de cerveza** brewer's yeast
levamisol *m* levamisole
levantamiento de pesas *m* weight lifting
levantar *vt* to raise, to lift; **Levante la pierna.**.Raise your leg; — **pesas** to lift weights (*work out*); *vr* to get up, to stand (up); — **de la cama** to get out of bed
leve *adj* (*herida*) slight, (*caso de enfermedad*) light, mild, (*fiebre, infección*) low-grade
levetiracetam *m* levetiracetam
levofloxacina *f* levofloxacin
levofloxacino *m* levofloxacin
levonorgestrel *m* levonorgestrel
levotiroxina *f* levothyroxine
Ley de Asistencia Asequible *f* Affordable Care Act (*US*)
Ley de Portabilidad y Responsabilidad del Seguro Médico *f* Health Insurance Portability and Accountability Act (HIPPA) (*US*)
LGV *See* **linfogranuloma venéreo**.
liberación *f* release; **de** — **controlada** controlled-release, timed-release; **de** — **lenta** slow-release; **de** — **prolongada** extended-release, slow-release; **de** — **sostenida** sustained-release; — **del túnel carpiano** carpal tunnel release
liberador -ra *adj* releasing, eluting; — **de cobre,** — **de hormona, etc.** copper-releasing, hormone-releasing, etc.;

— **de fármacos** (*stent*) drug-eluting
liberar *vt* to release, (*virus, etc.*) to shed
libido *f* libido
libra (lb) *f* pound (lb)
libre *adj* free; — **de gluten** gluten-free
libreta *f* log, booklet; — **de autocontrol** (*del diabético*) glucose log
licor *m* liquor
lidiar con *vi* to cope with
lidocaína *f* lidocaine; — **viscosa** viscous lidocaine
liendre *f* nit
lifting facial *m* (*Ang*) rhytidectomy (*form*), facelift
ligado -da *adj* linked; — **al cromosoma X** X-linked; — **al sexo** sex-linked
ligadura *f* ligation; — **de trompas,** — **tubárica** (*esp. Esp*) tubal ligation
ligamento *m* ligament; — **amarillo** ligamentum flavum; — **cruzado anterior** anterior cruciate ligament
ligar *vt* to ligate, to attach
ligero -ra *adj* light, slight; gentle
lima *f* file; (*fruta*) lime; — **de** *or* **para uñas** nail file
limar *vt* to file; *vr* — **las uñas** to file one's nails
limitar *vt* to limit
límite *adj* (*psych*) borderline; *m* limit; **dentro de los límites normales** within normal limits; — **inferior normal** lower limit of normal; — **superior normal** upper limit of normal; **por debajo de los límites normales** below normal limits; **por encima de los límites normales** above normal limits
limón *m* lemon
limpiador -ra de casas *mf* housecleaner
limpiador facial *m* facial cleanser
limpiar *vt* to clean; *vr* (*después de defecar*) to wipe (oneself)
limpieza *f* cleaning; (*aseo*) cleanliness; — **de colon** colon cleansing; — **dental** dental cleaning
limpio -pia *adj* clean
linaza *f* flaxseed
lindano *m* lindane
línea *f* line, streak; (*de una persona*) figure; **en** — online; — **de base** baseline; — **de la encía** gum line; — **del cuero cabelludo** hairline; — **media** (*del cuerpo*) midline (*of the body*)
linezolid *m* linezolid

linfa *f* lymph
linfadenitis *f* lymphadenitis
linfangitis *f* lymphangitis
linfático -ca *adj* lymphatic
linfedema *m* lymphedema
linfocito *m* lymphocyte; — **B (CD4, etc.)** B (CD4, etc.) lymphocyte
linfogranuloma venéreo *m* lymphogranuloma venereum (LGV)
linfoide *adj* lymphoid
linfoma *m* lymphoma; — **de células B** B cell lymphoma; — **de células T** T cell lymphoma; — **de tejido linfoide asociado a mucosas** mucosa-associated lymphoid tissue (MALT) lymphoma; — **(de) Hodgkin** Hodgkin's* lymphoma; — **MALT** MALT lymphoma; — **no Hodgkin** non-Hodgkin's* lymphoma

La forma no posesiva también se usa, sobre todo en la literatura médica.

linimento *m* liniment
linoleico -ca *adj* linoleic
liofilizado -da *adj* lyophilized, freeze-dried
liotironina *f* liothyronine
lipasa *f* lipase
lípido *m* lipid
lipodistrofia *f* lipodystrophy
lipoma *m* lipoma
lipoproteína *f* lipoprotein; — **de alta densidad** high density lipoprotein (HDL); — **de baja densidad** low density lipoprotein (LDL); — **de muy baja densidad** very low density lipoprotein (VLDL)
liposarcoma *m* liposarcoma
liposucción *f* liposuction
liquen plano *m* lichen planus
liquen simple crónico *m* lichen simplex chronicus
líquido -da *adj* liquid; *m* liquid, fluid; — **amniótico** amniotic fluid; — **cefalorraquídeo** (LCR) cerebrospinal fluid (CSF); — **corporal** *or* **del cuerpo** body fluid; — **pleural** pleural fluid; — **seminal** seminal fluid; — **sinovial** synovial fluid
liquor *n* licor *m*; **hard** — licor fuerte (*contenido de alcohol 50% o más*)
liraglutida *f* liraglutide
lisdexamfetamina *f* lisdexanfetamine
lisiado -da *adj* injured, disabled, crippled; *mf* injured person, disabled person, cripple; [*Note:* lisiado, *like* crippled *and* cripple, *can be offensive.*]
lisiar *vt* to injure, to disable; *vr* to become injured, to become disabled
lisina *f* lysine
lisinopril *m* lisinopril
lisis *f* lysis; — **de adherencias** lysis of adhesions
liso -sa *adj* smooth
lista de espera *f* waiting list
listeriosis *f* listeriosis
litio *m* lithium
litotricia, litotripsia *f* lithotripsy; — **extracorpórea por ondas de choque** extracorporeal shock wave lithotripsy
litro *m* liter
liviano -na *adj* light (*in weight*)
llaga *f* ulcer, sore
llama *f* flame
llamada *f* call; (*por buscapersonas*) page; — **de atención** wakeup call, red flag
llamado de atención *m* wakeup call, red flag
llamar *vt, vi* to call; (*por buscapersonas*) to page
llanto *m* cry; **el llanto del bebé**..the baby's cry
llenar *vt* to fill; (*un formulario*) to fill out (*a form*)
lleno -na *adj* full; **sentirse** — to feel full
llevar *vt* (*ropa, etc.*) to wear
llorando -da *adj* tearful
llorar *vi* to cry
lluvia radiactiva *f* (nuclear) fallout
lobar *adj* lobar
lobectomía *f* lobectomy
lobelia *f* (*bot*) lobelia
lobotomía *f* lobotomy
lobular *adj* lobular
lóbulo *m* lobe; (*de la oreja*) ear lobe
local *adj* local
localización *f* localization
localizado -da *adj* localized
loción *f* lotion; — **bronceadora** tanning *o* suntan lotion (*to increase tanning*); — **para manos** hand lotion
loco -ca *adj* crazy, insane; **volver (a alguien)** — to drive (*someone*) crazy; **volverse** — to go crazy; *mf* crazy person
locura *f* insanity, craziness

log₁₀ *m* log₁₀; **5 log₁₀ copias/ml** ..5 log₁₀ copies/ml

logopeda *mf* (*form*) speech language therapist (*form*), speech pathologist *o* therapist

logopedia *f* speech language therapy (*form*), speech pathology *o* therapy

logoterapeuta *mf* (*form*) speech language therapist (*form*), speech therapist

logoterapia *f* speech language therapy (*form*), speech therapy

lombriz *f* (*pl* -brices) worm, intestinal worm; — **solitaria** tapeworm

longevidad *f* longevity

longitud *f* length; — **de onda** wavelength

loperamida *f* loperamide

lopinavir *m* lopinavir

loquios *mpl* lochia

loratadina *f* loratadine

lorazepam *m* lorazepam

lordosis *f* lordosis

losartán *m* losartan

lote *m* (*pharm*) lot

lovastatina *f* lovastatin

lubricación *f* lubrication

lubricante *adj* & *m* lubricant

lubricar *vt* to lubricate

luces *pl of* **luz**

lucha *f* battle; — **contra el SIDA** battle against AIDS

lugar *m* place; — **de(l) trabajo** workplace

lumbar *adj* lumbar

lumpectomía *f* (*Ang*) lumpectomy

lunar *m* mole

lupa *f* magnifying glass, hand lens

lúpulo *m* (*bot*) hops

lupus *m* lupus; — **discoide** discoid lupus; — **eritematoso sistémico (LES)** systemic lupus erythematosus (SLE)

lúteo -a *adj* luteal

luto *m* grief (*due to death*)

luxación *f* dislocation

luxar *vt* to dislocate; *vr* to become dislocated

luz *f* (*pl* **luces**) light; — **solar** *or* **del sol** sunlight

M

macerar *vt* to macerate

macho *adj* male

machucadura *f* small crush injury

machucar *vt* to mash, crush

machucón *m* small crush injury

macizo -za *adj* (*persona*) heavyset

macrobiótico -ca *adj* macrobiotic

madrastra *f* stepmother

madre *f* mother; — **biológica** biologic mother; — **sustituta** *or* **portadora** surrogate mother

madrina *f* godmother

madrugada *f* early morning (*before dawn*)

madurar *vi* to mature; (*un absceso*) to come to a head

madurez *f* maturity; adulthood before old age

maduro -ra *adj* mature; (*fruta*) ripe

maestro -tra *mf* teacher

magnesio *m* magnesium

magro -gra *adj* lean, without fat

magullado -da *adj* bruised, sore

magulladura *f* bruise

magullar *vt* to bruise; *vr* to bruise, to get bruised

maicena *f* cornstarch

maíz *m* corn

mal *adj* See **malo**; *adv* bad, sick; **sentirse —** to feel bad, to feel sick; **Me**

siento mal por haberla ofendido..I feel bad for having insulted her...**Me siento mal del estómago**.. I feel sick to my stomach; *m* illness, sickness, ailment, disease; — **de mar** seasickness; — **de montaña** mountain sickness; — **de ojo** evil eye, pediatric folk illness believed to occur when a person with magical powers eyes an infant with ill intent (*in some areas this applies to adults as well*); — **de orín** (*fam*) urinary tract infection; — **de pinto** (*Mex*) pinta, tropical skin infection; — **de Pott** Pott's disease

malabsorción *f* malabsorption

mala praxis *f* malpractice

malaria *f* malaria

malatión *m* malathion

maléolo *m* malleolus; — **externo** lateral malleolus; — **interno** medial malleolus

malestar *m* malaise, vague illness

maletín del médico *m* doctor's bag

malformación *f* malformation; — **arteriovenosa** arteriovenous malformation

malignidad *f* malignancy

maligno -na *adj* malignant

malla *f* (*surg*) mesh

malnutrición *f* malnutrition

malnutrido -da *adj* malnourished

malo -la *adj* (**mal** *before masculine singular nouns*) bad

maloclusión *f* malocclusion

maloliente *adj* foul-smelling, that smells bad

malos tratos *See* **maltrato**.

maltodextrina *f* maltodextrin

maltratado -da *adj* abused, battered; **refugio para mujeres maltratadas** battered women's shelter

maltratar *vt* to abuse, mistreat

maltrato *m* maltreatment (*form*), abuse, mistreatment; — **a (los) adultos mayores** (*Amer*) elder maltreatment *o* abuse; — **a (los) niños** child maltreatment *o* abuse; — **a (las) personas mayores** elder maltreatment *o* abuse; — **físico** physical maltreatment *o* abuse — **infantil** child maltreatment *o* abuse; — **psicológico** psychological maltreatment *o* abuse; — **sexual** sexual maltreatment *o* abuse

malvavisco *m* (*bot*) marshmallow

mama *f* (female) breast

mamá *f* (*pl* **mamás**) mom, mother

mamadera *f* (*Amer, biberón*) baby bottle

mamar *vi* to nurse, to suck (*at mother's breast*); **dar de** — to breastfeed

mamario -ria *adj* mammary

mami *f* (*pl* **mamis**) mommy, mother

mamila *f* (*Mex, de un biberón*) nipple (*of a baby bottle*)

mamita *f* mommy, mother

mamografía *f* (*técnica*) mammography; (*estudio*) mammogram; — **digital** digital mammography; digital mammogram

mamoplastia *f* mammoplasty; — **de aumento** augmentation mammoplasty, breast augmentation surgery; — **de reducción** reduction mammoplasty, breast reduction surgery

mancha *f* spot, stain; — **en vino de Oporto** port-wine stain

manchado *m* (*gyn*) spotting

manchar *vt* to stain; (*gyn*) to spot, to have spotting; **He empezado a manchar**..I've begun to spot..I'm having spotting.

manco -ca *adj* one-handed, one-armed

mandíbula *f* mandible, lower jaw, jaw, jawbone; — **inferior** lower jaw, mandible; — **superior** upper jaw, maxilla

mandil *m* apron; — **de plomo** lead apron

mandrágora *f* (*bot*) ginseng

manejar *vt, vi* to manage; (*un vehículo*) to drive

manejo *m* management; — **de la ira** anger management; — **del dolor** pain management; — **del enojo** anger management

manga *f* sleeve; **camisa de** — **larga** long-sleeve shirt

manganeso *m* manganese

manguera *f* hose, tube

manguito *m* cuff; — **de los rotadores** rotator cuff; — **del tensiómetro** blood pressure cuff; — **rotador** rotator cuff

maní *m* (*pl* -**níes**) peanut

manía *f* mania

maníaco, maniaco -ca *adj* manic

maníaco-depresivo, maniaco-depresivo -va *adj* bipolar, manic-depressive (*ant*)

manicomio *m* (*ant*) psychiatric hospital, insane asylum (*ant*)

manicura *f* manicure

manifestación *f* manifestation

maniobra *f* maneuver; — **de Heimlich** Heimlich maneuver

maniobrar *vt, vi* to maneuver

manipulación *f* manipulation; — **de alta velocidad** high-velocity manipulation; — **espinal** *or* **de la columna** spinal manipulation

manipulador -ra *adj* manipulative; *mf* — **de alimentos** food handler

manipular *vt* to manipulate

mano *f* hand; **de** — (*dispositivo*) handheld; — **péndula** wrist drop

manometría *f* manometry

manta *f* blanket, light blanket; — **térmica** *or* **eléctrica** electric blanket

manteca *f* cooking grease, lard; — **de cacao** cocoa butter; — **de cerdo** lard

mantener *vt* to maintain

mantenimiento *m* maintenance; — **con metadona** methadone maintenance

mantequilla *f* butter; — **de maní** *or* **cacahuete** *or* **cacahuate** peanut butter

manual *adj* manual, handheld

manubrio *m* manubrium

manzana *f* apple; — **de Adán** Adam's apple

manzanilla *f* (*bot*) chamomile

mañana *adv* tomorrow; **pasado** — the day after tomorrow; *f* morning

mapache *m* raccoon

maquillaje *m* makeup, cosmetics

maquillarse *vr* to put on makeup

máquina de afeitar *f* (*manual*) razor, safety razor; (*eléctrica*) (electric) shaver

maquinilla *f* (*de afeitar*) razor, safety razor

maraviroc *m* maraviroc

marca *f* mark; — **de nacimiento** birthmark; **marcas de pinchazos** tracks (*fam*), scars due to intravenous drug use

marcador *m* marker

marcapasos *m* (*pl* **-sos**) pacemaker

marcha *f* gait

mareado -da *adj* dizzy, lightheaded, faint

mareo *m* dizziness, (*en avión*) airsickness, (*en barco*) seasickness, (*en vehículo*) carsickness, (*producido por el movimiento en general*) motion sickness; **dar(le)** — to make (*one*) dizzy; — **por movimiento** motion sickness;

tener — to feel dizzy

margarina *f* margarine

margen *m* margin, border, edge

marido *m* husband

mariguana, marihuana (*esp. Mex*) *f* marijuana, pot (*fam*), grass (*fam*); — **medicinal** medical marijuana

marisco *m* (*frec. pl*) shellfish

marrón *adj* brown

martillo *m* hammer; — **de reflejos** reflex hammer

más *adj* (*comp and super of* **mucho**) more; **más pastillas**..more pills; *adv* more, most; **una opción más conservadora**..a more conservative option... **la opción más conservadora de las tres**..the most conservative option of the three; *m* — **de** more than (*in number*); **más de 12**..more than 12...**más problemas de los que tenía antes**.. more problems than you had before; — **que** more than; **más que su hermano**.. more than his brother; [*Nota: Muchos adjetivos en inglés toman una forma comparativa en una sola palabra:* redder (*más rojo*), bigger (*más grande*), *etc. Lo mismo se aplica a las formas superlativas* (reddest, biggest, *etc.*)]

masa *f* mass, lump; — **muscular** muscle mass; — **ósea** bone mass

masaje *m* massage; **dar un** —, **dar** — (*esp. Mex*) to give a massage; — **cardíaco** cardiac massage; — **cardíaco externo** chest compressions

masajear *vt* to massage

masajista *m* masseur; *f* masseuse

máscara *f* mask, face mask; — **antigás** gas mask; — **con filtro** respirator; — **de gas** gas mask; — **de oxígeno** oxygen mask; — **quirúrgica** surgical mask

mascarilla *f* mask, face mask; — **con filtro** respirator; — **de oxígeno** oxygen mask; — **quirúrgica** surgical mask

mascota *f* pet

masculinidad *f* masculinity, manhood

masculino -na *adj* masculine, male

masivo -va *adj* massive

masoquismo *m* masochism

masoquista *adj* masochistic; *mf* masochist

mastectomía *f* mastectomy; — **radical modificada** modified radical mastec-

tomy
masticable *adj* chewable
masticar *vt, vi* to chew
mastitis *f* mastitis
mastocitosis *f* mastocytosis
mastoidectomía *f* mastoidectomy
mastoideo -a *adj* mastoid
mastoiditis *f* mastoiditis
masturbación *f* masturbation
masturbar *vt, vr* to masturbate
matar *vt* to kill
matasanos *mf* (*pl* **-nos**) quack, charlatan
materia *f* (*pus*) pus
material *m* material
maternal *adj* maternal, motherly
maternidad *f* maternity, motherhood, childbearing
materno -na *adj* maternal; **tío** — maternal uncle
matinal *adj* morning, in the morning
matricaria *f* (*bot*) feverfew
matrimonial *adj* marital; **problemas matrimoniales** marital problems
matriz *f* (*pl* **-trices**) matrix; (*útero*) uterus; — **ungueal** nail matrix
matutino -na *adj* morning, in the morning
maxila *f* (*Ang*) maxilla, upper jaw
maxilar *adj* maxillary; *m* (*fam*) maxilla, upper jaw; — **superior** maxilla, upper jaw
maxilofacial *adj* maxillofacial
maximizar *vt* to maximize
máximo -ma *adj* maximum, maximal; *m* maximum, peak; **alcanzar un** — to peak
mayor (*comp of* **grande**) *adj* (*más grande*) bigger, larger; (*de más edad*) older; (*anat, surg*) major; **gente mayor de 60 años**..people over 60 years old.. people over 60 (*fam*)
mear *vt, vi* (*vulg*) to urinate, to pee (*fam*), to piss (*vulg*)
meato *m* meatus
mebendazol *m* mebendazole
mecanismo *m* mechanism; — **de afrontamiento** coping mechanism; — **de defensa** defense mechanism
mecha *f* wick
meclizina, meclozina (*INN*), **meclicina** *f* meclizine, meclozine (*INN*)
meconio *m* meconium
media *f* stocking, sock; (*math*) mean

(*form*), average; **debajo de la** — below average; **encima de la** — above average; **medias de compresión, medias compresivas** (*esp. Esp*) compression stockings
medial *adj* (*anat*) medial
Media Luna Roja *f* Red Crescent
mediano -na *adj* medium (*size or degree*); (*nervio*) median; *f* (*stat*) median; — **de peso** median weight
mediastínico -ca *adj* mediastinal
mediastino *m* mediastinum
mediastinoscopia *f* mediastinoscopy
medicado -da *adj* (*champú, etc.*) medicated
medicamento *m* medication, medicine, drug; — **huérfano** orphan drug; — **recetado** prescription drug
medicar *vt* to medicate
medicina *f* (*campo*) medicine; (*medicamento*) medicine, medication; — **alternativa** alternative medicine; — **basada en la evidencia** evidence-based medicine; — **complementaria y alternativa** complementary and alternative medicine; — **de familia** family practice, family medicine; — **de la adicción** addiction medicine; — **deportiva** sports medicine; — **familiar** family practice, family medicine; — **física y rehabilitación** physical medicine and rehabilitation; — **holística** *or* **integral** holistic medicine; — **integrativa** integrative medicine; — **interna** internal medicine; — **laboral** occupational medicine; — **naturista** naturopathy; — **nuclear** nuclear medicine; — **occidental** Western medicine; — **ocupacional** occupational medicine; — **popular** traditional *o* folk medicine; — **preventiva** preventive medicine; — **recetada** prescription drug; — **regenerativa** regenerative medicine; — **socializada** socialized medicine; — **tradicional** traditional *o* folk medicine
medicinal *adj* medicinal
medición *f* measurement
médico -ca *adj* medical; *mf* physician, doctor, Doctor of Medicine (MD *o* M.D.); — **de atención primaria** primary care physician; — **de cabecera** family physician; personal physician; primary care physician; — **de familia**

family practice physician; family physician; — **de guardia** physician on call, on-call physician; — **de la familia** family physician; — **de turno** physician on call, on-call physician; — **familiar** family practice physician; — **forense** coroner; — **generalista** *or* **general** general practitioner; — **legista** (*esp. Mex*) coroner; — **personal** personal physician; — **primario** (*Esp*) primary care physician; — **privado** private physician; — **residente** resident (physician); — **tratante** attending physician, treating physician

medicolegal *adj* medicolegal

medida *f* measurement; measure; **(hecho) a la** — custom-fitted; **medidas heroicas** heroic measures

medidor *m* meter, measuring device, monitor; — **de glucosa** glucose meter *o* monitor

medio -dia *adj* half, half a, a half; middle, mid-; (*stat*) mean, average; **dedo** — middle finger; — **ciclo** mid-cycle; — **dormido** half asleep; — **hermana** half sister; — **hermano** half brother; — **pastilla** half a pill, a half pill; **peso** — mean *o* average weight; *m* middle; medium; **en medio de la noche**..in the middle of the night; — **ambiente** environment; — **de contraste** contrast medium, contrast (*fam*); *f* mean, average; **inferior a la** —, **por debajo de la** — below (the) average; **por encima de la** —, **superior a la** — above (the) average

mediodía *m* noon

medir *vt* to measure

meditación *f* meditation

meditar *vi* to meditate

medroxiprogesterona *f* medroxyprogesterone

médula *f* medulla; marrow; — **espinal** spinal cord; — **ósea** bone marrow

medular *adj* medullary

medusa *f* jellyfish

mefloquina *f* mefloquine

megacolon *m* megacolon

megadosis *f* (*pl* **-sis**) megadose

megestrol *m* megestrol

mejilla *f* cheek

mejor (*comp of* **bueno** *and* **bien**) *adj* & *adv* better

mejorar *vt* to improve, make better; *vi* to improve, get better

mejoría *f* improvement

melancolía *f* melancholy

melanina *f* melanin

melanoma *m* melanoma

melarsoprol *m* melarsoprol

melasma *m* melasma

melatonina *f* melatonin

melfalán *m* melphalan

mellizo -za *adj* & *mf* twin, fraternal twin

meloxicam *m* meloxicam

memantina *f* memantine

membrana *f* membrane, web; — **esofágica** esophageal web; — **mucosa** mucous membrane; — **timpánica** tympanic membrane

memoria *f* memory; — **a corto plazo** short-term memory; — **a largo plazo** long-term memory

menarquia, **menarca** *f* menarche

meninge *f* meninx; [*Nota: En inglés se usa casi siempre el plural*: meninges.]

meningioma *m* meningioma

meningitis *f* meningitis

meningocele *m* meningocele

meningocócico -ca *adj* meningococcal

meningococo *m* meningococcus

meniscal *adj* meniscal

meniscectomía *f* meniscectomy

menisco *m* meniscus; — **roto** torn meniscus

menopausia *f* menopause

menopáusico -ca *adj* menopausal

menor (*comp of* **pequeño**) *adj* smaller; least; (*de menos edad*) younger; (*anat, surg*) minor; **el menor tamaño**..the smaller size...**el menor riesgo posible**.. the least possible risk...**su hermana menor**..her younger sister; *mf* (*de edad*) minor; — **emancipado** emancipated minor

menos *adj* (*comp and super of* **poco**) less; **menos náuseas**..less nausea; *adv* less, least; **menos eficaz que el otro**.. less effective than the other...**el menos eficaz de todos**..the least effective of all; *m* — **de** less than (*in number*), fewer than; **menos de 70**..less than 70... **menos lesiones de las que tenía antes** ..fewer lesions than you had before; — **que** less than; **menos que lo esperado** ..less than expected

menstruación *f* menstruation, (menstrual) period
menstrual *adj* menstrual
menstruar *vi* to menstruate
menta *f* (*bot*) mint; — **verde** spearmint
mental *adj* mental
mente *f* mind
mentiroso -sa compulsivo *mf* pathological liar
mentol *m* menthol
mentón *m* chin
mentoniano -na *adj* mental, pertaining to the chin
menudo *adj* **a** — often, frequently
mepacrina *f* quinacrine (*USAN*), mepacrine (*INN*)
meperidina *f* meperidine (*USAN*), pethidine (*INN*)
meralgia parestésica *f* meralgia paresthetica
mercurio *m* mercury
meropenem *m* meropenem
mes *m* month
mesa *f* table, exam table; — **basculante** tilt table; — **de cirugía** operating table; — **de exploración** examination table, exam table (*fam*); — **de operaciones** operating table; — **inclinada** tilt table; — **quirúrgica** operating table
mesalamina, mesalazina (*INN*) *f* mesalamine (*USAN*), mesalazine (*INN*)
mescalina, mezcalina *f* mescaline
mesencéfalo *m* midbrain
mesentérico -ca *adj* mesenteric
mesenterio *m* mesentery
mesotelioma *m* mesothelioma
mesoterapia *f* mesotherapy
meta *f* goal
metabólico -ca *adj* metabolic
metabolismo *m* metabolism; — **basal** basal metabolism
metacarpiano -na *adj* & *m* metacarpal
metacualona *f* methaqualone
metadona *f* methadone
metal *m* metal; — **pesado** heavy metal
metálico -ca *adj* metallic
metanfetamina *f* methamphetamine, metamphetamine (*INN*)
metano *m* methane
metanol *m* methanol, methyl alcohol
metastásico -ca *adj* metastatic
metástasis *f* (*pl* -**sis**) metastasis

metastatizar *vi* to metastasize
metatarsiano -na *adj* & *m* metatarsal
metaxalona *f* metaxalone
meter *vt* (*insertar*) to insert; *vr* — **el dedo en la nariz** (*para sacarse los mocos*) to pick one's nose
metformina *f* metformin
meticilina *f* methicillin (*USAN*), meticillin (*INN*)
metilcelulosa *f* methylcellulose
metildopa *f* methyldopa
metilendioxianfetamina (MDA) *f* methylene dioxyamphetamine (MDA)
metilendioximetanfetamina (MDMA) *f* methylene dioxymethamphetamine (MDMA), ecstacy (*fam*)
metilfenidato *m* methylphenidate
metilprednisolona *f* methylprednisolone
metimazol *m* methimazole (*USAN*), thiamazole (*INN*)
metionina *f* methionine
metocarbamol *m* methocarbamol
metoclopramida *f* metoclopramide
método *m* method, technique; — **del ritmo** rhythm method; — **Lamaze** Lamaze method
metolazona *f* metolazone
metoprolol *m* metoprolol
metotrexato, metotrexate *m* methotrexate
metralla *f* shrapnel
metro *m* meter; — **cuadrado** square meter
metronidazol *m* metronidazole
mezcal *m* mescal
mezcla *f* mixture
mezclar *vt* to mix
mezquino *m* (*Mex, CA*) wart
mialgia *f* myalgia
miastenia grave, miastenia gravis *f* myasthenia gravis
miconazol *m* miconazole
micosis fungoide *f* mycosis fungoides
micótico -ca *adj* mycotic, fungal
microalbuminuria *f* microalbuminuria
microbiano -na *adj* microbial
microbicida *m* microbicide
microbio *m* microbe, germ (*fam*)
microbiología *f* microbiology
microcirugía *f* microsurgery
microdermoabrasión, microdermabrasión *f* microdermabrasion
microdiscectomía *f* microdiscectomy

micofenolato de mofetilo *m* mycophenolate mofetil

microflora *f* microflora

microgramo *m* microgram

micrometástasis *f* (*pl* -**sis**) micrometastasis

micronizado -**da** *adj* (*pharm*) micronized

micronutriente *m* micronutrient

microonda *f* microwave; **tomografía de microondas** microwave tomography

microondas *m* microwave oven, microwave (*fam*)

microorganismo *m* microorganism, germ (*fam*)

microscopia, microscopía *f* microscopy

microscópico -**ca** *adj* microscopic

microscopio *m* microscope; — **de luz** light microscope; — **electrónico** electron microscope

microvascular *adj* microvascular

midazolam *m* midazolam

midodrina *f* midodrine

miedo *m* fear; **tener** — to be afraid

miel *f* (*de abeja*) honey

mielina *f* myelin

mielitis *f* myelitis; — **transversa** transverse myelitis

mielodisplasia *f* myelodysplasia

mielodisplásico -**ca** *adj* myelodysplastic

mielofibrosis *f* myelofibrosis; — **primaria** primary myelofibrosis

mielografía *f* (*técnica*) myelography; (*estudio*) myelogram

mieloma múltiple *m* multiple myeloma

mielomeningocele *m* myelomeningocele

mieloproliferativo -**va** *adj* myeloproliferative

miembro *m* member; (*extremidad*) limb; — **de la familia** family member

mifepristona *f* mifepristone

migraña *f* migraine headache, migraine (*fam*)

migrar *vi* (*dentro del cuerpo, e.g., parásitos*) to migrate

milagro *m* miracle

milenrama *f* (*bot*) yarrow

milia *f* milia

miliar *adj* miliary

miliaria *f* miliaria, heat rash (*fam*)

miligramo *m* milligram

mililitro *m* milliliter

milímetro *m* millimeter

milirem *m* (*pl* -**rems**) (*rad, ant*) millirem (*ant*)

milisegundo *m* millisecond

milisievert *m* (*rad*) millisievert

mimar *vt* to pamper, coddle, spoil

mime *m* (*PR, SD*) biting gnat

mineral *adj* & *m* mineral

minero -**ra** *mf* miner

miniexamen del estado mental *m* minimental state examination

minimizar *vt* to minimize

mínimo -**ma** *adj* minimum, minimal; *m* minimum

minociclina *f* minocycline

minoxidil *m* minoxidil

minusvalía *f* disability (*esp. partial*)

minusválido -**da** *adj* disabled (*esp. partially*)

minuto *m* minute

miocárdico -**ca** *adj* myocardial

miocardio *m* myocardium

miocardiopatía *f* cardiomyopathy; — **dilatada** dilated cardiomyopathy; — **hipertrófica** hypertrophic cardiomyopathy; — **por estrés** stress-induced cardiomyopathy; — **restrictiva** restrictive cardiomyopathy

miocarditis *f* myocarditis

miofascial *adj* myofascial

mioglobina *f* myoglobin

mioma *m* leiomyoma, myoma; — **uterino** uterine leiomyoma *o* myoma, fibroid (*fam*)

miopatía *f* myopathy

miope *adj* myopic, nearsighted (*fam*)

miopía *f* myopia, nearsightedness (*fam*)

miositis *f* myositis

mirada *f* gaze

mirar *vi* to look; **Mire hacia abajo..** Look downward.

miringitis *f* myringitis

miringoplastia *f* myringoplasty

mirtazapina *f* mirtazapine

mirtilo *m* (*bot*) bilberry

miseria *f* misery

misoprostol *m* misoprostol

mitad *f* half; middle; **Tome la mitad de una pastilla..** Take half a pill..Take a half pill.

mito *m* myth

mitral *adj* mitral

mixedema *m* myxedema

mixoma *m* myxoma

mixto -ta *adj* mixed
moco *m* mucus
modafinilo *m* modafinil
modelo de conducta *m* role model
moderación *f* moderation
moderado -da *adj* moderate;
modificación *f* modification; — **de la conducta** behavior modification
modificador *m* modifier; — **de la respuesta biológica** biologic response modifier
modificar *vt* to modify
modulador *m* modulator; — **selectivo de los receptores estrogénicos** *or* **de estrógenos** selective estrogen receptor modulator
mofeta *f* (*esp. Esp*) skunk
moho *m* mold, mildew
moisés *m* (*pl* **-sés**) cradle, bassinet
mojar *vt* to wet; — **la cama** to wet the bed; *vr* to get wet
mola *f* (*obst*) mole; — **hidatiforme** *or* **hidatidiforme** hydatidiform mole
molar *adj* (*obst*) molar; *m* (*dent*) molar; **tercer** — third molar, wisdom tooth (*fam*)
molde *m* (*dent, etc.*) mold
moldeamiento *m* (*psych*) shaping
moldear *vt* to mold
molécula *f* molecule
molecular *adj* molecular
moler *vt* to grind, crush
molestar *vt* to bother, irritate, to upset; (*ped*) to tease; **Me molesta el brazo..** My arm is bothering me; *vr* to get *o* become annoyed *o* irritated, to get *o* become upset
molestia *f* discomfort, (*frec. pl*) trouble; **Tengo molestias en el pie..** I have trouble with my foot.
molesto -ta *adj* annoying, irritating; (*molestado*) annoyed, irritated, upset
mollera *f* fontanelle
molusco contagioso *m* molluscum contagiosum
mometasona *f* mometasone
monitor *m* monitor; — **cardíaco** cardiac monitor; — **de eventos** event monitor; — **fetal** fetal heart monitor; — **Holter** Holter monitor
monitorear *vt* to monitor, to follow
monitoreo *m* monitoring; — **electrocardiográfico ambulatorio** ambulatory ECG monitoring
monitorización *f* monitoring; — **electrocardiográfica ambulatoria** ambulatory ECG monitoring
monitorizar *vt* to monitor, to follow
monoclonal *adj* monoclonal
monofásico -ca *adj* (*pharm*) monophasic
monogamia *f* monogamy
monógamo -ma *adj* monogamous
monoinsaturado -da *adj* monounsaturated
mononucleosis *f* mononucleosis
monóxido de carbono *m* carbon monoxide
monstruo *m* monster; — **de Gila** Gila monster
montaña *f* mountain
montañismo *m* mountaineering
monte de Venus *m* mons veneris, pubic area (*of a female*)
montelukast *m* montelukast
montura *f* (*Esp, para lentes*) frames (*for eyeglasses*)
moqueo *m* nasal drainage; **tener** — to have a runny nose
moquera *f* (*Amer*) nasal drainage; **tener** — to have a runny nose
MOR *abbr* **movimientos oculares rápidos.** *See* **movimiento.**
morado -da *adj* purple; *m* (*fam, moretón*) bruise
moradura *f* bruise
moral *adj* moral; *f* morale
mórbido -da *adj* morbid
morbilidad *f* morbidity
mordedura *f* bite (*wound*)
morder *vt, vi* to bite; *vr* — **las uñas** to bite *o* chew one's nails
mordida *f* (*dent*) bite
moreno -na *adj* dark, (*azúcar, pan*) brown
morete *m* bruise
moretón *m* bruise; **hacerse(le)** *or* **salir-(le) moretones** (*a uno*) to bruise, get bruises, get bruised
morfea *f* morphea
morfina *f* morphine
morfología *f* morphology
morgue *f* morgue
morir *vi* (*pp* **muerto**) to die, expire, pass (away) (*euph*); — **de hambre** to starve
mormado -da *adj* (*Mex, fam*) congested, having nasal congestion

mortal *adj* fatal, deadly
mortalidad *f* mortality, death rate; — **infantil** infant mortality
mortinato -ta (*form*) *adj* stillborn; *m* stillborn infant, stillbirth
mosca *f* fly; — **doméstica** housefly; — **volante** (*ophth*) floater
mosquito *m* mosquito
mostrar *vt* to show
mota *f* (*de algodón*) cotton ball; (*Mex, CA; fam; mariguana*) marijuana, pot (*fam*), grass (*fam*)
motilidad *f* motility; — **espermática** or **de los espermatozoides** sperm motility
motivación *f* motivation
motivar *vt* to motivate
motivo *m* reason; — **de consulta** chief complaint, reason for seeing the doctor
moto *f* (*fam*) See **motocicleta**.
motocicleta *f* motorcycle
motoneta *f* scooter
motor -ra *adj* (*neuro*) motor
mover *vi, vr* to move, to wiggle; **No se mueva..**Don't move...**Mueva los dedos del pie..**Wiggle your toes.
móvil *adj* mobile
movilidad *f* mobility, motility; — **espermática** or **de los espermatozoides** sperm motility
movilización *f* mobilization; — **pasiva** passive mobilization
movilizar *vt* to mobilize
movimiento *m* movement, motion; **movimientos oculares rápidos (MOR)** rapid eye movements (REM); **rango de** — range of motion
moxibustión *f* moxibustion
moxifloxacina *f* moxifloxacin
moxifloxacino *m* moxifloxacin
muchacho -cha *m* boy, child; *f* girl
mucho -cha *adj* (*comp and super* **más**) much, a lot of (*fam*), (*plural*) many, a lot of (*fam*); **mucho dolor..** much pain ..a lot of pain...**muchas picaduras..** many bites..a lot of bites; *adv* much, a lot; **mucho peor..**much worse..a lot worse
mucinoso -sa *adj* mucinous
mucocele *m* mucocele
mucocutáneo -a *adj* mucocutaneous
mucolítico -ca *adj & m* mucolytic
mucormicosis *f* mucormycosis
mucosa *f* mucosa

mucosidad *f* mucus
mucoso -sa *adj* mucous
mudez *f* mutism
mudo -da *adj & mf* mute
muela *f* molar, back tooth (*fam*), tooth; — **del juicio,** — **cordal** third molar (*form*), wisdom tooth
muerte *f* death; — **cerebral** brain death; — **de cuna** crib death; — **digna** death with dignity; — **natural** natural death; — **piadosa** mercy killing; — **súbita** sudden death
muerto -ta (*pp of* **morir**) *adj* dead, deceased; *mf* dead person, corpse
muestra *f* sample, specimen
mujer *f* woman; (*fam, esposa*) wife
muleta *f* crutch
multidisciplinar *adj* multidisciplinary
multidisciplinario -ria *adj* multidisciplinary
multifactorial *adj* multifactorial
multifocal *adj* multifocal
multinodular *adj* multinodular
múltiple *adj* multiple
multiplicar *vt, vr* to multiply
multirresistente *adj* multidrug-resistant
multivitamínico -ca *adj & m* multivitamin
muñeca *f* wrist
muñón *m* (*anat*) residual limb (*form*), stump
mupirocina *f* mupirocin
murciélago *m* (*zool*) bat
muscular *adj* muscular (*pertaining to muscle*)
músculo *m* muscle; — **bíceps** biceps (muscle); — **cuádriceps** quadriceps (muscle); — **deltoides** deltoid (muscle); — **esquelético** skeletal muscle; — **gastrocnemio** or **gemelo** gastrocnemius (muscle); — **glúteo** gluteus (muscle); — **liso** smooth muscle; — **pectoral** pectoral (muscle); — **psoas** psoas (muscle); — **sóleo** soleus (muscle); — **trapecio** trapezius (muscle); — **tríceps** triceps (muscle)
musculoesquelético -ca *adj* musculoskeletal
musculoso -sa *adj* muscular (*having large muscles*)
músico -ca *mf* musician
muslo *m* thigh
mutación *f* mutation; — **BRCA** BRCA

mutation
mutante *adj & m* mutant
mutilación *f* mutilation

mutilar *vt* to mutilate
mutismo *m* mutism; **— selectivo** selective mutism

N

nabumetona *f* nabumetone
nacer *vi* to be born
nacido -da (*pp of* **nacer**) *adj* born; **— muerto** stillborn; **recién —** newborn; *m* (*forúnculo*) boil
nacimiento *m* birth; **ciego (sordo, etc.) de —** blind (deaf, etc.) from birth
nadar *vi* to swim; **ir a —** to go swimming
nafazolina *f* naphazoline
nafcilina *f* nafcillin
nailon *m* nylon
nalga *f* buttock
naloxona *f* naloxone
naltrexona *f* naltrexone
napalm *m* napalm
naproxeno *m* naproxen
naranja *adj* orange; *f* orange (*fruit*)
naratriptán *m* naratriptan
narcisismo *m* narcissism
narcisista *adj* narcissistic; *mf* narcissist
narcolepsia *f* narcolepsy
narcótico -ca *adj & m* narcotic
nariz *f* (*pl* narices) nose
nasal *adj* nasal; **voz —** nasal voice
nasofaringe *f* nasopharynx
nasogástrico -ca *adj* nasogastric
nata *f* cream
natación *f* swimming
natalidad *f* birth rate
natural *adj* natural
naturaleza *f* nature
naturismo *m* naturopathy
naturista *adj* naturopathic; *mf* naturopath
naturópata *mf* naturopath

naturopatía *f* naturopathy
naturopático -ca *adj* naturopathic
náusea *f* (*frec. pl*) nausea; **náuseas matutinas** (*form*), náuseas del embarazo morning sickness; **náusea(s) y vómito(s)** nausea and vomiting; **producir náusea(s)** to nauseate, make nauseated; **sentir náusea(s)** to feel nauseated; **tener náusea(s)** to be nauseated
nauseabundo -da *adj* nauseating
nebivolol *m* nebivolol
nebulizador *m* nebulizer; **— de mano** hand-held nebulizer
nebulización *f* nebulization; (*tratamiento*) breathing treatment
necesidad *f* need; **necesidades especiales** special needs
necesitar *vt* to need
necrobiosis lipoídica diabeticorum *f* necrobiosis lipoidica diabeticorum
necrofilia *f* necrophilia
necrofobia *f* necrophobia
necrólisis *f* necrolysis; **— epidérmica tóxica** toxic epidermal necrolysis
necropsia *f* autopsy
necrosante *adj* necrotizing
necrosis *f* necrosis
necrótico -ca *adj* necrotic
necrotizante *adj* necrotizing
nefrectomía *f* nephrectomy
nefrítico -ca *adj* nephritic
nefritis *f* nephritis
nefrogénico -ca *adj* nephrogenic
nefrógeno -na *adj* nephrogenic
nefrolitiasis *f* nephrolithiasis
nefrología *f* nephrology

nefrólogo -ga *mf* nephrologist
nefropatía *f* nephropathy; — **diabética** diabetic nephropathy
nefrosis *f* nephrosis
nefrostomía *f* nephrostomy
nefrótico -ca *adj* nephrotic
negación *f* denial
negativismo *m* (*psych., etc.*) negativism
negativo -va *adj* & *m* negative; **falso** — false negative; **verdadero** — true negative
negligencia *f* negligence, carelessness, neglect; — **médica** medical negligence, malpractice
negligente *adj* negligent, careless
negociación *f* (*etapa del duelo*) bargaining (*stage of grief*)
negruzco -ca *adj* dark, blackish
nelfinavir *m* nelfinavir
nemátodo, nematodo (*RAE*) *m* roundworm
nene -na *mf* (*fam*) baby, infant
neoadyuvante *adj* neoadjuvant
neomicina *f* neomycin
neonatal *adj* neonatal
neonato -ta *mf* neonate, newborn
neonatología *f* neonatology
neonatólogo -ga *mf* neonatologist
neoplasia *f* (*proceso*) neoplasia; (*tumor*) neoplasm
neoplásico -ca *adj* neoplastic
neostigmina *f* neostigmine
nervio *m* nerve; — **acústico** acoustic nerve; — **atrapado** entrapped nerve, pinched nerve (*fam*); — **auditivo** acoustic nerve; — **ciático** sciatic nerve; — **comprimido** entrapped nerve, pinched nerve (*fam*); — **craneal** cranial nerve; — **crural** femoral nerve; — **cubital** ulnar nerve; — **espinal** spinal nerve; — **facial** facial nerve; — **femoral** femoral nerve; — **frénico** phrenic nerve; — **mediano** median nerve; — **óptico** optic nerve; — **pellizcado** (*fam*) entrapped nerve, pinched nerve (*fam*); — **radial** radial nerve; — **raquídeo** spinal nerve; — **trigémino** trigeminal nerve; — **ulnar** ulnar nerve; — **vago** vagus nerve
nervios *mpl* (*fam, nerviosismo*) nervousness, nerves (*fam*); **Tengo nervios** ..I'm nervous.
nerviosismo *m* nervousness

nervioso -sa *adj* nervous, anxious; **estar** — to be nervous
neumocócico -ca *adj* pneumococcal
neumococo *m* pneumococcus
neumoconiosis *f* pneumoconiosis
neumología *f* pulmonology
neumólogo -ga *mf* pulmonologist
neumonectomía *f* pneumonectomy
neumonía *f* pneumonia; — **adquirida en la comunidad** community-acquired pneumonia; — **por aspiración** aspiration pneumonia
neumonitis *f* pneumonitis; — **por hipersensibilidad** hypersensitivity pneumonitis
neumonología *f* pulmonology
neumonólogo -ga *mf* pulmonologist
neumotórax *m* pneumothorax
neural *adj* neural
neuralgia *f* neuralgia; — **del trigémino** trigeminal neuralgia; — **postherpética** *or* **posherpética** postherpetic neuralgia
neurinoma *m* neurinoma; — **del acústico** vestibular schwannoma, acoustic neuroma (*fam*)
neuritis *f* neuritis; — **óptica** optic neuritis
neuroanatomía *f* neuroanatomy
neuroblastoma *m* neuroblastoma
neurocirugía *f* neurosurgery
neurocirujano -na *mf* neurosurgeon
neurofibroma *m* neurofibroma
neurofibromatosis *f* neurofibromatosis
neurofisiología *f* neurophysiology
neurogénico -ca *adj* neurogenic
neurógeno -na *adj* neurogenic
neuroléptico -ca *adj* & *m* neuroleptic
neurología *f* neurology
neurológico -ca *adj* neurological *o* neurologic
neurólogo -ga *mf* neurologist
neuroma *m* neuroma; — **(del) acústico** (*fam*) vestibular schwannoma, acoustic neuroma (*fam*); — **de Morton** Morton's neuroma
neuromuscular *adj* neuromuscular
neurona *f* neuron
neurooftalmología, neuro-oftalmología *f* neuroophthalmology *o* neuro-ophthalmology
neuropatía *f* neuropathy; — **diabética** diabetic neuropathy; — **periférica** peripheral neuropathy; — **sensorial** *or*

sensitiva sensory neuropathy

neurosífilis *f* neurosyphilis

neurosis *f* (*pl* -**sis**) (*ant*) anxiety disorder, neurosis (*ant*); — **de guerra** post-traumatic stress disorder (PTSD), shell shock (*ant*)

neurótico -**ca** *adj* (*ant*) crónica y excesivamente ansioso, neurotic (*ant*)

neurotóxico -**ca** *adj* neurotoxic

neutralizar *vt* to neutralize

neutro -**tra** *adj* (*chem, etc.*) neutral

neutrófilo *m* neutrophil

neutropenia *f* neutropenia

nevirapina *f* nevirapine

nevo *m* nevus; — **displásico** dysplastic nevus

niacina *f* niacin

niclosamida *f* niclosamide

nicotina *f* nicotine

niebla tóxica *f* smog

nieto -**ta** *m* grandson, grandchild; *f* granddaughter

nifedipina *f* nifedipine

nifedipino *m* nifedipine

nifurtimox *m* nifurtimox

nigua *f* chigoe, chigger

nilón *m* nylon

niñero -**ra** *mf* baby-sitter

niñez *f* childhood

niño -**ña** *m* boy, child; — **acogido** foster child; *f* girl; (*del ojo*) pupil (*of the eye*)

níquel *m* nickel

nistagmo, nistagmus *m* nystagmus

nistatina *f* nystatin

nitrato *m* nitrate; — **de plata** silver nitrate

nitrito *m* nitrite

nitrofurantoína *f* nitrofurantoin

nitrógeno *m* nitrogen; — **líquido** liquid nitrogen

nitroglicerina *f* nitroglycerin

nivel *m* level; **de tercer** — (*esp. Mex*) tertiary; — **de conciencia** level of consciousness; — **terapéutico** therapeutic level

nizatidina *f* nizatidine

nocardiosis *f* nocardiosis

noche *f* night, nighttime, late evening; **en** *or* **por** *or* **durante la** — at night, in the night

nocivo -**va** *adj* harmful; — **para la salud** bad for one's health

nocturno -**na** *adj* nocturnal

nodo (*card*) *See* **nódulo**.

nodriza *f* wet nurse

nodular *adj* nodular, lumpy (*fam*)

nódulo *m* nodule, lump (*fam*); (*card*) node; — **auriculoventricular** atrioventricular node; — **sinusal** *or* **sino-auricular** sinus o sinoatrial node

nombre *m* name, first name; — **de pila** first name

noradrenalina, norepinefrina (*INN*) *f* norepinephrine

noretindrona, noretisterona (*INN*) *f* norethindrone (*USAN*), norethisterone (*INN*)

norfloxacina *f* norfloxacin

norfloxacino *m* norfloxacin

norgestimato *m* norgestimate

norgestrel *m* norgestrel

norma *f* norm, standard; (*pauta*) guideline; — **de atención** *or* **cuidado** standard of care

normal *adj* normal

normalizar *vt* to normalize

normalmente *adv* normally, usually

nortriptilina *f* nortriptyline

nosocomio *m* (*Amer*) hospital, clinic

nostalgia *f* (*del hogar*) homesickness; **sentir** — to be homesick

nostálgico -**ca** *adj* (*del hogar*) homesick

notalgia parestésica *f* notalgia paresthetica

notar *vt* to notice, **No se notará**..It won't be noticeable.

notificación *f* notification; **enfermedad de** — **obligatoria** (*Amer*) reportable disease

notificar *vt* to notify

novio -**via** *m* fiancé; boyfriend; *f* fiancée; girlfriend

novocaína *f* novocaine, procaine

NR *abbr* no reanimar. *See* **reanimar**.

nublado -**da** *adj* cloudy, blurred, blurry; **visión nublada** blurred vision

nublarse *vr* (*la vista*) to blur, to become blurred *o* blurry (*one's vision*)

nuca *f* (*fam*) back of the neck

nuclear *adj* nuclear

nudillo *m* knuckle, joint of a finger

nudo *m* knot

nuero -**ra** *m* son-in-law; *f* daughter-in-law

nuez *f* (*pl* **nueces**) nut; — **de Adán** Adam's apple

número *m* number, (*recuento*) count; — **de glóbulos rojos (plaquetas, etc.)** red blood cell (platelet, etc.) count
nutricio -cia *adj* nutritional
nutrición *f* nutrition; — **enteral** enteral nutrition; — **parenteral total** (NPT) total parenteral nutrition (TPN)

nutricional *adj* nutritional
nutricionista *mf* nutritionist
nutriente *m* nutrient
nutriólogo -ga *mf* nutritionist
nutrir *vt* to nourish, to feed; to nurture
nutritivo -va *adj* nutritional, nutritious, nourishing

O

obedecer *vt* to obey, to mind
obesidad *f* obesity; — **central** central obesity; — **mórbida** morbid obesity
obeso -sa *adj* obese
objetivo *m* objective, goal; **orientado al logro de objetivos** goal-oriented
objeto *m* object; — **punzante** sharp object, sharp (*fam*)
oblicuo -cua *adj* (*rad, etc.*) oblique
oblongo -ga *adj* (*pharm, etc.*) oblong
obrar *vi* (*Mex, CA; defecar*) to have a bowel movement
obrero -ra *mf* worker
obscuro -ra *adj* dark, dim
observación *f* observation
obsesión *f* obsession
obsesionarse *vr* — **con** to become obsessed with, to fixate on
obsesivo-compulsivo -va *adj* obsessive-compulsive
obstetra *mf* obstetrician
obstetricia *f* obstetrics
obstétrico -ca *adj* obstetrical *o* obstetric
obstrucción *f* obstruction, blockage; — **de la(s) vía(s) aérea(s) superior(es)** upper airway obstruction; — **intestinal parcial,** — **parcial del intestino delgado** partial small bowel obstruction
obstructivo -va *adj* obstructive
obstruído -da *adj* obstructed, blocked
obstruir *vt* to obstruct, block; *vr* to become obstructed *o* blocked

obturación *f* (*dent, form*) filling
obturar *vt* (*dent, form*) to fill
occipital *adj* occipital
ocio *m* leisure
oclusión *f* occlusion
oclusivo -va *adj* occlusive
ocronosis *f* ochronosis
octogenario -ria *mf* octogenarian
ocular *adj* ocular
oculista *mf* (*optómetra*) optometrist, oculist; (*oftalmólogo*) ophthalmologist, oculist
ocultar *vt* (*signos, síntomas, etc.*) to mask
ocupación *f* occupation
ocupacional *adj* occupational
ocurrencia *f* occurence
odiar *vt* to hate
odio *m* hate
odontología *f* dentistry
odontólogo -ga *mf* dentist, Doctor of Dental Surgery (DDS *o* D.D.S.)
odontopediatra *f* pediatric dentistry
oficina *f* office
ofloxacina *f* ofloxacin
ofloxacino *m* ofloxacin
oftálmico -ca *adj* ophthalmic
oftalmología *f* ophthalmology
oftalmólogo -ga *mf* ophthalmologist
oftalmoscopio *m* ophthalmoscope
oído *m* ear (*organ of hearing*); (*audición*) hearing, sense of hearing; — **ex-**

terno external *o* outer ear; — **interno** inner ear; — **medio** middle ear; **oídos, nariz y garganta** ear, nose, and throat (ENT)

oír *vt, vi* to hear; — **voces** (*psych*) to hear voices

ojeras *fpl* dark circles under one's eyes

ojeroso -sa *adj* having dark circles under one's eyes

ojo *m* eye; — **morado** black eye; — **perezoso** amblyopia (*form*), lazy eye; — **rojo** conjunctivitis (*form*), pinkeye; — **vago** amblyopia (*form*), lazy eye

ola *f* wave; — **de calor** heat wave; — **de frío** cold snap, period of cold weather

olanzapina *f* olanzapine

olécranon *m* olecranon

oler *vt, vi* to smell; **No puedo oler**..I can't smell; — **a** to smell like; — **mal** to smell bad

olfativo -va *adj* olfactory

olfatorio -ria *adj* olfactory

oligoelemento *m* trace element

olmesartán *m* olmesartan

olmo americano *m* (*bot*) slippery elm

olor *m* odor, smell; — **corporal** body odor; — **de pies** foot odor

olsalazina *f* olsalazine

olvidadizo -za *adj* forgetful, absentminded

olvidar *vt* to forget

ombligo *m* umbilicus (*form*), navel, bellybutton (*fam*)

ombudsman *mf* ombudsman

omento *m* omentum

omeprazol *m* omeprazole

omóplato, omoplato *m* scapula, shoulder blade (*fam*)

OMS *abbr* **Organización Mundial de la Salud.** *See* **organización.**

oncocercosis *f* onchocerciasis

oncología *f* oncology

oncólogo -ga *mf* oncologist; — **radioterapeuta, — radioterápico** (*Esp*) radiation oncologist

onda *f* wave; — **cerebral** brain wave; — **de choque** shock wave

ondansetrón *m* ondansetron

ONR *abbr* **orden de no reanimar.** *See* **reanimar.**

onza (onz.) *f* ounce (oz.)

ooforectomía *f* oophorectomy

opacidad *f* opacity

opaco -ca *adj* opaque

opción *f* option; **opciones de tratamiento** treatment options

operable *adj* operable

operación *f* operation; — **cesárea** cesarean section

operar *vt, vi* to operate; **Tenemos que operarle (de) la mano**..We need to operate on your hand; — **maquinaria** to operate machinery; *vr* to have an operation

operatorio -ria *adj* operative

opiáceo -a *adj & m* opiate

opinión *f* opinion; **segunda —** second opinion

opio *m* opium

opioide *adj & m* opioid

oportunista *adj* opportunistic

opresivo -va *adj* (*dolor*) crushing

oprimir *vt* to press, to press down on, to squeeze

óptico -ca *adj* optical, optic; *mf* optician; *f* optics

optimismo *m* optimism

optimista *adj* optimistic

optimizar *vt* to optimize

óptimo -ma *adj* optimal, optimum

optómetra *mf* optometrist

optometría *f* optometry

optometrista *mf* (*Ang*) optometrist

oración *f* prayer

oral *adj* oral

orar *vi* to pray

órbita *f* (*anat*) orbit, eye socket

orbitario -ria *adj* orbital

orden *m* order; — **de nacimiento** birth order; *f* order (*by a doctor, etc.*); command; — **de no reanimar, — de no reanimación** Do Not Resuscitate (DNR) order; **seguir órdenes** to follow commands

ordenador *m* computer

ordenar *vt* to order

oreja *f* ear; **orejas de soplillo** (*Esp*) ears that stick out

orejeras *fpl* earmuffs

orfanato *m* orphanage

orfanatorio *m* orphanage

orfelinato *m* orphanage

orgánico -ca *adj* organic; **alimentos orgánicos** organic food(s)

organismo *m* organism; (*cuerpo*) body; **efecto sobre el organismo**..effect on your body; — **genéticamente modificado (OGM)** *or* **modificado genéticamente (OMG)** genetically modified organism (GMO)

organización *f* organization; **Organización Mundial de la Salud (OMS)** World Health Organization (WHO)

organizador de pastillas *m* pill organizer

órgano *m* organ; — **hueco** hollow organ; — **vital** vital organ

organoclorado *m* organochlorate

organofosforado *m* organophosphate

orgasmo *m* orgasm, climax

orgullo *m* pride

orgulloso -sa *adj* proud

orientación *f* orientation; (*consejería*) counseling, guidance; — **familiar** family counseling; — **matrimonial** marriage counseling; — **sexual** sexual orientation

orificio *m* orifice, hole; — **de entrada** entrance wound; — **de salida** exit wound; — **nasal** nostril

origen *m* source; — **étnico** ethnicity

orín *m* (*fam, frec. pl*) urine

orina *f* urine; — **de la mitad del chorro,** — **del chorro medio** midstream urine

orinadera *f* (*Amer, fam*) bout of frequent urination

orinal *m* urinal

orinar *vt, vi* to urinate; *vr* to urinate on oneself; — **en la cama** to wet the bed

orlistat *m* orlistat

oro *m* gold

orofaringe *f* oropharynx

orquiectomía, orquidectomía *f* orchiectomy *o* orchidectomy

orquitis *f* orchitis

ortesis *f* (*pl* -sis) orthosis, brace, orthotic device; — **de brazo (rodilla, etc.)** arm (knee, etc.) brace

ortesista *mf* orthotist

ortiga *f* (*bot*) nettle

ortodoncia *f* orthodontics

ortodóncico -ca *adj* orthodontic

ortodoncista *mf* orthodontist

ortomolecular *adj* orthomolecular

ortopedia *f* orthopedics *o* orthopaedics

ortopédico -ca *adj* orthopedic *o* orthopaedic

ortopedista *mf* orthopedist *o* orthopaedist; (*cirujano*) orthopedic *o* orthopaedic surgeon

oruga *f* caterpillar

orzuelo *m* sty

oscilaciones de humor *fpl* (*psych*) mood swings

oscilar *vi* to fluctuate, to vary

oscurecer *vt, vr* (*la piel, etc.*) to darken (*one's skin, etc.*)

oscuro -ra *adj* dark

oseltamivir *m* oseltamivir

óseo -a *adj* osseous (*form*), pertaining to bone; **médula** — bone marrow

ósmosis *f* osmosis

osteítis *f* osteitis; — **fibrosa quística** osteitis fibrosa cystica

osteoartritis *f* (*Ang*) osteoarthritis, degenerative joint disease

osteocondritis disecante *f* osteochondritis dissecans

osteofito *m* osteophyte

osteogénesis imperfecta *f* osteogenesis imperfecta

osteoma *m* osteoma

osteomalacia *f* osteomalacia

osteomielitis *f* osteomyelitis

osteonecrosis *f* osteonecrosis

osteópata *mf* osteopath, osteopathic physician, Doctor of Osteopathy (DO *o* D.O.)

osteopatía *f* osteopathy, branch of medicine which emphasizes a holistic approach and uses adjustments and massage for treatment

osteopático -ca *adj* osteopathic

osteopenia *f* osteopenia

osteoporosis *f* osteoporosis

osteosarcoma *m* osteosarcoma

ostomía *f* ostomy

ótico -ca *adj* otic

otitis *f* otitis; — **externa,** — **del nadador** (*fam*) otitis externa, swimmer's ear (*fam*); — **media** otitis media; — **media con derrame** otitis media with effusion; — **media serosa** secretory otitis media

otoesclerosis *f* otosclerosis

otoño *m* fall, autumn

otorrinolaringología *f* otolaryngology; ear, nose, and throat (ENT)

otorrinolaringólogo -ga *mf* otolaryngologist; ear, nose, and throat specialist

otosclerosis *f* otosclerosis

otoscopio *m* otoscope

ovárico -ca *adj* ovarian
ovariectomía *f* oophorectomy
ovario *m* ovary; — **poliquístico** polycystic ovary
ovulación *f* ovulation
ovular *vi* to ovulate
óvulo *m* ovum, egg (*fam*); (*supositorio vaginal*) vaginal suppository
oxalato *m* oxalate
oxcarbazepina *f* oxcarbazepine
oxibutinina *f* oxybutynin
oxicodona *f* oxycodone
oxidado -da *adj* rusty; **clavo** — rusty nail
oxidante *m* oxidant

óxido *m* oxide; — **de titanio** titanium oxide; — **de zinc** zinc oxide; — **nitroso** nitrous oxide
oxígeno *m* oxygen; — **domiciliario** home oxygen; — **hiperbárico** hyperbaric oxygen
oxigenoterapia *f* oxygen (*as therapy*); — **domiciliaria** home oxygen
oximetría *f* oximetry; — **de pulso** (*Amer*) pulse oximetry
oxímetro *m* oximeter
oximorfona *f* oxymorphone
oxitocina *f* oxytocin
oxiuro *m* pinworm
ozono *m* ozone

P

pabellón *m* (*de un hospital*) pavillion, ward
pacha *f* (*CA, biberón*) baby bottle
paciente *adj* patient; *mf* patient; — **ambulatorio** outpatient; — **hospitalizado** inpatient
paclitaxel *m* paclitaxel
padecer *vt, vi* to suffer, to have (*a disease, symptom, etc.*); **Padezco asma**..I suffer from asthma..I have asthma.
padecimiento *m* illness, ailment, affliction; (*sufrimiento*) suffering
padrastro *m* stepfather; (*en el dedo*) hangnail
padre *m* father, parent; **padres adoptivos** adoptive parents; **padres biológicos** biologic parents
padrino *m* godfather
paidofilia *f* pedophilia
paidopsiquiatría *f* (*form*) child psychiatry
pájaro *m* bird
palabra *f* word
paladar *m* palate, roof of the mouth

(*fam*); — **blando** soft palate; — **duro** hard palate
paladio *m* palladium
palangana *f* (wash) basin
paleta *f* (*fam, escápula*) scapula, shoulder blade (*fam*); (*depresor de lengua*) tongue depressor *o* blade
paletilla *f* (*fam, escápula*) scapula, shoulder blade (*fam*)
paliación *f* palliation
paliativo -va *adj* palliative
palidez *f* pallor
pálido -da *adj* pale
palidotomía *f* pallidotomy
palillo de algodón *m* (*Esp*) cotton swab
palma *f* (*anat, bot*) palm; — **enana americana** saw palmetto
palmada, palmadita *f* pat; **dar palmadas** *or* **palmaditas** to pat
palmar *adj* palmar
palpar *vt* to palpate
palpitación *f* palpitation
palpitar *vi* to palpitate
paludismo *m* malaria

pamplina *f (bot)* chickweed
pan *m* bread
panadizo *m* felon, whitlow
panarteritis nodosa *f (esp. Esp)* polyarteritis nodosa
páncreas *m (pl -creas)* pancreas
pancreatectomía *f* pancreatectomy
pancreático -ca *adj* pancreatic
pancreatitis *f* pancreatitis
pancrelipasa *f* pancrelipase
pandemia *f* pandemic
pandilla *f* gang
panhipopituitarismo *m* panhypopituitarism
pánico *m* panic; **ataque** *m* **de** — panic attack
panorámico -ca *adj (rad)* panoramic
pantaletas *fpl (Col, Mex, Ven)* (women's) underpants, panties
pantalla facial *f* face shield
pantalones *mpl* pants
panties *mpl (esp. Carib)* (women's) underpants, panties
pantimedias *fpl* pantyhose
pantoprazol *m* pantoprazole
pantorrilla *f (anat)* calf
panza *f (fam)* belly, paunch *(fam)*, tummy *(ped, fam)*
panzón -zona *adj* potbellied, having a potbelly; *m* potbelly
pañal *m* diaper; — **desechable** disposable diaper; — **de tela** cloth diaper
paño *m* towel, washcloth, compress; *(surg)* drape; *(derm)* melasma; — **frío** cool compress; — **quirúrgico** surgical drape
pañuelo *m (de papel)* tissue
papa *f (Amer)* potato
papá *m (pl papás)* dad, father
papada *f* double chin
papel *m* paper; *(rol)* role; — **higiénico,** — **sanitario** *(Mex, CA, Carib)*, — **de baño** *(Mex)* toilet paper
paperas *fpl* mumps
papi *m* daddy, father
papila *f* papilla; — **gustativa** taste bud
papilar *adj* papillary
papilomavirus *m (pl -rus)* papillomavirus; — **humano (PVH)** human papillomavirus (HPV)
papito *m* daddy, father
paquete *m (de cigarillos, etc.)* pack; — **blister** blister pack; **paquetes diarios**

packs per day; — **globular** *(Mex)* unit of packed red blood cells
par *m (neuro)* cranial nerve; *(igual)* peer; **grupo de pares** peer group; — **craneal** cranial nerve; **presión** *f* **de (los) pares** peer pressure
paracentesis *f* paracentesis
paracetamol *m* acetaminophen, paracetamol *(INN)*
paracoccidioidomicosis *f* paracoccidioidomycosis
parado -da *adj (de pie)* standing; **estar** — to stand, to be standing; *f (Esp)* arrest; — **cardíaca** cardiac arrest; — **respiratoria** respiratory arrest
paradójico -ca *adj* paradoxical
paraespinal *adj* paraspinal
parafilia *f* paraphilia
parafimosis *f* paraphimosis
paragonimiasis *f* paragonimiasis
parainfluenza *f* parainfluenza
parálisis *f* paralysis, palsy; — **cerebral** cerebral palsy; — **de Bell** Bell's palsy; — **del sueño** sleep paralysis; — **facial** facial paralysis
paralizador *m* stun gun
paralizante *adj* paralyzing
paralizar *vt* to paralyze
paramédico -ca *adj & mf* paramedic
paranasal *adj* paranasal
paranoia *f* paranoia
paranoico -ca *adj* paranoid
paranoide *adj* paranoid
paraparesia *f* paraparesis; — **espástica tropical** tropical spastic paraparesis
paraplejia, paraplejía *f* paraplegia
parapléjico -ca *adj & mf* paraplegic
paraquat *m* paraquat
pararse *vr* to stand (up)
parasimpático -ca *adj* parasympathetic
parasitario -ria *adj* parasitic
parásito *m* parasite
parasitología *f* parasitology
paratifoideo -a *adj* paratyphoid; **fiebre paratifoidea** paratyphoid fever; *f* paratyphoid fever
paratión *m* parathion
paratiroidectomía *f* parathyroidectomy
paratiroideo -a *adj* parathyroid
paratiroides *f (pl -des) (fam)* parathyroid gland
parche *m* patch; — **de nicotina** nicotine patch

parcial *adj* partial

parecerse *vr* to look like; **Te pareces a tu madre**..You look like your mother.

pared *f (anat)* wall; — **abdominal** abdominal wall; — **torácica** chest wall

paregórico *m* paregoric

pareja *f (compañero)* partner; *(dos personas)* couple; — **sentimental** life partner

parental *adj* parental

parenteral *adj* parenteral

paresia *f* paresis

parestesia *f* paresthesia

pariente *mf* relative; — **consanguíneo** *(form)* blood relative

parietal *adj* parietal

parir *vt, vi (Carib, fam)* to give birth

parkinsonismo *m* parkinsonism

paro *m* arrest; — **cardíaco** cardiac arrest; — **respiratorio** respiratory arrest

paromomicina *f* paromomycin

paroniquia *f* paronychia

parótida *f (fam)* parotid gland

parotídeo -a *adj* parotid

parotiditis *f* parotitis, *(paperas)* mumps

paroxetina *f* paroxetine

paroxismal *adj* paroxysmal

paroxismo *m* paroxysm

paroxístico -ca *adj* paroxysmal

parpadear *vi* to blink

parpadeo *m* blinking, blink

párpado *m* eyelid

parte *f* part; **cuarta** — quarter, fourth; **la cuarta parte de una tableta**..a quarter of a tablet; **partes íntimas** *(euph)* genitals, private parts *(euph)*; **partes por millón** parts per million; **partes por mil millones** parts per billion; **tercera** — third; **dos terceras partes**..two thirds

partero -ra *m* male midwife; *f* midwife

participación *f* participation, involvement

partícula *f* particle

partida *f* certificate; *(euph, muerte)* passing *(euph)*, death; — **de nacimiento** birth certificate

partido -da *adj* cracked, split, *(labios, piel)* chapped

partidura *f (Cuba, ortho)* fracture, break

partir *vt, vr* to crack, split, *(labios, piel)* to chap; *(Cuba, ortho)* to break

parto *m* birth, childbirth; delivery; **do-**

lores *mpl* **de(l)** — labor pains; **estar de** — to be in labor; — **de nalgas** breech birth; — **natural** natural childbirth; **ponerse de** — to go into labor; **sala de partos** delivery room, Labor and Delivery; **trabajo de** — labor

parvovirus *m (pl* **-rus)** parvovirus

pasado -da *adj* — **de peso** overweight

pasaje *m* passage; **pasajes nasales** nasal passages

pasajero -ra *adj (dolor, etc.)* fleeting, transient; *mf* passenger

pasar *vt (fam, una enfermedad)* to give; *(fam, tragar)* to swallow; **Me pasó el herpes**..He gave me herpes...**No puedo pasar las pastillas**..I can't swallow the pills; — **saliva** *(fam)* to swallow *(dry swallow)*; — **visita** to round, to make rounds; *vr* to wear off; **El dolor se le va a pasar**..The pain will wear off.

pasatiempo *m* pastime, hobby

pase de visita *m* rounds *(by doctors)*

pasiflora *f (bot)* passion flower

pasionaria *f (bot)* passion flower

pasivo -va *adj* passive

pasivo-agresivo -va *adj* passive-aggressive

paso *m* step; **dar un** — to step, take a step; **el próximo** — the next step; — **al acto** *(psych)* acting out

paspado -da *adj (los labios)* chapped

pasta *f* paste; — **dental** *or* **de dientes** toothpaste

pasteurizado -da *adj* pasteurized

pastilla *f* pill; — **para dormir** sleeping pill; — **para el dolor** pain pill

patada *f* kick; **dar una patada, dar patadas** to kick

pata *f (fam)* foot; **patas de gallo** *or* **gallina** crow's feet, wrinkles at the sides of one's eyes

pataleta *f* tantrum

patata *f (esp. Esp)* potato

patear *vt, vi* to kick

patela *f* patella, kneecap

paternal *adj* paternal, fatherly

paternidad *f* paternity, fatherhood

paterno -na *adj* paternal

pato *m (Amer, orinal)* urinal

patógeno *m* pathogen

patología *f* pathology

patológico -ca *adj* pathological *o* pathologic

patólogo -ga *mf* pathologist
patrocinador -ra *mf (AA, etc.)* sponsor
patrón -trona *mf* employer, boss; *m* pattern
pauta *f* guideline
peca *f* freckle
peces *pl of* **pez**
pecho *m* chest, breast; **dar —** to breastfeed
pectoral *adj* pectoral
pediatra *mf* pediatrician
pediatría *f* pediatrics
pediátrico -ca *adj* pediatric
pediculosis *f* pediculosis, louse infestation (*esp. of the head*)
pedicura *f* pedicure
pedo *m (vulg)* gas, fart (*vulg*); **tirarse pedos** *or* **tirarse un —** to pass gas, to fart (*vulg*)
pedofilia *f* pedophilia
PEG *See* **polietilenglicol.**
pegajoso -sa *adj* sticky
pegamento *m (como droga de abuso)* glue
pegar *vt* to strike, to hit
pegfilgrastim *m* pegfilgrastim
pegilado -da *adj* pegylated
peginterferón *m* peginterferon
peinar *vt* to comb; *vr* to comb one's hair
peine *m* comb
pelado -da *adj (la piel)* raw
pelagra *f* pellagra
pelarse *vr (la piel)* to peel; Me estoy pelando..**I'm peeling..My skin is peeling**
peligro *m* danger, hazard; **— biológico** biohazard
peligroso -sa *adj* dangerous, hazardous
pelo *m* hair; **— encarnado, — enterrado** (*esp. Mex*) ingrown hair
pelota *f* ball; (*fam, nódulo*) lump
peluca *f* wig
peludo -da *adj* hirsute (*form*), hairy
peluquero -ra *mf* barber, haircutter
pelviano -na *adj* pelvic
pélvico -ca *adj* pelvic
pelvis *f (pl -vis)* pelvis
pena *f* grief; (*vergüenza*) embarrassment
penciclovir *m* penciclovir
pendiente *adj* pending
pene *m* penis
peneano -na *adj* penile
penetración *f* penetration
penetrante *adj* penetrating

penetrar *vt* to penetrate
pénfigo *m* pemphigus
penfigoide *m* pemphigoid
peniano -na *adj* penile
penicilina *f* penicillin
pensamiento *m* thought, thinking; **un pensamiento..a** thought; **— concreto** concrete thinking; **— mágico** magical thinking
pensar *vi* to think
pentaclorofenol *m* pentachlorophenol
pentoxifilina *f* pentoxifylline
peor (*comp of* **malo** *and* **mal**) *adj & adv* worse
pepe *m (El Salv, Guat; chupete)* pacifier
pepsina *f* pepsin
péptico -ca *adj* peptic
pequeño -ña *adj* small, little
pera de goma *f* bulb syringe
percepción *f* perception; **— de la profundidad** depth perception
perclorato *m* perchlorate
percutáneo -a *adj* percutaneous
perder *vt* to lose; **— el conocimiento** *or* **la conciencia** to lose consciousness, pass out; **— la razón** to lose one's mind, to go crazy; **— la voz** to lose one's voice; **— peso** to lose weight
pérdida *f* loss; **— de audición** hearing loss; **— de peso** weight loss
perdonar *vt* to forgive
perfeccionismo *m* perfectionism
perfeccionista *adj & mf* perfectionist
perfenazina, perfenacina *f* perphenazine
perfil *m* profile
perforación *f* perforation
perforar *vt* to perforate, to pierce; (*dent*) to drill; **apéndice perforado** perforated *o* ruptured appendix
perfume *m* perfume
perfusión *f* perfusion
perianal *adj* perianal
periarteritis nodosa *f* polyarteritis nodosa
pericárdico -ca *adj* pericardial
pericardio *m* pericardium
pericarditis *f* pericarditis; **— constrictiva** constrictive pericarditis
periferia *f* periphery
periférico -ca *adj* peripheral
perifonear *vt (form)* to page (*overhead*)
perímetro *m (de una parte del cuerpo)*

girth
perinatal *adj* perinatal
perineal *adj* perineal
perinéfrico -ca *adj* (*Ang*) perinephric
periódico -ca *adj* periodic
período, periodo *m* period; **su último período**..your last period; **— de incubación** incubation period
periodoncia *f* periodontics
periodoncista *mf* periodontist
periodontal *adj* periodontal
perioral *adj* perioral
periorbitario -ria, periorbital *adj* periorbital
perirrenal *adj* perinephric
peristalsis *f* (*Ang*) peristalsis
peristaltismo *m* peristalsis
peritoneal *adj* peritoneal
peritoneo *m* peritoneum
peritonitis *f* peritonitis
periungueal *adj* periungual
perjudicar *vt* to damage, harm, impair
permanente *adj* permanent
permetrina *f* permethrin
permiso *m* permission, consent
peroné *m* (*pl* **-nés**) fibula
peroneal (*Ang*) peroneal
peroneo -a *adj* peroneal
peróxido *m* peroxide; **— de benzoílo** benzoyl peroxide; **— de carbamida** carbamide peroxide; **— de hidrógeno** hydrogen peroxide
perrilla *f* (*Mex, fam*) sty
perro *m* dog; **— guía, — lazarillo** guide dog, seeing eye dog
persistente *adj* persistent
persistir *vi* to persist
persona *f* person; **— con SIDA** person with AIDS; **de — a —** from person to person; *fpl* persons, people
personal *adj* personal; *m* staff, personnel; **el personal de la oficina**..the office staff
personalidad *f* personality; **— tipo A** type A personality (*See also* **trastorno.**)
pertussis, pertusis *f* (*Ang*) pertussis, whooping cough
pesa *f* (*deporte*) weight; **levantar pesas** to lift weights, weightlifting
pesadez *f* heaviness
pesadilla *f* nightmare
pesado -da *adj* heavy

pesar *vt, vi* to weigh; **¿Cuánto pesa Ud.?**..How much do you weigh?
pesario *m* pessary
pescado *m* fish (*after being caught, as food*)
pesimismo *m* pessimism
pesimista *adj* pessimistic
peso *m* weight; **con bajo —** underweight; **— al nacer** birth weight; **— corporal ideal** ideal body weight; **— corporal magro** lean body weight
pestaña *f* eyelash
peste *f* plague; **— bubónica** bubonic plague
pesticida *m* pesticide
PET *m&f* PET scan (*See also* **tomografía por emisión de positrones** *under* **tomografía.**)
petasita *f* (*bot*) butterbur
PET-CT *m* PET-CT scan (*See also* **tomografía por emisión de positrones-tomografía computarizada** *under* **tomografía.**)
petidina *f* meperidine (*USAN*), pethidine (*INN*)
petrolato *m* petroleum jelly, petrolatum
petróleo *m* petroleum
peyote *m* peyote
pez *m* (*pl* **peces**) fish; **— piedra** stonefish
pezón *m* (*anat*) nipple (*of a female*)
pezonera *f* nipple shield
pH *m* pH
pian *m* yaws
picada *f* (*de insecto*) bite, sting (*of an insect*)
picadura *f* (*de insecto*) bite, sting; (*pinchazo*) puncture, stick, prick
picante *adj* hot, spicy; **salsa —** hot sauce
picar *vt* (*insecto*) to bite, to sting; (*punzar*) to puncture, to stick, prick; *vi* to itch; **¿Le pica el brazo?**..Does your arm itch?; *vr* (*punzarse*) to puncture oneself, to stick *o* prick oneself
picaridina (*esp. Amer*) *f* icaridin, picaridin
picazón *f* itch, itching, itchiness; **sentir** *or* **tener —** to itch, to have itching, to have an itch; **Tengo picazón.**.I'm itching..I have itching..I have an itch.
pico *m* peak, maximum; **alcanzar un —** to peak
picor *m* burning in the mouth (*from*

eating hot peppers and the like); (*esp. Esp*) itch, itching, itchiness, (*de garganta*) tickle, irritation

pie *m* foot; **de —** standing; **estar de —** to stand, to be standing; **— caído** foot drop; **— de atleta** athlete's foot; **— diabético** diabetic foot; **— péndulo** foot drop; **pies planos** flat feet, fallen arches; **— zambo** clubfoot; **ponerse de —** to stand up

piedra *f* stone; **— en la vesícula** gallstone; **— en el riñón** kidney stone; **— pómez** pumice stone

piel *f* skin; **— de cordero** sheepskin; **— de gallina** goosebumps **— de oveja** sheepskin

pielografía *f* (*técnica*) pyelography; (*estudio*) pyelogram; **— intravenosa** intravenous pyelography; intravenous pyelogram (IVP)

pielograma *m* pyelogram

pielonefritis *f* pyelonephritis

piercing *m* (*Ang*) piercing

pierna *f* leg; **piernas arqueadas** genu varum (*form*), bowed legs; **con las piernas arqueadas** bow-legged

pigmentación *f* pigmentation

pigmentado -da *adj* pigmented

pigmento *m* pigment

pilar *adj* pilar

píldora *f* pill; **la —** (*fam, anticonceptivo*) the birth control pill, the pill (*fam*); **— anticonceptiva** birth control pill; **— del día siguiente** morning after pill

pillar *vt* (*Esp*) to mash; **Me pillé el dedo con la puerta**..I mashed my finger in the door.

pilocarpina *f* pilocarpine

pilonidal *adj* pilonidal

pilórico -ca *adj* pyloric

píloro *m* pylorus

piloroplastia *f* pyloroplasty

pimienta *f* pepper

pinchar *vt* to puncture, to stick, prick; *vr* to puncture oneself, to stick *o* prick oneself

pinchazo *m* puncture, stick, prick; **— en el dedo** fingerstick

pindolol *m* pindolol

pineal *adj* pineal

pinguécula *f* pinguecula

pinta *f* pinta

pintarse *vr* **— las uñas** to put on nail polish, to paint one's nails; **— los labios** to put on lipstick

pintura *f* paint

pinza *f* clamp; *fpl* tweezers

pinzamiento *m* impingement, pinching

pinzar *vt* to clamp

piña *f* pineapple

pioderma gangrenoso *m* pyoderma gangrenosum

piogénico -ca *adj* pyogenic

piógeno -na *adj* pyogenic

pioglitazona *f* pioglitazone

piojo *m* louse; **— de la cabeza** head louse; **— del cuerpo** body louse; **— del pubis** *or* **púbico** crab louse, pubic louse

piorrea *f* pyorrhea

pipa *f* (*para fumar*) pipe (*for smoking*)

pipí *m* (*esp. ped, fam*) (*orina*) urine, pee pee (*ped, fam*), pee (*fam*); (*pene*) penis, pee pee (*ped, fam*); **hacer —** to urinate, to go pee pee (*ped, fam*), to pee (*fam*)

piquete *m* puncture, stick, prick; (*de insecto*) bite, sting

pirantel *m* pyrantel

pirazinamida *f* pyrazinamide

piretrina *f* pyrethrin

piridoxina *f* pyridoxine

pirimetamina *f* pyrimethamine

piromanía *f* pyromania

pirsin *m* (*Ang*) piercing

pis (*fam or vulg*) *m* urine, pee (*fam*), piss (*vulg*); **hacer —** to urinate, to pee (*fam*), to piss (*vulg*)

piso *m* floor; **— de la boca** floor of the mouth; **— pélvico** pelvic floor

pispelo *m* (*El Salv*) sty

pistola *f* gun, handgun; **— paralizante** stun gun

pitar *vt* **pitar(le) (a uno) el pecho** (*esp. PR*) to wheeze

pitiriasis *f* pityriasis; **— alba** pityriasis alba; **— rosada** pityriasis rosea; **— versicolor** tenia *o* pityriasis versicolor

pito *m* (*Col*) kissing bug

pituitario -ria *adj* pituitary

placa *f* (*card, dent*) plaque; (*surg*) plate; (*rad*) film, x-ray; **— aterosclerótica** atherosclerotic plaque; **— bacteriana** bacterial plaque; **— dental** dental plaque

placebo *m* placebo

placenta *f* placenta; **desprendimiento prematuro de** — placental abruption; — **previa** placenta previa
placentario -ria *adj* placental
placer *m* pleasure
plaguicida *m* pesticide
plan *m* plan; — **de seguro colectivo** *or* **de grupo** group insurance plan
planificación familiar *f* family planning, planned parenthood
planificar *vi* to practice family planning, to use birth control
plano -na *adj* flat, level; **pies planos** flat feet, fallen arches; *m* plane
planta *f* (*del pie*) sole (*of the foot*); (*bot*) plant
plantar *adj* plantar
plantilla *f* insole
plaqueta *f* platelet
plasma *m* plasma; — **fresco congelado** fresh frozen plasma
plasmaféresis *f* plasmapheresis
plasmático -ca *adj* pertaining to plasma; **potasio** — plasma potassium
plástico *m* plastic
plata *f* silver
plátano *m* banana
platelminto *m* flatworm
platino *m* platinum
plazo *m* term; **a corto** — short-term; **a largo** — long-term
pleito *m* (*legal*) lawsuit
pletismografía *f* plethysmography
pleura *f* pleura
pleural *adj* pleural
pleuresía *f* pleurisy
pleurítico -ca *adj* pleuritic
pleuritis *f* pleuritis
plexo *m* plexus; — **solar** solar plexus
pliegue *m* fold, crease; — **cutáneo** skin fold; — **palmar** palmar crease; — **ungueal** nail fold
plomo *m* lead
pluma *f* pen; — **de insulina** insulin pen
población *f* population
pobreza *f* poverty
poco -ca *adj* little, not much, few, not many; **poco dolor**..little pain..not much pain...**unas pocas veces**..a few times; *m* little; — **a** — little by little
podagra *f* podagra
poder *m* power; — **notarial** power of attorney

podiatra *mf* podiatrist
podofilotoxina *f* podophyllotoxin, podofilox
podología *f* podiatry
podólogo -ga *mf* podiatrist
podrido -da (*pp of* **pudrir**) *adj* rotten
polen *m* pollen
poliangeítis *f* polyangiitis; — **microscópica** microscopic polyangiitis
poliarteritis nodosa, poliarteritis nudosa *f* polyarteritis nodosa
policarbófilo, policarbofilo *m* polycarbophil
policitemia *f* polycythemia; — **vera** polycythemia vera
policlonal *adj* polyclonal
policlorobifenilo *m* polychlorinated biphenyl (PCB)
policloruro de vinilo *m* polyvinyl chloride
polietilenglicol (PEG) *m* polyethylene glycol (PEG)
polietileno *m* polyethylene
polifarmacia *f* polypharmacy
poliinsaturado -da *adj* polyunsaturated
polimialgia reumática *f* polymyalgia rheumatica
polimiositis *f* polymyositis
polimixina B *f* polymyxin B
polineuropatía *f* polyneuropathy
poliomielitis, polio (*fam*) *f* poliomyelitis, polio (*fam*)
polipectomía *f* polypectomy
pólipo *m* polyp; — **adenomatoso** adenomatous polyp; — **hiperplásico** hyperplastic polyp; — **juvenil** juvenile polyp; — **nasal** nasal polyp
poliposis *f* polyposis; — **adenomatosa familiar** familial adenomatous polyposis
polipropileno *m* polypropylene
poliquístico -ca *adj* polycystic
poliquistosis renal *f* polycystic kidney disease
polisacarídico -ca *adj* polysaccharide
polisacárido *m* polysaccharide
polisomnografía *f* polysomnography
polivalente *adj* polyvalent
polivitamínico *m* (*Esp*) multivitamin
póliza *f* policy; — **de seguro** insurance policy
pollo *m* chicken
polución nocturna *f* nocturnal emission

polvo *m* dust, powder; **en —** powdered; **— casero** house dust; **polvos de talco** (*Esp*) talcum powder; **— doméstico** house dust; **— seco para inhalación** dry inhalation powder

pomada *f* cream, salve, ointment

pomelo *m* (*esp. Esp*) grapefruit

pomo *m* (*Mex, CA*) pill bottle

pompis *f* (*fam*) buttocks, bottom (*fam*)

pómulo *m* cheekbone

poner *vt* (*pp* **puesto**) to place; *vr* (*vestirse*) to put on; (*volverse*) to turn, to become; **Póngase esta bata..**Put on this gown...**¿Se le ponen blancos los dedos cuando hace frío?..**Do your fingers turn white when it gets cold?; **— de pie** to stand (up)

ponzoña *f* poison, venom

pool *m* (*Ang*) pool; **— genético** gene pool

poplíteo -a *adj* popliteal

popó *m* (*fam*) stool, bowel movement, poo poo (*ped, fam*); **hacer —** to have a bowel movement, to go poo poo (*ped, fam*)

por *prep* per; **— ciento** percent; **— día** per day; **— minuto** per minute

porcelana *f* porcelain

porcentaje *m* percentage

porcino -na *adj* porcine

porción *f* portion, serving; **porciones por envase** servings per container

porfiria *f* porphyria; **— cutánea tarda** porphyria cutanea tarda

poro *m* pore

porro *m* (*fam*) marijuana cigarette, joint (*fam*)

porta *adj* (*vena*) portal

portador -ra *mf* (*de un virus o una bacteria*) carrier; **— asintomático** asymptomatic carrier, (*amebiasis*) cyst passer; **ser —** to be a carrier, to have (*often chronically*); **El es portador de SARM..**He is an MRSA carrier; **Ella es portadora de un catéter epidural..** She has an (a chronic) epidural catheter.

portal *adj* portal

portal *m* portal; **— de entrada** portal of entry; **— del paciente** patient portal

portátil *adj* portable

posaderas *fpl* (*fam*) buttocks, bottom (*fam*)

posibilidad *f* possibility, chance

posible *adj* possible; **lo más posible..**as much as possible

posición *f* position; **poner en —** to position; **— fetal** fetal position; **— misionera** missionary position

positivo -va *adj* & *m* positive; **falso —** false positive; **verdadero —** true positive

posmenopáusico -ca *adj* postmenopausal

posnasal *adj* postnasal

posnatal *adj* postnatal

posos de café *mpl* coffee grounds

posparto *adj* & *adv* postpartum; **depresión** *f* **posparto** postpartum depression

posponer *vt* (*pp* **-puesto**) to postpone

posprandial *adj* postprandial, after meals

pospuesto *pp of* **posponer**

postemilla *f* (*Mex, CA; dent; fam*) abscess

posterior *adj* posterior

postexposición *adj* postexposure

postictal *adj* postictal

postizo -za *adj* prosthetic (*form*), artificial, false; **dientes postizos** dentures, false teeth (*fam*)

post mórtem *adj* & *adv* post-mortem

postnasal *adj* postnasal

postnatal *adj* postnatal

postoperatorio -ria *adj* postoperative

postparto *See* **posparto.**

postraumático -ca *adj* post-traumatic

postre *m* dessert

postura *f* posture

postural *adj* postural

potable *adj* potable

potasio *m* potassium

potencia *f* potency

potencial *adj* & *m* potential; **— evocado** evoked potential

potenciar *vt* to boost; **darunavir potenciado con ritonavir** ritonavir-boosted darunavir

potente *adj* potent, powerful, strong

povidona yodada *f* povidone iodine

PPD *m&f* PPD

práctica *f* practice; **— clínica** clinical practice

practicante *mf* (*de un deporte, una técnica, etc.*) practitioner, someone who practices (*a sport, technique, etc.*); (*de* *la medicina*) medical student, physician in training

practicar *vt* to practice; **— la medicina (la odontología, etc.)** to practice medicine (dentistry, etc.)

pramipexol *m* pramipexole

pramlintida *f* pramlintide

prasugrel *m* prasugrel

pravastatina *f* pravastatin

praziquantel, prazicuantel (*INN*) *m* praziquantel

prazosina *f* prazosin

prebiótico *m* prebiotic

precanceroso -sa *adj* precancerous

precaución *f* precaution; **por** *or* **como precaución**..as a precaution; **precauciones aéreas** (*fam*) airborne precautions; **precauciones de contacto** contact precautions; **precauciones de transmisión aérea** airborne precautions; **precauciones de transmisión por gotas** droplet precautions; **precauciones estándar** standard precautions; **precauciones por gotas** (*fam*) droplet precautions; **precauciones universales** (*ant*) universal precautions (*ant*)

precio *m* (*de un servicio médico*) charge

precisión *f* precision

preciso -sa *adj* precise

precordial *adj* precordial

precoz *adj* precocious, premature, early; **pubertad** *f* — precocious puberty

precursor *m* precursor

predecir *vt* (*pp* **-dicho**) to predict

prediabetes *f* prediabetes, borderline *o* early diabetes

predicho *pp of* **predecir**

predisponente *adj* predisposing

predisponer *vt* (*pp* **-puesto**) to predispose

predisposición *f* predisposition

predispuesto -ta (*pp of* **predisponer**) *adj* predisposed, prone

prednisolona *f* prednisolone

prednisona *f* prednisone

preeclampsia *f* preeclampsia

preembrión *m* fertilized ovum prior to implantation

preexistente *adj* preexisting

pregabalina *f* pregabalin

prehipertensión *f* prehypertension, borderline *o* early hypertension

preimplantacional *adj* pre-implantation

preimplantatorio -ria *adj* pre-implantation

preliminar *adj* preliminary; *mpl* (*sexuales*) foreplay

prellenado -da *adj* prefilled; **jeringa —** prefilled syringe

premaligno -na *adj* premalignant

prematuro -ra *adj* premature; *mf* (*fam*) premature newborn, preemie (*fam*)

premedicación *f* premedication

premenopáusico -ca *adj* premenopausal

premenstrual *adj* premenstrual

premolar *adj & m* premolar

prenatal *adj* prenatal

prensión *f* grip; **fuerza de —** grip strength

preñada *adj* (*fam*) pregnant

preñez *f* (*fam*) pregnancy

preocupación *f* worry, concern

preocuparse *vr* to worry; **¿Está preocupada?**..Are you worried?...**No se preocupe**..Don't worry.

preoperatorio -ria *adj* preoperative

preparación *f* preparation; **— quirúrgica** surgical prep, prep (*fam*)

preparado *m* (*pharm*) preparation

preparar *vt* to prepare

prepúber *mf* prepubertal child

prepuberal *adj* prepubertal

prepucio *m* foreskin

presbiacusia *f* presbycusis

presbicia *f* presbyopia

presbiopía *f* (*Ang*) presbyopia

présbita, présbite *adj* presbyopic

prescribir *vt* (*pp* **-scrito**) to prescribe

prescripción *f* prescription

prescrito *pp of* **prescribir**

presencia *f* presence

presentación *f* presentation; **— pelviana, — pélvica** (*Mex*), **— de nalgas** (*fam*) breech presentation

preservar *vt* to preserve, spare

preservativo *m* condom, rubber (*fam*)

presión *f* pressure; **— alta** hypertension (*form*), high blood pressure; **— arterial** (*form*) blood pressure; **— de grupo** peer pressure; **— de la sangre** (*fam*) blood pressure; **— del habla** pressured speech; **— diastólica** diastolic pressure; **— positiva con dos niveles de la vía aérea** bilevel positive airway pressure; **— positiva continua de la vía aérea** continuous positive airway pressure (CPAP); — **sanguínea** (*form*) blood pressure; — **sistólica** systolic pressure; — **social** social *o* peer pressure

presionar *vt* to press, to apply pressure; **Presione el botón.**.Press the button.

prestación *f* delivery; — **de servicios de salud** health care delivery

pretérmino *adj* preterm

prevalencia *f* prevalence

prevención *f* prevention; — **de las caídas** fall prevention, preventing falls

prevenible *adj* preventable; **enfermedad** — preventable disease

prevenir *vt* to prevent

preventivo -va *adj* preventive

previo -via *adj* previous

priapismo *m* priapism

primaquina *f* primaquine

primario -ria *adj* primary

primavera *f* spring

primero -ra *adj* first; **primeros auxilios** first aid

primidona *f* primidone

primitivo -va *adj* primitive

primo -ma *mf* cousin

principio *m* principle; (*pharm*) ingredient; — **activo** active ingredient; — **del placer** pleasure principle

prion, prión *m* prion

prisión *f* prison

privacidad *f* privacy

privación *f* deprivation; — **de andrógenos** androgen deprivation; — **de(l) sueño** sleep deprivation

privado -da *adj* private

probabilidad *f* probability

probablemente *adv* probably

probar *vt* to try, to test

probenecid *m* probenecid

probiótico *m* probiotic

problema *m* problem

probucol *m* probucol

procaína *f* procaine

procainamida *f* procainamide

procarbazina, procarbacina *f* procarbazine

procedimiento *m* procedure

procesado -da *adj* (*alimentos, etc.*) processed

proceso *m* process

proctitis *f* proctitis

pródromo *m* prodrome

producir *vt* to produce

producto *m* product; — **lácteo** *or* **de la leche** milk *o* dairy product; — **químico** chemical

pro-elección *adj* pro-choice

profecía autocumplida *f* self-fulfilling prophecy

profesional *adj* & *mf* professional; — **sanitario** *or* **de la salud** health care professional

profesor -ra *mf* (*en una escuela*) teacher

profiláctico -ca *adj* prophylactic; *m* condom

profilaxis *f* prophylaxis; — **postexposición** postexposure prophylaxis

profundidad *f* depth

profundo -da *adj* deep

progeria *f* progeria

progesterona *f* progesterone

programa *m* program

programar *vt* (*una cita, etc.*) to schedule (*an appointment, etc.*); **cirugía programada** elective surgery

progresar *vi* to progress

progresión *f* progression

progresivo -va *adj* progressive

progreso *m* progress

proguanil *m* proguanil

prolactina *f* prolactin

prolactinoma *m* prolactinoma

prolapso *m* prolapse; — **de la válvula mitral** mitral-valve prolapse; — **de recto (útero, vejiga, etc.)** prolapsed rectum (uterus, bladder, etc.); — **valvular mitral** mitral-valve prolapse

proliferación *f* proliferation

proliferar *vi* to proliferate

proliferativo -va *adj* proliferative

prolina *f* proline

prolongar *vt* to prolong

proloterapia *f* prolotherapy

promedio *adj* average; **la estatura promedio**..the average height; *m* average, mean (*form*); **en** — on average; **inferior al** —, **por debajo del** — below (the) average; **superior al** —, **por encima del** — above (the) average

prometazina, prometacina (*esp. Esp*) *f* promethazine

prometido -da *m* fiancé; *f* fiancée

prominencia *f* prominence

pronación *f* pronation

pronosticar *vt* to predict

pronóstico -ca *adj* prognostic; *m* prognosis

pronto *adv* soon

propagación *f* spread; **la propagación de enfermedades**..the spread of disease

propagar *vt, vr* to spread

propenso -sa *adj* prone, predisposed, susceptible; **propenso a infecciones**..prone to infections

propilenglicol *m* propylene glycol

propiltiouracilo *m* propylthiouracil

propiocepción *f* proprioception

propioceptivo -va *adj* proprioceptive

proporción *f* proportion

proporcionar *vt* to provide

propranolol *m* propranolol

proptosis *f* proptosis

prospecto *m* (*pharm, del envase*) package insert

prostaglandina *f* prostaglandin

próstata *f* (*fam*) prostate gland, prostate (*fam*)

prostatectomía *f* prostatectomy

prostático -ca *adj* prostatic

prostatismo *m* prostatism

prostatitis *f* prostatitis

prostituto -ta *mf* prostitute

proteasa *f* protease

protección *f* protection

protector -ra *adj* protective; *m* guard, shield; — **bucal** mouth guard, — **labial** lip balm; — **facial** face shield; — **solar** sunscreen

proteger *vt* to protect; — **contra** to protect against; — **de** to protect from; *vr* to protect oneself

proteico -ca *adj* pertaining to protein; **restricción proteica** protein restriction

proteína *f* (*frec. pl*) protein; **rico en proteínas**..rich in protein

proteinosis alveolar *f* alveolar proteinosis

protésico -ca *adj* prosthetic

prótesis *f* (*pl* **-sis**) prosthesis; — **dental** denture, false teeth (*fam*); — **mamaria** breast implant; — **total de cadera (rodilla)** total hip (knee) replacement

protocolo *m* protocol

protozoario -ria *adj* protozoan; *m* (*Amer*) protozoan

protozoo *m* protozoan

protruir *vi* to protrude

protuberancia *f* protuberance, bulge; (*anat, fam*) pons; — **anular** pons

proveedor -ra *mf* provider; — **de salud** health care provider

proveer *vt* to provide

pro-vida *adj* pro-life

provocación *f* challenge; — **con alergenos** allergen challenge

provocar *vt* to bring on, trigger, induce, provoke; **¿Hay algo en particular que le provoque los dolores?**..Is there anything in particular that brings on the pains?

próximo -ma *adj* next

proyección *f* (*psych, etc.*) projection

proyectil *m* projectile

prueba *f* test; trial, try; proof, evidence; **a — de agua, a — de niños, etc.** waterproof, childproof, etc.; **dosis *f* de —** test dose; — **cruzada** crossmatch; — **cutánea** skin test; — **de audición** hearing test; — **de cribado** (*esp. Esp*) — **de detección** screening test, screen; — **de drogas al azar** random drug test; — **de embarazo** pregnancy test; — **de esfuerzo** stress test; — **de función pulmonar** pulmonary function test; — **de guayacol en heces** stool guaiac test; — **de imagen** imaging study; — **de inclinación** tilt table test; — **del aliento** breath test; — **del interferón gamma** (*fam*) interferon gamma release assay; — **de mesa basculante** tilt table test; — **de(l) parche** patch test; — **del VIH** HIV test; — **de orina** urinalysis (*form*), urine test; — **de Papanicolaou** Papanicolaou smear (*form*), Pap smear; — **de radioalergoadsorción** radioallergosorbent test (RAST); — **de realidad** (*psych*) reality testing; — **de sangre** blood test; — **de sangre oculta en heces** fecal occult blood test; — **de tamiz** (*esp. Amer*) screening test, screen; — **de tolerancia oral a la glucosa** oral glucose tolerance test; — **de (la) tuberculina** tuberculin skin test (TST); — **de (la) tuberculosis** TB test; — **radioalergosorbente** radioallergosorbent test (RAST); — **tamiz** (*esp. Amer*) (*pl* **pruebas de tamiz**) screening test, screen; — **y error** trial and error

prurito *m* pruritus, itching

pseudoaneurisma *m* pseudoaneurysm
pseudoartrosis *f* (*ortho*) pseudoarthrosis, nonunion fracture
pseudociesis *f* pseudocyesis
pseudoefedrina *f* pseudoephedrine
pseudogota *f* pseudogout
pseudohipoparatiroidismo *m* pseudohypoparathyroidism
pseudoquiste *m* pseudocyst; — **pancreático** pancreatic pseudocyst
pseudotumor *m* pseudotumor; — **cerebral** pseudotumor cerebri
psicoactivo -va *adj* psychoactive
psicoanálisis *m* psychoanalysis, analysis (*fam*)
psicoanalista *mf* psychoanalyst, analyst (*fam*)
psicoanalizar *vt* to psychoanalyze
psicodinámico -ca *adj* psychodynamic; *f* psychodynamics
psicogénico -ca *adj* psychogenic
psicógeno -na *adj* psychogenic
psicología *f* psychology
psicológico -ca *adj* psychological
psicólogo -ga *mf* psychologist
psicomotor -ra *adj* psychomotor
psicópata *mf* psychopath
psicosis *f* (*pl* -sis) psychosis
psicosocial *adj* psychosocial
psicosomático -ca *adj* psychosomatic
psicoterapeuta *mf* psychotherapist, therapist (*fam*)
psicoterapia *f* psychotherapy
psicótico -ca *adj* & *mf* psychotic
psicotrópico -ca *adj* psychotropic
psilocibina *f* psilocybin
psique *f* (*psych*) psyche; (*alma*) soul
psiquiatra *mf* psychiatrist
psiquiatría *f* psychiatry
psiquiátrico -ca *adj* psychiatric
psíquico -ca *adj* psychic
psiquis *f* (*psych*) psyche
psitacosis *f* psittacosis
psoas *m* (*pl* psoas) psoas
psoraleno *m* psoralen; — **más luz ultravioleta A** psoralen plus ultraviolet A (PUVA)
psoriasis *f* psoriasis
pterigión *m* pterygium
PTI *abbr* púrpura trombocitopénica idiopática. *See* purpura.
ptosis *f* ptosis
PTT *abbr* púrpura trombocitopénica

trombótica. *See* **púrpura**.
púa *f* barb
puberal *adj* pubertal
pubertad *f* puberty
pubescente *adj* pubescent
pubiano -na *adj* pubic
púbico -ca *adj* pubic
pubis *m* (*región*) mons pubis, pubic area; (*hueso*) pubis, pubic bone
público -ca *adj* public
pudendo -da *adj* pudendal
pudrir *vt, vr* (*pp* **podrido**) to rot
puente *m* (anat, dent, etc.) bridge; (*neuro, fam*) pons; — **nasal** *or* **de la nariz** bridge of the nose; — **troncoencefálico** pons
puerco *m* pig; **carne** *f* **de** — pork
puerperal *adj* puerperal
puerperio *m* puerperium
puesto *pp of* **poner**
pujar *vi* to bear down, to strain (*at stool*); (*obst*) to push; **¿Tiene que pujar para defecar?**..Do you have to strain to have a bowel movement? ...**¡Respire profundo y puje!**..Take a deep breath and push!
pujo *m* tenesmus (*form*), frequent often painful urge to defecate without the ability to do so
pulga *f* flea
pulgada *f* inch
pulgar *m* (*de la mano*) thumb; (*del pie*) great toe (*form*), big toe
pulir *vt* (*dent, etc.*) to polish
pulmón *m* lung
pulmonar *adj* pulmonary, pulmonic
pulmonía *f* (*fam*) pneumonia (*See also* **neumonía**.)
pulpa *f* (*dent*) pulp
pulpectomía *f* (*dent*) pulpectomy
pulpejo *m* (*de un dedo*) finger pad
pulsar *vt* to pulsate; (*presionar*) to press
pulsera *f* bracelet; — **de alerta médica** medic alert bracelet; — **de identificación** identification (ID) bracelet
pulsioximetría *f* pulse oximetry
pulso *m* pulse; — **carotídeo (radial, etc.)** carotid (radial, etc.) pulse; — **de esteroides** pulse of steroids; **tomar(le) el** — (*a alguien*) to take (*someone's*) pulse
puna *f* mountain sickness
punción *f* puncture, tap; — **aspiración**

con aguja fina fine needle aspiration biopsy; — **digital** (*form*) fingerstick; — **lumbar** lumbar puncture, spinal tap; — **venosa** venipuncture (*form*), puncture of a vein for withdrawing blood or for injection or transfusion

puncionar *vt* to puncture, to tap

punta *f* tip; — **del dedo** fingertip; **puntas nasales** (*Mex*) nasal cannula *o* prongs; **tecnología (de)** — cutting edge technology, state of the art technology

puntaje *m* score; — **de Apgar** Apgar score; — **de calcio arterial coronario** coronary artery calcium score; — **de Gleason** Gleason score

puntiagudo -da *adj* sharp, pointed

punto *m* point; (*de sutura*) stitch; — **blanco** (*derm*) whitehead; — **ciego** blind spot; — **de corte** cutoff point; — **de presión** pressure point; — **gatillo**, — **hipersensible** trigger point

puntuación *f* score; — **de calcio en arterias coronarias** coronary artery calcium score; — **de Gleason** Gleason score; — **T** T-score; — **Z** Z-score

punzada *f* shooting pain, twinge, pang

punzante *adj* (*dolor*) sharp, shooting, jabbing, piercing; **herida** — puncture wound; **objeto** — sharp object

punzar *vt* to puncture, to stick, prick

puñalada *f* stab wound

puño *m* fist; **cerrar el** — to make a fist

pupa *f* (*Esp*) fever blister, cold sore

pupila *f* (*del ojo*) pupil (*of the eye*)

pupú *m See* **popó.**

puré *m* (*pl* **purés**) purée

purga *f* laxative, purge (*ant*), purgative (*ant*)

purgante *adj & m* laxative, purgative (*ant*)

purificación *f* purification

purificado -da *adj* purified

purificador *m* purifier

purificar *vt* to purify

purina *f* purine

puro -ra *adj* pure; *m* cigar

púrpura *f* purpura; — **de Henoch-Schönlein** Henoch-Schönlein purpura; — **trombocitopénica idiopática (PTI)** (*ant*) immune thrombocytopenia (ITP), idiopathic thrombocytopenic purpura (ITP) (*ant*); — **trombocitopénica trombótica (PTT)** thrombotic thrombocytopenic purpura (TTP)

pus *m* pus

pústula *f* pustule

PVH *abbr* **papilomavirus humano.** *See* **papilomavirus.**

Q

quebradizo -za *adj* fragile

quebrado -da *adj* broken, split

quebradura *f* break, split

quebrar *vt, vr* to break, fracture, split; **¿Cuándo se quebró la pierna?**..When did you break your leg?

quedar *vi* (*also* — **bien**) to fit; **Me queda (bien)**..It fits; *vr* — **dormido** to fall asleep, to go to sleep; — **en cama** to stay in bed

queilitis *f* cheilitis

queja *f* complaint

quejarse *vr* to complain

quelación *f* chelation

quelante *adj* chelating; *m* chelating agent; — **de(l) hierro** iron-chelating agent

queloide *m* keloid

quemador de grasa *m* fat burner
quemadura *f* burn; — **de primer (segundo, tercer) grado** first (second, third) degree burn; — **solar** sunburn
quemante *adj* burning
quemar *vt* to burn; *vr* to burn oneself, to get burned; (*con el sol*) to get sunburned **¿Se quemó?**..Did you burn yourself?..(*con el sol*) Did you get sunburned?...**¿Se quemó la mano?**..Did you burn your hand?
quemazón *f* burning; itching (*that burns*)
queratectomía *f* keratectomy; — **fotorrefractiva** photorefractive keratectomy (PRK)
queratina *f* keratin
queratitis *f* keratitis
queratomileusis *f* keratomileusis; — **in situ asistida por láser** laser-assisted in situ keratomileusis (LASIK)
queratosis *f* (*pl* -**sis**) keratosis; — **actínica** actinic keratosis; — **seborreica** seborrheic keratosis
queratotomía *f* keratotomy; — **radial** radial keratotomy
querer *vt, vi* (*amar*) to love
queso *m* cheese
quetiapina *f* quetiapine
quijada *f* mandible, lower jaw, jaw, jawbone
quilate *m* carat; **oro de 24 quilates** 24 carat gold
quimerismo *m* chimerism
químico -ca *adj* chemical; *f* chemistry
quimioprofilaxis *f* chemoprophylaxis
quimioterapia *f* chemotherapy; — **a dosis altas** high-dose chemotherapy; —

adyuvante adjuvant chemotherapy; — **de consolidación** consolidation chemotherapy; — **de inducción** induction chemotherapy; — **neoadyuvante** neoadjuvant chemotherapy
quinacrina *f* quinacrine (*USAN*), mepacrine (*INN*)
quinapril *m* quinapril
quinesiología *f* kinesiology
quinina *f* quinine
quinta enfermedad *f* fifth disease
quintillizo -za *mf* quintuplet
quirófano *m* operating room (OR)
quiropráctico -ca *mf* chiropractor; *f* chiropractic
quiropraxia *f* chiropractic
quirúrgico -ca *adj* surgical
quiste *m* cyst; — **de Baker** Baker cyst; — **del conducto tirogloso** thyroglossal duct cyst; — **de ovario** ovarian cyst; — **dermoide** dermoid cyst; — **epidermoide** epidermal inclusion cyst; — **hidatídico** hydatid cyst; — **ovárico** ovarian cyst; — **pilonidal** pilonidal cyst; — **poplíteo** popliteal cyst; — **sebáceo** (*fam*) sebaceous cyst (*fam*), epidermal inclusion cyst; — **sinovial** synovial cyst
quistectomía *f* cystectomy, removal of a cyst
quístico -ca *adj* cystic (*pertaining to a cyst*)
quitar *vt* to remove; *vr* (*ropa, etc.*) to take off; (*dolor, hábito, etc.*) to go away; **Quítese la camisa**..Take off your shirt...**No se me quita el dolor**..The pain won't go away.

R

rabadilla *f* (*Amer*) coccyx (*form*), tail-bone

rabdomiolisis, rabdomiólisis *f* rhabdomyolysis

rabdomioma *m* rhabdomyoma

rabdomiosarcoma *m* rhabdomyosarcoma

rabeprazol *m* rabeprazole

rabia *f* (*enfermedad*) rabies; (*ira*) rage

rabieta *f* tantrum

rabioso -sa *adj* (*con el mal de rabia*) rabid

ración *f* ration, (*esp. Esp, porción*) serving; **cantidad** *f* **por** — amount per serving; **raciones por envase** servings per container; **tamaño de** — serving size

racionalización *f* (*psych*) rationalization

racionalizar *vt, vi* (*psych*) to rationalize

radiación *f* radiation; **enfermedad** *f* **por** — radiation sickness; — **ionizante** ionizing radiation

radiactividad *f* radioactivity

radiactivo -va *adj* radioactive

radial *adj* (*anat*) radial

radical *adj* radical

radiculopatía *f* radiculopathy; — **cervical** cervical radiculopathy

radio *m* (*anat*) radius; (*elemento*) radium

radioactividad *f* radioactivity

radioactivo -va *adj* radioactive

radiocirugía *f* radiosurgery

radiografía *f* (*técnica*) radiography; (*estudio*) x-ray, film; — **de tórax** chest x-ray

radioisótopo *m* radioisotope

radiología *f* radiology

radiólogo -ga *mf* radiologist

radionúclido *m* radionuclide

radiooncología *f* radiation oncology

radiooncólogo -ga *mf* radiation oncologist

radioterapia *f* radiation therapy

radioyodo *m* radioiodine

radón *m* radon

raíz *f* (*pl* raíces) root; — **del cabello** hair root; — **del pelo** hair root; — **dental** tooth root, root of a tooth; — **de regaliz** (*bot*) licorice root; — **nerviosa** nerve root

ralo -la *adj* (*cabello*) thin

raloxifeno *m* raloxifene

raltegravir *m* raltegravir

rama *f* branch

ramipril *m* ramipril

rango *m* range; **en** — **normal** in normal range; — **de movimiento** range of motion; — **de valores** range of values

ranitidina *f* ranitidine

ranurado -da *adj* (*pharm*) scored

rapé *m* (*tabaco*) snuff

rápido -da *adj* rapid

raquídeo -a *adj* spinal

raquitis *f* rickets

raquitismo *m* rickets

raro -ra *adj* rare, unusual

rasburicasa *f* rasburicase

rascarse *vr* to scratch (oneself); **Trate de no rascarse..** Try not to scratch (yourself).

rasgo *m* trait; — **drepanocítico** *or* **falciforme** sickle cell trait; — **talasémico** thalassemia trait; *mpl* features

rasguñar *vt* to scratch

rasguño *m* scratch

rash *m* (*Ang*) rash

raspado *m* (*surg*) curettage

raspadura *f* abrasion, scrape (*fam*)

raspar *vt* to scrape, to skin (*fam*)

rasquiña *f* (*fam*) itching

rastreo *m* screening, screen; (*gammagrafía*) nuclear scan

rastrillo *m* (*de afeitar*) razor, safety razor

rasuradora *f* (*manual*) razor, safety razor; (*eléctrica*) (electric) shaver

rasurar *vt, vr* to shave

rata *f* rat

raticida *m* rat poison

rato *m* short time, short while

ratón *m* mouse

raya *f* streak; (*zool*) stingray

rayo *m* ray; **los rayos solares** *or* **del sol** the sun's rays; — **X** x-ray

raza *f* race (*of people*)

razón *f* reason; (*math*) ratio; **perder la** — to lose one's mind, to go crazy; — **normalizada internacional** international normalized ratio (INR)

RCP *abbr* **reanimación cardiopulmonar**. *See* **reanimación**.

reabsorber *vt* to resorb; *vr* to get resorbed

reabsorbible *adj* (*esp. Esp; sutura, etc.*) absorbable; **no** — nonabsorbable

reabsorción *f* resorption

reacción *f* reaction; — **adversa** adverse reaction; — **alérgica** allergic reaction; — **cruzada** cross reaction; — **de duelo** grief reaction; — **en cadena** chain reaction; — **en cadena de la polimerasa** polymerase chain reaction (PCR); — **ide** id reaction, autoeczematization; — **retardada** *or* **tardía** delayed reaction; — **transfusional** transfusion reaction

reaccionar *vi* to react

reactivación *f* reactivation

reactivar *vt* to reactivate

reactividad *f* reactivity; — **cruzada** cross-reactivity

reactivo -va *adj* reactive; *m* reagent

reagudización *f* exacerbation, flare

reagudizarse *vr* to get worse again, to flare

realidad *f* reality; **en** — actually

realimentación *f* refeeding

realizar *vt* (*pruebas, etc.*) to perform

realmente *adv* actually

reanimación *f* resuscitation; — **cardiopulmonar (RCP)** cardiopulmonary resuscitation (CPR); **no** — **(NR)** Do Not Resuscitate (DNR); **orden** *f* **de no** — **(ONR)** Do Not Resuscitate order, DNR order

reanimar *vt* to resuscitate, to revive; **no** — **(NR)** Do Not Resuscitate (DNR); **orden** *f* **de no** — **(ONR)** Do Not Resuscitate order, DNR order

reasignación *f* reassignment; — **de género** gender reassignment

rebote *m* rebound; **depresión** *f* **de** — rebound depression

recaer *vi* to relapse

recaída *f* relapse

recámara *f* (*esp. Mex*) bedroom

recepcionista *mf* receptionist

receptivo -va *adj* receptive

receptor -ra *mf* (*de una transfusión, un trasplante, etc.*) recipient; *m* receptor; **positivo para receptores de estrógeno** estrogen-receptor-positive

recesivo -va *adj* recessive

receta *f* (*pharm*) prescription

recetar *vt* (*pharm*) to prescribe, to order

rechazar *vt* to reject

rechazo *m* rejection; (*negación*) denial; — **de trasplante** transplant rejection

rechinar *vt* (*los dientes*) to grind (*one's teeth*)

reciclaje *m* recycling

reciclamiento *m* recycling

reciclar *vt* to recycle

recidivante *adj* (*hernia, etc.*) recurrent

recién nacido -da *mf* newborn

recientemente *adv* recently

recipiente *m* container

reclinable *adj* (*silla*) reclining

recobrar *vt, vr* to recover; — **el aliento** to catch one's breath

recoger *vt* (*una muestra, etc.*) to collect (*a sample, etc.*)

recolección *f* collection; — **de sangre** blood collection

recolectar *vt* (*sangre, muestra de heces, etc.*) to collect (*blood, stool sample, etc.*)

recolocar *vt* to reattach

recombinante *adj* recombinant

recomendación *f* recommendation

recomendar *vt* to recommend

reconectar *vt* to reconnect, reattach

reconocer *vt* to recognize; (*form, examinar*) to examine

reconocimiento *m* recognition; (*form, examen*) examination

reconstitución *f* reconstitution; — **inmune** immune reconstitution

reconstrucción *f* reconstruction

reconstructivo -va *adj* reconstructive

reconstruir *vt* to reconstruct

recordar *vt* to remember, recall; **No recuerdo el nombre del médico.** I don't remember the name of the doctor.

recordatorio *m* reminder

recostado -da *adj* recumbent, lying down

recostarse *vr* to lie down

recreación *f* recreation

recreativo -va *adj* recreational

recreo *m* recreation

recrudecer *vi, vr* to get worse again, to flare

rectal *adj* rectal

recto -ta *adj* straight; *m* rectum

rectocele *m* rectocele

recubrimiento *m* (*del estómago, etc.*) lining; (*de una pastilla*) coating

recubrir *vt* (*el intestino, etc.*) to line

recuento *m* count; — **bacteriano** *or* **de bacterias** bacterial count; — **de eritrocitos** red blood cell count; — **de espermatozoides** sperm count; — **de glóbulos blancos** white blood cell count; — **de glóbulos rojos, — de hematíes** (*esp. Esp, form*) red blood cell count; — **de leucocitos** white blood cell count; — **de pastillas** pill count; — **de plaquetas** platelet count; — **espermático** sperm count; — **plaquetario** platelet count; — **sanguíneo completo (RSC)** complete blood count (CBC)

recuerdo *m* (*capacidad para recordar*) recall

recuperación *f* recuperation, recovery; (*capacidad para recordar*) recall; **sala de** — recovery room

recuperar *vt* to regain, recover; **recuperar el uso del brazo**..to recover use of one's arm; — **el aliento** to catch one's breath; — **peso** to regain weight; *vr* to recuperate, recover; (*volver en sí*) to regain consciousness, to come to (*fam*)

recurrencia *f* recurrence

recurrente *adj* recurrent

recurso *m* resource; resort; **pacientes de bajo recursos**..low-income patients; **último** — last resort

red *f* net, network; — **de hospitales** network of hospitals; — **de seguridad** safety net

redondo -da *adj* round

reducción *f* reduction; — **abierta y fijación interna** open reduction and internal fixation; — **de senos** breast reduction; — **gradual** (*de la dosis de un medicamento*) taper; — **mamaria** breast reduction

reducible *adj* reducible

reducir *vt* (*ortho, etc.*) to reduce; — **gradualmente** (*la dosis de un medicamento, etc.*) to taper

reductible *adj* reducible

reemplazar *vt* to replace

reemplazo *m* replacement; — **articular** joint replacement; — **de válvula aórtica (mitral, etc.)** aortic (mitral, etc.)

valve replacement; — **total de cadera (rodilla)** total hip (knee) replacement; — **valvular aórtico (mitral, etc.)** aortic (mitral, etc.) valve replacement

reentrenamiento *m* retraining

reestenosis *f* (*pl* -sis) restenosis

referencia *f* reference

referido -da *adj* (*dolor*) referred

referir *vt* (*Ang, remitir*) to refer

reflejo *m* reflex; — **aquíleo** ankle jerk; — **condicionado** conditioned reflex; — **de eyección de la leche** (*obst, form*) letdown; — **de sobresalto** startle reflex; — **nauseoso** gag reflex; — **rotuliano, — patelar** (*Ang*) patellar reflex, knee jerk (*fam*)

reflexología *f* reflexology

reflujo *m* reflux; — **(de) ácido** acid reflux; — **gastroesofágico** gastroesophageal reflux

reforzar *vt* to reinforce, to strengthen

refracción *f* refraction

refractivo *adj* refractive; **error refractivo** refractive error

refresco *m* soft drink

refrigeración *f* refrigeration

refrigerador *m* refrigerator

refrigerar *vt* to refrigerate

refrigerio *m* snack

refuerzo *m* reinforcement; **dosis** *f* **de** — booster dose

refugio *m* shelter; — **para mujeres** women's shelter; — **para mujeres maltratadas** battered women's shelter; — **para personas sin hogar** homeless shelter

regaliz *m* licorice

regazo *m* lap

regeneración *f* regeneration

regenerarse *vr* to regenerate

regenerativo -va *adj* regenerative

régimen *m* (*pl* **regímenes**) regimen; (*dieta*) diet; **hacer** *or* **seguir un** — to diet, to be on a diet; — **adelgazante** (*Esp*) weight loss diet

región *f* region, area

regional *adj* regional

registrar *vt* (*anotar*) to record

registro *m* registry, record; (*de un ECG*) tracing; — **de tumores** tumor registry

regla *f* rule; (*período menstrual*) period; **bajar(le) (a uno) la** — (*fam*) to start one's period

regresión *f (psych)* regression
regulable *adj* adjustable
regular *adj* regular
regurgitación *f* regurgitation; *(valvular)* regurgitation, insufficiency; **— aórtica (mitral, etc.)** aortic (mitral, etc.) regurgitation *o* insufficiency
regurgitar *vt* to regurgitate
regusto *m* aftertaste
rehabilitación *f* rehabilitation
rehabilitar *vt* to rehabilitate; *vr* to become rehabilitated
rehidratación *f* rehydration
rehidratar *vt* to rehydrate
reinfección *f* reinfection
reinfectar *vt, vr* to reinfect
reír *vi, vr* to laugh
rejuvenecer *vt* to rejuvenate; *vr* to become rejuvenated
rejuvenecimiento *m* rejuvenation; *(derm)* resurfacing; **— (con) láser** laser resurfacing
relación *f* relation, relationship; **Busco una relación seria**..I'm looking for a serious relationship; **— médico-paciente** doctor-patient relationship; **relaciones sexuales** (sexual) intercourse, sex *(fam)*; **relaciones sexuales sin protección** unprotected intercourse *o* sex; **¿Puedo tener relaciones?**..Can I have intercourse?
relacionado -da *adj* related; **— con fumar** related to smoking
relajación *f* relaxation; **técnicas de —** relaxation techniques
relajante *adj* relaxing; *m* relaxant; **— muscular** muscle relaxant
relajar *vt, vr* to relax; **relajar el brazo**..to relax one's arm...**No puedo relajarme**..I can't relax.
relámpago *m* lightning
relevo *m* respite, relief
religión *f* religion
rellenar *vt (dent, fam)* to fill; *(un formulario)* to fill out *(a form)*
relleno *m (derm)* filling; *(Amer, dent, fam)* filling
reloj biológico *m* biologic clock
rem *m (pl* **rems)** *(rad, ant)* rem *(ant)*
remedio *m* remedy, cure; **— casero** home remedy; **— para** *or* **contra la tos** cough remedy
remisión *f* remission; *(a un especialista,*

etc.) referral; **entrar en —** to go into remission; **— completa** complete remission; **— espontánea** spontaneous remission; **— parcial** partial remission
remitir *vt (a un paciente)* to refer *(a patient)*
remoción *f* removal; **— de tatuajes** tattoo removal
remodelación *f* remodeling; **— cardíaca** cardiac remodeling; **— ósea** bone remodeling
remojar *vt* to soak
remordimiento *m* remorse
remover *vt* to remove
removible *adj* removable
renal *adj* renal
rendimiento *m* performance
renguear *vi* to limp
renovascular *adj* renovascular
renquear *vi* to limp
repaglinida *f* repaglinide
reparación *f* repair
reparar *vt* to repair, fix
repelente *m* repellent; **— de insectos** insect repellent
repente *m* **de —** suddenly
reperfusión *f* reperfusion
repetición *f* repetition
repetir *vt* to repeat
repetitivo -va *adj* repetitive
replicarse *vr (los virus)* to replicate
reponerse *vr* to recover; *(tranquilizarse)* to calm down
reportar *vt (declarar)* to report
reposabrazos *m* armrest
reposacabezas *m* headrest
reposapiés *m* footrest
reposar *vi* to rest
reposo *m* rest; **en —** at rest, resting; **frecuencia cardíaca en —** resting heart rate; **— del intestino** bowel rest; **— en cama** bed rest
representante *mf* representative; **— de servicio(s) al paciente** patient service representative (PSR)
represión *f (psych)* repression
reprimir *vt (psych)* to repress
reprobador -ra *adj* judgmental
reproducción *f* reproduction; **— asistida** assisted reproduction
reproducir *vt, vr* to reproduce
reproductivo -va *adj* reproductive
reproductor -ra *adj* reproductive

reprogramar *vt (una cita)* to reschedule *(an appointment)*

resabio *m* unpleasant aftertaste

resaca *f* hangover; **tener una —** to have a hangover, to be hungover

resbalar *vi, vr* to slip

rescatador -ra *mf* rescuer

rescatar *vt* to rescue

rescate *m* rescue; **inhalador** *m* **de —** rescue inhaler; **— aéreo** air rescue; **tratamiento de —** salvage therapy

resecar *vt (surg)* to resect, *(completamente)* to excise; *vr* to dry, get dry, dry out

resección *f* resection, *(total)* excision; **— transuretral de próstata (RTU)** transurethral resection of the prostate (TURP)

reseco -ca *adj* dry, dried, dried out

resectable *adj* resectable

resequedad *f* dryness

reserpina *f* reserpine

reserva *f* reserve, store

reservorio *m* reservoir

resfriado -da *adj* sick with a cold; **estar — to** have a cold; *m* cold *(illness)*; **— común** common cold; **— de cabeza** head cold

resfriarse *vr* to catch a cold

resfrío *m* cold

residencia *f* home, institution; **— de ancianos** skilled nursing facility, nursing home *(fam)*, board and care

residente *mf* resident; **— de medicina familiar** family practice resident; **— de medicina interna** medical resident; **— de cirugía** surgical resident

residual *adj* residual

residuo *m* residue; *mpl (desechos)* waste; **— médicos** medical waste; **— metabólicos** metabolic waste; **— peligrosos** hazardous waste

resina *f (dent, etc.)* resin

resincronización *f* resynchronization; **— cardíaca** cardiac resynchronization

resistencia *f* resistance; stamina; **— a la insulina** insulin resistance; **— cruzada** cross-resistance

resistente *adj* resistant; **— a (la) meticilina** methicillin-resistant; **— a múltiples fármacos** *or* **drogas** multidrug-resistant

resistir *vt* to resist

resollar *vi* to breathe; *(jadear)* to breathe hard, pant

resolución *f* resolution; **alta —** high resolution; **— de conflictos** conflict resolution

resolverse *vr (pp resuelto)* to resolve, to clear up

resonador magnético *m* MRI scanner

resonancia *f* resonance; **— magnética (RM)** *(técnica)* magnetic resonance (MR); *(estudio)* magnetic resonance imaging study, MRI *(fam)*; **una resonancia magnética de la rodilla..**an MRI of the knee; **— magnética abierta** open MRI; **— magnética nuclear (RMN)** *(ant)* magnetic resonance (MR), nuclear magnetic resonance *(ant)* (*See also* **imagen.**)

resorción *f* resorption

respaldo *m* backup; **— quirúrgico** surgical backup

respetar *vt* to respect

respeto *m* respect; **— hacia uno mismo** self-respect

respiración *f* respiration, breathing; breath; **una respiración profunda..**a deep breath

respirador *m (máscara)* respirator; *(ventilador)* respirator, ventilator

respirar *vt, vi* to breathe, to breathe in; **Respire profundo..**Breathe deeply.. Take a deep breath.

respiratorio -ria *adj* respiratory

respiro *m* rest, respite

responder *vi* to respond, to react

respuesta *f* response; **— completa** complete response; **— inmunológica** *or* **inmunitaria** immune response; **— parcial** partial response; **— sostenida** sustained response

restablecer *vt* to restore; *vr (de una enfermedad)* to recover

restablecimiento *m* recovery, restoration

restar *vt, vi (arith)* to subtract; **Reste 7 a 100..**Subtract 7 from 100.

restaurador -ra *adj (dent, surg)* restorative

restauración *f (dent, surg)* restoration

restaurar *vt (dent, surg)* to restore

restaurativo -va *adj (Ang)* restorative

resto *m* rest; **el resto de su convalecencia..**the rest of your convalescence

restricción *f* restriction

restringir *vt* to restrict; (*flujo sanguíneo*) to constrict
resucitación *f* (*Ang*) resuscitation
resucitar *vt* (*Ang*) to resuscitate
resuelto *pp of* **resolver**
resultado *m* result, outcome; **investigación** *f* **de resultados** outcomes research; — **de laboratorio** laboratory result, lab result (*fam*)
resultar *vi* to turn out; **¿Y si resulta positivo?**..And if it turns out positive?
retardado -da *adj* delayed
retardante de fuego *m* flame *o* fire retardant
retardar *vt* to delay
retardo *m* delay, retardation
retención *f* retention; — **urinaria** urinary retention
retenedor *m* (*ortodoncia*) retainer
retener *vt* to retain; — **agua** to retain water
retenido -da *adj* (*dent*) impacted
reticulocito *m* reticulocyte
retina *f* retina
retiniano -na *adj* retinal
retinitis *f* retinitis; — **pigmentosa** retinitis pigmentosa
retinoblastoma *m* retinoblastoma
retinoide *m* retinoid
retinol *m* retinol
retinopatía *f* retinopathy; — **diabética** diabetic retinopathy
retirada *f* (*de una sonda, etc.*) removal; (*de un producto defectuoso*) recall
retirar *vt* (*un catéter, etc.*) to remove; (*un producto defectuoso*) to recall
retiro *m* (*Amer, de una sonda, etc.*) removal
reto *m* challenge; **un reto diagnóstico**..a diagnostic challenge
retorcerse *vr* to writhe
retortijón, retorcijón *m* (*frec. pl*) abdominal cramp
retraído -da *adj* withdrawn
retraimiento *m* shyness
retrasado -da *adj* delayed, retarded; — **mental*** with (an) intellectual disability, intellectually disabled, mentally retarded[†]
**potentially offensive* [†]*potencialmente ofensivo*
retrasar *vt* to delay, to postpone; *vr* to lag

retraso *m* delay, lag; — **del crecimiento** (*ped*) failure to thrive; — **mental*** intellectual disability, mental retardation[†]
**potentially offensive* [†]*potencialmente ofensivo*
retrete *m* (*esp. Esp, inodoro*) toilet
retroalimentación *f* feedback
retrogusto *m* aftertaste
retrógrado -da *adj* retrograde
retroperitoneal *adj* retroperitoneal
retroviral *adj* retroviral
retrovírico -ca *adj* retroviral
retrovirus *m* (*pl* **-rus**) retrovirus
reuma, reúma *m&f* rheumatism
reumático -ca *adj* rheumatic
reumatismo *m* rheumatism; — **palindrómico** palindromic rheumatism
reumatoide, reumatoideo -a *adj* rheumatoid
reumatología *f* rheumatology
reumatólogo -ga *mf* rheumatologist
reusable *adj* (*Ang*) reusable
reutilizable *adj* reusable
revacunación *f* revaccination; additional vaccination (*in a series*), booster vaccination
revalorar *vt* to reevaluate
revaluar *vt* to reevaluate
revascularización *f* revascularization
reventar *vt, vr* to rupture, burst; **reventarse los granos** to squeeze pimples, pop pimples (*fam o vulg*)
reversible *adj* reversible
reversión *f* reversal; — **de la vasectomía** vasectomy reversal
revestimiento *m* (*del estómago, etc.*) lining
revestir *vt* (*el estómago, etc.*) to line
revisar *vt* to examine; (*chequear*) to check
revisión *f* (*corrección, ajuste*) revision; (*examen*) examination; — **médica** medical examination, checkup (*fam*); — **por sistemas** review of systems
revitalizador -ra, revitalizante *adj* revitalizing
revitalizar *vt* to revitalize
rezar *vi* to pray
ribavirina *f* ribavirin
riboflavina *f* riboflavin
ricina *f* ricin
rico -ca *adj* rich; — **en proteínas** rich in

protein

riesgo *m* risk, hazard; **correr el — de** to run the risk of; **de alto; de alto; de bajo —** low-risk; **de** *or* **en —** at risk; **en — de** at risk for; **factor** *m* **de —** risk factor; **— biológico** biohazard; **— calculado** calculated risk; **riesgos y beneficios** risks and benefits; **tomar un —** to take a risk

riesgoso -sa *adj* hazardous, risky

rifabutina *f* rifabutin

rifamicina *f* rifamycin

rifampicina, rifampina *f* rifampin (*USAN*), rifampicin (*INN*)

rifaximina *f* rifaximin

rigidez *f* rigidity, stiffness

rígido -da *adj* rigid, stiff

rigor mortis, rígor mortis (*RAE*) *m* rigor mortis

rilpivirina *f* rilpivirine

rimantadina *f* rimantadine

rímel *m* mascara

rinitis *f* rhinitis; **— alérgica** allergic rhinitis

rinofima *m&f* rhinophyma

rinoplastia *f* rhinoplasty

rinovirus *m* (*pl* **-rus**) rhinovirus

riñón *m* kidney; **— en herradura** horseshoe kidney

riñonera *f* emesis basin

risa *f* laugh

risedronato, risedronato sódico *m* risedronate, risedronate sodium (*USAN*), risedronic acid (*INN*)

risperidona *f* risperidone

ritidectomía *f* rhytidectomy, facelift

ritmo *m* rhythm; **método del —** rhythm method; **— biológico** biorhythm; **— circadiano** circadian rhythm

ritonavir *m* ritonavir

ritual *m* ritual

rituximab *m* rituximab

rivalidad *f* rivalry; **— entre hermanos** *or* **fraterna** sibling rivalry

rivaroxabán *m* rivaroxaban

rivastigmina *f* rivastigmine

rizatriptán *m* rizatriptan

RM *abbr* **resonancia magnética**. *See* **resonancia.**

RMN *abbr* **resonancia magnética nuclear**. *See* **resonancia.**

roble venenoso *m* (*bot*) poison oak

robótico -ca *adj* robotic

robusto -ta *adj* (*persona*) stocky, heavyset

rodenticida *m* rodenticide

rodilla *f* knee; **rodillas pegadas** genu valgum (*form*), knock knees

rodillera *f* kneepad

roedor *m* rodent

roflumilast *m* roflumilast

rojizo -za *adj* reddish

rojo -ja *adj* red

rollos *mpl* (*de grasa*) flab

romero *m* (*bot*) rosemary

romo -ma *adj* dull, blunt

romper *vt, vr* (*pp* **roto**) to break

ron *m* rum

roncar *vi* to snore

ronchas *fpl* urticaria (*form*), hives

ronchitas *fpl* (*derm, fam*) red spots, fine rash

ronco -ca *adj* hoarse; **estar —, tener la voz —** to be hoarse

rondas *fpl* (*Ang, por los médicos*) rounds (*by the doctors*)

ronquera *f* hoarseness

ronquido *m* (*frec. pl*) snoring, snore

roña *f* (*fam*) scabies

ropa *f* clothes, clothing; **— de cama** bedclothes, bedding; **— interior** underwear

ropinirol *m* ropinirole

rosado -da *adj* pink

roseola, roséola (*RAE*) *f* roseola, roseola infantum (*form*)

rosiglitazona *f* rosiglitazone

rostro *m* face

rosuvastatina *f* rosuvastatin

roto -ta (*pp of* **romper**) *adj* broken

rótula *f* patella, kneecap

rotura *f* rupture, tear; **— de menisco** meniscal tear; **— en asa de cubo** bucket handle tear; **— meniscal** (*esp. Esp*) meniscal tear; **— prematura de membranas** premature rupture of membranes

rozadura *f* abrasion (*due to chafing*)

rozar *vt* to chafe, rub; to graze; *vi* to chafe, rub

RSC *abbr* **recuento sanguíneo completo**. *See* **recuento.**

RTU *abbr* **resección transuretral de próstata**. *See* **resección.**

rubefacción *f* (*physio, form*) flush, flushing

rubeola, rubéola *f* rubella, German measles (*fam*)
rubio -bia *adj* blond; *m* blond; *f* blonde
rubor *m* (*form*) redness, flush, flushing; (*debido a la menopausia*) hot flash
ruborizarse *vr* to flush, to blush
rugir *vi* (*el estómago*) to growl
ruido *m* noise, sound; — **blanco** white noise; **ruidos cardíacos** heart sounds;

ruidos intestinales bowel sounds
rumiación *f* (*psych*) rumination
ruptura *f* rupture; (*de pareja*) breakup; — **prematura de membranas** premature rupture of membranes
rural *adj* rural
rutina *f* routine; (*bot*) rutin; — **diaria** *or* **cotidiana** daily routine
rutinario -ria *adj* routine

S

sábana *f* sheet, bedsheet
sabañón *m* chilblain
saber *vi* (*tener sabor*) to taste; — **a** to taste like; — **mal** to taste bad
sábila *f* (*bot*) aloe
sabor *m* flavor, taste; **con** — **a cereza**, **con** — **a plátano**, etc. cherry-flavored, banana-flavored, etc.
sacaleches *m* breast pump
sacar *vt* to remove, take out; — **aire** (*esp. Mex, CA; fam*) to breathe out; — **la lengua** to stick out one's tongue, to stick one's tongue out; — **sangre** to draw blood; *vr* — **los mocos** to pick one's nose
sacarina *f* saccharin
sacarosa *f* sucrose
sacerdote *m* priest
saciedad *f* satiety, fullness; — **precoz** *or* **temprana** early satiety
saco *m* (*anat*) sac; — **vitelino** yolk sac
sacro -cra *adj* sacral; *m* sacrum
sacroilíaco, sacroiliaco -ca *adj* sacroiliac
sacudida *f* (*muscular*) twitch
sacudir *vt* to shake; **sacudir a un bebé..** to shake a baby; *vr* — **la nariz** (*esp. Carib*) to blow one's nose
sádico -ca *adj* sadistic; *mf* sadist
sadismo *m* sadism

sadomasoquismo *m* sadomasochism
sadomasoquista *adj* sadomasochistic; *mf* sadomasochist
safeno -na *adj* saphenous
sal *f* salt; — **de Epsom** Epsom salt; **sales de rehidratación oral** oral rehydration salts; — **yodada** iodized salt; **sustituto de (la)** — salt substitute
sala *f* ward, room, suite; — **de emergencias** emergency room (ER); — **de endoscopia** endoscopy suite; — **de espera** waiting room; — **de exploración** (*form*), — **de examen** examination room, exam room (*fam*); — **de maternidad** maternity ward; — **de neonatología** (*form*) newborn nursery; — **de observación** observation ward; — **de operaciones** operating room (OR); — **de partos** delivery room, Labor and Delivery; — **de reanimación** recovery room; — **de recién nacidos** newborn nursery; — **de recuperación** recovery room; — **de urgencias** emergency room (ER)
salado -da *adj* salted, salty
salbutamol *m* salbutamol
salicilato *m* salicylate
salida *f* exit
salino -na *adj* saline
salir *vi* (*secreciones, etc.*) to drain; **¿Le**

sale pus?..Is it draining pus?; **salir(***le***)** (***a uno***) to appear, develop; **Me salió una úlcera**..An ulcer appeared (developed)..I developed an ulcer; **salir(***le***)** (***a uno***) **granos** to break out (*one's skin*); **Le están saliendo granos**..His skin is breaking out..He's breaking out; **salir(***le***)** (***a uno***) **los dientes** to teethe, to come in (*one's teeth*); **¿Le están saliendo los dientes?**..Is he teething?.. Are his teeth coming in?; *vr* to appear, develop

saliva *f* saliva, spit

salivación *f* salivation

salival *adj* salivary

salivar *adj* salivary; *vi* to salivate

salmeterol *m* salmeterol

salmonelosis *f* salmonellosis

salpingitis *f* salpingitis

salpingooforectomía, salpingo-ooforectomía *f* salpingo-oophorectomy

salpullido *m* rash, heat rash

salsalato *m* salsalate

saltar *vi* to hop; **Salte en un pie**..Hop on one foot; *vr* to skip; — **una comida** to skip a meal; **Me salté la cena**..I skipped dinner; — **un latido** to skip a beat; **Mi corazón se saltó un latido**..My heart skipped a beat.

salto *m* hop

salud *f* health; — **de la mujer** *or* **las mujeres** women's health; — **laboral** occupational health; — **mental** mental health; — **ocupacional** occupational health; — **pública** public health

saludable *adj* healthful, healthy

salvado *m* bran

salvamento *m* rescue

salvar *vt* to save, rescue, to salvage

salvia *f* (*bot*) sage

sanador -ra *mf* folk *o* traditional healer; faith healer

sanar *vt, vi* to heal

sanatorio *m* (*ant*) sanatorium (*ant*)

saneamiento *m* (*ambiental*) sanitation

sangrado *m* bleeding, bleed; — **gastrointestinal (alto, bajo)** (upper, lower) gastrointestinal bleed; — **menstrual** menstrual bleeding; — **nasal** *or* **por la nariz** nosebleed

sangrante *adj* bleeding; **úlcera** — bleeding ulcer

sangrar *vi* to bleed

sangre *f* blood; — **del cordón umbilical** cord blood; **poner** — (*fam*) to give a transfusion (*of blood*), to transfuse (*blood*); **¿Me van a poner sangre?**.. Are you going to give me a transfusion?; — **total** whole blood

sangría *f* therapeutic phlebotomy

sanguijuela *f* leech

sanguíneo -a *adj* pertaining to blood; **flujo** — blood flow

sanguinolento -ta *adj* (*form*) bloody; **esputo** — bloody sputum

sanidad *f* sanitation; (*salud*) health, healthiness; — **pública** public health

sanitario -ria *adj* sanitary; pertaining to health; **equipo** — health care team

sano -na *adj* healthy, in good health

sapo *m* (*PR, SD*) thrush

saquinavir *m* saquinavir

sarampión *m* measles; — **alemán** rubella (*form*), German measles

sarcoidosis *f* sarcoidosis

sarcoma *m* sarcoma; — **de Ewing** Ewing sarcoma; — **de Kaposi** Kaposi sarcoma

sarín *m* sarin

SARM *abbr* **Staphylococcus aureus resistente a meticilina**. *See* **Staphylococcus aureus**.

sarna *f* scabies; — **noruega** Norwegian scabies

sarpullido *m* rash, heat rash

sarro *m* (*dent*) calculus (*form*), tartar

sasafrás *m* (*bot*) sassafras

saturación *f* saturation

saturado -da *adj* saturated

saturar *vt* to saturate

sauna *m&f* sauna

saxagliptina *f* saxagliptin

scanner *m* (*Ang*) scanner

schwannoma *m* schwannoma; — **vestibular** vestibular schwannoma

scooter *m* scooter; — **para discapacitados** mobility scooter

SDRA *abbr* **síndrome de dificultad respiratoria del adulto**. *See* **síndrome**.

sebáceo -a *adj* sebaceous

sebo *m* sebum

seborrea *f* seborrhea

seborreico -ca *adj* seborrheic

secante *adj* drying

secar *vt* to dry; *vr* to dry, get dry, dry out

sección *f* section

seco -ca *adj* dry; **boca —** dry mouth

secreción *f* secretion, discharge; **— nasal** nasal drainage; **tener — nasal** to have a runny nose

secretar *vt* to secrete

secretario -ria *mf* secretary

secreto médico *m* doctor-patient confidentiality

secretorio -ria *adj* secretory

secundario -ria *adj* secondary

secundinas *fpl* afterbirth

sed *f* thirst; **dar —** to make thirsty; **tener —** to be thirsty

seda *f* silk; **— dental** dental floss

sedación *f* sedation; **— consciente** conscious sedation

sedante *adj & m* sedative

sedar *vt* to sedate

sedentario -ria *adj* sedentary

sedimento *m* sediment, deposit

segmento *m* segment

segregar *vt* (*form*) to secrete

seguido *adv* (*esp. Mex*) often; **¿Qué tan seguido le dan las contracciones?** ..How often are you having contractions?

seguimiento *m* follow-up

segundo -da *adj* second; *m* second

seguridad *f* safety; **— en uno mismo** self-confidence

seguro -ra *adj* safe, sure; **para estar —** to be sure; **sexo —** safe sex; *m* insurance; **— dental** dental insurance; **— médico** medical insurance, health insurance; **— privado** private insurance; **— sanitario** health insurance

selectivo -va *adj* selective

selegilina *f* selegiline

selenio *m* selenium

sello de oro *m* (*bot*) goldenseal

semana *f* week

semen *m* semen

semilla de lino *f* flaxseed

seminal *adj* seminal

seminoma *m* seminoma

semirrígido -da *adj* semi-rigid

sen *m* (*bot*) senna

sena *f* (*bot*) senna

senderismo *m* hiking

senectud *f* old age

senil *adj* senile

seno *m* (*pecho*) breast; (*paranasal, etc.*) sinus; **— esfenoidal** sphenoid sinus; **— etmoidal** ethmoid sinus; **— frontal** frontal sinus; **— maxilar** maxillary sinus; **— pilonidal** pilonidal sinus

sensación *f* sensation, feeling; **— de dolor** sensation of pain

sensibilidad *f* sensitivity; feeling, sensation; **— a la luz** sensitivity to light; **pérdida de la —** loss of feeling; **— táctil** light touch sensation

sensibilización *f* sensitization; awareness, sensitivity; **— a la leche** sensitization to milk; **— de VIH** HIV awareness

sensibilizar *vt* to sensitize; *vr* to become sensitized

sensible *adj* sensitive; susceptible; **piel** *f* **—** sensitive skin; **— al tratamiento** treatable

sensitivo -va *adj* sensory

sensorial *adj* sensory

sentaderas *fpl* (*esp. Mex, fam*) buttocks, bottom (*fam*)

sentadilla *f* squat, deep knee bend

sentado -da *adj* sitting; **quedarse —** to sit, to remain sitting; **Me quedé sentada más de una hora**..I sat for over an hour.

sentarse *vr* to sit (down), (*de una posición supina*) to sit up

sentido *m* sense; **— común** common sense; **— de(l) equilibrio** sense of balance; **— de la audición** sense of hearing; **— de la vista** sense of sight; **— del gusto** sense of taste; **— del humor** sense of humor; **— del oído** sense of hearing; **— del olfato** sense of smell; **— del tacto** sense of touch

sentimiento *m* feeling, emotion

sentir *vt* to feel (*something external*); (*lamentar*) to be sorry; **Va a sentir un poco de dolor**..You're going to feel a little pain...**Lo siento**..I'm sorry; *vr* to feel (*internally*); **¿Cómo se siente?**..How do you feel?...**¿Se siente cansada?**..Do you feel tired?; **— bien con uno mismo** to feel good about oneself

señal *f* sign, (*auditiva, visual, etc.*) cue; **— de advertencia** warning sign; **— de alerta** warning sign, wake-up call, red flag

separación *f* separation; (*de pareja*) separation, breakup

separado -da *adj* separate

separar *vt* to separate
sepsis *f* sepsis
septicemia *f* septicemia, blood poisoning (*fam*)
séptico -ca *adj* septic
septo *m* septum; — **interauricular** interatrial septum; — **interventricular** interventricular septum
septoplastia *f* septoplasty
sequedad *f* dryness; — **de boca** dry mouth
ser *m* being; — **amado** loved one; — **humano** human being; — **querido** loved one
seriado -da *adj* serial
sérico -ca *adj* pertaining to serum; **testosterona** — serum testosterone
serie *f* series
serina *f* serine
serio -ria *adj* serious
seroconversión *f* seroconversion
serología *f* serology
serológico -ca *adj* serologic
seronegativo -va *adj* seronegative
seropositivo -va *adj* seropositive
serotipo *m* serotype
serotonina *f* serotonin
serpiente *f* snake; — **de cascabel** rattlesnake
sertaconazol *m* sertaconazole
sertralina *f* sertraline
servicio *m* (*frec. pl*) service (*frec. pl*); **servicios de emergencia** emergency services; **servicios médicos** medical services, health care; **servicios sociales** social services; *mpl* (*baño*) restroom
seta *f* mushroom; — **venenosa** poisonous mushroom
seudoaneurisma *m* pseudoaneurysm
seudoartrosis *f* (*ortho*) pseudoarthrosis, nonunion fracture
seudoefedrina *f* pseudoephedrine
seudogota *f* pseudogout
seudohipoparatiroidismo *m* pseudohypoparathyroidism
seudoquiste *m* pseudocyst — **pancreático** pancreatic pseudocyst
seudotumor *m* pseudotumor; — **cerebral** pseudotumor cerebri
severidad *f* severity
severo -ra *adj* severe
sexo *m* sex, gender; — **oral** oral sex; — **seguro** safe sex

sexología *f* sexology
sexual *adj* sexual
sexualidad *f* sexuality
shigelosis *f* shigellosis
shock *m* shock; — **anafiláctico** anaphylactic shock; — **cardiogénico** cardiogenic shock; — **hipovolémico** hypovolemic shock; — **neurogénico** neurogenic shock; — **séptico** septic shock
sialoadenitis *f* sialoadenitis
sibilancia *f* (*form*) wheeze; **tener sibilancias** to have wheezing. to wheeze
sibutramina *f* sibutramine
SIDA *abbr* **síndrome de inmunodeficiencia adquirida**. *See* **síndrome**.
siempre *adv* always; **casi** — almost always; **como** — as usual
sien *f* (*anat*) temple
siesta *f* afternoon nap, nap; **tomar** *or* **dormir una** — to take a nap, to nap
sietemesino -na *mf* (*fam*) baby born at 7 months, premature newborn, preemie (*fam*)
sietillo -lla *mf* (*CA, fam*) baby born at 7 months, premature newborn, preemie (*fam*)
sievert *m* (*rad*) sievert
sífilis *f* syphilis
sifilítico -ca *adj* syphilitic
sigmoide *adj* sigmoid
sigmoideo -a *adj* sigmoid
sigmoides *m* (*fam*) sigmoid colon
sigmoidoscopia, sigmoidoscopía *f* sigmoidoscopy; — **flexible** flexible sigmoidoscopy
sigmoidoscopio *m* sigmoidoscope
significado *m* significance
signo *m* (*de enfermedad*) sign; **signos vitales** vital signs
siguiente *adj* next
silbido *m* (*en el pecho*) wheeze; **tener silbidos** to have wheezing, to wheeze
sildenafilo, sildenafil (*Amer*) *m* sildenafil
sílice *m* silica
silicona *f* silicone
silicosis *f* silicosis
silimarina *f* silymarin
silla *f* chair; — **con inodoro** commode; — **de coche para niño** (*Esp*) child car seat; — **de ducha** shower stool *o* seat; — **de ruedas** wheelchair; — **de ruedas eléctrica** electric wheelchair; —

de ruedas manual manual wheelchair; — de ruedas motorizada motorized wheelchair; — de ruedas plegable folding wheelchair; — inodoro commode; — reclinable reclining chair, recliner (fam)
sillón dental m dental chair
silodosina f silodosin
simbiosis f (psych, etc.) symbiosis
simeprevir m simeprevir
simeticona f simethicone, simeticone (INN)
simetría f symmetry
simétrico -ca adj symmetrical
simpatectomía f sympathectomy
simpático -ca adj (neuro) sympathetic
simulado -da adj factitious
simvastatina f simvastatin
sin prep without, free; — ánimo de lucro nonprofit; — azúcar, — sal, etc. sugar-free, salt-free, etc.; — dolor without pain, pain-free; — fines de lucro nonprofit; — olor odorless; — querer by accident
sinapsis f (pl -sis) synapse
síncope m syncope
sincronizar vt to synchronize
síndrome m syndrome; — alcohólico fetal fetal alcohol syndrome; — antifosfolípido antiphospholipid syndrome; — carcinoide carcinoid syndrome; — compartimental compartmental syndrome; — de abstinencia withdrawal; — de alcoholismo fetal fetal alcohol syndrome; — de asa ciega blind loop syndrome; — de Asherman Asherman's syndrome; — de choque tóxico toxic shock syndrome; — de colon irritable irritable bowel syndrome; — de Cushing Cushing's syndrome*; — de desgaste wasting syndrome; — de dificultad respiratoria del adulto adult respiratory distress syndrome (ARDS); — de discinesia apical (transitoria) apical ballooning syndrome; — de dolor regional complejo complex regional pain syndrome; — de Down Down syndrome; — de Ehlers-Danlos Ehlers-Danlos syndrome; — de fatiga crónica chronic fatigue syndrome; — de Felty Felty's syndrome*; — de Gilbert Gilbert's syndrome*; — de Gilles de la Tou-

rette Gilles de la Tourette syndrome; — de Guillain-Barré Guillain-Barré syndrome; — de hipoventilación por obesidad obesity-hypoventilation syndrome; — de inmunodeficiencia adquirida (SIDA) acquired immunodeficiency syndrome (AIDS); — de intestino corto short bowel syndrome; — de intestino irritable irritable bowel syndrome; — de Klinefelter Klinefelter syndrome; — de la piel escaldada estafilocócica staphylococcal scalded skin syndrome; — del asa ciega blind loop syndrome; — del colon irritable irritable bowel syndrome; — del corazón roto broken heart syndrome; — del intestino irritable irritable bowel syndrome; — del nido vacío empty nest syndrome; — del niño maltratado battered child syndrome; — del ocaso sundowning; — del túnel carpiano carpal tunnel syndrome; — de Marfan Marfan syndrome; — de muerte súbita del lactante or infantil sudden infant death syndrome (SIDS); — de Munchausen Munchausen syndrome; — de Osler-Weber-Rendu Osler-Weber-Rendu syndrome; — de ovario poliquístico polycystic ovary syndrome; — de Peutz-Jeghers Peutz-Jeghers syndrome; — de Pickwick obesity-hypoventilation syndrome, Pickwickian syndrome (ant); — de piernas inquietas restless legs syndrome; — de Reiter (ant) reactive arthritis, Reiter's syndrome (ant); — de Reye Reye's syndrome; — de Sheehan Sheehan's syndrome*; — de Sjögren Sjögren's syndrome*; — de sobrecarga overuse syndrome; — de Stevens-Johnson Stevens-Johnson syndrome; — de Turner Turner syndrome; — de vejiga hiperactiva overactive bladder syndrome; — de Wernicke-Korsakoff Wernicke-Korsakoff syndrome; — de Wolff-Parkinson-White Wolff-Parkinson-White syndrome; — hemolítico-urémico hemolytic-uremic syndrome; — hepatorrenal hepatorenal syndrome; — metabólico metabolic syndrome; — mielodisplásico myelodysplastic syndrome; — nefrótico nephrotic syndrome; — neuroléptico

maligno neuroleptic malignant syndrome; — **postconmocional** postconcussion syndrome; — **post-polio** post-polio syndrome; — **premenstrual (SPM)** premenstrual syndrome (PMS); — **respiratorio agudo severo (SRAS)** severe acute respiratory syndrome (SARS); — **vespertino** sundowning
La forma no posesiva también se usa, sobre todo en la literatura médica: Cushing syndrome, Felty syndrome, etc.

sinergia *f* synergy
sinérgico -ca *adj* synergistic
sínfisis *f* symphysis
sinoauricular *adj* sinoatrial, sinus
sinovial *adj* synovial
sinovitis *f* synovitis
sintético -ca *adj* synthetic
sintetizar *vt* to synthesize
síntoma *m* symptom
sintomático -ca *adj* symptomatic
sinus *m* sinus; — **pilonidal** pilonidal sinus
sinusal *adj* (*card*) sinoatrial, sinus
sinusitis *f* sinusitis
síquico -ca *adj* psychic
siringomielia *f* syringomyelia
sirolimús *m* sirolimus
sistema *m* system; — **cardiovascular** cardiovascular system; — **de salud** health care system; — **digestivo** digestive system; — **endocrino** endocrine system; — **esquelético** skeletal system; — **inmunológico, inmunitario** *or* **inmune** immune system; — **locomotor** musculoskeletal system; — **métrico** metric system; — **musculoesquelético** musculoskeletal system; — **nervioso autónomo** autonomic nervous system; — **nervioso central (SNC)** central nervous system (CNS); — **nervioso parasimpático** parasympathetic nervous system; — **nervioso periférico** peripheral nervous system; — **nervioso simpático** sympathetic nervous system; — **óseo** skeletal system; — **reproductor** *or* **reproductivo** reproductive system; — **respiratorio** respiratory system
sistémico -ca *adj* systemic
sistólico -ca *adj* systolic
sitagliptina *f* sitagliptin

sitio *m* site, place; — **quirúrgico** surgical site
SNC *abbr* **sistema nervioso central.** *See* **sistema.**
sobador -ra (*Mex, CA*) *mf* folk healer who employs manipulations and massage to treat dislocations and other orthopedic conditions
sobaco *m* (*fam*) axilla, armpit (*fam*)
sobandero -ra (*Col, Ven*) massage therapist
sobar *vt* (*Amer*) to rub, to massage
sobre *adv* (*por encima de*) over; **Su presión arterial es de 160 sobre 90..** Your blood pressure is 160 over 90.
sobrecarga *f* overload; — **de hierro** iron overload
sobrecargar *vt* to overload
sobrecompensación *f* (*psych, etc.*) overcompensation
sobrecompensar *vi* to overcompensate
sobrecrecimiento *m* overgrowth; — **bacteriano intestinal** bacterial overgrowth syndrome
sobredosis *f* (*pl* -sis) overdose
sobreexcitar *vt* to overexcite; *vr* to become overexcited
sobrellevar *vt* to endure, bear, to cope with
sobremordida *f* overbite
sobrepeso *m* excess weight
sobreproducción *f* overproduction
sobresalir *vi* to protrude, to stick out
sobreuso *m* overuse; **lesión** *f* **por —** overuse injury
sobreutilización *f* overutilization
sobreviviente *mf* survivor; — **del cáncer** cancer survivor
sobrevivir *vt, vi* to survive
sobriedad *f* sobriety; **recuperar la —** to sober up
sobrino -na *m* nephew; *f* niece
sobrio -ria *adj* sober
socio -cia *mf* (*profesional*) partner, associate
socioeconómico -ca *adj* socioeconomic
sociosanitario -ria *adj* pertaining to social and health needs of elderly and disabled persons
socorrista *mf* rescuer
socorro *interj* Help!; *m* help, assistance, (*después de un desastre*) aid, relief
sodio *m* sodium

sodomía *f* sodomy
sodomizar *vt* to sodomize
sofocación *f* suffocation
sofocar *vt* to suffocate
sofoco *m* (*debido a la menopausia*) hot flash
sofosbuvir *m* sofosbuvir
soja *f* soy
sol *m* sun; **tomar el** — to get sun, to sunbathe
solamente *adv* only
solar *adj* solar
soldado *mf* soldier
soldar *vi*, *vr* (*ortho*) to knit, to unite
sóleo *m* soleus
solicitar *vt* (*seguro, etc.*) to apply
solicitud *f* (*para seguro, etc.*) application
sólido -da *adj* & *m* solid
solifenacina *f* solifenacin
solitario -ria *mf* loner; *f* Taenia, tapeworm
solo -la *adj* only, (*sin otros*) alone; **de progestina sola** progestin-only; **sentirse** — to feel alone
sólo *adv* only; **sólo una vez**..only once
soltar *vt* (*pp* **suelto**) to loosen, free, (*fam, relajar*) to relax; **Suelte el cinturón**.. Loosen your belt...**Suelte la pierna**.. Relax your leg.
soltero -ra *adj* unmarried, single
soltura *f* (*Mex, fam*) diarrhea
soluble *adj* soluble
solución *f* solution; — **amortiguadora** buffer solution; — **de rehidratación oral** oral rehydration solution; — **electrolítica** electrolyte solution; — **salina normal** normal saline solution; — **tampón** buffer solution
solvente *m* solvent
somático -ca *adj* somatic
somatización *f* somatization
somatotropina *f* somatotropin
somatropina *f* somatropin
sombra *f* shadow; **sombras de** *or* **para ojos** eye shadow
sombrero *m* hat
someterse a *vi* to undergo
somnífero *m* sleeping pill
somnolencia *f* somnolence, sleepiness
somnoliento -ta *adj* somnolent, sleepy, drowsy
sonambulismo *m* sleepwalking
sonarse la nariz *vr* to blow one's nose

sonda *f* tube, (urinary) catheter; — **de alimentación** feeding tube; — **de gastrostomía** gastrostomy tube, G-tube (*fam*); — **Foley** Foley catheter; — **nasogástrica** nasogastric tube; — **pleural** (*esp Mex*) chest tube; — **vesical** urinary catheter
sondaje *m* placement *o* insertion of a tube; — **nasogástrico** placement of a nasogastric tube; — **vesical** bladder catheterization
sonido *m* sound; **sonidos cardíacos** heart sounds; **sonidos intestinales** bowel sounds
sonografía *f* (*técnica*) ultrasonography, ultrasound; (*estudio*) ultrasound, sonogram (*form*)
sonreír *vi*, *vr* to smile
sonrisa *f* smile
sonrojarse *vr* (*physio*) to flush, to blush
soñar *vt*, *vi* to dream; — **con** to dream of *o* about; — **despierto** to daydream
soñolencia *f* somnolence, sleepiness
soñoliento -ta *adj* somnolent, sleepy, drowsy
sopa *f* soup
soplar *vt*, *vi* to blow; *vr* — **la nariz** (*Carib*) to blow one's nose
soplo *m* (*card*) murmur; — **cardíaco** heart murmur
soportable *adj* tolerable, bearable
soportar *vt* to support, (*peso*) to bear (*weight*)
soporte *m* support; — **nutricional** nutritional support; — **vital** life support; — **vital básico** basic life support (BLS); — **vital cardíaco avanzado** advanced cardiac life support (ACLS)
sorber *vt* to sip
sorbitol *m* sorbitol
sorbo *m* sip; — **de jugo** sip of juice
sordera *f* deafness
sordo -da *adj* deaf; (*dolor*) dull; *mf* deaf person
sordomudez *f* deafmutism
sordomudo -da *adj* deaf and mute; *mf* deafmute
soroche *m* (*SA*) mountain sickness
sospechoso -sa *adj* suspicious; — **de cáncer** suspicious for cancer
sostén *m* brassiere, bra (*fam*)
sostener *vt* to support, to sustain
sotalol *m* sotalol

spa *m* spa, health resort; — **médico** medical spa, med spa (*fam*)

spinosad *m* spinosad

SPM *abbr* **síndrome premenstrual**. *See* **síndrome**.

spray *m* (*Ang*) spray; — **de pimienta** pepper spray; — **nasal** nasal spray

SRAS *abbr* **síndrome respiratorio agudo severo**. *See* **síndrome**.

Staphylococcus aureus, Staphylococcus aureus; — — **resistente a (la) meticilina (SARM)** methicillin-resistant Staphylococcus aureus (MRSA)

stent *m* (*pl* stent *or* stents) stent; — **de metal desnudo** bare-metal stent; — **liberador de fármaco(s)** drug-eluting stent

suave *adj* soft, (*pelo, piel*) smooth, (*jabón*) mild, (*toque*) light, gentle

suavizante *adj* (*una loción, etc.*) softening

suavizar *vt* (*la piel, etc.*) to soften

subacromial *adj* subacromial

subagudo -da *adj* subacute

subalimentación *f* undernourishment

subalimentado -da *adj* undernourished

subaracnoideo -a *adj* subarachnoid

subclavio -via *adj* subclavian

subclínico -ca *adj* subclinical

subconciencia *f* subconscious

subconjuntival *adj* subconjunctival

subconsciencia *f* subconscious

subconsciente *adj* subconscious

subcutáneo -a *adj* subcutaneous

subdural *adj* subdural

subespecialidad *f* subspecialty

subespecialista *mf* subspecialist

subir *vi* to go up, rise; Le subió el azúcar..Your sugar went up.

súbito -ta *adj* sudden

subletal *adj* sublethal

sublimación *f* (*psych*) sublimation

sublingual *adj* sublingual

subluxación *f* subluxation

submandibular *adj* submandibular

submarino -na *adj* underwater

submentoniano -na *adj* submental

subnormal* *adj* with (an) intellectual disability, intellectually disabled, mentally retarded[†]

*potentially offensive, [†]potencialmente ofensivo

subsalicilato de bismuto *m* bismuth sub-

salicylate

subtotal *adj* subtotal

subungueal *adj* subungual

subyacente *adj* underlying; **problema** *m* — underlying problem

succión *f* suction; — **del pulgar** (*form*) thumb sucking

suciedad *f* dirt

sucio -cia *adj* dirty

sucralfato *m* sucralfate

sucralosa *f* sucralose

sudamina *f* miliaria, heat rash (*fam*)

sudar *vi* to perspire, to sweat

sudor *m* perspiration, sweat

sudoración *f* perspiration, sweating; — **nocturna** night sweats

sudoroso -sa *adj* sweaty

suegro -gra *m* father-in-law; *f* mother-in-law

suela *f* sole (*of a shoe*)

suelo *m* floor; — **de la boca** floor of the mouth; — **pélvico** *or* **de la pelvis** pelvic floor

suelto -ta (*pp of* **soltar**) *adj* loose, free

sueño *m* sleep; dream; **dar** — to make sleepy; **mantener el** — to stay asleep; **persona de** — **ligero** light sleeper; — **húmedo** wet dream; **tener** — to be sleepy

suero *m* serum; (*fisiológico*) electrolyte solution, IV fluid(s) (*fam*); **¿Me van a poner suero?**..Are you going to give me IV fluids?; — **de rehidratación oral** oral rehydration solution

suero de leche *m* whey

sufentanilo *m* sufentanil

suficiente *adj* sufficient

sufrimiento *m* suffering

sufrir *vi* to suffer

sugerencia *f* suggestion

sugestión *f* (*psych*) suggestion; **poder** *m* **de la** — power of suggestion

sugestionabilidad *f* suggestibility

suicida *adj* suicidal; **gesto suicida** suicide gesture; **intento suicida** suicide attempt

suicidarse *vr* to commit suicide

suicidio *m* suicide; **intento de** — suicide attempt; — **asistido por un médico** physician-assisted suicide

sujeción *f* restraint; — **mecánica** mechanical restraint; — **química** chemical restraint

sujetador *m* brassiere
sujetar *vt* (*a un paciente*) to restrain
sulfacetamida *f* sulfacetamide
sulfadiazina, sulfadiacina *f* sulfadiazine; — **de plata** silver sulfadiazine
sulfafurazol *m* sulfisoxazole (*USAN*), sulfafurazole (*INN*)
sulfametoxazol *m* sulfamethoxazole
sulfas *fpl* sulfa drugs; [*Nota: En inglés se usa mucho la forma singular:* sulfa drug.]
sulfasalazina, sulfasalacina (*esp. Esp*) *f* sulfasalazine
sulfato *m* sulfate; — **de cobre** copper sulfate; — **de condroitina** chondroitin sulfate; — **de magnesio** magnesium sulfate, Epsom salt; — **ferroso** ferrous sulfate; — **magnésico** (*esp. Esp*) magnesium sulfate
sulfisoxazol *m* sulfisoxazole (*USAN*), sulfafurazole (*INN*)
sulfito *m* sulfite
sulfonamida *f* sulfonamide
sulfonilurea *f* sulfonylurea
sumar *vt* (*arith*) to add; ¿**Puede sumar 10 y 12?**..Can you add 10 and 12?
sumatriptán *m* sumatriptan
suministros médicos *mpl* medical supplies
superar *vt* to overcome; **superar miedos**.. to overcome fears
superdotado -da *adj* gifted
superego *m* (*psych*) superego
superficial *adj* superficial
superficie *f* surface
superior *adj* higher, greater; (*anat*) superior, upper; **brazo** — upper arm; **espalda** — upper back; **maxilar** *m* — upper jaw; **parte** *f* — **del cuerpo** upper body; — **a** higher than, greater than, above; **superior a 90**..higher (greater) than 90..above 90
supernumerario -ria *adj* supernumerary
superstición *f* superstition
supervivencia *f* survival
superviviente *mf* survivor; — **del cáncer** cancer survivor
superyó *m* (*psych*) superego
supinación *f* supination
supino -na *adj* supine
suplementario -ria *adj* supplemental, supplementary

suplemento *m* supplement; — **alimenticio** *or* **dietético** dietary supplement
supositorio *m* suppository; — **vaginal** vaginal suppository
suprarrenal *adj* adrenal; *f* (*fam*) adrenal gland, adrenal (*fam*)
suprarrenalectomía *f* adrenalectomy
supresión *f* (*psych, etc.*) suppression
supresor -ra *adj* suppressive; *m* suppressant; — **del apetito** appetite suppressant
suprimir *vt* to suppress, (*apetito, deseo*) to curb
supuración *f* suppuration (*form*), discharge, secretion (*of pus*)
supurar *vi* to suppurate (*form*), to form pus, to drain pus
supurativo -va *adj* suppurative
suramina *f* suramin
surco *m* (*de la sarna*) burrow (*of scabies*)
surfactante *m* surfactant
surtido *m* supply
surtir *vt* to supply, provide; (*un medicamento de acuerdo con una receta*) to fill (*a prescription*); — **de nuevo** (*un medicamento de acuerdo con una receta escrita previamente*) to refill (*a medication or prescription*); — **efecto** to take effect
susceptibilidad *f* susceptibility; (*irritabilidad*) sensitivity, irritability
susceptible *adj* susceptible; (*persona*) sensitive; **una enfermedad susceptible al tratamiento**..a treatable disease ...¿**Porqué eres tan susceptible?**.. Why are you so sensitive?
suspender *vt* (*un tratamiento, etc.*) to discontinue, to suspend
suspensión *f* suspension
suspensorio *m* athletic supporter, jockstrap (*fam*)
suspirar *vi* to sigh
suspiro *m* sigh
sustancia *f* substance, matter; — **blanca** white matter; — **gris** gray matter; — **química** chemical
sustitución *f* (*psych, etc.*) substitution; (*esp. Esp, reemplazo*) replacement; — **articular** joint replacement; — **de válvula aórtica (mitral, etc.)**, — **valvular aórtica (mitral, etc.)** aortic (mitral, etc.) valve replacement

sustituir *vt* to replace, to substitute; **Ud. puede sustituir la mantequilla por aceite de oliva**..You can replace butter with olive oil..You can substitute olive oil for butter; [*Nota: Observe que al traducir* sustituir *a* to substitute *el orden de los dos objetos mantequilla y aceite de oliva se invierte, lo cual no ocurre al traducirlo a* to replace.]

sustituto *m* substitute; — **de (la) sal** salt substitute; *mf* substitute; — **responsable de tomar decisiones** surrogate decision maker

susto *m* fright, scare; (*Amer*) folk illness manifest by anxiety and other symptoms and believed to be caused by a sudden fright

sutura *f* suture; — **absorbible**, — **reabsorbible** (*esp. Esp*) absorbable suture

suturar *vt* to suture, to stitch (up) (*fam*)

T

tabaco *m* tobacco; (*esp. Carib, puro*) cigar; — **de mascar** chewing tobacco; — **sin humo** smokeless tobacco

tábano *m* horsefly

tabáquico -ca *adj* pertaining to tobacco

tabaquismo *m* tobacco use, smoking

tabique *m* septum; — **desviado** deviated septum; — **interauricular** interatrial septum; — **interventricular** interventricular septum; — **nasal** nasal septum

tabla de Snellen *f* eye chart

tableta *f* tablet; — **dispersable** wafer

tablilla *f* splint

tabú *m* (*pl* -**búes**) taboo

taburete *m* stool

TAC *m&f* CAT scan (*See also* **tomografía axial computarizada** *under* **tomografía**.)

tacón *m* heel (*of a shoe*); **de** — **alto** high-heeled; **de** — **bajo** low-heeled

tacrina *f* tacrine

tacrolimus, tacrolimús (*INN*) *m* tacrolimus

táctil *adj* tactile

tacto *m* touch, sense of touch; — **fino** light touch sensation; — **rectal** rectal examination, rectal exam (*fam*)

tadalafilo *m* tadalafil

taladro *m* (*dent*) drill

tálamo *m* thalamus

talasemia *f* thalassemia

talco *m* talc, (*en polvo*) talcum powder

talidomida *f* thalidomide

talio *m* thallium

talla *f* (*altura*) height

taller *m* workshop; — **de entrenamiento en habilidades sociales para cirujanos** social skills training workshop for surgeons

tallo *m* (*del pelo, pene, etc.*) shaft; — **cerebral** *or* **encefálico** brainstem

talón *m* (*anat*) heel; — **de la mano** heel of the hand

talonera *f* (*para elevar el talón*) heel lift

tamaño *m* size; — **de porción** serving size

tambalear *vi, vr* to stagger

tamizaje *m* screening; — **del cáncer** cancer screening

tamoxifeno *m* tamoxifen

tampón *m* tampon; (*amortiguador*) buffer

tamsulosina *f* tamsulosin

tangencial *adj* (*psych*) tangential

tangencialidad *f* (*psych*) tangentiality

tanino *m* tannin

tanque *m* tank; — **de oxígeno** oxygen tank

tantalio *m* tantalum

tapa *f* (*de una botella*) cap (*of a bottle*); — **de seguridad** safety cap

tapado -da *adj* (*fam*) blocked, clogged, stopped up (*fam*); (*la nariz*) congested, stuffed up, stuffy; **Tengo la nariz tapada**..I'm congested..My nose is stuffed up.

tapar *vt* to cover; (*dent, fam*) to fill (*a cavity*); *vr* (*la nariz*) to stop up

tapentadol *m* tapentadol

tapiz rodante *m* (*esp. Esp*) treadmill

tapón *m* plug, packing; — **auditivo** earplug; — **de cerumen** cerumen impaction; — **de oído** earplug

taponamiento *m* tamponade; (*de una herida o cavidad*) packing; — **cardíaco** cardiac tamponade; — **nasal** nasal packing

taquicardia *f* tachycardia; — **paroxística supraventricular** paroxysmal supraventricular tachycardia

tarántula *f* tarantula

tarde *adj & adv* late; **más** — later; *f* afternoon, early evening

tardío -a *adj* late, delayed

tarea *f* task; — **de la vida** life task

tarjeta *f* (*del seguro, etc.*) card

tarsal *adj* tarsal

tarsiano -na *adj* tarsal

tartamudear *vi* to stutter, stammer

tártaro *m* (*dent*) calculus (*form*), tartar

TARV *abbr* **terapia** *or* **tratamiento antirretroviral**. *See* **terapia**.

tasa *f* rate; — **de metabolismo basal** basal metabolic rate; — **de mortalidad** death *o* mortality rate; — **de mortalidad infantil** infant mortality rate; — **de natalidad** birth rate; — **de sedimentación** erythrocyte sedimentation rate (ESR)

tatuaje *m* tattoo

taurina *f* taurine

tazaroteno *m* tazarotene

TB *See* **tuberculosis**.

TC *m&f* CT scan (*See also* **tomografía computarizada** *under* **tomografía**.)

TDAH *abbr* **trastorno por déficit de atención con hiperactividad**. *See* **trastorno**.

té *m* tea; — **verde** green tea

TEC *abbr* **terapia electroconvulsiva**. *See* **terapia**.

tecato -ta *mf* (*PR, fam*) heroin addict, junkie (*fam*)

tecnecio *m* technetium

técnico -ca *mf* technician; **técnico ortopédico** orthotist; *f* technique; — **aséptica** aseptic *o* sterile technique; — **de relajación** relaxation technique; — **estéril** sterile technique

tecnología *f* technology; — **(de) punta** cutting edge technology, state of the art technology

tejido *m* tissue; — **blando** soft tissue; — **cicatricial** scar tissue; — **conectivo** *or* **conjuntivo** connective tissue; — **de granulación** granulation tissue

tela *f* (*cinta*) tape; — **adhesiva** adhesive tape

telangiectasia *f* telangiectasia; — **hemorrágica hereditaria** hereditary hemorrhagic telangiectasia

telaprevir *m* telaprevir

telbivudina *f* telbivudine

telebobina *f* telecoil

teléfono *m* telephone, phone (*fam*); — **celular** cellular telephone, cell phone

telemedicina *f* telemedicine

telemetría *f* telemetry

telepate *m* (*El Salv, Hond*) bedbug

telmisartán *m* telmisartan

temazepam *m* temazepam

temblar *vi* to tremble, shake; **¿Le tiemblan las manos?**..Do your hands shake?

temblor *m* tremor; (*de tierra*) light earthquake; — **esencial** essential tremor

tembloroso -sa *adj* tremulous, shaky (*fam*)

temor *m* fear

temperamento *m* temperament

temperatura *f* temperature; — **ambiente** room temperature; — **axilar** axillary temperature; — **oral** oral temperature; — **rectal** rectal temperature; **tomar(le) la** — (*a alguien*) to take (*someone's*) temperature; **tomarse la** — to take one's (*own*) temperature

templado -da *adj* (*tibio*) lukewarm

temporada *f* season, time of year; — **gripal** flu season

temporal *adj* temporary; (*anat*) temporal

temporomandibular *adj* temporomandibular

temprano -na *adj & adv* early; **levantar-**

se más temprano..to get up earlier
tenacillas *fpl* tweezers
tenaza(s) *f or fpl* tweezers
tendencia *f* tendency, trend
tendinitis *f* tendinitis; — **calcificante** calcific tendinitis
tendón *m* tendon; — **de Aquiles** Achilles tendon; — **de la corva** hamstring
tendonitis *f* tendinitis
tener *vt* to have; **Tengo artritis**..I have arthritis.
tenesmo *m* tenesmus, frequent often painful urge to defecate without the ability to do so
tenia *f* Taenia, tapeworm
tenis *m* tennis
tenofovir *m* tenofovir
tenosinovitis *f* tenosynovitis
tensar *vt* (*los músculos*) to tense (*one's muscles*)
tensiómetro *m* blood pressure monitor
tensión *f* tension, strain; — **arterial** (*form*) blood pressure; — **nerviosa** nervous tension
tenso -sa *adj* tense; **ponerse** — to tense up, to get *o* become tense
teofilina *f* theophylline
teoría *f* theory
TEPT *abbr* **trastorno de estrés postraumático.** *See* **trastorno.**
terapeuta *mf* therapist; — **cognitivo conductual** cognitive behavioral therapist; — **conductual** behavioral therapist; — **del lenguaje** speech pathologist *o* therapist; — **físico** physical therapist; — **ocupacional** occupational therapist; — **respiratorio** respiratory therapist
terapéutico -ca *adj* therapeutic; *f* therapy
terapia *f* therapy; — **antirretroviral** *or* **antirretrovírica (TARV)** antirretroviral therapy (ART); — **antirretroviral de gran actividad (TARGA)** (*ant*) antiretroviral therapy (ART), highly active antiretroviral therapy (HAART) (*ant*); — **cognitiva** cognitive therapy; — **cognitivo conductual** cognitive behavioral therapy; — **combinada** combination therapy; — **conductual** behavioral therapy; — **con haz de protones** proton beam therapy; — **de calor** heat therapy; — **de consolidación** consolidation therapy; — **de grupo**

group therapy; — **de inducción** induction therapy; — **de la conducta** behavioral therapy; — **del habla** (*esp. Mex*) speech pathology *o* therapy; — **del lenguaje** language therapy; (*logoterapia*) speech pathology *o* therapy; — **de mantenimiento** (*oncología, medicina de las adicciones, etc.*) maintenance therapy; — **de masaje(s)** massage therapy; — **de protones** proton therapy; — **de quelación** chelation therapy; — **de reemplazo de nicotina** nicotine-replacement therapy; — **de reemplazo hormonal** hormone-replacement therapy; — **de rescate** salvage therapy; — **de resincronización cardíaca** cardiac resynchronization therapy; — **electroconvulsiva (TEC)** electroconvulsive therapy (ECT); — **física** (*Amer*) physical therapy; — **fotodinámica** photodynamic therapy; — **grupal** group therapy; — **hormonal** hormone *o* hormonal therapy; — **hormonal sustitutiva**, — **hormonal sustitutoria** (*Esp*) hormone replacement therapy; — **intensiva** (*cuidados intensivos*) intensive care; — **ocupacional** occupational therapy; — **respiratoria** respiratory therapy
terapista *mf* (*Ang*) therapist; — **físico** (*esp. Mex*) physical therapist; — **respiratorio** respiratory therapist
teratogenicidad *f* teratogenicity
teratogénico -ca *adj* teratogenic
teratoma *m* teratoma
terazosina *f* terazosin
terbinafina *f* terbinafine
terciario -ria *adj* tertiary
tercio *m* third; **dos tercios** two thirds
terconazol *m* terconazole
terfenadina *f* terfenadine
térmico -ca *adj* thermal
terminal *adj* terminal; **en fase** — endstage
terminar *vt* to finish; (*una relación*) to break up
término *m* term; **a** — at term; **embarazo a** — term pregnancy
termocoagulación *f* thermocoagulation
termómetro *m* thermometer; — **rectal** rectal thermometer
termoterapia *f* heat therapy
terremoto *m* earthquake
terrores nocturnos *mpl* night terrors

terso -sa *adj* (*piel, etc.*) smooth
testamento vital *m* living will
testicular *adj* testicular
testículo *m* testicle; — **no descendido** undescended testicle
Testigo de Jehová *m* Jehovah's Witness
testosterona *f* testosterone
teta *f* nipple, teat; [*Nota: teat, igual que teta, es un término veterinario que puede ser ofensivo al aplicarse a las personas.*]
tétanos *m* tetanus
tetero *m* (*Amer*) baby bottle
tetilla *f* nipple (*of a male*); (*del biberón*) nipple (*of a baby bottle*)
tetina *f* (*del biberón*) nipple (*of a baby bottle*)
tetraciclina *f* tetracycline
tetracloruro de carbono *m* carbon tetrachloride
tetrahidrocannabinol (THC) *m* tetrahydrocannabinol (THC)
tetralogía de Fallot *f* tetralogy of Fallot
tetraplejía, tetraplejia *f* tetraplegia, quadriplegia
tetrapléjico -ca *adj & mf* quadriplegic
tez *f* complexion
THC *See* **tetrahidrocannabinol.**
tía *f* aunt
tiabendazol *m* thiabendazole
tiagabina *f* tiagabine
tiamazol *m* methimazole (*USAN*), thiamazole (*INN*)
tiamina *f* thiamine
tiazida *f* thiazide
tibia *f* tibia, shinbone (*fam*)
tibio -bia *adj* lukewarm, slightly warm
tiburón *m* shark
tic *m* (*pl* **tics**) tic; — **doloroso** trigeminal neuralgia, tic douloureux
ticagrelor *m* ticagrelor
tiempo *m* time; weather; **¿Cuánto tiempo hace que se siente enferma?**..How long have you been feeling sick?... **cuando hace mal tiempo**..when the weather is bad; **ahorrar** — to save time; **con el** — eventually, in time; **mucho** — a long time; **poco** — a short time; — **de hemorragia** bleeding time; — **de ocio** leisure time; — **de protrombina (TP)** prothrombin time (PT); — **de sangrado** *or* **sangría** bleeding time; — **libre** free time; — **parcial de**

tromboplastina (TPT) partial thromboplastin time (PTT); **todo el** — all the time
tienda *f* tent; store; — **de oxígeno** oxygen tent; — **de productos naturales**, — **naturista** health food store, natural food store
tierra *f* ground
tieso -sa *adj* stiff
tifo *m* typhus
tifoideo -a *adj* typhoid; **fiebre tifoidea** typhoid fever; *f* typhoid fever
tifus *m* typhus
TIG *abbr* **transferencia intratubárica de gametos.** *See* **transferencia.**
tijeras *fpl* scissors; — **de** *or* **para uñas** nail scissors; — **para vendajes** bandage scissors; **unas tijeras**..a pair of scissors..a scissors
timectomía *f* thymectomy
timerosal *m* thimerosal (*USAN*), thiomersal (*INN*)
timidez *f* shyness
tímido -da *adj* timid, shy, bashful
timo *m* thymus
timol *m* thymol
timolol *m* timolol
timoma *m* thymoma
timpánico -ca *adj* tympanic
tímpano *m* (*anat*) eardrum
timpanoplastia *f* tympanoplasty
tina *f* (*de baño*) bathtub; — **de hidromasaje** (*esp. Mex*) whirlpool
tinción *f* (*micro*) stain; — **de Gram** Gram stain; — **de Papanicolaou** Papanicolaou smear
tinea tinea; — **capitis** tinea capitis, ringworm of the scalp (*fam*); — **corporis** tinea corporis, ringworm (*fam*); — **cruris** tinea cruris, jock itch (*fam o vulg*); — **pedis** tinea pedis, athlete's foot (*fam*)
tinidazol *m* tinidazole
tinnitus *m* (*frec. pl*) tinnitus
tinte *m* dye
tintura *f* (*medicina*) tincture; (*tinte*) dye
tiña *f* tinea; — **del cuero cabelludo** *or* **de la cabeza** tinea capitis (*form*), ringworm of the scalp; — **corporal** *or* **del cuerpo** tinea corporis (*form*), ringworm; — **inguinal** tinea cruris (*form*), jock itch (*fam o vulg*); — **versicolor** tenia *o* pityriasis versicolor

tío *m* uncle; *mpl* uncles, aunts and uncles
tiomersal *m* thiomersal, thimerosal
tiotropio *m* tiotropium
típico -ca *adj* typical
tipo *m* type; — de sangre A (B, O, etc.) blood type A (B, O, etc.); — de tejido tissue type
tipranavir *m* tipranavir
tiraleche *m* (*Mex*) breast pump
tiramina *f* tyramine
tira reactiva *f* (*para sangre*) test strip; (*para orina*) dipstick
tirita *f* (*esp. Esp*) small adhesive bandage
tiroglobulina *f* thyroglobulin
tiroidectomía *f* thyroidectomy
tiroideo -a *adj* pertaining to the thyroid gland
tiroides *m&f* (*pl* -des) (*fam*) thyroid gland, thyroid (*fam*)
tiroiditis *f* thyroiditis; — de Hashimoto Hashimoto's thyroiditis; — subaguda subacute thyroiditis
tirón *m* (*muscular*) pulled muscle, strain
tirosina *f* tyrosine
tirotóxico -ca *adj* thyrotoxic
tirotoxicosis *f* thyrotoxicosis
tirotropina, tirotrofina *f* thyrotropin, thyroid-stimulating hormone (TSH)
tiroxina *f* thyroxine
tisana *f* medicinal tea
titanio *m* titanium
titulación *f* titration
titulado -da *adj* titrated; (*certificado*) certified
titular *vt* to titrate
título *m* titer
tizanidina *f* tizanidine
toalla *f* towel; — facial washcloth; — sanitaria *or* femenina sanitary pad *o* napkin
toallita *f* (*facial*) washcloth; — íntima (*Esp*) sanitary napkin
tobillo *m* ankle
tocar *vt* to touch
tocoferol *m* tocopherol
tocólisis, tocolisis *f* tocolysis
tocolítico -ca *adj & m* tocolytic
tocología *f* obstetrics
tocólogo -ga *mf* obstetrician
tofo *m* tophus
tofu *m* tofu
tolerable *adj* tolerable, bearable
tolerancia *f* tolerance; alta (baja) — al dolor high (low) pain tolerance *o* tolerance of pain; alteración *f* de la — a la glucosa impaired glucose tolerance; — inmunológica immune tolerance
tolerante *adj* tolerant
tolerar *vt* to tolerate, stand, bear
tolnaftato *m* tolnaftate
tolteradina *f* tolteradine
tolueno *m* toluene
toma eléctrica *f* electrical outlet
tomacorriente *m* electrical outlet
tomaína *f* ptomaine
tomar *vt* (*una bebida*) to drink; (*medicamentos, etc.*) to take; Tome esta pastilla dos veces al día.. Take this pill twice a day; — aire (*fam, inspirar*) to inhale, breathe in
tomate *m* tomato
tomografía *f* (*técnica*) tomography; (*estudio*) tomogram (*form*), scan; — computarizada (TC), — axial computarizada (TAC) computed tomography (CT), computerized axial tomography (CAT); CT scan, CAT scan; — computarizada helicoidal spiral computed tomography, spiral CT (*fam*); spiral CT scan; — por emisión de positrones positron emission tomography (PET); PET scan; tomografía por emisión de positrones-tomografía computarizada (PET-CT) positron emission tomography-computed tomography (PET-CT); PET-CT scan
tomógrafo *m* (*form*) CT scanner
tónico *m* tonic, toner; — para la piel skin toner
tonificación *f* toning; ejercicios de — toning exercises
tonificar *vt* (*los músculos*) to tone (*one's muscles*)
tono *m* tone; tonos cardíacos heart sounds; — muscular muscle tone
tonsilectomía *f* (*Ang*) tonsillectomy
tonsilitis *f* tonsillitis
tópico -ca *adj* topical
topiramato *m* topiramate
toque *m* touch; — terapéutico therapeutic touch
toracentesis *f* (*pl* -sis) thoracentesis
torácico -ca *adj* thoracic
toracocentesis *f* (*pl* -sis) thoracentesis
toracoscopia, toracoscopía *f* thoracoscopy

toracoscópico -ca *adj* thoracoscopic
toracotomía *f* thoracotomy
torasemida, torsemida *f* torsemide (*USAN*), torasemide (*INN*)
tórax *m* thorax, chest
torcedura *f* sprain
torcerse *vr* to sprain, to twist; ¿**Cuándo se torció la muñeca?**..When did you sprain your wrist?
torcido -da *adj* crooked, twisted
tormenta tiroidea *f* thyroid storm
tornillo *m* (*ortho*) screw
torniquete *m* tourniquet
toronja *f* grapefruit
torpe *adj* clumsy
torrente sanguíneo *m* bloodstream
torsión *f* torsion; — **testicular** testicular torsion
torso *m* torso
tortícolis *f* torticollis
tortura *f* torture
torturar *vt* to torture
torunda *f* (*form*) cotton ball, pledget (*form*), soft material used for wound care or to stop hemorrhage
torus *m* (*pl* **torus**) torus; — **palatino** torus palatinus
torzón *m* (*Mex, fam*) abdominal cramp
tos *f* cough; **jarabe** *m* **para la** — cough syrup; **pastilla para la** — cough drop; — **ferina** pertussis (*form*), whooping cough; — **perruna** barking cough; — **seca** dry cough
toser *vi* to cough; **Tosa fuerte**..Cough hard.
tosferina *See* **tos ferina** *under* **tos**.
tostarse *vr* to tan, to get a tan
total *adj & m* total
toxemia *f* toxemia
toxémico -ca *adj* toxemic
toxicidad *f* toxicity
tóxico -ca *adj* toxic; **no** — nontoxic
toxicología *f* toxicology
toxicólogo -ga *mf* toxicologist
toxicomanía *f* drug addiction
toxicómano -na *mf* drug addict
toxina *f* toxin; — **botulínica** botulinum toxin
toxocariasis *f* toxocariasis
toxoide *m* toxoid; — **diftérico** diphtheria toxoid; — **tetánico** tetanus toxoid
toxoplasmosis *f* toxoplasmosis
TP *abbr* **tiempo de protrombina**. *See*

tiempo.
TPI *abbr* **trombocitopenia inmune**. *See* **trombocitopenia**.
TPT *abbr* **tiempo parcial de tromboplastina**. *See* **tiempo**.
trabajador -ra *mf* worker; — **social** social worker
trabajar *vi* to work; (*funcionar*) to function, to work
trabajo *m* work, job; — **corporal** bodywork; — **de parto** labor; **entrar en** — **de parto** to go into labor; **estar en** — **de parto** to be in labor; — **social** social work
tracción *f* traction
tracoma *m* trachoma
tracto *m* tract; — **digestivo** *or* **gastrointestinal** digestive *o* gastrointestinal tract; — **genital** genital tract; — **genitourinario** genitourinary tract; — **sinusal** sinus tract; — **urinario** urinary tract
traducir *vt* to translate
tragar *vt, vi* to swallow; — **saliva** to swallow (*dry swallow*)
trago *m* swallow; (*anat*) tragus
tramadol *m* tramadol
trancazo *m* (*fam*) (*influenza*) influenza, flu; (*dengue*) dengue
trance *m* trance
tranquilizante *adj* calming, sedative; *m* (*esp. vet*) sedative; (*ant, neuroléptico*) neuroleptic
tranquilizar *vt* (*esp. vet*) to sedate, to tranquilize (*esp. vet*); *vr* to calm down, quiet down
tranquilo -la *adj* calm
transaminasa *f* transaminase
transcatéter *adj* transcatheter
transcurso *m* (*de una enfermedad, etc.*) course (*of a disease, etc.*)
transcutáneo -a *adj* transcutaneous
transdérmico -ca *adj* transdermal
transexual *adj & mf* transsexual
transferencia *f* transfer; (*psych*) transference; — **embrionaria** embryo transfer; — **intratubárica de gametos (TIG)** gamete intrafallopian transfer (GIFT)
transferrina *f* transferrin
transformación *f* transformation
transfundir *vt* to transfuse
transfusión *f* transfusion; **hacer una** —

to transfuse, to give a transfusion; — **de glóbulos rojos (plaquetas, etc.)** transfusion of red blood cells (platelets, etc.)

transgenerismo m transgenderism

transgénero adj transgender; m transgender man, transgender person; f transgender woman

transición f transition

transicional adj transitional

transitorio -ria adj transient

translocación f translocation

transmisible adj transmissible, communicable

transmisión f transmission, spread; **de — aérea** airborne; **de — alimentaria** foodborne; **de — sanguínea** bloodborne

transmitir vt to transmit; **transmitido por el agua** waterborne

transpiración f perspiration, sweating

transpirar vi to perspire, to sweat

transportar vt to transport

transporte m transport

transposición f transposition

transrectal adj transrectal

transuretral adj transurethral

transvaginal adj transvaginal

trapecio m (anat) trapezius; (para una cama hospitalaria) trapeze (for a hospital bed)

tráquea f trachea, windpipe (fam)

traqueítis f tracheitis

traqueobronquitis f tracheobronchitis

traqueostomía f tracheostomy

traqueotomía f tracheotomy

trasbocar vi (SA, fam) to vomit, throw up

trasero m (fam) buttocks, bottom (fam), rear end (fam)

trasladar vt (a un paciente) to transfer, to move

traspié m stumble, slip; **dar un —** to stumble, trip, slip

trasplantar vt to transplant

trasplante m transplant; — **capilar** hair transplant; — **cardíaco** or **de corazón** heart transplant; — **de hígado** liver transplant; — **de médula ósea** bone marrow transplant; — **de órgano(s)** organ transplant; — **de pelo** hair transplant; — **de pulmón** lung transplant; — **de riñón** kidney transplant; — **he-**

pático liver transplant; — **pulmonar** lung transplant; — **renal** renal o kidney transplant

trastornado -da adj (molesto) upset, disturbed

trastornar vt to upset, disturb; vr to get o become upset o disturbed

trastorno m disorder, disturbance, disability; — **afectivo estacional** seasonal affective disorder; — **alimentario** or **alimenticio** eating disorder; — **anímico** mood disorder; — **antisocial de la personalidad** antisocial personality disorder; — **bipolar** bipolar disorder; — **ciclotímico** cyclothymic disorder; — **de adaptación** adjustment disorder; — **de ansiedad** anxiety disorder; — **de ansiedad por separación** separation anxiety disorder; — **de aprendizaje** learning disability; — **de estrés postraumático (TEPT)** post-traumatic stress disorder (PTSD); — **de la conducta** behavioral disorder; — **de la excitación sexual en la mujer** female sexual arousal disorder; — **de la personalidad** personality disorder; — **de la personalidad por dependencia** dependent personality disorder; — **de la personalidad por evitación** avoidant personality disorder; — **del aprendizaje** learning disability; — **del espectro autista** autism spectrum disorder; — **del estado de ánimo** mood disorder; — **del habla** speech disorder; — **del humor** mood disorder; — **del lenguaje** language disorder; — **del movimiento** movement disorder; — **del sueño** sleep disorder; — **de pánico** panic disorder; — **de personalidad** personality disorder; — **de somatización** somatoform disorder; — **dismórfico corporal** body dysmorphic disorder; — **esquizoide de la personalidad** schizoid personality disorder; — **esquizotípico de la personalidad** schizotypal personality disorder; — **histriónico de la personalidad** histrionic personality disorder; — **límite de la personalidad** borderline personality disorder; — **mieloproliferativo** myeloproliferative disorder; — **narcisista de la personalidad** narcissistic personality disorder; — **obsesivo-compulsivo** obsessive compulsive disorder; — **obsesivo-compulsivo de la personalidad** obsessive-compulsive personality disorder; — **paranoide de la personalidad** paranoid personality disorder; — **por atracón** binge eating disorder; — **por déficit de atención con hiperactividad (TDAH)** attention deficit hyperactivity disorder (ADHD); — **por estrés postraumático (TEPT)** post-traumatic stress disorder (PTSD)

tratable *adj* treatable
tratado -da *adj* treated; **no —** untreated
tratamiento *m* treatment, therapy; — **antirretroviral** *or* **antirretrovírico (TARV)** antiretroviral therapy (ART); — **antirretroviral de gran actividad (TARGA)** (*ant*) antiretroviral therapy (ART), highly active antiretroviral therapy (HAART) (*ant*); — **combinado** combination therapy; — **de conducto** root canal therapy (*form*), root canal (*fam*); — **de consolidación** consolidation therapy; — **de inducción** induction therapy; — **de mantenimiento** maintenance treatment *o* therapy; — **de rescate** salvage therapy *o* treatment; — **directamente observado** directly observed therapy
tratar *vt* (*una enfermedad*) to treat; (*un paciente*) to treat, to attend; *vi* — **de** to try; **Trate de no aislarse..**Try not to isolate yourself.
trauma *m* trauma
traumático -ca *adj* traumatic
traumatismo *m* trauma (*physical*)
traumatizar *vt* to traumatize
traumatología *f* traumatology
traumatólogo -ga *mf* trauma surgeon, traumatologist
travesti *mf* transvestite
travestido -da *mf* (*esp. Esp*) transvestite
travestismo *m* transvestism
travieso -sa *adj* mischievous
traza *f* trace; **elementos traza** trace elements; **trazas de proteínas..**trace(s) of protein
trazador *m* tracer
trazodona *f* trazodone
trébol rojo *m* (*bot*) red clover
trematodo *m* fluke
trementina *f* turpentine
treonina *f* threonine

tretinoína *f* tretinoin
triage *m* triage
triamcinolona *f* triamcinolone
triamterene *m* triamterene
triazolam *m* triazolam
tríceps *m* (*pl* **-ceps**) triceps
tricocéfalo *m* whipworm
tricomoniasis *f* trichomoniasis
tricotilomanía *f* trichotillomania, compulsion to pull one's hair out
tricúspide *adj* tricuspid
trifásico -ca *adj* (*pharm*) triphasic
trifocal *adj* trifocal
trigémino -na *adj* trigeminal
triglicérido *m* triglyceride
trigo *m* wheat; — **integral** *or* **entero** whole wheat
trihexifenidilo *m* trihexyphenidyl
trillizo -za *mf* triplet
trimestre *m* trimester
trimetoprim *m* trimethoprim
trimetoprima *m* trimethoprim
tripa *f* (*fam, frec. pl*) intestine, bowel, gut
tripanosomiasis *f* trypanosomiasis
tripsina *f* trypsin
triptófano *m* tryptophan
triquinosis, triquinelosis *f* trichinosis, trichinellosis
trismo *m* trismus
trisomía *f* trisomy; — **21** trisomy 21
triste *adj* sad
tristeza *f* sadness
triturar *vt* (*pharm, etc.; form*) to crush, to grind
trivalente *adj* trivalent
trocánter *m* trochanter
trocantéreo -a *adj* trochanteric
trocantérico -ca *adj* trochanteric
trombectomía *f* thrombectomy
trombo *m* thrombus
tromboangeítis obliterante *f* thromboangiitis obliterans
trombocitopenia *f* thrombocytopenia; — **inmune (TPI)** immune thrombocytopenia (ITP)
trombocitosis *f* thrombocytosis; — **esencial** essential thrombocytosis
tromboembolia *f* thromboembolism
tromboflebitis *f* thrombophlebitis
trombolisis *f* thrombolysis
trombolítico -ca *adj & m* thrombolytic
trombosis *f* (*pl* **-sis**) thrombosis; — **ve-**

nosa profunda (TVP) deep venous thrombosis (DVT)
trompa *f* tube; — **de Eustaquio** Eustachian tube; — **uterina,** — **de Falopio** (*ant*) fallopian tube
tronco *m* (*anat*) trunk; — **cerebral** *or* **encefálico** brainstem
tropezar *vi* to stumble, trip
tropical *adj* tropical
trotar *vi* (*forma de ejercicio*) to jog
tubárico -ca *adj* tubal
tuberculina *f* tuberculin
tuberculoide *adj* tuberculoid
tuberculosis (TB) *f* tuberculosis (TB)
tuberculoso -sa *adj* tuberculous; **infección tuberculosa latente** latent tuberculosis infection
tubería *f* tubing
tubo *m* tube; — **de drenaje** drainage tube; — **de ensayo** test tube; — **de gas-trostomía** gastrostomy tube, G-tube (*fam*); — **de tórax** chest tube; — **di-gestivo** digestive tract; — **endotra-**

queal endotracheal tube; — **torácico** chest tube
tubo-ovárico -ca *adj* tubo-ovarian
tubular *adj* tubular
túbulo *m* tubule
tuerto -ta *adj* blind in one eye
tularemia *f* tularemia
tumor *m* tumor; — **benigno** benign tumor; — **cerebral** brain tumor; — **desmoide** desmoid tumor; — **de Wilms** Wilms' tumor; — **maligno** malignant tumor
tumoral *adj* pertaining to a tumor; **tamaño** — tumor size
túnel *m* tunnel; — **carpiano** carpal tunnel; — **tarsiano** tarsal tunnel
tupido -da *adj* (*esp. Carib*) **con la nariz** — congested, having a stuffed up *o* stuffy nose
tutor -ra *mf* (*legal*) guardian, conservator
TVP *abbr* **trombosis venosa profunda**. *See* **trombosis**.

U

úlcera *f* ulcer, sore; — **de decúbito** decubitus ulcer, pressure sore; — **de estrés** stress ulcer; — **duodenal** duodenal ulcer; — **gástrica** gastric ulcer; — **péptica** peptic ulcer; — **por estrés** stress ulcer; — **por presión** pressure sore
ulceración *f* ulceration
ulcerado -da *adj* ulcerated
ulipristal *m* ulipristal
últimamente *adv* recently
último -ma *adj* last; **su última cirugía..** your last surgery
últimos ritos *mpl* last rites
ultrafiltración *f* ultrafiltration
ultrasónico -ca *adj* pertaining to ultra-

sound
ultrasonido *m* ultrasound (*diagnostic modality*); (*esp. Mex, estudio*) ultrasound (*study*), sonogram (*form*); — **terapéutico** ultrasound therapy, therapeutic ultrasound
ultrasonoterapia *f* ultrasound therapy, therapeutic ultrasound
ultravioleta *adj* ultraviolet
umbral *m* threshold; — **de audición** auditory threshold; — **de(l) dolor** pain threshold
uncinaria *f* hookworm
unción de los enfermos *f* anointing of the sick
ungueal *adj* ungual

ungüento *m* ointment, salve

único -ca *adj* only; **la única manera**..the only way

unidad *f* unit, department; **— coronaria** *or* **de cuidados coronarios** coronary care unit; **— de cuidados intensivos (UCI)** intensive care unit (ICU); **— de sangre** unit of blood; **— de terapia intensiva** intensive care unit (ICU); **— de urgencias** emergency department (ED), emergency room (ER); **— internacional** international unit

uniforme *adj* uniform; *m* uniform

unilateral *adj* unilateral

unión *f* (*ortho, etc.*) union

unir *vt, vr* to unite, join

universal *adj* universal

uno *m* **hacer del —** (*euph, orinar*) to urinate, to do number one (*euph*)

uña *f* nail; (*de la mano*) fingernail; (*del pie*) toenail; (*de una mascota*) claw; **— de caballo** (*bot*) coltsfoot; **— de gato** (*bot*) cat's claw; **— encarnada,** **— enterrada** (*esp. Mex*) ingrown nail

uñero *m* ingrown nail; (*panadizo*) whitlow, felon

uranio *m* uranium

urbano -na *adj* urban

urea *f* urea

uremia *f* uremia

urémico -ca *adj* uremic

uréter *m* ureter

ureteral *adj* ureteral

uretra *f* urethra

uretritis *f* urethritis; **— no gonocócica** non-gonococcal urethritis

urgencia *f* emergency; **sala de urgencias** emergency room (ER); **unidad** *f* **de ur-**gencias** emergency department (ED)

urgente *adj* urgent

urinario -ria *adj* urinary

urocinasa *f* urokinase

urocultivo *m* (*form*) urine culture

urodinámica *f* urodynamics

urogenital *adj* urogenital

urografía *f* (*técnica*) pyelography, urography; (*estudio*) pyelogram, urogram; **— excretora** excretory urography; excretory urogram; **— intravenosa** intravenous pyelography; intravenous pyelogram

urograma *m* pyelogram, urogram

uroquinasa, urokinasa, urocinasa *f* urokinase

urología *f* urology

urólogo -ga *mf* urologist

urosepsis *f* urosepsis

urticaria *f* urticaria, hives (*fam*)

usar *vt* to use

uso *m* use; **uso del brazo** use of the arm; **para — repetido** reusable; **— compasivo** (*pharm*) compassionate use; **— excesivo** excessive use

usual *adj* usual

usuario -ria *mf* user

uta *f* mild form of American cutaneous leishmaniasis

uterino -na *adj* uterine

útero *m* uterus; **en el —** in utero

UTI *abbr* **unidad de terapia intensiva**. *See* **unidad.**

utilizar *vt* to utilize, use

úvea *f* uvea

uveítis *f* uveitis

úvula *f* uvula

V

vaciamiento *m* emptying; — **ganglionar total** lymph node resection
vaciar *vt* to empty; — **la vejiga** to empty one's bladder, to void
vacío -a *adj* empty
vacuna *f* vaccine; vaccinia; — **antigripal** flu *o* influenza vaccine; — **antipoliomielítica oral** oral polio vaccine; — **atenuada** attenuated vaccine; — **BCG** BCG vaccine; — **conjugada** conjugated vaccine; — **contra (la) difteria, (el) tétanos y (la) tos ferina (DTP)** diphtheria, tetanus, and pertussis (DTP) vaccine; (*acelular*) tetanus, diphtheria, and acellular pertussis (Tdap) vaccine; — **contra el sarampión, las paperas y la rubéola** measles, mumps, and rubella (MMR) vaccine; — **contra el tétanos, la difteria y la tos ferina** (*Ang*) tetanus, diphtheria, and acellular pertussis (Tdap) vaccine; — **contra (el) Haemophilus influenzae tipo b** Haemophilus influenzae type b vaccine; — **contra la gripe** flu vaccine; — **contra la hepatitis B** hepatitis B vaccine; — **contra la influenza** influenza vaccine; — **contra la rabia** rabies vaccine; — **contra la varicela** varicella vaccine; — **contra la viruela** smallpox vaccine; — **contra (el) tétanos y (la) difteria** tetanus-diphtheria (Td) vaccine; — **inactivada** inactivated vaccine; — **meningocócica** meningococcal vaccine; — **neumocócica** pneumococcal vaccine; — **Sabin** Sabin vaccine; — **Salk** Salk vaccine; — **Tdap** (*Ang*) Tdap vaccine; — **triple viral** measles, mumps, and rubella (MMR) vaccine; — **viva** live vaccine
vacunación *f* vaccination, immunization
vacunado -da *adj* vaccinated; **no** — unvaccinated; *mf* vaccinee
vacunal *adj* pertaining to vaccination; **cobertura** — vaccination coverage
vacunar *vt* to vaccinate, to immunize; **sin** — unvaccinated
vagal *adj* vagal
vagina *f* vagina
vaginal *adj* vaginal

vaginitis *f* vaginitis
vaginosis *f* vaginosis; — **bacteriana** bacterial vaginosis
vago *m* vagus
vagotomía *f* vagotomy; — **selectiva** selective vagotomy
vaina *f* sheath; — **nerviosa** nerve sheath
valaciclovir *m* valacyclovir
valdecoxib *m* valdecoxib
valécula *See* **vallécula**.
valeriana *f* (*bot*) valerian
valgo -ga *adj* valgus
validación *f* (*psych, etc.*) validation
validez *f* validity
válido -da *adj* valid
valiente *adj* brave; **¡Sé valiente!**..Be brave!
valina *f* valine
vallécula *f* vallecula
valor *m* value; (*coraje*) courage; — **nutritivo** nutritional value; **valores personales** personal values
valoración *f* evaluation, assessment, testing
valorar *vt* (*evaluar*) to evaluate
valproato sódico, valproato *m* valproic acid, sodium valproate, valproate
valsartán *m* valsartan
valvulotomía *f* valvuloplasty, valvotomy
válvula *f* valve; — **aórtica** aortic valve; — **de escape** (*psych*) outlet; — **mitral** mitral valve; — **pilórica** pyloric valve; — **pulmonar** pulmonic valve; — **tricúspide** tricuspid valve
valvuloplastia *f* valvuloplasty
vancomicina *f* vancomycin
vapor *m* vapor, steam; **cocer al** — to steam cook, to steam
vaporización *f* vaporization
vaporizador *m* vaporizer
vardenafil, vardenafilo *m* vardenafil
varenciclina *f* varenicline
variable *adj & f* variable
variación *f* variation
variante *adj & f* variant; — **de enfermedad de Creutzfeldt-Jakob** Creutzfeldt-Jakob disease variant, variant of Creutzfeldt-Jakob disease
variar *vi* to vary, to fluctuate

varice, várice *f* varix, varicose vein (*fam*); [*Nota: El término* varix *se usa casi siempre en el plural:* varices.]
varicela *f* varicella, chickenpox (*fam*)
varicocele *m* varicocele
varicoso -sa *adj* varicose; **vena** — varicose vein
variz *f* (*pl* **varices**) (*esp. Esp*) *See* **varice**.
varo -ra *adj* varus
varón *m* male
vascular *adj* vascular
vasculitis *f* vasculitis; — **leucocitoclástica** leukocytoclastic vasculitis; — **necrotizante** *or* **necrosante** necrotizing vasculitis; — **por hipersensibilidad** hypersensitivity vasculitis
vasectomía *f* vasectomy
vaselina *f* petroleum jelly, petrolatum
vasija *f* basin, bedpan
vaso *m* vessel; glass; **un vaso de agua**..a glass of water; — **sanguíneo** blood vessel
vasoconstricción *f* vasoconstriction
vasoconstrictor *m* vasoconstrictor
vasodilatación *f* vasodilation, vasodilatation; [*Nota: Estos dos términos en inglés tienen la misma acepción.* Vasodilatation *es un poco más formal y se encuentra más que todo en la literatura médica.*]
vasodilatador *m* vasodilator
vasoespasmo *m* vasospasm
vasopresina *f* vasopressin
vasovagal *adj* vasovagal
VEB *abbr* virus Epstein-Barr. *See* **virus**.
vecindad *f* neighborhood
vecindario *m* neighborhood
vecino -na *mf* neighbor
vector *m* vector
veganismo *m* veganism
vegano -na *adj & mf* vegan
vegetación *f* vegetation
vegetal *adj & m* vegetable
vegetarianismo *m* vegetarianism
vegetariano -na *adj & mf* vegetarian
vegetativo -va *adj* vegetative; **estado** — **persistente** persistent vegetative state
vehículo *m* vehicle
vejez *f* old age
vejiga *f* bladder; blister; — **hiperactiva** overactive bladder; — **neurogénica**, — **neurógena** (*esp. Esp*) neurogenic bladder

vela de oído *f* ear candle
vello *m* body hair; — **axilar** axillary hair; — **corporal** body hair; — **facial** facial hair; — **púbico** pubic hair
velocidad de sedimentación globular (VSG) *f* erythrocyte sedimentation rate (ESR)
velo del paladar *m* (*form*) soft palate
vena *f* vein; — **antecubital** antecubital vein; — **femoral** femoral vein; — **porta** portal vein; — **safena interna** great saphenous vein; — **subclavia** subclavian vein; — **varicosa** varicose vein; — **yugular (externa, inerna)** (external, internal) jugular vein
vena cava *f* vena cava; — — **inferior** inferior vena cava; — — **superior** superior vena cava
vencer *vt* to overcome; — **miedos** to overcome fears
vencido -da *adj* (*pharm*) outdated, out of date
vencimiento *m* (*pharm*) expiration; **fecha de** — expiration date
venda *f* bandage, dressing (*before application*); dressing material, wrap; — **adhesiva** adhesive bandage; — **elástica** elastic bandage; — **elástica autoadherente** (*Amer*), — **elástica cohesiva** (*Esp*) self-adherent elastic wrap
vendaje *m* bandage, dressing (*after application*); — **adhesivo** adhesive bandage; — **compresivo** pressure *o* compression bandage *o* dressing; — **elástico** elastic bandage; — **funcional** taping; — **oclusivo** occlusive dressing; — **en ocho** figure-of-eight bandage
vendar *vt* to bandage, to dress (*a wound*)
veneno *m* poison, venom; — **para hormigas (ratas, etc.)** ant (rat, etc.) poison
venenoso -sa *adj* poisonous
venéreo -a *adj* (*ant*) sexually transmitted, venereal (*ant*)
venir *vi* to come; — **de familia** to run in one's family; *vr* (*fam or vulg, alcanzar el orgasmo*) to have an orgasm, to come (*fam o vulg*)
venlafaxina *f* venlafaxine
venografía *f* (*técnica*) venography; (*estudio*) venogram
venopunción *f* venipuncture, puncture of

a vein for withdrawing blood or for injection or transfusion

venoso -sa *adj* venous

venta *f* sale; **de — libre** over-the-counter, non-prescription

ventaja *f* advantage; **las ventajas e inconvenientes**..the advantages and disadvantages

ventilación *f* ventilation; **— mecánica** mechanical ventilation; **— no invasiva con presión positiva** noninvasive positive pressure ventilation

ventilador *m* electric fan; (*respirador*) ventilator

ventosear *vi* to pass gas

ventosidad *f* gas (*expelled from rectum*)

ventral *adj* ventral

ventricular *adj* ventricular

ventrículo *m* ventricle

vénula *f* venule

ver *vt, vi* (*pp* **visto**) to see; *vr* to look, to look like; **Se ve triste**..You look sad.

verano *m* summer

verapamilo, verapamil *m* verapamil

verbasco *m* (*bot*) mullein

verdadero -ra *adj* true

verde *adj* green

verdoso -sa *adj* greenish

verdugo, verdugón *m* welt, wheal

verdura *f* vegetable; *fpl* greens

vergüenza *f* shame, embarrassment

verruga *f* wart; **— genital** genital wart; **— plantar** plantar wart

vértebra *f* vertebra

vertebroplastia *f* vertebroplasty

vertical *adj* vertical

vértice *m* (*anat*) vertex

vértigo *m* vertigo

vesical *adj* pertaining to the bladder; **sonda —** bladder catheter

vesícula *f* vesicle, blister; (*fam*) gallbladder; **— biliar** gallbladder

vestibular *adj* vestibular

vestíbulo *m* vestibule

vestido *m* dress

vestir *vt* to dress; *vr* to dress (oneself), to get dressed

veterano -na *mf* veteran

veterinario -ria *adj* veterinary; *mf* veterinarian; *f* veterinary medicine

vez *f* (*pl* **veces**) time; **cuatro veces más grande**..four times as big...**dos veces al día**..two times a day, twice daily; **a**

veces at times; **cada —** each time, every time; **de — en cuando** from time to time, occasionally; **la primera —** the first time; **la próxima —** the next time; **la última —** the last time; **muchas veces** many times, often; **por primera —** first, for the first time; **raras veces** rarely; **una —** one time

VHB *abbr* **virus de la hepatitis B**. *See* **virus**.

VHC *abbr* **virus de la hepatitis C**. *See* **virus**.

VHS *abbr* **virus herpes simple**. *See* **virus**.

vía *f* tract, duct; route; **por — oral** by mouth; **vía(s) aérea(s) (inferior[es], superior[es])** (lower, upper) airway; **— biliar** bile duct, biliary tract; **vías biliares** biliary tract; **— de administración** route of administration; **vía(s) digestiva(s)** digestive tract; **— lagrimal** lacrimal duct, tear duct (*fam*); **vías nasales** nasal passages; **vía(s) respiratoria(s) (inferior[es]** *or* **baja[s], alta[s])** (lower, upper) respiratory tract

viable *adj* viable

viajes *mpl* travel; **— al extranjero** foreign travel

vial *m* vial

víbora *f* viper, (type of) poisonous snake

vibración *f* vibration

vibrador *m* (*juego sexual*) vibrator

vicio *m* bad habit

víctima *f* victim

vida *f* life, lifetime; **— asistida** (*esp. Esp*) assisted living; **de por —** for life, lifelong, indefinitely; **— media** half-life; **— sexual** sex life; **— social** social life

vidarabina *f* vidarabine

video, vídeo (*RAE*) *m* video

videotoracoscopia *f* video-assisted thoracoscopy

vidrio *m* glass; **un pedazo de vidrio**..a piece of glass

viejo -ja *adj* old; *m* old man, old person; *f* old woman

viento *m* wind

vientre *m* belly, abdomen; (*fam, útero*) womb

vigabatrina *f* vigabatrin

vigilancia *f* surveillance, monitoring; (*estado de alerta*) alertness

vigor *m* stamina
vigoroso -sa *adj* vigorous, strong; (*actividad*) strenuous
VIH *abbr* **virus de la inmunodeficiencia humana**. *See* **virus**.
vinagre *m* vinegar
vinblastina *f* vinblastine
vinchuca *f* (*Arg, Bol, Chile, Ur*) kissing bug
vincristina *f* vincristine
vínculo *m* (*obst, psych, etc.*) bond, connection; **establecer un vínculo (afectivo), establecer vínculos (afectivos)** to bond
vino *m* wine; — **blanco** white wine; — **tinto** red wine
violación *f* (*sexual*) rape
violar *vt* (*sexualmente*) to rape
violencia *f* violence; — **con armas de fuego** gun violence; — **doméstica** *or* **conyugal** domestic violence; — **vial** road rage
violento -ta *adj* violent
violeta de genciana *f* Gentian violet
viral *adj* viral
viremia *f* viremia
virgen *mf* virgin
virginidad *f* virginity
vírico -ca *adj* viral
virilidad *f* virility, manhood
virilización *f* virilization
virología *f* virology
virológico -ca *adj* virologic *o* virological
virtual *adj* virtual; **endoscopia** — virtual endoscopy
viruela *f* smallpox
virulencia *f* virulence
virulento -ta *adj* virulent
virus *m* (*pl* **virus**) virus; — **atenuado** attenuated virus; — **de la gripe** flu virus; — **de la hepatitis B (VHB)** hepatitis B virus (HBV); — **de la hepatitis C (VHC)** hepatitis C virus (HCV); — **de (la) influenza** influenza *o* flu virus; — **de (la) inmunodeficiencia humana (VIH)** human immunodeficiency virus (HIV); — **del Nilo Occidental** West Nile virus; — **del papiloma humano (VPH)** human papillomavirus (HPV); — **Epstein-Barr (VEB)** Epstein-Barr virus (EBV); — **gripal** influenza *o* flu virus; — **herpes simple (VHS)** herpes simplex virus (HSV); — **linfotrópico**

humano de células T human T-lymphotrophic virus; — **Norwalk** Norwalk virus; — **respiratorio sincitial,** — **sincitial respiratorio,** — **sincicial respiratorio** respiratory syncytial virus; — **varicela-zóster** varicella-zoster virus; — **vivo** live virus
víscera *f* organ; — **hueca** hollow organ
visceral *adj* visceral
viscosidad *f* viscosity
viscoso -sa *adj* viscous
visible *adj* visible
visión *f* vision; — **borrosa** blurred vision; — **cercana** near vision; — **de túnel** tunnel vision; — **doble** double vision; — **en túnel** tunnel vision; — **lejana** far vision; — **nocturna** night vision; — **periférica** peripheral vision; — **túnel** tunnel vision
visita *f* visit; — **al médico** visit to the doctor, doctor's visit; — **domiciliaria** house call, visit to a patient's home; — **médica** doctor's visit; — **no programada** unscheduled visit, drop-in (*fam*)
visitante *mf* visitor
visitar *vt* to visit
vista *f* sight, eyesight, vision; (*radiografía, etc.*) view; **a simple** — with the naked eye; — **cansada** (*fam*) presbyopia; — **corta** nearsightedness; — **panorámica** panoramic view
visto *pp* *of* **ver**
visual *adj* visual
visualización *f* visualization
visualizar *vt* to visualize
vital *adj* vital
vitalidad *f* vitality
vitamina *f* vitamin; — **A (B₁₂, etc.)** vitamin A (B₁₂, etc.); — **hidrosoluble** water-soluble vitamin; — **liposoluble** fat-soluble vitamin
vitamínico -ca *adj* pertaining to vitamins; **contenido** — vitamin content
vitíligo, vitiligo *m* vitiligo
vítreo -a *adj* vitreous
viuda negra *f* black widow
viudo -da *adj* widowed; *m* widower; *f* widow
vivir *vi* to live; **vivir con sida..** to live with AIDS
vivo -va *adj* alive, (*virus, vacuna*) live
vocal *adj* vocal
voltear *vt* (*a un encamado*) to turn; *vr* to

turn over, roll over; ¿Me volteo?.. Should I turn over?

voltio *m* volt

volumen *m* volume; — **corriente** tidal volume

voluntad *f* will; **contra su** — against your (his, her) will; **fuerza de** — will power; **por propia** — of one's own free will; **(documento de)** — **anticipada** advance directive

voluntario -ria *adj* voluntary; *mf* volunteer

volver *vi* (*pp* **vuelto**) — **en sí** to regain consciousness, to come to (*fam*); *vr* — **loco** to go crazy, to flip out (*fam*)

vólvulo *m* volvulus

vomitar *vt, vi* to vomit, to throw up (*fam*)

vomitivo -va *adj & m* emetic

vómito *m* (*frec. pl*) vomit; vomiting; **vómitos del embarazo** morning sickness; vómito(s) en proyectil, vómitos en escopetazo (*Esp*) projectile vomiting

voriconazol *m* voriconazole

voyeurismo *m* voyeurism

voz *f* (*pl* **voces**) voice, speech; **hablar** *or* **decir en** — **baja** to whisper; **perder la** — to lose one's voice

VPH *abbr* **virus del papiloma humano**. *See* **virus**.

VSG *abbr* **velocidad de sedimentación globular**. *See* **velocidad**.

vuelta *f* turn; **darse media** — to turn around; **darse** — to turn; (*voltearse*) to turn over, roll over; **dar vueltas** (*girar*) to spin; **Todo me da vueltas**..Everything's spinning.

vuelto *pp of* **volver**

vulnerable *adj* vulnerable

vulva *f* vulva

W

warfarina *f* warfarin

X

xantoma *m* xanthoma

Y

ya visto *m* déjà vu
Y de Roux, Roux-en-Y; **derivación gástrica en Y de Roux** Roux-en-Y gastric bypass
yema *f* yolk; (*del dedo*) pad (*of the finger*); — **de huevo** egg yolk
yerba *See* **hierba.**
yerbabuena *f* (*bot*) peppermint
yerbatero -ra *mf* herbalist, person who sells or prescribes herbs
yerbero -ra *mf* herbalist, person who sells or prescribes herbs
yerna *f* (*esp. Carib*) daughter-in-law

yerno *m* son-in-law
yeso *m* (*ortho*) cast; plaster (*for a cast*); — **removible** removable cast
yeyunal *adj* jejunal
yeyuno *m* jejunum
yo *m* (*psych*) ego
yodado -da *adj* iodized
yodo *m* iodine
yoga *m* yoga
yogur *m* yogurt
yohimbina *f* yohimbine
yuca *f* (*bot*) yucca
yugular *adj* jugular

Z

zafirlukast *m* zafirlukast
zalcitabina *f* zalcitabine
zaleplón, zaleplon *m* zaleplon
zanahoria *f* carrot
zanamivir *m* zanamivir
zancudo *m* (*Amer*) (type of) mosquito
zapato *m* shoe; **zapatos ortopédicos** orthopedic shoes
zarzaparrilla *f* (*bot*) sarsaparilla
zen *adj* & *m* zen
zidovudina *f* zidovudine
zigomicosis *f* zygomycosis
zigoto *m* zygote
zinc *m* zinc; **óxido de** — zinc oxide
ziprasidona *f* ziprasidone
zoledronato (*esp. Esp*) zoledronic acid,
zoledronate
zolmitriptán *m* zolmitriptan
zolpidem *m* zolpidem
zombi, zombie *m* zombie
zona *f* zone, area; *m* (*zóster*) herpes zoster, shingles; — **afectada** affected area; — **de confort** *or* **comodidad** comfort zone
zoofilia *f* zoophilia
zorrillo *m* (*esp. Amer*) skunk
zumaque *m* (*bot*) poison sumac
zumba *f* (*ES, Guat; fam*) binge
zumbido *m* (*de oído, etc.*) ringing, buzzing
zumo *m* (*esp. Esp*) juice
zurdo -da *adj* left-handed

DIALOGUES

DIÁLOGOS

HISTORY AND PHYSICAL/
HISTORIA CLÍNICA Y EXAMEN FÍSICO

PRESENT ILLNESS / ENFERMEDAD ACTUAL

Good morning. I'm Dr. Jones. / Buenos días. Soy la Dra. Jones.
Good afternoon. I'm Dr. Smith. / Buenas tardes. Soy el Dr. Smith.
Have a seat, ma'am. / Siéntese, señora.
How can I help you? / ¿En qué puedo servirle?
What brings you here today? / ¿Qué lo trae por aquí?
Do you have pain? / ¿Tiene Ud. dolor?
Where is the pain exactly? / ¿Dónde está el dolor exactamente?
Can you show me? / ¿Puede enseñarme?
Does the pain move to other areas? / ¿Se le mueve el dolor a otros lados?
Does the pain stay here? / ¿Se le queda aquí el dolor?
What is the pain like? / ¿Cómo es el dolor?
Sharp? / ¿Agudo?
Dull? / ¿Sordo?
Does it burn? / ¿Le arde?
Like quick jabs? / ¿Como punzadas (piquetes)?
Like pressure? / ¿Como una opresión?
Is it a severe pain? / ¿Es un dolor severo?
Moderate? / ¿Moderado?
Mild? / ¿Leve?
When did the pain begin? / ¿Cuándo le empezó el dolor?
When was the first time you ever had this pain? / ¿Cuándo fue la primera vez que sintió este dolor?
Did it go away for a while? / ¿Se le quitó por un tiempo?
By itself? / ¿Por sí solo?
When did it begin again? / ¿Cuándo le empezó de nuevo?
Does the pain come and go? / El dolor, ¿va y viene?
Is it a constant pain? / ¿Es un dolor constante?
When it comes, how long does it last? / ¿Cuando le viene, cuánto tiempo le dura?
How often do you get the pain? / ¿Cada cuánto tiempo le viene el dolor?

In the last week, how many times have you had the pain? / ¿En la última semana, cuántas veces ha tenido el dolor?

What were you doing when the pain came on? / ¿Qué estaba haciendo cuando empezó el dolor?

What time of day does the pain come on? / ¿A qué hora del día empieza el dolor?

Do you get it more often in the morning? / ¿Le viene más en la mañana?

In the afternoon? / ¿En la tarde?

Anytime? / ¿A cualquier hora?

Is it worse after you eat? / ¿Empeora después de comer?

Is it worse when you exert yourself? / ¿Empeora al hacer esfuerzos?

Is there anything which makes the pain worse? / ¿Hay algo que le agrave el dolor?

Is there anything which makes the pain better? / ¿Hay algo que le alivie el dolor?

Does it get better with exercise? / ¿Se alivia con el ejercicio?

It gets worse? / ¿Se pone peor?

Have you tried medications? / ¿Ha probado medicamentos?

Did it help? / ¿Le ayudó?

Are there relatives or friends who have the same problem? / ¿Hay familiares o amigos que tienen el mismo problema?

What do you think is causing the problem? / ¿Qué cree que está causando el problema?

Have you seen a doctor before for this problem? / ¿Ha consultado a un médico por este problema antes?

What did he say you had? / ¿Qué le dijo que tenía?

Did he do any studies? / ¿Le hizo estudios?

Did he draw blood? / ¿Le sacó sangre?

When was this? / ¿Cuándo fue esto?

What's the name of the doctor? / ¿Cómo se llama el médico?

Do you know his telephone number? / ¿Sabe su número de teléfono?

Why did you come to the hospital today instead of some other day? / ¿Porqué vino al hospital hoy en vez de cualquier otro día?

Do you have any other problems? / ¿Tiene algún otro problema?

How long have you been in the United States? / ¿Hace cuánto que está en los Estados Unidos?

When was the last time you left the country? / ¿Cuándo fue la última vez que salió del país?

Where did you go? / ¿A dónde fue?

By the way, how old are you? / ¿A propósito, cuántos años tiene Ud.?

PAST MEDICAL HISTORY / ANTECEDENTES MÉDICOS

How long have you had diabetes? / ¿Hace cuánto que tiene diabetes?

Who takes care of you for your diabetes? / ¿Quién lo trata por su diabetes?

Do you have a regular doctor? / ¿Tiene algún médico a quien consulta regularmente?

Where is he located? / ¿Dónde está ubicado?

Is he a private doctor? / ¿Es un médico privado?

When was the last time you saw a doctor? / ¿Cuándo fue la última vez que consultó a un médico?

Have you ever been hospitalized? / ¿Ha sido hospitalizado alguna vez?

Have you ever had surgery? / ¿Ha sido operado alguna vez?

Have you ever had any serious illness? / ¿Alguna vez ha tenido alguna enfermedad grave?

Have you ever had emotional problems? / ¿Ha tenido alguna vez problemas emocionales?

MEDICATIONS / MEDICAMENTOS

Are you taking any medications? / ¿Está tomando algún medicamento?

Have you taken any over-the-counter medications? / ¿Ha tomado algún medicamento que se vende sin receta médica?

Are you taking birth control pills? / ¿Está tomando píldoras anticonceptivas?

Do you have your medications with you? / ¿Trae sus medicamentos?

What color are the pills? / ¿De qué color son las pastillas?

Are they tablets or capsules? / ¿Son tabletas o cápsulas?

How many times a day do you take them? / ¿Cuántas veces al día las toma?

Who prescribed the pills for you? / ¿Quién le recetó las pastillas?

Do you take them every day or do you forget every now and then? / ¿Las toma todos los días o se le olvida de vez en cuando?

For example, in a week how many times do you forget to take the pills? / Por ejemplo, durante una semana, ¿cuántas veces se le olvida tomar las pastillas?

When was the last time you took this pill? / ¿Cuándo fue la última vez que tomó esta pastilla?

How many of these did you take yesterday? / ¿Cuántas de estas tomó Ud. ayer?

Show me exactly which pills you took this morning. / Muéstreme exactamente cuáles pastillas tomó esta mañana.
When did you run out of pills? / ¿Cuándo se le acabaron las pastillas?

ALLERGIES / ALERGIAS

Are you allergic to penicillin? / ¿Es Ud. alérgico a la penicilina?
Have you ever taken penicillin? / ¿Ha tomado penicilina alguna vez?
Are you allergic to any medication? / ¿Es Ud. alérgico a algún medicamento?
Have you ever had a bad reaction to a medicine? / ¿Ha tenido alguna vez una mala reacción después de tomar una medicina?
What happened? / ¿Qué le pasó?
Can you tolerate aspirin? / ¿Tolera bien la aspirina?

SOCIAL HISTORY / ANTECEDENTES SOCIALES

What type of work do you do? / ¿Qué tipo de trabajo hace Ud.?
How long have you been out of work? / ¿Hace cuánto que no trabaja?
Why haven't you been able to work? / ¿Porqué no ha podido trabajar?
What kind of work did you use to do? / ¿Qué tipo de trabajo hacía Ud.?
Were there toxic chemicals or other hazards where you worked? / ¿Había sustancias químicas tóxicas u otros peligros donde trabajaba?
What do you do during the day? / ¿Qué hace Ud. durante el día?
Do you eat well? / ¿Come bien?
Do you sleep well? / ¿Duerme bien?
Do you have a place to live? / ¿Tiene dónde vivir?
Who do you live with? / ¿Con quién vive Ud.?
Do you smoke? / ¿Fuma Ud.?
Did you use to smoke? / ¿Fumaba?
How many packs a day did you use to smoke? / ¿Cuántas cajetillas fumaba al día?
When did you quit smoking? / ¿Cuándo dejó de fumar?
Do you drink alcohol? / ¿Toma bebidas alcohólicas?
Wine? / ¿Vino?
Beer? / ¿Cerveza?
Did you use to drink? / ¿Tomaba?
How long has it been since you quit drinking? / ¿Hace cuánto que no toma?

When was the last time you had a drink? / ¿Cuándo fue la última vez que tomó un trago?

How much can you drink when you have a mind to? / ¿Cuánto puede tomar cuando tiene ganas?

Do your hands ever shake when you quit drinking? / ¿Le tiemblan las manos cuando deja de tomar?

Have you ever had the d.t.'s when you quit drinking? / ¿Ha delirado alguna vez cuando ha dejado de beber?

Have you ever had seizures when you quit drinking for a few days? / ¿Alguna vez ha tenido convulsiones al dejar de beber por unos días?

Have you tried to quit drinking? / ¿Ha tratado de dejar de tomar?

Have you ever used drugs? / ¿Ha usado drogas alguna vez?

Have you ever used I.V. drugs? / ¿Se ha inyectado drogas alguna vez?

How often do you use it? / ¿Cada cuánto la usa?

Do you share needles? / ¿Comparte agujas?

Have you had relations with other men? / ¿Ha tenido relaciones con otros hombres?

With prostitutes? / ¿Con prostitutas?

Did you use condoms? / ¿Usó preservativos (condones)?

Have you ever received a blood transfusion? / ¿Ha recibido alguna vez una transfusión de sangre?

Have you been tested for AIDS? / ¿Le han hecho la prueba del SIDA?

What was the result? / ¿Cuál fue el resultado?

FAMILY HISTORY / ANTECEDENTES FAMILIARES

Are there any diseases which run in your family? / ¿Hay enfermedades que vienen de familia?

Are there family members who have had colon cancer? / ¿Hay familiares que han tenido cáncer del colon?

Are your parents still living? / ¿Aún viven sus padres?

Does your mother have any medical problems? / ¿Tiene algún problema médico su madre?

What did your father die of? / ¿De qué murió su padre?

How old was he when he died? / ¿Qué edad tenía cuando murió?

REVIEW OF SYSTEMS / REVISIÓN POR SISTEMAS

General / General:

Has your weight changed recently? / ¿Ha cambiado de peso recientemente?
How many kilograms have you gained? / ¿Cuántos kilos ha ganado?
How many pounds have you lost? / ¿Cuántas libras ha perdido?
Over what period of time? / ¿En cuánto tiempo?
Do you have as much energy as usual? / ¿Tiene la misma energía de siempre?
How long have you felt tired? / ¿Hace cuánto que se siente cansado?
Have you had fever? / ¿Ha tenido fiebre?
Night sweats? / ¿Sudores durante la noche?

Skin / Piel:

Do you have problems with your skin? / ¿Tiene problemas con la piel?
Rash? / ¿Erupción? (¿Sarpullido?)
Itching? / ¿Comezón? (¿Picazón?)
Sores? / ¿Úlceras? (¿Llagas?)
How often do you bathe? / ¿Cada cuánto se baña?
For how long? / ¿Por cuánto tiempo?
Do you use hot water? / ¿Usa Ud. agua caliente?
What type of soap do you use? / ¿Qué tipo de jabón usa Ud.?

Head / Cabeza:

Do you have headaches? / ¿Tiene dolores de cabeza?
Have you hurt your head recently? / ¿Se ha lastimado la cabeza recientemente?

Eyes / Ojos:

Can you see well? / ¿Puede ver bien?
Do you wear glasses? / ¿Usa lentes?
Does your vision get blurry at times? / ¿Ve borroso a veces?
Do you ever see double? / ¿Ve doble a veces?
Do you have cataracts? / ¿Tiene cataratas?
Glaucoma? / ¿Glaucoma?
Do you see halos around lights at night? / ¿Ve Ud. halos (círculos) alrededor de las luces en la noche?
Have you ever had your vision tested? / ¿Le han revisado la vista alguna vez?

When was the last time you saw an eye doctor? / ¿Cuándo fue la última vez que consultó a un médico de los ojos?

Ears / Oídos:

Do you hear well? / ¿Oye bien?
Do you hear equally well in both ears? / ¿Oye igual de bien con los dos oídos?
Has your hearing gotten worse recently? / ¿Oye menos últimamente?
Do you have an earache? / ¿Tiene dolor de oído?
Have you had ear infections? / ¿Ha tenido infecciones del oído?
Is there liquid draining from your ear? / ¿Le sale líquido del oído?
Do you feel as though the room were spinning around you? / ¿Siente como si el cuarto le estuviera dando vueltas?

Nose / Nariz:

Do you get a lot of nosebleeds? / ¿Le sangra la nariz frecuentemente?
Are you allergic to pollen? / ¿Es Ud. alérgico al polen?
Do you have sinusitis? / ¿Tiene sinusitis?
Do you get a lot of colds? / ¿Le dan resfriados frecuentemente?
Can you smell all right? / ¿Puede distinguir bien los olores?

Oropharynx / Orofaringe:

Do any of your teeth hurt? / ¿Le duele algún diente?
Do you have false teeth? / ¿Tiene dientes postizos?
How often do you brush your teeth? / ¿Cada cuánto se cepilla los dientes?
Do your gums bleed easily? / ¿Le sangran con facilidad las encías?
When was the last time you saw a dentist? / ¿Cuándo fue la última vez que vio a un dentista?
Is your throat sore? / ¿Le duele la garganta?
Do you get canker sores frequently? / ¿Le salen pequeñas llagas en la boca frecuentemente?
Has your voice changed recently? / ¿Le ha cambiado la voz recientemente?

Neck / Cuello:

Is your neck sore? / ¿Le duele el cuello?
Do you have any lumps in your neck? / ¿Tiene bolitas en el cuello?

Breasts / Mamas (Senos):

Do you have any lumps in your breasts? / ¿Tiene algunos nódulos (bolitas) en los senos?

Have you ever had a mammogram? / ¿Le han hecho una mamografía alguna vez?

Do your nipples ever secrete milk? / ¿Le sale leche de los pezones a veces?

Lungs / Pulmones:

Do you have trouble breathing? / ¿Tiene dificultad para respirar?

Are you short of breath? / ¿Le falta el aire?

Can you climb stairs? / ¿Puede subir escaleras?

Do you have to stop to catch your breath? / ¿Tiene que parar para recuperar el aliento?

How may blocks can you walk without stopping? / ¿Cuántas cuadras puede caminar sin parar?

Do you use oxygen at home? / ¿Usa oxígeno en casa?

Do you have a cough? / ¿Tiene tos?

Are you bringing up phlegm? / ¿Le sale flema(s)?

Have you coughed up blood? / ¿Ha tosido sangre?

Do you have wheezing? / ¿Tiene sibilancias (silbidos) en el pecho?

Do you have asthma? / ¿Tiene asma?

Is there anything that brings on the asthma attacks? / ¿Hay algo que le provoque los ataques de asma?

Does it have anything to do with the time of year? / ¿Tiene algo que ver con las estaciones del año?

Do you have allergies? / ¿Tiene alergias?

Is there a lot of dust in your home? / ¿Hay mucho polvo en su casa?

Are there animals in your home? / ¿Hay animales en la casa?

Have you ever had a TB test? / ¿Le han hecho alguna vez la prueba para la tuberculosis?

What was the result? / ¿Cuál fue el resultado?

Have you ever had a chest x-ray? / ¿Le han tomado una radiografía (placa) de tórax alguna vez?

Heart / Corazón:

Do you have heart problems? / ¿Tiene problemas de corazón?

High blood pressure? / ¿Presión alta?

How do you know you have high blood pressure? / ¿Cómo sabe que tiene presión alta?

Do you ever have chest pain? / ¿Ha tenido dolor de pecho alguna vez?

Do you use pillows when you sleep? / ¿Usa Ud. almohadas cuando duerme?

What happens when you don't use pillows? / ¿Qué le pasa cuando no usa almohadas?

Have you ever woken up in the middle of the night with a smothering sensation? / ¿Alguna vez se ha despertado en la noche con una sensación de ahogo?

Have you ever been told you had a heart murmur? / ¿Le han dicho alguna vez que tiene un soplo cardíaco?

When you were a child, did you have a disease called rheumatic fever? / Cuando era niño, ¿le dio una enfermedad llamada fiebre reumática?

Gastrointestinal / Gastrointestinal:

Do you have trouble swallowing? / ¿Tiene dificultad para tragar (pasar) alimentos?

Does food stick in your throat? / ¿Se le atraganta (atora) la comida?

Do you have trouble swallowing liquids too? / ¿Tiene dificultad para tragar (pasar) líquidos también?

Do you have heartburn? / ¿Tiene acidez?

Nausea? / ¿Náusea(s)?

Vomiting? / ¿Vómito(s)?

Did you vomit blood? / ¿Vomitó sangre?

Do you have a stomachache? / ¿Tiene dolor de estómago?

Are there certain foods that bring on the pain? / ¿Hay ciertas comidas que le provoquen los dolores?

Do you have trouble going to the bathroom? / ¿Tiene problemas para ir al baño?

Are you constipated? / ¿Está Ud. estreñido?

Do you have diarrhea? / ¿Tiene Ud. diarrea?

Have you noticed blood in your stool? / ¿Ha notado sangre en sus heces (popó, caca)?

Have you had stools that were black like asphalt? / ¿Ha tenido heces negras (popó negro, caca negra) como el asfalto de la calle?

Do you have hemorrhoids? / ¿Tiene hemorroides (almorranas)?

Have you had your gallbladder taken out? / ¿Le han sacado la vesícula?

Have you had hepatitis? / ¿Ha tenido hepatitis?

Has your skin ever turned yellow? / ¿Se le ha puesto la piel amarilla alguna vez?

Genitourinary / Genitourinario:

Do you have problems urinating? / ¿Tiene problemas para orinar?
Are you urinating more often than usual? / ¿Orina más a menudo que de costumbre?
Do you have to get up in the middle of the night to urinate? / ¿Tiene que levantarse durante la noche para orinar?
Does it burn when you urinate? / ¿Le arde al orinar?
Have you ever had a urinary tract infection? / ¿Ha tenido alguna vez una infección de la orina?
Have you ever noticed blood in your urine? / ¿Ha notado sangre en la orina alguna vez?
Have you ever passed a stone? / ¿Ha eliminado un cálculo (una piedra) en la orina alguna vez?
Have you ever had a sexually transmitted disease? / ¿Ha tenido alguna vez una enfermedad de transmisión sexual?
Were you treated by a doctor? / ¿Recibió tratamiento de un médico?
Do you have any sexual problems? / ¿Tiene algún problema sexual?

(Men) / (Hombres)
Do you have to strain to get your urine out? / ¿Tiene que esforzarse para que salga la orina?
How is your stream? / ¿Cómo está el chorro?
Do you have problems with dribbling? / ¿Gotea después de haber terminado?
Do you have sores on your penis? / ¿Tiene llagas (heridas, úlceras) en el pene?
Do you have a discharge from your penis? / ¿Le sale alguna secreción por el pene?

(Women) / (Mujeres)
Do you ever lose your urine accidentally? / ¿Se le escapa la orina a veces sin querer?
When you laugh or cough? / ¿Cuando se ríe o tose?
Do you still have periods? / ¿Todavía menstrua?
When was your last period? / ¿Cuándo fue su última menstruación (período, regla)?
Was it normal? / ¿Fue normal?
Do you have pain with your periods? / ¿Tiene dolor con las menstruaciones?
Do you bleed a lot during your periods? / ¿Sangra mucho durante las menstruaciones?
How many sanitary napkins do you use? / ¿Cuántas toallas sanitarias

usa?

Do you use tampons? / ¿Usa tampones?

Are your periods regular? / ¿Sus menstruaciones son regulares?

Have you had bleeding between periods? / ¿Ha sangrado entre las menstruaciones?

How old were you when you had your first period? / ¿A qué edad le vino la primera regla?

When did you go through menopause? / ¿Cuándo le vino la menopausia?

Have you had bleeding since then? / ¿Ha sangrado desde entonces?

Do you get hot flashes? / ¿Le vienen sofocos (bochornos)?

How many children have you had? / ¿Cuántos hijos ha tenido?

Did you have problems with any of your pregnancies? / ¿Tuvo problemas con alguno de sus embarazos?

Have you had any abortions or miscarriages? / ¿Ha tenido algún aborto?

An abortion or a miscarriage? / ¿Provocado o espontáneo?

When was the last time you had sexual relations? / ¿Cuándo fue la última vez que tuvo relaciones sexuales?

Are you using any birth control? / ¿Usa algún método anticonceptivo?

The pill? / ¿La píldora?

Condoms? / ¿Preservativos (condones)?

Could you be pregnant? / ¿Podría estar embarazada?

Do you have a vaginal discharge? / ¿Tiene secreción (flujo) vaginal?

As usual or different? / ¿Como siempre o diferente?

What is it like? / ¿Cómo es?

Do you have sores on your genitals? / ¿Tiene llagas (heridas, úlceras) en los genitales?

Do you have itching? / ¿Tiene comezón (picazón)?

Does it hurt when you have intercourse? / ¿Le duele cuando tiene relaciones?

Musculoskeletal / Musculoesquelético:

Do you have joint pains? / ¿Tiene dolores de las articulaciones (coyunturas)?

Do your joints swell up? / ¿Se le hinchan las articulaciones?

Do you feel stiff in the morning? / ¿Se siente rígido (tieso) en la mañana?

Does your back hurt? / ¿Le duele la espalda?

Do you feel weak? / ¿Se siente débil?

Do you have trouble climbing stairs? / ¿Le dificulta subir escaleras?

Getting up from a chair? / ¿Levantarse de una silla?

Combing your hair? / ¿Peinarse?

Neurological / Neurológico:

Which hand do you write with? / ¿Con cuál mano escribe Ud.?
Have you had a stroke? / ¿Ha padecido un ataque cerebral (derrame, embolia)?
Has a single part of your body ever turned weak, like your arm or your leg? / ¿Se le ha puesto débil una sola parte del cuerpo alguna vez, como el brazo o la pierna?
Has your vision in one eye ever gone black? / ¿Se le ha puesto negra la vista en un solo ojo alguna vez?
Does any part of your body feel numb? / ¿Siente adormecida alguna parte del cuerpo?
Do you have tingling? / ¿Tiene hormigueo?
Do your hands shake? / ¿Le tiemblan las manos?
Do you have trouble remembering things? / ¿Tiene dificultad para recordar cosas?
Do you get dizzy at times? / ¿Tiene mareos a veces?
As if you were going to faint? / ¿Como si fuera a desmayarse?
Have you fainted? / ¿Se ha desmayado?
Have you ever had a seizure? / ¿Ha tenido alguna vez una convulsión?

Mental status / Estado mental:

What's your name? / ¿Cómo se llama Ud.?
Do you know where you are? / ¿Sabe dónde está?
What type of building are we in? / ¿En qué tipo de edificio estamos?
What's the date? / ¿Cuál es la fecha?
What year is it? / ¿Qué año es?
Do you know who I am? / ¿Sabe quién soy yo?

Psychiatric / Psiquiátrico:

Would you say you are a nervous person? / ¿Diría que Ud. es una persona nerviosa?
Is something bothering you? / ¿Hay algo que le molesta?
Would you say you suffer from depression at times? / ¿Diría que padece de depresión a veces?
Have you ever seen a psychiatrist? / ¿Ha visto alguna vez a un psiquiatra?
Did it help? / ¿Le ayudó?
Have you ever thought of killing yourself? / ¿Ha pensado alguna vez en suicidarse?
Have you thought about how you would do it? / ¿Ha pensado en cómo lo haría?

Have you thought of hurting someone else? / ¿Ha pensado en hacerle daño a otra persona?

Do you think you can take care of yourself? / ¿Cree que puede valerse por sí mismo?

Are you going to be able to manage? / ¿Va a poder arreglárselas?

Endocrine / Endocrino:

Do you have thyroid problems? / ¿Tiene problemas de tiroides?

Did a doctor tell you? / ¿Se lo dijo un médico?

Do you feel hot frequently? / ¿Siente calor muy a menudo?

More than usual? / ¿Más que de costumbre?

Do you feel cold a lot when others don't? / ¿Siente frío muchas veces cuando los demás no lo sienten?

Are you thirsty a lot? / ¿Tiene mucha sed?

Have you always been thirsty or is this something new? / ¿Siempre ha tenido sed o es algo nuevo? /

Are you eating a lot? / ¿Está comiendo mucho?

PHYSICAL EXAMINATION / EXAMEN FÍSICO

General Examination / Examen General

Have a seat on the exam table. / Siéntese en la mesa (de exploración).

Take off your jacket. / Quítese la chaqueta (chamarra).

I need to take your blood pressure. / Necesito tomarle la presión.

Roll up your sleeve please. / Súbase la manga, por favor.

Let your arm fall; I will hold it up. / Deje caer el brazo; yo se lo sostengo.

Your blood pressure is one hundred thirty over seventy. / Su presión es de 130 sobre 70.

Take off your clothes from the waist up please. / Desvístase de la cintura hacia arriba, por favor.

Take off all your clothes except your underwear. / Quítese toda la ropa menos la ropa interior.

Put on this gown with the opening at the back. / Póngase esta bata con la abertura hacia atrás.

Sit facing this wall please. / Siéntese mirando hacia esta pared, por favor.

Sit with your legs dangling. / Siéntese con las piernas colgando.

Let me take your pulse. / Déjeme tomarle el pulso.

Follow my finger with your eyes without moving your head. / Siga mi dedo con los ojos sin mover la cabeza.

Look at my nose. / Míreme la nariz.

Stare at that point on the wall. / Fije la vista en aquel punto en la pared.

Keep staring at it even if I get in the way of one eye. / Siga mirándolo aún cuando yo bloquee su visión en un ojo.

Try not to move your eyes. / Trate de no mover los ojos.

Now look directly at the light. / Ahora mire directamente a la luz.

Raise your eyebrows. / Levante las cejas.

Frown. / Frunza el ceño.

Wrinkle your nose. / Arrugue la nariz.

Smile. / Sonría.

Show me your teeth. / Enséñeme los dientes.

Clench your teeth. / Apriete los dientes.

Raise your shoulders against my hands. / Levante sus hombros contra mis manos.

Look up at the ceiling. / Mire al techo.

Open your mouth. / Abra la boca.

Stick your tongue out. / Saque la lengua.

Move it from side to side. / Muévala de lado a lado.

Say "Ah." / Diga "A."

Swallow. / Trague.

Breathe quietly through your nose while I listen your heart. / Respire suavemente por la nariz mientras le escucho el corazón.

Don't talk for a moment. / No hable por un momento.

Lean forward. / Inclínese hacia adelante.

Cross your arms. / Cruce los brazos.

Take deep breaths through your mouth while I listen to your lungs. / Respire profundo por la boca mientras le escucho los pulmones.

I need to examine your breasts. / Necesito examinarle las mamas (los senos).

Do you examine your breasts regularly? / ¿Examina Ud. sus mamas regularmente?

Place your hands on your hips and push inward. / Ponga las manos en la cadera y empuje hacia dentro.

Lift your arms above your head like this. / Levante los brazos arriba de la cabeza así.

Now lie down. / Ahora acuéstese.

Face up. / Boca arriba.

I'm going to examine your abdomen. / Le voy a examinar el abdomen (la barriga).

Arrange yourself straight on the table. / Acomódese recto en la mesa.

Relax your muscles. / Relaje los músculos.

Let your head rest. Don't try to lift it. / Descanse la cabeza. No trate de levantarla.

Tell me if it hurts. / Dígame si le duele.

I have to do a rectal examination. / Necesito hacerle un tacto rectal.

Do you know what a rectal exam is? / ¿Sabe Ud. qué es un tacto rectal?

I need to examine your rectum with my finger, using a glove. / Necesito examinar su recto con mi dedo, usando un guante.

Roll over onto your left side. / Voltéese a su lado izquierdo.

Bend your knees toward your chest. / Doble las rodillas hacia el pecho.

Bear down as if you were having a bowel movement. / Puje como si estuviera defecando.

Squeeze my finger. / Apriete mi dedo.

I need to examine you for a hernia. / Necesito examinarle para ver si tiene una hernia.

Cough please. / Tosa, por favor.

Pelvic Examination / Examen Pélvico

I need to do a pelvic examination. / Necesito hacerle un examen pélvico.

Put your feet in the stirrups. / Coloque los pies en los estribos.

Move forward. / Muévase hacia adelante.

Separate your legs. / Separe las piernas.

I'm going to insert the speculum. / Voy a introducirle el espéculo.

I'm going to do a Pap test. / Voy a hacerle una citología (prueba de Papanicolaou).

The exam is almost over. / Falta poco para terminar el examen.

I need to examine you with my fingers, using a glove. / Necesito examinarla con mis dedos, usando un guante.

Now I am going to examine your vagina and rectum and the tissue in between. / Ahora le voy a examinar la vagina, el recto y el tejido entre ellos.

Neurological Examination / Examen Neurológico

Close your eyes. / Cierre los ojos.

Do you smell anything? / ¿Huele algo?

What does it smell like? / ¿A qué huele?

I am going to examine your peripheral vision. / Voy a examinarle la visión periférica.

Cover your left eye and with your right eye look in my eye. / Tápese el ojo izquierdo y con el derecho mire mi ojo.

Now tell me "Yes" the moment you see my finger wiggling. / Ahora diga "Sí" al momento que vea mover mi dedo.

Don't look at my finger. / No mire mi dedo.

Keep looking at my eye. / Siga mirando mi ojo.

Close your eyes and don't let me open them. / Cierre los ojos y no permita que se los abra.

Can you hear the sound of my fingers rubbing? / ¿Puede escuchar el sonido de mis dedos frotando?

Close your eyes and tell me the moment you hear my fingers rubbing. / Cierre los ojos y dígame al momento que escuche mis dedos frotando.

On which side does the tuning fork sound louder? / ¿En cuál lado suena más fuerte el diapasón?

Or does it sound the same on both sides? / ¿O suena igual en los dos lados?

Which sound seems louder: this? / ¿Cuál sonido le parece más fuerte: este?

Or this? / ¿O éste?

(For additional dialogue concerning the cranial nerves see GENERAL EXAMINATION above.) / *(Para diálogos adicionales sobre los pares craneales, vea el EXAMEN GENERAL arriba.)*

Stand please. / Levántese, por favor.

Walk toward the door. / Camine hacia la puerta.

Now walk toward me. / Ahora camine hacia mí.

Walk on your toes. / Camine de puntillas.

Walk on your heels. / Camine con los talones.

Walk in a straight line, putting one foot directly in front of the other, like this. / Camine en una línea recta, poniendo un pie directamente enfrente del otro, así.

Hop on one foot. / Salte en un pie.

Now on the other one. / Ahora en el otro.

Squat down. / Póngase en cuclillas.

Now get up without using your arms. / Ahora levántese sin usar los brazos.

Stand with your feet together and your arms extended in front of you, palms up, like this. / Párese con los pies juntos y los brazos extendidos enfrente, las palmas hacia arriba, así.

Keep your arms extended. / Mantenga los brazos extendidos.

Close your eyes. / Cierre los ojos.

I won't let you fall. / No lo voy a dejar caer.

Sit here please. / Siéntese aquí, por favor.

Squeeze my fingers as hard as you can. / Apriete mis dedos lo más fuerte que pueda.

Separate your fingers like this and don't let me close them. / Separe los dedos así y no permita que se los cierre.

Make a circle like this and don't let me break it. / Haga un círculo así y no permita que se lo rompa.

Pull against my hand. / Jale contra mi mano.

Push against my hand. / Empuje contra mi mano.

Harder. / Más fuerte.

Make a fist. / Haga un puño.

Flex your wrist against my hand. / Flexione (Doble) la muñeca contra mi mano.

Raise your arms against my hands. / Levante los brazos contra mis manos.

Extend your leg against my hand. / Extienda la pierna contra mi mano.

Pull it back. / Jálela hacia atrás.

Push your foot against my hand. / Empuje el pie contra mi mano.

Bend your foot upward. / Doble el pie hacia arriba.

Raise your leg against my hand. / Levante la pierna contra mi mano.

Touch your nose with your finger. / Tóquese la nariz con el dedo.

Now touch my finger. / Ahora toque mi dedo.

Keep on touching your nose and my finger, back and forth, as rapidly as you can. / Siga tocando su nariz y mi dedo repetidamente lo más rápido que pueda.

Touch your knee with the heel of your other leg. / Tóquese la rodilla con el talón de la otra pierna.

Now slide your heel down your shin to your foot. / Ahora con el talón recorra la espinilla hasta el pie.

Can you feel the tuning fork vibrating? / ¿Siente vibrar el diapasón?

Now it isn't vibrating. / Ahora no está vibrando.

Can you tell the difference? / ¿Siente la diferencia?

Close your eyes. / Cierre los ojos.

Is it vibrating or not? / ¿Está vibrando o no?

Now? / ¿Ahora?

Can you feel when I touch you with this piece of cotton? / ¿Puede sentir cuando le toco con este algodón?

Close your eyes and tell me "Yes" each time you feel the cotton. / Cierre los ojos y diga "Sí" cada vez que sienta el algodón.

The moment you feel it, tell me. / Al momento que lo sienta, me dice.

I'm going to use this pin to test your sensation of pain. / Voy a usar este alfiler para examinar su sensación de dolor.

This is sharp. / Esto es agudo.

This is dull. / Esto es romo.

Can you feel the difference? / ¿Siente la diferencia?

Close your eyes and tell me "Sharp" or "Dull" each time I touch you. / Cierre los ojos y dígame "Agudo" o "Romo" cada vez que lo toque.

Did you feel anything? / ¿Sintió algo?

Do you feel this point? / ¿Siente esta punta?

Do you feel these two separate points? / ¿Siente estas dos puntas separadas?

Close your eyes and tell me "One" or "Two" according to how many points you feel. / Cierre los ojos y dígame "Una" o "Dos" según cuantas puntas sienta.

I am going to check your reflexes. / Voy a examinarle los reflejos.

Relax. / Relájese.

Relax your leg. / Relaje la pierna.

NURSING / ENFERMERÍA

Orientation / Orientación:

Hello. I'm Lee. I'll be your nurse today. / Hola. Me llamo Lee. Voy a ser su enfermera (enfermero) hoy.

Let me show you how your bed works. / Permítame mostrarle cómo funciona su cama.

This button here raises your head and this other one raises your legs. / Este botón aquí eleva su cabeza y este otro eleva sus piernas.

This works the T.V. / Esto hace funcionar la televisión.

If you need me, press this button here. / Si me necesita, presione este botón aquí.

If you want to make a call, dial nine first. / Si quiere hacer una llamada, marque el nueve primero.

You need to put on this gown. / Tiene que ponerse esta bata.

You can put your clothes in this drawer. / Puede poner su ropa en este cajón.

Do you have any valuables with you? / ¿Lleva algo de valor consigo?

Do you want us to lock it up? / ¿Quiere que se lo guardemos bajo llave?

I need to take your vital signs. / Necesito tomarle sus signos vitales.

Relax your arm. / Relaje su brazo.

Hold this thermometer under your tongue. / Mantenga este termómetro bajo su lengua.

Please step on this scale; I need to weigh you. / Por favor párese sobre esta balanza; necesito pesarlo.

I need to start an IV on you. / Necesito ponerle suero.

Make a fist. / Cierre el puño.

You're going to feel a stick. / Va a sentir un pinchazo (piquete).
Don't forget you're attached to this IV now. / No olvide que ahora está conectado a este suero.
Visiting hours are from nine in the morning to eight in the evening. / Las horas de visita son de las nueve de la mañana a las ocho de la noche.

Comfort / Comodidad:

Are you cold? / ¿Tiene Ud. frío?
Would you like an extra blanket? / ¿Quisiera otra cobija más?
An extra pillow? / ¿Otra almohada más?
Are you too warm? / ¿Tiene demasiado calor?
Are you comfortable? / ¿Está cómodo?
Are you having pain? / ¿Tiene dolor?
How bad is your pain on a scale from 1 to 10? / ¿Qué tan intenso es su dolor en una escala de 1 a 10?
Where is the pain? / ¿Dónde siente el dolor?
What do you usually take for the pain? / ¿Qué es lo que acostumbra tomar para el dolor?
I'll call your doctor and see if he can prescribe something for the pain. / Voy a llamar a su médico para ver si le puede recetar algo para el dolor.

Nourishment / Alimentación:

Here's a menu showing your choices for dinner. / Aquí tiene un menú de lo que puede escoger para cenar.
You can order something from the cafeteria if you like. / Puede pedir algo de la cafetería si gusta.
Are you on any kind of special diet? / ¿Está Ud. en alguna dieta especial?
Are you diabetic? / ¿Es diabético?
Do you have high blood pressure? / ¿Tiene presión alta (hipertensión)?
Do you need help eating? / ¿Necesita ayuda para comer?
After midnight you won't be able to eat or drink anything because of the study they are going to do in the morning. / Después de la medianoche no va a poder comer ni tomar nada debido al estudio que le van a realizar en la mañana.
Try to drink more fluids. / Trate de tomar mas líquidos.
Your doctor doesn't want you to eat in case you need surgery. / Su médico no quiere que coma en caso de que necesite cirugía.
Would you like ice chips? / ¿Quisiera pedacitos de hielo?
You're getting plenty of fluids through your IV. / Está recibiendo suficientes líquidos a través del suero.

Here's a basin in case you need to throw up. / Aquí tiene una riñonera (un recipiente) en caso de que necesite vomitar.

I need to pass a tube through your nose down into your stomach. / Necesito pasarle un tubo por la nariz hasta el estómago.

It will be a little uncomfortable but it shouldn't be painful. / Le será un poco incómodo, pero no debería ser doloroso.

When I tell you, I'm going to want you to swallow. / Cuando yo le avise, voy a querer que trague.

Swallow. / Trague.

Good. / Bien.

Elimination / Eliminación:

Do you have diarrhea? / ¿Tiene Ud. diarrea?

Do you want something for constipation? / ¿Quiere Ud. algo para el estreñimiento?

I need to give you an enema. / Necesito ponerle un enema (una lavativa).

Are you going to be able to walk to the bathroom? / ¿Va a poder caminar al baño?

Do you want me to bring you a bedpan? / ¿Quiere que le traiga una cuña (chata, bacinica, bacinilla)?

I can bring you a urinal. / Puedo traerle un orinal (pato).

You need to urinate in this container. / Necesita orinar en este recipiente.

I'm going to need a sample of your stool. / Necesitaré una muestra de sus heces (su popó, su caca).

Let me close the curtain. / Permítame cerrar la cortina.

Your doctor has ordered a catheter. / Su médico le ha indicado (ordenado) una sonda.

I'm going to pass this tube through your urethra, that is, through the opening just above your vagina. / Le voy a pasar esta manguerita por su uretra, o sea, por la abertura justo arriba de su vagina.

I'm going to pass this tube through your penis into your bladder. / Le voy a pasar esta manguerita por su pene hasta la vejiga.

It's not as bad as it sounds. / No es tan malo como suena.

Just relax. / Simplemente relájese.

Be sure not to pull this out. / Asegúrese de no sacarse esto.

Medication / Medicamentos:

What medications do you take at home? / ¿Qué medicamentos toma Ud. en casa?

Are you allergic to any medicines? / ¿Es alérgico a alguna medicina?

Here are your medicines. / Aquí tiene sus medicinas.

Drink this liquid please. / Tome este líquido, por favor.

Would you like a pill to help you sleep? / ¿Quisiera una pastilla que le ayude a dormir?

Would you like another injection for the pain? / ¿Quisiera otra inyección para el dolor?

I need to give you a suppository. / Necesito darle un supositorio.

It's a medicine that is placed in your rectum. / Es un medicamento que se coloca en el recto.

Activity / Actividad:

You need to walk around in order to regain your strength. / Necesita caminar para recuperar su(s) fuerza(s).

I'll help you. / Yo le ayudo.

Your doctor wants you to sit up in a chair for a while. / Su médico quiere que se siente en una silla por un rato.

Ask for help before getting out of bed. / Pida ayuda antes de levantarse de la cama.

Do you feel dizzy when you stand up? / ¿Se siente mareado cuando se levanta?

Your doctor doesn't want you to get out of bed. / Su médico no quiere que Ud. se levante de la cama.

You need to rest. / Necesita descansar.

I will be coming in every couple of hours to turn you. / Voy a regresar cada par de horas para cambiarlo de posición (voltearlo).

Hygiene / Higiene:

Would you like to take a shower? / ¿Quisiera ducharse (tomar un baño de regadera)?

I'm going to give you a sponge bath. / Voy a darle un baño de esponja.

Here's a toothbrush and toothpaste. / Aquí tiene un cepillo de dientes y pasta dental.

Here's a washcloth and towel. / Aquí tiene una toallita facial y una toalla.

Here is a container for your dentures. / Aquí tiene un recipiente para sus dientes postizos.

Respiratory / Respiratorio:

Are you short of breath? / ¿Le falta el aire?

You need to keep your oxygen mask on. / Necesita mantener puesta su máscara de oxígeno.

Don't remove your nasal cannula. / No quite su cánula nasal.

Take a deep breath. / Haga una respiración profunda.

You're due for another breathing treatment. / Es hora para otra nebulización.

Put this mouthpiece in your mouth and suck in air. / Coloque esta boquilla en la boca y chupe aire.

Make the ball go as high as you can. / Haga que la bolita suba lo más alto que pueda.

You need to do this every hour or so. / Tiene que hacer esto cada hora más o menos.

I need you to spit into this container. / Necesito que escupa en este recipiente.

There's no smoking in the hospital. / Está prohibido fumar en el hospital.

If you need to smoke, you can use the patio on the second floor. / Si tiene que fumar, puede usar el patio en el segundo piso.

Discharge Planning / Planes para dar de alta:

Who do you live with? / ¿Con quién vive Ud.?

Is there someone who can help you? / ¿Hay alguien que pueda ayudarle?

Do you have a wheelchair at home? / ¿Tiene una silla de ruedas en su casa?

A hospital bed? / ¿Una cama de hospital?

Who prepares your meals? / ¿Quién le prepara la comida?

Your doctor says you can go home now. / Su doctor dice que ya puede regresar a su casa.

You can call your family and tell them to come pick you up. / Puede llamar a su familia y pedirles que vengan a recogerlo.

Miscellaneous / Miscelánea:

You better ask your doctor the next time you see her. / Es mejor que le pregunte a su doctora la próxima vez que la vea.

Mr. Gomez, can you hear me? / Sr. Gomez, ¿puede oírme?

Open your eyes. / Abra sus ojos.

Squeeze my hand. / Apriete mi mano.

I'm sorry to wake you up, but I need to take your blood pressure and temperature. / Disculpe que lo despierte, pero necesito tomarle la presión (de la sangre) y la temperatura.

I need to prick your finger to measure your sugar. / Necesito pincharle (picarle) el dedo para medirle el azúcar.

Would you like the hospital chaplain to visit you? / ¿Quisiera que el capellán (sacerdote) del hospital lo visite?

PEDIATRICS / PEDIATRÍA

Your baby is fine. / Su bebé está bien.

He's a little jaundiced, but we can fix that with light treatments. / Se ve un poco amarillo, pero podemos arreglar eso con tratamiento de luz.

Are you going to breastfeed or use a bottle? / ¿Va a darle el pecho o le va a dar biberón (mamadera, pacha)?

You need to burp him after each feeding. / Necesita hacerlo eructar después de cada comida.

Don't dilute the formula. / No diluya la fórmula.

You shouldn't put your baby to bed with a bottle of milk. / No debe acostar a su bebé con un biberón de leche.

Have you weaned her yet? / ¿Ya la ha destetado?

She is ready to eat solids. / Ya puede comer alimentos sólidos.

Don't give her food that could make her choke, like beans or peanuts. / No le dé comida con la que se pueda atorar, como frijoles o maníes (cacahuetes, cacahuates).

Make sure your children aren't eating chips of paint off the walls. / Asegúrese de que sus hijos no estén comiendo pedacitos de pintura de las paredes.

Who cares for your baby when you are at work? / ¿Quién cuida a su bebé cuando Ud. está en el trabajo?

Does your son coo? Squeal? Laugh? Babble? Say any words? Talk? / ¿Hace su hijo sonidos como una paloma? ¿chilla? ¿ríe? ¿balbucea? ¿dice algunas palabras? ¿habla?

Can he lift his head up? Sit up? Crawl? Walk? / ¿Puede levantar la cabeza? sentarse? ¿gatear? ¿caminar?

Don't worry, he's developing fine. / No se preocupe, se está desarrollando bien.

Many children his age can't talk yet. / Muchos niños a su edad todavía no pueden hablar.

Tantrums are normal at this age. / Los berrinches son normales a esta edad.

There's nothing wrong; she's just teething. / No hay ningún problema; solamente que le están saliendo los dientes.

Has she been pulling on her ear lately? / ¿Ha estado jalándose la oreja últimamente?

Ear infections are common among children her age. / Las infecciones del oído son comunes en niños de su edad.

Does she have asthma? Allergies? A heart murmur? / ¿Tiene ella asma? ¿alergias? ¿un soplo cardíaco?

Has he ever had seizures? Eye problems? Pneumonia? / ¿Ha tenido alguna vez convulsiones? ¿problemas de los ojos? ¿neumonía?

Do you have a record of your child's immunizations? / ¿Tiene una tarjeta de vacunas de su niño?

You need to lower the temperature of the water coming out of your faucets. / Necesita bajar la temperatura del agua que sale del grifo (de la llave).

You need to put all poisons out of reach of your children. / Necesita poner todas las sustancias tóxicas fuera del alcance de sus niños.

Do you have a car seat for your child? / ¿Tiene un asiento de seguridad en el carro para su niño?

Is there a working smoke alarm on each floor of your house? / ¿Hay un detector de humo operativo en cada piso de su casa?

Would you like to attend a class on parenting? A class on cardiopulmonary resuscitation (CPR)? / ¿Quisiera asistir a una clase para padres? ¿una clase de reanimación cardiopulmonar (RCP)?

Does your daughter know her street address? / ¿Sabe su hija la dirección de su casa?

Can she brush her own teeth? Dress herself? Comb her hair? / ¿Puede cepillarse los dientes ella misma? ¿vestirse? ¿peinarse?

She will probably quit sucking her thumb on her own eventually. / Con el tiempo, es probable que deje de chuparse el dedo.

I wouldn't worry about it. / No me preocuparía por eso.

How long has she been acting listless? / ¿Hace cuánto que ha estado decaída?

Do you think she has been molested? / ¿Cree que ha sido abusada?

How often does your son wet the bed at night? / ¿Con qué frecuencia moja la cama su hijo?

It's normal for him to feel jealous of his younger brother. / Es normal que su hijo tenga celos de su hermano menor.

Has he had problems behaving? / ¿Ha tenido problemas de conducta?

How do you punish him? / ¿Cómo lo castiga?

Has he been missing school a lot? / ¿Ha faltado mucho a la escuela?

To the patient: / Al paciente:

How are you doing in school? / ¿Cómo te va en la escuela?

Do you have trouble paying attention? / ¿Se te hace difícil prestar atención?

What grade are you in? / ¿En qué grado estás?

Do you smoke cigarettes? / ¿Fumas cigarrillos?

Have you tried any drugs? / ¿Has probado alguna droga?

Are you sexually active? / ¿Eres sexualmente activo?..¿Has tenido relaciones sexuales recientemente?

Do you use birth control? / ¿Usas algún método anticonceptivo?

Do you have any questions regarding sexual matters? / ¿Tienes algunas preguntas sobre asuntos sexuales?

Are you unhappy about your appearance in any way? / ¿Por algún motivo te sientes descontento con tu apariencia?

Do you get along with your parents? / ¿Te llevas bien con tus padres?

Do you feel you can talk to them about personal things? / ¿Sientes que puedes hablar con ellos acerca de cosas personales?

What do they do that bothers you? / ¿Qué hacen que te molesta?

What do you do that makes them angry? / ¿Qué haces que los hace enojar?

What do you do during your free time? / ¿Qué haces en tu tiempo libre?

Do you spend a lot of time alone? / ¿Pasas mucho tiempo solo?

Are you involved in sports? / ¿Participas en deportes?

Do you belong to a gang? / ¿Eres miembro de una pandilla?

Have you had any trouble with the law? / ¿Has tenido problemas con la ley?

What do you plan to do after high school? / ¿Qué piensas hacer después de terminar la preparatoria?

DENTISTRY / ODONTOLOGÍA

When was the last time you saw a dentist? / ¿Cuándo fue la última vez que vio a un dentista?

Do you brush your teeth after each meal? / ¿Se cepilla los dientes después de cada comida?

Do you floss regularly? / ¿Usa hilo dental regularmente?

You need to brush more along the gum line. / Necesita cepillarse más en la linea de la encía.

Open really wide now. / Ahora abra bien la boca.

Open part way. / Ábrala un poco.

Bite down. / Muerda.

Close your mouth around this as though it were a straw. / Cierre la boca alrededor de esto como si fuera un popote (una bombilla, un pitillo).

Rinse your mouth and spit. / Enjuáguese la boca y escupa.

Turn your head toward me. / Voltée la cabeza hacia mí.

Are you feeling any pain? / ¿Está sintiendo algún dolor?

You have a loose filling. / Ud. tiene un empaste suelto.

I'm going to replace it with an acrylic filling. / Se lo voy a reemplazar con un empaste acrílico.

You need a root canal. / Necesita una endodoncia (un tratamiento de conducto).

I need to remove one of your teeth and put in a bridge. / Necesito sacarle uno de sus dientes y colocarle un puente.

Is there someone who can drive you home afterward? / ¿Hay alguien que lo pueda llevar a su casa después?

Have you ever had to take antibiotics before a dental procedure? / ¿Alguna vez ha tenido que tomar antibióticos antes de un procedimiento dental?

The only part that hurts is when I give you the numbing medication. / Solo le va a doler cuando le ponga el anestésico.

It will only hurt for a minute or so. / Solo le va a doler por un minuto más o menos.

You're going to feel a little stick. / Va a sentir un pequeño pinchazo (piquete).

You may feel a little burning. / Puede sentir un poco de ardor.

Bite down hard. / Muerda fuerte.

When you bite does it feel as though your tooth is too high? / Al morder, ¿siente que su diente está demasiado alto?

You have some staining on your front teeth. / Tiene un poco manchados los incisivos.

Would you be interested in a treatment which would make your teeth whiter? / ¿Le interesaría un tratamiento que le hiciera más blancos los dientes?

Swish this around for a minute and then spit it out. / Enjuáguese la boca con esto por un minuto y luego escúpalo.

You shouldn't eat, drink or rinse your mouth for half an hour. / No debe comer, beber, ni enjuagarse la boca por media hora.

RADIOLOGY / RADIOLOGÍA

Could you be pregnant? / ¿Podría Ud. estar embarazada?

How do you know? / ¿Cómo lo sabe?

When did you last eat? / ¿Cuándo fue la última vez que comió algo?

Are you able to sit up? Stand? Walk? / ¿Es capaz de sentarse? ¿levantarse? ¿caminar?

Stand here. / Párese aquí.

Put your hands on your head. / Ponga sus manos en la cabeza.

Put your chin here. / Ponga su mentón (barbilla) aquí.

Take a deep breath and hold it. / Respire profundo y no suelte el aire.

Don't move. / No se mueva.

Relax. / Relájese.

Go ahead and breathe. / Ya puede respirar.

Get on the table, please. / Súbase en la mesa, por favor.

You can get dressed now. / Ahora puede vestirse.

Come this way please. / Venga por acá, por favor.

Are you allergic to seafood? / ¿Es Ud. alérgico a los mariscos?

I'm going to inject the contrast now. / Le voy a inyectar el medio de contraste ahora.

You may feel a little warmth. / Puede que sienta un poco de calor.

You may get a metallic taste in your mouth. / Puede que sienta un sabor metálico en la boca.

That is normal. / Eso es normal.

Do you have any metal in you? / ¿Tiene Ud. algo de metal en su cuerpo?

No pacemaker? Hip replacement? Rods or pins? / ¿Nada de marcapasos? ¿prótesis de cadera? ¿grapas? ¿barras o clavos?

Have you ever had brain surgery? Inner ear surgery? / ¿Alguna vez ha sido operado del cerebro? ¿del oído interno?

Have you ever worked in welding or grinding? / ¿Alguna vez ha trabajado en soldadura o amoladura?

Do you ever get claustrophobic? / ¿Padece a veces la claustrofobia?

Does it bother you to be in a small, cramped place? / ¿Le molesta estar en un lugar pequeño y apiñado?

You're going to hear a lot of noise. / Va a escuchar mucho ruido.

Remove everything metallic from your clothes and your body. / Quite toda cosa metálica de su ropa y su cuerpo.

Like earrings, bracelets, and watches. / Como aretes, brazaletes, y relojes de pulsera.

CODE STATUS DISCUSSION /
HABLANDO DE REANIMACIÓN

Lastly, there is a question I ask of all my patients. / Por último, hay una pregunta que le hago a todos mis pacientes.

What would you like us–the medical team–to do in the very unlikely event that your heart should stop or you should stop breathing? / ¿Qué quería que hiciéramos nosotros–el equipo médico–en el caso muy improbable en que se le pare el corazón o que Ud. deje de respirar?

Would you like us to do everything reasonable to try to resuscitate you? / ¿Quería que hiciéramos todo lo razonable para reanimarlo?

Would you like us to let you die in peace? / ¿Quería que lo dejáramos morir en paz?

If we thought you had suffered brain damage, would you like us to continue resuscitation efforts anyway? / ¿Si creemos que ha padecido daño cerebral, quería que continuáramos con la reanimación?

Would you like us to continue resuscitation efforts as long as we thought there was a reasonable likelihood that you could get back to how you are now? / ¿Quería que continuáramos con la reanimación mientras creámos que hay una posibilidad razonable de que Ud. pudiera recuperarse, como está ahora

Would you like to name a family member or close friend who could advise us regarding your care in case you become unable to communicate? / ¿Quisiera designar a un familiar o a un amigo cercano quien pudiera avisarnos acerca su cuidado en caso de que Ud. se vuelva incapaz de comunicarse?

Have you filled out an advance directive? / ¿Ha llenado un documento de voluntad anticipada?

An advance directive is a document that describes what you want your doctors to do if you become seriously ill and can no longer tell them yourself. / Un documento de voluntad anticipada es un documento que describe lo que Ud. quisiera que sus médicos hicieran si Ud. se pone grave y ya no puede decírles Ud. mismo.

So that I'm sure I understand you, if your heart stops beating, you want us to let you die. / Para que nos entendamos bien, si se le para el corazón, Ud. quiere que le dejemos morir.

You can always change your mind. / Siempre puede cambiar su decisión.